Italian Literature

Italian Literature

Roots and Branches

ESSAYS IN HONOR OF
Thomas Goddard Bergin

Edited by Giose Rimanelli and
Kenneth John Atchity

New Haven and London, Yale University Press

Published with assistance from the
foundation established in memory
of James Wesley Cooper
of the Class of 1865, Yale College.

Designed by John O.C. McCrillis
and set in Times Roman type.
Printed in the United States of America by
The Murray Printing Co., Forge Village, Massachusetts.

Published in Great Britain, Europe, and Africa by
Yale University Press, Ltd., London.
Distributed in Latin America by Kaiman & Polon,
Inc., New York City; in Australasia
by Book & Film Services, Artarmon, N.S.W., Australia;
in India by UBS Publishers' Distributors Pvt.,
Ltd., Delhi; in Japan by John Weatherhill, Inc., Tokyo.

Contents

v

Contributors

Kenneth John Atchity, Assistant Professor of English and Comparative Literature, Occidental College

Gian-Paolo Biasin, Professor of Italian and Comparative Literature, University of Texas at Austin

Glauco Cambon, Professor of Italian and Comparative Literature, University of Connecticut

A. Robert Caponigri, Professor of Philosophy, University of Notre Dame

Franco Fido, Professor of Italian Studies, Brown University

A. Bartlett Giamatti, Professor of English and Comparative Literature, Yale University

Thomas M. Greene, Professor of English and Comparative Literature, Yale University

Erich Köhler, Professor of Romance Philology, University of Freiburg

Lowry Nelson, Jr., Professor of Comparative Literature, Yale University

Stephen G. Nichols, Jr., Professor of Comparative Literature and Romance Languages, Dartmouth College

William D. Paden, Jr., Associate Professor of French and Italian, Northwestern University

Mary T. Reynolds, Visiting Lecturer in English, Yale University

Giose Rimanelli, Professor of Italian, State University of New York at Albany

T. K. Seung, Professor of Philosophy, University of Texas at Austin

Michael Vena, Assistant Professor of Foreign Languages, Southern Connecticut State College

James J. Wilhelm, Professor of Comparative Literature, Livingston College of Rutgers University

Preface

These sixteen essays were written by former students and colleagues of
Thomas Goddard Bergin specifically to honor him on the occasion of
his retirement from full-time teaching at Yale University. Yet their
coherence in this volume is much more substantial than that generally
associated with the traditional Festschrift. The editors were determined
from the outset to avoid the typical European-style *miscellanea* which
so frequently amounts to no more than a random collection of off-the-
desk articles submitted—often still in their various tongues —by harried
contributors responding almost by rote to yet another casual invita-
tion, and which therefore produces as its chief result, a memorial library
book of doubtful integrity and dubious interest except to the person
being honored or to the curious bibliophile. The world of scholarship
can no longer afford such self-indulgent luxuries.

Our purpose, instead, was to assemble in one cohesive volume several stylistically sound and scholarly essays dealing with almost the
entire panorama of Italian literature from its Provençal roots to its
most modern branches, for the immediate, productive use of students
and scholars of Italian, Provençal, and comparative literature. It was,
and remains, our belief that the most meaningful way to pay tribute to
Thomas Bergin's distinguished career is to have *his* students present the
best fruits of their labors to *their* students. The present readers of these
essays, then, are in effect Bergin's academic grandchildren.

Bergin's contribution to the status and growth of Italian studies in
America, fully documented in the bibliography at the end of this
volume, is incontestable and widely recognized. His introductions to
Petrarch, Dante, and Vico have long been appreciated by English-
reading students of these great Italian authors. His concordance to
Dante and his anthology of Provençal troubadours are invaluable
reference works. Bergin's translations, collections, and reviews of modern Italian fiction and poetry have been no less influential in furthering
the expansion and enhancing the image of Italian literary studies in this
country. Most recently, his translations of Petrarch from the Latin,

ix

coinciding with the six-hundredth anniversary of that poet's death, have added to his stature in the scholarly world.

Bergin once wrote of Petrarch: "As old men will and as he had good reason to, he grew increasingly pessimistic about the state of the world and its future. But his spirit still glowed; he still found joy in conversation, in friendship, and above all in writing." No words fit Bergin himself any better, for his life as an all-round man of letters has been a true *imitatio Petrarchae*. With Petrarch, Bergin would insist that "there is no lighter burden, nor more agreeable, than a pen." Bergin grumbles about the burdens, self-imposed, of his literary endeavors. But his pen does not falter; nor is his genial general pessimism particularly applicable to the consequences of his lifelong penmanship. The products of Bergin's pen are both a solid monument to his literary interests and industry, and a shining example to all who know them and him.

The divisions of this book not only match the various fields in which Bergin has toiled so fruitfully but also—so all-inclusive have been his interests—correspond to the major periods of Italian literary development. The book is a critical survey of that development. It begins with the Provençal heritage, not only because *it* is important to an introduction to Italian literature in general, but also because the great Renaissance scholarship taught us that Provençal was the recognized basis of the material and stylistic developments that would culminate in the poetry of Dante. Erich Köhler's subject is the definition of the *descort*, a troubadour genre in which the masochistic aspects of courtly love are celebrated. Köhler locates this genre's position in the system of genres in general, and in particular in relationship to the *canso*. The contradiction between text and melody that is definitive to the descort integrates this genre into the system of courtly love by way of cultivating the martyrdom of loving hearts. Stephen G. Nichols examines the extent and nature of formalism in the troubadour lyric. In the face of recent claims that the Old Provençal and Old French lyric traditions are "totally objectified," he sets out to determine whether one can realistically speak of an individual and identifiable creative physiognomy in early troubadour lyric. Studying the ways in which Guilleme IX and Marcabru utilized similar forms, Nichols concludes that the claim for a collective, "totally objectified" lyric tradition cannot be sustained.

Bridging the lyric traditions, William D. Paden, Jr., investigates Bertran de Born's literary fortunes in Italy. Paden's research reveals why Dante's close acquaintance with the almost immediately legendary troubadour was based upon knowledge that was, without exception, inaccurate. Three Provençal poems, involving imitation of Bertran's meters and allusions to his legend, are edited at the end of Paden's essay. Finally, James J. Wilhelm's comparative approach widens the scope of literary influence to show how the influence of Arnaut Daniel is apparent in the critical writings of Dante, who in turn passed ideas of poetic composition on to Ezra Pound, the founder of modern imagism. Essentially, Arnaut's ideas focus upon highly original diction, variant rhythmics, dramatic sound combinations, and an abhorrence of clichés that can be found in the epic writings of his Italian and American successors.

Although the shift to Dante is a natural one at this point, justification of Dante criticism is always a delicate matter. Why only three essays? Why these three? The editors have sought to present approaches to Dante that were both original and freshly revealing, and also representative of more general trends in Dante criticism. Atchity's study of the *Purgatorio* is a definitively modern approach that takes into account the existential self-awareness inherent in all poetry and particularly manifest in the second canticle of the *Commedia*, where the self-realization of the poem, searching for its own image in contexts of fictional art, forms a continuum with the self-fulfillment of Dante's "optimum reader." Atchity emphasizes the inextricable unity of the moral and the aesthetic in Dante.

T. K. Seung's is a cultural, contextual viewpoint that separates two independent claims in Auerbach's figural realism—namely, literal fundamentalism (the literal sense of the *Commedia* is true) and figural allegorism (its allegory is meant to be figural). He argues that the first claim is historically untrue and inconsequential for interpretation; and he shows how the second claim has not always been honored, although it is the only significant one. Then Seung demonstrates that this hypothesis can be fulfilled by accepting Bonaventure's Trinitarian exemplarism in its figural mode, in place of Thomistic dualism.

The Dante section, too, concludes with a study of influences, specifically, the impact of Dante's art upon a great twentieth-century author. Thus Mary T. Reynolds provides a close textual explication of the "Sirens" episode from Joyce's *Ulysses* to demonstrate how greatly indebted Joyce was to Dante, both in general theme and in detailed execution. The bewildering breadth of Joyce's literary knowledge is revealed at the same time that the importance of Dante is recognized in its true perspective—as equaled only by that of Homer. For Dante's presence in Joyce, though it may be more subtle, is just as definitive as Homer's.

Following the traditional division of Renaissance from Middle Ages, we have separated Petrarch and Boccaccio from their great contemporary, Dante. In this section the Renaissance period is given its widest possible definition, from Petrarch to Ariosto. It is distinguished from the preceding one as an age of exploration, of business, until the predominance of the bourgeoisie was eventually to lead to the high Renaissance. On the one hand, we have Boccaccio's absolutely pure language, a model of realistic, contemporary linguistic expression; on the other, we have Alberti's attempt to extend the social revolution to the invention of a literary language that would overcome the division between the spoken and the written tongues.

According to Thomas M. Greene, Petrarch's habit of contemplating landscape in terms of a buried historical layer can be assimilated to his reading of ancient poetry and his creative composition of poetry; both involve the recognition of half-buried layers of historical realities. The reader's discernment of these layers as organic parts of the literary object is termed by Greene "subreading," and is described as a humanist alternative to older medieval, hermeneutic methods. In the sixth day of the *Decameron*, Boccaccio's storytellers speak of witty sallies—that is, of characters interesting chiefly because they know how to speak. Franco Fido's study of the ten stories of this *giornata* reveals the *ars narrandi* that governs the whole book: a blend of conformity to a given theme, and freedom of stylistic invention, through which storytelling becomes a noble, self-rewarding exercise of *savoir parler*, and yet at the same time a way to salvage in terms of pleasure and wisdom—that is, of culture—all the civilized experiences and values which the various plagues of history would otherwise destroy.

In "Alberti's Linguistic Innovations," Michael Vena offers a contribution to Italian linguistic history, concentrating on Alberti the writer and fashioner of a linguistic medium of expression, neither in Latin nor in dialect but in the evolving "standard" Italian. The subject of the essay is important both for the conception of the vernacular and for the configuration of ideas in early Italian humanism of the Renaissance. Vena's essay points out this worthy attempt at lexical and conceptual synthesis.

The final Renaissance essay is concerned with the epics of Pulci, Boiardo, and Ariosto and with the way these poets confront the activity they are engaged in. A. Bartlett Giamatti's theme is the alternation of restraint and release in Renaissance epic poetry; his fundamental image for this dialectic is the figure of the "cavallo sfrenato," the unchecked horse and his powerless rider. After a brief glance at earlier epic uses of the unrestrained horse, Giamatti offers readings of these three Italian Renaissance epics in terms of this figure and all it implies.

Giambattista Vico, going beyond Descartes, is the proper figure to introduce "the modern world." The purpose of Robert Caponigri's essay is to establish the relevance of the *New Science* to contemporary philosophy of culture by the identification of its problematic, the development of its method, and the description of its substantive doctrine. Most critical comment on Leopardi's poetry is concerned with the so-called idylls, early and "great." Lowry Nelson, Jr., seeks to evaluate historically and critically two poems, successful in various measure, that come before and after the idylls: "All'Italia" and "La Ginestra." Both are "rhetorical" or "parenetic" in ways that demand complex historical and aesthetic understanding, as Nelson's essay demonstrates.

Gian-Paolo Biasin's essay describes the alienated "anti-heroes" of Svevo, Pirandello, and Montale in their consecutive aspects, with particular consideration for thematic and stylistic traits; his analysis aims to show the structural correlation between social and artistic alienation, as well as between novel and poetry. As a writer writing about another writer, Giose Rimanelli blends criticism and personal recollection. Pavese's *Diario* is so personal, so forbidden, that it demands a private analysis of its author and his work by someone who knew and knows them both intimately. The question of whether Pavese committed suicide in a decadent way is probed in Rimanelli's essay, which concludes that Pavese saw his action as the only way to overcome the impotence of history.

Finally, our panorama of criticism reaches to the present time in Glauco Cambon's essay on the lyrical aesthetic of Ungaretti. His essay on "Lindoro di Deserto" first of all discovers the rich, elusive poem in its own right, and then descries its correlation to the rest of *L'Allegria*. In so doing, Cambon reveals how much the vitality of Ungaretti's poetics in this memorable first phase of his career depends on the element of playfulness—a playfulness that articulates the free, plurilinear structure of the whole composition as well as its lexical and iconic-semantic cells. Cambon shows that this playfulness enhances, rather than neutralizes or weakens, the "high seriousness" of the poem, which turns out to be both an exercise in verbal freedom and an existential statement. The *uomo di pena* was also an acrobat of *allegria*.

The editors wish to acknowledge with gratitude the careful assistance of Elissa Rabellino, Eric K. Marcus, and Deborah Lloyd, and the support of H. P. Salomon. We are also grateful to Occidental College, the State University of New York at Albany, and the University of Texas at Austin for financial support in the preparation of this volume.

G.R.
K.J.A.

Albany, New York
Los Angeles, California
May 8, 1974

Italian Literature

1

Deliberations on a Theory of the Genre of the Old Provençal Descort[1]

Erich Köhler

Although it may be more and more neglected nowadays, the study of the Old Provençal language has its special rewards for all those concerned with literary provenance. In the tenth and eleventh centuries, a rich literature developed in the *langue d'oc* that was to become the cultural heritage of Italy, and eventually of all Europe. It was in the south of France that the earliest and most influential vernacular lyric was born and flourished, in the "courtly love" poetry of the troubadours. The Provençal lyric, moreover, was, directly or indirectly, normative for all later lyric poetry. This essay seeks to define a particularly interesting form of the Provençal lyric, the descort. Because the descort relates to and modifies the whole genre system in Old Provençal, careful attention to its autonomous generic status is demanded.

If the descort were to be judged only in terms of its contents, there would be no reason not to consider it as anything other than a variant of the *canso* and to relate it to this genre, granting it at most the status of a "subgenre," similar to the *chanson de change* or the *comjat*. "All descorts deal with courtly love: their subject is always an amorous request or complaint, and they involve a great number of clichés and hackneyed phrases."[2] But there are two reasons why, in spite of all this, the descort must be given the status of an independent lyrical genre: first of all, the poets themselves looked upon the descorts in this way; and secondly, the descort's metrical and musical structure distinguishes

1

it (as well as the lay) quite clearly from the canso. "Generally speaking, every stanza of a descort has its own individual metric formula (and an individual melody), whereas the stanzas of strophic songs are strictly isometrical."[3]

Sometimes the pithy definitions of Provençal poetics—treatises that appeared long after the flourishing of Provençal poetry—have hindered research rather than promoting it, even though these definitions apparently try to emphasize distinguishing characteristics of both content and form. One of these definitions is in the *Doctrina de compondre dictatz*:

> Si vols far discort deus parlar d'amor com a hom qui n'es desemparat e com a hom qui no pot haver plaser de sa dona e viu turmentatz. E que en lo cantar, lla hon lo so deuria muntar, que·l baxes; e fe lo contrari de tot l'altre cantar. E deu haver tres cobles e una o dues tornades e responedor. E potz metre un o dos motz mes en una cobla que en altra, per so que mils sia discordant.[4]

> [If you want to make a descort, you have to speak of love like a man whom it has abandoned and like someone who cannot enjoy his lady and lives in pain. And in his song the melody must fall where it is expected to rise and it has to run quite counter to any other song. And the descort normally has three stanzas and one or two tornadas and a *responedor* [i.e. recurrence of the same musical phrase as half- or full cadence at the end of each section of the tune]. And you might add one or two words more to one stanza than to the other, in order to make them more discordant.]

The definition of the *leys d'amors* also proves to be as clear in its characterization of the content as the *Doctrina*'s, but it is equally misleading in the determination of the formal structure. Rather than clarifying the descort's structure, the remarks in the *leys d'amors* on the tornada, and the comparison with the "vers," make the descort's structure difficult to understand—especially since the instructions concerning the use of several languages generalize the exceptional case of the famous multilingual descort of Raimbaut de Vaqueiras. The following statement, it is true, is ambiguous:

> las . . . coblas devon esser singulars, dezacordablas e variablas en acort, en so et en lengatges . . . E deu tractar d'amors o de lauzors

o per maniera de rancura: "guar midons no mi ama aissi cum sol,"
o de tot aisso essems, qui·s vol.[5]
[the . . . stanzas must be singulars, discordant and variable in
harmony, melody and words. And [the descort] must deal with
love, either praising it or in the manner of complaint: "for Milady
does not love me as she was wont to do," or with all of it together,
as you like.]

The comment of Donat Proensal, "cantilena habens sonos diversos,"[6]
only confirms that the descort is a musically complete form.

Even though the poetics (whose authors are apparently not in active
contact with a tradition, which is dead anyway) cannot yield much information, they have again and again troubled our investigations which,
in the case in question, cannot do without the assistance of a music
historian. The definition of the genre, as proposed by Jean Maillard, is
based on the analysis of preserved melodies for the Provençal and
French descort and lay:

> A descort is a poetic composition of a personal character, which is
> essentially meant to be sung to an original melody. This melody
> may be played casually on an instrument. The casuistry of the
> descort amounts to an amorous complaint and request, which
> provoke an imbalance in the soul and the thoughts of the poet. The
> structure of the descort is complex and, like the lay, it presents a
> variable number of asymmetrical strophes of different length, gener-
> ally from five to eleven lines. Sometimes the principle of metric
> repetition, which can also be observed in the lay, can be found in
> the descort. The strophes themselves consist of couplets with
> frequent enjambements. The structural scheme of the melody is
> different from the poetic scheme, although they closely coincide;
> this is the essential principle of this lyrical genre.[7]

Descort means "dissension," "discord," "disharmony." This feeling is
expressed: (a) as far as the content is concerned by an appropriate spectrum of motifs, which will be treated later on; (b) by the disparity of the
strophe structure; (c) by the contradiction between words and melody.
Raimbaut de Vaqueiras and his imitators add to these elements the
discord of languages. Is the descort, with its distinctive "irregularity,"
to be considered as an "anti-chanson" (according to R. Baum), a

counterpart of the *acort* in the canso, which Ferdinand Wolf classifies as the "pure homogeneous art form reproducing itself in a typical way"?[8]

The *discordantia* of sequential music, in contrast to the *concordantia* of strophe, had, by the eleventh century, already become marked.[9] The terminology of poetics that deals with vernacular language, however, seems to be motivated by poetic content rather than by liturgical music, although there is no doubt that the origins do lie in liturgical music. An unknown poet (Pillet-Carstens 461, 5) begins his descort: "A chantar m'er un descort/per mi don,/puois ab leis noi trob acortz/cui hom son" ("I shall compose a descort because of Milady, for I do not find *acort* with her whose man [servant] I am"). Guillem de Salignac (P.-C. 235, 2) says: "Ja non feira descort/s'eu acort/e bon acordansa trobes ab leis" ("I shall not make a descort, if I find *acort* and good accordance with her").

Descort, as opposed to *acort*, describes the remoteness from the relative and precarious "peace" of the loving poet, who can be sure at least of hope, if not of fulfillment. In one descort, which was much imitated because it seemed to include all elements of the genre in an exemplary way, Aimeric de Peguillan sighs in a state of *amar desamatz* (P.-C. 10, 45): "Patz en volgr' et acort" ("I would like to have peace and *acort* from her"). Deprived of confidence, Raimbaut de Vaqueiras writes his famous *descort d'amor*, "Eras quan vey verdeyar" (P.-C. 392,4), using five different languages (Provençal, Italian, French, Gascogne, and Galician-Portuguese). He explains this in the following way:

> qu'una dona·m sol amar,
> mas camjatz l'es sos coratges,
> per qu'ieu fauc dezacordar
> los motz e·ls sos e·ls lenguatges.

[5–8]

[For a certain lady was wont to love me, but her heart has changed, and so I produce discordance in the rhymes, melodies, and languages.]

Raimbaut's descort has its location in a cycle of songs that belong to different genres. These songs (written between 1197 and 1202) express

the "story" of some love,[10] and Raimbaut's descort occupies the place
of the extreme *desacordansa* in this "context." Presumably, Raimbaut
was inspired by his own invention of a (fictive) bilingual tenso with a
lady from Genoa (P.-C. 392,7). His procedure was adopted by other
poets.[11]

Raimbaut's second descort, "Engles, un novel descort," dedicated to
the Marquis Boniface of Montferrat, is one of remembrance because the
state of mind that provided the basis for the emotional tone of the
descort no longer prevails. The beloved lady has realized her fault in the
mal'acordansa and has, for her part, initiated reconciliation—in other
words, she has reestablished the *acort* (v. 15). One cannot but draw a
line from there to the song "Bella dona cara" (P.-C. 461,37), which is
remarkable in many respects. The unknown author has explained his
intention of writing an *acort*, it is true, as opposed to a descort, whose
form, nonetheless, he still maintains:

> Amors, ben es mos acortz,
> Que acortz
> S'apel mos cantz totz tems mays
> Entre'ls fins aimans verais
> Cui plas solatz e deportz,
> Que descortz
> Non deur' far qui non s'irais·
> Per qu'ieu lais
> Descortz
> Per far acortz gays
> Entre·ls gais.
>
> [str. 6]

[Love, good is my accord, for *acortz* my song is always called
among fine and true lovers who enjoy pleasure and gaiety, whereas
a descort should only be made by one who is vexed [by Love];
that is why I reject the descort in order to make joyous *acort*
among joyous people.]

The attempt to contrast the genre of the descort to the genre of the
acort was bound to fail,[12] as this must lead back to the genre from which
the descort itself separated, namely, the canso. Carl Appel is certainly
justified in saying that it is absurd to sing about the unity of love in a

discordant form.[13] But talk about "degeneration" is ruled out by the logic used by the unknown author when drawing his conclusion from the fact that the descort-writer accustoms himself to a state of resignation that cannot be endured unless one abandons courtly love as such. No one, however, would agree with this opinion. Every protest remained limited to a verbal and formal *desacordanza*.

If the descort played the role of an "anti-chanson," the acort, being an "anti-descort,"[14] was bound to return to the affirmative canso. Only such dialectics between the "schismatic deformity" (Wolf) of the descort and the "art-form" of the acort (or canso) make possible the precious word-play with which Na Lombarda answers the courtship of Bernart d'Armagnac:

> Car lo mirailz e no ueser descorda
> Tan mon acord c'ab pauc no·l desacorda;
> Mes can record so qu·l meus noms recorda,
> En bon acord totz mons pensars s'acorda;

[For the mirror and the absence of view trouble my *acord* in such way that they almost discord it, but when I recall what my name reminds me of, all my thinking accords in good *acort*.]

The appearance of the acort as anti-descort, no matter how ephemeral, may still allow conclusions with respect to the character of the descort as anti-canso. Discord is the law of this genre, in direct and challenging contrast to the *acort* of the canso. It is primarily the task of a "gay" melody to create this discord. "En aquest gai son leugier/ faz descort ses alegransa" ("In this joyous, light melody I compose a descort without joy") is the beginning of a descort written before 1200 by an anonymous poet (P.-C. 461, 104). A few years later, Peire Raimon de Tolosa (P.-C. 355, 1) emphasizes, "Ab son gai, plan e car/ faz descort leu e bon" ("I compose a light and good descort in a gay, simple, and lovely melody").

The *Doctrina de compondre dictatz* seems to mean nothing other than this very inherent contradiction between melody and words when it says, "lla hon lo so deuria muntar, que·l baxes; e fe lo contrari de tot l'altre cantar" (cf. p. 2). *Gai descort*, according to Pons de Capduoill, Aimeric de Belenoi, Albert de Sisteron, Elias de Barjols (Elias Cairel: *gai so*), is an oxymoron including the whole misery and desperate hope of love—a love that notes its failure without being able to renounce longing for that "acort," the only hope of fulfilling the purpose of life. A gay melody, and a complaint that stops before arriving at complete resignation, demonstrate in the totality of their contradiction the discord of the poet's soul, which by being integrated into the system of the genre is therefore mastered and appeased.

Key words, themes, and motives of the descort give information concerning its relations to the canso. In the last verses of his song, "Pus Amors vol qu'en faça sa comanda" (P.-C. 434a, 49), Cerveri de Girona not only summarizes the preceding thoughts but also summarizes all the themes of the descort as such, in a valid formula: "A, madon', ades denan vos fenis!/ Pero viure volri'ab que·n jausis!" ("Ah Lady, I always die in your presence! And yet I long to live in joy with you!").

To die living and to live dying— this fundamental paradox of courtly love reaches its peak in the descort. In a stylized form this paradox can be enjoyed. The "fins amanz e merceiaire" (fine lover and petitioner")— Bonifaci Calvo, Guillem de la Tor, and others—accepts it as an affirmed destiny, from which it is impossible to escape (estraire). There is hardly any poet who, in his poems, does not speak of mort, morir, aucir, sufrir, and who does not consider himself a martire. Also, there is hardly any poet who would not rather perish before the eyes of the beloved lady than seek comfort in the jauzimen (enjoyment) of another. Even the certainty of having to suffer endless pain cannot stop the poet from devoting himself to the one lady who alone can promise happiness (Aimeric de Peguillan, Guiraut de Calanson). All attempts to free himself from the pain of unfulfilled longing by turning to another, less disdainful lady are in vain (Guillem Augier Novella, Cerveri de Girona). The borderline between the descort and the "chanson de change" (song of change), otherwise so strictly observed, is crossed only once, and that is by Elias Cairel (P.-C. 133, 10). He invokes the poetic quality of the descort in order to convince the newly chosen lady of the true feelings of the loving poet ("que mon servizi prenda/ e mon descort entenda/ e·l gai so"—"that she might accept my service and listen to my descort and its joyous melody").

Among the different themes of the descort, there is not a single one that does not also occur in the canso, not even the theme of dissension itself. But this very theme has become so dominant and inherent for the descort that it reduces the number of possible themes considerably.[15]

It is not surprising that it still nearly always leaves enough room to praise the qualities of the beloved lady; occasionally, it also includes a (mostly contrastive) "Natureingang" (Guillem Augier Novella, Raimbaut de Vaqueiras, Elias Cairel), and—more rarely—it incorporates the theme of the *lauzengiers*, "slanderers," (Raimbaut de Vaqueiras, Guiraut de Salignac, P.-C. 461, 70). But the dominant element is the vocabulary, which gives expression to a delightfully cultivated martyrdom of the loving heart. The descort almost suspends the process that leads from hope, postponed again and again, to total resignation—a process that remains in the self-tormenting and yet sweet sadness of frustrated yearning and confers distinction by the readiness to suffer the torture of a permanent death of love. The descort isolates, cultivates, and neutralizes the masochistic aspect of courtly love.

If this interpretation of the character and function of the descort is accepted, then not only its relations to the canso but also the fact of its presumed development in the eighties of the twelfth century (the period of full blossoming of the system of troubadour genres) becomes understandable. It is difficult, however, to trace the history of this genre. But the assertion in the *Vida* of Garin d'Apchier[16]—which credits this troubadour with having written the first descort—could be true only if a second and earlier poet by the same name could be found.[17] The majority of the anonymous descorts withstand any attempt to determine their date of composition. Only the two descorts of Raimbaut de Vaqueiras and the anonymous descort "En aquest gai son leugier" (P.-C. 461, 104) can be established with some certainty as having been extant before 1200. About or shortly after the turn of the century, Guiraut de Salignac, Peire Raimon de Tolosa, and Guiraut de Calanson (two pieces) wrote their descorts. The descorts of the troubadours Pons de Capduoil, Aimeric de Belenoi, Aimeric de Peguillan, Elias de Barjols (two pieces), Elias Cairel, and Guillem Augier Novella (three or four pieces) fall in the first quarter of the thirteenth century. Guillem de la Tor and Albertet de Sisteron can be considered as their younger contemporaries. The interest in descorts, visibly decreasing toward the middle of the century, was somewhat revived by Bonifaci Calvo, Peire Cardenal, Cerveri de Girona (fourteen pieces), Joan Esteve, and Giraut Riquier, the poets of the late epoch.

Like the canso, the descort also requires a stanzaic structure and a melody of its own. It involves "Kontrafakturen" (melodic imitations) only very rarely. It is odd that these exceptions only occur in a single poem, the descort "Qui la ve en ditz" by Aimeric de Peguillan (P.-C., 10, 45). This descort is one of the four representatives of the genre whose melodies have been preserved as well. Of course, only one of the four imitations can be considered as a real descort, namely, the anonymous song "Sill qu'es caps e guitz" (P.-C. 461, 67a). Peire Cardenal's song (P.-C. 335, 36) is, according to its content, a *sirventes*; Joan Esteve's descort (P.-C. 226, 8) is a religious song, and Guillem Raimon's, an exchange of couplets with Ferrari de Ferrera—a later reminiscence that occurs at the beginning of the fourteenth century. Contextual borderings on other genres, such as those mentioned above, and even transitions into other genres may be noted already in the case of a song by Elias Cairel (P.-C. 133, 10, cf. above), which is a chanson de change. Guillem Augier Novella (P.-C. 205, 6) calls a song, of which unfortunately only fragments still exist, "sirventés avols e descortz."[18]

The problem of defining the descort and its relationship to the lay still has to be examined more carefully.[19] Of course, in this essay I must set aside any discussion of the question of origin.[20] The *Doctrina de compondre dictatz* defines the lay according to its piously edifying content and its penitent contrition, prescribing for it, as for the descort, the same number of stanzas and tornadas that are demanded in the canso. However, this very definition cannot be applied to the three Provençal lays that have been handed down to us.[21] The definition, nevertheless, contains a noteworthy remark: "ab so novell e plazen, o de esgleya o d'autra manera" ("with a new and pleasing melody, either liturgical or of some different kind"). This means that a genuine and pleasant melody, perhaps adapted to the content (in contrast to the descort) is required. This melody may be of sacred or secular origin. Bonifaci Calvo's song, "Ai Deus! s'a cor que·m destreigna" (P.-C. 101, 2, which the poet himself called a lay), the "Lai Markiol" (P.-C. 461, 124, which may have been written fairly early, about 1200, and whose form—and melody—is identical with that of a French and a Latin poem), as well as the also anonymous "Lai nonpar" (P.-C. 461, 122), are of definitely courtly character. Their spectrum of motifs can even be clearly associated with the descort. Are "descort" and "lay" only different names for the same artistic genre?

It is true that Jeanroy's opinion, according to which the "pieces with different names" are "one single genre,"[22] has a respectable tradition.

But Wolf has already made the reservation that the different names of the genre were given "depending on whether their popular character, their irregularity, or their inner disunity (the discord) as opposed to the stable regularity of the purely artistic songs (cansos, chansons), was to be emphasized."[23] What has come down to us of Provençal songs, though small in volume, seems to confirm Maillard's observation—which he made surveying the French scene—that generally poets of descorts are known, whereas many poets of lays remain anonymous.[24] Even if the literary historian wishes to adhere to the Celtic origin of the lay, he still has to submit himself to the unanimous judgment of musicology, which advocates the thesis that the form of the lay developed from a sacred sequence. The same is true for the descort.

The differences, however, are evident. What differentiates Bonifaci Calvo's lay, the "Lai Markiol," and the "Lai non-par" (in spite of their congruent content) from the descort, is the habit of giving the first and last strophe the same metrical and musical structure; this is a characteristic of the lay that nearly became a law for this genre. The descort, however, tends to approach the canso, chiefly by adopting the principle of the tornada.[25] An original comparison made by Bertran de Born, which, by the way, shows that "lay" as a name for a genre was a perfectly current expression for the troubadours in the year 1184, proves that the congruency of the first and last strophe was considered to be a characteristic of the lay.[26] According to Appel, one can add to the above-mentioned distinctive characteristics, the fact that the rhymes in the lay change more often than in the descort; "that the strophes are divided much more distinctly than in some lays"; that the form of the lay can be derivative, whereas the form of the descort cannot.[27] Appel's interesting statement regarding a numerical architecture of the descort—in other words, a clear tendency toward having a round number of verses—is unsuitable as a definitive criterion so long as there is no proof or probability showing that the lays to which these characteristics also refer have been influenced by the descort.[28]

There is still no definite answer to the question of whether the descort is "an offshoot of the lay"[29] or, what is more probable, whether it originated in the south independently of the lay, though also on the basis of the sequence. The most recent proposition, offered by Baum, recommends itself by the conclusion it draws from this difficult situation. He says the common denominator for a type of song that is to be considered as "anti-canso" is "irregularity" acting as a principle of composition. According to this proposition, the sequence, the lay, and the descort "are therefore expressions differing in space and time of an evolving poetical principle."[30] However, to imply that it is therefore unnecessary to answer the question of whether or not the lay and the descort represent one and the same genre, is to fail to see the problem of the functions which the undeniably different arrangements of the "principle" assume in the system of medieval lyrical genres. The domain of the lay is northern France. The descort has offshoots among the trouvères, and among the Italian and the Galician-Portuguese poets.

NOTES

1. Translated by Wolfgang Fehlberg and Ruth Callahan; editorial assistance: Lowry Nelson, Jr., and Michel-André Bossy.
2. Jean Maillard, *Evolution et esthétique du lai lyrique des origines à la fin du XIVème siecle* (Paris, 1963), p. 128. R. Baum offers a historical sketch of evaluations of the descort in his book, *Le descort ou l'anti-chanson* (Liège: Mélanges Jean Boutière, 1971), pp. 75 ff.
3. István Frank, *Répertoire métrique de la poésie des troubadours* (Paris, 1953), 1: xci.
4. John Henry Marshall, *The "Razos de Trobar" of Raimon Vidal and Associated Texts* (London: Oxford University Press, 1972), pp. 97 and 139 n. The author of the *Doctrina* goes on to say: (l.c. 98) "Discort es dit per ço discort cor parla descordament e reversa; e es contrari a totz altres cantars, cor gita de manera ço que diu" ("It is called descort because a dejected heart speaks discordantly and reversedly; and it is the contrary of any other song, the heart expressing everything it says in irregular verse-form").
5. Quoted from Carl Appel, *Provenzalische Chrestomathie* (Leipzig, 1930), pp. 198 ff.
6. *The Donatz Provesals of Uc Faidit*, ed. John Henry Marshall (London, 1969), p. 230.
7. Maillard, *Evolution et esthétique*, pp. 143 ff.
8. Ferdinand Wolf, *Über die Lais, Sequenzen und Leiche* (Heidelberg, 1941), p. 131; Baum, *Le descort*, p. 97.
9. Hans Spanke, *Sequenz und Lai, Studi Medievali* 11 (1938): 34; cf. Freidrich Gennrich, *Grundriss einer Formenlehre des mittelalterlichen Liedes* (Halle, 1932), p. 140; Baum, *Le descort*, pp. 90 ff.
10. Cf. Joseph Linskill, *The Poems of the Troubadour Raimbaut de Vaqueiras* (The Hague, 1964), pp. 21 ff.

11. Cf. the trilingual poem by Bonifaci Calvo (P.-C. 101,2); the *cobla* of Cerveri de Girona (P.-C. 43a, 40), in six languages; and the trilingual (French, Latin, Italian) descort "Ai! fals rics," believed to be written by Dante, cf. Dante Alighieri, *Rime*, ed. Gianfranco Contini (Turin, 1965), pp. 239–42.

12. After all, a second anonymous poet followed him (P.-C. 461,194): "E plaz's vos mon acort" (v.47).

13. ZRPh 11 (1887), p. 218.

14. Cf. Jean Maillard, "Notes sur l'acort provençal," *Revue de Langue et de Littérature provençales* 3 (1960): 48.

15. As to the significance of the "dominant" for the determination of genres, and as to a theory of genres in general, cf. H. R. Jauss, "Theorie der Gattungen und Literatur des Mittelalters," in *Grundriss der romanischen Literaturen des Mittelalters* 1 (Heidelberg: H. R. Jauss and E. Köhler, Généralités, 1972): 107–38.

16. Jean Boutière and A.-H. Schutz, *Biographies des Troubadours* (Paris, 1950), p. 417.

17. Cf. Carl Appel's unsuccessful attempt, ZRPh 11 (1887): 221 ff.

18. Jean Maillard, *Problèmes musicaux et littéraires du descort*, in *Mél. de linguistique et de littérature romanes à la mémoire d'I. Frank* (Saarbrücken, 1957), p. 392, considers it to be a descort, whereas Frank excludes it.

19. Baum, *Le descort*, pp. 92 ff, claims this rightly.

20. As to the most recent results of research, see G. Aarburg, in *Die Musik in Geschichte und Gegenwart* (Basel, London, New York, 1960), pp. 81–87; cf. Maillard, *Evolution et esthétique*, and R. Baum, "Les troubadours et les lais," ZRPh 85 (1969): 1–44.

21. Ed. J. H. Marshall, *The "Razos de trobar" and Associated Texts*, p. 95: "Si vols fer lays, deus parlar de Deu e de segle, o de eximpli o de proverbis, de lausors ses feyment d'amor, qui sia axi plazent a Deu co al segle; e deus saver que·s deu far e dir ab contriccio tota via, e·ab so novell e plazen, o de esgleya o d'autra manera. E sapies que·y ha mester ayantes cobles com en la canço, e aytantes tornades; e segueix la raho e la manera axi com eu t'ay dit" ("If you want to make a *lai* you have to speak of God and of the world, or of examples or proverbs, or of praise of love without pretence, so that it be pleasant both to God and to the world; and you must know that contrition must always be expressed, and with a new and pleasing melody, either liturgical or of some other sort. And you must know that there have to be as many stanzas as in the canso, and as many tornadas, and you must follow the subject-matter and the metrical construction just as I have told you").

22. Alfred Jeanroy, Louis Brandin, and Pierre Aubry, *Lais et descorts français du XIIIe siècle* (Paris, 1901), p. vi; cf. H. Spanke, *Sequenz und Lai, Studi Medievali* 11 (1938): 34: "The *descort* is a courtly, scholarly term for the same thing which more modestly was called lay."

23. Wolf, *Über die Lais*, p. 130.

24. Maillard, *Evolution, et esthétique*, p. 128.

25. Cf. Appel, "Vom Descort," p. 230; Baum, "Les troubadours," p. 33.

26. In the sirventes "Puois lo gens terminis floritz" (P.-C. 80,32), it is said about Alfons II of Aragon: "Sos bas paratges sobreissitz/Sai que fenira coma lais/E

tornara lai don si trais" (vv. 10–12—"I know that his miserable family will end like a *lai* and will turn back where it came from"). Cf. Appel, "Zur Formenlehre des provenzalischen Minnesangs," ZRPh 53 (1958): 161. Cf. also the canso "S'al cor plagues" of Folquet de Marseille, written only shortly afterwards (P.-C. 155,18); for both excerpts, see also Baum, "Les troubadours," p. 33. Of course, Appel's remark (ibid., p. 168, n. 2) concerning Bertran de Born, is also true for both excerpts. It says that it is possible that the term *lay* "may in fact refer to the northern French genre."

27. Appel, "Vom Descort," p. 230.
28. Appel, "Zur Formenlehre," pp. 162 ff.; cf. also Baum, *Le descort*, pp. 87 ff.
29. Maillard, *Evolution et esthétique*, p. 379.
30. Baum, *Le descort*, pp. 97 ff.

2

Toward an Aesthetic of the Provençal Lyric II:
Marcabru's *Dire vos vuoill ses doptansa*
(BdT 293, 18)

Stephen G. Nichols, Jr.

In a radical application of formalism to the northern French lyric of the twelfth and early thirteenth centuries, Paul Zumthor postulates the concept of "register," "formally conceived as a set of paradigms and the corpus of songs as a set of syntagmatic features."

> What I have called 'register' is the only perceptible referent to poetic language which the tradition provides for us, since other living cultural connections are lacking. It is what at once provokes and satisfies the reader's expectations. In the register are rooted the conventions which determine what one may call the stylistic sensibility. While in modern poetry the connotations of the work permit us to infer that extratextual thing called History, those of the *grand chant courtois* refer only to the *text*—which is the register. It is at that level that the 'classemes' of the semantic constitution are determined. Register can be formally conceived . . . as a complex of motivations, as a pre-existent network of lexical, rhetorical, and even syntactic probabilities; as a system of pre-established equivalences, register constitutes the basis of the poetic expression of the *trouvère*: it provides him with a set of predetermined poetic requirements.[1]

It is this register that provides the text, for Zumthor, with poetic coher-

15

ence, and in doing so, operates as much on the level of interpretation as on the level of performance or creation.

Register assumes the existence of a socially homogeneous situation—namely, an encoder, the poet, and a decoder, the audience, who share the same ideological and axiological situation—in short, the same tradition. The creation/performance of the lyric, for Zumthor, is an almost simultaneous social act, a dual act of creation/encoding-listening decoding, very much akin to the act of language itself:

> As long as the tradition of the *grand chant courtois* continued in its prime, register could be defined interchangeably either from the viewpoint of the encoder (the poet) or of the decoder (his public): their viewpoints coincided.[2]

Zumthor, then, sees the medieval lyric tradition as anonymous and collective. Even when we know the names of particular poets, he denies that we really know anything more than their names, perhaps a few approximate dates, and what appears in the texts of their poems. Indeed he points out that what appears in the poems of known poets differs little from the form and content of anonymous ones. There is no subject, no subjectivity in this lyric. The role of the poet qua individual in the genesis of any given poem is secondary. We are, he asserts, "in the presence of an almost totally objectified poetry: I mean by that a poetry whose subject escapes us."[3]

As Zumthor makes clear in his distinction between the modes register and *écriture*, it is impossible to speak of an individual poetic style before the second half of the thirteenth century. He uses écriture for what is not register rather than the Saussurian *langue* or the Hjelmslevian *schéma* for its more exact correspondence to the literary object.[4] The relation of register to écriture, is defined as follows:

> Register is a feature of *écriture* . . . that of a state of language possessing a certain autonomy, an 'interior essence' with its own generative rules, to be distinguished from language on the one hand and individual style on the other . . . . Despite the 'I' who programmatically controls the poem, the writing appears to be divested completely of personal origin.[5]

But writing cannot be divested of personal origin without a corresponding renunciation on the part of the audience: there can be no personal identification of the listener with the "I" of the poem, no fiction of participating in the experience. The act of decoding, for Zumthor, was, like the act of creation, a collective one: a dialectic between the conventional, "individual" voice of the register and the "interior essence" of the *écriture*.

That Zumthor is referring to the northern French lyric tradition in his theory is perfectly clear, but he assumes this theory to have originated with the earliest troubadours:

> As we know, the *canso* was created in Old Provençal by the troubadours of the first half of the twelfth century . . . [the *trouvères*] inherited the *canso* after it had reached its point of equilibrium, at the moment of its classic flowering, already beyond the fuss and conflicts occasioned in the course of its progressive development. [The *trouvères*] received it as a dynamic body of mental and expressive tendencies, and of rules of structural formation. They did little more than adapt the basic terminology to their own language, which, as a matter of fact, was already close enough to the original. The functions of the French terms thus substituted for their Provençal originals remained the same.[6]

It is clear from this quotation, and others one could cite, that Zumthor's range is sweeping and of great import for the traditionally held notions of the medieval poet. Despite the little that is known of the poets responsible for creating the medieval lyric, their individual creative physiognomies have been seen and felt in their works in a way that has not been possible, for example, regarding the anonymous poets of the epic tradition. If Zumthor's theories prevail, all this must be revised. There will be only individual songs and a collective canso tradition; the shadowy figures of the master poets long cherished, however imperfectly known, will be relegated to the role of identifying labels.

If this be necessary in the name of the progress of literary science, then by all means let us forgo sentiment and reform our mode of perception accordingly. But first it may be prudent to test some of the assumptions of Zumthor's radical formalism. Rather than following his example in taking the whole for the part, let us reverse the process and take a small part, or ultimately a series of small parts, to see what insight may be gained regarding the nature of the whole lyric tradition.

In other words, let us substitute metonymy for synecdoche, the micro-scope for the wide-angle lens.

The twelfth-century troubadour Marcabru, who wrote between 1130 and 1150, offers an excellent starting point for such an undertaking. He is not the first troubadour, and so may be considered in light of an emergent, if not established, tradition. On the other hand, he belongs indisputedly to that exclusive and elusive category of artists whom Pound called "inventors"—"men who found a new process, or whose extant work gives us the first known example of a process."[7] He "invented" the pastourelle as we know it; he gave us the most striking early examples of crusade songs; he was the first to make consistent use of compound word-formations, to exploit the poetic potential of rarer forms of familiar words, and to specialize in rich rhymes—all devices that Arnaut Daniel later made his stock-in-trade, thereby earning for himself Dante's famous accolade. All of these facts have won for Marcabru a special place among the early troubadours, giving him the possibly unjust distinction of singularity. This traditional view was most pungently summed up by Alfred Jeanroy:

> When approaching Marcabru, one has the feeling of meeting a true poet, a vigorous and original temperament; but a persistent obscurity, a bizarreness which it is difficult not to attribute to willfulness, makes the reading of his poetry a tedious task.[8]

Not the most grateful of appreciations, and not even true by con-temporary standards, but Jeanroy's opinion does serve notice that even to his detractors, Marcabru presented a definite image of individuality. In short, it has been accepted dogma that one could speak of a partic-ular style as identifiably Marcabru's own. If Zumthor's theories are to be corroborated by practical criticism, one should attempt to demon-strate that what has heretofore been considered idiosyncratic or original in Marcabru's poetry belongs, rather, to the "pre-established network of lexical, rhetorical and syntactic possibilities" which Zumthor calls "register."

Looking broadly at the formal characteristics of Marcabru's oeuvre, uniqueness and variety stand out as characteristics of his metrical repertory. One does not find in his work the architectonic complexity of subsequent troubadours, such as Bernart de Ventadorn, Raimbaut d'Aurenga, or Arnaut Daniel, with whom the almost baroque intricacies of *coblas capcaudadas* and the rest are commonplace. Rather, one finds an imaginative variation within a limited repertory of stanzaic patterning.

Of the forty-one songs ascribed to Marcabru in the long out-moded, but still the only complete critical edition by Dejeanne,[9] almost half, seventeen to be precise, have unique metric schemes—that is, they have separate entries in Frank's *Répertoire métrique de la poésie des troubadours*.[10] Another eighteen songs, while sharing a main entry with other troubadours, have separate subentries, indicating significant variation in metrical pattern from the other songs listed in the same entry. These eighteen may thus be considered unique as well.[11] In all, then, thirty-five of Marcabru's forty-one poems show significant variation from the rest of the troubadour canon in their metrical structures; four of these are sufficiently problematical in their structural patterning to have occasioned different interpretations of the metrical scheme in Dejeanne and Frank.[12]

Taking the rhyme patterns of Marcabru's forty-one songs, we find still further deviation from the norms. Hendrik Van der Werf calculated recently that "the troubadours chose either *abba* . . . or *abab* . . . as the rhyme scheme of the *frons* [first section of the traditional medieval lyric strophe] for about two-thirds of their poems, with the former pattern being slightly more common than the latter."[13] In Marcabru, less than one-half of the poems show this kind of patterning (fifteen out of forty-one), and of those that do, four-fifths have precisely the rhyme scheme, *abab* . . . , found by Van der Werf to be the less common. Van der Werf asserts that stanzaic division into the two parts *frons* and *cauda* was so common in troubadour and trouvère poetry as to have constituted "a stereotyped form."[14] Marcabru conforms only grudgingly to this stereotype. While a majority of the poems do allow a bipartite stanzaic division (twenty-seven of the forty-one), only eleven of them have the form—four lines + three/six—suggested by Van der Werf's statistics; three others show a 4/2 variant of that form, while five more have an exact 4/4 division in which the cauda is a mirror image of the frons. Eight of the twenty-seven show a precise 3/3 division not uncommon with the troubadours.[15]

On this very superficial, statistical level of formal structure, Marcabru does possess a certain singularity. But to understand the nature of troubadour poetry, one must, as I have pointed out elsewhere, examine the stanzaic structure itself, for it is the *cobla* that constitutes the essence of the poem.[16] In this respect, Marcabru's coblas reveal what would seem to be an interesting intention. As in the coblas of the first troubadour, Guillaume IX, we find little emphasis upon obvious external form, that is, complex interstanzaic patterning, end-rhyme schemes— the sort of thing, in short, which led ultimately to the creation of the sestina by Arnaut Daniel. Marcabru's coblas appear, rather, to emphasize a formal virtuosity at the level of audio-visual verbal interplay; it is *within* the cobla that we find Marcabru expending his poetic energy to achieve formal effects not often found in other troubadours.

The vast majority of Marcabru's songs have the kind of stanza linking which stresses the individual cobla. Twenty-nine of the forty-one songs are either *coblas singulars* or *coblas unissonans* (thirteen have the former, sixteen, the latter).[17] The remaining twelve songs may be broken down into eight *coblas doblas*, a form that stresses pairs of stanzas— again emphasizing a structural unit smaller than the whole song; and four *coblas alternadas*, a form that divides the song into two sets of coblas unissonans.

Rarely do we find a troubadour with a corpus as extensive as Marcabru's yet with so restrained a repertory of stanzaic patterning. To some extent, this fact must be ascribed to choice rather than to Marcabru's place near the beginning of the tradition. For when he does choose to use a complex stanzaic patterning, as with the coblas alternadas, we do not find an awkward adumbration but, on the contrary, a sophisticated execution of the form. Similarly, the virtuoso verbal interplay characteristic of many of his coblas, linked formally by the simple *singulars* or *unissonans* forms, exhibits a sophistication which belies any thought that we are dealing with a naïve or unskilled poet.

Turning from the general to the specific, let us consider the structural formation of the cobla as illustrated by Marcabru's sirventes, *Dire vos vuoill ses doptansa* (BdT 293, 18). The song has attracted little critical attention despite the fact that it is fairly well known for the "biographical information" offered in the last stanza:

> Marcabrus, lo fills Na Bruna
> fo engenratz en tal luna
> qu'el sap d'amor cum degruna.
> Escoutatz!

> Quez anc non amet neguna
> ni d'autra non fo amatz.

[ll. 73–78][18]

> [Marcabru, the son of Lady Bruna
> was begotten under such a moon
> that he knows how love goes to seed.
> Listen!
> For he never loved any woman
> nor was he ever loved by any.]

Yet it offers an invaluable focal point for our purposes for two excellent reasons: it is one of the four songs of Marcabru for which we still possess musical notation; and it is precisely one of the songs whose metrical form is not entirely unique. It thus allows us to study the dialectic between preexisting form and individual use.

The formal coordinates of the cobla are a six-line stanza rhymed *aaaBab*. There is a clear-cut frons/cauda division—which for the moment we shall call 4/2—seemingly rendered more emphatic by the *B*-rhyme line which is a refrain word, *Escoutatz*! The basic pattern, *aaabab* is also used by Marcabru in number XXIX of Dejeanne's edition, *L'autrier, a l'issida d'abriu*, but with metrical variations.

Fortunately, we can discover something about the preexistent nature of this cobla form because Guillaume IX, whose stanza forms Marcabru utilized in other songs,[19] employed varying forms of the same pattern for three of his twelve songs.[20] Bernard Marti, a troubadour traditionally seen as a disciple of Marcabru, also accounts for one of the subentries under this heading in Frank. Among them, these three early troubadours account for six of the nine variants of this metrical scheme.

All three of the examples in Guillaume IX utilize lines of mixed length, as does Marcabru's *Dire vos vuoill*, and of these three, two have markedly different line-lengths (eight syllables and four). Like Marcabru, Guillaume IX uses coblas singulars. Perhaps the most useful for purposes of comparison with Marcabru's song is Guillaume's *Farai un vers de dreyt nien*. I quote the first stanza.

> Farai un vers de dreyt nien
> Non er de mi ni d'autre gen
> Non er d'amor ni de joven

Ni de ren au
Qu'enans fo trobatz en durmen
Sobre chevau.

[ll. 1–6, Jeanroy ed.]

[I'll make a poem about pure nothing
Not of me nor you nor other being
Neither love's nor youth's praise will it sing
Nor subject larger
For it's a song composed while sleeping
Astride my charger][21]

An analysis of the three categories of sound, syntax, and vocabulary should allow a fairly complete description of stanzaic structure and has the added advantage, for the purposes of our inquiry, of corresponding to the categories Zumthor used. As may be seen, the stanza's basic metrical scheme is

$$\frac{\text{a a a b a b}}{\text{8 8 8 4 8 4}}$$

The rhymes are all masculine, and there is a clear 4/2 frons/cauda division even though, syntactically, the stanza constitutes a single period.[22] Lines 1–3 divide precisely into hemistiches of equal length (4 + 4); and line 4, the first short line, is—syntactically as well as metrically—a mirror-image of the second hemistiches of lines 2–3. The end-rhyme sounds of the frons and cauda are –en and au. The alternation of the b-rhyme au with the a-rhyme –en is anticipated as early as the second line, where the two sounds appear in quick succession at the end of the line: au (tre) gen. The use of internal syllables to anticipate or echo end-rhyme sounds is a technique Marcabru employs frequently, as we shall have occasion to see. Like Marcabru, Guillaume uses the alternating sounds within the same line as a kind of phonic counterpoint. Thus the au (tre) gen of line 2 (an a-rhyme line) is reversed in line 4, the first b-rhyme line: ren au. Line 5, the first line of the cauda—and its only a-rhyme line—has as many en sounds as the three a-rhyme lines of the frons:

Qu'enans fo trobatz en durmen.

Here, rather than an alternation of a/b rhyme sounds, we find an emphatic repetition of the same rhyme sound, as though to stress the identity of this line with the *a*-rhyme lines of the frons (and indeed, like line one, the content refers to the creative act).

The frons, then, contains four examples of the *a*-rhyme sound (one used internally), while the cauda has three (two internal). Similarly, and as though to stress the primacy of the frons (four lines) over the cauda (two lines), we find there two examples of the *b*-rhyme sound (one internal) as opposed to a single occurrence in the cauda. There will be much to say about the structural use of internal rhyme in Marcabru's song, but what we have already seen in Guillaume's piece demonstrates that Jeanroy's laconic assertion that "internal rhyme is a refinement appearing only occasionally in a work"[23] is just another example of his failure to accord the phonic structure of the cobla its full value.

Another set of binary sound alternations may be discerned in the frons: the higher pitched *i* and the lower pitched *en*. *Nien*, the rhyme word of line 1, introduces this phonic alternation, which is immediately reinforced at three stressed points in line 2: at the caesura, at the beginning of the second hemistich, and in rhyme position, *mi ni . . . gen*. The pattern is repeated in the same positions of the second hemistich of line 3 and, with only the variation necessary to accommodate the new rhyme, in line 4: *ni de joven/ ni de ren*.

Another, less extensive sound pattern is the alliterative system created by the anaphora of the first hemistiches of lines 2–3; *non er de mi/ non er d'amor*. In both lines, the alliteration of the first hemistich is echoed in the second and carried over into line 4: . . . *ni d'autre gen/ . . . ni de joven/ ni de ren*.

In the cauda, it is line 5, already remarked for its internal echoing of the *a*-rhyme, that provides still another set of internal rhymes and assonances: *fo tro(b)–* and *–ans . . . atz*. Finally, we might note en passant, that the internal rhymes *fo tro(b)–* are echoed by *so(b)–* of line 6.

The tightly organized sound-patterning of the cobla, especially the frons, is facilitated by a syntactic feature: the extensive anaphoric structure of lines 2–4. This structure creates a 1 + 3 division in the frons in which the main clause, announced in line 1, is paratactically prolonged by parenthetical "fillers" that extend or clarify the sense of the main clause without taking it further—at least not in a strict narrative sense. The subordinate clause introduced by *que* constitutes the cauda. Note how closely the cauda mirrors in miniature the syntax of the frons: just as the frons has one line of "business" followed by three lines of paratactic expansion, so the cauda has one line of essential information followed by a line of commentary expanding on the first. Thus, at the levels of sound and syntax, the frons establishes a pattern to be followed by the cauda. This will be extremely important for Marcabru's stanza conception in *Dire vos vuoill*.

Unavoidably, we have already come into contact with lexical features in discussing the sound and syntax of this stanza. Given the repetitions characteristic of the sound-patterning and the syntactic features that make them possible, it is hardly surprising to find, in examining the vocabulary, recurring adverbs and conjunctions in the frons: *non . . . ni/ non . . . ni/ni*. These recurring negative particles create a semantic charge in which the idea of absence dominates, a spinning out of the idea of *nien* in line 1. Because of them, all of the nouns or noun substitutes in the stanza, with the exception of *vers* (l. 1) and *chevau* (l. 6) are evoked negatively, or rather their absence is evoked positively and emphatically. The two principal verbs, the one of the main clause, the other of the subordinate, are affirmative and refer to the act of creating.

We have, then, affirmative verbs of creation acting upon negative noun locutions, precisely as affirmed by the first line. Something and nothing, the challenge half-humorously, half-seriously issued in this first line, has been realized in the tension of opposites carried through the stanza at every level. If the tension is resolved in favor of the something—the created stanza—this too was foreseen. But it is less the content that concerns us here than the fact that the stanzaic structure of this cobla—repeated with varying degrees of success throughout the remainder of the song—was generated by a dialectic of form and language consciously and deliberately manipulated by a knowing subject— more than that, a known subject. In this stanza, we perceive a poetic self-consciousness capable of creating a song in the absence of conventional subject matter—a song whose subject matter is the creative act itself and whose purpose is the creation of pure poetic object. At the risk of romanticizing, one cannot but discern the shade of a poet asking: what is poetry? But that is matter for another essay. Let me turn back from my excursion into Guillaume's domain to that of Marcabru.

Keeping in mind the first stanza of *Farai un vers de dreyt nien*, let us look at the beginning of Marcabru's song:

> Dire vos vuoill ses doptansa
> d'aquest vers la comensansa;
> li mot fan de ver semblansa
>   Escoutatz!
> Qui ves proessa balansa
> semblansa fai de Malvatz.
>
>   [ll. 1–6]

> [I want to tell you without fear
> about this song's beginning;
> the words are truth revealed.
>   Listen!
> He who would from valor waver
> reveals his evil nature.]

The most obvious difference between the appearance of this stanza and that of Guillaume is the alternation of feminine and masculine rhymes and the differing line-lengths, particularly the use of the refrain word as the short line. The latter is rhythmically, visually, and emotionally the most obvious feature of the cobla. Both in the original and in translation, the interjection of *Escoutatz!* in mid-stanza tends to break the rhythmical flow. Guillaume's cobla encouraged that flow by the use of syntax and sound-patterning. Other songs by Guillaume utilized variations of the same syntactic method to bind the frons and cauda into a progressively flowing unit. If the syntax of his coblas was paratactic, it was also sequential. The eruption of *Escoutatz!* in the middle of Marcabru's stanza dramatically separates it into two parts without obvious linkage between them. *Escoutatz!* even modifies the expected 4/2 frons/cauda division clearly authorized by the rhyme scheme, for it stands between the two parts of the stanza rather than serving as the final line of the frons. In short, *Escoutatz!* divides the stanza into two mini-poems.

This suggests an emergent dialectic between form and language—a tension, such as we saw in Guillaume's song, that will generate the structure best able to resolve the tension. A formal element—the refrain word, which is also, syntactically, an apostrophe without obvious connection to what precedes or follows it, and which, finally, happens to have a harsh phonic value—divides the stanza. Yet the stanza remains a poetic unit which, as such, must be cohesive. So other formal elements are called upon to generate, under the imposed conditions, a new means of order capable of incorporating the divisive element without destroying its value.

There is an obvious circularity here, in which form creates the problem that form must resolve; but it is the circularity of the creative process generally. The specific formal problem posed by the stanza divided in this particular way is new; the situation of this song and no other. To solve the problem, the poet must draw at once upon the preexisting tradition—what he has learned and assimilated from others —and upon his own talent as a poet, a talent revealed and refined in just such situations. The circularity thus begins and ends in the poet's consciousness, proving that he is indeed there and may be known.

Looking at the metrical scheme of the stanza, we begin to see how Marcabru created the elements of order by which to overcome the initial impression of fragmentation. The lines are unequally distributed between seven-syllable feminine *a*-rhymes and masculine *b*-rhymes of two different lengths (three syllables and seven syllables). An almost identical stanza configuration may be seen in another of Guillaume IX's songs, *Farai chansoneta nueva* (BdT 183, 6). Here too, we find feminine *a*-rhymes alternating with masculine *b*-rhymes, but the stanza does not have any problematical formal element to disrupt it. Not having Marcabru's problem of unity, Guillaume IX has only two of the coblas singulars of *Farai chansoneta nueva* rhyme on variants of the sound *a*.

In *Dire vos vuoill*, on the other hand, we find that all of the coblas singulars are rhymed on variants of *a*: *-ansa, -isa, -uia, -igna, -era, -ega, -osca, -eigna, -una*. Since the *b*-rhyme *-atz* is constant throughout, doubly emphasized, in fact, by the refrain word, we are justified in seeing in the song a phonic modulation on the sound *a*.[24] This pattern of tonal unity is confirmed by Friedrich Gennrich's modern interpretation of the musical notation for the song preserved in Manuscript R (Paris, Bibl. Nat., franç, 22543).

In Gennrich's text, one finds the syllables in *a*, in the first stanza, receiving over half of the notes, while of the ten neumes in Gennrich's transcription, six of them correspond to *a* syllables.[25] (See p. 27).

As Gennrich's transcription shows, the modulation on *a* is not confined to the end rhyme, though it is strongest there. It figures as part

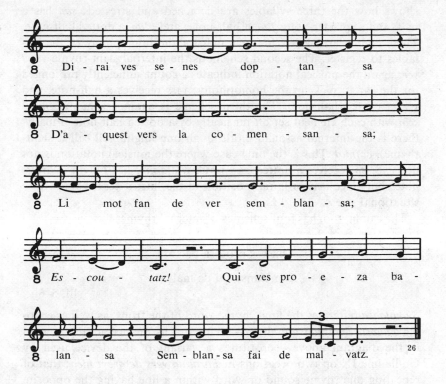

of a larger system of sound-patterning which constitutes a salient aspect of the stanza structure. This sound-patterning contains a number of elements, the most prominent being the internal rhyme/assonance and alliteration. The internal rhymes and assonances form both "vertical" and "horizontal" patterns, visually speaking, since they are found in two or more lines as well as within the same one. Often, both vertical and horizontal patterns are used in close association. In lines 2–3, for example,

d'aquest vers la comensansa
li mot fan de ver semblansa

we find four schemes of internal rhyme and assonance. First, *fan* echoes *san* of *comensansa* and *blan* of *semblansa*. The musical notation shows how the three syllables are detached and stressed: *san* has a half- and a quarter-note: *fan*, a half-note; and *blan*, a dotted half-note. These counts are clearly long enough for the homophony of the syllables to register. The second scheme is the internal slant-rhyme *vers/ver*: again the musical notation indicates a count sufficiently prolonged for the ear to pick up the homophony; *vers* receives a half-note, and *ver*, a dotted half-note. The third scheme is again assonantal, *men/sem* with each element set off musically by a dotted half-note. Finally, there is the internal assonance (although one might well call it slant-rhyme), *co/mot*. This is the only case where the musical notation is not decisive: *co* receives a dotted half-note, while *mot* has only a quarter-note; but since it is in initial position in the line, it receives a certain situational stress.

The cauda, too, has four schemes of internal rhyme:

3   3 2 4 1 2
Qui ves proessa balansa
1 2   4
semblansa fai de malvatz

[ll. 5–6]

Semblansa reiterates the final rhyme word of the frons, as well as echoing *balansa*. Semblansa/malvatz—an internal assonance not represented in the diagram above—constitutes a variant of the device used by Guillaume IX on two occasions in *Farai un vers de dreyt nien*: that of repeating one rhyme sound or word within a line having the opposite rhyme in terminal position. The device may be used to anticipate the introduction of the opposite rhyme, as in line 2 of *Farai un vers*; to signal a transition from one rhyme to the other, as in line 4 of the same song; or to give a kind of final recapitulation of the rhymes at the end of a stanza, as in this case.[27] The device is particularly striking here, since *semblansa* not only repeats a whole *a*-rhyme word, but follows hard upon the final *a*-rhyme, *balansa*. The musical notation corroborates the importance of this combination, since *balansa/semblansa* are set off by neumes, thereby giving them a lengthened count of at least a whole measure apiece (the first *semblansa* takes up a measure and a half).

As may be seen from the diagram of lines 5–6, above, *balansa* and *semblansa* also participate in other internal rhyme patterns. *Proessa/balansa/semblansa* all terminate with the syllable *-sa*. *Ba-* of *balansa*

makes at least an assonance with *mal-* of *malvatz*, although the anticipated *l* which begins the second syllable of *balansa*, makes the assonance in this case almost a full rhyme. The same may be said of *ves/
pro-e-ssa* in line 5. These last two cases are of interest, for when taken
with *fan/blan* (l. 3) and *vers/ver* (ll. 2–3), they demonstrate a technique
for a musical intensifying of the homophony. In each case, the first
rhyme element introduces the sound with a quarter—or a half-note,
while the repeated, second element receives a longer count (or in the
case of *mal-*, l. 6, a neume). Before abandoning this part of the analysis,
we should note that *ves/pro-e-ssa* include yet another element in their
pattern, since they rhyme internally with the first syllable of *Es-cou-
tatz!*, the refrain word.

Alliteration is the last major category we must consider in studying
the sound-patterning of this stanza. Martin Scholz was the first scholar
in the twentieth century to make a full-fledged study of alliteration in
the poetry of the troubadours, and his work still remains the only major
study.[28] Of all the early troubadours, Marcabru has the highest per-
centage of alliteration, according to Scholz. Although not concerned
with the role of sound-patterning as a structural device, Scholz did note
the existence of alliterative chains over several lines.

The first three lines of *Dire vos vuoill* contain several alliterative
chains, some of which run throughout the frons while others exist only
in single lines. The frons contains four chains:[29]

   1. d/t: *Dire* . . . *do*t*ansa/d'aques*t . . . */mo*t . . . *de* [ll. 1–3]
   2. v/f: *vos vuoill* . . . */vers* . . . */fan* . . . *ver* [ll. 1–3]
   3. q/c: *aquest* . . . *comensansa* [l. 2]
   4. s/z: *vos* . . . *ses doptansa/aquest vers* . . . *comensansa/* . . .
      semblansa [ll. 1–3]

Three of these chains, d/t, q/c, and s/z, are echoed in the refrain word
E*s-cou-*t*atz!* Moving to the cauda, we also find four alliterative chains,
three continued from the frons and one new one.

   1. s/z: *ves proessa balansa/semblansa* . . . *malvatz.*
   2. v/f: *ves* . . . */ . . . fai de malvatz.*[30]
   3. q/c: *Es-cou-tatz/Qui* . . .
   4. p/b: *proessa balansa*

Alliteration in this stanza falls into two categories: major chains recurring over two or more lines and generally carried through from frons to cauda—in several cases via the refrain word—and minor alliterative associations occurring only in one line. The major chains join the other elements of sound-patterning to establish an identifiable network of relationships that we may call the phonic physiognomy of the stanza. That the cohesiveness of the stanza should be so dependent on a strong phonic physiognomy, an aural image as it were, should hardly be surprising when one recalls that the songs could not have had the visual impact in the Middle Ages that they have for us who use modern critical editions. It is not impossible that Marcabru himself never saw his songs written out. The coblas really needed a strong phonic physiognomy, a writing in the ear, if not in the air, as it were. If the sound-patterning seems excessive to modern taste, we may put it down to a need to "overwrite" so that the major sound patterns could be recognized. In fact, it should not seem strange to us; strong sound-patterning has become a major force in the contemporary poetic sensibility, and not only in such poets as Gerard Manley Hopkins or Dylan Thomas.[31]

The fragmented cobla we began with has now attained its proper image of harmony and cohesiveness, thanks to our understanding of its tightly unified sound structure. Perhaps because the challenge to unity was so much stronger, Marcabru's cobla attains a more sophisticated sound-patterning than Guillaume's, even though the latter possessed at least an adumbration of all the elements found in Marcabru. Whether this should be ascribed to individual choice and talent, or rather to technical advances in the art, cannot be determined. Given the proximity of the two, the former factor would seem at least as likely as the latter, although a combination of the two might be nearer the truth.

Strong as it is, the sound-patterning does not entirely abolish the tension between harmony and fragmentation with which we began. The sound-patterning exists in a dialectical relationship with the syntax, the source of the fragmenting impulse in this cobla. All of the stanzas in the song consist of two periods, corresponding to the frons/cauda division, with the refrain-word apostrophe interjected between them. This syntactic pattern accords very well with the nature of the periods, a series of didactic apothegms. Whereas Guillaume's song possessed at least an embryonic narrative, *Dire vos vuoill* does not. The stanzas are, rather, a series of assertions, two per stanza, which on inspection turn out to be carefully balanced. We have, thus, something of the opposite situation to what we found in Guillaume. In his song, there was binary opposition at the level of sound, but harmony in the syntax; here there is harmony in the sound-patterning, thanks mainly to the prevailing modulation on *a*, while syntax creates a binary opposition between the two parts of the cobla.

It would thus seem characteristic of the troubadour stanza, at least at this stage of its history, to contain within itself dialectical elements, opposing forces subdued into a general unity in which they remain perceptible but are contained. This fact may well constitute one of the constants in troubadour songs, an element of écriture, an expectation of poet and audience alike that figures in the process of creation and completion or, to use Zumthor's terms, encoding and decoding.

Marcabru's syntax is hypotactic, in keeping with the nature of the sirventes, a genre representing the world both as appearance and as reality. In Marcabru's case, this meant representing the world as he saw it and as he thought it should be. Gnomic or proverbial sayings are generally straightforward declarations, and this is precisely what we encounter here, with certain inversions of word order to accommodate poetic exigencies. Elsewhere, I have described the poetic experience offered by the gnomic mode as expressed in the cansos of Arnaut Daniel.[32] The essence of this mode is dispassionate observation. Although the question of emotional tone is more properly the province of the semantic than the syntactic structure, let us note here that the syntax of this sirventes does establish the kind of rhetorical distance appropriate to the gnomic mode.

By splitting the cobla into three distinct statements, Marcabru creates a balanced unit of commentary, in which the frons presents a specific image, while the cauda offers a generalized apothegm, a truism capable of being cited out of context. The connection made between the two statements, at the level of syntax, is more apparent than real, the result of the refrain-word, an I-thou intervention by the poet directing the listener's attention to the maxim which follows. We are left to assume that the maxim has been elicited by the image given in the frons, but this rapport is certainly not inevitable.

To understand to what extent the relationship between the frons and the cauda is a necessary one—as the sound-patterning suggests—one must look, not to the syntax but to the vocabulary. For it is here that the words assume their conceptual meaning, in the way they interact in the context of a given cobla, in the work as a whole, and by comparison with the preexisting tradition. In the last respect, Marcabru's vocabulary has a reputation for idiosyncrasy.[33]

Like *Farai un vers de dreyt nien*, Marcabru's song begins with reference to itself and its content. Guillaume refused to admit external reference to his song, even claiming that it was conceived at a moment when he could not have been in touch with external reality. Marcabru, on the other hand, makes just the opposite assertion. He wants to begin a song whose words will represent the truth; that is, his song will offer a faithful mimesis of external reality, at least as he sees it. Since he also says that he will declaim his verse "without fear," we are led to expect that the mimesis will be unvarnished enough to arouse sensibilities, if not tempers.

All these impressions spring from the interplay of five substantives in the frons, substantives we have already encountered in the sound-patterning. They are the three end-rhyme words, *doptansa, comensansa, semblansa* (to which we join the verb *fan*, already associated with them by the sound-patterning), and the internally rhymed pair, *vers*, "song"/ *ver*, "truth." *Li mot*, "the words," is the only other substantive in the frons, and it is syntactically joined to *ver* and *semblansa*.[34]

Both Guillaume's and Marcabru's opening stanzas thus postulate an axis of reality/revelation of reality, and that axis controls the nature of the vocabulary for the rest of the song, just as the poetic form determines the form of subsequent stanzas or, a fortiori, the musical form requires subsequent stanzas to be sung to it. Once again, we encounter the circularity discussed earlier. The poetic positioning of vocabulary creates the semantic field, which in turn determines the nature of the reality revealed. But it is the revealed reality—that is, the signified— which determines the reality valuation of the signifier. Marcabru's *mot* ("words") cannot help but *fan de ver semblansa* because they *are* the *semblansa* (the "representation" or "manifestation")[35] and the *ver*. Hence the brilliance of the internal rhyme *vers/ver*, which now becomes more than a rhyme, a *calembour* as well. The *vers* is *ver* because it *is*,— that is, by virtue of existing as poetic assertion. In the *vers*, Marcabru will create a world that will then be a *semblansa de ver*, presumably as opposed to the unrepresented world which is *semblansa de malvatz*. In other words, the poem is a mimesis of metamorphosis, the metamorphosis being the transformation of preexisting potential signifiers into a *real* signifier, the poetry.[36]

We now have the means to refine our understanding of the relationship of the frons and the cauda. The two are connected on a conceptual axis of metamorphosis/mimesis. The frons is the place of metamorphosis, the forge where potential signifiers become concrete signifier, thereby constituting a signified, a transformed image of "reality"—the reality of the poetic image. On this axis, the cauda is a mimesis of the transformed reality of the frons. The proverbial character of the cauda statement, its air of collective wisdom, gives an imprimatur to the frons. We cannot *not* assent to the wisdom of the cauda, and therefore we approve the truth of the frons of which the cauda is a mimetic representation. Frons and cauda thus exist in a signified/signifier relationship, in which the truth object or signified is the frons; the signifier, the cauda. Between the two stands the magical word *Escoutatz*! exhorting us to attend to the poet's conjurations.

Back again to our starting point, we see that we have been discovering answers to the initial questions all along. The opening stanzas of Guillaume's and Marcabru's songs are important for more than what they have to tell us about their relationship to the rest of the song. Because they are the models on which subsequent stanzas must be based, they stand in relation to the latter much as the song is said, by formalists, to stand in relation to the preexisting tradition. But even with so domesticated a version of the Zumthorian hypothesis, one feels uneasy. For how are those subsequent stanzas to be generated if not by the same knowing consciousness that created the model?

If this be so, how much more difficult it is, then, to imagine these first, paradigmatic stanzas being generated in any way other than by the interplay of a creative imagination with a preexisting but still potential tradition. It requires the kind of vision we saw in Guillaume IX and Marcabru to see what is not *yet* there, what has not *yet* been done with that tradition, and to transform this vision into a song as rich as *Dire vos vuoill ses doptansa.*

The potential elements for Marcabru's song preexisted in the poems of Guillaume IX. But Guillaume's songs do not have the same voice as Marcabru's; they do not have the portentous *Escoutatz*!, with all that we found to depend on and issue from it. Guillaume did not conceive of the axis of metamorphosis/mimesis that Marcabru uses so effectively.

The potential elements of Marcabru's song may have existed in Guillaume, but the vision and experience which transformed them came from elsewhere. And that elsewhere can only have been in the consciousness of the creator known to us imperfectly, but concretely, as Marcabru.

NOTES

1. "Style and Expressive Register in Medieval Poetry," in *Literary Style: A Symposium*, ed. Seymour Chatman (London: Oxford University Press, 1971), p. 273.

2. "Aussi longtemps que s'était maintenue, dans sa vigueur première, la tradition du grand chant courtois, le registre pouvait se définir indifféremment du point de vue de l'encodeur (le poète) ou des décodeurs (son public): ses points de vue coïncidaient." Paul Zumthor, *Essai de poétique médiévale* (Paris: Seuil, 1972), p. 267.

3. ". . . nous sommes en présence d'une poésie presque totalement objectivée: je veux dire dont le sujet nous échappe." "La littérature médiévale," in *L'Enseignement de la littérature*, ed. Serge Doubrovsky and Tzvetan Todorov (Paris: Plon, 1971), p. 62. On the same page, he further asserts: "la littérature resta longtemps au Moyen Age, beaucoup plus qu'á d'autres époques, conditionnée par l'existence collective et que *les contemporains n'attachèrent qu'une importance relativement secondaire au rôle de l'individu dans la genèse du texte*" (my italics).

4. Roland Barthes includes *écriture* as one aspect of his concept of idiolect: "the language of a linguistic community, that is a group of persons who all interpret in the same way all linguistic statements: the idiolect would then correspond roughly to what we have attempted to describe . . . under the name '*écriture*'." *Elements of Semiology*, trans. Annette Lavers and Colin Smith (London: Jonathan Cape, 1967), p. 21.

5. Zumthor, "Style and Expressive Register," p. 267.

6. "La chanson, on le sait, fut créé en langue occitane, par les troubadours de la première moitié du XIIᵉ siècle. . . . [Les trouvères] reçurent la chanson parvenue à son point d'équilibre, dans son épanouissement classique, par-delà les remous et les conflits qu'avait provoqués sa progressive formation. Ils la reçurent comme un ensemble dynamique de tendances mentales et expressives et de règles de structuration. Ils ne firent guère qu'en adapter à leur propre langue, très proche, il est vrai, de l'originale, la couverture lexicale. Le fonctionnement des termes français ainsi substitués aux occitans resta le même." Zumthor, *Essai de poétique médiévale,* pp. 190–91.

7. Ezra Pound, *ABC of Reading* (New York: New Directions, 1960), p. 39.

8. "On a le sentiment, quand on aborde Marcabru, d'avoir affaire à un véritable poète, à un tempérament vigoureux et original; mais une obscurité, une bizarrerie

constantes, qu'il est bien difficile de ne pas attribuer à un parti pris, font de la lecture de ses vers une rebutante corvée." *La poésie lyrique des troubadours* (Toulouse: Privat, 1934), 2:24.

9. *Poésies complètes du troubadour Marcabru*, translation, notes, and glossaries by J-M.L. Dejeanne (Toulouse: Privat, 1909). A contemporary edition has been undertaken by the Italian scholar Aurelio Roncaglia. A half-dozen of Marcabru's songs edited by Roncaglia have been published so far.

10. István Frank, *Répertoire Métrique de la poésie des troubadours,* vol. 1, in *Bibliothèque de l'école des Hautes Etudes* 302 (1953). The poems in Dejeanne's edition are as follows (the numbers in parenthesis refer to the listings in Frank). I (54,1), II (733,1), IV (211,1), V (157,1), IX (190,1), XI (649,1), XVII (118,1), XIX (204,1), XXV (84,1), XXVI (84,2; these two songs have the same metrical scheme, but Marcabru is alone in using it), XXXI (371,1), XXXII (266,1), XXXV (456,1), XXXVI (282 a, 1; inadvertently omitted in Frank; I give the number of the *Répertoire* it should have), XXXVII (669,1), XL (167,1), XLIV (40,2; 40,1 is an anonymous fragment of only two stanzas).

11. III (476,3), VII (5,18), XIIbis (538,3), XIII (407,16), XIV (864,6), XV (91,8), XVIII (55,9), XXbis (193,8), XXI (223,5), XXII (91,9), XXIV (196,2), XXVIII (376,16), XXX (51,5), XXXIII (223,4), XXXIV (405,5), XXXVIII (430,6), XXXIX (405,6), XLII (376,13).

12. These are numbers IX, XXIV, XXXII, and XL.

13. *The Chansons of the Troubadours and Trouvères: A Study of the Melodies and their Relation to the Poems* (Utrecht: A. Oosthoek, 1972), p. 60.

14. Ibid.

15. Jeanroy, *La poésie lyrique,* 2: 71.

16. Stephen G. Nichols, Jr., "Toward an Aesthetic of the Provençal *Canso,*" in *The Disciplines of Criticism,* ed. Peter Demetz, Thomas Greene, and Lowry Nelson, Jr. (New Haven: Yale University Press, 1968), pp. 249–73. Van der Werf, *The Chansons of the Troubadours,* chaps. 3 and 4, finds the same thing. Zumthor, *Essai de poétique médiévale,* p. 193. says: "Le message que transmet la chanson ne peut être perçu qu'en tant qu'unité complexe, aux parties convergentes et à finalité expressive propre. Le lieu de convergence dans le grand chant courtois est la strophe plutôt que la chanson comme telle. Cette tendance de la poésie médiévale chantée, à se constituer en série d'unités relativement autonomes, atteint ici sa perfection, et s'accentue plutôt qu'elle ne se relâche à mesure qu'on avance dans le temps."

17. In *coblas singulars,* each stanza has a different rhyme-sound although, as in the songs we will examine shortly, a minority rhyme may remain the same from stanza to stanza. Thus, in number XVIII, the *a*-rhyme (4 lines) changes in each stanza, while the *b*-rhyme (2 lines) remains the same. *Coblas unissonans* are stanzas (*cobla*-stanza) having the same rhyme-sounds throughout the song.

18. The text of this stanza and stanza 1, to be discussed shortly, are taken from *Introduction à l'étude de l'ancien provençal,* ed. Hamlin, Ricketts, and Hathaway (Genève: Droz, 1967), pp. 67, 69. Hamlin et al. give the manuscript as it appears in MS A (Rome: Vatican Library 5232).

19. Five of Marcabru's songs share listings in Frank with Guillaume: IX, XVIII, XXIII, XXIV, XXIX. These five correspond to eight of the eleven extant songs of Guillaume.

20. These are numbers VIII, IV, and VII of Jeanroy's edition, *Les chansons de Guillaume IX*, 2d ed. (Paris: Champion, 1927).

21. Thomas G. Bergin has given a considerably freer rendition of this cobla: "I'll make some verses just for fun, / Not about me nor anyone, / Nor deeds that noble knights have done, / Nor love's ado— / I made them riding in the sun / (My horse helped, too.)" In *An Anthology of Medieval Lyrics*, ed. Angel Flores (New York: Modern Library, 1962), p. 6.

22. All of the stanzas but stanza 3 constitute a single period, and all show the same 4/2 division.

23. "La rime intérieure est un raffinement qui peut n'apparaître que ça et là dans une pièce; il n'est pratiqué systématiquement, à l'époque classique, que par Borneil et Daniel." *La poésie lyrique*, 2: 72–73.

24. The adumbration of such a phonic modulation exists in *Farai chansoneta nueva* where the *b*-rhymes are *-am*, but it is not carried through.

25. I use *neume* to mean "a group of a few notes sung over one syllable" (see Van der Werf, *Chansons of the Troubadours and Trouvères*, p. 157).

26. Musical texts from Erhard Lommatzsch, *Leben und Lieder der provenzalischen Troubadours*, with a musical supplement by Friedrich Gennrich (Berlin: Akademie Verlag, 1959), 2: 161.

27. In stanza 10 of *Dire vos vuoill*, Marcabru uses the reverse of this device in somewhat the same manner as Guillaume did in line 5 of *Farai un vers*—that is, we find internal repetition of the terminal rhyme: *leg'en lega* (l. 58); *etz dejus o disnatz* (l. 60, here slant rhyme). Lines 55 and 61 have examples of the obverse, i.e. internal *a*-rhyme in *b*-rhyme line and vice versa.

28. "Die Alliteration in der altprovenzalischen Lyrik," *Zeitschrift für romanische Philologie* 37 (1913): 385–426.

29. Scholz admits a wide variety of alliterative combinations: near-sound alliteration, internal syllabic alliteration, and so on. See his general introduction, ibid., pp. 386–410.

30. This chain is carried over into the first line of the second stanza: *Jovens faill e fraing e brisa* (l. 7).

31. M. L. Rosenthal has discussed this phenomenon cogently in *The New Poets* (London: Oxford University Press, 1967).

32. Nichols, "Toward an Aesthetic," pp. 366–73.

33. Thus Jeanroy: "Dans ses mots composés, qui ont tout l'air de créations personnelles, dans ses alliances de mots et ses métaphores, il y a d'étonnantes trouvailles." *La poésie lyrique*, 2: 29.

34. The substantives in the frons are structured on a vertical and horizontal axis of association / revelation. *Comensansa*, the longest of the three *a*-rhyme words of the frons, is three syllables plus the final feminine ending, which is traditionally not counted metrically although it does receive a lengthy count in the musical notation. *Doptansa* (2 syllables +) cannot be taken semantically by itself, because it makes a

semic unit with *ses* (it is *ses doptansa* that is revealed, not *doptansa*). *Ses doptansa* gives us the same count (3 syllables +) as *comensansa*. *Semblansa*, like *doptansa*, is also a 2-syllable- + count, and also like *doptansa* it makes a semic unit with *ver*, which immediately precedes it. *Ver semblansa* gives us the same 3-syllable- + count as in the two preceding lines. Vertically, then, we have a perfectly symmetrical terminal-rhyme series in the frons. To this symmetrical vertical axis of revelation must be joined a horizontal one, the individual lines themselves: each of these makes an assertion about "saying," "poem," and "words," and thus, when viewed schematically, together create a horizontal series whose meaning joins that of the vertical series. The horizontal and vertical axes compose a concrete image (both aural and visual) reinforcing the sequential meaning.

35. Susan M. Olson, in her study, "Marcabru's Psychomachy: The Concept of Vice and Virtue in the Twelfth-Century Troubadour" (Ph. D. diss., Yale University, 1969), p. 8.

36. I have previously discussed the problem of self-awareness in troubadour language and the concept of metamorphosis in my study, "Rhetorical Metamorphosis in the Troubadour Lyric," in *Mélanges de langue et de littérature médiévales offerts à Pierre Le Gentil* (Paris: SEDES, 1973), pp. 569–85.

3

Bertran de Born in Italy

William D. Paden, Jr.

The memorable figure of Bertram dal Bornio, who appears in the *Inferno*, canto 28 carrying his severed head before him by the hair, functions as a dramatis persona within the structure of the *Commedia*; through him Dante expresses certain dramatic and intellectual forces instrumental to the poem.[1] Only Bertram names the principle governing all the punishments of Hell, the *contrapasso*, using a term from Aquinas's commentary on the *Ethics* of Aristotle. Other sowers of discord whom Dante the pilgrim has encountered earlier in the ninth *bolgia* are guilty of dividing father from son, or king from nation. Bertram sums them up, since he declares he made the father and the son rebel against each other—that is, he caused the dispute between Henry II Plantagenet and his son Henry: *Io feci il padre e'l figlio in sé ribelli* (*Inferno* 28.136). Bertram conforms to the stylistic texture of the *poema sacro* by likening himself to Achitophel, who turned Absalom against David (2 Kings 15–18), and by echoing Lamentations 1:12 in line 132.

In none of these particulars does the damned soul faithfully represent the troubadour Bertran de Born, who flourished during the last two decades of the twelfth century. An awareness of eternity, gained through death and damnation, explains the biblical allusions and scholastic terminology (which have no precedents in Bertran's Provençal verse) but cannot account for the discrepancy between the grandeur of the sin which the soul confesses and the modest proportions of the living troubadour's true political influence. Bertran de Born did not make Henry Curtmantel, the Young King, revolt against his father, nor did

39

he make Henry II revolt against his son. If anyone besides Young Henry and Old Henry caused the disputes between them, more likely it was Eleanor of Aquitaine, old Henry's wife and Young Henry's mother —as Old Henry believed— or the other sons, Richard and Geoffrey.

The trouble between the two principals can be traced back to 1170, when Henry II unwisely crowned his oldest surviving son king of England in name alone, and their military conflicts reached a first culmination in 1173. None of Bertran's songs can be dated before 1181. In the spring of 1183 Bertran urged the Young King to assume leadership of a revolt of the barons of Aquitaine against Richard (Pillet-Carstens 80,13),[2] but by his own testimony his prodding was ineffectual. After Young Henry died suddenly in June of the same year, the revolt collapsed. Richard and Alfonso of Aragon besieged Bertran de Born in his castle of Autafort; after they drove him out of it, Richard and Old Henry jointly gave it back (80,20). This is the only episode we know of in which Bertran exerted political force—or rather felt it exerted upon himself. The scale of his influence in Europe is reflected by the calendar of chroniclers who mention his name: it appears in Geoffrey of Vigeois, a local historian of his native Périgord, who narrates the siege of Autafort; in the cartulary of the abbey of Dalon where Bertran retired; and in a note by the librarian of Saint-Martial in Limoges, recording the price of a candle burned in his memory (the wax sold for three sous).

Dante's other allusions to Bertran are imprecise too. In *De Vulgari Eloquentia* 2.2.9, he honors him as an illustrious vernacular poet of arms. A great war-poet Bertran certainly was, but not in the sense of *arma* which Dante carefully explains—that is, as the necessary means to gain *salutem*, "security." This is war as Virgil sang it; Bertran's motive was the opposite, an explosive élan which found expression in imagery of destruction. Security he disdained. In *Convivio* 4.11.14, Dante presents Beltram dal Bornio as an example of generosity, among others such as Alexander the Great and Saladin. And although it is true the troubadour praised this virtue in others, for lack of wealth he did not practice it himself.

These imprecisions are the more surprising because Dante knew Bertran's poetry in the text. In praising him as poet of arms he cites the first line of *No posc mudar mon chantar non esparga* (80, 29: "I can't keep myself from bringing out a song"). In this poem Bertran rejoices that war makes stingy leaders generous but complains that he has no means to make distant war himself. Dante draws upon various poems by Bertran for inspiration in *Inferno* 28. He echoes the theme of cleavage that runs through many of Bertran's poems in describing the dismemberment of the souls of the violent, among them Bertran's.[3] The periodic structure of the sentence with which Dante enters his subject (ll. 7–21) imitates the beginning of the *planh* for the death of the Young King, which Dante probably attributed to Bertran, as scholars continued to do until recently (80,41). Dante's coinage *accisma* ("he dresses") (l. 37) echoes Provençal *acesmatz*, as in Bertran's most famous ode to war (80, 8a, l. 27). Dante expresses violence throughout canto 28 in language reminiscent of Bertran's martial verse: "I concentrate" becomes *m'attacco* (l. 28), "let him prepare" becomes *s'armi* (l. 55), "good conscience" becomes *l'asbergo del sentirsi pura* (l. 117).

The paradox of Dante's precise textual acquaintance with Bertran, and his persistent inaccuracy in alluding to him, can be resolved only by a general enquiry into Bertran's literary fortunes in Italy. Hitherto Dante's references, particularly in the *Commedia*, have usually been explained by the influence of the first Provençal *vida*, which declares that he was master of Old Henry and his son, whenever he wished, and that he constantly urged them to fight. Critics have restricted Dante's knowledge of Bertran to this vida and a few *sirventes*, which they suppose he read, perhaps, in some single manuscript now lost. The contact between the poets has been judged narrow and bookish. But this view is improbable on the face of it, since Bertran inspired Dante to write the stirring passage in canto 28 and to allude to him repeatedly, in various ways, there and elsewhere; moreover, this view ignores the demonstrable fact that Bertran de Born was widely known throughout northern Italy before and during Dante's time. In the culture to which Dante was born Bertran had become a figure of legendary stature.

We have no reason to believe that Bertran visited Italy. Italian affairs were not one of his chief concerns; nevertheless he was alive to them, especially as they influenced his interests closer to home, and he referred to them in a number of passages that have hitherto been left unexplained. He recalled "the good man of Tarantais," Archbishop Peter of Tarentaise in Savoy, who had striven as papal legate to maintain order among the Plantagenets during the early 1170s, and who was soon to be canonized (80, 2); later he slurred the men of Savoy as ill-smelling woodsmen (80, 17)

In 1182 Bertran sneered at "that fox of an Emperor," Frederick

Barbarossa, because of the effortless skill with which Frederick had just dispossessed Henry the Lion, Duke of Saxony, and his wife Mathilda Plantagenet. Bertran cheered for the Lombard League and celebrated their courageous building upstream from Cremona—that is, the construction of Alessandria, the fortress whose resistance to Frederick had been the prelude to his defeat at Legnano (80, 11). It appears that Bertran attended the court held by Henry II at Argentan, in Normandy, late in 1182, and there composed two songs in honor of the exiled Duchess Mathilda. He found her more precious than Ravenna, a wealthy member of the defiant league (80, 9—but the reading is uncertain), and said that the Roman crown would be honored if she wore it (80, 19). (She never did, but the son she probably bore at Argentan was to become Otto IV.)

In 1183 Bertran likened the rebellious barons of Aquitaine to the Lombard League, speaking once of the Gascons (80, 14) and once of Limoges (80, 39). The following year he exulted in his lady's favors, saying she had made him wealthier than the king of Palermo (80, 28)— that is, than William II of Sicily. This monarch rarely emerged from his palace at Palermo, where he led the life of an oriental potentate, fluent in Arabic, served by eunuchs, and surrounded by a harem of Moslem women, among them his wife, Joanna Plantagenet. After Jerusalem fell to Saladin in 1187, Bertran sang the heroism of Conrad of Montferrat in the defense of Tyre (80, 17 and 80, 4). Frederick Barbarossa died during the Crusade that ensued; while returning from Jerusalem, Richard Plantagenet was captured, eventually to be ransomed by Frederick's son and successor, Henry VI, who used his ill-gotten gains to finance the conquest of Apulia and Romagna. Bertran decried this ignoble deed (80, 8). Even after retiring to Dalon in 1196, he continued to sing the joys of war and love with characteristic irony. His shapely young lady, he says, has a pact with him like the one between Pisa and Genoa—cities whose bitter enmity had burst into open conflict in the mid-1190s (80, 22).

Yet Bertran was to influence the development of Italian poetry through several indirect connections. It was probably he, despite the uncertainty of the attribution, who composed a violently satirical sestina (233, 2) in response to the prototypical amorous one of Arnaut Daniel (29, 14), and so contributed to the early diffusion of the form that was to be carried on by Dante and Petrarca. It was Bertran who inspired the genre of the *enueg*, or enumeration of annoyances, which in turn inspired the *noie* from Cremona. The Monk of Montaudon, who invented the genre, set one of his enueg to a melody borrowed from Bertran, while developing the antithesis of enueg and *plazer* as he found it in the same poem and others by him.[4] The monk was imitated in Italian by Girardo Patecchio, who flourished around 1228, and in two matched responses to Girardo by Ugo di Perso.[5] Their examples were to be followed by a long line of fretful Italians.[6]

Bertran's most pervasive influence on Italian poetry was a more general one, and one underlying both these particular cases. It was he who first established among the troubadours the practice of adopting his rhyme sounds, as well as his rhyme scheme from another poem; more significantly still, it was Bertran who first employed imitation of rhyme scheme and meter in a poem thematically unrelated to its model. In doing so he expanded upon the more restricted practice of answering a sirventes in its own form.[7] The importance of these innovations for the concept of fixed form requires little elaboration. When Italian poets of the thirteenth century returned time and time again to the form of the sonnet, first introduced by Giacomo da Lentino (fl. 1215–33), they were carrying to its logical conclusion the principle of formal imitation which Bertran de Born had been instrumental in developing.

Bertran's own words found echoes in the poetry of various troubadours who visited Italy or were Italians themselves and wrote in Provençal. Peire Vidal, who was to travel to the courts of Montferrat and the Malaspina in the 1190s, probably imitated Bertran's *escondich* in his splendid *gap* beginning *Drogoman senher* (364, 18 from 80, 15). The rhyme schemes and meters are identical, as are the rhymes, except that Peire substitutes *–au* for *–ar*. He develops at length the image of the ridiculous knight from Bertran's sixth stanza, and in conclusion threatens the *lauzengiers*, or malicious gossips, just as Bertran elsewhere threatened Poitevin soldiers (80, 44, ll. 36–42). Bertran probably wrote this last poem in July 1182, and from internal evidence Avalle has dated Peire's text before December of the same year. Peire's *gap* later served as the model for an exact imitation by Sordello, in 1240–41 (437, 28). Elias de Barjols was linked with the house of Savoy around 1219. It was probably in the early 1190s that he imitated Bertran's imaginary lady, the *domna soiseubuda* (80, 12), in composing an imaginary knight (132, 5); he asked to borrow from Bertran the wit, *sen*, of which he had boasted (80, 20 and 44). The domna soiseubuda was probably also the model for a canso written about 1220 by Aimeric de Péguilhan, who frequented the court of the Este, among others (10, 40); the last stanza gives a punning list of the lady's virtues that recalls Bertran's enumeration.

During the late 1250s and the 1260s a company of Italian poets sang the violent affairs of their country in language reminiscent of Bertran's.[8] Most of them recall the great ode to war, Be·m platz lo gais temps de pascor (80, 8a: "The gay time of spring pleases me well"), or the Miez· sirventes (80, 25: "Half a sirventes"), or both among other texts. In 1259 the Genoese Percivalle Doria, a poet in both Provençal and Italian, rejoiced at the prospect of war between Richard of Cornwall and Alfonso of Castile (371, 1); in 1260 Bonifaci de Castellane commemorated Charles of Anjou's inroads into Piedmont (102, 2); in 1261 an anonymous Ghibelline poet mocked kings and praised the emperor (461, 164a). About 1264 another Genoese, Luchetto Gattilusi, reminded Charles of Anjou that his ancestor Charlemagne had conquered Apulia—an event Bertran mentions too (290, 1: cf. 80, 29, v. 24), while Raimon de Tors warned Charles to beware of perfidious priests in a style so close to Bertran's as to deceive two sixteenth-century Italian scribes, who attributed the poem to him (410, 2). One Aicart del Fossat, otherwise unknown, used the meter and rhymes of the anonymous sirventes of 1261, and language from several of Bertran's poems, to greet Conradin's ill-starred challenge to Charles of Anjou in 1266 (7, 1). Perhaps it was around this time that, in Provence, Blacasset imitated Bertran's descriptions of war (96, 6).

The mode of formal imitation in which Bertran had played a pioneering role was applied to his own works by numbers of later troubadours having some connection with Italy. Gaucelm Faidit, whose nickname "the Exile" indicates the breadth of his travels, imitated Bertran about 1188 (167, 58 from 80, 10, written in 1182), and about 1196 Raimbaut de Vaqueiras, the intimate of Boniface of Montferrat, did the same (392, 15 from 80, 25, written 1190). It would appear that Bertran's planh for the Young King (80, 26) inspired Peire Raimon de Tolosa (355, 9), and not vice versa, as we have no other firm evidence that Peire was active before 1196; the case is an interesting one, since it suggests that a canso could indeed be modeled on one of the lesser genres. Peire was acquainted with the houses of Savoy, Este, and Malaspina, and with the Italian troubadour Rambertino Buvalelli of

Bologna. Around 1220 Aimeric de Péguilhan imitated Bertran in form
(10, 32 from 80, 28) as well as in substance. A troubadour named
Fortunier, of whom we know very little, mentions Sir Aimeric—perhaps de Péguilhan—in a cobla imitating Bertran (158, 1 from 80, 18).

Around 1227, Folquet de Romans imitated the ode to war, urging
Frederick II to go on Crusade just as Bertran had urged Richard (156,
11 from 80, 8a). He wrote this poem in Provence, and it was in Provence
about ten years later that Sordello used the meter of the same poem as
well as Bertran's general manner (437, 25). Again in 1240–41, Sordello
drew upon Bertran for everything but the rhyme sounds of a stinging
invective against Peire Bremon Ricas Novas (437, 20 from 80, 33). But
Sordello got worse than he gave: at about the same time he was the butt
of a grossly vulgar sirventes by Joan d'Aubusson and of a jeering
anonymous cobla, both fashioned after Bertran (265, 3 and 461, 80,
from 80, 34). The troubadour of Venice, Bertolome Zorzi, who flourished around 1268–71, imitated the form of one of Bertran's love-songs
(74, 17 from 80, 9) and repeated in a sestina the rhyme words Bertran
and Arnaut Daniel had used before him in theirs (74, 4 like 233, 2).

This wealth of varied evidence for the diffusion of Bertran's poems
in Italy finds confirmation in the Italian manuscripts containing them.
We owe the preservation of his songs chiefly to Italian scribes.[9] Of the
twenty extant medieval manuscripts and fragments with poems by
Bertran, twelve were written in Italy, five in the south of France, and
three in Cataluña; five Italian manuscripts (and only one other) contain more than twenty poems by Bertran apiece. The earliest of the
Bertran de Born manuscripts date from the thirteenth century: five are
Italian, among them MS D from 1254; two are from Cataluña, and
one from Provence.

The diffusion of Bertran's texts carried with it the germ of his
legend. His reputation for wit is attested by Elias de Barjols. He must
have been known for prowess as a lover, too, if it is true that Arnaut
Daniel in his sestina addressed Bertran as *Desirat, cui pretz en cambra
intra* (29, 14, 39), which we may loosely render as "Hotshot, brave in
the bedroom." In any case, the late fourteenth-century Italian scribe
of MS H believed that Desirat was Bertran, as he noted in his margin.
The legend of Bertran flourished in three media: in the Provençal
razos and *vidas*, in the miniature paintings that adorn several manuscripts, and in thirteenth-century Italian prose tales.

All of the razos for Bertran are found in manuscripts written in Italy;

vida 1 is in four Italian manuscripts and one from either Italy or Provence, and vida 2 is in two from Languedoc. None of the razos concerning Bertran or any other troubadour refer to events later than 1219, according to Favati, except certain ones concerning the troubadour Uc de Saint-Circ; since we know that Uc himself wrote some razos which include his name, and that Uc traveled from Provence to Italy in 1219–20, Favati hazarded the hypothesis that he brought materials for the razos with him and composed in Italy all those we have. Favati believes that the vidas were composed in Italy during or after the 1230s.[10] The latest editors, Boutière and Schutz, maintain that the two genres were invented simultaneously, partly in *pays d'Oc* and partly in Italy, where they concede the significant role played by Uc de Saint-Circ.[11]

Most critics agree, however, that the razos and vidas were composed for the sake of entertainment, not scholarship. They contain factual statements here and there, generally concerning the place a troubadour came from, his social status, or the circumstances of his death, but their more imaginative elements are not reliable. This is particularly true of their gossip about the poets' love affairs; and it is true, too, of their tales of political intrigue and adventure. The razos invent a mistress for Bertran de Born out of thin air and marry her to a husband who never existed either, while giving her a father who was real enough, as Stroński proved in 1914. In one razo Bertran shows signal generosity, furnishing his old friend Alfonso of Aragon with the supplies he needed to continue the siege of Autafort; in another, Bertran extricates himself cleverly from a tight spot, winning the sympathy of Henry II by saying he has lost his *sen* in grief for the death of the Young King. The razos say Bertran wanted the Young King to fight Richard, and that Old Henry blamed Bertran for his son's defiance, but they do not say Old Henry was right. This was left for the vidas, which both say Bertran caused the trouble between father and son. One characterizes Bertran as a *bons cavalliers . . . e bons guerrers e bons domnejaire e bons trobaire e·savis e ben parlanz* ("a good knight and a good warrior and a good lover and a good poet and wise and eloquent"); the other, as an *azautz hom e cortes* ("a clever and courtly man").[12]

The miniature paintings concerning Bertran were all executed in Italy: we have five that date from the thirteenth century, and one from

the fourteenth.[13] The artist's intention to illustrate the poem before him
is plain in MS I, folio 174v, where a picture of two knights jousting represents the tourney which Bertran anticipates with glee (80, 23). In
the closely related MS K, folio 160r, the same poem shows a knight
mounted, his lance raised and his head covered; but it would be arbitrary to assume this is a figure of Bertran, particularly since he speaks
of fighting in this poem only in the first-person plural. A badly smeared
miniature in MS M (fourteenth century), folio 227r, shows a knight on
horseback charging forward, raising his right arm to deliver a blow of
the sword. The design admirably illustrates these lines from the poem:

> A Peiregos pres del muraill
> tant cant poirai gitar ab maill,
> volrai anar sobre Baiart.
> E se·i trob Peitavin pifart,
>   sabra de mon bran cum tailla—
> que sus el cap li farai bart
>   de cervel mesclat ab mailla.

                                   [80, 44]

[At Périgueux, near the wall, I'll ride out on my Bayard as far as I
can throw a club. And if I find some pot-bellied Poitevin, he'll
learn how my blade cuts—on top of his head I'll make him a slop
of brains mixed with mail.]

In the Frammento Romegialli, a painting of a knight on horseback,
armed, before a walled gate illuminates the poem in which Bertran
proclaims with pride and defiance that he has regained possession of
Autafort (80, 20). This gate clearly represents Bertran's castle, regardless of the fact that it is a conventional element of design used elsewhere
for other purposes.[14]

    The remaining miniatures portray the poet more independently of
his words. Bertran says he got Autafort back because the king—that
is, Henry II—and Count Richard pardoned him, and exults over the
decision of his lord the king (80, 20). A razo in the Frammento Romegialli elaborates on these matters. In its initial there is a miniature showing
two men: one seated, crowned, raising his right arm and extending his
index finger in a gesture of summons or command; before him the
other, on his knees. These must be Henry and Bertran. Through the

mediation of the razo, the picture has given to Bertran's words a dramatic form which the poet did not express himself.

In MS A, in the upper margin of folio 189r, we may read an instruction in Italian from the scribe to the miniaturist: *·j· bel caualler ben armado a cauall cũ. ·j· scudo a collo & la lança soto braço* ("a handsome knight well armed on horseback with a shield at his neck and his lance under his arm"). The legend of Bertran as *bel caualler* inspired this instruction, not the following poem, which depicts no knight-at-arms. At the end of the poem, Bertran declares with heavy irony that he will no more make war for love of Sir Ademar, whom he despised (80, 21). Yet the instruction may reflect a detail from the verses transcribed a few folios away, where Bertran speaks of carrying his shield at his neck (80, 15, ll. 31–32 and 80, 29, l. 16). However that may be, the miniaturist ignored his instruction to put the shield *a collo* and the lance *soto braço*: instead the knight carries his shield at the ready, on his arm, and raises his lance in his hand. Other details in the painting contradict Bertran: the pennant is blue, whereas Bertran mentions a white one (80, 29), and the horse is dappled, not a bay (80, 44). However, the knight wears a curious headgear having precisely the shape of a late thirteenth-century *capel*, a protective hat of iron or leather that Bertran once mentions wearing (*capel en ma testa*, 80, 29, v. 16).[15] If the miniaturist made any effort to illustrate the poetry here, it was a slight one. The image of Bertran de Born which he transmitted is a stereotyped one of the fair knight, armed and vigorous.

The collection of Italian prose tales known as the *Novellino* was assembled by an anonymous Florentine, probably during the last twenty years of the thirteenth century.[16] Here Bertran again boasts of his wit, and once more moves Old Henry to tears and clemency by his grief for his son. The Young King makes war upon his father through Bertran's counsel and dies in a castle belonging to Bertran—as vida 2 had erroneously claimed. The *Novellino* is the first text we have which specifies that Bertran advised the Young King to demand of his father all the treasure that was rightfully his.

It is curious that the *Novellino* nowhere mentions that Bertran was a poet; neither do the *Conti di antichi cavalieri*, which were written about the same time.[17] Here Bertran is simply identified as the *maestro del Re giovene* ("the master of the Young King"). After hearing wonderful tales of the virtues of Saladin, Bertran determines to visit his court.

There he instructs the Saracen prince in the refinements of courtly love, with devastating effect. The tale is similar to numerous others in which various Christian knights or poets persuade Saladin to adopt the norms of chivalry. Bertran has here become a full-blown figure of legend, free to move within the legendary sphere, no longer bound by biographical or textual fact.

The diffusion in Italy of texts and legends concerning Bertran de Born provides the historical context that is necessary to an understanding of the three poems edited below. The first and third reproduce the meter and the rhymes of Bertran's poem *Mailoli, joglar malastruc* (80, 24: "Mailolin, you miserable minstrel"), and echo rhyme words, expressions, and thoughts from various others. The first resembles Bertran's work so closely, in fact, that many scholars regard it as his own. However, the reasons they have advanced for doing so are far from sufficient.

In the sole manuscript containing the poem M, which was written during the fourteenth century in Italy, the rubric for the poem attributes it to Ser Lantelmet de l'Aguilhon; so does the table of contents. The claim first made by Chabaneau, that Bertran wrote the poem, rests on nothing but its similarities to his authentic canon—the very evidence that it is an imitation of him, like the numerous Italian imitations of his forms and language we have surveyed. Nor is the imitation so perfect as to become indistinguishable from its original. This poet is heavy-witted. Bertran is more nimble when he jokes abrasively with the joglars Mailolin (80, 24) or Fuilhetas (80, 16 and 17), when he ridicules Sir Ademar (233, 2)—even when he slanders Alfonso of Aragon (80, 32 and 35). This poet, who plainly should be called Lantelmet, describes his poem as a catapult loaded to batter bad barons, and the metaphor fittingly captures its numbing impact.

Who was Lantelmet de l'Aguilhon? We find his name nowhere else. Chabaneau suggested he might have been a native of Aiguillon (Lot-et-Garonne). He may have had an ancestor in the Esteve Agullo, who appears in a deed of about 1140 from Rouergue, and a descendant in the Guiraut d'Aguilo, mentioned in 1274 by Cerveri de Girona—but more likely this Guiraut was called "D'Aguilo" from the locality of that name in the district of Montblanch, province of Tarragona.[18] Then again, some or all of these men may have been called *agulho* ("goad, needle") because they needled their enemies with stinging words, as Lantelmet does in the poem. Indeed, Bertran de Born uses the word this way in one of the poems to which Lantelment alludes:

> Un sirventes fatz dels malvatz barons,
> e ja mais d'els no m'ausiretz parlar;
> qu'en lor ai fraiz mais de mil agulions,
> q'anc no·n puoic far un correr ni trotar. . . .

[80, 43]

[I'll make a sirventes about the bad barons, and you'll never hear me speak of them again. On them I have broken more than a thousand goads, but I have never been able to make a single one run, or even trot. . . .]

Many joglars took professional names advertising their trade, like Pistoleta (Little Epistle) and Esquileta (Little Bell). Other surnames designating the bearer's character that we find in the characters are Raimun Auriol (Raymond the Bird-Brain), Guiral Balb (Gerald the Stammerer), Matfre Laricson (Manfred the Rich Man), and Gillem d'Alciacamba (William the Leg-Lifter).

Since the diminutive ending was used freely in Provençal proper names,[19] Lantelmet de l'Aguilhon might well be the same man as a certain Lantelm, of whom we have two poems. One of these is addressed to Lanfranc Cigala, the Genoese poet and judge who flourished from about 1235 until 1270; Lantelm needles him for folly, avarice, malevolence, ignorance, and injustice (283, 1). The other is a playful *joc partit* (French *jeu parti*) with a man named Raimon (283, 2). In the joc partit Lantelm asks Raimon this question: if a worthy lady grants her love to a true lover, but then her husband finds out and puts a stop to it, which of the three endures the greatest suffering? Raimon answers that the lady and the lover suffer more than the husband does, so Lantelm argues the contrary, and the two poets vie in witty disputation.

This joc partit must have gained some notoriety, since it is referred to in the second poem edited below. Here Guillem Raimon defends what Rei has said in a song, namely, that it is no good to separate two lovers (ll. 4–6). Rei must have been a nickname suggesting "King of the Joglars," and Guillem Raimon defends him like a man defending himself, as De Bartholomaeis perceived; the reference to the joc partit clearly indicates that Guillem Raimon and Raimon were the same man. (Of course, Rei also puns on Raimon.)

Toward the end of the second poem, Guillem Raimon says that when he came from Hungary Sir Aicelis laughed at him, but if the tables were turned Aicelis would look more ridiculous than the poet, "even though he pretends to be a Solomon." It has generally been supposed that this Aicelis is Ezzelino (Azzolino) da Romano. De Bartholomaeis dated the text before 1259 for no other reason than Ezzelino's death in that year. But the identification is an incongruous one: far from being reputed for laughter and wisdom, Ezzelino da Romano was the infamous tyrant whom Dante finds boiling in blood in the circle of the violent (*Inferno* 12. 110), and who Uc de Saint Circ, a familiar of the Romano court, accused of capturing children, knifing virgins, burning women, and setting fire to convents, crosses, and altars (457, 8, ll. 37–43).

There are several reasons to believe, rather, that Sir Aicelis is Azzo VII, called *il Novello*, marquis of Este from 1215 until his death in 1264 and a patron of troubadours and joglars.[20] Any Azzo could be called by the diminutive Aicelis, as Azzo VI was called Azzolino,[21] and the byname Novello has a diminutive force. We have long believed that Guillem Raimon speaks of Azzo VII in another poem, a *tenso* with Aimeric de Péguilhan (229, 2); he there calls him *aqest* novel *marqes*, according to the plausible emendation adopted by Shepard-Chambers. Azzo VII was chief of the Guelph party, which took its name from one of his ancestors. He is said to have won the love of his people through his generosity and justice, and to have gained such respect from his enemies that they grieved for him when he died.[22]

Moreover, this hypothesis leads to a second one which provides a general understanding of the poem's cultural setting. As Guillem Raimon concludes with Aicelis, he begins with Sir Obs de Biguli, whom he ridicules for his hypocritical indignation at the faintly libertine claim made by Raimon in the joc partit. Obs de Biguli has been linked to the Bigoli family of Piacenza by Schultz, and to the Bigolini of Padua by Bertoni, but there is no Obs (Italian Obizzo) in either. De Bartholomaeis suspected that Biguli could be a pun on *un noto vocabolo del dialetto milanese* ("a well-known word in the dialect of Milan")—by which we may suppose he meant *beg*, "worm, idiot, penis" (Italian *baco*).[23] If we approach the problem from the other direction, we find that Obizzo was not an unusual name: Obizzo I and II di Malaspina ruled during the late twelfth century; Obizzo I d'Este preceded Azzo VI, and Obizzo II followed Azzo VII, ruling from 1264 until 1293. Obizzo II d'Este had a curious nickname, according to Benvenuto da Imola:

> Fuerat enim monoculus, non a natura, sed a casu, cum hastiluderet ob amorem cuiusdam dominae; ideo denominatus est marchio Obizo ab oculo.[24]

> [He had lost the use of one eye, not by nature, but by an accident, when he was jousting for the love of a certain woman; for that reason he was called Marquis Obizzo the one-eyed.]

Ab oculo could easily have produced *de Biguli* by word-play on *beg* or a related form, or on Sienese *bigollo*, "spinning top," the child's toy.[25] Since in Provençal *ops de* meant "for the sake of," we may roughly translate *N'Obs de Biguli* as "Sir Plays-With-Himself." By a similar process Ponzio Amato was deformed into Porc Armat in a contemporary poem (236, 11, l. 6).

If Guillem Raimon jeered at Obizzo d'Este for being stuffy in a matter of sexual morality, he had good reason. Not only did Obizzo lose an eye for a woman of no station; the bastard grandson of Azzo VII, he was the first marquis of Este to be born illegitimately, and he distinguished himself by his dedication to the most unbridled libertinage.[26] A chronicler who is frankly hostile toward him says he spared neither maidens nor wives, noble nor common, not even—according to gossip—his wife's sister and his own sisters;[27] for violence such as this, no doubt, as well as for more varied forms of despotism, Dante put him in Hell beside Ezzelino da Romano (*Inferno* 12.111). The same chronicler goes on to say that *joculatores* ridiculed Obizzo as the bastard son of an ignoble mother.

One such joglar was Guillem Raimon. He takes up the cudgels with glee: Obizzo, he says, pretends to be more *senatz*, "virtuous," than any figure of legendary *sen* he can think of. Simply to hear loose talk he suffers terribly, enduring greater outrage than Roland, who with all his sen came to disaster at Roncevaux, or than Bertran, who said it was by sen that he fell from a high (*aut*) platform—he didn't say he was pushed. This Bertran must be recognized as the poet of Autafort. When Bertran de Born celebrates the regaining of his castle, he boasts of his cleverness in escaping Count Richard and King Alfonso—who, he neglects to mention, had driven him out of it after a week-long siege, on 6 July 1183:

> Ges de far sirventes no·m tartz,
> anz lo fauc senes totz affans,
> tant es sotils mos geins e m'artz.
> Que mes m'en sui en tal enans
>   e s'ai tant de sort
>   qe ve·us m'en estort,
>   qe comte ni rei
>   no·m forssan ni grei.
>
> [80, 20, ll.1–8]

[I'm not slow at sirventes—I make 'em without the least effort, so subtle are my wit and my art. I've got so far ahead and I'm so lucky that I escape like magic: neither counts nor kings nor cares can bother me.]

This is the poem that was illuminated twice in the Frammento Romegialli. We have seen Bertran's reputation for sen in Elias de Barjols, in the razos, and in the *Novellino*. Roland and Bertran were supposed to have sen, just as Obs pretends to be senatz, and Guillem Raimon delights in recalling that they were disgraced. He then refers to Obs's grandfather Azzo, who used to laugh at him. Even though Azzo pretends to be a Solomon of sen, says Guillem Raimon, he would have looked ridiculous too if things had been different.

This interpretation requires a careful analysis of the poem's date. If it was written while Azzo VII was alive, it must have been written during Obizzo's adolescence. Obizzo was born in 1247, and so was only seventeen years old when he succeeded to the title; but he was mature enough to have married in the preceding year.[28] To judge by his later reputation, he must have been an unruly young man. Two questions remain. If the poem was written half a century after Bertran's death, how could Guillem Raimon say Bertran told him—*zo·m dis*—he fell by his sen? By a figure of speech meaning that Guillem Raimon heard or read Bertran's poem on the subject. He refers to Bertran as living legend. Through a related conceit Petrarch wrote epistles to Virgil and Homer.

We could hardly take the statement literally in any case, since we have no reason to believe Bertran visited Italy. Secondly, is it reasonable to believe that Guillem Raimon was still active in the 1260s, considering that he spoke of Azzo VII as *joves* in his *tenso* with Aimeric de Péguilhan? Yes it is. Since Azzo was born around 1206, a court poet could have called him "young" considerably later than 1215, when he became marquis.[29] We suppose Aimeric lived until around 1230, and possibly longer. There is nothing unlikely in the claim that Guillem Raimon's poetic career stretched from the young manhood of Azzo VII down to the first excesses of Obizzo II.[30]

The third poem edited here is an exchange of scurrilities between Guillem Raimon and a joglar known as Mola (Whetstone), in which the contestants imitate the meter and rhymes of Bertran's poem to Mailoli and of Lantelmet's imitation, while picking up expressions from both. Mola confirms that Rei was a nickname for Guillem Raimon (vv. 11–12), and Guillem Raimon speaks once more of Bertran de Born as though he were alive (vv. 2–7). He challenges Mola to combat, and Bertran too (if Mola can get such an ally), insulting Bertran as a hatcher of treasons—*Io feci il padre e'l figlio in sé ribelli*—and as a pauper without a coat of mail. He drew the latter slur from one of Bertran's poems (80, 36, vv. 15–19):

> Nos em tal trenta gerrier—
> chascus ha capa traucada—
> tuich seignor e parsonier
> per cor de gerra mesclada,
> c'anc no·n cobrem dinairada.

[We are about thirty warriors—each one has a cape full of holes— all lords and partners for love of a pitched battle, for we never made a dime.]

Guillem Raimon wishes that Bertran had been a coward since Mola claims to be his equal. Lantelmet said (ll. 15–17) that the man he hated closed his eyes to his enemies but saw with both to deceive his friends; similarly, Guillem Raimon tells Mola to shut his other eye as well as the first if he wants to survive their scuffle.

Mola answers at once with a skillful stroke, repeating a rhyme word from Lantelmet (l. 8) while recalling in coarser language Bertran's memorable image of the slop of brains mixed with mail (80, 44). He berates this Rei as Bertran berated the Young King and King Alfonso (v. 12), adding for good measure that Guillem Raimon loves a woman in whom he has more allies than Milan has in battle. He alludes to that city's leading role from the 1160s onward in the Lombard resistance to the emperor.

The facts that Guillem Raimon imitated Lantelmet (poem three), and that Raimon and Lantelm shared in a joc partit, provide support for the hypotheses that Guillem Raimon equals Raimon (poem two) and that Lantelmet equals Lantelm (poem one). The two hypotheses reinforce one another. Lantelmet and Guillem Raimon maintained a close poetic association which took the form of imitation in the third poem below, and of dialogue in the joc partit. Together with Mola and Aimeric de Péguilhan, they form a group of poets linked to the court of the Este and sharing an admiration for Bertran de Born. By dating the second poem in the early 1260s, we put it at the moment when Bertran's influence on poets writing in Italy was at its height.

To summarize these proposals: Lantelmet's poem (284, 1) should be returned to him, and he should be recognized as Lantelm (283). The Raimon with whom Lantelm participated in the tenso (283, 2) should be recognized as Guillem Raimon (229). The Bertran whom Guillem Raimon mentions twice (229, 3 and 4) is Bertran de Born, who inspired both these poems.

The legendary status which Bertran de Born had attained in Italian culture accounts for the imprecisions in Dante's references to him. Dante spoke not of the twelfth-century troubadour we know but of a figure descended from him, a character who played on the literary stage of Dante's time. Bertram dal Bornio differed from his ancestor the troubadour by the volatility which is a privilege of myth: he could be— now a symbol of generosity, now of warfare for the sake of security, now of discord, even though Bertran de Born had been none of these things, and despite the perceptible contradictions among these roles. Yet the figure of legend continued to draw sustenance from the texts of his ancestor's poetry, which circulated widely in Dante's Italy and which Dante certainly read.

This is not to say that Dante knew each phase in the development of the legend as we have recovered it. In *De Vulgari Eloquentia* 2.2.10, he says he can find no Italian who has sung of arms, so it appears he was unaware of the war poetry written in Provençal by Italians imitating Bertran. It has been claimed that he cannot have read vida 2, for he would then have learned that Bertran ended his days as a monk, not a sower of discord; but the pious last years of Guido da Monteféltro were not enough to keep him from the eighth *bolgia*, nor did the high offices of a crowd of priests and popes save them from *Inferno*.[31] From the vidas Dante may have gotten his idea that Bertran caused the conflict between Old Henry and his son, and from the razos that he was generous.

The razos concerning Bertran may also have exerted on Dante another and far greater influence. Since by their sheer bulk they dominate the razos on all the other troubadours; since they are linked together, at least by their common reference to Bertran; and since they offer a sequence of prose commentaries on lyric verse written in a vernacular language (unlike the meters of Boethius), it is no idle claim that they may have underlain the form of the *Vita Nuova*.[32] The miniature in the Frammento Romegialli showing a knight before a gate could have led a reader, perhaps Dante himself, to think that Bertran de Born fought for the security of a city. But we have no reason to restrict Dante's acquaintance with Bertran to any such particular contacts. On the contrary, we have strong evidence that in Dante's world Bertran was a living legend.

After his appearance in the *Inferno*, Bertran's lasting celebrity was assured. Among commentators on the *Commedia* he assumed the shape of a Gascon knight or of an Englishman. Eventually Bornio was misunderstood as *borgno*, and he lost an eye.[33] Such are the defigurations of myth.

Bertran's legendary afterlife is not without parallel. Another troubadour who entered the timeless realm was Jaufre Rudel, whose merits as a lover came to be disputed in the same breath as those of worthy Pyramus (255, 1). Just as in the fictional year 1300 Dante encountered the shade of Bertran, he also met an Arnaut Daniel, who had rejected the historical poet's attitudes about love and language, and a Folquet de Marseille, who had modified the political opinions he held in this world.[34] Petrarch traced his poetic genealogy from the Greek and Roman lyricists through the troubadours, then to Italian poets, in the fourth *Trionfo d'Amore*. An early redaction of the text included the name Bertrando,[35] and it must have been the war-poet of whom Petrarch thought when he spoke of *molti altri . . . a cui la linqua/ lancia e spada fu sempre e targia ed elmo* ("many other troubadours for whom their tongues were always lance and sword and targe and helm," ll. 56–57). It is true that Petrarch imitated Bertran's *escondich* in his canzone beginning *S'i'l dissi mai, ch'i' vegna in odio a quella* ("If ever I said it, may I be hateful to her").[36] However, he must have felt that the warpoet would be ill-at-ease among softer voices such as that of Bernart de Ventadorn, and so he replaced his name with that of Aimeric de Péguilhan. Petrarch's own textual acquaintance with Bertran de Born seemed to be contradicted by the legend of the war-poet, and it was the legend which dominated. From our more distant perspective we must distinguish the legend from the troubadour—not a generous Alexander, not a warlike Aeneas, not a discordant Achitophel, but a brilliant and influential poet.

TEXTS

1. Lantelmet de l'Aguilhon, *Er ai ieu tendut mon trabuc* MS M, fol. 246. Istvan Frank, *Répertoire métrique de la poésie des troubadours* (Paris: Champion, 1953–57), 673:3.

Scheme: a b b c b b c

8 8 8 7' 8 8 7'

Rhymes *uc, os, alha*. 5 *coblas unissonans*.

Pillet-Carstens 284, 1. Partial ed. J. F. M. Raynouard, *Choix des poésies originales des troubadours* (rpt. Osnabrück: Biblio, 1966), 5: 248. Ed. Chabaneau, *Revue des Langues Romanes* 25 (1884): 231–33; discussion A. Stimming, *Bertran von Born* (Halle: Niemeyer, 1913), pp. 49–50; Giulio Bertoni, *Trovatori d'Italia* (Modena: Orlandini, 1915), p. 134; Carl Appel, *Nachrichten von der Gesellschaft der Wissenschaften zu Göttingen, Philologisch-Historische Klasse* (1930), pp. 55–56. Ed. Appel, *Lieder Bertrans von Born* (Halle: Niemeyer, 1932), no. 41a; cf. L. E. Kastner, *Modern Language Review* 32 (1937): 217–19. Appel's text is reproduced by Martín de Riquer, *Lirica de los Trovadores* (Barcelona: Escuela de Filología, 1948), pp. 453–54, and by Suzanne

Méjean, *La Chanson satirique provençale au moyen-âge* (Paris: Nizet, 1971), pp. 137–38.

I.   Er ai ieu tendut mon trabuc
       don sueilh trair' als malvas baros,
       e trayrai n'a un de cor blos,   3
          vueiz d'onor, plen de nuailha,
       lausengier, bausador, janglos,
       avar ric croy, vueig de fatz bos,
          plen d'enjan, vil en batailha.   7

II.   Malvas es dels pes tros q'al çuc
       e flacs del cap tros q'als talos;
       e sos conseills es de garsos,   10
          sa cortz de paupra vitailha,
       sos solatz pesanz e iros,
       e sei don paupr' e sofrachos.
          Sei fach van con fuecs de pailha.   14

III.   Als enemics son sei hueilh cluc
       e contra·ls amics ve d'amdos,
       per far enjans e tracïos.   17
          E per tan no tem far failha;
       q'el ditz, e no·n es vergoinhos,
       qe sos parenz fo Ganeilhos—
          per o no·il cal qe·l trasailha.   21

IV.   Anc als enemics no fes truc
       qe no·i laises sos compainhos,
       e·ls cavals e las garnisos.   24
          E fa mal qan porta mailha
       ni armas, mas los esperos,
       qe mais ll'an valgut a sasos
          qe lança ni branz qe tailha.   28

V.   Al baro plus cau d'un säuc,
       sirventes, vai tost e cochos;
          e no si' en luec tan rescos   31
          qe tu as auta sonailha
       no·l digas, "Ieu vieinh çai a vos."

> Pero lai vay a reculos,
>> q'enaissi tainh c'om l'asailha.   35

I. Now I've loaded the catapult I always shoot at the bad barons, and I'm going to shoot one who is without a heart, empty of honor, full of flab, a lying, cheating, jabbering, stingy rich wretch, empty of good deeds, full of trickery, cowardly in battle.

II. He's bad from toe to top and imp from head to heel; his advice is that of a thug, his feast one of meager food, his sport heavy and sad, and his gifts meager and miserly. His deeds pass away like a straw-fire.

III. To enemies his eyes are closed, but against his friends he sees with both, for playing tricks and treason. Yet he's not afraid of going wrong, for he says that his ancestor was Ganelon, and he isn't ashamed of it—so he doesn't care if he's got the jump on that traitor.

IV. He never has given his enemies a blow without abandoning his comrades and their horses and equipment. He does wrong to wear mail and arms, except his spurs—they have done him more good sometimes than lance or slashing sword.

V. Go quick and fast, sirventes, to the baron who is hollower than an elder tree; and no matter where he hides, you tell him with a loud ring, "Here I come for you." But go there backwards, for that's the way he has to be assaulted.

Rubric Ser lantelmet de laguilhon. *Table Ser* lantelmet de laguglo.

1 *trabuch* Table.
3 *tray* M, with an illegible superscript.
12 *pensanz* M, first *n* expunctuated.
16 *contra*] first two letters partially erased.
21 *noil* M, *non* Chab., Ap.
21 *qel* M, *q'el* Chab., Ap.
21 *Trasalhir* v.a. "sauter au delà de, transgresser," Levy, *Petit Dictionnaire provençal-français*. "There is no need for him to be untrue to his stock," Kastner. "No es preciso que salte," Riquer ("verso poco claro").
24 *cavals*] lower half of *1* missing.
31 *sia en tan luec* M.

32   *Sonalha* was glossed as "Getön, Klang" in this passage by Levy, *Supplement-Wörterbuch*, 7: 813. "Tú, que tienes alta voz," Riquer.
2. Guillem Raimon, *N'Obs de Biguli se plaing* MS H, fol. 55. Frank, 719:1 (unicum), erroneously gives the second *c*-rhyme 7 syllables. Scheme:

$$a\ b\ b\ c\ c\ d\ d\ e\ e\ f\ f\ e\ e\ g\ g$$
$$\overline{7\ 7\ 7\ 7\ 5\ 5\ 5\ 7\ 7\ 5'\ 5'\ 7\ 7\ 7\ 7}$$

Rhymes *anh, ens, ir, atz, ans, ia, os.* One *cobla* with two *tornadas* of six and two lines.

Pillet-Carstens 229, 3. Transcriptions in *Archiv für das Studium der Neueren Sprachen und Literaturen* 34 (1863): 413, and *Studi di Filologia Romanza* 5 (1891): 537, no. 233. Discussion by O. Schultz, *Zeitschrift für romanische Philologie* 7 (1883): 231–35; Bertoni, *Annales du Midi* 20 (1908): 223–24. Partial ed., Bertoni, *Trovatori*, p. 69. Ed. Vincenzo de Bartholomaeis, *Poesie Provenzali Storiche* (Roma: Istituto Storico Italiano, 1931), 2: 193–94.

I.   N'Obs de Biguli se plai*n*g
         (ta*n*t es iratz e dolenz)
         a Deu e pois a las genz
         del Rei, car chantan vol dir   4
            qe ges bon partir
            no fai dos privatz.
            Et es tan senatz
         N'Obs qe locs no sai en cha*n*z: 8
         a sofert plus c'us Rolanz
            sofrir no poria,
            c'ab sen enqeria
         gerras, trebailh *et* affanz;   12
         e *p*er sen, zo·m dis Bertrans,
         cazet d'un aut solar jos—
         no dis pas q'enpeinz en fos.

II.   Qant eu ving d'Ongria   16
            N'Aicelis rizia,
         car *p*er saluz e *p*er manz
         er' eu folz; mas si l'enchanz
         q'eu sai d'autra color fos,   20
         e seria *p*er un dos

III.   plus ras de mi, e plus tos,
       se tot s'en feing Salamos.

I. Sir Obs de Biguli cries out to God and the people, he is so upset by what the king says in a song—that it is no good to separate two lovers. Sir Obs is more *senatz* than anyone I know in songs: he has endured more than Roland could, whose *sen* was for war, toil, and torment; and Bertran told me it was by *sen* that he fell from a high platform—he didn't say he was pushed.

II. When I came from Hungary Sir Aiceli laughed at the way greetings and messages drove me crazy; but if the sale I know about were of another kind, he would be twice as

III. Shaved and shorn as I am, even though he pretends to be a Solomon.

Rubric Guillems *raimon.*

8   Cf. *loc* "Stelle in einem Buch," *Supplement-Wörterbuch*, 4: 417.

8   *sai* H, em. *hai* deB. "Che non ci è da meravigliare," DeB.

9   Bertran de Born refers to Roland in both his *planhs*, the one for the Young King (80, 26, v. 47) and the one for Geoffrey (80, 6a, v. 20).

12   *trebaillz* Archiv, Studi, DeB.

15   *en peiz* (z ill-formed) H, DeB. "E dice che non si fece in pezzi," DeB, thinking of the word *pesa*, "piece."

16   Initial om. H.

16   *Ongaria* H, em. DeB.

18   *manz* "strette di mano," DeB.

19   *L'enchanz* has not been explained.

19   *mas*] *s* broken.

21   *E* H, "zur Einleitung des Nachsatzes dienend," *Supplement-Wörterbuch*, 2: 311–12; em. *El* DeB.

3. Guillem Raimon and Mola, *coblas*

MS H, f. 54. Frank, 673:2 and 4.

Scheme: a b b c b b c
        8̄ 8̄ 8̄ 7̄′ 8̄ 8̄ 7̄′

Rhymes *uc, os, alha.* Exchange of single *coblas* with *tornadas* of three lines.

Pillet-Carstens 229,4 and 302,1. Transcriptions in *Archiv* 34 (1863): 412, and *Studi di Filologia Romanza* 5 (1891): 534–35, nos. 224–25. Partial eds.: Raynouard, *Choix*, 5: 267, and M. Milá y Fontanals, *De los Trovadores en España*, ed. C. Martínez and F. R. Manrique (Barcelona: Consejo Superior, 1966), p. 408. Mola cannot be identified as a poet named elsewhere by the Monk of Montaudon, as Milá proposed, because that poet's name is correctly understood as Tremoleta—cf. Frank M. Chambers, *Proper Names in the Lyrics of the Troubadours* (Chapel Hill: University of North Carolina Press, 1971), ss.vv. Ed. de Bartholomaeis, *Poesie Provenzali*, 2: 194–95.

Guillems Raimons al Mola:

I. On son mei guerrier desastruc
  Mola e Bertrams pedollos?
  L'us pugna de far tracïos,   3
   pero meinz es d'una mailla.
  Ab sol qe l'autre meinz i fos
  plagra·m, e qe fos timoros
   Bertrams—qe ab lui s'egailla. 7

II. Mola, se fos l'autre balcos
  serratz, vos foratz plus gignos
   e plus seürs en batailla.   10

Mola li respondet aisi:

I. Reis feritz de merda pel çuc,
  Reis aunitz, Reis dels enoios,
  per qe voletz ab me tenzos? 13
   Noca volgr' ab vos barailla.
  Pero drutz es, e fos espos
  de tal don avetz compagnos
   plus qe Milans en batailla. 17

II. Noca, s'anc jorn fui pedollos,
  de lei apris dont es zellos
   en un veill sacon de pailla. 20

Guillem Raimon to Mola:

I. Where are my unlucky attackers, Mola and Bertran full of lice? The second strives to spread treachery, but he's missing a coat of mail. If only the first were missing too I'd be pleased, and if Bertran had been cowardly—for Mola claims to be his equal.

II. Mola, if you shut your other peeper too, you'd be even trickier, and safer in battle.

Mola answered him this way:

I. King struck with shit on the skull, King put to shame, King of the dull, why do you want a fight with me? I'd never want a brawl with you. But you are the lover of a woman—and I wish you were her husband—in whom you have more allies than Milan has in battle.

II. Never, if ever I caught lice, have I learned anything on an old sack of straw from the woman who makes you jealous.

Rubric Raimon *Studi*, DeB.
1   Initial omitted by rubricator, but indicated in left margin
1   *desastruc*] cf. *malastruc*, 80,24, v. 1.
2   *pedollos*] cf. *ez a's maior cor uns soiros*, 80, 24, v. 23.
4   *d'*] om. H, DeB.; *mens de* "ohne," *Supplement-Wörterbuch*, 5: 197. "Però è piú piccolo di una maglia," DeB.
5   *autra* H, em. DeB.
5   *eser mens* "fehlen," *Supplement-Wörterbuch*, 5: 199. "Sol che l'altro fosse da meno [*di lui*]," DeB.
6   *plagra me* Milá.
6   *qel* II, DeB.; *qu'el* Milá.
6   *timos* H, DeB.; *ticnós* Milá. "E che fosse dello stesso peso," deB., apparently interpreting *timos* as the noun meaning "forte balance à plateaux de bois" (*Petit Dictionnaire*).
7   *se gailla* Milá.
8   *balcos* "balcone [= occhio?]" DeB. No such slang usage is mentioned in Raynouard, *Lexique Roman*; the word is omitted by *Supplement-Wörterbuch* and *Petit Dictionnaire*. Cf. W. von Wartburg, *Französisches Etymologisches Wörterbuch*, s.v. *balko*, the senses "chassis dormant, ou vitre fixée dans la couverture d'une maison pour éclairer le grenier;" "volet."
11   Initial omitted by rubricator, but noted in right-hand margin.
12   Cf. *enuios* at the rhyme in 80,24 v. 9; *reis . . . aunitz*, 80,32 v. 8; *sia reis dels malvatz*, 80,13 v. 8.
14   *Nocra* H, *Nonca* Raynouard, DeB; cf. *Lexique Roman*, 2: 81.
14   *volgra ab* H.
14   Cf. *barailla*, 80,44 v. 12, and *baralhur*, 80,44 v. 36.

18 *Muca* H, *Nunca* DeB. "Se mai fui pidocchioso, presi [*i pidocchi*] da lei," DeB.

20 Cf. *palharda*, "femme de mauvaises moeurs" (*Petit Dictionnaire*), and so on.

NOTES

1. See Thomas Goddard Bergin, "Dante's Provençal Gallery," *Speculum* 40 (1965): 15–30, reprinted in his *A Diversity of Dante* (New Brunswick, N.J.: Rutgers University Press, 1969), pp. 87–111. A useful bibliographical study is François Pirot, "Dante et les troubadours," *Marche Romane* 15 (1965): 213–19.

2. In this way I identify Provençal poems by reference to Alfred Pillet and Henry Carstens, *Bibliographie der Troubadours* (Halle: Niemeyer, 1933). For my discussion of Bertran de Born in particular, I draw texts, translations, and various opinions from the forthcoming edition of *The Poems of the Troubadour Bertran de Born*, ed. William D. Paden, Jr., Tilde Sankovitch, and Patricia Harris Stablein. I wish to thank my collaborators for their help with the texts which I edit here.

3. See Hayden Boyers, "Cleavage in Bertran de Born and Dante," *Modern Philology* 24 (1926–27): 1–3.

4. The Monk's poem (305,10) adapts the *so de la Rassa* from 80,37. Compare also 80,15, the *escondich*; 80,7 and 80,24a, on old and young; 80,27 against rich peasants; and 80,16,17, and 24 against joglars. Most of these correlations were observed by Carl Appel in *Nachrichten von der Gesellschaft der Wissenschaften zu Göttingen, Philologisch-Historische Klasse* (1929), p. 253.

5. These texts are readily available in *Poeti del duecento*, ed. Gianfranco Contini (Milan and Naples: Ricciardi, n.d. [1960]), 1: 585–95.

6. See Angelo Monteverdi in *Giornale Storico della Letteratura Italiana* 82 (1923): 165, n.1.

7. See Frank M. Chambers, "Imitation of Form in the Old Provençal Lyric," *Romance Philology* 6 (1952–53): 104–20. The texts are 80,13 (from Guiraut de Borneill's *so de n'Alamanda*) and 80,34 (from Guillem de Saint Didier), both written in 1183.

8. Most of these imitations were pointed out by Vincenzo de Bartholomaeis in "I Trovadori e la Storia d'Italia," in his *Poesie provenzali storiche relative all'Italia*, 2 vols. (Rome: Senato, 1931), 1: vii–lxxx.

9. I follow Clovis Brunel, *Bibliographie des manuscrits littéraires en ancien Provençal* (Paris: Droz, 1935), and Pillet-Carstens; for MS Mh, Silvio Pellegrini, "Frammento inedito di canzoniere provenzale," *Studi Mediolatini e Volgari* 15 (1967): 89–99.

10. Guido Favati, ed., *Le biografie trovadoriche* (Bologna: Palmaverde, 1961).

11. Jean Boutière and A.-H. Schutz, eds., *Biographies des troubadours: textes*

provençaux des XIIIe et XIVe siècles, 2d rev. ed. Jean Boutière and I.-M. Cluzel (Paris: Nizet, 1964), pp. xliii -xliv. I base my discussion of the prose texts upon the texts and notes of this edition.

12. Ibid., pp. 65, 68.

13. See J. Anglade, "Les Miniatures des chansonniers provençaux," *Romania* 50 (1924): 593–604, and Pio Rajna, "Bertran de Born nelle bricciche di un canzoniere provenzale," *Romania* 50 (1924): 233–46. I have verified Anglade's observations against microfilm. Rajna provides a facsimile of the Frammento Romegialli.

14. It is used in MS K for Raimon de Miraval (fol. 52v) and Gui d'Uissel (fol. 73r), though in K, Bertran does not have it (Rajna, p. 245).

15. I do not agree with Guy de Poerck that in this line Bertran offers to help without fighting. See his edition in *Romanica Gandensia* 7 (1959): 49–63, and the note on p. 59. On the *capel*, see E. Viollet-le-Duc, *Dictionnaire raisonné du mobilier français* (Paris: Gründ et Maguet, n.d.), 5: 266–67 and fig. 3. Anglade described this *capel* as a *casque à salade* (p. 595); but Rajna recognized as a *cappello* the article of identical shape shown in the Frammento Romegialli, where it is colored red (p.245).

16. Ed. Cesare Segre in *La prosa del duecento*, ed. Cesare Segre and Mario Marti (Milan and Naples: Ricciardi, n.d. [1959]); references to Bertran in chapters 19 and 20, pp. 814–17.

17. The relevant *conto* is in ibid., pp. 548–50.

18. Esteve Agullo: Clovis Brunel, *Les Plus Anciennes Chartes en langue provençale* (Paris: Picard, 1926), item 32,1. Guiraut d'Aguilo: Wilhelmina M. Wiacek, *Lexique des noms géographiques et ethniques dans les poésies des troubadours des XIIe et XIIIe siècles* (Paris: Nizet, 1968), s.v. Aguilo.

19. See Stanislaw Stroński, ed., *Le Troubadour Folquet de Marseille* (Krakow: Académie des Sciences, 1910), p. 5* n. 1, and cf. P-C 14, 16, 143, 238, 458.

20. See Celestino Cavedoni, "Delle accoglienze e degli onori ch'ebbero i trovatori provenzali alla corte dei Marchesi d'Este nel secolo XIII," in *Memorie della Real Accademia di Scienze, Lettere e d'Arti di Modena* 2 (1858): 268–312.

21. Alfonso Lazzari, "Il Marchese Obizzo II d'Este signore di Ferrara nel poema di Dante e nella storia," *Giornale Dantesco* 39 (1938): 125–50, esp. 125.

22. Ibid., p. 133.

23. I am indebted for this information to my colleague Gianna Panofsky. Cf. Ettore Galli, *Dizionario pavese-italiano* (Pavia: Istituto Lombardo di Scienze e Lettere, 1965), s.v. beg.

24. Benvenuti de Rambaldis de Imola, *Comentum super Dantis Aldigherij Comoediam*, ed. Jacobo Philippo Lacaita (Florence: Barbèra, 1887), 1: 411. The episode is also mentioned by Fra Salimbene (n. 27 below), but he does not mention the nickname.

25. Cecco Angiolieri, *Qualunque giorno non veggio '1 mi' amore*, v.3.

26. Lazzari, "Il Marchese Obizzo II d'Este," p. 137.

27. *Cronica Fratris Salimbene de Adam Ordinis Minorum*, ed. Oswaldus Holder-Egger, Monumenta Germaniae Historica, Scriptorum vol. 32 (Hanover and Leipzig: Hahniani, 1905–13): 168.

28. Luigi Simeoni, "L'elezione di Obizzo d'Este a signore de Ferrara," *Archivio Storico Italiano* 93 (1935): 165–88.

29. Though it seems unlikely, it is not impossible that this marquis was Obizzo II. See Tommaso Casini, "I trovatori nella marca trivigiana," *Il Propugnatore* 18 (1885): 149–87, esp. 183–84.

30. On the other hand, since Guillem Raimon was a contemporary of Aimeric de Péguilhan, he can hardly have been the same as the Raimon Guillem who exchanged coblas (229,1a) with Ferrari di Ferrara—if Ferrari died after 1330, as Jeanroy says.

31. The old argument of Jeanroy and Santangelo has been repeated by F. Pirot (n. 1 above), p. 216. It was refuted by Olin H. Moore in *The Young King: Henry Plantagenet (1155–83), in History, Literature and Tradition* (Columbus: Ohio State University, 1925), pp. 74–75.

32. Cf. Thomas G. Bergin, *Dante* (New Tork: Orion, 1965), pp. 80–81.

33. These materials were collected by Moore, *The Young King*, pp. 65–73 (summary), 90–95 (texts).

34. Cf. Bergin, "Dante's Provençal Gallery" (n. 1 above).

35. See N. Zingarelli, "Petrarca e i trovadori," in *Provenza e Italia*, ed. Vincenzo Crescini (Florence: Bemporad, n.d. [1930]), p. 106.

36. Because of his Romantic conception of originality, Zingarelli denies that Petrarch imitated Bertran, but it is acknowledged as a matter of course by, for example, F. Neri, in his edition of Francesco Petrarca, *Rime, trionfi e poesie latine* (Milan and Naples: Ricciardi, n.d. [1961]), p. 272. On the mythic function of the troubadours in Petrarch's thought, see Luigi Peirone, "La prospettiva occitanica del Petrarca," *Giornale Italiano di Filologia* 20 (1967): 235–41.

4

Arnaut Daniel's Legacy to Dante and to Pound

James J. Wilhelm

The troubadour Arnaut Daniel exercised a strong influence on the work and thought of Dante Alighieri and Ezra Pound. Although this influence is apparent, it is not always easy to understand. Most modern critics, even when trying hard to embrace Daniel, find it difficult to avoid making negative comments about his work. Maurice Bowra, for example, points out how Daniel taught Dante that "he must employ both rough and smooth elements to break the softness and ease into which Italian verse too readily falls," but elsewhere Bowra cannot resist mentioning the troubadour's "brusque Provençal" and his "boldness and his violence."[1] T. G. Bergin spoke of the troubadour more positively when he noted that to Dante and to Pound Arnaut was first and foremost a "maker of words," as the word *trobaire* indicates in its derivation from *trobar* ("to find," "to invent").[2] This essay will attempt to justify Arnaut further by an examination of his diction, imagery, meter, and sound patterns, first in relation to Dante and then to Pound.

Perhaps the most striking feature of Daniel's poetry is his diction, which is complex, facile, witty, and rather contrived. Its influence on Dante is obvious from the frequent references to Arnaut in the *De Vulgari Eloquentia*; but when one moves from theory to practice, it is not easy to observe any close connections between the two poets. If we put a song of Daniel's that Dante praises in *De Vulgari* 2.6 next to one of the *Vita Nuova* lyrics like the following poem from chapter 8, we see more differences than similarities:

Morte villana, di pietà nemica,
di dolor madre antica,
giudicio incontastabile gravoso,
poi che hai data matera al cor doglioso
ond'io vado pensoso,
di te blasmar la lingua s'affatica.[3]

[Villainous death, enemy of compassion,
ancient mother of grief,
heavy judgment without any appeal,
since you've given my sad heart reason
why I should go with woe,
my tongue will never tire of blaming you.]

[my translation]

A typical Daniel poem translated by Pound shows a marked contrast:

Sols sui qui sai lo sobrafan quem sortz
Al cor d'amor sofren per sobramar,
Car mos volers es tant ferms et entiers
C'anc no s'esduis de celliei ni s'estors
Cui encubic al prim vezer e puois:
Qu'ades ses lieis dic a lieis cochos motz.
Pois quan la vei non sai, tant l'ai, que dire.

[I only, and who elrische pain support
Know our love's heart o'er borne by overlove,
For my desire that is so firm and straight
And unchanged since I found her in my sight
And unturned since she came within my glance,
That far from her my speech springs up aflame;
Near her comes not. So press the words to arrest it.][4]

Pound himself spelled out the basic differences in his youthful critical study, *The Spirit of Romance*: "The Provençal canzone can be understood when sung. Tuscan canzoni often require close study in print before they will yield their meaning."[5] He thus established a useful critical stance in 1910, long before the work of most of the esteemed modern critics, such as Erich Auerbach, who would add that Italian lyric poetry pursues rational patterns of organization, unlike the troubadour poem, which moves in an irrational way reflecting Platonic love-mania.[6]

But if the overall patterns are different, Arnaut and friends are close to Dante in terms of basic poetic techniques: rhyme, rhythm, and diction. In order to grasp the essentials of the *dolce stil nuovo* or "sweet new style" with which he was associated, one must turn to *Purgatorio* 24.43 ff., where Bonagiunta of Lucca, a second-rate poet of an older generation, is speaking:

"Femmina è nata, e non porta ancor benda,"
cominciò el, "che ti farà piacere
la mia città, come ch'om la riprenda . . .
Ma dì s'i'veggio qui colui che fore
trasse le nove rime, cominciando
'Donne ch'avete intelletto d'amore.' "
E io a lui: "I'mi son un che, quando
Amor mi spira, noto, e a quel modo
ch'è ditta dentro vo significando."[7]

["A woman's born who's not yet wearing a wimple,"
began he, "and she will give you comfort in my city,
though others will upbraid her for it . . .
But tell me—do I see here the man
who brought out that new-sounding rhyme
beginning *Ladies who have intellect of love?*"
And I to him: "I am the kind of man
who, when Love breathes upon me, note—and in that mode
he dictates in me, I go making meanings."]

[my translation]

Bonagiunta is praising the poem of *Vita Nuova* 19, which Dante analyzes in the following way. He says that it was written under the direct force of love, with inspiration (*mi spira*). It was composed didactically, so that not a single line could be changed: *ditta dentro*[8] ("dictates within me"). It was also composed in a serious manner, with an eye toward philosophy: *significando* ("making meanings"). We may gather from these remarks that an opposing style, such as that practiced by Bonagiunta and Guittone d'Arezzo, would be unphilosophical, loosely romantic, and probably hollowly rhetorical.

Dante's contempt for Guittone d'Arezzo was clearly expressed in *Purgatorio* 26.115 ff., when Guido Guinizelli passes over the earlier Italians and Guiraut de Bornelh, and says of Arnaut Daniel:

> "O frate," disse, "questi ch'io ti cerno
> col dito," e additò un spirto innanzi,
> "fu miglior fabbro del parlar materno."

> ["O brother, that man where I am pointing—"
> and he pointed out a figure up ahead—
> "*he* was a better craftsman of our mother tongue."]

[my translation]

The striking phrase is *miglior fabbro*, "better craftsman." It is obvious that Dante, like Pound—and also like Eliot, who used this phrase as his dedication line to Pound for *The Waste Land*—thought of the poet as the highest form of artisan. After the birth of imagism, an emphasis on precision became almost synonymous with Pound's name.

The word *dolce*, "sweet," in the phrase *dolce stil nuovo* from *Purgatorio* 24 causes the major problem precisely because it sounds more Victorian than Poundian. Here the treatise *De Vulgari Eloquentia* provides some insight.[9] In part 2, chapters 6 and 7, Dante outlines the range of rhetorical styles that extend in words from the humble *mamma*, which he uses himself in *Purgatorio* 30.44–45 ("quale il fantolin corre a la mamma/quando ha paura": "like the little babe who runs to his Mamma/whenever he's afraid") to the exalted, polysyllabic *amore* or *disio*, "love" or "desire," which are high-sounding and basic in love poetry.

At the level of the complete sentence, the mundane style can be demonstrated by: *Petrus amat multum dominam Bertam*, ("Peter loves Lady Bertha very much"). On a more complex level, Dante settles on the following sentence as one that is *sapidus* ("full of good flavor"): "Eiecta maxima parte florum de sinu tuo, Florentia, nequicquam Trinacriam Totila secundus adivit" ("Having chased away the greater part of the flowers from your bosom, O Florence, in vain did Totila the Second go away to Sicily"). This sentence may sound artificial in my English rendering, but it is possible to see what Dante is working toward: he is trying to combine the metaphor of flowers with common, realistic words like *eiecta* and *adivit*. There is a definite musical rise and fall that begins with the ablative absolute, works through the refrain of *florum* in *Florentia*, moves over the dental alliterations, and halts in the stop-word *adivit*. The sentence shows a mean between rhetorical elaboration and forceful, direct expression. .

Dante mentions some poets who have managed to mix rhetorical idealism with the precision of prose, citing Arnaut Daniel along with himself for his *Amor che ne la mente mi ragiona* ("Love that reasons to me in my mind") of *Convivio* 3. Dante suggests that critics study Virgil, Ovid, Statius, and Lucan for poetry, and prose writers like Livy and Pliny. He levels still another criticism at Guittone d'Arezzo for *plebescere*, "being plebeian." We would have to conclude that the negative poles in poetic composition are artificial rhetoric and trite, common rhetoric.

If we take a cursory look at Guittone d'Arezzo's work, we find that he oscillates between artificial hollowness and vague, indirect, forever abstract expressiveness; at his best, he is close to prose, as Pound often suggested that poets ought to be.[10] In the twentieth century, in fact, Pound railed against these very same excesses: the full-blown, artificial styles of the highly fashionable Victorian and Edwardian poets like Tennyson and his imitators; and the equally artificial folksiness that was popular in America in such writers as Sandburg, Lindsay, and Masters. The poles themselves are not necessarily to be avoided; indeed, Pound repeatedly pointed out that Dante had divided words into "shaggy" (*hirsuta*) and "combed" (*pexa*) groups, among others, and insisted on the usability of all categories. It was merely an excess that had to be shunned.

Dante, for example, always shows a complete respect for the "tragic" or elevated style of the *Aeneid*, but when it came time to pen his own epic, he followed the advice of Guido Cavalcanti, as expressed in *Vita Nuova* 30, and stayed with the tongue and the style of the people. His work is called a comedy largely because of this basic stylistic decision—not because of its happy ending. In the very same way, Pound in the *Cantos* never veered away from the cracker-barrel rhetoric of his favorite persona, Uncle Ez, as in Cantos 12 and 16; but he also tried to hew out passages of metaphysical power and beauty throughout the work.

This same variety can be detected in Daniel, whose diction combines pleasant connotations with the grotesque, and whose sound patterns combine sharp dentals and sibilants with soft liquids and nasals. Let us look at an outstanding example, the third stanza of canso 12, *Doutz brais e critz* ("Sweet cries and cracks"):

> Ben fui grazitz
> E mas paraulas coutas,
> Per so que jes al chausir no fui pecs,
> Anz volgui mais prendre fin aur que ram,
> Lo jorn quez ieu e midonz nos baizem
> Em fetz escut de son bel mantel endi
> Que lausengier fals, lenga de colobra,
> Non o visson, don tan mals motz escampa.
>
> [*Translations*, p. 172]

Pound's translation reads:

> Welcome not lax,
>   and my words were protected
> Not blabbed to other, when I set my likes
> On her. Not brass but gold was 'neath the die
> That day we kissed, and after it she flacked
> O'er me her cloak of indigo, for screening
> Me from all culvertz' eyes, whose blathered bluster
> Can set such spites abroad; win jibes for wages.
>
> [*Translations*, p. 173]

This translation, although a bit belabored, conveys the general sense. In the original, words such as *pecs*, *escut*, and *colobra* are either dissonant in sound or negative in meaning ("stupid," "shield," "serpent"). Monosyllabic fricatives like *fui* ("I was"), *fetz* ("she made"), and *fals* ("false") are modulated by soft palatals, by nasals and diphthongs, culminating in the line that haunted Pound: *Em fetz escut de son bel mantel endi*, which might be rendered literally: "and made for me a shield with her lovely cloak of indigo." Here the warlike shield is countered by the soft, sensuous suggestion of the cloak, and the color indigo is used to bathe the entire scene in a magic glow.

Clearly Daniel, like Dante and Pound, is a rhetorical nominalist, delighting in names, both to expand a frame of reference and to enrich sound values. Canso 12 in the *Translations* contains the following extraordinary catalogue: Saint Guillem, blind Longinus, Rome (*Roam*),

Jerusalem, Dobra, Pampeluna (*Luna-pampa*), Galicia, as well as the names of some Spanish nobles. Many of these words rhyme with others, and thus unite the familiar with the strange. The exotic allusions undoubtedly irked some of Daniel's readers, just as Pound's Chinese allusions annoy many today, but there is also a countering value in that the sound pattern is extremely varied. Daniel detests the trite and the ordinary in the same way Pound and Dante do. One can say, furthermore, that Daniel is international in his scope, as are his Italian and American successors.

Any apologist for Daniel must eventually face the broader question of his relationship to the practice of *trobar clus*, the "closed" or "hermetic" style of composition, which existed alongside the plain or simple style called *trobar leu* or *trobar pla*. There is no space here for an intellectual consideration of trobar clus, for this would take us into the realm of biblical exegesis on the one hand and Manicheanism or witchcraft on the other—topics that can be handled properly only in books.[11] This essay will continue to restrict itself to a consideration of rhetoric.

First of all, one must say firmly that not all of Daniel's poems *are* written in an obscure or difficult manner. Secondly, one must admit that Daniel's most frequently cited poem in this style, *Lo ferm voler* ("The firm desire"), is rather naïvely constructed. Pound usually viewed this work as an embarrassing bit of juvenilia.[12] In fact, Pound pursued a sensible course in his examination of Daniel's work by at first limiting himself exclusively to the poems cited by Dante in the *De Vulgari*. Since Dante was examining these poems in a rational manner, Pound adopted a similar approach; and as a result, the Daniel who emerges from Pound's translations is remarkably lucid:

> Lancan son passat li giure
> E noi reman puois ni comba,
> Et el verdier la flors trembla
> Sus el entrecim on poma,
> La flors e li chan eil clar quil
> Ab la sazon doussa e coigna
> M'enseignon c'ab joi m'apoigna,
> Sai al temps de l'intran d'april.

> [When the frosts are gone and over,
> And are stripped from hill and hollow,

When in close the blossom blinketh
From the spray where the fruit cometh,
The flower and song and the clarion
Of the gay season and merry
Bid me with high joy to bear me
Through days while April's coming on.]

[*Translations*, pp. 152–53]

Another stanza, the sixth of Canso 11, shows diction and rhythms that are more complex, but still very much held in control. A literal translation by me follows because the one offered by Pound facing the text is truncated:

Pensar de lieis m'es repaus,
E tragam ams los huoills crancs
S'a lieis vezer nols estuich;
El cor non crezatz qu'en tuoilla,
Car orars ni jocs ni viula
Nom pot de leis un travers jonc
Partir . . . C'ai dig? Dieus, tum somertz
Om peris el peleagre!

[The thought of her is my repose,
And may my two eyes weak constrain me
If they aren't summoned to her sight;
And my heart—don't think it veers off,
For prayers nor jests nor violining
Could ever move her away from me
A reed's breadth . . . What? God! You sank me
Like one who's lost in a lagoon!]

[*Translations*, p. 170]

In this extraordinary stanza we move from the tranquil vision of love, through erotic madness, to drowning. The tortured quality of the rhythm helps to break up a linear presentation, and in no way interferes with the thought. In fact, the twisted exposition stresses the tangled intellect behind it. Perhaps only an accomplished rhymester like John Skelton or a lyricist-musician like Edmund Waller or Thomas Campion could imitate this fractured, contradictory, highly sophisticated frame of mind. The troubadour music, when performed, must have been extremely elastic to bear these thrusts and lunges.

In his codas Daniel is fully capable of emerging from his miasmic surfaces, as in the celebrated close of *En cest sonet coind'e leri* ("In this little song pretty and gay"):

> Ieu sui Arnautz qu'amas l'aura,
> E chatz la lebre ab lo bou
> E nadi contra suberna.[13]

> [I am Arnaut, who amasses the wind
> And chases the rabbit with the bull
> And swims against the rising tide.]
>
> [my translation]

For a time Pound seemed to be biased against this poem because it was a *sonet* (his dislike of the full-fledged sonnets of Petrarca being almost legendary). He rendered it rather lamely as an addition to the *Translations* (p. 423), where he mistook *amas* ("amass") as a form of *amar* ("love"), and dulled the sharp imagery of the bull and the hare by throwing in an ox-cart.

If these lines create an unforgettable picture of the rebellious artist running counter to the spirit of his time and bucking the popular taste—how like those exiles of Rapallo and Ravenna!—the opening lines of the poem create the equally memorable contrast of the classical troubadour hewing away at his work like a Romanesque sculptor:

> En cest sonet coind'e leri
> Fauc motz e capuig e doli,
> E serant verai e cert
> Quan n'aurai passat la lima

> [Though this measure quaint confine me,
> And I chip out words and plane them,
>   They shall yet be true and clear
> When I finally have filed them.]
>
> [*Translations*, p. 421]

In the *Vita Nuova*, Dante shows similar care in selecting the proper word. For example, he goes so far as to print two openings for the poem of chapter 34, and in chapters 24 and 40, he makes important distinctions between words, with pun value. Again and again he proves himself to be a verbal artisan, and this also shows in the way that he approaches his own poems in the commentaries. Many critics, especially of the nineteenth century, have regarded these remarks as flaws or embarrassments, while others, especially today, have defended them as imitations of biblical exegesis; they suggest that Dante is a Scholastic treating his own work as if it had a hieratic value, like the Bible.[14] This point of view is not entirely wrong, for Dante does take his work very seriously, but we must also examine the action in the light of aesthetics.

Obviously Dante wrote the commentaries to show the reader the great care that had gone into every phase of their construction. The analyses are always mechanical rather than conceptual, for Dante is preoccupied with poetic methodology. If we think back to *Vita Nuova* 25, we may recall that Cavalcanti mentioned that most of the masses, especially women, did not have a knowledge of Latin; they were therefore not only cut off from poetry itself, but also from the rhetorical handbooks describing it. As a result, Dante had to begin in a way that sounds primitive to the modern reader. But Pound also adopted a patient, pedagogical approach in his highly influential essay "How to Read," and in his critical texbook, *The ABC of Reading*. Both writers are in some ways teachers, whether they care to admit it or not. Both express a love for the profession in their works: Dante in his sensitive handling of Brunetto Latini, and Pound in his memories of teachers from Hamilton and the University of Pennsylvania. Poetry to Pound was a major stroke in the general cultural ideogram; to Dante it was the brook that encircled and defended his *nobile castello*, "noble castle" (*Inferno* 4.106), the symbolic center of secular wisdom.

A vivid, dramatic opening for lyric poems is still another idea bequeathed by the troubadour to his successors. Daniel's own poems begin this way in Pound's translation: *En breu brisaral temps braus* (*Trans.*, p. 168), "Briefly bursteth season brisk" (p. 169); *L'aura amara/ Fals bruoills brancutz/ Clarzir* (p. 160), "The bitter air/ Strips panoply/ From trees" (p. 161); *Doutz brais e critz,/ Lais e cantars e voutas* (p. 172), "Sweet cries and cracks/ and lays and chants inflected" (p. 173). These poems do not dally; from the start, they move. Similarly, the lyrics of the *Vita Nuova* show a distinct flair for the dramatic: *Cavalcando l'al-tr'ier per un cammino*, "Riding the other day upon a highway" (chap. 8); *Ne li occhi porta la mia donna Amore*, "My lady carries Love within her eyes" (chap. 21); *Voi che portate la sembianza umile,* "You who bear the semblance of humility" (chap. 22); and *Deh peregrini che pensosi andate*, "Alas, pilgrims, who move so thoughtfully" (chap. 40). Pound's early poetry is similarly dramatic and visual. The opening lines of his monologues of Cino of Pistoia and Bertran de Born both show a tendency to delve into the heart of the poetic matter.

Pound discovered his interest in Daniel through Dante, and thus all three poets are linked in their poetic theories.[15] Using the *De Vulgari* as his guide, Pound discussed the troubadours in chapters 2 and 3 of his *Spirit of Romance* almost entirely from the perspective of Dante's criticism. In his presentation Daniel emerges as the chief singer of Provence. Pound follows Dante's lead and relates the two poets closely, as when he says of the Italian:

> His vividness depends much on his comparison by simile to particular phenomena; this we have already noted in the chapter on Arnaut Daniel; thus Dante, following the Provençal, says, not "where a river pools itself," but "As at Arles, where the Rhone pools itself."[16]

Even the citation of a simile from *Paradiso* 26.85 leads Pound to credit Daniel for the inspiration, as far as presentation goes.[17] Dante showed his respect for Daniel by letting him speak his own tongue in *Purgatorio* 26, a decision that Pound duly noted. Pound went even further by attributing most of his basic critical ideas to the troubadour; and thus Daniel looms as a genius behind twentieth-century imagism, since a lucid use of the visual image was a cornerstone of the school's belief, and Pound was its direct promoter.

In a series of articles written for the economist-editor A. R. Orage, Pound spelled out the importance of Daniel for himself and for the modern world. He cited Daniel's "style," concentrating on poetic diction, on the handling of the visual image, on the wedding of rhythm to sound and sense—in short, the points already covered in this essay. He went on to cite "the beauty to be gotten from a similarity of line-terminations" that "depends not upon their multiplicity, but upon their action the one upon the other; not upon frequency, but upon the manner of sequence and combination."[18] Obviously he had in mind a poem like the celebrated *L'aura amara*, in which the first stanza contains a series of clipped rhymes that force the thought forward in leaps and bounds:

L'aura amara
Fals bruoills brancutz
Clarzir
Quel doutz espeissa ab fuoills,
Els letz
Becs
Dels auzels ramencs
Ten balps e mutz,
Pars
E non-pars

[The bitter air
Strips panoply
From trees
Where softer winds set leaves,
And glad
Beaks
Now in brakes are coy,
Scarce peep the wee
Mates
And un-mates.]

[*Translations*, pp. 160–61]

There is no doubt that much of the troubadour poetry written after Daniel during the Albigensian period is boring. The rhyme schemes are tired and overworked, the rhythmic schemes are predictable, the thought is pedestrian, and the visual images, insofar as they exist, scarcely rise above the trite. None of these objections can be raised against Daniel, for even when he is using a rather worn trope—such as saying that he would not exchange his lady for a rich city—he selects a novel place like Lucerne rather than the overused Pisa and Rome. The same can be said about his use of rhythm and rhyme as they interact in the stanza above. Instead of the dull, end-stopped lines with insistent paratactic construction that recur constantly in Guiraut de Bornelh, Daniel employs a hopping, leaping sound—much like the movement of a bird.

It is the duty of every great poet to correct the excesses of his predecessors. Pound fought to break the stranglehold of the sonnet form and the heave of the iambic, in addition to overembellished diction.

Dante, as Bowra observed, had to contend with the insidious tendency of the Italian language to turn into a saccharine confection. Daniel was valuable to both, for in addition to a novel use of words and musical sounds, he offered a fresh approach to poetic beat, the pulse of the poem. In the following stanza the rhythm breaks up the tendencies of the words to fall into patterns that are too fixed, as the interior caesuras help to augment the stops and stresses at the ends of the lines. What we have here is a poetic beat working with and against the musical rhythm (the line being more a musical entity than a poetic one):

> Autet e bas entrels prims fuoills
> Son nou de flors li ram eil renc
> E noi ten mut bec ni gola
> Nuills auzels, anz braia e chanta
> Cadahus
> En son us:
> Per joi qu'ai d'els e del tems
> Chant, mas amors mi asauta
> Quels motz ab lo son acorda.
>
> [*Translations*, p. 156]

Pound's translation also creates a poetic medium that defeats the insistent beat of the metronome, just as it tosses the "book of fixed tropes" out of the window:

> Now high and low, where leaves renew,
> Come buds on bough and spalliard pleach
> And no beak nor throat is muted;
> Auzel each in tune contrasted
> Letteth loose
> Wriblis [warblings] spruce.
> Joy for them and spring would set
> Song on me, but Love assaileth
> Me and sets my words t'his dancing.
>
> [*Translations*, p. 157]

It might be hard to find an equivalent in the lyrical Dante, but the poems written about the Rock Lady (*la donna petrosa*) catch some of the mysterious quality of composition that Daniel had perfected earlier, and certainly the bulk of the writing in the *Commedia* shows a mastery over rhythm. Dante, no less than Pound, did not let the poetic line dominate him, and here again Daniel hovers somewhere in the background.

The final point that Pound makes about Daniel's genius concerns the man's visual eye and his general intellect:

> For that fineness of Arnaut's senses which made him chary of his rhymes, impatient of tunes that would have distorted his language, fastidious of redundance, made him likewise accurate in his observation of Nature.[19]

This is indeed high praise. Its origin can be traced to a passage where Daniel presents the following picture of his beloved:

> God who did tax
>   not Longus' sin, respected
> That blind centurion beneath the spikes
> And him forgave, grant that we two shall lie
> Within one room, and seal therein our pact,
> Yes, that she kiss me in the half-light, leaning
> To me, and laugh and strip and stand forth in the lustre
> Where lamp-light with light limb but half engages.
>
>   [*Translations*, pp. 173 ff.]

The last two lines in Provençal read:

> Quel seu bel cors baisan rizen descobra
> E quel remir contral lum de la lampa.
>
>   [*Translations*, p. 174]

The image of the woman in the candlelight is indeed a thousand times more explicitly suggestive than almost any other image of a woman in Provençal poetry. Pound was haunted by the phrase *e quel remir* ("and that look"), using it in Cantos 7 and 20 in contexts that mention incandescent human beauty.[20] One feels in Daniel's lines a rising of the physical into the metaphysical in a way that is consummated in Dante. Daniel almost alone of the troubadours can offer us such a development. His contemporaries are neither exact enough nor suggestive enough to compete with him in this respect. The preceding stanza, with the mention of the "cloak of indigo" that his beloved throws around him as a shield, does the same thing. Daniel's handling of light imagery was bound to affect Pound, who was already very interested in Neo-platonic light philosophers like Grosseteste, Scotus Erigena, and Plotinus. Perhaps one of the most beautiful passages in Daniel's poetry deals precisely with a rain of golden sunlight:

> Bertran, non cre de sai lo Nil
> Mais tant de fin joi m'apoigna
> Tro lai on lo soleills ploigna,
> Tro lai on lo soleills plovil.
>
> [Sir Bertran, sure no pleasure's won
> Like this freedom naught so merry
> 'Twixt Nile 'n' where the suns miscarry
>   To where the rain falls from the sun.]
>   [*Translations*, pp. 154–55]

An echo of this passage occurs in Pound's own poetry in a paradisal context:

> Thus the light rains, thus pours, *e lo soleills plovil*
> The liquid and rushing crystal
>   beneath the knees of the gods.
>   [Canto 4, p. 15]

In *The Cantos* Pound never loses sight of Daniel as a master crafts-man. He mulls over the words *ongla* (nail) and *oncle* (uncle) from Daniel's sestina *Lo ferm voler* in Canto 6 (p. 21), and he debates the meaning of the puzzling word *noigandres* from Daniel's *Er vei vermeills* ("Now I see green") in Canto 20 (pp. 89–90). He even made a special trip to Freiburg to speak with the Provençal lexicographer Emil Levy to try to establish a precise interpretation. Pound in effect recreates the craftsmanlike care of Daniel by retracing his steps through the creative process. In fact, he devoted many months of his life to translating the troubadour, against the advice of several of his friends.

Possibly the most interesting way in which Pound regards Daniel concerns the troubadour's closeness to nature. Pound sees him as a hymner of Natura. The modern poet could hear the calls of birds again and again in Daniel's lines, and struggled (somewhat in vain) to reproduce them:

> Mas pels us
> Estauc clus
>
> Burns profuse,
> Held recluse
>
> [*Translations*, pp. 156–57]

or again:

> Anz sui brus
> Et estrus
>
> And no truce
> But misuse
>
> [*Translations*, pp. 158–59]

In Canto 29, Pound places Daniel in the position of a man who is studying the wave-patterns in the castle at Excideuil.[21] Daniel's interest in the undulatory patterns of the ocean is as important as his receptivity to the cry of the bird. Beneath the mystical tidal wave of the Middle Ages, Daniel kept the worship of the goddess Natura alive. Is there not a similar acknowledgment in Dante's placing of Daniel among the Lustful, just one rung beneath the Earthly Paradise? In the *Commedia*, Daniel is as close to heaven on earth as a sinner can get.

As an artist, Daniel was viewed by both Dante and Pound as a supreme classicist, a hewer and shaper and planer of every word; but as a man of his time, he was viewed by both Dante and Pound as a nature-loving romantic. The reader who returns to Daniel and who is willing to overcome any preconceived notions about strange words and variant patterns and explosive sounds will find that these judgments—by two of the greatest poets of their own ages—are, in the last analysis, convincing.

NOTES

1. "Dante and Arnaut Daniel," *Speculum* 27 (1952), 469, 474; see Salvatore Santangelo, *Dante e i trovatori provenzali* (Catania: Giannota, 1921).
2. "Dante's Provençal Gallery," *Speculum* 40 (1965), 20.
3. *La Vita Nuova*, ed. N. Sapegno, 2d ed. (Milan: Mursia, 1968), p. 12.

4. *Translations*, rev. ed. (New York: New Directions Paper, 1963), p. 178, for Provençal; p. 179 for English. All translations of Daniel are by Pound, unless otherwise stated. Essay follows Pound's texts of Daniel in *Translations*, reprinted from editions of R. Lavaud, *Annales du Midi* 22 (1910), 77 ff., and U. A. Canello (Halle: Niemeyer, 1883), unless otherwise indicated. Pound's works are reprinted with the permission of New Directions, Faber & Faber, and Peter Owen.

5. (New York: New Directions, n.d.), p. 113.

6. *Dante: Poet of the Secular World*, trans. R. Manheim (Chicago: University of Chicago Press, 1961), pp. 24 ff.

7. *La Commedia*, ed. Giorgio Petrocchi, 4 vols. (Milan: Mondadori, 1966–67).

8. *Ditta* can mean simply "poetize," as in Latin *dictare*. For the work of Dante's predecessors, see *Poeti del duecento*, ed. G. Contini, 2 vols. (Milan: Ricciardi, 1960).

9. Ed. A. Marigo, rev. P. G. Ricci, 3d ed. (Florence: Le Monnier, 1968).

10. *Rime*, ed. F. Egidi (Bari: Laterza, 1940); cf. the trickery of nos. 12, 13, with the tractate quality of no. 20.

11. See Leo Pollman, "Trobar clus," *Bibelexegese und Hispano-Arabische Literatur* (Munster: Aschendorff, 1965) and Ulrich Mölk, *Trobar clus, Trobar leu* (Munich: Fink, 1968).

12. *The Spirit of Romance*, p. 36.

13. *Anthology of Provençal Troubadours*, ed. R. T. Hill and T. G. Bergin (New Haven: Yale University Press, 1957), pp. 78–79; not in *Translations*.

14. Exegetical approaches by C. S. Singleton, *Essay on "Vita Nuova"* (Cambridge: Harvard University Press, 1949); J. E. Shaw, *Essays on "Vita Nuova"* (Princeton: Princeton University Press, 1929); cf. Karl Vossler, *Mediaeval Culture*, tr. W. C. Lawton, 2 vols. (rpt. New York: Ungar, 1958), 2: 164.

15. See Stuart Y. McDougal, *Ezra Pound and Troubadour Tradition* (Princeton: Princeton University Press, 1973), esp. pp. 8 ff.

16. *The Spirit of Romance*, p. 159.

17. Ibid., p. 150.

18. *New Age*, 10 (1911–12): 179.

19. Ibid.

20. *The Cantos* (New York: New Directions, 1972), pp. 26, 90.

21. Ibid., p. 145. For the interesting news that the actual person described in this incident is T. S. Eliot, see Hugh Kenner, *The Pound Era* (Berkeley: California, 1972), pp. 336–37.

5

Dante's *Purgatorio*: The Poem Reveals Itself

Kenneth John Atchity

One dimension of the *Purgatorio* is "the inward-turning self-reflexive-ness" by which the middle canticle of Dante's "poema sacro" comments upon its own nature so fully that artistic introspection becomes a major theme. As the *Purgatorio* unfolds, this theme expands until the "optimum reader"[1] is compelled by the poem's own view of its impact on his life. Dante's impact, both moral and artistic, chiefly derives from the equivalence between the demands he makes on his reader for study and self-reflection, and the studied artistic self-reflexiveness of his great poem.

For us, then, Dante-the-narrator[2] plays the role of Beatrice, return-ing to Hell in order to allow us to go there—and beyond. The descent we undertake, our reading of the poem, is as vivid as the pilgrim's journey (recalled by the narrator, the pilgrim returned). And we are meant to investigate the corners of the poem, the narrator's account, as earnestly and meticulously as the pilgrim himself explored the landscape of his journey. As he is helped by others within the fiction, so the narrator helps us to reenter the fiction of the *Commedia* as critical readers.

The self-image of the *Commedia* is revealed most insistently in the numerous passages within the *Purgatorio* that deal, in one way or another, with art. Their frequency identifies this canticle as the one most concerned with its own poetic nature. Such passages can be viewed as analogues of the poem itself, both as a whole and in its diverse aspects, so that analyzing their effects upon the fictional realm and upon the

85

pilgrim may suggest the way in which the *Commedia* means to affect both the world of its reader and the reader himself. The *Purgatorio*, as the canticle in which time and eternity coexist in the souls as well as in the pilgrim, is the appropriate place for defining the spiritual potential of human art in terms of the human insufficiency for divine creation.

Adam, in *Paradiso* 26. 130 ff., is not the first one to recognize the paradox of "transhumanizing . . . in words" [*Par*. 1.70–71]—of seeking unchanging truth by means of an ever-fluid medium. Nonetheless, language is man's main means of communication, and the pilgrim's purpose in eternity is to learn how to shape words so that they will become, despite their physical basis, spiritually effective. If *we* are to see the beatific vision, we shall see it, then, in Dante's poem. Only then will Dante have succeeded in advancing *our* cause, as the pilgrim, by his prayers, can advance the cause of Manfred [*Purg*. 3.142–45] and the others in Purgatory once he has returned from Paradise. In the *Purgatorio*, more emphatically than in any other work of the Middle Ages, the reader is drawn into the fiction, so that he, like the pilgrim, can perfect his own reality once he has returned to time from the timeless moral and artistic experience.

Thomas G. Bergin has noted that the *Purgatorio* is preoccupied with art;[3] indeed, so replete is this canticle with references to art that we hardly know where to begin. Perhaps it will help to enumerate several different devices through which the poem declaims its own aesthetic and moral. These devices fall into three chief categories: (1) statements, by the pilgrim or the narrator, to characters within the fiction or to the reader; (2) narrative presentation of other arts; and (3) contacts with other poets. Associated with these three types of devices are certain verbal and phraseological patterns, as well as a number of specific motifs and images. This essay, however, concerns itself only with the three main categories, because they are the most definitive revelations of the poem's self-image.

In a poem that ultimately proclaims its own self-image by comparing the universe itself to a book, "legato con amore in un volume" ("bound in one volume by love," *Par*. 33.82),[4] it is not surprising that artistic self-consciousness should be progressive. So the contrast between Purgatory and Hell is borne out by the univocal psalms that never leave our ears on this mountain, the opposite of the cacophony of the *Inferno*, just as Purgatory is the geometrically opposite extroversion of that conically introverted, empty Hell. Moreover, Purgatory is the gate of Paradise [9.128], as its poetic language is the gateway to the reader's personal inspiration and salvation.

No wonder the purpose of the *Commedia* is touched upon so often in the *Purgatorio*. That purpose is as manifold as the text itself. The unrenewed pilgrim tells the gathering souls that "quinci su vo per non esser piú cieco" ("Upward I go to be no longer blind," 26.58), proving his final acceptance of Cato's early injunction (2.122–23). A more selfless purpose is revealed when he tells the souls in canto 5:

> ma s'a voi piace
> cosa ch'io possa, spiriti ben nati,
> voi dite, e io farò per quella pace
> che dietro a' piedi di sí fatta guida
> di mondo in mondo cercar mi si face.
>
> [5.59–63]

> [but if I can do aught
> To bring you solace, spirits born to good,
> Say but the word; I'll do it for that peace
> Which bids me seek it out from world to world,
> Close following in the steps of such a guide.]

Dante will eventually discover that " 'n la sua volontade è nostra pace" ("in His will is our peace," *Par.* 3.85), but already here he realizes that men must find peace as a community, helping one another (through language) as he helps himself. Moreover, just as this speech connects the narrator-to-be with the souls in eternity—by offering to serve them with his future speech—so the pilgrim's question of Marco Lombardo links those souls with us in time: "Ma priego che m'addite la cagione,/ Sí ch'i' la veggia, e ch'i' la mostri altrui" ("But I would have you indicate the cause/ That, seeing it, I may make others see," 16.62–63). Here the pilgrim clearly foresees his narrative role. Later, he is even clearer in specifying the exact artistic medium of his future telling (*significando*): "ditemi, acciò ch'ancor carte ne verghi" ("tell me, so I may further leaves inscribe," 26.64). He may *see* and understand and be saved; we must *read* the record of his vision as our way to salvation. The power that compels Dante's personal pilgrimage becomes, when he returns, the power that inspires his art—inspiring, that is, the *inspiring* account of his journey (3.97–99).

That power comes not from within but from God, moving from the ultimate outside to within, so that the outgoing force of Dante's art is both his own—that is, human—and also divine. That is what he means to tell Bonagiunta in canto 24. The *Commedia* is, in effect, art transformed into effective prayer because its author has heard and has been heard in Paradise (cf. *Purg.* 4.133–35). That is why the narrator can do what John and Paul, as the letter to Can Grande explains, could not do—*trasumanar significar per verba* ("signify going beyond the human in words," *Par.* 1.70)—because his words have been ordered miraculously by God to become revelation incarnate. The new law allowing this journey explains why even the *pilgrim's* words have such force in eternity.

(1) Important revelations of the poem's aesthetic are the addresses of the narrator to the reader, of the pilgrim to Virgil, of Virgil to the pilgrim (who, then, becomes analogous to the student-reader), and direct statements about art by the pilgrim and the narrator. These multiple distinctions in persona are necessitated by the poem—which posits *three* Dantes. When, for example, the pilgrim modestly protests, "Io non Enea, io non Paulo sono" ("Aeneas am I not, nor am I Paul," *Inf.* 2.32), we must ascertain which Dante is saying what. The pilgrim's disclaimer means one thing, the narrator's another, and the poem's self-irony (the author's) a third.

For in the last case the poem's self-consciousness considers itself as indeed superior to Aeneas or to Paul, as, in fact, more nearly analogous to Beatrice or to Christ—inasmuch as its accurate account of eternity leads us to the divine vision. The intentional fallacy notwithstanding, Dante has made it so that his poem subsumes his self, encompassing his internal inspiration thereby to express it externally. He is proud, then, not for himself but for his poem. And we must accept this clever subterfuge to appreciate the *Commedia* which, almost like God's creation, is the embodiment of its maker's artistic, creative self—aimed at elevating our spirits to its own sublime level. The addresses must be understood holistically, in this light: that the journey narrated is a true one.

Erich Auerbach marks the absence of direct address from classical epic poetry;[5] and Nelson notes that there are more addresses in the *Purgatorio* than in the other two canticles.[6] In canto 8 the narrator interrupts his description of the univocal, prayerful singing of the souls to insure our participation: "Aguzza qui, lettor, ben li occhi al vero,/ ché 'l velo è ora ben tanto sottile, / certo che 'l trapassar dento è leggero" ("Your sight here, reader, sharpen to the truth, / For now indeed so tenuous is the veil / It were not hard to penetrate within," 8.19–21). What follows is an extended metaphor for man's middle position in the war between good and evil, as the angels come to secure the Valley of the Princes from the serpent.[7] Evil is still a danger because the perfection of the circle is not accomplished until the spiral terraces of Purgatory are left behind.

If this admonition of the narrator is moral, the following one is artistic: "Lettor, tu vedi ben com'io innalzo / la mia matera, e però con piú arte / non ti maravigliar s'io la rincalzo" ("Reader, well may you mark how I exalt / My story's substance, therefore wonder not / If now I strengthen it with higher art," 9. 70–72). Other addresses ask the reader to use his memory to aid imagination in a process of reinforcement analogous to the pilgrim's aesthetic reaction to the divine artistry he sees in cantos 10 and 12 (17.1–18), and direct the reader to supplementary reading in the interest of narrative economy (29.97–102), concomitantly enhancing the divine authority of his account through scriptural allusions. Still another asks us to empathize with the pilgrim—in a statement that applies as much to our reaction to the *Commedia* as it does to the pilgrim's reaction to the divine bas-reliefs:

> Pensa, lettor, s'io mi maravigliava,
>   quando vedea la cosa in sé queta,
>   e nell'idolo suo si trasmutava.
>
> [*Purg.* 31.124–26]
>
> [Consider, Reader, how I was amazed
>   Seeing the thing itself stay motionless
>   And in its image ever changing shape.]

Direct addresses are complemented by direct statements from both pilgrim and narrator to insure the complicity of the reader. One of the most fascinating of such passages occurs when the pilgrim compares his effect on the siren [19.10 ff.] to that of the sun as it motivates life both on earth and in Purgatory. The narrator is reminding us that the pilgrim himself is, throughout his poem, the outward force that provokes the speech of those he meets in eternity—just as, he tells Bonagiunta, love is the force that moves him (cf. 19.15, 24.53). What is lacking here, as the shocking end of the siren passage reveals, is that absolute correspondence between artistic *mover* and artistically *moved* that differentiates Dante's art from hers.

The verbal echoes—"io son"—make the contrast evident (cf. 19.19; 24.51 ff.), just as, thematically, the siren episode recalls the misused art that damned Paolo and Francesca to eternal sorrow in *Inferno* 5. Once the narrator uses a strange body-reading metaphor to describe the emaciated visages he sees (23.32–33), so we know that he, too, is a practiced reader. He even asks us rhetorical questions, to draw us into his view and his experience so that it becomes as real to us as our own reality (5.19 ff.). Unlike Boccaccio (and later Renaissance writers like Rabelais and Nashe), however, Dante refers to us always in the singular (*lettor*). He does so because he assumes that, as we educate ourselves in his poem, we will grow to be increasingly like him morally and artistically, until we become reduced to the single "optimum reader," with one definable common character. The narrator will even admit partial ignorance to convince us of our equivalence to him (18.127 ff.).

Four times Dante interrupts his narrative to "comment in his fully 'educated' voice—his voice from the world."[8] (1) The opening invocation, "o sante Muse," proclaims the combination of Christian morality with classical artistry (1.6–12), their accompaniment (*seguitando*) suggesting the bilateral components of his poetic expression (*significando*). (2) In canto 17, Dante invokes abstract imagination, instructing us about the divine source of its sensual impact (17.13–18). (3) The narrator's second invocation of the Heliconian Muses combines formality with a hint of the poet's personal sacrifices for his art (29.40 ff.), begging strength "forti cose a pensar mettere in versi" ("to set in verse things mighty to conceive," 29.42). (4) The closing lines of the *Purgatorio* are remarkable for their self-reflexive evocation of complicity with the reader, as the narrator speaks of the writing material which the reader presently holds in hand:

> S'io avessi, lettor, piú lungo spazio
>   da scrivere i' pur cantere' in parte
>   lo dolce ber che mai non m'avría sazio;
> ma perché *piene son tutte le carte*
>   ordite a questa cantica seconda,
>   non mi lascia più ir lo fren dell'arte.

[33.136–41]

[If I had, Reader, more abundant space
   To write, I would sing here at least in part
   Of that sweet draught which ne'er could satiate me.
But inasmuch as *all the sheets* ordained
   For this my second canticle *are filled*,
   The curb of art will let me go no further.]

Here indeed is a happy congruence between the moral and the artistic. *Ordite* (138) reveals that third Dante—or the "self" of the poem—who is the lord of its own creation. The authority of the narrator's sense of closure insists that we, too, find here the proper ending to our moral and aesthetic purgatorial experience. And the ultimate effect of the narrator's explicit reference to himself, in his envoi, as a writer, is the reinforcement, in Auerbach's words, of "a fiction so fused with reality that one easily forgets where its realm begins."[9] That is, we accept the narrator's word for his sudden restriction as if that restriction were indeed real—and not self-imposed by the poem. The triangle of reader, narrator, and fictional character (pilgrim-becoming-narrator) is changed into a continuous circle that predicts the union of all discrete points in the pilgrim's ultimate experience: in the final lines of the artistic vision (of the *Paradiso*) the reader's mind will become literally involved with the mind of Dante, as the pilgrim's was with the mind of God.

Finally, we must not fail to note that Dante, in this ending of the *Purgatorio*, definitely *leads* us; he does not give his reader a choice of remaining behind but directs him upward with the pilgrim. He tells us that we, too, are ready for Paradise, whether we agree or not: "The reader, as envisioned by Dante . . . is a disciple. He is not expected to discuss or judge, but to follow; using his own forces, but the way Dante orders him to."[10] That *ordite* applies to the reading as well as to the writing. Our Virgil, Dante-the-narrator, *forces* us to turn the page.

We come now to those marvelously evocative images that demonstrate Dante's love for a favorite rhetorical device of the classical world, *ecphrasis*, or the poetic description of material objects of art, exemplified by Homer's description of Achilles' shield (*Iliad* 18), by Virgil's of Aeneas's shield (*Aeneid* 8), or by the paintings on the walls of Carthage (*Aeneid* 1).[11] The marble carvings on the walls of Purgatory in canto 10 can be compared more profitably with Homer's shield of Achilles than with Keats's "Grecian Urn." Both these instances of ecphrasis represent pictorial perfection as the ideal. But for Keats ideality is associated with interrupted, uncompleted action; the figures on his urn are frozen forever in arrested mobility.

The figures on Homer's shield, on the other hand, move and speak in a paradox of continual yet immutable change that transcends the graphic art form (bronze-forging) being depicted. To Dante, as to Homer, perfection implies constant life; and life means motion. As the pilgrim's learning eyes comprehend those figures on the wall and bring them to life, the narrator reassembles them vividly for our perusal. We, in turn, must breathe into the printed images our share of communicative vitality, across the abyss of time between us and Dante, to make his words, as we reread them, live ever and again. Just as the poem finds its reflection in allegorized reality, likening itself to a little ship (cf. 1.1 and 32.129), so in canto 10 it reveals its countenance in fictional artistry.

The first thing the narrator tells his reader is that the carvings are superior to man's art, and even to nature's (10. 32–33). They are as extraordinary as is his pilgrimage. What do these carvings represent— beyond their literal moral meaning? It is not as crucial to decide whether the inspiration for this passage lay in Dante's impression of the realistic sculpture of Giovanni Pisano or the painting of Giotto as it is to agree that Dante means to present these sculptures as miraculous.[12] The divine images demonstrate the inadequacy of human sculpture to convey the essentially sacred with the same degree of authenticity as it can be conveyed in this, Dante's, art of words.[13]

So the carvings must be considered a poetic microcosm, an analogue of the poem itself, not as moral substance but as pure mimetic form. Gabriel, in the first scene, "non sembiava imagine che tace," ("appeared to be no wordless image but as real as life," 10.39). And Mary's response, "Ecce ancilla Dei" ("Behold the handmaid of the Lord," 10. 44), is not carved literally into the stone—as it is actually inscribed, for example, on the "Annunciation" of Arnolfo di Cambio—but instead "in atto" ("in her gestures," 10.43). The pilgrim's educated eye is necessary to *realize* this artistic communication. The repeated reference to vision in this canto emphasizes that he must be prepared to interpret what he sees, bringing his perspective to bear upon the evidence provided by his senses.

Demanding the same degree of involvement in each case, the realism of the fictional art to the pilgrim is analogous to the realistic impression the poem itself intends to make upon the reader. Urged by Virgil to move his eyes (46), as he has so often urged him to move his body along the road, Dante makes his eyes disposed (54) to read the other "storia nella roccia" ("storied stone," 52). Although only the pilgrim's eyes are *really* involved, Dante dramatically explains the way in which his other senses are no less forcefully involved *imaginatively* (55 ff.). Trajan's bannered eagles even seem to flutter in the wind (80), as if the eye itself were being deceived—or rather, were seeing through the static surface to the essential vitality latent in the art form and waiting to be released by the imaginative observer.

There follows the narrator's description of the poignant confrontation between the poor widow and the emperor, with every word recorded for us to see as the pilgrim must have accurately imagined them. He is able to *hear* the sculpted exchange, not only because he knows the famous legend discursively, but also because his celestial mission has made him the ideal observer who can pierce the veil—i.e. the silent images, like the poetically discursive words that must be pierced by the ideal reader—to the intuited vision underneath. Having described the scene as the pilgrim experienced it, the narrator makes a most significant comment:

> Colui che mai non vide cosa nova
> produsse esto visibile parlare,
> novello a noi perché qui non si trova.
>
> [10.94–96]

> [He to whose timeless vision naught is new
> Produced this kind of speech made visible,
> Novel to us, since here it is not found.]

Such sensually combined communication is also found, of course, in the poem itself, where *visibile parlare* is produced through the interaction between the author's words and the reader's visual imagination, between the inspiring and the inspired. The "new things" theme runs through this passage to disjoin and conjoin at once the positions of the reader, the narrator, the pilgrim, and God. The last (and furthest from us) is defined as "he who has never seen a new thing," a definition that does not apply to the staring pilgrim or the intent first reader but does apply, we suddenly notice, in some sense to the narrator —who has, by the time his narration commences, now seen everything—and to the second reader, in other words, the reader who travels through the poem more than that first, naïve time.

Lines 103–04 are no less definitive of the distinction between divine and human art. For here Dante-the-narrator identifies himself as poet with the remark, "li occhi miei ch'a mirare eran contenti/ per veder novitadi ond' e' son vaghi" ("my eyes, which were well satisfied to look,/ Desirous as they [were] to see new things"). Certainly the tense of *eran* is poignantly ambiguous—since the narrator's eyes must be satisfied now only by imagining others (namely, his readers) seeing new things. The selflessness at the base of this poem's self-image is that its writer does not luxuriate in its making; or, put more positively, he enjoys creating the poem in the same sense that God enjoyed creating the universe—not for himself alone, but for himself because for others.

A close juxtaposition of God's images (98) with Dante's (100 ff.) indicates the kind of artistry whose *dolce stil novo* thrives on new things. The narrator then intervenes between the "fabbro" of the sculptures and his own inspired knowledgeability, to reassure the still benighted reader (106–11). Finally, however, as the canto ends, *our* role is brought to the level of God's and Dante's own:

> Come per sostentar solaio o tetto,
>   per mensola tal volta una figura
>   si vede giugner le ginocchia al petto,
> la qual fa del non ver vera rancura
>   nascere 'n chi la vede; cosí fatti
>   vid' io color, quando puosi ben cura.
> Vero è che piú e meno eran contratti
>   secondo ch'avíen piú e meno a dosso;
>   e qual piú pazienza avea nelli atti,
> piangendo parea dicer: "Piú non posso."
>
>   [130–39]

> [As to support a ceiling or a roof
>   Sometimes a corbel figure is seen shaped
>   With breast bowed down to touch the very knees—
> Which though unreal creates a real distress
>   In the observer—even so I saw
>   Those souls bent down, when I looked carefully.

> In truth they were bent over more or less
> According to the burden on their backs
> And those who seemed most patiently disposed
> Still seemed to say in tears, "I can no more."]

The caryatids, like God's sculptures, are morally as well as artistically effective (133)—and are therefore another analogue of the poem. But unlike the divine sculptures, the caryatids here are made (134) by the pilgrim-becoming-narrator—since they are admittedly inadequate (136) figures of the images he really saw. *We* must intuit the truth they represent, must see through the veil of Dante's words. God has weighed these souls down but it is Dante who has made them into similes, for the purpose of presenting them to us.

The similes, however, make them all seem the same; but the narrator himself warns us that each, as is appropriate in the moral scale of things, is weighed down differently, individual by individual (which would not, of course, work well with corbels). The last two lines echo the description of the first sculptured scene, both verbally and psychologically (cf. 38 ff.). We are told by the narrator how to interpret these "atti"— with his final *imagined* words. But we are not told what these specific *atti* themselves are. Instead we are asked to become involved artistically, by ourselves imagining what these gestures must be—just as the pilgrim must imagine the gestures of Michol (10.68–69). And, as we agree to become so involved, we see all the more clearly the correspondence between God as artist and Dante as artist, the one creating Purgatory, the other fashioning the *Purgatorio*. For if we have succeeded in seeing those patient gestures, we have been inspired to the vision by Dante. Dante's art depends upon our involvement. Although the *Commedia* is full of images commonly perceived, its ideal reader is constantly creating his own particular images based on Dante's provocative, guiding words.

Equally complex are the pavement images in canto 12. As the sculptures showed the exaltation of the humble, these images illustrate the condemnation of the proud. Virgil's opening direction to Dante may easily be read as the narrator's instruction to the reader: "Volgi li occhi in giúe:/ buon ti sarà, per tranquillar la via,/ veder lo letto delle piante tue" ("Downward bend your eyes:/ For solace of your journey it will serve/ To see the bed your soles are treading on," 12.13–15). The act of seeing (*veder*) is here again emphasized throughout this remarkable ecphrasis, which begins with a simile so inward-turning and self-re-flexive as to leave no doubt that the art to be described is meant to reflect the poem's own:

Come, perché di lor memoria sia,
  sovra i sepolti le tombe terragne
  portan segnato quel ch'elli eran pria,
onde lí molte volte si ripiagne
  per la puntura della rimembranza,
  che solo a' pii dà delle calcagne;
sí vid'io lí, ma di miglior sembianza
  secondo l'artificio, figurato
  quanto per via di fuor del monte avanza.

[12.16–24]

[Just as on the ground above those buried,
  That they may be remembered, tombstones
  Carry carvings showing who they were before,
So that men many times lament for them
  From the piercing pain of recollection,
  Which goads only those who are compassionate:
Such saw I imaged there—but of a closer
  Resemblance from better workmanship—
  Upon the road that jutted from the mountain.]

Because, moreover, the technique of this divine art is superior (22–23), its effectiveness depends not upon the previous internal disposition of the observer (21) but only upon the reader's persisting vision. Dante's poem does not convince us of its divine authority; it merely shows divinity to us so clearly that only willful aesthetic and moral blindness can obviate its impact. The images themselves, recounted with those strange acrostic terzinas (*VOM*), are a recapitulation of Hell and of the *Inferno* that is associated with both creators, God and Dante, simul-taneously. The ecphrasis ends with the narrator's revealing recollection in excitement:

Qual di pennel fu maestro o di stile
  che ritraesse l'ombre e' tratti ch'ivi
  mirar farieno uno ingegno sottile?

Morti li morti e i vivi parean vivi:
non vide mei di me chi vide il vero,
quant'io calcai, fin che chinato givi.

[64–69]

[Was ever master of the brush or chisel
To reproduce the lines and shades that there
Would waken wonder in the subtlest wit?
Dead seemed the dead, the living seemed alive:
I saw as well as the true witnesses
The scenes I trod on, as I walked bowed down.]

Is not the poem's intention here to insist upon its veracity as a representation—not a pale imitation, but a true mimesis—of reality?
Consider the rich ambiguity and ambience of *il vero* (68)—referring to
(1) the mythical and biblical events depicted, on a literal level that does
not even itself remain strictly literal; (2) the sculpted images here in
Purgatory; (3) the Dantesque images of the *Purgatorio*; and (4) back to
the paradoxical realism of the opening simile (20–21). For it is the
sottile ingegno of the nascent poet that marvels here, at the same time
that the complicated narration challenges *our* "sottile ingegno" to
involve ourselves imaginatively in his vision. The paradox reverberates
back and forth between our time and Dante's eternity, both shared by
us and also by Dante: the dead live and the living we see are dead (67).

The pilgrim's mere attentive vision, as in canto 10 (10.49–51), re-
vitalizes the pavement sculptures in exactly the same way as the act of
opening this book does. Reading brings the poem's marvelous images
alive. We finally understand, then, how to interpret the narrator's subsequent disclaimer about his ability to describe the way the next group
of souls are singing (12.111; Cf. *Par*. 1.71). He means that human art
is insufficient without both divine inspiration and *our own* inspired
artistic perception. The reader himself must envision the sweetness of
the psalm, exactly as the reader is made to imagine the gestures that end
canto 10. So the solace that the poem provides us, like that which the
sculpted images provide the pilgrim (12.14), is one that comes from
within ourselves as much as from outside—the solace of our own active
imaginations.

Psalms resound harmoniously from page to page, from terrace to
terrace, of this poetic place inhabited by happily chanting souls, angels,

and blessèd ladies. A glance at their melodious presence will serve as transition to the third category, that of the poets. From the "Te lucis ante" of canto 8.13 ff. to the *dolce salmodia* of canto 33.2, these religious songs provide the pilgrim with the experience of a new sweetness (*dolcezza*), religiously hortatory and not secularly amorous—very different from that of Casella's singing (2.112–14). Religious singing in the *Purgatorio* reveals five characteristics. (1) It is univocal, thus marking a unanimity in striking contrast with the cacophonous disharmony of infernal chants. Compare *Purgatorio* 16.19–21—"una parola in tutte era ed un modo,/ sí che parea tra esse ogni concordia" ("All were as one in measure and in word,/ So among them sweet concord seemed to reign")—with *Inferno* 7.125–26—"Quest'inno si gorgoglian nella strozza/ ché dir nol posson con parola integra" ("This [hymn] they gargle in their throats since they cannot form sound words"). (2) It is characterized, appropriately, by loving sweetness, which recalls Dante's description of his own singing in the Bonagiunta episode ("Cantando come donna innamorata," "He, singing like a woman rapt in love," 29.1 ff.; cf. 9.139–41). (3) The singing makes a purposeful contribution to the souls' upward movement (for example, 13.28–30; 28.80–81; 30.92–94); and (4) it displays supernatural beauty, like that of the sculptures (see 27.8 ff.). (5) The narrator overtly assumes the knowledgeable participation of the reader's education and memory by describing the psalms in shorthand notation—namely, by giving only the first few words. The air of Purgatory is filled with orderly notes (29.22 ff.),[14] and the pilgrim learns to listen carefully to these righteous and harmonious songs (29.36). However, because he is not yet fully instructed, even in Purgatory, he cannot entirely comprehend the meaning of the singing he hears in the earthly paradise (32.61 ff.).

The pilgrim's still insufficient instruction is the key to understanding his encounter with the professional singer Casella, an occasion of secular singing that makes the whole of canto 2 perhaps the most intricate self-reflexive passage in the *Purgatorio*. The canto begins with a simile describing Virgil and Dante standing in confusion at the foot of the mountain, "come gente che pensa a suo cammino,/ che va col cuore e col corpo dimora" ("Like folk who, studying their journey's road,/ Set forth in spirit while the body stays," 2.11–12)—an ominous comparison, in this canticle obsessed with the necessity for constant movement. The simile is proleptic within the canto; it will be less exactly, but nonetheless generally, appropriate when the encounter with Casella stills the progress of both "cuore" and "corpo."

As Virgil and Dante wait, the radiant angel appears [16 ff.] to guide us all—Virgil, Dante, the souls, the reader—into the canto, as Cato will direct us brusquely out of it. The angel's wings, as Virgil describes them (31–36), form an imagistic commentary on the difference between divine and human art. His wings, eternally pointed upward, cause temporal change but are not themselves changed. They are therefore the true opposite of Satan's wings which, eternally flapping up and down, have no effect except to perpetuate their owner's sameness. Only Dante's immutable divine language can succeed in changing the status of his reader, because Dante's "argomenti" are not solely "umani" (31). The angel is too bright for Dante's as yet unperfected vision (39) and the pilgrim must avert his eyes. But his sense of hearing is not impaired or incapable, neither here as he listens to the choral unanimity of the embarked souls' psalm (45 ff.), which he describes with a reference to the written text (48), nor later when he hears the single voice of Casella. Disembarked, the crowd marvels at the "nove cose" of the purgatorial shore (54). They turn to Virgil and Dante for direction, but Virgil tells them, "ma noi siam peregrin come voi siete" ("but we are pilgrims even as you are," [63]), and concludes with his prophetic description of the climb to come that will prove, by canto's end, to be wrong-headed (calling it *gioco*, "sport" [66], compared to the hellish descent).[15]

Now begins a remarkable structural parallel with the subsequent meeting with Casella. As Virgil speaks, the souls suddenly realize that Dante, himself quite a "new thing" indeed, is alive:

> E come a mesagger che porta ulivo
>   tragge la gente per udir novelle,
>   e di calcar nessun si mostra schivo,
> così al viso mio s'affisar quelle
>   anime fortunate tutte quante
>   quasi obliando d'ire a farsi belle.
>
> [70–75]

> [And, as around a messenger who bears
>   The olive branch, the folk press close for news,
>   None slow to tread on others' heels to hear,

> Even so these happy souls, forgetting now
> To go their way and make themselves more fair,
> Fastened, each one, his gaze upon my face.]

Here we see that it is life-defining *time*—as the simile, like the pilgrim's very presence, links earth and Purgatory—which makes people ever anxious for *news* (71). The blessed souls focus ignorantly on the living Dante exactly as they, along with him and Virgil, will focus on the dead Casella (cf. 115 ff.). Their curiosity is vain because it does not contribute to their salvation. So watching Dante is no more effective now—because he is not yet the divine author—than are his own attempts to embrace Casella (76 ff.), themselves foreshadowing the encounter between Statius and Virgil in its poignant naïveté—even to the detail of the wondering smiles they exchange (82–84).

As Casella expresses the continuity of his secular love for Dante (not its religious sublimation), Dante rewards him with a statement of the personal purpose of his journey: "Casella mio, per tornar altra volta/ là dov'io son, fo io questo viaggio" ("Casella mine, this course I run/ So that I may return to where I am," 91–92). Perhaps the sober soundness of Casella's explanation of his own puzzling status (94 ff.) reminds Dante that he may not know his old friend now as well as he once did. At any rate, his request is couched in terms that bespeak a dawning consciousness of the newness of this realm, as they suggest the self-awareness of the *Purgatorio* itself:

> E io: "Se nuova legge non ti toglie
>   memoria o uso all'amoroso canto
>   che mi solea quetar tutte mie voglie,
> di ciò ti piaccia consolare alquanto
>   l'anima mia, che, con la mia persona
>   venendo qui, è affannata tanto!"
>
> [2.106–11]

> [I said: "If no new law denies to you
>   Memory or usage of that song of love
>   Which soothed all my desires in days of old,
> Console a little with it, if you will,
>   My soul that hither having borne the weight
>   Of flesh and blood, is spent with weariness."]

Does the pilgrim suspect that his old love songs are forbidden in eternity? And, in view of this singing's outcome, why has Casella *not* forgotten or been denied such practice? Why do Virgil, the pilgrim, and the souls with them listen? But, even more importantly, why does the narrator still, in his post-Paradise present, confirm the "dolcezza" of music that only provokes Cato?

Answering these questions leads us deeper than ever into the paradoxical self-image of the *Purgatorio*. Perhaps Casella can still sing because the "nuova legge" does not affect him yet—or does not command his full understanding and commitment. These newly arrived souls, we might say, are still more caught up by earthly time than by eternity. Virgil's fault—if indeed his listening is as grave an impropriety as Cato's reaction would have him and us believe[16]—may be explained, morally, by the fact that he is, after all, technically one of the damned. As for the pilgrim, he is as yet unredeemed. And the souls, still forgetful of their fairness-to-be, despite the angel, have not yet begun the process of purification that seems always to include the *willing* participation of the sufferer (their will being analogous to the reader's active imagination).

But the aesthetic attraction of the singing cannot be explained away so easily: "cominciò elli allor sí *dolcemente*,/ che la *dolcezza* ancor dentro mi sona" ("then he began to sing so sweetly that the sweetness sounds still within me," 2.113–14). So compelling is Casella's song that the adverb describing it as the pilgrim experiences it is solidified in the abstract noun that defines the narrator's still affected memory—giving scant evidence that he truly wants to return, as the pilgrim had told Casella (91–92), to a place deprived of song. Although he has been to Paradise, the narrator has not himself forgotten "memoria o uso" of the love song and clearly feels that it still provides some kind of spiritual solace. Why, then, is Cato so severe? Why does he imply (his *gridando* so different from Casella's *dolcezza* or even from the poet's *significando*) that the art of singing is among the scales that must be cast off before man can see God (122)? The answer lies in that much quoted line from the *Paradiso*: "'n la sua volontade è nostra pace" (3.85), and its relationship to the singing of Casella as here requested by the pilgrim. For the moving will of Casella's song, like that of Francesca's love, is not divine but only human; and the peace it brings is therefore temporary.

The *Purgatorio* explicates in this passage the distinction between the content, and the function and form, of art. Despite Irma Brandeis's conclusion that Dante's old song is toylike,[17] "Amor che ne la mente mi ragiona" is in fact among the finest odes of the *dolce stil novo*—and probably later than "Donne ch'avete intelletto d'amore," which Bonagiunta praises without apology in canto 24. Moreover, the ode deals with a theme indigenous to the *Commedia*, the insufficiency of human speech to express love.[18] What is wrong is the pilgrim's *use* of the song, both in his previous life where it distracted his will from pursuit of the good (108), and here where it makes him forget his destined journey (109–11; 116–17) toward that peace which alone provides proper haven for man. The song, as it functions here, contrasts with the art works of cantos 10 and 12, which provide a consolation that effectively expedites the journey. Purgatory is constituted by nature to demand the ceaseless pursuit of that peace-bestowing divine will by the wills of its temporary inhabitants, whenever that will, represented by the sun, beckons them onward.

Cato is insisting on what Spenser's Redcrosse and Sir Calidore learn through hard experience—that the *quest* cannot be slowed by improper *rest*—and he thereby indicates the epic quality of the *Commedia*. The only rest that can be justified is one that contributes directly to the quest—as do the divine sculptures (or as would even this precise song, had its listeners paid as much attention to its content as they do to the mesmerizing beauty of its form). Formal beauty taken alone, because it does not lead to action, is as pernicious as the siren's song. As for Casella, his fault is that his singing is moved by personal, temporal love (88–90) instead of by the eternal, divine love that moves the universe—and the master of the *dolce stil*. In this scene Casella (and all his company) is like the man who has not put away childish things, and Cato sternly plays the spoilsport role of St. Paul.

The sharpness of the narrator's memory and account, then, is justified by the function canto 2 itself performs as an anti-exemplum in the poem contrasting with cantos 10 and 12 where art is used toward good. The narrator's artistic recollection does not contradict his moral purpose because, unlike the pilgrim's guide, he does not allow *us* to forget the road to Paradise.[19] After all, he is recording not Casella's song—of which only one line is noted—but, rather, the impact of his singing. The final involuted irony of this exquisitely complex canto is that the narrator stops reciting in the same breath in which his characters stop singing (132).[20]

We come, now, to those memorable meetings between poets, the pilgrim's and Virgil's contact with Sordello (cantos 6–7), Statius (21–22), Bonagiunta da Lucca (24), Guinizelli (26), and Daniel (26). All these dramatic relationships, as Bergin has noted, have special interest.[21] Nor must we overlook the constant and constantly evolving relationship between Dante and Virgil. No moment in the *Commedia* is more poignant than that when the pilgrim turns around to discover the sudden absence of his "dolcissimo padre" (30.50).[22] It is Virgil who never fails to offer the pilgrim "quel dolce pome" ("that fruit so sweet," 27.115) for which he always hungers. Virgil leads the pilgrim to the top of the mountain "con ingegno e con arte" (27.130) and thus is his prototypical redeemer—a Christ-figure. But, as he does for Statius so too for Dante, Virgil plays a double role—aesthetic as well as moral—in effect turning the naïve pilgrim into the fully instructed narrator. Both Virgil and Dante seem to be aware of the latter's destined poetic task, so that Virgil's reply to Cato's question about their infernal journey is ironic: "Com' io l'ho tratto, saría lungo a dirti" ("How I have led him would be long to tell you," 1.67). For that telling belongs, Virgil knows, both to another artist and to another audience—to Dante, who will have seen Paradise to make the telling complete and possible, and to Dante's reader, who has the chance to profit morally from his account.

Virgil's perceptive relationship with Dante need not be labored. Suffice it to contrast Virgil's warmth with the relatively chilly guidance of Beatrice, who tells Dante that there will be a time hereafter for him to lament the departure of that "antica fiamma" (30.48, 54), chiding the pilgrim for his emotional upheaval even before he can express it. And indeed, Dante does lament Virgil "later," in the narrator's delicate characterization that makes his *maestro* seem closer to us for his humanity than the sainted *donna* who dismisses Virgil as imperiously and abruptly as she commissions him. Nor does the reader mistake the analogy—between the *Commedia* and Virgil, as moral poetry—in the narrator's description of the journey's start: "i' mi ristrinsi alla fida compagna:/ e come sare' io sanza lui corso?/ chi m'avria tratto su per la montagna?" ("I stayed and drew/ The closer to my faithful partner's side;/ Without him how should I have taken flight?/ Who would have led me up the mountain slope?," 3.4–6). As the pilgrim clings to Virgil, so the living reader must cling to Dante's Virgilian poetry as his only sure guide up the mountain.

Brandeis has well remarked that the meetings with the poets form a series, to be "experienced as *one* thing, somewhat greater than the sum of its parts."[23] She rightly sees these meetings as an evolving expression of brotherly love; yet they are equally important as a gradual revelation of the poem's self-image. Sordello, Virgil's fellow citizen, comes first, to express the strength of communal brotherhood. Appropriately, it is Sordello's informing gaze, his leonine eyes, that the narrator recalls to introduce his fellow craftsman to us (6.61 ff.). Sordello's failure to respond to Virgil's question is oddly in contrast to the usual behavior of the eternal souls. And his sudden burst of excitement—"O Mantovano, io son Sordello" (6.74)—leads to an equally extraordinary embrace (since Statius later proves unable to embrace Virgil) (75).

The narrator's long invective against Italy (76 ff.) suggests that Sordello, because of his initial self-centered silence, serves here as an anti-exemplum to teach the wrongness of an inordinate attachment to temporal goods—that is, to a temporal, imperfect community rather than to the eternal community at peace in God's will. Sordello's behavior, in fact, parallels that of Dante and Virgil with Casella; and here it is the *narrator* who plays Cato's castigating role. Remember that the *pilgrim*, however, is not yet instructed enough to play that role himself, not yet understanding the impropriety of Sordello's speech— which is evoked not by their need but initially for his own gratification. It is Dante-returned whose retrospective vision effectively enacts for us the role that the poets on his journey played for him.

So we view Sordello from two perspectives; for canto 7 begins where canto 6.76 breaks off to allow the narrator's exclamation. Sordello, who had announced his own name so eagerly after questioning the pilgrims' provenance (6.70–71) ("io son" [74] is a phrase echoed by Dante to Bonagiunta, by Daniel to Dante, as well as by the siren), only then thinks to ask Virgil's name. The ensuing exchange between them, now as poet to poet, is gracious and noble. Sordello's reaction to Virgil's identity is a striking parallel to Dante's reaction to the wall sculptures:

> Qual è colui che cosa innanzi a sé
>   subita vede ond' e' si maraviglia
>   che crede e non, dicendo 'Ella è . . non è . . '
> tal parve elli . . .
>
> [7.10–13]

> [As one who all at once beholds a thing
>   Before him whence he marvels, half in doubt
>   And half believing, saying ' 'Tis—'Tis not,'
> So he appeared . . .]

And Sordello's eulogy of Virgil (7.16 ff.), weighing the pre-Christian poet's glory against his own redeemed worth, is allowed to stand without contradiction as Virgil explains to Sordello his eternally unhappy state (7.23 ff.) marked primarily by the *vision* he will never command (26–27)—a further ironic commentary on the present limitation of Sordello's vision. In effect, Sordello is, for that reason alone, a closer analogue to Dante than to Virgil—although the pilgrim will see Paradise both before and after the Provençal poet. The reader, consequently, is related to Sordello in an equally ambivalent manner, since we, too, will see Dante's vision before he does. The next poet we meet, however, will beat us there.

That is, of course, Statius, whose presence in the *Purgatorio* is monumental in its radiation. Like the poem itself, Statius's words are a constant affirmation of the unity between the moral and the artistic, between faith and poetry (22.65 ff.). Mario Sansone has noted the resemblance between this meeting and Christ's encounter with the disciples on the road to Emmaus.[24] Indeed, this poetic context, more than any other, is concerned specifically with Christology. To begin with, Statius's intellectual humility contrasts sharply with Sordello's political pride and is truly Christlike, as it unquestioningly accepts the divine will. Brandeis marks the confluence of the motion theme with the aesthetic and moral significance of Statius's presence: "The three do not pause at all . . . but rather continue . . . questioning and answering one another as they go."[25] In fact, the connection between the motion theme and artistic self-revelation is made explicitly in the context of Statius, when the narrator remarks, "Né 'l dir l'andar, nè l'andar lui più lento / facea" ("Stride slackened not for speech nor speech for stride," 24.1). Dante will soon be telling Bonagiunta that his own poetic style combines *going* (*vo*) and *speaking (significando)*, newly enforced by Statius's example.[26]

Statius's attitude toward Virgil, reminiscent of Sordello's, merits close examination for the way it expresses paradoxically a tension between the moral and the artistic realms. His artistic debt to the *Aeneid* recalls, as he expresses it, the pilgrim's own declaration in the proem (*Inf.* 1.79 ff.), but goes even further:

> "dell'Eneida dico, la qual mamma
> fummi e fummi nutrice poetando:
> sanz'essa non fermai peso di dramma.
> E per esser vivuto di là quando
> visse Virgilio, assentirei un sole
> piú che non deggio al mio uscir di bando."
>
> [21.97–102]

> [I speak of the *Aeneid*, which to me
> Was as a mother, as a nurse in art,
> Without it not a jot did I compose.
> To have dwelt yonder while yet Virgil lived
> I would consent to spend another sun
> In exile, added to my rightful debt.]

Here, surely, Dante reveals through Statius his own view of Virgil's poetry. But it is not a simple view. Statius's declaration clearly affords Virgil a superior position in his own regard. Yet that Dante has Statius, instead of the pilgrim, make the most expansive tribute to Virgil's literary influence, just as surely implies Dante's awareness of his own superiority to both Virgil and Statius—neither of whom limits *his* art. Certainly the narrator could not concur with the statement in line 99; his primary inspiration is divine.

Nonetheless, the purpose here is to praise Virgil. Accordingly, once again a seeming contradiction is allowed to stand unchallenged by either pilgrim or narrator, as the unforgettable recognition scene, catalyzed by the pilgrim's badly muffled smile, immediately unfolds. As that scene demonstrates anew the intimacy between Virgil and Dante, Statius's apparent attitude leaves us uneasy, on purely moral grounds. Is not Statius's attitude toward art as disorderly as Casella's in canto 2? After all, the *Aeneid* is a pagan poem and should not be considered currency among the eternal goods of Purgatory.

Statius's exaggerated hypothetical offer, then, must be intended again to tell us something about the distinction between the content and origin, and the function, of poetry. The *Aeneid* converted Statius to

Christianity—and that is all that matters. As far as he is concerned, he owes his salvation to it and therefore would spend an extra year in torment if only he could have known its author, a morally understandable artistic self-indulgence. He does not view Virgil's poem as Dante viewed Casella's song—as an instrument of forgetfulness. For Statius it is, as poetry should be, the vehicle that carried him toward his present happy state.

Virgil's relationship to Statius, then, is a past analogue to his present relationship to the pilgrim—whose epic is yet unborn. Past and present come together through the temporally ambivalent pilgrim, as Dante introduces Statius to Virgil as "questi che guida in alto gli occhi miei" ("this same spirit who now leads my eyes on high," 21.124). And the interplay of three pairs of visionary eyes is perfected in Statius's declaration of love (135–37) that ends the canto by its own agency—no Cato needed. As the conversation continues, everything Statius tells Virgil about his inspiration tells us about Virgil's influence on Dante as well, both in and out of the *Commedia* (22.65 ff.). Virgil is the light that shines in the darkness (67–68), untouched by anything but illuminating all. And the Virgilian theme Statius invokes is that of the *new* age (22.70).

Indeed, the writing of the *Commedia* introduces another "nova età" ("new age," 16.122), as Dante's divinely inspired art makes the divine experience accessible to man, just as Virgil's art, though without realizing it, effected Statius's salvation. The act of reading Dante's poem begins a "vita nova" ("new life," 30.115) for us just as its fictional experience did for the pilgrim. Here we see the very process by which pilgrim becomes redemptive poet:

> Elli givan dinanzi, ed io soletto
>   di retro, e ascoltava i lor sermoni,
>   ch'a poetar mi davano intelletto.
>
> [22.127–29]

> [They went ahead, I in my solitude
>   Behind them, listening to their discourse
>   Which gave me wisdom in poetic lore.][27]

This time Virgil need not tell the pilgrim to listen. Our role, we understand here, is to read as carefully as the pilgrim listens, or as carefully as Statius read his Virgil (22.37 ff.). Later, for Virgil's sake, Statius answers Dante's question about the spiritual corporeality of the souls, admonishing him to listen carefully (25.31 ff.), as the narrator often exhorts the reader. The presence of Statius is a glowing testimony to the moral power of poetry which, for him, is as worthy of love as God is—since the two are linked directly. His wish to know Virgil (he says not "*I would have* assented" but "*I would* assent") is fulfilled in Dante's vision of eternity so that it becomes, in the last analysis, the aegis of Dante the poet under which this fictional trio stands. Dante, by finishing his divine poem, has himself replaced Virgil, assuming his master's place in the moral history of poetry.

It is no wonder, then, that Virgil and Statius remain in the background during the last two encounters with poets. Poetic self-reflexiveness, in the encounter with Bonagiunta da Lucca, is at the very heart of Dante's art. The pilgrim himself singles out Bonagiunta from the crowd and asks him earnestly to speak louder (24.35–42). The old man's prophetic beginning remains, perhaps, as abstruse as his poetry was; and Dante may have made it purposefully so. But Bonagiunta's question to the pilgrim is clear:

> Ma di' s' i' veggio qui colui che fore
> trasse le nove rime, cominciando
> *"Donne ch'avete intelletto d'amore."*

[24.49–51]

> [But tell me, do I see before me him
> Who brought forth the new rhymes, beginning thus:
> *"Donne ch'avete intelletto d'amore."*]

The poet from Lucca is referring here to the first canzone of the *dolce stil novo*, the first ode in the *Vita Nova*—explicated by Dante in the *De Vulgari Eloquentia* (2.8,12), where he says that in writing it, "my tongue spoke as though moved by itself."[28] The pilgrim's reply, studied by every generation of Dante critics, reveals the secret of this new style:

> E io a lui: "I' mi son un, che quando
> Amor mi spira, noto, e a quel modo
> ch' è ditta dentro vo significando."

[52–54]

> ["I am," I answered, "one who, when inspired
> By Love, takes note and afterwards expounds
> Accordingly as he dictates within."]

There is modesty here as well as conviction—and a straightforward, simple theory of inspiration.[29] Francis Fergusson is right to emphasize the "laconic under-emphasis" of the pilgrim's reply. The same critic also notes the implicit reproof of Bonagiunta's preoccupation with style,[30] a criticism now quite familiar to the pilgrim since his meetings with Casella and Sordello.

Dante's own poetry, instead, combines formal inner stasis, or receptivity (*noto, ditta dentro*), and external influential motion (*vo significando*). The one (*vo*) balances the other (*noto*) in a dynamic tension that allows sincerity and conviction to be born from the mystical vision. Bonagiunta, in fact, recognizes the meaning in its very expression; the pilgrim's brief but definite words exemplify the "dolce stil novo ch' i' *odo*" ("the sweet new style which now I *hear*"). That is because the words fit perfectly into their ordered place in this great master tapestry (*ordite*, 33.140), the *dentro* harking back to the dead central stillness of Hell (cf. *Inf.* 7.9), the *vo* to the present movement up the mountain, and the *significando* to the philosophical exegeses of the *Paradiso*'s discursive poetry. Fergusson expresses it well:

> When he speaks of the dictation of "love" he means the countless
> analogous voices in which Love has spoken up to this point, and
> he assumes that, in his further ascent, love will speak in other
> voices still . . . just as the love of God is hidden behind every
> mode of mortal love, and includes them all, even the Hellish, so
> that Dante's inspiration includes every other authentic source of
> poetry, and transcends them all.[31]

Beatrice, for example, is this loving muse, as she tells Dante to watch and write (32.104–05; cf. 33.52 ff. 75–81), showing him that properly functioning art is permitted. There is nothing more complicated to it than this, as Bonagiunta himself points out (24.60–61). A Dantesque poet *listens* carefully to his inspiration, observes his vision clearly, and allows it to flow freely through his pen (58–59) to inspire his reader.

Appropriately enough, our next meeting is with the immediate predecessor of Dante's *stil novo*, Guido Guinizelli of Bologna. Once again Virgil and Statius leave the stage to Dante for this meeting with the other poet, whom he calls "il padre/ mio e delli altri miei miglior

che mai/ rime d'amore usar dolci e leggiadre" ("Mine and my betters'
father, sire of all/ Who ever dealt in sweet and gallant rhyme," 26.96–
98). Dante's reaction here should be compared to those of Sordello and
Statius to Virgil's name. Guinizelli tells Dante that his words are so
clear, so well-ordered, that Lethe shall not obliterate them (107–08).
And this allows us to understand, now, how the narrator has been able
to remember "la dolcezza" of Casella's song, since Casella sings Dante's
poem, fashioned from divinely inspired words that alone can transcend
the human. As for himself, Guinizelli continues, he cannot understand
the delight Dante displays in seeing him, even when Dante explains that
Guido's verse is still alive (112–14). His humility contrasts touchingly
with the narrator's modest self-assurance; but then, Dante would say,
Guido is not Dante, after all. Guinizelli's declination of praise recalls
that of Oderisi (11.82). The Bolognese poet then motions toward a man
he calls a "miglior fabbro"—recalling Dante's praise of the divine
artistry of the pavement images in canto 12.22–23—the Provençal
poet Arnaut Daniel. The reader looks forward to this new encounter
at the same time that he admires the quiet nobility of Guido Guinizelli,
who halts to speak with Dante without moving from the refining fire.

And indeed, as Brandeis says, Arnaut "seems to speak for himself,
for Guido, for every soul burning there"—including Dante.[32] Daniel
speaks his unique terzinas, as Dante the disciple does homage to another of his masters by employing his own "parlar materno" ("mother
tongue") within the bounds of the poem's terza rima. And he begins
"liberamente" ("freely," 139), responding to Dante's "cortes deman"
("gentil curteisyë," 140). Two lines in Daniel's speech should be re-
emphasized: "Ieu sui Arnaut, que plor e vau cantan" ("Arnaut am I,
that wepe and alwey singë," 142); and the last line: "sovenha vos a
temps de ma dolor!" ("in after tyme remember my dolour," 147).[33]
The first line is another phraseological echo of the narrator's self-
description. Dante had told Bonagiunta that he was one who "takes
heed" and "goes explaining;" but, for Daniel, song is connected not
with present inspiration but with the weeping caused by his "passada
folor" ("past folyë," 143). The implication is that his inspiring love was
not the same as Dante's,[34] but more like that of Paolo and Francesca,
although Daniel followed its dictates with equal artistic fidelity.

Nonetheless, Dante pays tribute to his stylistic master by fashioning for him a closing line of graceful, purposeful ambiguity. For line 147 can be translated to mean several things, depending ultimately upon the will of its translator, or upon the imagination of the reader, like that of the listening pilgrim. It can mean that the pilgrim should remember Daniel's suffering at the right time, in other words, in Paradise where he might intercede to shorten it; or back in time, on earth where he might report it to caution others but also to have them pray for Daniel; or to pray for him himself; or in time, for his own personal salvation; or all of these. With characteristic elusiveness, Daniel, the master of the *trobar clus*, and the last poet we meet in the *Purgatorio*, retreats into the flame.

As Statius and Virgil guide the pilgrim, so Dante guides us, introducing us to Sordello, Bonagiunta, Guinizelli, and Daniel, not only to suggest the persistence of fragile human art in the temporal eternity of Purgatory, but also to suggest that Virgilian art, as used by Statius and as augmented by Dante himself, is superior by its inspiration and function to an art moved by less than the eternal love—however beautiful that lesser art may be in formal eloquence. The poetry of the *Purgatorio*, its self-image revealed in these passages, is a "union of wisdom and beauty, of exquisite rhetoric and intellectual and moral understanding."[35]

The tension between human and divine art may not be resolved in the *Purgatorio*—as, indeed, it cannot be—but it is stabilized dynamically and made to bear moral and artistic fruit. The poem's desire to have a transcendent, intuitive, divine effect on its reader is linked decisively with its ability to make a temporal, discursive, human impression through its well-ordered, pleasing words and images. That dependency—of moral intuition upon poetic discourse—is basic to the aesthetic self-image of the *Purgatorio*. It is central to the moral effectiveness the poem intends to continue exercising beyond the present— the present which, after all, escapes before the poet's ink is dry.

The passages we have examined show that the *Purgatorio* considers itself both didactic and pleasurable. The analogy between its reader and the student-pilgrim is inescapable. As it fashions the pilgrim into the poet after its own image, the poem clearly makes him a communal servant. Manfred's parting words have wider significance than he knows.

"Vedi oggimai se tu mi puoi far lieto,
    revelando alla mia buona Costanza
    come m'hai visto, e anche esto divieto;
ché qui per quei di là molto s'avanza."

[3.141–44]

[You see now how happy you can make me
    By letting my good Constance know that you
    Have seen me, and also of this stipulation:
That those back there can greatly benefit those here.][36]

This individual and specific relationship, of prayer between the living
and those in Purgatory, is also a generic one that is parallel to the poet's
service to the community, in reverse. The community can help them
now; in Paradise, they can help the community. Only their temporality
makes the circuit between earth and eternity a transmitting one. Similarly, only the poet's *return* from eternity into time makes him com-
munally effective—as well as, for Manfred, individually effective. The
poem conceives its narrator as an intermediary between man and God,
and between temporal man and man in eternity. Dante's, then, is the
"imaginativa" ("imagination," 17.13) whose aesthetic impact has been
commissioned specifically by God's will for moral purposes (17.17–18).
So it is, paradoxically but nevertheless definitely, his own talent, albeit
God-supported, that the narrator invokes in canto 17.

Art, though a suspension of ordinary action (12.77–78), is therefore
permitted when it is moral art. But it functions, like any other art,
through its pleasurable attraction. Fergusson comments that "that act
of spirit whereby the song was held and enjoyed is accepted as good,
but not *the* Good."[37] Yet it is the only means at man's disposal to reach
the Good. The sensual impact of the poem does not contradict, but in
fact serves, the divine effect. The pleasure it brings must simply be trans-
lucent and mediatory rather than opaque and terminal. Virgil tells
Dante that, "Matto è chi spera che nostra ragione/ possa trascorrer la
infinita via" ("Only a madman could hope that our reason/ Might follow on the pathway infinite," 3.34–35); and indeed rational, discursive,
secular words alone will not suffice. Only divinely inspired poetry, with
its interplay between the senses and the imagination, can lead to intuition of the eternal vision.

The poem conceives of its function as that of grace. In this regard the *Commedia* is as unfathomable to the merely reasonable, secular reader as is the Trinity (3.36), of which its form is an avatar. Its essence must ultimately be intuited (3.37). Yet that intuition, like the pilgrim's faltering desire, is activated only by words (4.49): poetic words that embody moral spirit. Art is necessary to man in time; and the temporality of the *Purgatorio* explains its preoccupation with art. It sees its own art and asks its optimum reader to understand and react to it as the second incarnation of the divine love that moves the universe, its motivating force the same force that moves the pilgrim and all souls from time to eternity.

NOTES

1. The terms "inward-turning self-reflexiveness" and "optimum reader" are those of Lowry Nelson, Jr., "The Fictive Reader and Literary Self-Reflexiveness," in *The Disciplines of Criticism*, ed. Peter Demetz, Thomas Greene, and Lowry Nelson, Jr. (New Haven and London: Yale University Press, 1968), p. 175. I am grateful to Lowry Nelson, Jr. and to Lewis Owen for critical suggestions; also to the National Endowment for the Humanities for research in Florence supporting this essay.

2. For a discussion of Fergusson's distinction among the "three Dantes," see Kenneth John Atchity, "*Inferno VII*: The Idea of Order," *Italian Quarterly* 12, nos. 47–48 (Winter-Spring 1969): 50.

3. *Dante* (Boston: Houghton Mifflin, 1965), p. 275.

4. Edition of Natalino Sapegno, *La Divina Commedia* (Florence: "La Nuova Italia" Editrice, 1955/1964). All references are to the text of this edition. Translations are generally those of Thomas G. Bergin, *The Divine Comedy*, 3 vols. (New York: Grossman, 1969).

5. See Erich Auerbach, "Dante's Addresses to the Reader," in Robert J. Clements, ed., *American Critical Essays on the Divine Comedy* (New York: New York University Press, 1967), pp. 37–51.

6. Nelson, "The Fictive Reader," p. 186; ibid., p. 37.

7. See my discussion of the symbolism of this passage, "*Inferno VII*," p. 21.

8. Irma Brandeis, *The Ladder of Vision: A Study of Dante's Divine Comedy* (New York: Doubleday, 1960), p. 84, refers to 6.76 ff.

9. Cf. Auerbach, "Dante's Addresses," p. 42.

10. Francis Fergusson, *Dante's Drama of the Mind: A Modern Reading of the Purgatorio* (Princeton: Princeton University Press, 1953), p. 26.

11. See Donald L. Clark, *Rhetoric in Greco-Roman Education* (New York: Columbia University Press, 1957), p. 203, who refers to Philostratus' specialty of depicting paintings and sculptures in words.

12. Francesco T. Roffarè, *Il Canto X Del "Purgatorio"* (Florence: Le Monnier, 1968), pp. 12–13.

13. Cf. Francesco Tateo, *Teologia e "Arte" Nel Canto X Del Purgatorio* (Rome, 1966), p. 72.

14. Helmut Hatzfeld, "The Art of Dante's *Purgatorio*," *Studies in Philology* 49 (1952): 45, notes the omnipresence of music juxtaposed with silence. He calls music a healing medicine for the souls' wounds.

15. There may be a double-edged ironical reference here to Virgil's own lines in the *Aeneid* 6.126 ff.: "facilis descensus Averno."

16. The narrator terms Virgil's slip a "small" one, in 3.8.

17. Brandeis, *Ladder of Vision*, p. 80.

18. See *The Odes of Dante*, trans. H. J. Vere-Hodge (Oxford: Clarendon Press, 1963), p. 120; the author points out that Dante explicated this ode in the third book of the *Convivio* and referred to it with praise in the *De Vulgari Eloquentia* 2.6.6.

19. This disagrees with Brandeis's interpretation, *Ladder of Vision*, p. 79.

20. Fergusson, *Dante's Drama of the Mind*, p. 154, says the conflict in canto 2 is between poetry "and morally responsible action" instead of between moral poetry and purely aesthetic poetry.

21. *A Diversity of Dante* (New Brunswick: Rutgers University Press, 1969), p. 18.

22. For a fuller discussion of Virgil, see Thomas M. Greene, "Dramas of Selfhood in the *Comedy*," in Thomas G. Bergin, ed., *From Time to Eternity: Essays on Dante's Divine Comedy* (New Haven: Yale University Press, 1967), p. 129.

23. Brandeis, *Ladder of Vision* pp. 67, 80; her series starts with Casella; see also Bergin, "Dante's Provençal Gallery," in *Diversity of Dante*, especially 93 ff. (Daniel) and 103 ff. (Sordello).

24. *Il Canto XXI Del Purgatorio* (Florence: Le Monnier, 1968), pp. 10, 18.

25. Brandeis, *Ladder of Vision*, p. 90.

26. Here is an instance where the pilgrim and narrator can be separated clearly from the author. The pilgrim, we may say, has learned from Statius's example, so that the narrator's art is a confirmation of the validity of the pilgrim's art. But it was the third Dante, the author, who made Statius exemplary in the first place—so that, from this viewpoint, Statius's character here is based on Dante's example.

27. Cf. *Inf.* 4.94, where he follows the five poets but overtly learns nothing.

28. "Donne ch'avete intelletto d'amore" was written in 1289, according to Kenneth McKenzie, ed., *La Vita Nuova di Dante Alighieri* (Boston: D. C. Heath, 1922), p. 99.

29. I owe this observation to Sapegno, *La Divina Commedia*, p. 272 n., and to Lowry Nelson, Jr.

30. Fergusson, *Dante's Drama of the Mind*, pp. 29, 253; see also his explanation on p. 157.

31. Ibid., p. 153.

32. Brandeis, *Ladder of Vision*, p. 110.

33. See Greene, "Dramas of Selfhood," p. 127; and Bergin, "Dante's Provençal Gallery," p. 94, who points out that the Provençal verse here is stylistically more characteristic of Dante than of Daniel.

34. Cf. Fergusson, *Dante's Drama of the Mind,* p. 169.

35. Translation by Louis Biancolli, *The Divine Comedy. II* (New York: Washington Square Press, 1966), p. 12.

36. Fergusson, *Dante's Drama of the Mind*, pp. 24, 155; see *Purg.* 4.1 ff., for the way attraction works on the senses.

6

Bonaventure's Figural Exemplarism in Dante

T. K. Seung

If there is anything indisputable about *La Divina Commedia*, it is the assumption that this medieval epic is an allegorical work. But the precise nature of Dante's allegory that has long been taken for granted is now coming to be recognized as a problem no less perplexing than any other medieval mystery. It is to this perplexing problem that Robert Hollander has lately addressed his *Allegory in Dante's Commedia*.[1]

Hollander reports that Dante's *Commedia* had been interpreted as a personification allegory from the time of its publication to the beginning of our century, and claims that this way of reading it is really in conflict with Dante's own precepts as expressed in his letter to Can Grande. He further claims that only in our century has the true nature of Dante's allegory begun to be appreciated through the labor of Erich Auerbach and Charles Singleton.[2] Thus, at the outset, Hollander declares his unmistakable allegiance to the Auerbach-Singleton school of figural realism. What is unique about Hollander's book is that it elevates the debate—between the school of personification allegory and that of figural allegory—to the fully theoretical level. Hence it can be said to mark a new stage of theoretical consciousness in Dante scholarship.

Hollander assumes that Dante himself had clearly in mind the distinction between these two types of allegory when he made use of the distinction between the allegory of poets and the allegory of theologians in his *Convivio*. He further assumes that Dante's allegory of poets is the same as personification allegory, and that his allegory of theologians is the same as figural allegory.[3]

117

Personification allegory is exemplified in such works as *Psycho-machia, The Romance of the Rose, The Faerie Queene,* and *The Pilgrim's Progress.* Its modus operandi is to represent a certain universal or moral by the use of fictitious persons or events; fables and parables largely function in this mode of signification. Figural allegory or typology has been developed as an instrument of biblical exegesis—namely, to establish the connection between the Old and New Testaments. Its modus operandi is to represent one person by another, or one event by another, by virtue of the similarity of the one to the other (for example, Isaac is a Christ-figure, since the sacrifice of the former resembles that of the latter).

These two types of allegory may reflect two different types of ontological or epistemological outlook: nominalism and realism.

Personification allegory cannot function without presupposing the reality of universals, at least in two modes. The first of these is the existence of the universal or moral (*universalis ante rem*) as the object of allegorical representation. The same universal or moral must also be reflected or manifested in the medium of allegorical representation, and this reflected being of the universal (*universalis in re*) is its second mode of existence. Thus, the universal appears twice in personification allegory, first in its own being and then in its being represented.

Figural allegory does not require the existence of universals in either of these two modes, since the representing and the represented are both particulars in this type of allegory. The representational or allegorical link of these particulars is established, not by some universals that stand above them, but by the similarity that is immediately present between the particulars themselves. This immediate similarity-relation constitutes the essence of the only universal that nominalists can admit, namely, the intramental universal (*universalis in mente*), or the *unreal* universal.

Some particulars in figural allegory may function like universals. Christ may be represented not only by one but by many figures, not only by Isaac but also by Joseph and Jonah. But even these cases do not presuppose the existence of the extramental universals, because the one-to-many relation in each of these cases is meant to reflect not the common essence shared by the particulars involved but only their many-termed similarity or resemblance relation. That is, there can be neither the Platonic Form of Christhood that stands above Christ and all the Christ-figures, nor the Aristotelian essence of Christhood that is shared by them. If there were such a Form or such an essence, Christ would be a derivative reality rather than an ultimate one. Not to recognize the ultimate reality of Christ would repudiate one of the central tenets in Christian teaching.

All that can be admitted about the relation of Christ to Christ-figures is that the latter resemble the former in some respect, which can be specified only in a nominalistic stipulation. Hence, only particulars are admitted in figural allegory for the functions of representing and of being represented, just as only the reality of particulars is accepted in the nominalistic account of being and being known.

The relation of the signifying and the signified in personification allegory is the vertical relation of the lower (or sensible) and the higher (or supersensible) worlds; in figural allegory it is the horizontal relation of the earlier and the later events of one and the same sensible world. The vertical relation is the relation of a copy or shadow and its original; the horizontal relation is the relation of promise and its fulfillment. One is a temporal or historical relation; the other is an atemporal or ahistorical relation.

Personification allegory reflects the highly atemporal Hellenic sensibility ("the timeless essence of things"); figural allegory manifests the highly temporal Hebraic sensibility ("the fullness of time").

As Robert Hollander points out, personification allegory was already used in Homeric criticism in the fifth century B.C.[4] Plato makes extensive use of it in his "mythical account" of the higher truths, and then the Neoplatonists firmly establish it as a central method of exposition and instruction. Most of the great works of personification allegory, from *Psychomachia* to *The Faerie Queene*, have been written within the ambience of Neoplatonism.

As Beryl Smalley says, Philo of Alexandria was the first to adopt personification allegory for the exegesis of the Old Testament. As a Hellenized Jew who spoke and wrote not in Hebrew but in Greek, he was too sophisticated to accept the literal truth of some biblical stories. Since these stories in their literal sense appeared to him either superstitious or fabulous, he tried to save their religious sanctity by reading them as the allegorical rendering of some Platonic truths.[5]

Smalley also says that, as a practising Jew, Philo accepted the literal meaning of some biblical stories as well as their allegorical one. Thus,

Philo's biblical allegories fall into two groups: (1) the fabulous, and (2) the literal or historical. The former is a straightforward adoption of Hellenic allegory; the latter is its adaptation for the Judaic tradition. Philo's example of the former is Genesis, and of the latter, Samuel. The former story has only allegorical significance; the latter describes a historical personage who probably lived as a compound of soul and body, but allegorically represents a mind rejoicing in the service and worship of God.[6]

Even Philo's historical allegory is more firmly grounded in the Hellenic realistic ontology than in the Judaic nominalistic one. Like a true Platonist, he acknowledges only the *probable* truth of the historicity of the biblical events ("Probably there was an actual man called Samuel"). He expects to find universal and certain truths only on the Platonic allegorical level.[7]

The difference between Philo's fabulous and historical allegories cannot become a matter of serious concern for Platonists. For they believe that the historical events of the corporeal world have no true reality: the corporeal world is no more than a copy or a shadow of the supersensible world. Since true fables (or lies) are also shadowy manifestations of the same supersensible reality, the Platonists' distinction between fabulous and historical allegories amounts to no more than a distinction of one type of shadowy picture from another.

Hence, as Smalley says, there is always the queer sense of an Alice-in-Wonderland logic hovering over Philo's demarcation between those biblical passages which are only fabulously true and those which are literally as well as allegorically true.[8] This Alice-in-Wonderland maneuver is a source of irritation and frustration only for those who presuppose the complete reality of history and the complete unreality of fictions. But what counts for Platonists is not which of these two sets of shadowy entities has a greater semblance of reality, but how well they portray the true reality.

Since the question of historical truth and untruth is largely irrelevant for the efficacy of personification allegory, Philo's two kinds of allegory can be readily combined into a hybrid form. As Hollander points out, Prudentius does this in his *Psychomachia* by including at least one historical person in each of its episodes, for example, the appearance of Job in the train of Patientia during her struggle with Ira.[9]

As Hollander intimates, the function of personification allegory can be regarded as that of exemplification as manifested in the Roman rhetoricians' notion of exemplum. Ernst Robert Curtius says that Cicero and Quintilian urge the orator to gather his exempla not only from history but from myth and legend.[10] "Exemplification allegory" is a little more accurate label than "personification allegory." Although most works of personification allegory happen to employ persons rather than animals or things, it is not always persons per se that perform the function of exemplification. That function often falls not on persons but on events.

It has often been pointed out, especially by the champions of figural allegory, that personification allegory tends to be abstract while figural allegory tends to be concrete. We may invite some serious confusion in this matter unless we distinguish the concreteness or abstractness of the rind (the signifying) of allegory from that of its core (the signified). This medieval distinction between rind or shell (*cortex*) and core or kernel (nucleus) comes from Alanus de Insulis.[11]

It is obvious that the core of personification allegory is bound to be abstract since it is only an idea or a moral. What is not obvious is that the rind of personification must also be abstract. To be sure, the fictitious persons in personification allegory do tend to be abstract simply because they are drawn only to portray abstract ideas. But historical persons used in personification allegory need not—and cannot—be any less concrete than historical persons appearing in figural allegory.

Even the fictitious entities in personification allegory need not always be abstract since they can be rendered as concrete as historical entities. Hence, we should bear firmly in mind that the concreteness or abstractness of the rind of personification allegory has no inherent connection with its factualness or fictitiousness. The same is true of the rind of figural allegory.

While Philo adopts personification allegory for the Platonic reading of the Old Testament, St. Paul introduces figural allegory as his Christian way of seeing the relation of the Old to the New Testament. According to Paul's figural vision, the things of the Old Testament are figures or types for the things of the New Testament. The two sons of Abraham prefigure the two Covenants, one of freedom and the other of bondage (Gal. 4:21–31); Adam is a Christ-figure (1 Cor. 15:21–22); The Crucifixion is the fulfillment of the animal sacrifices of the Jewish high priests (Heb. 9: 11–14). To see everything in the context of the figure and its fulfillment is engrained in the Pauline sensibility—so firmly engrained, in fact, that its operation is unmistakable even in cases where the word *typos* and its cognates are not even mentioned (e.g. 1 Cor. 15:21–22).

The figural way of seeing things does not remain a Pauline monopoly but becomes a common heritage of all the first Apostles of Christ. We can feel its presence not only in Acts (see 8:32), but even in the synoptic Gospels. For example, the long genealogy of Jesus at the beginning of Matthew clearly carries the sense of promise and its fulfillment; the relation of John the Baptist and Christ is cast in the context of preparation and achievement (Matt. 11:2–9; Luke 7:18–35). According to Luke, the first act of Jesus after his Resurrection was to give his disciples a figural account of himself: "And beginning with Moses and all the Prophets, he interpreted to them in all the Scriptures things referring to himself" (Luke 24:27). The very notion of the Messiah had been built up as a figural way of perceiving Providence in history.

The conversion of Philo's vertical scheme of personification allegory into Paul's horizontal scheme of figural allegory was dictated by the this-worldly ethos of the Hebraic tradition. Yahweh is the god of this world, who knows no other world; his covenant with Abraham is to be fulfilled in this world of mortality, whose perpetuation is the only form of immortality known to the Hebrews. The Hebraic sensibility is so inexorably history-oriented that all the sacred writings of the ancient Jews have been cast in the form of historical chronicles. The horizontal schema of promise and fulfillment has grown out of this historical sensibility.

The decisively new element which the Christians bring into this figural sensibility is their firm belief in the Messiah—that is, fulfillment is no longer to be looked for in the future because it is already here and now ("in the midst of us"—cf. Matt. 11:2–9; Luke 7:18–35). The moment of fulfillment which has been cast in the future tense for the Jews is now recast in the present-perfect tense by the Christians. Thus, the uniquely Christian principle of figural allegory takes its general form: the Old Testament prefigures the New Testament (*omnia in figura contingebant illis*).

The Pauline legacy received its further elaboration in two different cultural contexts: The Greek East and the Latin West.

The Fathers of Alexandria did not hesitate to retain both the Philonian and the Pauline methods of allegorical exegesis. As Erich Auerbach tells us, Origen is too much of a Platonist to believe in the bodily presence of the Lord. He is willing to admit that some biblical stories, including even those from the New Testament, are no more than fabulous representations of the supersensible reality.[12] Side by side with this Philonian sensibility, Origen also develops the Pauline typology, by classifying all biblical types in four categories: (1) Christ and his Coming; (2) the Church and her sacraments; (3) the Last Judgment and the Kingdom of Heaven; and (4) the relation between God and the individual soul.[13]

As Auerbach shows, Tertullian puts a decisive stamp on the Pauline sensibility in the Latin West. He uses the Latin word *figura* for Paul's Greek word *typos*: Joshua is a Christ-figure. From Auerbach's documentation, it appears likely that Tertullian adopted the word *figura* from Quintilian's distinction between tropes and figures.[14] He may have thought that *figura* could be effectively used for the Christian notion of typology since *tropos* had been so closely associated with the Hellenic sensibility of personification allegory.

In relentless opposition to the Alexandrian view of the Incarnation, Auerbach tells us, Tertullian argues that the Lord has come truly in flesh and blood.[15] This literally carnal conception of the Incarnation compels Tertullian to retain only figural allegory by completely dissociating it from personification allegory. Thus he restores the Pauline figural sensibility to its original purity by cleansing it of its Philonian accretion. With the triumph of Tertullian's position in the West, Auerbach says, both feet of Christian allegory came to be firmly anchored in historical reality, and the sense of reality and concreteness was fully restored to the Christian conception of history.[16] Through Tertullian, the this-worldly sensibility of the Latin tradition came to reinforce the this-worldly sensibility of the Hebraic tradition in its waning days.

Although figural allegory has been indelibly stamped with the sign of historical reality, both in its rind and its core, since the time of Tertullian, it would be a mistake to assume that there is absolutely no room for poetic fiction in figural allegory. In the case of personification allegory, we have seen, its rind can be made of historical persons or events rather than fictitious ones. Conversely, we can see the possibility of using fictitious persons or events rather than historical ones for the rind of figural allegory. This type of allegory may be called fictitious or poetic figuralism. The most prominent example of this type of figural allegory for the medieval Christians was the Song of Solomon; pious Christians from Augustine to Bernard of Clairvaux read it as a figural representation of the relation of Christ and his Church.

Fictitious figuralism has survived as an important element in the novel tradition to our own day: we can witness it in Thomas Mann's *Doctor Faustus*, a figural allegory of the decadent Faustian man, and in Günter Grass's *The Tin Drum*, a figural allegory of the Nazi superman.

In contrast with the abstract tendency of personification allegory, the concrete tendency of figural allegory has been well recognized. But the concreteness in question should be distinguished from historical reality. The core of figural allegory is always concrete since it is always historically real. However, the rind of figural allegory, which need not be historically real, nevertheless may take on as concrete a texture as any other form of fiction.

It has been Auerbach's signal thesis that the *Commedia* is written not as a personification allegory, and not even as a fictitious figural allegory, but as a historically true figural allegory. At first sight this appears to be an implausible thesis. The *Commedia* is assuredly written as a poem, which belongs to the domain of fiction rather than that of historical records. To give this thesis some air of plausibility has been the chief task for Auerbach and his followers.

Auerbach was, of course, the first courageous soul to try his hand at this impossible task. In recollection of his own performance in "Figura," he says,

> In the case of three of its most important characters—Cato of Utica, Virgil, and Beatrice—I have attempted to demonstrate that their appearance in the other world is a fulfillment of their appearance on earth, their earthly appearance a figure of their appearance in the other world.[17]

In Auerbach's interpretation, the historical Virgil is the figure and Dante's Virgil in the *Commedia* is its fulfillment. In order to maintain his figural realism, he advances the absurd view that Dante's Virgil is as real as the historical Virgil. It is one thing to grant the concreteness of Dante's Virgil, but quite another thing to claim his reality.

Following Charles Singleton, Robert Hollander sensibly makes one concession in his own valiant attempt to defend Auerbach's position:

the persons and events of the *Commedia* are not truly real or historical, but they are presented as though they were.[18] What he calls "fictional pretense" is the only thing that is truly real in the *Commedia*. But unfortunately this admission of the "as-if" tone or fictional pretense gives away the whole show. It is precisely the as-if tone of reality or fictional pretense that gives a fiction its fictitious character. I know of neither a fiction that is not written as if it were a true story, nor a fiction that is written as if it were a false story. To say that the *Commedia* has the as-if tone of reality is to admit that it is a fictitious work.

Hollander tries to inject some spirit into Auerbach's limp thesis by citing, on the authority of Ulrich Leo's *Sehen und Wirklichkeit bei Dante*, the amazingly frequent use of the word *see* and its cognates, which occurs over four hundred times, an average of more than four per canto.[19] But the word *see* can be used in the pretense of seeing as well as in the real act of seeing. The use of perception words never guarantees the reality of the perception in question. One sees in dream and fiction as much as one does in real life. The domain of *Sehen* is not always coextensive with the domain of *Wirklichkeit*. The designation of the perceptual contexts is never made by the perception words themselves, but always by their adjectival or adverbial qualifiers. Dante's extensive use of the word *see* would be a solid piece of evidence against Marshall McLuhan's thesis ("The medieval culture is more aural than visual"), but it is clearly irrelevant to the proving of Auerbach's.

Even such a staunch follower of Auerbach's literal fundamentalism as Robert Hollander admits the patently fictitious character of the first two cantos of the *Commedia*, namely, Dante's getting lost in the dark wood, his encounter with the beasts of the mountainside, the coming of Virgil to his rescue, etc. Except for this brief interval, he is ready to uphold the literal truth and historical reality of Dante's journey on the ground that the *Commedia* takes on an unmistakable aura of realism from the third canto on—that is, from the moment Dante and Virgil step into the Inferno.[20]

In my view, the aura of Dante's Hell does not appear to be any less or more realistic than that of the first two cantos. Virgil's behavior inside Dante's Hell cannot be considered as any less fictitious than his behavior outside, just as the beasts outside cannot be considered any less realistic than the beasts and monsters inside. Indeed, most of these monsters have been pronounced to be only fabulous or fictitious by the Church authorities. According to Hugh of Saint-Victor, they belong to the category of *pictura*, an artificial and lying configuration of elements on the literal level.[21]

The difference between the first two cantos and the rest of the poem is not that the former are fictitious while the latter is realistic. This way of reading would only introduce a grievous textual fissure into the *Commedia*. Probably for this erroneous reason, Charles Singleton regrets "that somehow a curtain does not fall at the end of Canto II *Inferno* to mark off the first two cantos of the poem for the prologue which they are."[22]

The real difference between the two parts of the *Commedia* in question is that Dante provides clear enough pointers for the fictitious texture of his poetic world in the first two cantos, while he does not continue to do so after entering the gate of the Inferno. And he provides those pointers in the first two cantos because they indeed constitute the prologue for the *Commedia*. The function of the prologue, however, is not to be marked off, but to mark off Dante's poetic world from the world of reality. The prologue constitutes the frame for the world of Dante's poetic imagination, as it were.

That many of Dante's characters are derived from history makes no difference to their fictitious character; the Job of *Psychomachia* is as fictitious as any other of its characters. Their historical origins may indeed add to the concreteness they gain in the fictitious world, but the sense of concreteness should never be mistaken for the sense of true historical reality.

Singleton and Hollander try to shore up their position by citing Dante's own authority; they believe that Dante himself clearly stated the nature of his own allegory once and for all in his letter to Can Grande. According to this letter, the *Commedia* is a fourfold allegory that has the following senses: the literal, the allegorical, the moral, and the anagogical sense.[23] They assume that this fourfold allegory is the same as what Dante has called the "allegory of theologians." This assumption is prima facie justifiable, not only because Dante's fourfold eschem appears to be only a recapitulation of St. Thomas's doctrine of the fourfold allegory in biblical exegesis, but also because Dante himself uses the fourfold exegesis of a Psalm (*In exitu Israel de Aegypto*) in his illustration of the fourfold allegory of his *Commedia*.

If this is so, not to accept the literal truth of the *Commedia* would be reading Dante's work in contradiction of his own intention. Hence

Singleton may be right in believing that to avoid this apparent contradiction has been the ulterior motive lurking behind the repeated
attempt to prove the inauthenticity of Dante's letter to Can Grande.[24]
Unfortunately, I have no textual competence to address myself to the
question of the letter's authorship, but I do know which is the more
sensible option to take if I am given the choice between the authenticity
of that letter and the factuality of the *Commedia*.

Even if Dante's authorship of this problematic letter were conclu-
sively established, I believe, it would be still of no use in justifying
Singleton's position unless the link between paragraphs 7 and 8 of that
document is rigidly construed. Paragraph 7 of the letter enumerates the
four different senses in biblical exegesis and illustrates them by the
fourfold reading of the Psalm *In exitu Israel de Aegypto*. Paragraph
8 shows how the fourfold allegory applies to the reading of his own
poem.

Singleton and his followers take this application of fourfold
allegory to the *Commedia* in an obstinately rigid way; the *Commedia*
must be literally true in the same way the Bible is believed to be. In fact,
this sense of rigidity has been the hallmark of the Auerbach-Singleton
school and even its stumbling block. In that school, the vice of rigidity
is usually mistaken for the virtue of consistency. One can see a historical
irony in this rigidity of the Auerbach-Singleton school if one knows the
historical fact that the chief motive for devising allegorical interpretation was to free the sacred and the profane texts from the rigid trap of
literalism and fundamentalism. To be flexible and subtle is the life of
allegorical sensibility; to be rigid and obtuse is its death.

We can avoid many evils of rigidity by taking the link between paragraphs 7 and 8 in a flexible way: Dante is proposing an adaptation of
fourfold biblical allegory to the reading of his own poem. All he has
to do to make this adaptation is to change the literal or historical sense
into the fictitious or poetic one; he can leave the other three senses
intact. To be sure, Dante does not say as much in paragraph 8; but once
the fictional framework of Dante's poem is understood, the adaptation
in question shows itself as too obvious to be mentioned.

The adaptation of fourfold allegory to the reading of poetic works
is not even new for Dante. He already tried it in the *Convivio*, where he
explains fourfold allegory as a way of composing his own commentaries on his canzoni. He says that these commentaries will be made on

four different levels of signification—that is, the literal, the allegorical, the moral, and the anagogical. Here Dante does not use the word *adaptation*. But what he does in his explanation of the four senses is clearly an act of adaptation. He explains the first two senses by taking an example from Ovid's story of Orpheus: it hides a truth or a fable ("the wise man with the instrument of his voice maketh cruel hearts tender and humble") behind a mantle of fiction ("Orpheus with his lyre made wild beasts tame"—*Conv.* 2:1).[25]

Then Dante goes on to point out that the second sense in this case is quite different from the second sense in the practice of theologians. But he does not take the trouble to explain the difference in question, probably because he regards it as too obvious. Whereas the second sense in the allegory of theologians refers to some concrete historical entities— let us be clear on this—the second sense in his allegorical scheme conveys some abstract ideas or morals.

Dante's main purpose in this *Convivio* passage has been mistaken by many Dante scholars; he is often assumed to be establishing the distinction between the allegory of poets and that of theologians. To be sure, he does introduce the distinction in question; but it is introduced not as a matter of theoretical comparison but as part of his practical proposal for the adaptation of fourfold allegory to the reading of his canzoni. His is a proposal for the ramification of personification allegory— namely, that the allegory of poets be expanded to the same fourfold scheme as that of the allegory of theologians. This is a noteworthy proposal to make, since the allegory of poets has been assmued to be limited to only two levels of signification. If so, Dante's proposal is probably meant to render personification allegory as complex and as resourceful as figural allegory.

What is noteworthy in this proposal is that, on the level of literal sense, he does not even mention the difference between the allegory of poets and that of theologians. There is a slim chance that he might have done it in the famous textual lacuna, but this chance appears to be so slim that we may safely discount it; this remote possibility is not seriously entertained in any of the restoration works of that lacuna.

Since Dante does not assert the difference between the two types of allegory on the literal level, should we then assume that Dante sees no difference between the literal sense of his canzoni and that of the Bible? It is just too obvious for him to assert that his canzoni have only the fictitious literal sense because they are poetic works. And if this point is too obvious for him to belabor in the case of the *Convivio*, it cannot be any less obvious in the case of the *Commedia*.

The Auerbach-Singleton school has the tendency to assume that "the literal sense" in medieval usage was synonymous with "the literal and historical sense." To be sure, this was the usual rule in the field of biblical exegesis. But the expression "literal sense" enjoyed a far wider currency than this restricted one among biblical commentators. In its general usage, "the literal sense" just meant the immediate meaning of a sentence or a text, which can be obtained by simply knowing the ordinary meaning of its words and their grammatical connection. The question of meaning in this general usage is completely divorced from that of truth. The latter question is always an extratextual problem; the former is an intratextual one.

The distinction between the intratextual problem of meaning and the extratextual problem of truth is equivalent to the distinction made by Hugh of Saint-Victor between the meanings of words and the meanings of things. He says that the meanings of words can be determined by the disciplines of the trivium while the determination of the meanings of things requires the disciplines of the quadrivium.[26]

Hugh of Saint-Victor is evidently assuming that the disciplines of the trivium are the logical sciences of semantics and syntactics in the purely verbal domain, and that the disciplines of the quadrivium are the empirical sciences of real things and their relations in the factual domain. This division of labor is presumably applicable to the reading of not only pagan but also sacred writings. To be exact, the determination of the historical truth of the Sacred Texts requires more than the use of the disciplines of the quadrivium, since it ultimately rests on the act of faith and revelation. Nonetheless, these extra elements surely belong not to the intratextual but to the extratextual domain.

At any rate, the literal sense in its general usage should be understood as the common stage that one has to go through in reading both pagan and sacred writings. The understanding of the literal sense is the first step one has to take whether one is a poet or a historian, a rhetorician or a theologian. Hence even St. Thomas, who adamantly refused to accept any allegorical interpretation of pagan writings, readily recognized their literal sense.[27]

The literal sense as a genus is context-neutral; it has no inherent connection either with the context of fiction or with that of fact. Only with the ascription of a respective differentia does it produce such species as the fictitious literal sense, the historical literal sense, or even the rhetorical literal sense. If Dante is using the literal sense in this generic and neutral way in his *Convivio*, and if he assumes that the differentiae of its various species are dictated by the relevant contexts, he has every reason to expect us to understand that the literal sense of the Bible is the historical literal one, and that the literal sense of his canzoni is the fictitious literal one. Thus, he sees no need to mention the difference between the allegory of poets and the allegory of theologians on the literal level.

Dante's adaptation of fourfold allegory in the *Convivio* amounts to replacing the first two senses of biblical allegory with the two senses of personification allegory. He appears to leave intact the other two senses of biblical allegory as they stand in the practice of theologians. Whereas he draws his examples from the pagan personification allegory in explaining the literal and the allegorical sense, he derives his examples from biblical exegesis when he explains the moral and the anagogical senses. But the appearance in question hides a subtle change that Dante installs in the last two senses of fourfold allegory.

According to Dante's account of the third sense, the biblical story that Christ took with him to the occasion of his transfiguration only three of his twelve disciples, conveys the moral "that in the most sacred things we should have but few companions" (*Conv.* 2:1). This third sense belongs to personification allegory as much as Dante's second sense; the function of both is to convey some moral that can be expressed in the form of a universal proposition. Their only difference appears to be that Dante's third sense conveys a religious moral while his second sense conveys a nonreligious one.

According to his account of the fourth sense, the Exodus story expresses the spiritual meaning "that when the soul goeth forth out of sin, it is made holy and free in its power" (*Conv.* 2:1). A technical question we have to face is whether the quoted clause is meant to contain a universal or a particular proposition. If it refers to a particular, existing soul, it is meant to contain a particular proposition describing some particular historical event; if it refers to *any* soul, it is meant to contain a universal proposition setting forth a universal truth. The sentence in question is ambiguous enough to be read either way, but in this case I am

inclined to take it as a universal proposition. As is often the case, the
definite article here operates as a universal quantifier. Thus, Dante's
fourth sense, along with his second and third, conveys a universal truth
and can be readily accommodated within Philo's scheme of biblical personification allegory just as much as Dante's second and third senses.
Dante's fourth sense is not only religious but also concerns the affairs
of the other world, or rather "the supernal things of eternal glory"
(*Conv.* 2:1).

Dante's adaptation of fourfold allegory in the *Convivio* assumes,
in brief, the following form: his first sense is literal and poetic; his
second is nonreligious personification allegory; his third is religious
personification allegory concerning this world; and his fourth is religious personification allegory concerning the other world. Through
this adaptation he completely assimilates the fourfold biblical allegory
into the Philonian scheme of personification allegory.

Since all three spiritual senses in Dante's new fourfold scheme are
given the form of personification allegory, they are hardly distinguishable from one another in their formal properties. Dante's distinction of
the three spiritual senses may indeed appear to be a distinction with
little difference. As many Dante scholars have pointed out, he seldom
appears to use the third and fourth senses in his own commentaries on
the canzoni. Yet it may be closer to the truth to say that the third and
fourth senses in his own practice are only formally indistinguishable
from the second, for they can be materially distinguished.

When Dante comes to make another attempt toward adaptation in
his Can Grande letter, he appears to reject his previous attempt. It is
hard to detect anything like that attempt to transform figural allegory
into personification allegory. In fact, the Can Grande letter gives the
impression that Dante accepts the biblical fourfold scheme in its
entirety for the reading of the *Commedia*. Hence Singleton and Hollander are led to cite this letter in support of the literal fundamentalism
in their interpretation of the *Commedia*.

I am still convinced that Dante is using "the literal sense" in its
generic and context-neutral way in this letter, and that he leaves us to
see its specific meaning in the light of the relevant contexts. This is
precisely the way he handled the matter in the *Convivio*; he regards this
point as no less obvious in the Can Grande letter than in the *Convivio*.
In the seventh paragraph of this letter, Dante describes the first sense of

the fourfold scheme as literal *(literalis)* and defines it as the meaning conveyed by the letter *(per literam)*. The meaning conveyed *per literam* is what I have called the "intratextual" meaning.

Toward the end of paragraph 7, where he demarcates the three spiritual senses from the first sense, Dante calls the first sense not merely literal but historical, *a literali sive historiali*. This designation of the first sense may appear to be a casual restatement of St. Thomas's designation of it as *historicus vel literalis*—and may be taken as textual evidence to conclude that Dante's first sense in the Can Grande letter is meant to designate the sense that is historically true, just as St. Thomas believes it to be in the Bible. Thus the phrase *a literali sive historiali* appears to be the philological clincher for the argument of the Auerbach-Singleton school. In fact, such reputable translations as that of the Temple Classics or Singleton translate the phrase in question as "the literal and historical [sense]."[28]

But the would-be clincher fails to clinch the argument; it has neither the muscles nor the teeth. The Latin word *historia* does not always mean "history"; its usual meaning is synonymous with the English word *story*. When Dante uses the Italian word *istoria* in the first treatise of the *Convivio* (*la litterale istoria*), he is using it as the Italian counterpart of the Latin *historia*. Since *historia* is context-neutral just as "the literal sense" is, the former is used simply as a synonym of the latter in Dante's *a literali sive historiali*. Thus, his *sive* is the same as the English *or* of synonymity as it is translated by Paget Toynbee.[29]

To be sure, St. Thomas may have placed *historicus* before *literalis* in his *historicus vel literalis* in order to emphasize the historicity of Sacred Scripture by implicitly exploiting the special connotation of the word *historia*. If so, it is equally plausible that Dante has reversed the order of the two words in his *a literali sive historiali* in order to restore or retain the neutrality of the first sense. Probably for the same purpose, he has completely dropped the word *historialis* on two of the three occasions where he names the first sense. None of these probable conjectures can be confirmed by appealing to the textual evidence because the text of the letter is hopelessly ambiguous.

Auerbach's thesis concerning Dante's figuralism has two features: (1) the literal sense of the *Commedia* belongs to history and not to fiction (his literal fundamentalism); and (2) its spiritual senses are figural and not of personification allegory (figural allegorism). Auerbach has assumed that these two features are inseparable from each other in figural allegory as in biblical exegesis. This assumption stems from an overgeneralization. Literal fundamentalism has never been maintained by theologians for every passage of the Bible; in fact, some of its passages have been read only figurally, while others have been read both literally and figurally.

St. Augustine provides a flexible guideline for distinguishing these two types of biblical passages from each other in his motto of the promotion of charity—that is, whenever the literal reading of a biblical passage is not conducive to the promotion of our love of God and neighbors, its meaning should be taken only on the figurative level.[30] Since then, very few pious Christians have thought that the literal meaning of the Song of Solomon is very conducive to promoting their charity.

Thus, literal fundamentalism and figural allegorism are not only distinguishable but also separable. We have already seen the implausibility of maintaining literal fundamentalism for the *Commedia*. But this should not mislead us to neglect the second feature of Auerbach's figural realism, since the core of figural allegory can be enclosed within a fictitious rind as well as within a historical one. So we shall undertake to examine the figural interpretation of the *Commedia* without undue concern with its literal sense.

At the outset we must not be confused about our own motives. Some have favored the figural interpretation of the *Commedia* on the ground that it is a more interesting way to read the poem than seeing it as a personification allegory. This is just an expression of subjective preference; personification allegory should, indeed, be a more interesting way for Platonists to read it than figural allegory. Subjective preferences and interests should have no place at all in our endeavor to find the right approach to reading the *Commedia* only in light of its allegorical texture.

We cannot accept the traditional interpretation of Dante's Virgil as a personification of reason, not because we are adverse to personification allegory, but because, as Singleton rightly says, "Virgil can not and does not always speak and act as Reason."[31] The most troublesome anomaly of Virgil as a representation of natural reason is that he guides Dante not only through Inferno but right up to the top of Purgatorio.

According to the Christian faith, Purgatory as a realm of grace is inaccessible to natural reason. One may counter this objection by saying that Virgil performs this and many other acts of grace as the personification of natural reason instructed and assisted by divine grace. But this rejoinder simply magnifies the initial anomaly: natural reason can not but cease to be natural as soon as it is instructed and assisted by divine grace. To receive grace in nature is the very essence of the infusion of grace into nature; there is, in fact, no other vessel for the reception of grace than nature.

It is quite easy to point out the unsatisfactory consequneces of viewing Dante's Virgil as a personification allegory, but it is very hard to provide a figural interpretation of him. Auerbach proposes a simple solution: The historical Virgil is a figure of Dante's Virgil, or rather the latter is the fulfillment of the former.[32] The obvious trouble with this solution is the reversal of figure and fulfillment. Within Dante's poetic world, his Virgil must be a figure that carries the literal sense, whatever figural senses it may also contain.

Even such an enthusiastic follower of Auerbach as Singleton cannot accept this reversal of figure and fulfillment. He is content to accept the traditional view that Dante's Virgil is the rind (figure) of his allegory and not its core (fulfillment). He is even willing to accept the traditional interpretation of Dante's Virgil as an allegorical representation of natural reason, in spite of his vehement protest that Dante's Virgil is far from exhausted ("sometimes but not always") by this allegorical function.[33]

The excessive allegorical residual of Dante's Virgil—too much of him is left out in his interpretation—is indeed a reliable sign that his Virgil should be read not as personification allegory but as figural allegory. For the literal sense of figural allegory tends to have a greater amount of allegorical residual than that of personification allegory. But nowhere does Singleton try to provide a figural interpretation of Dante's Virgil.

Thus, Singleton's commitment to Auerbach's figural realism remains half-hearted in his handling of Dante's Virgil. Figural realism as conceived by Auerbach requires two solid wings, historical reality and figural allegorism. In Singleton's manipulation of it for the case of Dante's Virgil, it cannot even take off the ground since it has to flutter on a pair of mismatched wings: historical reality and personification allegory.

The need for a figural interpretation of Beatrice is not any less urgent than the need for that of Virgil. As the personification of revelation, her appearance at the top of Purgatorio would mean that revelation does not come to mankind until it regains the lost Paradise, or that mankind is not given revelation until it completes its purgatorial works. This is a strange view of revelation for any Christian. Read as a personification allegory, the allegorical residual of Dante's Beatrice is as obtrusive as that of his Virgil. Hence some critics, such as Pierre Mandonnet, have been tempted to see her allegorical role on a much broader scale (*ordre surnaturel*) than that of revelation.[34]

In his figural interpretation of Beatrice, Auerbach is more sensible than in that of Virgil. He does not insist on Dante's Beatrice being the fulfillment of the historical Beatrice: he readily admits her function in the *Commedia* as a figure rather than a fulfillment. He calls her a *figura* or *idolo Christi*.[35] But to regard Beatrice as a figure is quite inconsistent with his view that Dante's Virgil is a fulfillment and not a figure. Perhaps to amend this inconsistency, Auerbach in a subsequent essay insists on Beatrice's role as a fulfillment, along with Virgil's corresponding role.[36]

Singleton almost develops a fixation with Auerbach's notion of Beatrice as a Christ-figure. There is something bizarre about this figural view of Beatrice: a feminine creature is singled out as the figural representation of a singularly masculine figure. Medieval theologians have always placed heavy stress on the amsculine image of Jesus Christ, since Augustine consigned the feminine portion of mankind to a lowly place somewhere between man and beasts. To the medieval understanding, Christ was the man of all men; he was the second Adam, the perfection of the first Adam, the first man. To the best of my recollection, I do not know of a single woman to be included among the numerous Christ-figures—such as Adam, Isaac, Joseph, David, Solomon, Jonah, etc.—by medieval biblical commentators.

I have singled out the two cases of Virgil and Beatrice because they are about the best touchstones for evaluating any allegorical theories proposed for the reading of the *Commedia*. For Virgil as the personification of reason and Beatrice as that of revelation are certainly the best-known examples of interpreting the *Commedia* as a personification allegory.

We have yet to consider the source of still greater embarrassment,

Dante's third guide. Auerbach and Singleton are no different from many other Dante scholars in passing over this third guide in silence. He is seldom even mentioned in the voluminous allegorical exegeses on Virgil and Beatrice; he has long entered the realm of oblivion. I mean St. Bernard, who waits for Dante's arrival in the Heaven of the Empyrean and brings his journey to its consummation.

Virgil and Beatrice have been established so firmly as the two focal points for the interpretation of the *Commedia* that some scholars have even come up with the thesis of a bipartite plan for the poem. For example, C. A. Robson seriously entertains the idea that Dante's original master plan for the composition of the *Commedia* was bipartite, the realm of Virgil and the realm of Beatrice, while the tripartite plan was only a matter of surface adornment.[37] If Robson's thesis were true, it would surely offer reasonable justification for the burial of Dante's third guide in the realm of silence and oblivion.

That the apparent triadic surface of the *Commedia* hides its truly dyadic structure has indeed become a widely shared premise even among those Dante scholars who would not openly embrace Robson's thesis; for they stand on this very premise, often unwittingly, when they subscribe to one of the most enduring assumptions in Dante scholarship —namely, that St. Thomas provides the substantive theological ideas for Dante's poetic ornamentation. The fundamental pattern of the Thomistic system is dualistic as manifested in his various dichotomies, such as the natural vs. the supernatural and the rational vs. the irrational. Of course, this pervasive dualistic pattern is the Aristotelian legacy. On some occasions, to be sure, the Angelic Doctor makes use of Plato's triadic pattern, but its role in the Thomistic system is no less incidental than in the Aristotelian one. If the content of Dante's epic derives from the dualistic Thomistic system, that epic is bound to have a dyadic structure despite its triadic surface form.

In contrast to St. Thomas's dyadic sensibility, St. Bonaventure's is thoroughly molded in the triadic pattern. The Seraphic Doctor sees everything in triple focus and feels everything in triple rhythm. It is for this reason that I have called special attention to his *Journey of the Mind to God* as one of the striking models for Dante's epic journey.[38] Since very few have seriously taken up this suggestion of mine, let me stress once more the indispensability of the Seraphic Doctor's mystical theology for comprehending the triadic structure of Dante's *Commedia*.

I myself have had to make a tortuous detour before coming to appreciate the prodigious significance of St. Bonaventure for understanding not only Dante but also the entire Gothic culture. I have had much difficulty freeing myself from the prevalent view that St. Thomas's achievement was the theological summation of the Gothic ethos. Only recently have I come to realize that this view gravely distorts the real character of Gothic culture. It was not St. Thomas and his Dominican brethren, but St. Bonaventure and the Franciscans who constituted the mainstream of the Gothic ethos. The Angelic Doctor's contribution was no more than a tributary feeding the fresh currents of the Arabian influence into this mainstream. These tributary currents were often so overwhelming as to require a series of extraordinary surveillances culminating in the Condemnation of 1277. St. Thomas's dualistic system is simply incongruous with the very texture of the Gothic ethos. The Gothic cathedral is not a two-storied edifice but a one-storied structure despite its many-tiered windows—just like St. Bonaventure's mystical corpus.

The distorted view of St. Thomas's achievement has been an inevitable consequence of the Council of Trent, which adopted him as the official theologian of the Counter-Reformation. This view was further confirmed as "official" by the encyclical *Aeterni Patris* in 1879, and since then the exaltation of this official distortion has been the ultimate task of most contemporary Thomists, especially under the aegis of Étienne Gilson.

Although here I cannot fully establish St. Bonaventure's as the central voice of the Gothic age, I will try to show that his mystical theology has a far closer affinity with Dante's epic than the dialectical theology of St. Thomas. The Seraphic Doctor's is a theology of allegory; the Angelic Doctor's is a theology of analogy. In spite of the instinctive assumption that allegory and analogy must somehow be intimately related, the precise nature of their relation still remains one of the most baffling medieval mysteries yet to be explored. Since we cannot here delve into this mystery, let us be content to observe one obvious difference: allegory is an intuitive mode, analogy a discursive one.

Analogy is the predominant form in the organization of St. Thomas's system, while allegory is given only a subsidiary role in it. The insignificant role of the allegorical mode in his works is fully attested by the fact that he devotes only one article of his *Summa Theologiae* to the explanation of this mode; and even that lone article is tucked away into the first question of the first part, which is only a preface to his *Summa*. In his other *Summa*, the topic of allegory fails to receive even this sort of cursory treatment. The only place where St. Thomas discusses the nature of allegory as an independent topic is his *Quodlibet*—that is, the haphazard assemblage of his miscellaneous ideas; even there he gives it only three articles (q.vii, aa. 14–16).

The intuitive mode of allegory is what places St. Bonaventure's works securely in the tradition of mystical theology. The allegorical mode is not only his chief form of perception and exposition in his mystical *opuscula*, but is extensively used even in his *Breviloquium*, one of his obviously discursive works. He devotes the entire prologue to this work to an inquiry into the nature of biblical allegory, and St. Thomas's exposition of fourfold allegory, which we have cited from his *Summa Theologiae*, appears to be no more than a summary of this intricate exposition. In *De reductione artium ad theologiam*, Bonaventure exalts fourfold allegory as the universal schema for interpreting all human experience, ranging from sense perception to mechanical arts to natural and moral philosophy.

The allegorical mode is the very essence of Bonaventurian exemplarism, in which every creature is viewed as either a shadow (*umbra*), a vestige (*vestigium*), or an image (*imago*) of God. These three forms for the reflection of God come under the general category of resemblance or similitude (*similitudo*), which we have cited as the ontological foundation for figural sensibility. Throughout the prologue to the *Breviloquium* Bonaventure clearly assumes the antonymity of 'the figural sense' to 'the literal sense' and its synonymity to 'the spiritual sense' on all levels.

In his figural perception, St. Bonaventure sees all of creation as the mirror of the divine perfections, or rather the poe mthat God writes with real things rather than with words. This is what is meant by "God's way of writing," which can be read only in the allegorical mode.[39] St. Bonaventure's mystical theology is to provide the proper way of reading this divine poem in allegory, and Dante consummates this mystical tradition with his allegorical epic.

It is this sense of the Bonaventurian trinitarian structure that compelled me to take Dante's third guide, St. Bernard, seriously in my *Fragile Leaves of the Sibyl: Dante's Master Plan*. Following the Bonaventurian triadic schema, in which the third always plays the crucial role of bringing the first two into union, I was then convinced that the allegorical interpretation of Virgil and Beatrice could never be complete without tying it in with that of St. Bernard. As a matter of fact, the function and labor of the first two guides in the *Commedia* would amount to nothing until and unless they were consummated in the function and labor of the last guide. Thus I came to attempt a joint figural interpretation of all three guides by proposing the simple thesis that they are figural representations of the Three Persons of the Holy Trinity.[40]

In my figural interpretation, Dante's Virgil is seen as a representation of the Second Person. Virgil comes to Dante lost in the *selva obscura*, just as Christ comes to mankind lost in this sinful world. Virgil shows Dante how to die in the world of sin (Inferno) and how to be reborn in the world of grace (Purgatorio)—that is, the way of the Crucifixion and the Resurrection. At Virgil's first appearance, Dante the poet gives us two rather prominent clues to indicate his function as a Christ-figure. Virgil tells Dante that he was born *sub Julio* (*Inf.* 1:70). Virgil's birth *sub Julio* is meant to be a veiled reference to the mission of the Second Person, from the Nativity (*nacqui*) to the Crucifixion (*sub Julio*—cf. *sub Pontio Pilato passus, et sepultus est*—the Nicene Creed). After Virgil's self-introduction, Dante describes him as "that fountain [*fonte*] which pours forth so rich a stream of speech [*parlar*]" (*Inf.* 1:79–80).[41] Since the Gospel according to John, the Son has been known as the Logos, the Primordial Word—or the Fountain of Speech.

Lest we may have missed these clues, Dante gives us one final pointer right after Virgil's departure: "Virgil, to whom I have given myself for my salvation [*mia salute*]" (*Purg.* 30:51). As Hollander alertly points out, Dante does not use the word *salvation* lightly.[42] As a Christian, Dante knows that there are no other agents of salvation than the Three Persons of the Holy Trinity. To deliver himself to Virgil for his salvation would be a blatant act of idolatry or stupidity on Dante's part unless his Virgil were conceived as a figure of one of the Three Persons.

The emphatic stress on Virgil's being a man of nature and not of grace may appear to be an insurmountable obstacle for his identification as a Christ-figure. But in truth, the unmistakable stamp of nature on him is an indispensable figural means to convey the idea of the Incarnation; the human or natural aspect of the Son is as essential as his divine aspect in the dogma of Christ's dual nature.

In contrast to his relation with the ethereal Beatrice, the outstanding feature of Dante's relation with Virgil is its earthy dimension. As my mentor T. G. Bergin loves to remind me, Dante's Beatrice is in marked contrast with Petrarch's Laura. The latter is tangibly carnal; the former is thoroughly spiritual. Whereas Dante never grabs or hugs Beatrice, he is pushed and pulled by Virgil. This physical dimension of their relationship reflects Virgil's bodily nature. The same physical or carnal dimension of the Second Person is the essence of the Incarnation: "Behold, the virgin shall be with child, and shall bring forth a son; and they shall call his name Emmanuel; which is interpreted, 'God with us' " (Matt. 1:23). Through his physical dimension the Second Person comes to dwell among us and to be called Emmanuel. Dante's Virgil is a figure of Emmanuel.

From the fourth century through Dante's own time Virgil's Fourth Eclogue has been believed to be the secular version of the sacred prophecy of the virgin birth of Emmanuel. Statius tells Virgil that he became not only a poet but also a Christian by following Virgil, and cites the prophetic passage from the Fourth Eclogue (*Purg.* 22:70–73). He regretfully adds that Virgil himself did not benefit from his own light, which guided other people. Even this expression of his regret carries a subtle reference to the role of Virgil as a Christ-figure. Christ neither draws any benefit from his own Incarnation, nor becomes a Christian by following himself. Christ is not a Christian. Thus Statius's description of his relation to Virgil turns out to be a deliberate case of figural or allogorical irony.

In my figural interpretation, Beatrice is viewed as a figure of the Third Person of the Holy Trinity. She comes to Dante after the departure of Virgil; the Holy Spirit comes after the departure of the Son. Christ explained this relation between the Second and the Third Persons:

> "But I speak the truth to you; it is expedient for you that I depart. For if I do not go, the Advocate will not come to you; but if I go, I will send him to you. And when he has come he will convict the world of sin, and of justice, and of judgment." [John 16:7–9]

On her arrival in the Terrestrial Paradise, Beatrice convicts Dante of his sin and judgment. After the ascension of the Griffin, she is adorned with the seven lights or gifts of the Holy Spirit while guarding the

Chariot. This is clearly a figural representation of the Holy Spirit entrusted with the task of guiding the Church.

Auerbach and Singleton have just mistaken this Spirit-figure for a Christ-figure. This misidentification can be readily exposed by the presence of the Griffin, the mythical animal that comes to the Terrestrial Paradise with Beatrice. With its dual nature (half lion and half eagle), the Griffin clearly represents Christ in his dual nature. Beatrice as a Christ-figure would therefore duplicate the allegorical function of the Griffin, a duplication that would offend our sense of order and elegance since Beatrice and the Griffin come together in the same procession.

The error of mistaking a Spirit-figure for a Christ-figure largely reflects two significant points in Christian theology which often fail to come to most Dante scholars' attention. First, there is always an intimate connection between Christ-figures and Spirit-figures, which in turn reflects the integral relation between the Second and the Third Persons. Second, there is a marked contrast between the medieval and the modern conception of God. Whereas the latter has been almost exclusively reduced to Christology, the former was always systematically amplified to Trinitarianism.

When the error of identification in question reflects the first of these two causes, it may produce some excusable consequences. However, when it reflects the second of the two it can become a serious problem, since the initial error may lead to a still graver one—as in the pathetic case of mistaking Beatrice's procession on the top of the Purgatorio as the center of the entire *Commedia*. Christ may indeed be regarded as the center of the Christocentric conception of God. But in the Trinitarian conception, he cannot be taken to be any more of a center than the Father or the Spirit.

In the Heaven of the Sun, Beatrice becomes the center around which revolve the three circles of theologians under the inspiration of the Holy Spirit: "Oh vero sfavillar del Santo Spiro" ("Oh, the very sparkling of the Holy Spirit"— *Par.* 14:76; also cf. *Par.* 10:65). In the Heaven of the *primum mobile*, she herself explains the nine orders of the angelic ministers for the invisible mission of the Holy Spirit, while she leaves the task of explanation to some other blessed souls in the other Heavens.

When Beatrice is relieved of her mission and goes back to her seat in the Mystical Rose, Dante changes the form of his address from *voi* to *tu*. This change is accompanied by a corresponding change in the syllabification of her name. While she stands as a figure for the Holy Spirit, *Beatrice* is syllabified as in *beatus* and *beati*. As soon as she returns to her private role, the first two vowels of *Beatrice*, *e* and *a*, are contracted into one syllable as in the normal pronunciation of Beatrice as a human name.

Virgil in Limbo assumes the mission of guiding the lost Dante at the request of Beatrice, who is sent to Virgil by the Virgin Mary. This is probably meant to be a figural reference to the Miraculous Conception of the Son by the Holy Spirit: *Qui propter nos homines, et propter nostram salutem descendit de caelis. Et incarnatus est de Spiritu Sancto ex Maria Virgine*—"Who for us men, and for our salvation came down from Heaven and was made flesh, by the Holy Spirit of the Virgin Mary" (the Nicene Creed).

In my figural scheme of reading the *Commedia*, St. Bernard is understood as a figure of the First Person. The Father alone remains in the Kingdom of Heaven, while sending his Son on the visible mission and his Spirit on the invisible mission. St. Bernard waits for Dante's arrival in the highest heaven, while he is being recovered from the dark wood by Virgil and brought to the Empyrean by Beatrice. St. Bernard not only looks like a tender father, *tenero padre*, but he is addressed as the holy father, *santo padre* (*Par.* 32:100).

The visible mission of the Son is to establish faith: Virgil constantly talks of faith. The invisible mission of the Spirit is to strengthen hope; Beatrice comes crowned with olive and her eyes are emerald. The function of the Father is to consummate the missions of his Son and his Spirit by receiving the sanctified soul into the bower of love. In this world St. Bernard was already well known as an eloquent exegetical expert on the nature of love, through his *Sermons on the Song of Songs* and *On Loving God*. Thus the Three Persons in their functioning are related to the three theological virtues of faith, hope, and love.

On his first appearance, St. Bernard tells Dante that his intention is to bring Dante's journey to its consummation. This should remind us of the promise which Father Benedict, another Father-figure, gave Dante in the Heaven of Saturn—that is, to grant Dante's wish to see his face unveiled (*Par.* 32: 61–63). To see the Holy Father's face unveiled is the very essence of Dante's beatific vision, which brings his love to its consummation.

In *The Fragile Leaves of the Sibyl*, I present this figural interpretation of Dante's three guides not as being complete in itself but as an integral part of my systematic figural reading of the entire *Commedia*. In this program I maintain the thesis that every person and every event in the three realms of Dante's other world are figural representations of the Holy Trinity in their works of salvation on the macrocosmic and microcosmic levels. The figural roles of the three guides constitute only one (surely the most prominent) fragment of this overall figural re-presentation of the Three Persons throughout the entire epic. I do not set forth my figural reading of various persons and incidents one after another in an ad hoc sequence, but show how Dante introduces them in a systematic sequence of three successive circles: the Son in his visible mission, the Spirit in his invisible mission, and the Father in his mansion.

The figural way of seeing the Holy Trinity in their works of salvation is to see the history of mankind from the perspective of Providence. The providential perspective had been firmly engrained in the medieval sensibility since Augustine's *City of God* and *On the Trinity*. In contrast to the Eastern Fathers' abstract doctrines of the Trinity, the unique feature of Augustine's Trinitarian doctrine is its concreteness, which reflects his figural sensibility. He tries to show us the nature and function of the Trinity as figurally manifested in the history of mankind.

It is such a figural view of God in history that Dante adopts from St. Augustine for the spiritual sense of his *Commedia*. The *Commedia* is ostensibly a literal account of the other world ("the state of souls after death"), but its spiritual sense is meant to be a "story of the living world," as Bergin says in his succinct restatement of Dante's own intention in his letter to Can Grande. "A story of the living world" is precisely the history of mankind referred to in the opening line of the *Commedia*: "Nel mezzo del cammin di nostra vita" ("Midway along the journey of our life").[43] As in St. Thomas's fourfold allegory, the history of mankind functions in the *Commedia* as the common prototype for all three levels of figural signification: the macrocosmic, the micro-cosmic, and the supersensible.

Dante's figural vision of the Trinity turns out to be a poetic version of Augustine's figural view of God and His Providence. Hence Augustine's *City of God* and *On the Trinity* are as prominent models for Dante's epic as Virgil's *Aeneid*. Perhaps Dante adopted the *Aeneid* as one of his models mainly because he looked upon it as a secular forerunner of his own poetic version of Augustine's providential vision.

My figural reading of the *Commedia* leads to the astonishing conclusion that the actions of the Trinity constitute the ultimate theme of Dante's epic. As long as one does not accept this, one has to conclude instead that the *Commedia* is an epic devoid of an epic hero. Chiefly to forestall such an absurd consequence, critics have often presented Dante the traveler as the epic hero who allegorically represents the Christian or even mankind.

But Dante the traveler makes an awkward epic hero. Whereas the traditional function of an epic hero is to perform a sustained heroic action, Dante's chief function is to see and report, the function of a traveling reporter. Of course, there are a few things he does on his own, but all of them are the instinctive kinds of behavior one can expect from any attentive, involved observer. It is in perfect accord with the medieval conception of a true Christian primarily as a receiver of grace that Dante the traveler plays the passive role of observer rather than the active one of a gallant hero. As Meister Eckhart says, "We are made perfect by our passivity rather than by our activity."[44] So the *Commedia* is bound to remain essentially a travelogue without an epic hero as long as we fail to see the action of the Trinity as its main theme. To be sure, Virgil's *Aeneid*, one of the conscious models for Dante's work, is also cast in the form of a travelogue. But Virgil's is a travelogue not of a mere traveler but of an epic hero. The failure to see the epic action of Aeneas in the *Aeneid* would be the same gross oversight as the failure to see the epic action of the Divine Trinity in the *Divina Commedia*.

Once the epic model of the *Commedia* is understood and is placed in the Pauline figural sensibility, my thesis that the Trinity is the epic hero for Dante's epic shows itself to be inevitable. In a perceptive review of my *Fragile Leaves*, Father Kenelm Foster of Cambridge University grants this point:

> If Dante's poem is about God and man, we should expect it to present the divine nature as the dominant ordering principle of the whole. And so in fact it does; and in this sense Mr. Swing [Seung] is perfectly right to say that the Trinity is the 'main theme of

Dante's epic.' Few critics, however, have ever said this of the *Comedy*; and none that I know, apart from Swing, has made anything like a convincing effort to show that it is true.[45]

To see the figural presence of the Trinity in Dante's poetic mirror is indeed a novel way of reading his epic, but it is by no means incompatible with the traditional way. To be sure, even the traditional way has its own mode of seeing the Trinity in Dante's poetic world by observing the pervasive effect of the divine power and justice. But that mode provides only an indirect reflection of God in Dante's mirror, while the other mode presents his direct reflection in it. To see God's reflection through his effect is an indirect mode; to see his reflection in his action is a direct mode. And it is these two modes of seeing the divine reflection that St. Bonaventure systematically employs in his use of the "mirror" of the whole world. According to him, the direct reflection is to see God "in the mirror" (*in speculo*), while indirect reflection is to see him "through the mirror" (*per speculum*). Furthermore, to see God through the mirror is only the preparatory stage for seeing him in the mirror. Thus, to see the working or effect of God's justice in the *Commedia* is no more than the stage preparatory to seeing God's reflection through Dante's poetic mirror, which must be perfected by the last stage of seeing God's figural presence and action in that mirror.

To see the figural presence of the Trinity in the *Commedia* is as hard as to see it in the history of mankind. Augustine stresses the obscurity of this figural reflection: the reflection of God in the mirror of mankind or its history is obscure (*aenigma*) because the mirror (*speculum*) is an obscure one (*De Trinitate*, 15:8 and 9). Dante's *Commedia* as a mirror of divine reflection is not any less obscure than the mirror of human history. Both are so obscure that the figural reflection of the Trinity is supposedly visible only to the eyes of the faithful. Even to have a fleeting glimpse of it is meant to be an act of faith and a gift of grace.

Dante is keenly conscious of this obscurity of his poetic mirror. Throughout the *Commedia*, in fact, he is almost obsessed with the fear that the vivid realism of his poetic creation may mislead his readers to mistake it for an ultimate reality and fail to perceive its obscure figural function. In order to forestall this grievous misunderstanding on our part, he ceaselessly draws our attention to the "veiled" (*ombra*) or "figural" (*figura*) character of his visionary world.

For the sake of consistency in my figural reading, I do not make the obstinate claim that there is no personification allegory in the *Commedia*. I readily admit that Dante's three worlds are organized in accordance with the medieval table of seven natural virtues (humility, mercy, meekness, fortitude, liberality, temperance, chastity) and three supernatural virtues (faith, hope, and love), and their contraries. In that respect, Dante's epic belongs to the medieval tradition of representing virtues and vice in personification allegory. Dante's unique contribution to this tradition has often been pointed out—namely, Dante gives his regions of virtue and vice a strong sense of concreteness by filling them with concrete people and their behavior. But this concerns the concreteness of the rind of Dante's allegory; I have shown the concreteness of its core by demonstrating that the abstract attributes of virtue and vice are not the ultimate but only the proximate core of Dante's figural allegory—which in turn figurally represents, severally or jointly, the Three Persons of the Trinity.

These virtues and sins can be interpreted on three different allegorical planes: (1) as independent entities ascribed to no particular persons either human or divine, (2) as attributes of human beings, and (3) as attributes of the divine being. The first of these three positions is taken when one reads the *Commedia* as a personification allegory, while either the second or the third position can be taken in its figural reading. The first position is incompatible with the central tenet of Christian ontology, since it exalts abstract entities as the ultimate reality. This is one of the overriding reasons that forbids the personification reading of the *Commedia* and dictates its figural reading on the ultimate level of its signification. The second position would indeed provide a figural reading, but would render the *Commedia* an epic of humanity rather than one of divinity. This is roughly the direction in which Robert Hollander moves by emphasizing the role of universal history in his figural reading of the *Commedia*.

The role of humanity and its universal history are indeed important in the *Commedia*, but they should be taken as the proximate core of its figural sense rather than its ultimate core, if we are to preserve the *Commedia* as an epic of divinity rather than converting it into an epic of humanity. Thus, the third position alone is left as a viable way of reading the *Commedia*, since it alone regards the virtues and sins in

Dante's three worlds as a figural representation of the virtues and actions of the Three Persons of the Holy Trinity. It is this figural reading
of the virtues and vices that I have systematically presented in my
Fragile Leaves of the Sibyl.

The table of virtues and vices that is used as the ground plan for
the construction of the Inferno, Purgatorio, and Paradiso, constitutes
the ladder of grace for Dante's descent and ascent. This triple ladder
of grace consists of two sections, the natural and the supernatural.
The seven natural virtues and their contraries become the seven rungs
of the natural section; the three supernatural virtues and their contraries
become the three rungs of the supernatural section. The natural section
of the ladder is used for separate representations of the Three Persons
in the following figural schema: the first and second rungs (humility
and mercy) for the Son; the third and fourth rungs (meekness and fortitude) for the Spirit; and the fifth, sixth and seventh rungs (liberality,
temperance, and chastity) for the Father.[46] The supernatural section of
the ladder is used for joint representations of the Trinity in the following
figural schema: the eighth rung (faith) for the Son with the Father; the
ninth rung (hope) for the Spirit with the Father; and the tenth (love)
for the Father with the Son and the Spirit.[47]

Even such attentive readers as Hollander may have received the misleading impression that the ultimate objective in my Dante book is to
clarify the topography of virtues and vices in the three realms of Dante's
other world.[48] But the clarification of the topography in question is only
a means, a methodic framework, to provide a systematic figural reference of the *Commedia* as a whole. Without such a systematic framework
as mine, the figural interpretation of Dante's epic always turns into an
arbitrary succession of fragmentary illuminations of one scene after
another, one episode after another, in the endless course of which Dante's vision in its totality is likely to recede further and further into
obscurity.

The same thing can be said of the traditional way of seeing Virgil and
Beatrice as personification allegories. It is sometimes feasible to see
Virgil as a personification of reason, because he is a figure of the Son,
whose attribute is wisdom or reason; it is also sometimes possible to
see Beatrice as a personification of revelation, because she is a figure
of the Holy Spirit, in whose province lies the function of revelation.

Nevertheless, as long as one remains on this abstract personification level, one has mistaken the proximate core of Dante's allegory for its ultimate core.

Now it should be instructive to compare my figural program for the interpretation of the *Commedia* with that of the Auerbach-Singleton school. We have already seen that Auerbach's own program has two elements: (1) the carnal sense of Dante's epic must be construed as historically true, and (2) its spiritual senses must be construed as figural allegory rather than personification allegory. He wants to maintain the indispensibility of both elements even at the expense of reversing figure and fulfillment.

Singleton is as emphatic as Auerbach in maintaining the historical truth of the carnal sense, but he is willing to accept some personification allegory along with figural allegory on the level of spiritual senses (in other words, Virgil does sometimes represent reason). In our discussion of Dante's letter to Can Grande, we entertained the possibility that his fourfold scheme in that letter may consist of both figural and personification allegory on the level of spiritual senses. Singleton understands Dante's fourfold scheme in this hybrid form when he takes it as Dante's own explanation of the nature of his allegory in the *Commedia*.

Singleton's hybrid version is a considerable revision of Auerbach's own program, which leaves no room for personification allegory on any level of interpretation. Robert Hollander subscribes to Singleton's revised version rather than Auerbach's original program, generously admitting other kinds of allegory than that of figuralism for the *Commedia*.[49] Freely accepting the personification allegory of Beatrice as theology and that of Virgil as reason, Hollander fully acknowledges "the mixture of the two kinds of allegory."[50] He also assumes that the moral sense in Dante's allegory belongs to the abstract allegory of personification.[51]

Hollander's unique stand in the furtherance of Auerbach's figural program is his insistent stress on the importance of illuminating the figural references of the *Commedia* to the secular tradition. This persistently shows up in most of his ingenious figural interpretations, for example, the figural reference of *Inferno* 1 and 2 to Aeneas's shipwreck in the *Aeneid* 1, and that of *Paradiso* 2 to Jason's voyage.[52] His performance almost counterbalances that of Singleton, whose chief concern has been to elucidate Dante's figural references to the sacred tradition.

In the *Divina Commedia* the traditions of the sacred and the profane are two complementary features of one universal history: I have already stressed this point as an expression of Dante's universal spirit in *The Fragile Leaves of the Sibyl*. Hollander's truly remarkable contribution lies in rounding out Dante's vision of universal history by illuminating its secular dimension, which is usually overshadowed by its sacred dimension in most commentators' exegeses. He appropriately calls the central chapter of his book "The Roots of Universal History."[53] His secular-oriented figural reading will long remain as durable a guide for Dante readers as Singleton's sacred-oriented, figural reading.

My identification of Dante's Virgil as a Christ-figure should have been welcomed by Hollander in his interpretation of the *Commedia*, but he has not given it a serious thought in his reading of my book. Instead, he proposes the hypothesis that Virgil is a figure of John the Baptist.[54] This hypothesis is a natural consequence of accepting the Auerbach-Singleton thesis that Beatrice is a Christ-figure: Virgil may appear as the harbinger to the coming of Beatrice just as John the Baptist was to the coming of Christ. In support of this hypothesis, Hollander cites Dante's first words describing Virgil, "Quella fonte/che spandi di parlar sì largo fiume" ("that fountain which pours forth a river of speech").[55] Then he entertains the idea that this "river of speech" may be figurally related to the River Jordan where John was baptized. Unfortunately, he fails to see that what cannot fit into this apparently neat figural schema is the most important phrase in Dante's description of Virgil, *quella fonte*. Dante calls Virgil not simply a river of speech, but its very fountain. This metaphor of the fountain, especially in conjunction with that of rivers, has long enjoyed the unique function of representing God, the fountain of all creation, in the Christian Neoplatonic sensibility. It would simply be sacrilegious to use that metaphor to describe the role of the Baptist.

So Virgil's preparation of Dante for the coming of Beatrice should be understood as a figural representation of the mission of the Second Person preparing for the coming of the Third Person. Perhaps in order to avoid any misunderstanding of this figural relation, Dante presents both Virgil and Beatrice as the agents of salvation, as Hollander carefully observes:

> The last words of Dante concerning Virgil (*Purgatorio* xxx, 51) are these: "Virgilio a cui per mia salute die'mi" ("Virgil, to whom I gave myself up for my salvation"). And, contained in Dante's last words to Beatrice are these: "O donna . . . che soffristi per la mia salute/in inferno lasciar le tue vestige" ("O lady . . . who for the sake of my salvation bore the leaving of thy footprints in Hell") (*Paradiso* xxxi, 79–81).[56]

Mia salute ("my salvation") is the common element that appears in Dante's last words to Virgil and Beatrice. We should once more repeat Hollander's astute observation that Dante does not use the word *salute* lightly. For it is the crux of the Christian *Credo* that the agents of salvation are none other than the Three Persons of the Holy Trinity.

The one element that revisionists Singleton and Hollander share with their master Auerbach is their insistence on the historical truth of the *Commedia* on the level of literal sense. Evidently, Singleton and Hollander believe that the first of the two elements in Auerbach's program is far more important than the second: they assume that the historical truth of literal sense is the sine qua non of figural realism.

In diametrical opposition to these revisionists' position, I dismiss as inessential the first element in Auerbach's program and retain the second element as the only essential one. I fully grant the fictitious character of Dante's epic on the level of literal sense, but always insist on finding the figural interpretation of every passage on all three levels of spiritual senses. Whenever I find personification allegory in any part of the poem, I assume that the interpretation in question is bound to be only provisional or proximate.

In my figural program, all three spiritual senses revolve around the Three Persons of the Holy Trinity: the allegorical sense is the figural representation of their works in this world (the macrocosmic dimension); the moral sense is the figural representation of their works in the individual soul (the microcosmic dimension); and the anagogical sense is the figural representation of their works in the Kingdom of Heaven (the supracosmic dimension).

My thoroughgoing figuralism is not meant to neglect the significance of the poem on its carnal (literal) level. On the contrary, the literal sense of the poem should be stressed as the very foundation on which the superstructure of spiritual senses stand. Furthermore, figural allegory assures the existence of sufficient allegorical residual, whose chief function is to remind us that the poem as a carnal entity has its own independence and can never be exhausted by any assemblage of spiritual readings. This perpetual tug-of-war between the carnal and the spiritual senses, which may be called allegorical dissonance, is the same kind of simultaneous relation of attraction and repulsion or dependence and independence that one can find in St. Thomas's conception of the natural and the supernatural orders, in the musical relation of the tenor (lower voice) and the upper voice(s) in the organum, or in the medieval interaction of the Empire and the Church. It is this inner tension (war of love and love of war) that gives Dante's work its unique vitality and its inexhaustible fascination.

After reading through my systematic figural interpretation of the *Commedia* and generously calling it "a grand design," Kenelm Foster says, with his usually astute perception, "There are obscurities in the *Comedy* which resist—I would rather not say contradict—the critic's system [i.e. my interpretative system]."[57] These obscurities and resistance are precisely the manifestations of the conflict between the carnal sense of the poem and its spiritual sense. They can be generated neither by a wrong-headed interpretation which can produce a patent contradiction with the text of the poem, nor by a superficial interpretation which can assure a hollow harmony with it. It is only a profound interpretation can induce and sustain the perpetual tug-of-war. So the allegorical obscurity functions just like Socratic ignorance: its presence can be distinctly felt only under penetrating illumination.

We may call my figural program of interpretation "figural fictionalism" or "figural poeticism" in order to distinguish it from Auerbach's figural realism. Figural poeticism is precisely the way St. Bernard reads the Song of Solomon in his *Sermons*. This is why I said that his *Sermones in Cantica Canticorum*, along with his other works, constitutes a "chief model for the architectonic construction of Dante's *Cantica* of divine love."[58] In truth, it is almost impossible to think of a more appropriate model for the composition of Dante's own *cantica* of divine love than the *Cantica Canticorum* as explicated in St. Bernard's *Sermons*.

In the *Commedia*, Dante gives clear enough indications of his own conception of poetic figuralism. First, Dante the poet is welcomed into the elect company of the classical poets in the Noble Castle (*Inf.* 4: 101). Then, in the Heaven of the Sun he is accepted into the sacred school of theologians by virtue of his being with Beatrice, around whom the circles of theologians revolve (*Par.* 10:65 ff.). By this joint affiliation with poets and theologians, he is asking us to understand the *Commedia* as a fusion of the allegory of poets (fictionalism) and the allegory of theologians (figuralism)—that is, his work is a theological poem. It is perhaps to stress the importance of understanding the dual nature of his poem that Solomon, the father of all theological poems, is given the role of explaining the equal importance of body (carnal sense) and soul (spiritual sense) in human nature (*Par.* 14:34 ff.).

In my reading of the *Commedia* I have spared no efforts in trying to peel off every layer of its rind and to find its innermost figural sense. In this I have followed Meister Eckhart's advice. "If you want the kernel, you have to break the shell" (Sermon 11). I have adopted my figural program not as an end in itself but as the necessary means for grasping the ultimate meaning of the *Commedia*. With my conviction of the inseparability of form and content, I have assumed that there can be no other way into the sanctum sanctorum of Dante's allegorical domain than that of figural understanding. Thus, by simply following this figural path to the innermost core of Dante's allegory, I have, at the same time, come to see the Trinity as epic hero and as the ultimate spiritual sense of his epic. I am now convinced that his *Divina Commedia* is the finest embodiment of Bonaventure's exemplarism in its figural mode, which enables us to see God not only *through* but also *in* the mirror of divine reflection.[59]

NOTES

1. (Princeton, 1969).
2. Ibid., pp. 3 ff.
3. Ibid., pp. 29 ff.
4. Ibid., pp. 8 ff.
5. Beryl Smalley, *The Study of the Bible in the Middle Ages* (Oxford, 1952), pp. 2–4.
6. Ibid., p. 3.
7. Ibid.

8. Ibid., p. 5.

9. Hollander, *Allegory*, p. 255.

10. Ibid.; E. R. Curtius, *European Literature and the Latin Middle Ages* (New York, 1958, 1963), p. 60.

11. Cf. D. W. Robertson, "Some Medieval Literary Terminology, with Special Reference to Chrétien de Troyes," *Studies in Philology* 48 (1951): 677.

12. Auerbach, "Figura," trans. Ralph Manheim, in *Scenes from the Drama of European Literature* (New York, 1959), p. 36.

13. Smalley, *Bible in the Middle Ages*, p. 7.

14. Cf. Auerbach, "Figura," p. 28 ff.

15. Ibid., p. 34 ff.

16. Ibid., p. 36.

17. Erich Auerbach, *Mimesis* (Princeton, 1953), p. 195.

18. Hollander, *Allegory*, pp. 76, 258.

19. Ibid., pp. 62–63.

20. Ibid., pp. 70 ff.

21. Cf. Robertson, "Some Medieval Literary Terminology," p. 684.

22. Charles Singleton, *Dante Studies 1: Commedia: Elements of Structure* (Cambridge, Mass., 1954), p. 9.

23. Ibid., pp. 1 ff. and pp. 84 ff.; Hollander, *Allegory*, pp. 40 ff.

24. Singleton, *Dante Studies 1*, p. 86.

25. *Convivio* 2:1 translated from the Temple Classics.

26. Cf. Robertson, "Some Medieval Literary Terminology," p. 680.

27. Cf. *Quodlibet*, q 7, a 16.

28. *Translations of the Latin Works of Dante Alighieri* (The Temple Classics: 1904) p. 348; Singleton, *Dante Studies 1*, p. 14.

29. *Dantis Aligherii Epistolae: The Letters of Dante* (Oxford, 1920), p. 199.

30. *On Christian Doctrine*, 3:10.

31. Singleton, *Dante Studies 1*, p. 91.

32. Auerbach, "Figura," p. 71.

33. Singleton, *Dante Studies 1*, p. 91.

34. Cf. Auerbach, "Figura," p. 75.

35. Ibid.

36. Cf. Auerbach, *Mimesis*, p. 195.

37. Cf. "Dante's Use in the *Divina Commedia* of Medieval Allegories on Ovid," in *Centenary Essays on Dante* by Members of the Oxford Dante Society (Oxford, 1965), pp. 22 ff.

38. *The Fragile Leaves of the Sibyl: Dante's Master Plan* (Westminster, Md., 1962), pp. 124, 130.

39. There are two senses to "God's way of writing." St. Bonaventure says, "Now, God speaks not with words alone, but also with deeds, for with Him saying is doing and doing is saying." (*Brevil.*, prol. (4), 4, trans. José de Vink, in *The Works of Bonaventure*, Paterson, N. J. [1963], 2: 15.) When God writes with words, he gives us the Sacred Scripture. When he writes with deeds, he creates the whole world. Hence there are two divine volumes: the Bible and the Book of Creation. These two

divine books dictate two allegories: the scriptural allegory and the universal or cosmic allegory.

40. T. K. Swing [Seung], *Fragile Leaves of the Sibyl*, pp. 390 ff.

41. Trans. John D. Sinclair, *Dante's Inferno* (Oxford, 1961).

42. Hollander, *Allegory*, p. 261.

42. Cf. Singleton, *Dante Studies 1*, p. 57.

43. Trans. T. G. Bergin, in *The Divine Comedy* (New York, 1955).

44. Sermon 2. Translation is mine.

45. Kenelm Foster, O. P., "A Propos of a New Book on Dante," *Blackfriars* 43, no. 509 (November 1962): 480.

46. T. K. Swing, pp. 168, 190, 217, 240, 263, 289, 312.

47. Ibid., pp. 359, 372, 407.

48. Cf. Hollander, *Allegory*, appendix 4, pp. 308 ff.

49. Ibid., pp. 233 ff.

50. Ibid., p. 251.

51. Cf. ibid., p. 259.

52. Ibid., pp. 81 ff. and 220 ff.

53. Ibid., p. 57.

54. Ibid., p. 261.

55. Ibid.

56. Ibid.

57. Foster, "New Book on Dante," p. 483.

58. Swing, *Fragile Leaves of the Sibyl*, p. 12.

59. In his appraisal of the various efforts made to interpret the *Commedia* figurally, Hollander singles out "one German and one American" for special praise (p. 18). I was disappointed to find that he had not even recognized my *Fragile Leaves of the Sibyl* as an endeavor toward the figural reading of the *Commedia*—in truth, the only comprehensive and consistent reading up to this day. That the consummation of the figural reading of the *Commedia* may even take one Korean, may be seen as an eloquent testimony to the universality of Dante's genius.

7

Dante's Francesca and James Joyce's "Sirens"

Mary T. Reynolds

No admirer of Dante can be unresponsive to the central theme of the *Divine Comedy*, the power of love. James Joyce, who once said, "I love Dante almost as much as the Bible; he is my spiritual food, the rest is ballast,"[1] certainly had a full awareness of Dante's treatment of this theme. Joyce's pervasive irony has made his readers wary of claiming for him an affirmative treatment of love in his fiction. Nevertheless, any appraisal of Dante's influence on Joyce must accept as a central challenge the determination of what use Joyce made of his reading of Dante's treatment of love; and indeed, any fair-minded reading of Joyce's work as a whole will turn up indicators, oblique and scattered but not at all casual, that Joyce had a sensitive appreciation of Dante in precisely this area. But it was a silent force. Joyce's admiration was expressed, not in critical exegesis, but in deep absorption and complex transformation.

To begin with, there is some evidence that Joyce had a particular interest in the Francesca episode of the *Inferno*. An investigation into his reading of this great love story can well begin by describing the fragmentary allusions and references to Dante's *Inferno* 5, which are found in Joyce's fiction and letters, and in the reports of his contemporaries. This review will be followed by a detailed comparison of Dante's hundred lines with Joyce's artistic construction in the Sirens episode of *Ulysses*, the eleventh of eighteen episodes into which the novel is divided. The Sirens chapter is not the only place, but it is clearly one place, where the theme of love is pervasive, significant, and treated by Joyce with seriousness as well as with irony.

155

The Sirens chapter is also one the writing of which made exceptional demands on Joyce's verbal skills—a point that underlines a possible ground for comparison with Dante. Joyce, in the schema for *Ulysses*, specified the "art" of this chapter as music; in his fulfillment of this intention he has manipulated language to produce effects commonly associated with music and poetry. "The poet, for Dante, is a musician with words; his special effect on them is a *legame musaico*. Poets are defined as those who make harmony with words, *armonizantes verba*."[2] This comparison, therefore, will focus on Joyce's verbal techniques where they seem to reflect his reading of Dante.

In the comparison we will search out and demonstrate the essence of two important rhetorical modes, by a review of certain syntactical and structural patterns. In the first section, the rhythms of Joyce's chapter, which apparently he intended to *be*, not merely seem to be, a fugue in some sense of this musical term, will be compared with Dante's use of rhythm and rhyme; and the tenor of discourse will be examined for similarities in Dante's and Joyce's use of tone and vocabulary to create verbal progressions in which multiple meanings are conveyed. The second section will be an inspection of structural patterns for congruent elements of plot, with special attention to the construction of an extended metaphor—literature in *Inferno* 5 and music in Joyce's Sirens chapter.

As a preliminary exercise, then, let us briefly review the evidence that Joyce had a particular interest in the Francesca episode. Here, Dante accomplishes a formidable compression of intellectual and emotional material. Joyce's interest in the rhetorical effects of this canto is reported by one of his contemporaries, Oliver St. John Gogarty.

> Joyce had a nose like a rhinoceros for literature. From his appreciations and quotations I learned much . . . Virgil's "procumbit humi bos" he would compare to Dante's "Cade [*sic*] como corpo morte [*sic*], cade." He tried not unsuccessfully *to form his style on the precision and tersity of Dante*. [Italics mine][3]

Gogarty's imperfect knowledge of Italian suggests that his reporting of the incident may also be less than reliable. (He is the original of Buck Mulligan in *Ulysses*, and is an unsympathetic critic of Joyce's work.) But even making due allowance for possible deficiencies in understanding Dante, or Virgil, or Joyce's views of either, we must admit that

Gogarty has nevertheless reproduced with the ring of authenticity one of Joyce's critical observations.

Joyce habitually memorized whatever appealed to him strongly in poetry or prose, a practice that has left in the record of his life and works many lines from *Inferno* 5—more, in fact, than from any other single area of Dante's writings. Joyce's use of these and other quotations reveals a highly individual reading of Dante. Joyce's critical insights, expressed in the early years of the twentieth century, anticipate the postwar modernist innovators both in modern poetry and in Dante criticism; in the latter especially, Joyce is more avant-garde than, for example, T. S. Eliot or Ezra Pound.

An illuminating report comes from Joyce's biographer Richard Ellmann. On Joyce's desk in Trieste, in 1914, stood a picture, cut from an exposition catalog, showing the sculptured figure of an old woman, naked and ugly, under which Joyce had placed two lines from *Inferno* 5:

> Elena vedi, per cui tanto reo
> tempo si volse...

> [Helen, mark, for whom so long a term
> of wasteful war was waged.]
> > [*Inf.* 5:64–65, trans. T.G. Bergin]*

Joyce's pupil, Oscar Schwartz (possibly thinking of the third act of *Faust II*), was distressed at this assault on the traditional image of the beautiful woman and asked, "Why Helen?"

> For answer Joyce made a rapid calculation of the number of years Helen lived with Menelaus before she met Paris, of the time she spent at Troy, and of the time she had been back in Sparta when Telemachus met her; he then calculated the age she must have been when Dante saw her in the Inferno.

Schwartz, moved by mingled anger and scorn, charged his teacher with having "killed Helen"; at which, Ellmann reports, "Joyce laughed and repeated several times, as though approvingly, 'Killed Helen'!"[4]

Other quotations by Joyce suggest a deep absorption in the poetry of *Inferno* 5. He wrote in a 1900 college essay, "Those whom the flames of too fierce love have wasted on earth become after death pale phantoms

*Hereafter, verse translations are from T. G. Bergin (N.Y., 1953); prose from Temple ed. (London, 1900).

among the winds of desire"—a paraphrase of lines 31–49 of *Inferno* 5 that foreshadows Joyce's later use of Dante's lines. In *Finnegans Wake*, his last and densest work, a marginal note says "Undante umoroso," at a passage that recalls Francesca's response when Dante the pilgrim asks her how, "al tempo de' dolce sospiri," ("in the time of sweet sighs") love first made the fateful couple aware of their "dubbiosi desiri," their equivocal desires. Francesca says,

> . . . Nessun maggior dolore,
> che ricordarsi del tempo felice
> ne la miseria; e ciò sa 'l tuo dottore.

> [. . . There is no greater woe
> Than happiness recalled in misery,
> And that your learned doctor well should know.]

> [*Inf.* 5: 121–23]

Joyce renders the spirit of this passage and gives the final line verbatim:

> Is a game over? The game goes on. . . . The beggar the maid the bigger the mauler. And the greater the patrarc the griefer the pinch. And that's what your doctor knows. O love it is the commonknounest thing how it pashes the plutous and the paupe. [*FW*:269]

In another chapter of *Finnegans Wake*, Joyce alludes to the seduction of Paolo and Francesca by their reading together the story of Lancelot:

> he'd be good tutor two in his big armschair lerningstoel, and she be waxen in his hands. Turning up and fingering over the most dantellising peaches in the lingerous longerous book of the dark. Look at this passage about Galilleotto. I know it is difficult but when your goche I go dead. . . . 'Twas ever so in monitorology since Headmaster Adam became Eva Harte's teacher . . . with man's mischief in his mind. [*FW*: 251]

Dante's line, "Love, that quickly captures the gentle heart," appears in *Finnegans Wake* in a more ambiguous context. Joyce describes an aspect of "Shem the Penman":

> As though he, a notoriety, a foist edition, were a wrigular writher

neonovene babe:—well diarmuee and granyou and Vae Vinctis, if
that is what lamoor that of gentle breast rathe is intaken seems
circling out yondest (it's life that's all chokered by that batch of
grim rushers) heaven help his hindmost. [*FW*:290]

"Shem the Penman" is part of Joyce's continuing effort to construct a
portrait of the artist, putting himself into *Finnegans Wake* as Dante the
pilgrim-poet is a personage in the *Divine Comedy*. It is possible that the
"grim rushers" may be the souls of the lustful who are whirling forever
around the Second Circle of Dante's Hell, "circling out yondest."
There is, at any rate, no doubt about the origin of "lamoor that of
gentle breast rathe," nor is there any doubt that Joyce believed he had
made use of the *Divine Comedy* in a significant way in *Finnegans Wake*.
He encouraged the production of a book of critical essays at an early
stage when his new work was being published only in fragments, and
later he acknowledged to Valéry Larbaud that he had "directed the
research" of the twelve critics. Two of these, Samuel Beckett in an
essay entitled, "Dante . . . Bruno . . . Vico . . . Joyce," and Thomas
McGreevy, in "The Catholic Element in *Work in Progress*," drew explicit parallels between Joyce's work and Dante's presumably at
Joyce's instigation.[5]

Of these parallels, one is especially important for the present study.
Assuming Beckett's essay to be based on conversations with Joyce, it
becomes clear that Joyce had read both the *De Vulgari Eloquentia* and
the *Convivio* and saw himself as Dante's disciple, particularly in the
area of linguistic innovation. What compelled Joyce's interest however,
was nothing so simple as word coinage or the fracturing of syntax; it
was a concern with the ultimate reality of language, with its most
fundamental and most general principles. This was what led Joyce to
create the language of *Finnegans Wake* which, as one realizes immediately on hearing the recorded voice of the author reading his own work,
is English in syntax, Irish in cadence, and multilingual in vocabulary;
and in all this it is a continuation of experiments begun in *Ulysses* and
even earlier—a fulfillment of tendency. Beckett writes that between
Dante and Joyce "there exists considerable circumstantial similarity.
They both saw how worn out and threadbare was the conventional
language of cunning literary artificers, both rejected an approximation
to a universal language. . . . If English is not yet so definitely a polite

necessity as Latin was in the Middle Ages, at least one is justified in declaring that its position in relation to other European languages is to a great extent that of medieval Latin to the Italian dialects."[6]

Here, Beckett is making the point that Dante's development of a vernacular adequate to encompass the range of his poem's design followed from his decision, or gradual realization, that neither Tuscan nor its rival dialects provided an adequate literary form; and the "circumstantial similarity" obviously reflects Joyce's view of his own problems in fashioning a verbal medium that would render the night-time life of the mind. Dante's ultimate mastery of language came with his narration of an experience which is not a dream yet is somehow beyond the mind's waking life; Joyce, who once said, "I can do any-thing with words,"[7] also saw the dreaming consciousness as a chal-lenge and sought a literary form in which he could represent it. Joyce worked for seventeen years on *Finnegans Wake* and certainly wished it to be read. Thus it is interesting to find the youthful Beckett, under Joyce's inspiration, writing of Dante's conclusion that, "he who would write in the vulgar must assemble the purest elements from each dialect and construct a synthetic language that would at least possess more than a circumscribed local interest . . . that *could* have been spoken by an ideal Italian who had assimilated what was best in all the dialects of his country."[8]

To Joyce's European outlook this approach to language was irresis-tible. As he began the writing of his universal history, his hero—Universal Man—was required to "possess" all the Indo-European lan-guages, very much in the way that linguistic science has now demon-strated that infants possess the physical equipment for making any sound (that is, producing any phoneme) in any language. The extent to which Joyce realized his construct is indicated by the many lists of linguistic elements found in *Finnegans Wake*, including short lists in Hebrew and Basque as well as the classical languages, Sanskrit, Dutch, Scandinavian, German, and Gaelic. For the last three, book-length glossaries have now been compiled.[9] *Finnegans Wake*, among other things, is a vocabu-lary of mutations: Joyce's compounds in *Ulysses* were recognizably English; in *Finnegans Wake* they are polyglot. Leaving aside the many arguable features of the book, this determination to force language into a new range is testimony to Joyce's most ambitious and deliberate imitation of Dante.[10]

Joyce also quoted and paraphrased lines from *Inferno* 5 in conversation and in letters, a common enough practice. In 1938 he wrote to Ezra Pound, "I don't think I ever worked so hard, even on Ulysses," and added the line, "Galeotto è il libro e chi lo scrive," ("Galeotto [i.e., a pander] is the book and he who writes it"). Another letter, to Valéry Larbaud, ended with the line, "E come i gru van cantando lor lai" ("As the cranes go, chanting their lays," *Inf.* 5:46).[11] These lines are not among the cliches of the *Divine Comedy*, and they were quoted in the original—a practice widely reported by Joyce's contemporaries.

Such allusions and quotations can safely be taken as evidence of knowledgeable attachment to the canto; and they supply pertinent insight into the workings of Joyce's mind. In these respects they illuminate another cluster of direct quotations from the *Divine Comedy* that provide more compelling evidence of Joyce's special interest in *Inferno* 5. His most substantial direct reference to Dante's poem occurs in *Ulysses*, in the Aeolus chapter, which is set in a newspaper office. Here, in an unspoken or monologue passage, Stephen Dedalus' interest in Dante is shown to be an interest in his craftsmanship; and it is canto 5, its rhymes and cadences, which becomes the starting point for a mental review by the young poet of Dante's art. In a silent review of Dante's choice of rhyme-words, Stephen surveys critically the subtle artifice that ties the long poem together.

Ulysses, a long novel set in Dublin and limited in its action to a single day, has three main characters: Leopold Bloom, a Jewish advertising canvasser (the chief protagonist); his unfaithful wife Molly, who is a concert soprano; and Stephen Dedalus, a twenty-two-year-old teacher and would-be writer, who is the first of the three to be introduced. Three chapters of the novel focus the reader's attention on the mind of Stephen Dedalus, each dealing with the young man's potential as a creative artist. Each of these chapters gives a direct view of Stephen's thoughts; each contains a direct quotation from Dante (among a great deal of other literary and philosophical material), demonstrating—if nothing else—Stephen's close reading and easy recall of the *Divine Comedy*. In the first, the Proteus chapter (the eighteen episodes of *Ulysses* are named for the sections of Homer's *Odyssey*), Stephen thinks of Aristotle, who is identified by Dante's line, "maestro di color che sanno" ("Master of all them who know," *Inf.* 4:131).[12] In the second, the Aeolus chapter, and in the third, Scylla and Charybdis, the reader is made more explicitly aware of Stephen's admiration for Dante. It becomes apparent that the young man has a firm critical knowledge of the *Divine Comedy*.

This young poet has a new and eccentric view of Hamlet, which he proposes (in "Scylla") to some members of the Dublin literary establishment gathered in the National Library.[13] As Stephen does this, the text gives both his spoken words and his unspoken thoughts. Into the latter comes a silent thought of Dante, a quotation from the *Divine Comedy*.[14] Now Stephen is the only character in Joyce's novel who is presented as being capable of such juxtaposition—the only individual in that group of literati who is able to quote extensively, who is perhaps even capable of understanding, *both* Dante and Shakespeare. It is therefore noteworthy that Joyce has selected for association in such a context the Hamlet love-triangle and the Francesca story.

The reader has been prepared for this by the long passage from the *Divine Comedy* quoted by Stephen—again silently—in the Aeolus chapter. Here, while he waits for an interview with the newspaper editor, Stephen listens to the windy conversation of his elders; to escape his depressing surroundings, he thinks of love, of literature, and particularly of Dante's skill as a poet. The text of the chapter is divided up by headlines (taken together these form a kind of commentary; the voice is unidentifiable), and the headline of what may be called the "Dante section" is "RHYMES AND REASONS."[15] As he looks at the editor's twitching mouth, Stephen wonders, "Would anyone wish that mouth for her kiss? How do you know? Why did you write it then?"— a reference to rhymes he has jotted down, "mouth to her mouth's kiss," earlier that morning in the Proteus chapter. Stephen recalls some commonplace rhymes, then a fragment of Dante's poetry:

> . . . la tua pace
> . . . che parlar ti piace
> . . . mentre che il vento, come fa, si [*sic*] tace.
> [*Inf.* 5:92, 94, 96]

These are among Francesca's opening lines. But the terzina, thus placed, seems at first reading to have no direct connection with the theme of love; rather, these lines deal with wind, the great wind of Hell which sweeps the carnal sinners through canto 5, and which is briefly lulled so that Dante can hear Francesca's story:

> . . . thy peace
> . . . if thee to speak it please,
> while the wind, as now, for us doth cease.

Aeolus, the newspaper office in Joyce's chapter, is Homer's Cave of the Winds. Dante's lines cut through the windbags. Stephen's mental retreat into Dante's poem has momentarily stilled for him the winds of editorial bombast.

But now Stephen shows himself to be a discriminating reader of the *Divine Comedy*, a poet himself and one who understands Dante's craftsmanship. Apparently Stephen knows the poem. or much of it, by heart; as he reflects on Dante's skill in rhyming, and especially on the "reasons" for Dante's choice of rhyme-words, the young man is able to draw examples from widely separated sections of the *Comedy*. (Dante, in *Inferno* 1, similarly makes the point that he had memorized Virgil's poem.)[16] Rhymes, says Stephen to himself, are "two men dressed the same, looking the same, two by two"; and one man, "he," saw them "three by three"—a tidy specification of Dante's terza rima.

Stephen summons to mind what he knows of Dante's use of color-words as rhyme-words. Francesca's triple rhyme becomes a visual image of approaching girls: "He saw them three by three." This moves his mind to canto 29 of the *Purgatorio*, where Dante first has the vision of seven ladies approaching at the wheel of the gryphon's magic chariot. Three of them are brightly clad, Stephen remembers, "in green, in rose . . . in russet entwining." He knows that the other four are purple, and the associative force of each thought sets off a new impulse: "*per l'aer perso*, in mauve, in purple," he thinks. *Persse*, a kind of murky purple, is the color of the air in Francesca's region of Hell; and it is also the color of the streamlet which trickles into the marshes of the Styx and the color of one of the three great stone steps at Purgatory's gate. But only in canto 5 of the *Inferno* is *perso* used as a rhyme-word. Here Dante makes it a somber image set in contrast, by the other rhymes in its terzina, with omnipotent goodness, the power of "il Re de l'Universo," whom—if she were able—the gentle Francesca would ask to grant Dante "la tua pace" because he feels compassion for her sad fate, her "mal perverso."

If the reader recalls, as Stephen seems to be doing, the "Reasons" for Dante's use of rhyme-words, Dante's color choices in the canto of the dancing ladies extend these associations still further. Red is one of their colors, and the third of the stone slabs at Purgatory's gate is a flaming blood-red.[17] But the word that Stephen renders as "green" is not the simple *verde* which Dante uses twenty-one times and three times as rhyme-word. It is *smeraldo*, used only once as a rhyme—in the climactic passage at the close of *Purgatorio* 31, where the eyes of Beatrice are first unveiled to Dante:

> posto t'avem dinanzi a li smeraldi
> ond' Amor già ti trasse le sue armi.
>
> [We have set thee now before the emeralds
> when Love drew the shafts he loosed against thee.]
> [*Purg.* 31:116–17]

At this point in the poem Dante is escorted by the four ladies in penitential purple, while the other three, singing, urge Beatrice to turn her eyes upon Dante—"al tuo fidele" ("thy liegeman"). It is the moment when he reaches the highest possible level of human love.

Stephen's last color word is *oriafiamma*, which he sees as gold. Dante uses this rhyme-word at another emotional apex: the conclusion of *Paradiso* 31, where amidst dancing angels, the vision of the Virgin Mary's matchless beauty is revealed:

> così quella pacifica oriafiamma
> nel mezzo s'avvivava . . .
>
> [so that great oriflamme of peace
> shone at the center mightily]
> [*Par.* 31:127–28]

Now Stephen, who has probably repeated silently the whole of this passage—the last sixteen lines of canto 31—ends his foreshortened overview of the *Divine Comedy* with the last line of canto 31, expressive of St. Bernard's love for Mary and of Dante's contemplation of Bernard's vision:[18]

> Bernardo, come vide li occhi miei
> nel caldo suo calor fissi ed attenti,
> li suoi con tanto affetto volse a lei,
> che i miei di rimirar fe' più ardenti.

> [Bernardo, seeing that my eyes were fixed
> upon the shining source of his own warmth,
> with such devotion turned his eyes upon her
> as to make mine more ardent in their gaze.]
>
> [*Par.* 31: 139–42]

In only ten lines, Joyce has allowed Stephen to connect three distinct and widely separated examples of the *Comedy*'s theme, the role of love in human destiny, and thus to demonstrate how Dante uses language to lock together his poem's three major divisions. Joyce's passage is one of great economy:

RHYMES AND REASONS

Mouth, south. Is the mouth south someway? Or the south a mouth? Must be some. South, pout, out, shout, drouth. Rhymes: two men dressed the same, looking the same, two by two.

> . . . la tua pace
> . . . che parlar ti piace
> . . . mentre che il vento, come fa, si tace.

He saw them three by three, approaching girls, in green, in rose, in russet, entwining, *per l'aer perso* in mauve, in purple, *quella pacifica oriafiamma*, in gold or oriflamme, *di rimirar fe' più ardenti*. But I old men, penitent, leadenfooted, underdarkneath the night: mouth south: tomb womb. [*U*: 136–37]

Stephen's interest in canto 5 is rhetorical but not narrowly so; his regard for Dante goes to the root of his use of language. "Mouth, south. Is the mouth south someway? . . . Must be some."—the missing words being, in effect, "*reason*, which makes all the difference in the choice of each word the poet selects." To the extent that the fictional Stephen Dedalus resembles in some characteristics the young Joyce of 1904, this passage demonstrates what was involved in the mature Joyce's admiration for "the precision and tersity" of Dante.

In the novel, the way has been opened for exploration of Dante's theme; and the reader's ear will also be prepared for linguistic interlocking of the three major sections of *Ulysses*. An important critical observation about Dante has been made, in the Aeolus chapter, in the voice of Stephen Dedalus. Joyce, who composed with a carefulness almost equal to Dante's, is not likely to have made a casual election of *Inferno* 5 for Stephen's demonstration. Of course the Francesca story is so well known that the names of Paolo and Francesca are familiar even to people who have never read a line of the *Divine Comedy*. With Joyce, quite otherwise: his borrowings from Dante are not merely the catchwords but are spread throughout the *cantiche*. When, therefore, he chooses canto 5 as the focus of a disquisition on poetic expertness and power, there may be good warrant for closer examination of its appearance in other parts of the book.

So much, then, for the evidence of Joyce's interest in *Inferno* 5, which appears to have included both the canto's theme and its verbal devices. We can now turn to a direct comparison. However, before examining syntactical patterns in the two works, something must be said about the general problem of adapting Dante's story (or any other legend or myth) to fit a modern setting, and some preliminary indication given of Joyce's complex methods of maneuver, both in *Ulysses* generally and in the Sirens chapter.

A major challenge to Joyce in using Dante's poem was the difficulty of connecting it with an improbable protagonist. But, to reverse the terms, the integrity of Joyce's design repeatedly demanded some kind of enlargement or extension of Mr. Bloom to fit the context of Homer, Shakespeare, Goethe, and others, as well as Dante. The construction of many subtle connections between Bloom, who is uneducated but intellectually curious, and Stephen, who is erudite by any standard, works to this end. Operating with a gentle contrapuntal irony (for after all, Mr. Bloom's intellectual limitations are not of his own making), the author nudges them closer to each other. Cumulatively the pattern becomes important—as patterns of human action always do—very much in the manner that Dante makes little patterns of personal relations echo and vibrate with repetition.

The Sirens chapter, all else apart, is a demonstration of verbal skill. In this respect it is consistent with the mind of Stephen Dedalus, as the reader observes it in action in the three chapters where he silently quotes Dante. But the Sirens episode is *all* Bloom. Stephen does not appear, nor does the chapter contain any direct quotations from Dante. On the other hand, in the Aeolus chapter Mr. Bloom does appear; he sees Stephen without speaking to him,[19] and later on in "Sirens" Mr. Bloom recalls the newspaper office.[20] A similar crossing of paths occurs in the Scylla and Charybdis episode in the National Library.[21] Both chapters focus on the writer's craft, though differently; and both suggest Bloom's interest in it and Stephen's character as writer. Stephen's relationship to Bloom is a matter of central importance in the novel; yet it is never explicitly described and must be apprehended holistically from the reader's acceptance of a multitude of verbal clues.

Note that, in the episode of *Purgatorio* 31 which Stephen silently recalls, a notable exchange of personalities occurs: the silent disappearance of Virgil at the moment when Beatrice first appears. The context is Dante's confession of waywardness in love; weeping, he admits that as soon as she had died, "Le presenti cose / col falso lor piacer volser mici passi" ("the things of the moment, with their false allurement, turned aside my steps," *Purg.* 31: 34–35).[22] Beatrice warns him, "e perchè l'altra volta / udendo le Serene sie più forte" ("another time hearing the Sirens be thou of stouter heart," *Purg.* 31: 44–45). Something of the flavor of the interplay of Dante's three personages pervades the near-meetings, both physical and psychic, of Stephen and Bloom in the two episodes, first in the newspaper office and then in the library, in which each is shown pursuing, so to speak, his chosen vocation and finally in the Wandering Rocks chapter, where each is engaged in bookbuying—a literary activity too, and one in which these two alone among the novel's characters engage.

In "Wandering Rocks," which immediately precedes the Sirens chapter, a pronouncement is made on each of the protagonists. Stephen is the subject of discussion between his enemy Mulligan and the English visitor, Haines. In Mulligan's disparaging remarks a contrast appears between his and Stephen's views of Dante:

> —They drove his wits astray, he said, by visions of hell. He will never capture the Attic note. The note of Swinburne, of all poets, the white death and the ruddy birth. That is his tragedy. He can never be a poet. [*U*: 245]

In Mulligan's estimation Swinburne eclipses Dante. "Visions of hell" are not the stuff of poetry; the sense of the passage is that Stephen, because of his ingrained Catholicism, is incapable of following the lead of Yeats, Russell, and the group of Dublin intellectuals who wish to Celticize Homer—to graft onto native Irish themes the "Attic note" of classical Greece. Neopaganism and paganism both exclude the kind of psychological and spiritual quest that Dante provides.

> —Eternal punishment, Haines said, nodding curtly. He can find no trace of hell in ancient Irish myth. . . . The moral idea seems lacking, the sense of destiny, of retribution. Rather strange he should have just that fixed idea. Does he write anything for your movement? [*U*: 245]

But Stephen, unsuspected by the Dublin cult, is following Dante's lead—the example of the poet who, with skills comparable only to Shakespeare's, made use in an original fashion of classical themes and patterns. Mulligan's scornful answer is equivocally met by Haines:

> —Ten years, he [Mulligan] said, chewing and laughing. He's going to write something in ten years.
> —Seems a long way off, Haines said, thoughtfully. Still, I shouldn't wonder if he did after all [*U*: 246]

A remarkably similar pronouncement is made, in the same chapter, on Bloom. Lenehan and M'Coy, two Dublin parasites, see Mr. Bloom bookhunting, "a darkbacked figure scanned books on the hawker's cart." M'Coy says that he has seen Bloom purchase a book on astronomy, but M'Coy thinks that Bloom is only a bargain hunter, "dead nuts on sales." They gossip idly about Bloom's wife, but then Lenehan makes a more serious judgment:

> —He's a cultured allroundman, Bloom is, he said seriously. He's not one of your common or garden . . . you know. . . . There's a touch of the artist about old Bloom. [*U*: 231–32]

Both Bloom and Stephen are praised by persons who might be expected only to disparage them.

It is with this background that the Sirens chapter begins to look like a critical turn in Joyce's novel, related to its other parts as *Inferno* 5 is related to Dante's *Purgatorio* and *Paradiso*. The *Divine Comedy* would lie far outside the range of reading that realistically would be possible for Mr. Bloom. (On the other hand, he has made a great effort, "aided by a glossary," with Shakespeare.) But the theme of the Sirens chapter, like that of the *Divine Comedy*, is human love—its part in man's destiny. And the chapter's narrative form and focus, like the

Francesca episode, concerns an adulterous triangle. Stephen, who is never shown to have any awareness of Bloom's predicament, is nevertheless seen by the reader—and by no one else—making a mental connection between Shakespeare's Hamlet triangle and Dante's Francesca. Stephen Dedalus has a fine critical understanding of Dante's treatment of this theme, but the young man has not yet known love in his limited experience of life. Mr. Bloom has, however; and in "Sirens" his unspoken thoughts pass in review what he has learned about love. On the evidence, the Sirens episode in its many resemblances to Dante's *Inferno* 5 seems to be one more of those instances in which Joyce has Mr. Bloom "act out" a more pragmatic, Ulyssean version of ideas and attitudes expressed by Stephen Dedalus—ideas which, transformed by Bloomesque experiential realities, are often sounder and more defensible than the younger man's verbal formulations.

Turning now to stylistics, let us examine Joyce's fugue as a response to his admiration for Dante's terza rima. Joyce's manipulation of language in "Sirens" bears many resemblances to Dante's linguistic maneuvers; it becomes clear that Joyce had a craftsman's understanding of Dante's invention of the terza rima and his achievement in using it for such a long poem. Dante's rhyme choices usually have an unforced, effortless quality; yet nine times out of ten he uses the rhyme-word to emphasize or even carry his idea. The rhyme-word is the important word in the line not only for sound but for sense; not just for the pleasure it gives the ear but for the progress of Dante's argument. Most of the sentences in the *Divine Comedy* coincide with the terzina; some are just three lines long, but sentence length is varied to avoid mechanical rhythm. Since the middle verse of a terzina prepares the ear for the sound of the rhyme-word to come in the next terzina, Dante has used his rhymes as a structural tool of great force. They lock the parts of his poem together as firmly as the great blocks of some ancient stone wall.

A suggestion, necessarily subjective, of close "fit" of acoustic and semantic properties is important everywhere in Joyce's prose. In the Sirens chapter, this quality is tightly controlled to produce the circular pattern often used in the musical fugue.[23] One of Dante's notable effects in the *Divine Comedy* is the linkage of sound and meaning, and a comparable achievement lies at the heart of Joyce's technical accomplishment in "Sirens." Here, two things can be observed and related to each other. First, there is the selection of words in which phoneme and morpheme are so related as to make possible chains of linked sound that can be made to echo in the ear as rhymes do, and that can be made to carry overtones of defined meaning. Second, there is the effort Joyce made to prune and cut back syntactic structures so that sound values could be brought forward and woven into a verbal counterpoint.

In the first endeavor Joyce has created identifiable voices—in the musical sense of the term *voice*—a total of seventeen. In the second, by a skillful manipulation of connectives, he has tied together long passages made up of several voices. The prose moves the reader's eye and ear from one meaning to the next, as a composer passes from note to note and from chord to chord. The effect is not unlike Dante's use of the terza rima to move his lines through transitions both musically and intellectually meaningful.

Joyce had also observed and admired Dante's manipulation of stress and rhythm by rhyme choices. This is apparent in his selection and placement of the three lines quoted by Stephen Dedalus: ". . . la tua pace/. . . che parlar ti piace/. . . mentre che il vento, come fa, ci tace." In the novel, only the last of these three verses is quoted in full; thus the reader is made aware of the cumulative rhythm by Stephen's silent recall of the complete phrase rather than just the rhyme-word. The manner of recall suggests an interest in Dante's use of the terza rima in the control and ordering of cadence. Cadence is a notable feature of *Inferno* 5. It is a term which can indicate any measured movement of sound, and may be taken here as "intonation," especially as that modulation of tones which produces a sense of movement toward a conclusion. In their context the rhyme-words build a cumulative emotional progression (in the musical sense) and the final rhyme, coming at the end of the last of the series of terzine in which we are introduced to Francesca, accomplishes one of Dante's impressive effects. Geoffrey Bickersteth describes it as bringing a long, drawn-out melody to a full close.[24]

Joyce (whose own verses are perhaps the least part of his achievement) transferred this metrical effect to prose, using repetitive sound patterns to perform the function of rhyme in placing and interweaving the stresses. The ear (while the eye goes on reading for the literal sense of the line) perceives a triple effect, as recurring sound patterns in the

opening pages of "Sirens" identify the fugal voice, involve it in a duet
with a second identifiable voice, and move the reader's attention musically through a statement.

A bit of detail will be enlightening. In the first fifty-six lines of connected discourse, Joyce introduces the "Subject"[25]—which in the chapter is the Sirens' song—and briefly combines it with the "Answer,"
stated by Mr. Bloom. This initial passage opens and closes with a
sentence that is a verbal equivalent of the tonic in music: "Bronze by
gold, Miss Douce's head by Miss Kennedy's head, over the crossblind
of the Ormond bar heard the viceregal hoofs go by, ringing steel"
(*U*: 253). The rhythm is established and carried forward beyond the
opening sentence by a succession of aspirates:

> head . . . head . . . heard . . . hoofs . . . her . . . his

The fugal subject is heard for the first time through the notation of
two barmaids, Miss Douce and Miss Kennedy, who work in the Ormond Hotel and are the sirens of the chapter. For their characterization, or musical voice, Joyce develops a pattern of sibilants and alliterative *l* sounds, combined with light vowel sounds and the light
plosive *t*.

It is important to distinguish the fugal *subject* from the fugal *voice*:
the former is carried into effect through the content of the *words*, the
latter by the *sound*. Thus the Sirens' song as the fugal subject is flirtatious, falsely welcoming, insincerely promising, mendacious; but these
qualities cannot be attributed to phonemic combinations. Moreover,
the fugal subject, after its first announcement by the two barmaids, is
taken up by other characters present in the Ormond bar, each of whom
speaks and is otherwise represented by an individualized sound pattern,
his own fugal *voice*.

The barmaids' fugal voice is based on these words:

> Miss Douce . . . bronze . . . Miss Kennedy's. . . gold . . .
> ladylike . . . eagerly

In the consonance of partial rhyme and alliteration, their sibilants and
vowel sounds become repetitive stress patterns. Miss Kennedy's rhythm, like her surname, is dactyllic, and the barmaids' voices, though
differentiated from each other, are not dissimilar as they disappear
into the prose and reappear:

flower . . . I'll . . . long . . . ladylike . . .
she . . . teacup tea . . . teapot tea . . . reef . . . teas . . . teas.

The choice of *reef* suggests mermaids, the reiterated *teas* carries a double meaning, and Miss Kennedy's light front vowel *e*, a soprano sound, becomes through the narrator's descriptive terms more firmly established as part of the barmaids' *l*-laden fugal voice. The opening passage concludes (as each successive statement does, following the musical convention) with a return to the tonic. Joyce repeats in a new intermixture the sounds of the opening sentence, giving a sense of circular movement: "Yes, bronze from anear, by gold from afar, heard steel from anear, hoofs ring from afar, and heard steelhoofs ringhoof ringsteel."

In similar fashion, Joyce selected for each of the "speaking" characters in the episode a pattern of sounds which, like the resonance of the barmaids' fugal voices, vibrate simultaneously in the ear and in the mind. These distinctive sound patterns, each one carefully introduced, are combined in duets, trios, and quartets of mixed conversation, monologue, and descriptive (presumably authorial) fact or comment. A narrative pattern is constructed on the fugal model of statement and restatement.

In the opening pages of the chapter, then, distinctive rhythms are established; like every verbal composition it is constructed of rhythms. Dante's canto 5, just on the face of things, is assumed to be composed of rhythms. Moreover, most admirers of Dante's poetry have noted that the determinants of rhythm are not the metronomic beats of absolute time but the phrasal rhythms and the movement of the line as a whole, in groupings of stresses that are related to the sense of the passage. As Bickersteth notes, in English verse too it is the accentual relation of word-values to one another which determines the rhythm. Joyce inspired Stuart Gilbert, in his book *James Joyce's Ulysses*, to call attention specifically to the importance of "the rhythm of the prose" in "Sirens." The first three pages of this section of Gilbert's exegesis are set off from the rest, and in the introduction it is claimed that these pages "reproduce word for word, information given me by Joyce."[26] Attention is called to "rhythm as one of the clues to the meaning,"[27] and to the fact that each character has "his appropriate rhythm."[28] If Joyce was thus sensitive to the uses of rhythm, it is hard to believe that he was unaware of its use to individuate the foremost personage of canto 5. Let us now examine some aspects of this complex question.

Mode and tenor of discourse, and also choice of speaker, in the hands of a craftsman like Dante or Joyce, become important stylistic tools; through them the reader is given delicate shades of meaning and wide-ranging connections and contrasts. The modulations of speech in Dante's *Inferno* 5 are developed with some ambiguity. The story, told in melodious language while the great wind of Hell is stilled, seems out of place, an intrusion. Dante the traveler responds to the sad tale and to the inflections of the gentle narrator with such compassion that at its conclusion he falls, fainting. Dante the poet has placed in eternal torment one of his most sympathetic portraits; in terms of the poem as a whole, he has committed the lyric voice to the unfolding of a theme, the power of love, which seems not to belong in Hell since it is, for Dante, the force that draws man upward to Paradise. Linguistically as well as explicitly, love in the moral structure of the *Divine Comedy* is identified with Beatrice, who brought Dante out of the Dark Wood.

Some of the linguistic subtleties of Dante's construction are also discernible in Joyce's "Sirens." First, modern critics have noted that *amore*, a word reserved by Dante for the *Purgatorio* and *Paradiso*, appears a minimal number of times in the *Inferno* but is a key word in Francesca's story. This word, *love*, is certainly a *voussoir* also in the rhetorical structure of the Sirens chapter. Joyce's manipulation of vocabulary, in fact, is as carefully precise as Dante's.[29]

Second, Joyce's selection of the fugue, with its potential for complicated interweaving of ideas and its recurrent summaries and restatements, becomes a powerful rhetorical implement. It offers a flexible verbal system in which the author can show his protagonist's thoughts moving back and forth between two poles—in this case, between the Dantesque themes of love and death. The chapter becomes a kind of dramatization of Dante's line, "e più di mille / ombre mostrommi, e nominommi, a dito / ch' amor di nostra vita dipartille" ("and a thousand yet / and still more . . . he pointed to / and named, whom love from our life did separate"). Dante's meaning in this line is not, of course, simply physical death; it is the eternal death of the souls consigned to damnation. Joyce, in this chapter, invests the idea of death with multiple significance but always centers it on the *waste of life*: it may be the purposeless ending of life before one has fully lived; or the careless squandering of vitality in dissipation; or, especially, the moral death of despair, which he associates with degradation, brutality, or venality.

These are matters of rhetoric, and in the Sirens episode Joyce's principal weapon is his use of the contrapuntal technique to pair contrasting aspects of his subject of discourse. Dante's line, "Amor condusse noi ad una morte" ("Love led us to one death"), is the controlling idea of Joyce's "Sirens" as it is in the Francesca episode. It is not simply "Love "which is the object of inquiry, but that perverse aspect, willfully misguided love, through which men and women are drawn down to eternal death. It is *not* human passion that is punished in canto 5, nor is it simple lust nor broken marriage vows. The mortal quality of the sin of Paolo and Francesca lay in their abandonment of reason, highest of human faculties, as a guide to action. Their punishment was to continue forever thus; losing their power of free movement, subject to their master "Amor" for all eternity.

Joyce's critical reading of this story is reflected in his identification of the Sirens' song as the *mendacious* promise of love which leads men to death—literally in the Homeric original, morally in Joyce's view, as also in Dante's. The Dantesque view is made explicit near the end of the novel, in the Eumaeus chapter, as Stephen Dedalus and Mr. Bloom walk home together, "continuing their tête à tête . . . about sirens, enemies of man's reason" (*U*:649.26).

Third in Joyce's rhetorical maneuvers is the control of tone and atmosphere in the episode. Dante in canto 5 has portrayed Francesca entirely by the suggestive potential of the lyric voice. Elsewhere in the *Divine Comedy*, in a striking simile or by some telling descriptive phrase, the author sketches a character in brief, decisive strokes; he has not done so with Francesca. She comes through to the reader as a presence, a gentle and modest noblewoman; we know her attributes through the tone of voice with which the poet has endowed her.

The two girls who are the Sirens of Joyce's episode seem to present themselves to us directly; but by subtle and sharp contrasts of tone, Joyce creates an ironic negative metaphor. In their self-images Miss Douce and Miss Kennedy resemble Francesca, but the reader sees them both through their own utterances and also in the private view where the spurious self-image is deflated. These two see themselves as "ladylike" but in fact they are vulgar in speech and action. They see themselves as generous and kindly but in fact they are hostile and venal. Confidently they assume their own feminine attractiveness; in fact, their flirtatious relationship to the patrons of the Ormond is trivial and transient.

A similar but more ambitious effect is Joyce's portrait of Mr. Bloom's mind, which is rendered without overt comment, by controlling the tone of his silent monologue and setting this in contrast to the conversations and remarks of the other patrons of the Ormond.

In the case of Mr. Bloom, the resemblance to *Inferno* 5 stems from the moral and rhetorical uncertainties of Dante's construction, especially his placing of the gentle, loving Francesca in Hell. Dante's awareness of the fatal flaw comes in the terzina where he asks Francesca how the lovers came to their sad plight:

> Ma dimmi: al tempo de' dolci sospiri
> a che e come concedette amore
> che conosceste i dubbiosi desiri?

> [But tell me: in the season of sweet sighs
> what sign made Love that led you to confess
> your vague desires? How opened he your eyes?]
>   [*Inf.* 5:118-20]

Up to this point Dante has been altogether sympathetic. But now the tone changes: as Francesca recounts their self-seduction through their reading of the tale of Lancelot, she enlarges the perspective, saying, "Our Gallehaut [pander] was the book, and he who wrote it" ("Galeotto fu il libro e chi lo scrisse"), indicating their awareness of mortal sin. Now the pathos is enhanced by a parallelism of Paolo's involvement in the story.

At the end of the first segment of Francesca's recital, Paolo appears —but only in the use of the plural pronoun, "da lor" ("from them"): "Queste parole da lor ci fur porte" ("These words were borne to us from them"). The next line, set off by a full stop from the preceding one, is believed by some critics to be spoken *by Paolo*: "Caïna attende chi a vita ci spense" ("Caina waits for him who shed our blood [took our lives]," *Inf.*5:108). The tone of this line, hostile and grim, has often been remarked upon as being out of character for Francesca; Dante was not likely to refer to Francesca's story with a plural pronoun, "da loro," if the words had been spoken by a single character; and there is the matter of the full stop, which seems to set these words apart.

But in any case, the *contrast of tone* of this line seems essential to the characterization of Francesca; rhetorically, it is a basic element in the total effect:

> Mentre che l'uno spirto questo disse
> l'altro piangea sí che di pietade . . .

> [While the one spirit said this, throughout the tale
>   so piteous were the tears the other shed . . .]

[*Inf.* 5:139]

As Francesca describes the lovers' first fatal kiss, in the closing terzina, Paolo silently weeps; and Dante swoons in pity: "E caddi, come corpo morto cade" ("and I fell, as a dead body falls," *Inf.* 5:142).

Joyce, by a comparable manipulation of tone, gives a sympathetic portrait of the mind of his protagonist engaged in reflection on the same problem that Dante encounters in canto 5: the causes and complications of misdirected love. Mr. Bloom asks himself, as Dante the traveler asks Francesca, "How does adultery come about?" The compassionate and humane quality of Bloom's reflections and conclusions are a kind of critical comment on *Inferno* 5; as Dante begins with compassionate curiosity (*l'affettuoso grido*) but ends with a deep involvement of pity, *pietà*, so Mr. Bloom exhibits something of Dante's relentless rationality. And the last line of the canto suggests a strong personal identification with this sin: like Mr. Bloom, Dante is *un homme moyen sensuel*.

Bloom's reflections center on his obsessive jealousy, fueled by the thought of his wife's probable infidelity with her concert manager, Blazes Boylan; his thoughts are counterpointed with his silent observations on the lives and personalities of the other patrons of the Ormond. At the core of the chapter is the tale of the wronged husband, the erring wife, and the wife's lover. The rhetorical strategy uses the associative force of songs to force Mr. Bloom to recall, one after another, circumstances associated with his wife. Extended by the development of Joyce's fugal web, the origins of Bloom's predicament unfold, as Francesca's tale unfolds, in a few sharply defined sequences.

Like the terza rima, the fugal form enriches while it constrains. The requirements, even when loosely observed (as usually also in musical

compositions—the strictest canon compositions are the least interesting), are a confining influence. The form arrests the motion of language,
as the author concentrates on producing a verbal equivalent of imitative
counterpoint. But this effect in turn strengthens the inner movement.
Within each statement, four in Joyce's chapter, an emotional climax is
precisely built; a new aspect of Mr. Bloom's dilemma is set forth, as his
silent monologue is related to the story—briefly summarized—of
another character. The complexities of narration are firmly held by the
fugal pattern.

More especially, the imitative quality of the fugal writing creates a
resonance, a challenge recurrently suggested yet concealed. The rigid
form, that is, also holds in check the portrayal of complexities of personality. Contradictory glimpses are given of the principal voices, and
especially of Mr. Bloom. These are held in an undetermined state; they
are invested with expectation, their precise meanings never identified.
Meanings are examined but apparently not governed by the author.

Here the resemblance to Dante's canto 5 evokes the three-line statement of Francesca which reveals that she and her lover were killed *in
flagrante delicto* by her husband. It was this event, cutting off the guilty
pair from any possibility of repentance of mortal sin, which determined
their damnation.[30] It poses a moral problem that Dante deals with later
in the poem and is central to the artistic question of why he demands
our sympathy for Francesca. The suggestion is made that a force more
powerful than reason has been implanted in human nature—and divinely. Dante contains this meaning in a single line, which he introduces
first in Francesca's terzina:

> Amor, ch' al cor gentil ratto s'apprende,
>   prese costui de la bella persona
>   che mi fu tolta, e 'l modo ancor m'offende.

> [Love, which quickly captures the gracious heart,
>   took him with the fair body which was taken from me;
>   and the manner in which 'twas done still offends me.]
>   [*Inf.* 5: 100–02]

Biographical details that are somewhat sordid and brutal are here
stated with a gentle reticence—almost the voice of innocence.

As in Dante's canto, Joyce's rhetoric shades the tone and atmosphere, creating emotional progressions. *Inferno* 5 begins with storm, and as Francesca speaks, the wind explicitly ceases; but within her tale, the use of gentle terms such as *desire* and *peace* contrast with the brutality of the central event. There are two progressions, the first describing Francesca's birth and upbringing, her meeting with Paolo and their love for each other, and their murder; the second tells with great brevity and rising emotion how their love developed into the sin of adultery. Both sections of the story, on different moral levels, move from innocence to catastrophe, from love to death.

Joyce's four fugal statements within the chapter are, taken as a whole and also internally, a progression from the simplicity of unthinking guile to the complex moral catastrophe of wasted life. First, in a brief exposition of the fugal theme, the reader is introduced to the siren barmaids and the ear is prepared for an apparent confrontation of Mr. Bloom and his rival, the seducer Blazes Boylan. The fugal technique requires repetition of the original theme, always with a difference. Thus, with the barmaids' flirtatious maneuvers being the "subject" of the fugue, Mr. Bloom's version of the Sirens' song will be the "answer," and Boylan's version the countersubject. Immediately the dimensions are widened by this formal pattern, of which the essence is contrast. The reader is invited to look for resemblances which are defined by the *differences* that appear when things are set alongside each other.

The fugal web develops our knowledge of three Dublin characters who, with Bloom, Boylan, and the barmaids, are the major personages of the chapter. Each is a study in failure; three lives have been ruined by dissipation. Simon Dedalus, father of Stephen, once had talent and still has charm; but we learn that conviviality was pursued at the expense of his family. His wife has died of overwork, his children are ragged and hungry. Richie Goulding, Stephen's maternal uncle, is a member of a Dublin business firm and carries himself as "a prince"; but in fact he is a spendthrift, is slowly dying of Bright's disease, and is estranged from his brother-in-law, whom he nevertheless continues to flatter. Ben Dollard, once a wealthy ships' chandler but now in a home for derelicts, is an alcoholic bankrupt, the clearest example of failure through dissipation. Like Homer's original, the chapter's vehicle of enticement is music; these three men are notable in Dublin as vocal performers.

In the four fugal statements that make up the chapter's narrative, the intermingling of these characters becomes more complex and the account of failure and wasted life becomes increasingly specific. This progression is matched by the music (each of these characters "performs" in turn) which identifies and marks out each statement, and also by the internal rhetoric. Within each presentation there is also a movement, as the tale is told, from the idea of love to the idea of death.

While the singing of Dedalus and the conversation of Goulding elicits from Bloom a thin trickle of direct reply and a great deal of silent monologue, the reader watches the progress of Bloom's silent reflections about his wife. As Dante, the listener in *Inferno* 5, wishes to hear from Francesca what first steps led to the downfall of the lovers, so Joyce's protagonist now reviews in his mind his courtship of Molly, their early love, and the circumstances of her involvement with Boylan. Joyce's passage is a kind of model, a demonstration of an admired predecessor's deployment of rhetorical devices. Observe the resemblances between the tone of Dante's request and the opening passages of Bloom's reminiscences. First there is a pattern of question and answer, speaker and listener, combined with a promise of revelation.

Canto 5	"Sirens"
E cominciai: 'Francesca, i tuoi martiri/a lacrimar mi fanno tristo e pio. Ma dimmi: al tempo de' dolci sospiri,/a che e come concedette amore che conosceste i dubbiosi desiri?'	The voice of Lionel returned, weaker but unwearied. It sang again to Richie Poldy Lydia Lidwell also sang to Pat open mouth ear waiting, to wait.
["Francesca," I began,/"Your martyrdom calls forth compassion's tears;/But tell me, in the time of love's sweet sighs,/What stratagem of passion urged you on,/And wakened guilty yearning in your heart?"] [*Inf.* 5:116–19]	How first he saw that form endearing, how sorrow seemed to part, how look, form, word, charmed him Gould Lidwell won Pat Bloom's heart. [*U*:270]

The fugal subject, answer, and countersubject are set against each other, as Bloom's monologue moves from the innocent joy of first love to the "loss" of love in estrangement, seduction, or death.

Now, through manipulation of vocabulary, a change of atmosphere in the Ormond bar recalls the change of tone that introduces Francesca's story:

Canto 5	"Sirens"
Di quel che udire e che parlar vi piace/noi udiremo e parleremo a vui,/mentre che 'l vento, come fa, ci tace.	Through the hush of air a voice sang to them, low, not rain, not leaves in murmur, like no voice of strings of reeds [Mr. Bloom's own words now briefly interpolated—italics mine] *or whatdoyoucallthem dulcimers*, touching their still ears with words, still hearts of their each his remembered lives. [*U*: 269]
[Of that which it pleases thee to hear and to speak we will hear and speak with you, while the wind, as now, for us is silent. [*Inf.* 5:94–96]	

The passage from the *Divine Comedy* will be recognized as the one quoted earlier by Stephen Dedalus in the Aeolus chapter; it is notable that Mr. Bloom hears the voice as a medieval instrument. Now the repetition of *still* and the associated terms, *hush, low,* and *murmur,* suggests the change of tone in canto 5 that comes at this point when the hellish blast, "la bufera infernal," ceases so that Dante may hear the lovers' story. Dante and Virgil listen to the tale of Francesca and Paolo; similarly, the personal application of "Love's Old Sweet Song" will be recalled for each of the characters in the Ormond bar—especially for Mr. Bloom.

The song that Simon Dedalus sings, "M'appari," is rendered in English, but not fully, the title indicating that the translation comes from the Italian (the aria is from Flotow's opera *Martha,* originally written in German). As the song begins, the word *love* is repeated three times in two lines. This suggests the triple repetition of *amor* in Francesca's story, as the initial word of three successive terzine:

Canto 5	"Sirens"
Amor, ch' al cor gentil ratto s'apprende, ... Amor, ch' a nullo amato amar perdona, ...	Good, good to hear: sorrow from them each seemed to from both depart when first they heard. When first they saw, lost

Amor condusse noi ad una morte

. . . .

[Love, that soon makes the noble
heart its own, ...
Love, that from loving lets off none
beloved, ...
Love led us to one death. . . . .]
        [*Inf.* 5:100, 103, 106]

Richie, Poldy, mercy of beauty,
heard *from a person wouldn't ex-*
pect it in the least [Mr. Bloom's
own words in italics], her first
merciful lovesoft oftloved word.
Love that is singing: love's old
sweet song . . . Love's old
sweet sonnez la gold. [*U*: 269]

Joyce's language in the line, "Her first merciful lovesoft oftloved word,"
seems also to echo Dante's triple repetition, "Amor . . . amato amar,"
which heightens the emotional quality of the central terzina.[31]

The next sentence includes the Dantesque word *fourfold*, inviting
multiple interpretations while the complexity of Bloom's thoughts is
suggested; and the contrapuntal movement of the chapter is recapitu-
lated by the use of musical terms: "Bloom wound a skein round four
forkfingers, stretched it, relaxed, and wound it round his troubled double, fourfold, in octave, gyved them fast" (*U*: 269).

The passage concludes with a restatement of Mr. Bloom's fugal
answer. The note of death is struck as he imagines the breakup of his
marriage and Molly's subsequent abandonment by her seducer.

> Thou lost one. All songs on that theme . . . Cruel it seems. Let
> people get fond of each other: lure them on. Then tear asunder.
> Death. Explos. Knock on the head. Outtohelloutofthat. Human
> life . . . Gone. They sing. Forgotten. I too. And one day she
> with. Leave her: get tired. Suffer then. Snivel. Big Spanishy eyes
> goggling at nothing. [*U*: 273]

He repeats the theme of the Sirens' song, "Let people get fond of each
other: lure them on," as the musical convention requires: but with the
notable difference (which characterizes Mr. Bloom as the fugal answer)
of the added element of compassion: "Cruel it seems." The verbal
counterpoint juxtaposes with this the fugal subject, which at this stage
in the development has become a batsqueak of sensuality: "Lydia for
Lidwell squeak scarcely hear so ladylike the muse unsqueaked a ray of
hope" (*U*: 270).

The chapter as a musical composition ends with a coda, introduced
in Bloom's words by the musical sign, "da capo." The bright-eyed gal-

lantry has whirled to a *stretto*; but it has been contradicted rhetorically and the coda takes on a pensive tone. There is no longer any sound of piano or song; the chapter's sounds are now only thumps, taps, pom-poms, and growls. Mr. Bloom, though he could not possibly quote Dante as Stephen Dedalus has done, nevertheless is allowed a Dante-sque conclusion to his monologue. His digestion is disturbed by flatu-lence from his luncheon drink: "Gassy thing that cider" (*U*: 283). With the musical signs of forte, *Ff*, and fortissimo, *Fff*, and corresponding signs of *piano* and *pianissimo*, the growling *Rr* of Bloom's flatulence ends the chapter, as Dante ends a canto of the *Inferno*: "Ed egli avea del cul fatto trombetta" ("and he of his rump made a trumpet"). This line, moreover, is the line silently quoted by Stephen in *his* silent reflections in the National Library, the Scylla and Charybdis chapter. Joyce now ends the Sirens chapter on triple forte:

    Pprrpffrrppfff

with the last word being the Italian musical sign or direction *Fine* ("Done").

    Structural maneuvers, no less than modes of speech, in the hands of Dante and Joyce become active agents for the control and rendering of meaning. Two relevant devices will be examined here: congruence of plot and construction of an extended metaphor. To begin with, if Joyce indeed meant to focus the Sirens episode on a narrative pattern that would reflect the Francesca story, the endeavor is in itself Dantesque; Dante gave a new ending to the Ulysses story in *Inferno* 26, and other traditional stories in the *Divine Comedy* are told with a new ending or from a unique point of view. Claiming the ubiquity of plot and of the underlying realities in human relationships, Dante and Joyce assert their own vision. The triangular relationship which structures the narrative of *Ulysses* resembles the Francesca episode, but with an important difference. In Dante's canto 5, Virgil and the poet-pilgrim listen, Francesca speaks, and Paolo silently weeps; but the wronged husband is only a pronoun—"Caïna attende chi a vita ci spense" ("Caïna waits for him who took our lives"). For their murder, and still more for encompassing their damnation, the jealous husband will be consigned to the deepest circle of Hell—frozen Caïna.[32]

    Joyce's twist to this pattern first of all gives the wronged husband the center of the stage. Mr. Bloom, the principal voice in Joyce's fugue, has

more than three times as many lines as any other character; his unspoken thoughts are the chapter's vehicle for narrative advance.
Bloom's wife Molly is present—like Francesca's husband—only in the
mind of her spouse and in the lazily scurrilous gossip of the patrons of
the Ormond bar. The adulterous usurper, Boylan, does appear and
speak in person, as the prospect of a confrontation opens the chapter.
And there is a confrontation: but it takes place wholly in Bloom's
mind. He and his rival are in adjoining rooms in these crucial moments
before Boylan goes to the rendezvous. Mr. Bloom stays out of sight,
watches Boylan leave, considers going home to break it up, but in the
end does not do so. Thus the chapter becomes an exploration in depth
of the feelings of the wronged husband. As a rejection of the irrational
wrath that produces murder, "Sirens" preserves the substance and
moral stance of *Inferno* 5.

Joyce's novel is at its most un-Dantean in its exploration of domestic-
ity. This is a matter to which Dante, whose own wife never appears in
the *Divine Comedy*, makes only the most incidental reference. Dante
offers no encomium on the steadfast husband, no invective against the
shrewish wife. In the seventh cornice of Purgatory, the souls in the
purging fire sing of husbands and wives who were chaste, "come virtute
e matrimonio imponne" ("as virtue and strict wedlock point the way,"
Purg. 25:135). There are occasional fragments on the happiness of
parenthood, as in Cacciaguida's account of old times and old families
in Florence, but these focus on the parent-child rather than the hus-
band-wife relationship; and except for Cacciaguida's remarks, they are
stated from the viewpoint of the child. Even the happiness of parenthood is qualified, as Dante notes that the same fond, obedient child who
runs trustfully to the parent at the stage of lisping and babytalk, when
he reaches the age of mature speech turns from his mother and wishes
for her death.

But the core of the narrative in *Ulysses* is the stripping away of
sentimentality from the relationship between husband and wife. In the
Sirens chapter, where a moment of crisis focuses the protagonist's action, it is revealed to Mr. Bloom that he is a husband. He is the life-
partner; Boylan, the casual companion in lust.

Finally, let us examine another device, the structural use of metaphor.
Music as the art of the Sirens chapter is more than technique; it becomes an extended metaphor. Mr. Bloom says, "Words? Music? No:

it's what's behind." What he means, we learn from his silent monologue, is that music, the "language of love," is a vehicle for human
communication. In this broader sense it has the functional importance
in the chapter that literature holds for Dante's canto 5.[33]

The characters in Joyce's chapter respond to music with a mindless
sentimentality which is also revealed as their response to the problems
of life. Music is seductive; but they meet it more than halfway, using
music as a drug might be used. Their inadequacy in the musical dimension both stands for and is part of their other insufficiencies. The
showing forth of this falsely sentimental quality of contemporary
Dublin goodfellowship becomes the true business of the chapter.

Dante's lovers in *Inferno* 5 were enticed into adultery by reading
together the story of Lancelot and Guinevere. By the use of this tale, the
Francesca episode invokes (as Dante also does in other parts of the
poem) an older literary tradition; and Francesca's use of the cadences
of Dante's own poetry in turn invokes the *dolce stil novo* (which is
also used in other sections of the *Comedy*). Readers today are apt to
overlook this aspect of *Inferno* 5 because, over seven centuries, Paolo
and Francesca have themselves become legendary. But Dante makes
these lovers, protagonists in a contemporary scandal, say that they
were enticed into adultery by reading together the older legend. The
book was their pander, "and he who wrote it." Dante, poet and pilgrim, disciple of the troubadours, is shocked by the element of menace
to his artistic authority, as well as by his compassion for the lovers;
this increases Dante's personal involvement and is represented by his
final swoon. Through the metaphorical extension of literature's enchantment to include the role of seducer, the true business of the canto
thus becomes the poet's broadened understanding of the nature of love
and the requisite adjustment of this knowledge in his art.

In Joyce's chapter, music is the predominant art and is a seductive
influence in exactly the way that literature is in *Inferno* 5. Mr. Bloom's
wife Molly is a concert artist and Boylan, her seducer, has arranged
concerts for her. Thus brought together in the first place by music, the
ostensible purpose of their appointment on this fatal day is a rehearsal
for a forthcoming concert. On the piano in Bloom's house, the sheet
music for "Love's Old Sweet Song" is, as Bloom himself sees at the
end of the day, "open at the last page;" these words suggest the presence of a rhetorical model focused on the conclusion of Dante's little

drama, and the word *page* directly connects Francesca's book with Molly Bloom's music.

Observe the imitative movement of Joyce's design. The piano is functionally connected with "Sirens" by a descriptive term, *coffin* (*U*:259:20), which also associates this passage with *Inferno* 5 by echoing a note of death. As the objects on the piano are enumerated, an emerging visual image of Boylan playing and Molly singing begins to resemble Dante's account of the seductive reading that entrapped Francesca —the song of love, the book of love. The convention of musical directions permits the Italian language to be used in Joyce's "final indications" of the musical duet; his chosen terms do not apply to the banal composition on the piano, but they do convey the emotional quality of Francesca's closing lines. Thus Joyce's final word, *close*, becomes a compressed expression of the equivalent moment in canto 5, which Dante has emphasized by understatement and by setting it off grammatically in a separate sentence occupying exactly one line: "quel giorno più non vi leggemmo avante," ("that day we read no further," *Inf.* 5:138)

Inferno 5	*"Ithaca"*
But if thou hast such desire to learn the first root of our love, I will do as one who weeps and tells.	What occupied the position originally occupied by the sideboard?
One day, for pastime, we read of Lancelot, how love constrained him; we were alone, and without all suspicion.	A vertical piano (Cadby) with exposed keyboard, its closed coffin supporting a pair of long yellow ladies' gloves and an emerald ashtray containing four
Several times that reading urged our eyes to meet, and changed the colour of our faces; but one moment alone it was that overcame us.	consumed matches, a partly consumed cigarette and two discoloured ends of cigarettes, its musicrest supporting the music in the key of G natural for voice
When we read how the fond smile was kissed by such a lover, he, who never shall be divided from me,	and piano of *Love's Old Sweet Song* (words by G. Clifton Bingham, composed by J. L.
Kissed my mouth, all trembling; the book and he who wrote it was	Molloy, sung by Madam Antoinette Sterling) open at the

a Galeotto; that day we read in it no further.

[*Inf.* 5: 124–38]

last page with the final indications ad libitum, forte, pedal animato, sustained, pedal, ritirando, close. [*U*: 691]

This particular arrangement of data, in its carefully composed sequence, tells the story of the exact moment of Molly's consent to her seducer; the visual image thus conveyed corresponds to the graphic recital by Francesca of the same moment in her story. (Perhaps it should be explained that this quotation is typical of the Ithaca chapter, which is rendered entirely in the narratorial voice and in which, throughout, information is given in the driest question-and-answer form.) The song, of course, is a prominent feature of the Sirens chapter. Since Bloom has been told by Molly at an early stage in the novel that she is going to meet Boylan for a rehearsal of this very song, when the reader reaches the Sirens episode he is aware that the mere thought of the title is enough to make Bloom think of the seduction enacted in his absence. As Dante connects *Inferno* 5 with other parts of his poem, so Joyce extends Sirens twice to establish important connections in the novel: first, by the talk between Bloom and Stephen about "Sirens, enemies of man's reason," in Eumaeus (*U*:649:26), and now by this evocation of Molly in Bloom's mind, in Ithaca.

Bloom's recall of the title in "Sirens" comes at the beginning of Simon Dedalus's rendition of Lionel's aria, "M'appari." This is a passage which, as shown above, in placement and in rhetoric echoes *Inferno* 5, with an additional Dantesque implication in the use of *fourfold* to describe Bloom's winding of an elastic band round his fingers. This band later becomes a "musical instrument," when the singing has ended and Bloom has "ungyved his crisscrossed hands," but at this earlier point it must be intended as reinforcing imagery for the direction and complexity of Bloom's thoughts. It is an emotional climax both in the chapter and in the novel as a whole, where an unironic view is given —momentary but quite clear—of Bloom as he considers "Love's bitter mystery" with that knowledge of life which has thus far been denied to young Stephen Dedalus. And it is in this passage that Bloom articulates the metaphor of music as the "language of love":

Words? Music? No: It's what's behind.
Bloom looped, unlooped, noded, disnoded.

[*U*: 270:21–22]

The verbs *noded* and *disnoded* seem almost to be Joycean inventions produced to fit the musical convention of his fugal pattern; but they also echo the *Divine Comedy*, where Dante twice uses *disnodare*, a word taken directly from Latin and as rare in Italian as it is in English.

As Dante does with literature, so Joyce with music as his figurative vehicle builds a complex progression. The principal characters of the episode are presented in terms of the music they hear; and the chapter explores the implications of the musical compositions that are presented and used in a variety of ways, always with extended significance. Both in the Francesca episode and in "Sirens," there are two sides to the metaphor, and in both works the negative and positive aspects are hedged with ambiguity. In Joyce's chapter, while the negative thrust of the maneuver represents the music as seductive and weakening—not absolutely but potentially—this is only part of the picture; as a vehicle of human communication, music is also made to stand for an affirmation of vitality, of the deep wellsprings of life. To the extent that a parallel with Dante's metaphor can be accepted, this suggests a sensitive reading of *Inferno* 5. Dante's statement, "Our Galeotto was the book and he who wrote it," would have none of the force with which it comes through to the reader, placed as it is at the conclusion and climax of Francesca's tale, had it not been preceded by the moving and impressive representation in the lyric voice, Francesca's own words, of the enchantment of the poet's art.

In the positive dimension of the extended metaphor, the association of literature and music with love suggests that sensuality in human nature is not an evil impulse but rather one of the good things of life. It puts the sparkle in the eye, the spring in the step. It is God-given, and becomes reprehensible only when wrongly used: the line to be drawn between lust and love is a distinction to be made by man's reason.

Dante deals with this theme in more than one area of the *Divine Comedy*. In canto 26 of the *Purgatorio*, where Dante himself must undergo the purgation of lustful impulses, he requires the utmost urging from Virgil and Statius to enter the cleansing fire. Here he meets, not any of the great lovers of history, but *the singers of love*: Guido Guinizelli and Arnaut Daniel. The fire imagery, which extends into canto 27, begins on the ascent to the seventh cornice with Statius's explanation of the creation of the body and soul, heart and mind. Dante here describes man as the fair work of the Primal Mover, self-aware and full of power, and he uses two strikingly sensuous figures:

generation as the sun's heat being turned into wine, and God's finished work as a little flame that follows the fire wherever it turns: "e simigliante poi a la fiammella / che segue il foco là 'vunque si muta" ("like the little flame that follows the fire / wheresoever it moves," *Purg.* 25: 97–98). The imagery is used by Joyce in the Sirens chapter, as noted above, at an emotional apex where Bloom's reaction to the music reaches a peak of sensual excitement: "Braintipped, cheek touched with flame, they listened feeling that flow endearing flow over skin limbs human heart soul spine" (*U*:260). The association of ideas, of course, is not uncommon. But Joyce also used Dante's figure, perhaps by coincidence, in a 1909 letter to his wife Nora: "carrying always with her in her secret heart the little flame that burns up the souls and bodies of men."[34]

Dante's treatment of sensuality in the *Paradiso* extends this structure of meaning. Whom do we find in the Heaven of Venus? Not the chaste husbands and wives, but two reformed rakes, one a man and the other a woman; the woman is Cunizza, and the man is Folquet de Marseille, another troubadour. The suggestion of *Inferno* 5, that the lovers' damnation was determined less by their sin than by their lack of time to repent, is here explicitly reinforced by these happy souls of *Paradiso* 9.

The fire imagery of *Purgatorio* 25 is picked up by Cunizza's description of herself. She describes her ancestor as a firebrand and says that she "shines" here in the heaven of Venus because on earth she had been conquered, *vinse* (Francesca says *prese*, "seized") by the light of that star.[35] Nor is she ashamed to admit this but gladly acknowledges it, Lethe having washed away all sense of guilt. She says, "ma lietamente a me medesma indulgo / la cagion di mia sorte, e non mi noia" ("Yet joyfully within me I approve / the occasion of my lot, nor am displeased," *Par.* 9: 34–35). Folquet makes the same point, and more strongly—for after all he is a poet—saying that he is now stamped with the rays of this heaven as he was on earth, and he blazed fiercely "infin che si convenne al pelo" ("so long as it matched my hair")—that is, until age overtook him (*Par.* 9:99).

Folquet's speech to Dante is a long one, more involved and obscure in its language than Folquet's poetry was on earth, yet in the Provençal tradition. At its conclusion the troubadour reveals to Dante that the spirit highest in this order of beatitude is Rahab, the harlot of Jericho, redeemed by her good deed of sheltering Joshua's spies. Following this train of thought, Folquet remarks on the pope's neglect of the Holy Land (at the end of his life Folquet became a bishop and a Crusader), and Dante ends the canto with the word *l'adultero* ("adultery") applied, with a kind of reverse emphasis recalling the shock of finding the words *amor* and *pace* in *Inferno* 5, to the corruption of the papal curia. Thus Dante makes a strong rhetorical statement for sensuality, allowing the adulterers to be received into heaven, and describing as unlawful intercourse the actions of the papal regime.

In Joyce's chapter the association of music with love, and specifically with sensual love, is less explicit than Dante's association of love poetry with an affirmation of sensuality. The extended metaphor is perfectly clear in both; but Joyce's metaphor is encompassed by ironic qualifications. The ambiguities lie particularly in the role of Bloom in this paradoxical tension, and of course also in the underlying question of just how much of Joyce's construction depended on his reading of Dante.

Yet there are indications that Joyce's portrayal of Bloom, though extensively qualified, includes a positive role for his protagonist. First, Bloom is allowed to articulate the metaphor. We are thus encouraged toward sympathetic identification with him, exactly as we are drawn to Francesca. Joyce's chapter, like Dante's canto, could easily have been written otherwise; but both protagonists make this important point in voices that are recognizably their own. Second, to whatever extent music as the language of love is the chapter's controlling figure, there is a good deal of evidence to affirm Bloom's musicianship.

Joyce has used every kind of musical association, in this chapter, to convey meanings beyond the surface context. By implication, sensuality is represented as the underlying reality without which there can be no human "music," no real communication. The Sirens, male and female, have their due measure of this. The vigorous rhythms of Blazes Boylan and the siren barmaids bring particular liveliness and color to the suggestion of sensuality in their briefly glimpsed actions. Joyce's best metaphors, like Dante's, continue to shine in the imagination long after the book has been closed.

It is Bloom who says that music is "all a kind of attempt to talk," and he is perceived as being able to distinguish rationally between "music" and mere clamor. It is Bloom, cuckold but also "unconquered hero" (*U*: 260:34), whose sensibility associates sensuality with the "language of love." Moreover, in his own words Bloom adds the dimension of joyfulness to sensuality, on the analogy of Mozart's Minuet from *Don Giovanni*:

> Nice, that is. Look: look, look, look, look, look: you look at us. That's joyful I can feel. Never have written it. Why? My joy is other joy. But both are joys. Yes, joy it must be. Mere fact of music shows you are. (*U*:277: 34)

Bloom is also the channel of figurative expression through whom a progressive differentiation is made between the Sirens' song and the larger universe of discourse which is music: if the Sirens' song leads to death, as drunkenness and brutality lead to degradation and despair, nevertheless, sensuality transformed by kindness and steadfastness is on the side of life. Through adroit syntactical choices, the songs heard in the Ormond bar are made to suggest a counterpoint of brutality with compassion, mendaciousness with veracity, venality with benevolence and integrity, folly with reason, hatred and force with love, despair and death with hope and life.

Repeatedly the voice of the episode conveys an impression of one sort which is contradicted by the appearance of the character in his own fugal voice; his individuating combination of words and rhythms is supplemented by direct discourse and by comment. Boylan's rhythms are consistently trochaic, a jaunty jingling, but there is a denial of this impression by what the reader learns elsewhere from description, comment, and Boylan's own flat tones in dialogue. Bloom says, "he can't sing for tall hats" (*U*:270). This might only be an indication that Bloom is an unreliable narrator; but another impression comes to us when Bloom says, "There's music everywhere. Ruttledge's door: ee creaking. No, that's noise," and we are thus reminded that one of Boylan's distinctive words is *creaking* (*U*:277; and 260:29, 263:07, 272:04).

Other characters are portrayed with more straightforward irony. There is clearly less warm life in Simon Dedalus, Richie Goulding, Bob Cowley, and Ben Dollard than in the portrayal of Boylan, the barmaids, and Bloom. And two minor characters, the deaf waiter Pat and the quarrelsome, grunting Boots, errand boy of the Ormond, suggest

yet another kind of deprivation, an almost total inability to hear music
and to make music.

As the question of Bloom's musicianship within the metaphor begins
to seem important, evidence accumulates that he is sensitive and discriminating in his understanding of music—that he is, though untutored, in some sense musically competent. To begin with, Bloom is a
careful listener with a good ear. He knows at once that the piano has
been tuned, and he appreciates a competent performer. "Nice touch,"
he thinks. "Must be Cowley. Musical. Knows whatever note you play."
Though he does not use the term *absolute pitch*, the accuracy of Bloom's
observation about Cowley is shortly confirmed when Simon Dedalus
sits down at the keyboard: "No, Simon. Father Cowley turned. Play it
in the original. One flat. The keys, obedient, rose higher" (*U*:267). Still
more important, Mr. Bloom recognizes the equivalent of perfect pitch
in human communication, and defines this as the instinctive response of
person to person.[36] It is a quality that he associates with his erring wife;
he realizes that she could comprehend the Italian hurdygurdy boy "without understanding a word of his language." "With look to look: songs
without words. . . . She knew he meant the monkey was sick. . . .
Gift of nature" (*U*:281).

Bloom's preferred area of critical interest is the mechanics of music,
and here his formulations seem knowledgeable and to the point. He
rates above any mechanical instrument, "the human voice, two tiny
silky chords. Wonderful, more than all the others." Though untrained,
his understanding includes an intelligent interest in the theoretical basis
of harmony: "Numbers it is. All music when you come to think. . . .
Vibrations: chords those are. One plus two plus six is seven" (*U*:274).
From this choice of words it is clear that Bloom recognizes, perhaps
intuitively, the construction of a musical seventh: unison plus second
plus sixth.[37] He calls this "musemathematics" (*U*:274); his views are
original and expressed with directness and vigor. When he thinks of
girls learning the piano, playing scales up and down, he imagines the
sound as "two together nextdoor neighbors" (*U*:274); this formulation,
so comparable to Stephen Dedalus' description of rhymes as "two men
dressed the same, looking the same, two by two," may be a deliberate
parallelism.

On the other hand, Bloom does have many deficiencies and weak points, most of them in the realm of musicology. He refers to the compositions he has heard in the Ormond as "all that Italian florid music" (*U*:274), apparently not realizing that "M'appari" and the minuet from *Don Giovanni* are the work of German composers. He is also mistaken about the authorship of his favorite oratorio, "The Seven Last Words," which he attributes sometimes to Mercadante, sometimes to Meyerbeer. He expresses a preference for "the severe classical school such as Mendelssohn" (*U*:645), though that composer is a pillar of the romantic tradition. At the end of the day, as Bloom walks home with Stephen Dedalus, many such irrelevant and ridiculous comments are voiced. It becomes clear that Bloom is no scholar and could never win an argument about music.

But in the reader's wholly private view another hypothesis is offered: that Bloom's posturings are accident rather than substance. Music, despite all the ironic qualifications, seems to be Bloom's aesthetic métier. In comparison with his Dublin contemporaries, and still more in comparison with his own excursions into literature, he seems less of a purely comic figure as we share his desultory thoughts in the Ormond bar.

In the previous chapter Lenehan has said seriously, "There's a touch of the artist about old Bloom." Bloom's fund of intellectual curiosity has led him into exploration of scientific and philosophical questions, and he has had some slight and unmethodical literary ambitions. He has made an effort with literature, but nowhere does he show any literary discrimination comparable to the accuracy and sensitivity of his reflections about music. He is a comic figure as he daydreams of writing for a magazine or as he seeks earnestly in the works of Shakespeare a solution to the problems of life. In contrast, in the Sirens chapter he seems on firm ground of his own choosing when he says, "Words? Music? No: it's what's behind."

The Sirens chapter has been much discussed, and is a kind of touchstone for the two major lines of interpretation of *Ulysses* and estimation of the author. The influence of Dante on Joyce has also been noted, not comprehensively but in scattered references, ever since Ezra Pound read the manuscript of *Ulysses*, and more confidently after the publication of Beckett's essay.[38] Here, we have merely noted the Dantean parallels—

which, like all parallel lines, coincide without converging—in one of Joyce's chapters. Dante continued his treatment of the theme of love into the *Purgatorio* and *Paradiso*, finally uniting it with the Beatific Vision. Joyce's protagonist, and still more his protagonist's wife, are personages humanly different from those of the *Divine Comedy*; yet he claims for them a sensibility on this one level equal to that of Dante and Beatrice: that is, their common humanity. They may not compare in the expression of their love, but their possession of this important experience makes Joyce's treatment of Dante's theme more than a reasonable facsimile. Joyce does not say that Bloom is Dante (nor that Bloom is Joyce), but he does say that all three have shared and given expression to a common human experience of love. The important question is whether Joyce intended to create a reductive parody of Dante; and on the evidence of the Sirens chapter, it would appear that his reading of the *Divine Comedy* is more comprehensive and more subtle, and his treatment of the theme far more serious, than can be allowed to the merely parodic.

The closing passages of the *Divine Comedy* and *Ulysses* have in common the final affirmation of each author's most deeply rooted beliefs, and placement of a poetic affirmation of life in Joyce's final pages is not accidental. Dante, at the same point in his poem, is approaching the Beatific Vision. Joyce gives to Molly, wife of Mr. Bloom, the lines which surround that declaration—" O that awful deepdown torrent" (*U*: 768)—with a crescendo of rose symbolism, so that the closing, climactic, unpunctuated words of the monologue develop strikingly their own tangled beauty. (The final chapter is written entirely in the first person; there is no narrational voice.) The words just quoted parallel Bloom's mental representation of sexual intimacy in "Sirens", which was indicated above. Molly is a sensualist, as is her husband, and her impulses and experiences have earlier in this final chapter been expressed by her in the crudest terms, the very nadir of lust. But Joyce, with delicate verbal brushwork, turns the tide of her soliloquy and moves her thoughts steadily upward until, as she recalls the details of "the day I got him to propose to me," her mind, like that of Dante's Cunizza, shows its highest sensibilities as it becomes possessed and absorbed by the knowledge and sensations, no longer of lust but of love. Molly Bloom's acceptance of her greatest moment is characteristically offhand and unsentimental: "I thought well as well him as another" (*U*:768). But the impact of this remark is once more ironic rather than negative.

What is sometimes overlooked, partly because of the didactic impulses of the *Divine Comedy* in general and the *Paradiso* in particular, is the significance of Dante's continuing into Heaven his affirmation of sensuality. (It is no accident that we find Solomon there.) It is the effort to express with equal force the two faces of love—one spiritual, one sensual—that marks both the aspiration and the achievement of Dante's treatment of this theme. Joyce's version is marked by the insistence that the same qualities be admitted to humble personages. They are full of faults, unintellecutal, erring and comical, but what they are not is brutish—Bloom and Molly are fully and rationally human. Joyce, we must conclude, understood that the force of Dante's art in *Paradiso* 27 (where Beatrice and Dante together look down for the last time at "our little threshing floor" [*Par.* 22: 151], centered on Ulysses' narrow pass, the straits of Gibraltar), depends on the continued *human* quality of his protagonists even here in the highest spiritual realm.

Joyce's grasp of Dante's intention is indicated not only by his giving Stephen Dedalus the line, "che i miei di rimirar fe' piu ardenti," "so that mine eyes became more ardent in their gaze" (thus marking the point at which Dante finally passes beyond Beatrice), but still more by Joyce's decision to have Molly born in Gibraltar. This fact is surely an indication, as Ellmann has said, that Joyce must have planned the Dante parallels very early.[39] The Ulyssean reference in *Paradiso* 27 is a final reminder to the reader that Dante created his own version of this story; and *Paradiso* 27 must be connected geographically, for full understanding, with *Paradiso* 22. Similarly, in the last paragraphs of *Ulysses* Molly remembers "Gibraltar as a girl" (*U*:768) and thinks of an adolescent love, "how he kissed me under the Moorish wall" (*U*:768). Here minor loves merge with the major love, her husband, exactly as occurred in "Sirens" at the climax of Bloom's thoughts about love. As the reader watches Dante and Beatrice looking down from Heaven, so also Joyce's reader receives from the close of the book a sense of Molly Bloom united with her husband and looking at life from the farthest perspective of which she is capable.

Dante, by multiple references, emphasizes the connectedness of the separate cantiche in the poem's entirety and makes a last allusion to his imaginative use of pagan materials: Joyce underlines the interrelatedness of his separate episodes and also gives a final indication of the structural dependence of his work on the *Divine Comedy*. The effect of these verbal echoes, in both works, is reinforcement of meanings by the careful linguistic connection of parts with the whole. It is not necessary to make a comprehensive judgment on *Ulysses* in order to recognize the seriousness of purpose with which Joyce approached Dante's treatment of love in the *Divine Comedy*. Manifestly, his assimilation of *Inferno* 5 was deep and issued in wide-ranging imitative maneuvers. We can at the very least admit the adequacy of Joyce's reading of Dante and acknowledge his technical success in imaginative reconstruction of Dante's treatment of a major theme.

NOTES

1. A. Francini-Bruni, *Joyce Intimo Spogliato in Piazza*, quoted in Richard Ellmann, *James Joyce* (New York: Oxford University Press, 1959), p. 226.

2. Kenelm Foster, O.P. and Patrick Boyde, *Dante's Lyric Poetry* (Oxford: Clarendon Press, 1967), p. xvi. Father Foster cites Dante's *De Vulgari Eloquentia* 2.8. 5, and goes on to say that in this passage, "the poet is perhaps distinguished from the musician proper by a light stress on the noun *verba*."

3. Oliver St. J. Gogarty, *It Isn't This Time of Year at All* (1954), reprinted in Robert Scholes and Richard M. Kain, *The Workshop of Daedalus* (Evanston, Ill.: Northwestern University Press, 1965), p. 215.

4. Ellmann, *James Joyce*, p. 392.

5. Samuel Beckett, et al., *Our Exagmination Round His Factification for Incamination of Work In Progress* (Paris: Shakespeare and Co., 1929; Norfolk, Conn: New Directions, 1939, 1962), pp. 1–22, 117–28.

6. Beckett et al., *Exagmination*, pp. 17–18.

7. Ellmann, *James Joyce*, p. 475.

8. Beckett, et al., *Exagmination*, p. 18.

9. The most comprehensive treatment of Joyce's language is Anthony Burgess, *Joysprick* (London: André Deutsch, 1973). Also useful are: Bernard Benstock, *Joyce-Again's Wake* (Seattle: University of Washington Press, 1965), chap. 3, "Comic Seriousness and Poetic Prose"; Derek Bickerton, "James Joyce and the Development of Interior Monologue," *Essays In Criticism*, 18 (1968): 32–46; Wayne Booth, *The Rhetoric of Fiction* (Chicago: University of Chicago Press, 1961), chap. 11, "The Price of Impersonal Narration," especially pp. 323–38; Gerhard R. Kaiser, *Proust, Musil, Joyce* (Frankfurt am Main: Athenaum Verlag, 1972), chap. 4, "Joyce, *Ulysses*," especially pp. 221–25, which deal with the use of *Inferno* 5 in "Aeolus";

Eberhard Kreutzer, *Sprache und Spiel im Ulysses von James Joyce* (Bonn: Bouvier, 1969), pp. ix, 307; Joseph Prescott, *Exploring James Joyce* (Carbondale: Southern Illinois University Press, 1964), chap. 1, "James Joyce: A Study in Words"; Ulrich Schneider, *Die Funktion der Zitate im Ulysses von James Joyce* (Bonn: Bouvier, 1970); Erwin R. Steinberg, *The Stream of Consciousness and Beyond in Ulysses* (Pittsburgh: University of Pittsburgh Press, 1973), especially parts 2 and 3.

10. Glauco Cambon refers to Joyce as one of the "Dante-inspired moderns." *Dante's Craft* (Minneapolis: University of Minnesota Press, 1969), p. 199.

11. Letter to Valéry Larbaud, 30 July 1929, in *Letters of James Joyce*, ed. Stuart Gilbert (New York: Viking, 1947) 1:283–84; here, the line reads "Siccome [*sic*] i gru van cantando lor lai." In the letter to Ezra Pound (9 February 1939; *Letters* 3:415 and n., ed. Richard Ellmann, 1959), Joyce has deliberately changed the tense of Dante's line from past to present, the original being "Galeotto fu il libro e chi lo scrisse" ("Galeotto was the book and he who wrote it.").

12. *Ulysses*, 38:08. (All quotations from *Ulysses* are from the Modern Library Edition, Random House, 1946, and later printings that have pagination to match the *Word Index to Ulysses*, ed. Miles Hanley.)

13. *Ulysses*, pp. 185–94.

14. "Ed elli avea del cul fatto trombetta" ("And he made of his rump a trumpet," *Inf.* 21: 139), *Ulysses* 182:37.

15. *Ulysses*, pp. 136–37.

16. *Inferno* 1: 82–87.

17. Stephen, although he is aware of the allegorical aspect of Dante's color choices, is thinking of them here as rhetorical maneuvers. Unless we want to rule out altogether the association of "approaching girls" with the dancing nymphs of *Purg.* 29, we must note that Stephen omits white, the color of one of their robes and also of one of the stone steps. That he does this, and furthermore that in his thoughts he alters Dante's "rossa" (red) to "rose," and then immediately to "russet," argues against the simple association of the sentence in the context of the Aeolus chapter with the traditional identification of Dante's red, white, and green as faith, hope, and charity.

18. *Ulysses*, 137:06.

19. *Ulysses*, p. 144.

20. *Ulysses*, p. 256.

21. In the Library chapter, Stephen's silent thoughts produce the words, "In a rosery of Fetter Lane of Gerard, herbalist, he walks, greyedauburn. An azured harebell like her veins. Lids of Juno's eyes, violets. He walks. One life is all, One body. Do. But do" (*U*: 199:32). Part of this is repeated in the Sirens chapter: "In Gerard's rosery of Fetter Lane he walks, greyedauburn. One life is all. One body. Do. But do" (*U*:276:7). Bloom is thinking here of Shakespeare, but the sentence about Gerard is not in his diction; yet the four short expressions that follow are clearly Bloom's voice, for his next words (silently) are "Done anyhow." In the Eumaeus chapter, one of the topics of conversation as Stephen and Bloom walk home together is "the lutenist Dowland who lived in Fetter Lane near Gerard the herbalist" (*U*: 646: 02).

22. Joyce used this phrase, no doubt by coincidence, in a statement on aesthetics: "The classical temper . . . chooses to bend upon *these present things* [italics mine] and so to work upon them and fashion them that the quick intelligence may go beyond them to their meaning which is still unuttered." *Stephen Hero*, ed. Theodore Spencer (Norfolk, Conn. and New York: New Directions, 1944, 1955), p. 78.

23. Some readers have been unsympathetic to Joyce's effort, others have approved it. Professor Sternfeld's reading of the chapter found in the fluid sequences of the prose a *movement* and a *progression* in which verbal sounds had, in his opinion, been successfully manipulated in the manner of a composer's production of musical patterns. Luigi Dallapiccola, a contemporary composer, writes that he learned much about technique from reading *Ulysses*; he points out examples of Joyce's placement of recurring words and syllables so that cadence is controlled and progressions of sound in the fugal pattern are created. Frederick W. Sternfeld, "Poetry and Music— Joyce's *Ulysses*," in *Sound and Poetry*, ed. Northrop Frye, English Institute Essays 1956 (New York: Columbia University Press, 1957), pp. 16–54; Luigi Dallapiccola, "On the 12-Note Road," *Music Survey* 4, no. 1 (1951): 318–32.

Stuart Gilbert's chapter on "Sirens" took a defensive attitude, answering a penetrating but unsympathetic essay by Ernst Curtius, in which Joyce's mastery of artistic expression was praised but his "experiment" declared a failure. Ernst Robert Curtius, "Technique and Thematic Development of James Joyce," trans Eugene Jolas, *transition*, nos. 16–17 (June, 1929), pp. 310–25; Stuart Gilbert, *James Joyce's Ulysses* (London: Faber & Faber, 1930; 1952, 1969), pp. 211–25. Harry Levin, calling the episode "a poem about music," noted that the strict treatment of canon had not been satisfied, but that the chapter's value did not depend on its form alone: *James Joyce, a Critical Introduction*, 2d ed. (London: Faber & Faber, 1960), p. 89; Stanley Sultan and William Y. Tindall bypassed the problem of the chapter as a musical structure, the former finding in the episode the climax and turning point of the narrative, while the latter noted that "words and notes, having rhythm, sound and feeling in common when put together, are not unrelated." Stanley Sultan, *The Argument of Ulysses* (Columbus: Ohio State University Press, 1964), pp. 220–31; W. Y. Tindall, *A Readers Guide to James Joyce* (New York: Noonday Press, 1959), pp. 184–87.

The first full technical examination of the fugal structure in the chapter is made in Lawrence L. Levin, "The Sirens Episode as Music: Joyce's Experiment in Polyphony," *James Joyce Quarterly* 3, no. 1 (1965): 12–24; and a complete review of the music used in the chapter is made in Zack Bowen, "The Bronzegold Sirensong: A Musical Analysis of the Sirens Episode in *Ulysses*," *Literary Monographs* 1, ed. Eric Rothstein and Thomas K. Dunseath (Madison: University of Wisconsin Press, 1967), pp. 247–98, 319–20.

24. Geoffrey Bickersteth, *The Divine Comedy* (Cambridge: Harvard University Press, 1965), p. xxxi, passim. Professor Bickersteth's long introduction to his excellent translation includes a discussion of Dante's artistic use of the terza rima. See also Father Kenelm Foster's introduction to *Dante's Lyric Poetry*, ed. and trans. Kenelm Foster, O.P. and Patrick Boyde (Oxford: Clarendon Press, 1967), pp. ix–xliii; and the detailed discussion of Dante's style in Patrick Boyde, *Dante's Style in his Lyric Poetry* (Cambridge: Cambridge University Press, 1971), pp. 1–51.

See also T. G. Bergin, *A Diversity of Dante* (Englewood Cliffs, N.J.: Prentice-Hall, 1971), "The Ship and the Pilot," pp. 96–105; *Perspectives on the Divine Comedy* (New Brunswick, N. J.: Rutgers University Press, 1967), "The Design of the Comedy," pp. 37–70; and *Dante* (New York: Orion Press, 1965), "The Commedia: Tools and Tactics," pp. 278–98. Philip McNair, "The Poetry of the 'Comedy,'" in *The Mind of Dante*, ed. U. Limentani (Cambridge: Cambridge University Press, 1965), pp. 17–46; Glauco Cambon, *Dante's Craft* (Minneapolis: University of Minnesota Press, 1969), esp. chap. 3, "Francesca and the Tactics of Language," pp. 46–66; Luigi Pirandello, "The Poetry of Dante," in *Dante*, ed. John Freccero (Englewood Cliffs, N.J.: Prentice-Hall, 1969), pp. 14–22.

25. The musical term Joyce used to describe the "technique" of the chapter is *fuga per canonem*, which simply means a composition contrapuntally written, utilizing in part canon passages. Contrapuntal writing occurs in other forms of musical composition; but in the fugue the element of circularity adds a dimension, as the fugal theme, or "Subject," is initially stated in two parts, as one would write a sentence with two clauses. This is accomplished by the second voice taking up the theme while the first goes on with a "Reply" or fugal "Answer." Subject and answer are necessary to each other as sections of a circle. Subsequent variations on the theme take their cue alternately from the one and the other. When the subject and answer have been announced, a second theme, the countersubject, may be introduced. It is the combination of these three that creates the fugal counterpoint. Lawrence Levin's article indicates the ways in which Joyce weaves thematic material into the counterpoint, and Zack Bowen reviews extensively Joyce's "Orchestration" of the chapter.

26. Stuart Gilbert, *James Joyce's Ulysses*, pp. 10, 210–25.

27. Ibid., p. 213. It should be noted that this comment was applied to *Finnegans Wake* as well as to the Sirens chapter.

28. Ibid.

29. Cambon, *Dante's Craft*, p. 58, and chap. 3, passim.

30. As Cambon has noted (*Dante's Craft*, p. 48), Hamlet also wishes to kill his uncle at a moment when his unshriven death will bring damnation. In *Ulysses*, following the quotations from Dante, Stephen's next thought (triggered by a mention of fratricide) is a quotation from Hamlet, "And in the porches of mine ear [*sic*] did pour. By the way [*how* presumably suppressed here] did he find that out? He died in his sleep. Or the other story, beast with two backs?" (*U:* 137–38). Stephen's gloss on the line, a reference to Hamlet's words in act 3, scene 4, appears to connect the Hamlet quotation with the Francesca episode.

31. This passage builds up an emotional progression, the culmination of which must be noted here since the meaning of Joyce's fugue and the interpretation of the chapter depends on it. This apex is a brief rendition of the thoughts of Bloom in the narratorial voice, as the music brings his recollections of his wife to a state of violent sexual excitement. The passage quoted above, which actually begins with "Brain-tipped, cheek touched with flame, they listened feeling that flow endearing flow over skin limbs human heart soul spine," marks the author's direction of Bloom's thoughts toward an understanding of his central problem. The source of all his trouble with his wife (a fact not revealed until the Ithaca chapter) is the eleven-year suspension of

full sexual relations; in the Sirens chapter the music, forcing its way into Blooms' thoughts about Molly, produces a complete recollection of their sexual intimacy. The passage ends as follows:

> Now! language of love.
> . . . *ray of hope.*

The first word is Bloom's own voice, the rest of the first line is in the narratorial voice; the second line comes from the song. Immediately thereafter, Joyce makes an ironic qualification, first indicating that the rest of the listeners in the Ormond have been similarly affected (the irony is assisted by the low artistic level of the music—the Liebestod would have commanded too much respect for Joyce's purpose), then indicating a momentary change in direction of Bloom's thoughts. But this effect, one that Joyce uses constantly, merely checks the flow of Bloom's reminiscence, which immediately returns, and affectionately, to his wife. It is like the harmonic note of a stringed instrument, a momentary arrest which heightens rather than diminishes the emotional force of the passage. Meanwhile an important point has been made, the association of sexual intimacy with love. See Cambon, *Dante's Craft*, p. 57; Sultan, *Argument*, p. 225.

32. Cambon, *Dante's Craft*, p. 48.

33. Ibid., p. 52.

34. Ellmann, *Letters*, 2: 266, 19 November 1909. For a discussion of Dante's imagery, see T. G. Bergin, *Perspectives*, pp. 66–68, and *Diversity*, pp. 101–02; K. Foster, "Dante's Idea of Love," in Bergin, ed., *From Time to Eternity* (1966), pp. 65–101, and "Dante and Eros," *Downside Review*, 1967; and John Freccero, "Casella's Song," *Dante Studies* 91 (1973): 73–80.

35. Cambon, *Dante's Craft*, p. 58.

36. Gilbert, *Ulysses*, p. 224; and Bowen, "Bronzegold Sirensong," p. 260.

37. For this insight, and for enlightenment on the technical construction of the musical fugue that extended to scoring the musical entrances of the voices in Joyce's "Sirens," I am indebted to Professor Edgar M. Hoover, formerly of the University of Pittsburgh, and his wife and musical colleague, Mary Hoover. My interest in Joyce's manipulation of sound values was initially stimulated and also greatly extended by conversations with Professor W. Freeman Twaddell, of Brown University.

38. Parallels between Joyce and Dante have been noted for many years. Among the more extensive and circumstantial discussions are: W. Y. Tindall, "Dante and Mrs. Bloom," *Accent* 11 (1951): 91; W. B. Stanford, *The Ulysses Theme* (Oxford: Blackwell, 1954), chap. 15, "The Re-integrated Hero," pp. 211–46; Barbara Seward, *The Symbolic Rose* (New York: Columbia University Press, 1954), chap. 7, "Joyce and Synthesis," pp. 187–221; Verson Hall, *Explicator* 10 (June 1952); Stanley Louis Jedynak, "Epiphanies and Dantean Correspondences in Joyce's *Dubliners*," Ph.D. diss. University of Syracuse, 1962; Warren Carrier, "*Dubliners*: Joyce's Dantean Vision," *Renascence* 17 (1965): 211–15; Florence L. Walzl, "Gabriel and Michael: The Conclusion of The Dead," *James Joyce Quarterly* 4, no. 1 (1966): 17–31; Howard Helsinger, "Joyce and Dante," *ELH* 35 (1968): 591–605; Mary T. Reynolds, "Joyce's Planetary Music: His Debt to Dante," *Sewanee Review* 76, no. 3 (1968):

450–77; Robert Boyle, S. J., "Swiftian Allegory and Dantean Parody in Joyce's 'Grace'," *James Joyce Quarterly* 7, no. 1 (1969): 11–21; Sharon G. B. Mancini, "Finnegans Cake as Dante's Purgatorio," Ph.D. diss. Kent State University, 1971; Tibor Classics, "Nota su Dante nell' *Ulisse*," *Rivista di Letterature Moderne e Comparate* 24 (1971): 151–154; Vittoriana Villa, "Figure Paterne nel *Portrait* e nell' *Ulysses* di James Joyce," *Annali* 15 (Naples, 1972): 127–144; and Marion Montgomery, *The Reflective Journey Toward Order* (Athens, Ga.: University of Georgia Press, 1973), pp. 138–141 and *passim*.

Joyce's use of Dante was also explored in Richard Ellmann, *James Joyce* (1959), and every report of Joyce's personal interest in Dante has been recorded there; Ellmann has also indexed all references and quotations in Joyce's letters, following volume 3, and he makes an appraisal of Dante's influence on *Ulysses* in *Ulysses on the Liffey* (London: Faber & Faber, 1972) at several points.

39. See *Ulysses on the Liffey*, p. 172.

8

Petrarch and the Humanist Hermeneutic

Thomas M. Greene

A well-known letter from Petrarch to Giovanni Colonna di San Vito evokes a promenade the two men had made together through the wilderness of ruins then covering most of Rome. As he recalls to his friend the sites they had visited, the poet identifies them not as they appeared to the naked eye but as they prompted his historical imagination: "Each step," he writes, "stirred our tongue and mind" ("Aderat . . . per singulos passus quod linguam et animum excitaret"). The organization of the long touristic catalogue that ensues bears no relation to the disposition of historic sites in Rome—most of which were lost or so overgrown as to be unrecognizable—but follows rather the course of ancient Roman history: "Hic Evandri regia . . . hic Caci spelunca; hic lupa nutrix" ("Here was the dwelling of Evander . . . here the cave of Cacus, here the nourishing she-wolf"),[1] and so on through the early kings, the republic, the empire, and the Christian martyrs. Since neither Petrarch nor his friend could identify more than a fraction of the actual scenes where the historical or legendary events were supposed to have been enacted, the letter exhibits the imaginative projection onto a landscape of a historical coherence which that landscape could only begin to suggest. Petrarch essentially *read* an order into the Roman wilderness, intuited a plan beneath the shattered temples and grazing sheep whose overwhelming human drama rendered the surface accidents of the city merely evocative pretexts. Oblivious like all his contemporaries to the atmospheric appeal of ruins in themselves, Petrarch might be said to have divined the subterranean plan of a living city in

201

the way a scholar might puzzle out conjecturally the precious and nearly obliterated text of a palimpsest whereon a debased modern text had been superimposed.

The pursuit of a deeper historical reality beneath unpromising modern appearances leaves its mark on many of Petrarch's works, and especially on those letters that reflect his touristic curiosity. Thus the young Petrarch describes his pleasure in the city now called Cologne as having stemmed from the fanciful reconstructions it provoked:

> Proximis aliquot diebus a mane ad vesperam civitatem iisdem ducibus circumivi, haud iniucundum exercitium, non tam ob id quod ante oculos erat, quam recordatione nostrorum maiorum, qui tam procul a patria monumenta Romanae virtutis tam illustria reliquissent. [*Fam.* 1:5]

> [During the next few days I wandered about the city from morning to night under the guidance of my friends. It was a very pleasant occupation, not so much because of what I actually saw, as from the recollection of our ancestors, who left such illustrious memorials of Roman virtue so far from the fatherland.]

A few years later, during his first visit to Rome, he wrote that he had been actually hesitant to arrive, "metuens ne quod ipse michi animo finxeram, extenuarent oculi et magnis semper nominibus inimica presentia" ("fearing that the sight of actuality would bring low my high imaginations. Present reality is always hostile to greatness," *Fam.* 2:14). But in this case, he added, the present was greater than he expected. It was greater, of course, precisely because it offered sufficient stimulus for the imagination to win its contest with the diminished present.

A long letter to Philippe de Vitry about the itinerary of Cardinal Gui de Boulogne through Italy evokes this prelate's future visit to Rome in terms of the Christian relics he will find there, each of which preserves intact the memory of a past event. The letter then turns to the pagan past of Rome which also awaits the traveler, and here Petrarch's prose blends almost inextricably the objects of common sight with the objects of the mind's eye:

> Mirabitur septem colles unius muri ambitu circumclusos, cuntis olim terris ac montibus et pelagis imperantes, et latas vias captivorum agminibus tunc angustas; arcus suspiciet triumphales

subactorum quondam regum ac populorum spoliis honustos;
Capitolium ascendet omnium caput arcemque terrarum, ubi olim
cella Iovis fuerat, nunc est Ara Coeli, unde, ut memorant, Augusto
Cesari puer Cristus ostensus est. [*Fam.* 9:13]

[He will gaze in wonder at the seven hills enclosed within a single
wall, once supreme over all lands, seas, and mountains; and the
broad streets, all too narrow for the hordes of captives. He will
look up at the triumphal arches, once loaded with the spoils of
subjugated kings and peoples. He will ascend the Capitoline hill,
the world's head, the citadel of all lands, where aforetime was
Jove's seat, where now stands the *Ara Coeli*. There, they say, the
infant Christ was displayed to Caesar Augustus.]

In each instance the eye rushes past the contemporary appearance into
the imaginative image of history or legend, situated by the adverbs
tunc, quondam, olim. The present condition of the arches seems almost
irrelevant to the contemplation of their once magnificent function. In
still other texts, Petrarch's historical vision strives unsuccessfully to
discern the tokens of a prestigious past now concealed too effectively by
the modern landscape. This at any rate seems to be the case when, as
the verse letter to Virgil describes it, Petrarch visited supposedly Virgilian haunts near Mantua:

> Hinc tibi composui quae perlegio, otia nactus
> Ruris amica tui; quonam vagus avia calle
> Fusca sequi, quibus in pratis errare soleres
> Assidue mecum volvens, quam fluminis oram
> Quae curvi secreta lacus, quas arboribus umbras,
> Quas nemorum latebras collisque sedilia parvi
> Ambieris, cuius fessus seu cespitis herbam
> Presseris accubitu, seu ripam fontis amoeni;
> Atque ea praesemtem mihi te spectacula reddunt.
>
> [*Fam.* 24: 11]

[It is in this city [Mantua] that I have composed what you now are
reading. It is here that I have found the friendly repose of thy rural
fields. I constantly wonder by what path you were wont to seek
the unfrequented glades in thy strolls, in what fields were wont to
roam, what streams to visit, or what recess in the curving shores of

the lake, what shady groves and forest fastnesses. Constantly I wonder where it was that you rested upon the sloping sward, or
that, reclining in moments of fatigue, you pressed with your elbow
the grassy turf or upon the marge of a charming spring. Such
thoughts as these bring you back before my eyes.][2]

At first the questing imagination seems to wander unappeased; and yet
the ultimate goal is attained, since Virgil's human presence emerges as
a reality—*praesentem*—even from the random questioning of stream
and wood.

This habit of seeking out everywhere the latent vestiges of history is
shared today by every tourist, but in Petrarch's century it was a momentous acquisition. His inquisitions of landscape reveal him in the act of
discovering history, and they reveal how creative, how inventive was
this act for which he is properly famous.[3] The letters and poems that
reflect the exercise of his historical imagination exhibit him in the process of living through this discovery, not only in his study but also in
the daily experiences of his peripatetic life. To say that Petrarch "discovered" history means, in effect, that he was the first to notice that
classical antiquity was very different from his own medieval world, and
the first to consider antiquity more admirable. Even if anticipations of
these attitudes may be found, he was the first to publicize them so
effectively as to influence profoundly his immediate posterity.

Thus Petrarch took more or less alone the step an archaic society
must take to reach maturity: he recognized *the possibility of a cultural
alternative*. With that step he established the basis of a radical critique
of his culture: not the critique that points to a subversion of declared
ideals, but rather the kind that calls ideals themselves into question. It
is this immense shift of perspective that is signaled by Petrarch's original way of looking at places, and especially his view of Rome. Before
him, writes Peter Burke, the Roman ruins were noticed, but their historical significance was scarcely perceived.

> They were thought of as 'marvels,' *mirabilia*. But they were taken
> as given. People seem not to have wondered how they got there,
> when they were built, or why the style of architecture was different
> from their own. The most they will do is to tell "just so stories"
> or explanatory myths about the names of places.[4]

With the rare exception of such a proto-humanist as Hildebert de

Lavardin, this statement is true; its accuracy can be measured by the continuing use, well after the age of Petrarch, of the twelfth-century "guidebook" *Mirabilia urbis Romae*, whose mingling of Christian miracle and topographic error betokens an incapacity or unwillingness to perceive the passage of history. To gauge the originality of Petrarch, one can set against the *Mirabilia* the extended passage in book 8 of the *Africa* which evokes the edifices of republican Rome with loving detail and reverent prolixity, even if not with archaeological precision. It was this Rome that Petrarch had gone to see and did see, despite the hostility of "present reality."

The effort of the imagination that produced these pages of the *Africa* reversed, in a sense, the imaginative effort behind the eighth book of the *Aeneid*—and to a lesser extent the treatment of place throughout that poem. For the *Aeneid* systematically introduces places as yet unfamiliar to its heroes but deeply charged for the Roman reader: Actium and Carthage, Cumae and Avernus, the Forum and the Janiculum. The *Aeneid* requires of its reader a simultaneous double vision that superimposes the past landscape on the present, thus providing a peculiar pleasure compacted of recognition and nostalgia. This process is sustained most continuously in lines 337–61 of book 8, lines which follow Evander and Aeneas as they walk from the Carmental shrine to what was to become the Forum, and which stress repeatedly the modest pastoral simplicity of each hallowed site:

> Hinc ad Tarpeiam sedem et Capitolia ducit
> aurem nunc, olim silvestribus horrida dumis.
>
> > [*Aeneid* 8: 347–48]

[From there he conducted them to Tarpeia's Place and the Capitol, which is now all gold, but was once wild and ragged, covered with woodland undergrowth.][5]

The reader is required to hold before his eyes two plans, two historical incarnations at once, and to shift his focus so quickly from the upper to the lower and back again that he grasps with a thrill the staggering impetus of time. Petrarch's eighth book makes no explicit reference to the city of his own age, to the Capitol once again "silvestribus horrida dumis," but the late medieval reader could not fail to perceive the Rome of the *Africa* as an archaeological construct. He

would retrace in his mind the same promenade taken by the poet and
Giovanni Colonna: he would superimpose present decay upon past
glory and measure now the ironies of history. More painfully, he would
confront a cultural alternative that appeared to dwarf his own crude
and divided Christendom. For Petrarch, refusing Hildebert's conception of a fortunate Roman fall—"Maior sum pauper divite, stante
iacens" ("I am greater in poverty than in wealth, prostrate than erect")
—saw the vestigial text of the Roman palimpsest as still more precious
than its rude overlay.

Similar uses of landscape appear elsewhere in Petrarch's work where
history is not at issue. The beautiful canzone that begins "Chiare
fresche e dolci acque" (*Canzoniere* no. 126) situates the speaker in a
landscape by a stream where once he had seen Laura bathing and
where he repeatedly returns to recapture this privileged moment. He
even pictures her, in his fantasy, returning some day to seek *him*, only
to find his grave. The poem thus depends on two distinct superpositions
of presence upon absence, past upon present. Several of the poems
in morte will also represent the poet seeking and finding Laura present
in the places she once frequented:

> Così comincio a ritrovar presenti
> le tue bellezze a' suoi usati soggiorni.
>
> [no. 282]

> [Thus I begin to discover again the presence of your beauty in its
> accustomed haunts.]

Fantasies like these constitute a kind of erotic, or perhaps narcissistic,
complement to the fanciful re-creation of a historical site.

To move from these uses of the actual landscape to less literal interests and unearthings was only a small step for Petrarch, as it would be
for the humanist movement he unknowingly fathered. The image that
propelled the humanist Renaissance and that still determines our perception of it, was the archaeological, necromantic metaphor of *disinter-
ment*, a digging up that was also a resuscitation or a reincarnation or
a rebirth. The discovery of the past led men literally to dig in the
ground, and the recovery from it of a precious object needed only a
touch of fancy to be regarded as a resurrection. But the resurrection of
buried objects and buildings could not be sharply distinguished from
the resurrection of literary texts as they were discovered, copied, edited,

disseminated, translated, and imitated by the humanist necromancer-scholar. Petrarch found it natural to use the term *ruinae* for the lost or fragmentary literary remains of antiquity,[6] and he himself would be praised by later humanists for having brought the Latin language back to the light of day from among the ruins with which it had been entombed.[7]

This commonplace Renaissance equation between the literal unearthing of antiquities and the unearthing or resurrection of ancient culture was already current during Petrarch's lifetime. Benvenuto of Vicenza (died 1323) celebrated the discovery of a manuscript of Catullus by composing a poem "de resurectione Catulli poete Veronensis."[8] Boccaccio employed the same metaphor in at least three separate contexts in order to praise three great trecento artists: Dante, Giotto, and Petrarch himself.[9] Filippo Villani, writing a short time after Petrarch's death, praised Giotto for having "revived the bloodless and almost extinct art of painting."[10] Several passages in Petrarch's work can be associated with the same image.[11] Thus the effort to decipher and re-create the buried reality of a place can be assimilated to the re-creation of a culture that was buried in various literal and progressively figurative ways. The title of a work by Valla—"Repastinatio," a digging up again—might have been used appropriately for any number of humanist writings.[12]

Vestigial traces of necromantic superstition are by no means absent from the awe that produced this imagery. We catch an echo of it in the canzone "Spirto gentil" (*Canzoniere* no. 53), which evokes a senile Rome overcome by sleep, to be awakened perhaps by the unnamed hero who is being addressed. The call for Rome's reawakening is followed immediately by a vision of the ancient walls, the tombs of Roman heroes, the entire ruined city, and the souls beneath the earth of the Scipios, Brutus, and Fabricius, hoping and rejoicing at the prospect of an imminent *renovatio*: "tutto quel ch'una ruina involve, / per te spera saldar ogni suo vizio" ("All that a ruin envelops, hopes through you to remedy every loss"). The allusions to an underworld of heroes and the metaphoric portraits of a stupefied or widowed Rome waiting to be revived, contain in germ the full-blown necromantic imagery of the later Renaissance. Petrarch, like Boccaccio, situated the otherness of the past beneath his feet and formulated his hopes of renewal in terms of a return to life.

The force of this necromantic superstition at the heart of the humanist enlightenment gave rise to a curious artistic phenomenon. It produced buildings and statues and poems that have to be scrutinized for subterranean outlines or emergent presences or ghostly reverberations. Renaissance art requires us to penetrate its visual or verbal surface to make out the vestigial form below, a revived classical form or a medieval form transmuted by a classicizing taste. Sir Kenneth Clark remarks that the Venus of Botticelli's *Primavera* "raises her hand with a gesture of a Virgin Annunciate; and the figure of Spring, fleeing from the icy embraces of the East Wind, is a Gothic nude."[13] Anthony Blunt, discussing Lescot's design for the façade of the Cour Carrée of the Louvre, points out that the "triple repetition of the pavilion seems to be an echo, probably unconscious, of the late medieval chateau façade divided by three round towers, to be seen for instance at Josselin or Martainville."[14]

Other examples from the visual arts would be easy to find. But it is above all the humanist literature of the Renaissance that requires an "archaeological" scrutiny, a decipherment of the latent or hidden or indecipherable object of historical knowledge beneath the surface. I propose to call this activity "sub-reading." In the case of Petrarch, we can follow the ways in which sub-reading the landscape came to resemble sub-reading a culture. The crucial moment occurs when the poet turns from landscape to the literary remains of antiquity and struggles to pierce their verbal surfaces to reach the living particularity of the past they bear within them. This sub-reading seems to me to be a central activity of Petrarch's mind, an activity that can be distinguished from medieval hermeneutics and that he bequeathed to his humanist heirs.

Sub-reading an ancient text involved first of all an intuition of its otherness,[15] an intuition that neither filial reverence nor fraternal affection could altogether dim. It also involved a dynamic and continuous interplay between the reader and the distant voice whose very accent and idiom he sought to catch. The first and essential discipline created by the humanist movement was the science of philology, which was designed to deal systematically with the otherness and distinctiveness of ancient literature. Philology, queen of the *studia humanitatis*, testified to the humanist discovery that cultural styles and verbal styles alter with time, like languages. Thus the first problem for the humanist was to deal with the temporal, cultural, and stylistic gap between the text and himself. Fully to bridge that gap required an effort of sub-reading that would unearth the alien presence carried by a text in all its subtle integrity. More arduous even than the reading of ruins is the intimate, delicate, and subtle conversation with a voice of the ancient past. The sub-reader tries to catch the inflections of a remote idiom, the cultural and personal quiddities obscured by millennial history. Petrarch's own capacity to sub-read is proven by his distinction as a gifted textual scholar. Writing to Boccaccio about the cult of Virgil on the part of Giovanni Malpaghini, his copyist and an aspiring poet, he remarks that he understands the seduction that the young man feels, rapt with the sweetness of another's wit—"alieni dulcedine raptus ingenii." We will not greatly distort the meaning of this phrase if we link the sweetness with the *alien* character of Virgil's genius. Petrarch himself was perhaps the first modern man to be intoxicated by this sweetness.

The reading of poetry before Petrarch had been described in terms of a different activity: not the bridging of time but the piercing of a veil. The activity of sub-reading needs to be distinguished from the conventional medieval hermeneutic methods with which it would at first coexist and which it would later progressively replace. It resembles neither the fourfold method of scriptural exegesis adapted by Dante and described in his letter to Can Grande, nor the Alexandrian method that presumed a poetic truth concealed by an allegorical veil. Petrarch himself echoes this latter presumption in several works, including his coronation address and the ninth book of the *Africa*: "sub ignoto tamen ut celentur amictu, / nuda alibi, et tenui frustrentur lumina velo" ("[Poets may] conceal in an unfamiliar garment things which otherwise are bare, and may baffle our vision with a fine veil," 9.100–01). But he also expressed doubts about the propriety of this presumption in the interpretation of Virgil: once through the mouth of Augustine in the *Secretum*, and again at greater length in the late letter to Federico Aretino containing an allegorical interpretation of the *Aeneid*, which he there assigns to his youth and which he is no longer prepared to support.[16] Petrarch never explicitly recognized the disparity between the traditional hermeneutic presumptions and the presumptions that emerge in other works of his, most notably in the three letters to Boccaccio on imitation (*Fam.* 1:8; 22:2; 23:19). But we can perceive these rhetorical and philological presumptions silently challenging the allegorical in his own mind, as we can follow this challenge or tension or split dividing humanist theory of the next two centuries.

The two hermeneutics are by no means mutually exclusive, but they do bring sharply dissimilar expectations to the literary text. The older method presupposed a fullness of knowledge awaiting the successful interpreter—knowledge that is whole and entire because it can be unlocked by a single operation of the appropriate intellectual key. This method aligned author and reader in a single universe of discourse wherein no cultural distance could exist because, with the sole exception of the Christian revelation, historical change was virtually unknown. The new "archaeological" hermeneutic, on the other hand, presupposed a considerable distance and withheld a single all-divulging key. Instead of a relation between "veil" and "truth" that, once discovered, is easily grasped and formulated, there emerges an interplay of entities that resists total description because it operates in the elusive domain of style. Style by definition cannot be described perfectly even if it can be categorized. And the poetic substance enmeshed in, or half-buried beneath, the verbal surface is now perceived as reaching the reader from far off, from a remote and prestigious world radically unlike his own.

Examples of the older method are not difficult to find in the corpus of Petrarch's work. It will be useful to choose one of the least convincing. De Nolhac reproduces a page from the manuscript of Virgil which Petrarch kept with him throughout his life and which he annotated copiously.[17] On the folios containing the first eclogue, he inserted an interlineated gloss based on a mechanical and reductive interpretation inspired by Donatus but now spelled out with a relentlessly heavy hand. If, as Donatus suggested, the figure of Tityrus represents Virgil enjoying the leisurely *otium* granted him by Augustus, Petrarch's gloss takes the *flumina* of Virgil's countryside to be students, the *fontes sacros* to be their masters, the *frigus opacum* to be restful study, the *saepes* to be chronicles immortalizing the poet's name, and so on for the length of the poem. In this particular instance, the effort of sub-reading failed; misled by a risky hermeneutic convention, Petrarch's literary intelligence could not locate the alien poetic substance latent in the words on his codex. The reductive hermeneutic presuppositions that underlay his gloss were supported by reverend authority and would continue to exercise an influence on literary theory as late as the seventeenth century. But their influence on the actual composition of poetry would decline sharply after the trecento, and Petrarch himself followed them systematically only in his *Bucolicum carmen*.

What in fact Petrarch did choose repeatedly to do as poet was to write verse that could itself be sub-read and demanded to be sub-read, verse bearing within it the latent presence of an ancient author. In so doing, of course, he again anticipated the course of the humanist imagination. We move here from the humanist sub-reading of an ancient text to the sub-reading required by a modern humanist text. Each activity, though distinct, can illuminate the other. The composition of humanist poetry can best be approached through the term *imitation*, a term that was to spark a series of quarrels during the high Renaissance.[18] Petrarch's fullest and most interesting discussion of it occurs in the letter to Boccaccio already cited (*Fam.* 23:19), which begins by portraying Giovanni Malpaghini. Petrarch goes on to describe himself as pleased with Giovanni's poetic progress but fearful that too crude a fidelity to their common master Virgil might vitiate his verse:

> Curandum imitatori, ut quod scribit simile non idem sit, eamque similitudinem talem esse oportere, non qualis est imaginis ad cum cuius imago est, quae quo similior eo maior laus artificis; sed qualis filii ad patrem, in quibus cum magna saepe diversitas sit membrorum, umbra quaedam et quem pictores nostri aerem vocant, qui in vultu inque oculis maxime cernitur, similitudinem illam facit, quae statim viso filio patris in memoriam nos reducat, cum tamen si res ad mensuram redeat, omnia sint diversa; sed est ibi nescio quid occultum quod hanc habeat vim. Sic et nobis providendum, ut cum simile aliquid sit, multa sint dissimilia, et idipsum simile lateat, nec deprehendi possit, nisi tacita mentis indagine, ut intelligi simile queat potius quam dici. Utendum igitur ingenio alieno, utendumque coloribus, abstinendum verbis. Illa poetas facit, haec simias. [*Fam.* 23:19]

[A proper imitator should take care that what he writes resemble the original without reproducing it. The resemblance should not be that of a portrait to the sitter—in that case the closer the likeness is the better—but it should be the resemblance of a son to his father. Therein is often a great divergence in particular features, but there is a certain suggestion, what our painters call an "air," most noticeable in the face and eyes, which makes the resemblance. As soon as we see the son, he recalls the father to us, although if we should measure every feature we should find them all different. But there is a mysterious something there that has this power. Thus we writers must look to it that with a basis of similarity there should be many dissimilarities. And the similarity should be planted so deep that it can only be extricated by quiet meditation. The quality is to be felt rather than defined. Thus we may use another man's conceptions and the color of his style, but not his words. In the first case the resemblance is hidden deep; in the second it is glaring. The first procedure makes poets, the second makes apes.]

In this admirable passage, more enlightened than most discussions of the subject by later theorists, Petrarch is describing an object of knowledge that, unlike the "truth" represented by medieval allegory, cannot by definition be fully and succinctly delimited. The resemblance of a poem to its model or series of models will never be fully articulated, even supposing that it will be fully grasped. Rather, one sub-reads, patiently and intuitively, the dim, elusive presence of the model in the modern composition. This presence can no more be circumscribed than can the mysterious resemblance of a son to a father, or the confused relations between the levels of a buried city. Petrarch himself says this in one crucial sentence of the passage just quoted: "Sic et nobis providendum, ut cum simile aliquid sit, multa sint dissimilia, et idipsum simile lateat, nec deprehendi possit, nisi tacita mentis indagine, ut intelligi simile queat potius quam dici." This silent searching of the mind, "tacita mentis indagine," is considered never to complete its meditative investigation. That is because the object of knowledge is perceived to be composed not by a kernel of moral, religious, or philosophic wisdom, but by what might be called a *moral style*—a texture of feeling, thought, rhetoric, and tone defining itself allusively against a ground of literary tradition.

Petrarch's letter itself needs to be sub-read since its central comparison—likening the goal of proper literary imitation to the resemblance of a son to his father—bears just this resemblance to a much briefer simile in Seneca.[19] As we sub-read the father's features, indistinctly but unmistakably, in his son's, so we sub-read Seneca in this letter, and so we sub-read Virgil in the *Africa* and other poems. We pursue the diffused, the incomplete, the latent, even as we recognize that their presence cannot fully be violated by verbal definition. Petrarch points to this fleeting latency when he uses the word's etymological ancestor: "ut . . . idipsum simile lateat." The interplay between the surface text and the antecedent or sub-text involves subtle interpenetrations, an interflowing and tingeing, an exchange of minute gradations, that cannot be measured wholly or formulated. If the allegorical meaning participated in being, this humanist interplay is forever becoming. Reading and sub-reading it means dealing with the implicit, the incipient, the virtual, and the inexpressible—"ut intelligi simile queat potius quam dici."

The humanist poet's interplay with antiquity also involves what might be called a sub-reading of the self. As Petrarch warned Malpaghini, the very sweetness of otherness constitutes a risk, since it may change the poet into an ape; it may so fill the spirit with another's presence that one's own selfhood will be dimmed. Here he seems to adumbrate the idea that true respect for another's wit requires a certain reciprocity. As the ultimate symbols of this reciprocity, we might take his epistles in prose and verse to the ancient authors who mattered most to him, epistles that characteristically reflect a certain humility but do not lack traces of their author's pride and, in the case of Cicero, his disapproval. Petrarch read (and sub-read) the ancients with less risk, with fuller appreciation, and with sharper philological acuity than Malpaghini not only because he was a great poet but also because he was a great egoist. This means that he brought to his reading a mind blessed with or condemned to compulsive self-questioning, a mind greedy of experience and quick to change its tenor, a mind forever in the process of becoming, obsessed with its own movements and turnings but intermittently open nonetheless to other minds and worlds.

If Petrarch was the first great humanist, his primacy can teach us that the fullest apprehension of otherness requires a continuous circle of adjustments. The subject who attempts to sub-read must be ready to play with subjective styles of perception, must question and test himself as he sharpens his intuitions, must finally sub-read his own consciousness to discern that inner likeness, that virtual disposition capable of conversing with a voice from the depths of time. Only thus can he taste without risk that sweetness of the alien that will wither the unguarded and the pallid self. Renaissance anthologies are full of poems by the

Malpaghinis who never mastered this humanist circle of continuing adjustments. In the poetry of mature humanism, sub-reading the alien text required sub-reading the range of potential styles of response in one's innermost being, imitation with the inner ear and then imitation with the pen. Imitation at its most powerful pitch required a profound act of self-knowledge and then a creative act of self-definition.[20] Of course the reverse requirement is equally stringent: the definition or creation of literary voices, literary styles, required the progressive apprehension of voices and styles from outside the self.

This process of dynamic self-discovery is adumbrated in another, somewhat earlier letter to Boccaccio that also deals with imitation. Here the analogy is sartorial:

> Alioquin multo malim meus michi stilus sit, incultus licet atque horridus, sed in morem toge habilis, ad mensuram ingenii mei factus, quam alienus, cultior ambitioso ornatu sed a maiore ingenio profectus. . . . Omnis vestis histrionem decet, sed non omnis scribentem stilus; suus cuique formandus servandusque est, ne . . . rideamur. . . . Et est sane cuique naturaliter, ut in vultu et gestu, sic in voce et sermone quiddam suum ac proprium, quod colere et castigare quam mutare cum facilius tum melius atque felicius sit. [*Fam.* 22:2]

> [I much prefer that my style be my own, rude and undefined, perhaps, but made to the measure of my mind, like a well-cut gown rather than to use someone else's style, more elegant, ambitious, and ornamented, but suited to a greater genius than mine. . . . An actor can wear any kind of garment; but a writer cannot adopt any kind of style. He should form his own and keep it, for fear we should laugh at him. . . . Certainly each of us has naturally something individual and his own in his utterance and language as in his face and gesture. It is better and more rewarding for us to develop and train this quality than to change it.]

The perfunctory and quite insincere formulas of modesty need not detain us, but the perception that literary composition requires a lucid estimate of the self is important and valuable, and cuts deeper than the corresponding passage in Quintilian. Petrarch sees that a man's style is as personal as his face, and that both reflect the essential core of selfhood—"quiddam suum et proprium"—that makes him unique. Only after grasping his own selfhood can the artist create (*formare*) and preserve his literary style. Actually, the conception of selfhood shifts slightly but significantly in the course of this passage. The sartorial analogy implies a conception that is basically static. The gown I wear either fits or fails to fit; I may choose between gowns but I cannot alter the fit once I put one on. But the argument that follows this analogy allows us to glimpse a more dynamic self-cultivation. By recognizing our capacity to develop and train (*colore et castigare*) not only our style but also our essential individuality, Petrarch recognizes the potentially creative interplay between the alien and the self. Thus, for the humanist poet the beginning of creativity does not lie in a *cogito*, a *prise de conscience*, as it must, according to Georges Poulet, for the modern poet; it lies, rather, in a double groping—toward the otherness of the ancient text and toward a modern sensibility, a modern voice, that can mediate the ancient. And we as readers of humanist poems have to follow the interplay of that mediation, shifting our focus back and forth from the surface text to the fragments buried below it.[21]

Thus these two letters on imitation can be made to yield a kind of embryonic theory of humanist composition, a theory that is clarified by other passages and other images in these same texts. Both letters make use of an apian analogy which was to become a humanist cliché but which in these Petrarchan contexts retains a fresh power of suggestion.

> Standum denique Senecae consilio, quod ante Senecam Flacci erat, ut scribamus scilicet apes mellificant, non servatis floribus, sed in favos versis, ut ex multis et variis unum fiat, idque aliud et melius. [*Fam.* 23:19]

> [This is the substance of Seneca's counsel, and Horace's before him, that we should write as the bees make sweetness, not storing up the flowers but turning them into honey, thus making one thing of many various ones, but different and better.]

The analogy with bees, whose ancient sources are cited correctly,[22] implies a capacity for absorption and assimilation on the part of the poet, a capacity for making one's own the external text in all its otherness. That Petrarch did, in fact, perceive this process to be crucial in his own creative experience is clear:

> Legi apud Virgilium apud Flaccum apud Severinum apud Tullium;

nec semel legi sed milies, nec cucurri sed incubui, et totis ingenii
nisibus immoratus sum; mane comedi quod sero digererem, hausi
puer quod senior ruminarem. Hec se michi tam familiariter inges-
sere et non modo memorie sed medullis affixa sunt unumque cum
ingenio facta sunt meo, ut etsi per omnem vitam amplius non
legantur, ipsa quidem hereant, actis in intima animi parte radici-
bus. [*Fam.* 22:2]

[I have read Virgil, Horace, Livy, Cicero, not once but a thousand
times, not hastily but in repose, and I have pondered them with all
the powers of my mind. I ate in the morning what I would digest
in the evening; I swallowed as a boy what I would ruminate upon
as a man. These writings I have so thoroughly absorbed and fixed,
not only in my memory but in my very marrow, these have become
so much a part of myself, that even though I should never read
them again they would cling in my spirit, deep-rooted in its
inmost recesses.]

Here the analogy is digestive, and it too can be traced back to Seneca
as well as forward at least to Francis Bacon,[23] but the formulation here
corresponds to something of moment in the poet's own artistic formation. It betokens an intimacy of conversation with the ancient text, a
habitual interiorization of its letter and essence, and a freedom to transform, to re-create this sweetness of an alien wit into the honey of one's
own personal creation.

One might argue that already in these digestive and apian analogies
there lies in germ the obsessive analogy of a rebirth. The metamorphosis
of the ancient into renewed modern life within the poet's consciousness
constitutes a kind of renascence. This metamorphic implication is more
visible in a much earlier usage of the bee simile:

Neve diutius apud te qualia decerpseris maneant, cave: nulla quidem esset apibus gloria, nisi in aliud et in melius inventa conver-
terent. Tibi quoque, siqua legendi meditandique studio repperis,
in favum stilo redigenda suadeo. [*Fam.* 1:8]

[Take care that the nectar does not remain in you in the same state
as when you gathered it; bees would have no credit unless they
transformed it into something different and better. Thus if you
come upon something worthy while reading or reflecting, change it
into honey by means of your style—author's translation.]

Petrarch seems already to see that this kind of assimilation must occur if the modern text is truly to recall its paternal model imprecisely but unmistakably. Only this profounder and more secret act of "imitation" permits the authentic sub-reading of a latent otherness in the modern work and invests it with its unique historical depth. The alien text has been absorbed so thoroughly that its presence *haunts* the polyvocal modern text, slowly reveals itself to the silent searching of the mind, resonates faintly in the third ear. In that resonance lies its renascence. The reader divines a buried stratum, as a visitor to Rome divines the subterranean foundations of a temple.

In Petrarch's own poetry, this latent stratum can be felt only intermittently, and more commonly in the Latin works than in the vernacular. Neither body is lacking in pseudo-imitation, in perfunctory assimilation and distorted self-definition. Most noticeably, the *Africa* is marred by failings that from our perspective can be attributed to a double incapacity: first, to grasp the alien substance of ancient epic in its artistic fullness; and second, to gauge lucidly the character of the writer's own poetic vocation. In fact, Petrarch's most successful and influential poetry needs to be sub-read less consistently than does the poetry of his great humanist successors—Poliziano and Tasso, Ronsard and Du Bellay, Jonson and Milton, among them. Yet there are instances of "imitation" in something like the creative sense we have been considering, and these instances, however scattered and brief, are full of interest; in terms of the history of European poetry, they are highly significant.

One such instance appears in sonnet 164 of the *Canzoniere*, which opens with a nightscape deriving from Virgil:

> Or che 'l ciel e la terra e 'l vento tace,
> e le fere e gli augelli il sonno affrena,
> notte il carro stellato in giro mena
> e nel suo letto il mar senz' onda giace;   4
> vegghio, penso, ardo, piango, e chi mi sface
> sempre m' è inanzi per mia dolce pena;
> guerra è 'l mio stato, d'ira e di duol piena,
> e sol di lei pensando ò qualche pace.   8

[Now that the heavens and the earth and the wind are silent, and the wild beasts and the birds are bridled by sleep, night leads its starry car upon its round and without one wave the sea lies in its bed; I see, think, burn, and weep; and she who is my undoing is always before me to my sweet pain: my state is one of war, full of rage and grief; and only in thinking of her do I have some peace.]

[*Oxford Book of Italian Verse*]

Of the several nightscapes in the *Aeneid*, the closest to this one in imagery and dramatic force is the passage in book 4 which evokes the nocturnal anxiety of Dido:

> Nox erat, et placidum carpebant fessa soporem
> Corpora per terras, silvaeque et saeva quierant
> Aequora; quum medio volvuntur sidera lapsu,
> Quum tacet omnis ager pecudesque pictaeque volucres   4
> Quaeque lacus late liquidos quaeque aspera dumis
> Rura tenent, somno positae sub nocte silenti.
> At non infelix animi Phoenissa, neque unquam
> Solvitur in somnos oculisve aut pectore noctem   8
> Accipit: ingeminant curae.

[4:522–31]

[It was night, and tired creatures all over the world were enjoying kindly sleep. Forests and fierce seas were at rest, as the circling constellations glided in their midnight course. Every field, all the farm-animals, and the colorful birds were silent, all that lived across miles of grassy mere and in the wild country's ragged brakes, lying still under the quiet night in a sleep which smoothed each care away from hearts which had forgotten life's toil. But not so the Phoenician queen. Her accursed spirit could not relax into sleeping, or welcome darkness into her eyes or brain. Instead, her torment redoubled.]

In instances like this one, the Virgilian fragment juts clearly through the surface; for our purposes, its visibility will only increase its exemplary usefulness. Nothing in the culture of the trecento resembled the august sorrow and specious majesty of Virgil's mature manner; nothing resembled the balance of a moral vision that registered at once the beauty and grandeur of the world, the pain visited randomly on noble and ignoble alike, the ineluctable course of a history which is both cruel and redemptive. Petrarch's use of this fragment succeeds because it leaves room between the Virgilian note and its own; it ac-

cepts the gap. The shift of verb tenses publicly exchanges epic distance
for lyrical immediacy—not "Nox erat" but "Or," *now*. The four verbs
of line 5, their impact heightened by asyndeton, crash upon the noc-
tural stillness with a harsh intrusiveness that sets off Virgil's more discursive turn at his seventh line. *His* night is primarily a repose of living
things, of birds and beasts (line 4), of the *corpora* (2) with its richly suggestive vagueness, and the even vaguer "Quaeque . . . quaeque" (5).
This impression of a densely inhabited quietude gives way in Petrarch
to an *elemental* stillness, wherein living creatures are noticed a little
neutrally in only a single line, but where the cosmic presence of heaven,
earth, and wind are at rest, where the starry carriage of a personified
Night follows its orderly circuit, and where a universal quiescence
culminates in the arresting fourth line with the immense peace of the
sea. The imperial imagination of Roman epic, whose vocation was the
ordering of history and space, yields to a private intuition of natural
forces, an intuition entertained no longer by a transparent narrator but
by a speaker who is chief actor and sufferer and mythic center. There
is also a shift from the broad narrative psychology of Dido, which
unfolds progressively and spaciously, so to speak, to the analytic psychology of Petrarch and its proto-modern play with paradox and oxymoron, its denser, more perverse subtleties and traps (which the sestet
will continue to probe). The interplay of surface text and sub-text involves a *distancing* of Virgil and demonstrates the originality of his
imitator; but this specific originality could only come into being, and
could only be perceived, against the fixed greatness of a model, now
firmly apprehended as it was not by the author of the *Africa*. Petrarch's
sonnet, unlike an epic, does not represent history, but like all successful
humanist imitations, it incorporates the movement of history and
implicitly asserts a freedom over history.

   The echoing of ancient Latin poetry was not of course unknown in
medieval literature, but it could not truly incorporate this movement of
history because the very sense of historical change was so largely deficient. E. P. M. Dronke has analyzed, with interesting results, a passage
from the *Waltharius* (ninth- to tenth- century) to show the number of
its borrowings from Virgil and the richness of their poetic effect.[24] The
effect is beyond dispute. But there is no implication in this passage of
a historical distance from its model so wide that the echo involves a
renascence. There is no distance built into the poem, no controlled

movement from one culture to another, no historical polyvocality, no awareness of a dead period intervening between the model and its renascence. This awareness does emerge in Dante, who describes Virgil's voice as hoarse from long silence ("per lungo silenzio parea fioco") and who imitates him magnificently in such rare passages as *Inferno* 13:31 ff. and the simile at *Inferno* 3:112–17, but who does not practice imitation as a constant technique.[25]

Despite distant anticipations in a figure like Mussato, only with Petrarch can one speak of imitation as a poetic principle; only his poems in the trecento come to us asking to be sub-read. In canzone no. 50 of the *Canzoniere* ("Ne la stagion che 'l ciel") almost the entire verbal texture is interwoven with images of reverberating Roman resonance; sonnet 159 deftly encases a Horatian allusion in the manner of the *dolce stil novo*: "non sa come Amor sana e come ancide / chi non sa come dolce ella sospira / e come dolce parla e dolce ride" ("He does not know how Love heals and kills, who does not know how sweetly she sighs, and sweetly speaks, and sweetly laughs").[26] In the exquisite sonnet 311 ("Quel rosignuol che si soave piagne") we catch, beyond the accents of native and Provençal convention, the sorrow of Virgil's Orpheus and the virile melancholy of the *Georgics* (4:511–15). A single electric phrase in the great canzone 129 ("Di pensier in pensier")—"lì medesmo assido me freddo, pietra morta in pietra viva" ("at that very place I seat myself, chilled, dead stone on living stone")—receives part of its charge from a buried Ovidian image and a buried allusion to Ovid's Ariadne.[27] In these last two examples, as in the nightscape of no. 164, an archaeological reading brings to light a smuggled transfer to mythic energy.

The poetry initiated by Petrarch in these brief and scattered instances was to become a major current of Renaissance literature, a current whose signal successes amid the perennial mediocrity proved that the double quest of the humanist artist could fecundate the imagination. Before the current spent itself, Petrarch's poetry was itself to achieve the status of a classic; after the dead poetic interval of the earlier quattrocento, and after the genuine poetic renewal of the full European Renaissance, his work joined the ancients' as the object of innumerable attempted resuscitations, some of them splendidly successful. The poems of this current, enriched by a new and subtle polyvocality, might be described as *chronomachias*, battlegrounds for a conflict of eras, a struggle of period styles. In an authentic struggle, the contemporary always wins—which is to say that the poetic voice learns from the baptism of otherness to find its own unique salvation. Merleau-Ponty has written:

> True history . . . gets its life entirely from us. It is in our present that true history gets the force to refer everything else to the present. The *other* whom I respect gets his life from me as I get my life from him. A philosophy of history does not deprive me of any rights and privileges. It simply adds to my personal obligations the obligation to understand situations other than my own and to create a path between my life and the lives of others, that is, to express myself.[28]

It was this arduous route which the great humanists of the Renaissance chose—and Petrarch first of all—in their momentous search for a self-expression that was, then as always, self-discovery.

NOTES

1. All quotations from Petrarch's correspondence, unless otherwise identified, are taken from *Le familiare*, ed. Vittorio Rossi and Umberto Bosco, 4 vols. (Florence, 1933–42). Letters will be identified by volume and number according to Petrarch's original division. Translations of the correspondence, unless otherwise identified, are taken from *Letters from Petrarch*, trans. Morris Bishop (Bloomington and London, 1966).

2. Mario Emilio Cosenza, ed. and trans., *Petrarch's Letters to Classical Authors* (Chicago, 1910), pp. 138–39 (slightly altered).

3. Among the many discussions of Petrarch's perception of history, a few of particular interest can be cited: Theodor Mommsen, "Petrarch's Concept of the Dark Ages," *Speculum* 17 (1942): 226 ff.; Erwin Panofsky, *Renaissance and Renascences in Western Art* (Stockholm, 1960), pp. 8 ff.; Beryl Smalley, *English Friars and Antiquity in the Early Fourteenth Century* (New York, 1960), pp. 292–98; Peter Burke, *The Renaissance Sense of the Past* (London, 1969), pp. 21 ff.; Roberto Weiss, *The Spread of Italian Humanism* (London, 1964), pp. 23–28.

4. Burke, p. 2.

5. Translations of the *Aeneid* are those of W. F. Jackson Knight, *Virgil: The Aeneid* (Baltimore, 1956).

6. "Inter humanarum inventionum tot ruinas litterae sacrae stant cum maiore hominum studio, tum vel maxime protegente sua sancta poemata, suas sanctas historias, divinasque suas leges, auctore illarum deo . . . . Reliquarum nobilissimae

pereunt, et iam magna ex parte periere." *De remediis utriusque fortune*, 1:43, quoted by Conrad H. Rawski in Petrarch, *Four Dialogues for Scholars* (Cleveland, 1967), pp. 36–37.

7. See, for example, the tribute by Francesco Florido: "Immo et plurimum laudis inter eos meruit Petrarcha qui primus apud Italos (nisi fallor) latinam linguam diu sepultam ex ruderibus et vetustate in lucem afferre adortus est." *Apologia in linguae latinae calumniatores* (Basel, 1540), fol. 106. Quoted by Franco Simone, *La Coscienza della rinascita negli umanisti francesi* (Rome, 1949), p. 65.

8. Cited by B. L. Ullman, *Studies in the Italian Renaissance* (Rome, 1955), p. 13.

9. On Dante; "Per costui la morta poesia meritamente si può dire suscitata"— *Vita di Dante*, ed. Carlo Muscetta (Rome, 1963), p. 7. On Giotto: "avendo egli quella arte ritornata in luce che molti secoli . . . era stata sepulta"—*Decameron*, fifth story of the sixth day. On Petrarch: "poeticum diffundit nomen a se in lucem et latebra revocatum"—letter to Jacopo Pizzinghe, *Lettere edite e inedite*, ed. F. Corazzini (Florence, 1877), p. 196.

10. *Liber de origine civitatis Florentiae et eiusdem famosis civibus*, quoted in J. von Schlosser, *Quellenbuch zur Kunstgeschichte des Abendländischen Mittelalters* (Vienna, 1896), p. 370.

11. In the *De Vita solitaria*, Petrarch writes of demonstrating gratitude to the ancients by "nomina illorum vel ignota vulgare, vel obsolefacta renovare, vel *senio obruta eruere*." Imagery of revival recurs frequently in the exhortation to Cola di Rienzo (*Epistolae variae XLVIII*). One example: "Italia, quae cum capite aegrotante languebat, sese iam nunc erexit in cubitum." Rome, in *Fam.* 2:9, is seen as a "desertam effigiem." Compare the metrical epistle (2:5) to Clement VI, where Rome is represented as a widow crying: "My wounds are as numerous as my churches and fortified palaces; the walls of the city, thickly strewn with ruins, reveal but the remnants of a stately and lamentable city, and move all spectators to tears." Quoted in *Petrarch. A Humanist Among Princes*, ed. and trans. David Thompson, p. 70.

12. See Valla's *Scritti filosofici e religiosi*, ed. and trans. G. Radetti (Florence, 1953), p. 445, n. 1.

13. Sir Kenneth Clark, *The Nude* (New York, 1956), pp. 96–97.

14. Anthony Blunt, *Art and Architecture in France 1500 to 1700* (Baltimore, 1957), p. 46.

15. The term *otherness*, as used in this essay, is limited to cultural and historical distance and is thus considerably more restricted than the term *altérité*, as used passim in the admirable study by Arnaud Tripet, *Pétrarque, ou La connaissance de soi* (Geneva, 1967).

Readers of Michel Foucault will perceive that the literal and metaphoric applications of the word *archaeology* here diverge from those in his *Les Mots et les choses* (Paris, 1966) and *L'Archéologie du savoir* (Paris, 1969).

16. On the subject of "poetice narrationis archana," the Augustine of the *Secretum* wonders whether in fact Virgil thought of them as he wrote or whether he was not totally remote from any such thought: "sive enim id Virgilius ipse sensit, dum scriberet, sive ab omni tali consideratione remotissimus." Francesco Petrarca, *Prose*, ed. G. Martellotti et al. (Milan and Naples, 1955), p. 124. In the *Senili* 4:5, Petrarch asks:

"Who is there, in dealing with such doubtful matters, daring to affirm with assurance that the intention of those authors was absolutely this rather than that, in works which they composed a thousand years ago?" Author's translation.

17. Pierre de Nolhac, *Pétrarque et l'Humanisme* (Paris, 1907), 1: 145–57.

18. On Renaissance theory of imitation, see Izora Scott, *Controversies over the Imitation of Cicero* (New York, 1910); F. Ulivi, *L'Imitazione nella poetica del Rinascimento* (Milan, 1959); Cesare Vasoli, "L'estetica dell'Umanesimo e del Rinascimento," in *Momenti e problemi de storia dell'estetica* (Milan, 1959), 1: 325–433; H. Gmelin, "Das Prinzip der Imitatio in den romanischen Literaturen," in *Romanische Forschungen* 46 (1932): 83–360; Nancy Struever, *The Language of History in the Renaissance* (Princeton, 1970), pp. 154 ff.; Robert J. Clements, *Critical Theory and Practice of the Pléiade* (Cambridge, Mass., 1942); G. Castor, *Pléiade Poetics* (Cambridge, 1964); Harold White, *Plagiarism and Imitation during the English Renaissance* (Cambridge, Mass., 1935); Jerome Mazzaro, *Transformations in the Renaissance English Lyric* (Ithaca and London, 1970), pp. 73–107.

19. *Epistulae morales LXXXIV*: "Etiam si cuius in te comparebit similitudo, quem admiratio tibi altius fixerit, similem esse te volo quomodo filium, non quomodo imaginem; imago res mortua est." Richard M. Gummere, (London and New York: Loeb Classical Library, 1930), 2: 281.

20. "Quel che scrive non si riveste soli di cultura, ma nasce di cultura: la letteratura . . . è il tramite attraverso il quale l'esperienza gli si tramuta in sentimento." Umberto Bosco, *Petrarca* (Turin, 1946), p. 149.

21. The same implication seems to emerge briefly in a passage of the *De vita solitaria* (1:3), exhorting each man to "qualem eum natura, qualem ipse se fecerit." *Prose*, p. 330.

Compare Struever: "Under the rubric of imitation the Humanist forms a notion of identity; nor is this a theoretical discussion only: if freedom is the foundation of his achievement, his rhetorical-critical activity fills this concept of freedom with concrete activity, and exercises his convictions in quotidian employment. *Imitatio* is a source of freedom." *The Language of History*, p. 150.

22. Seneca, *Epistulae morales* 84,3–5; Horace, *Carmina* 4:2, 27–32. For the history of this image, see J. von Stackelberg, "Das Bienengleichnis," *Romanische Forschungen* 68 (1956): 271–93.

23. Seneca, *Epistulae morales*, 84,6–7; Bacon, "Of Studies": "Some books are to be tasted, others to be swallowed, and some few to be chewed and digested."

24. "Functions of Classical Borrowings in Medieval Latin Verse," in *The Classical Heritage and its Beneficiaries*, ed. R. R. Bolgar (London, 1963), pp. 159–64.

25. Commenting on *Inferno* 1:85 ff., Curtius writes: "For Dante . . . Virgil is the master of rhetoric in the late antique and medieval sense." *European Literature and the Latin Middle Ages* (New York and Evanston, 1963), p. 357. Dante's brief references to the value of studying and imitating ancient authors in the *De vulgari eloquentia* (2:4:3 and 2:6:7) might be said to be pre-humanist.

26. On Petrarch's transformation of the Horatian model, see the sensitive comments by Bosco, p. 162.

27. *Heroides* 10:49–50. The insight of Thomas G. Bergin is relevant to all these

examples: "[Many of the *Rime*] bespeak an ease and familiarity with the classics—and one may say *the intent of the classics*—which adds a new element to the traditional love lyric" (my italics)—*Petrarch* (New York, 1969), p. 157.

28. Maurice Merleau-Ponty, *Signes* (Paris, 1960), p. 93. Cited from *The Prose of the World*, trans. John O'Neill (Evanston, 1973), p. 86.

9

Boccaccio's *Ars Narrandi* in the Sixth
Day of the *Decameron*

Franco Fido

Many critics today seem to share a basic notion of literature, and of fiction in particular, according to which, in the words of one of them,

> any work, any novel tells, through the events of its plot, the story of its own creation, that is, its own story. . . . The sense of a work consists in telling about itself, in speaking to us of its own existence . . . the very existence of a novel is the last link in the chain of its plot: where the story that is narrated ends, is precisely where the story that narrates, the literary story, begins.[1]

This statement, or at least the last part of it, seems so true that it hardly needs to be expounded further or commented upon. At the same time, behind the idea that "the sense of a work consists in telling about itself" one feels the critic's determination to deal with homogeneous, purely literary materials, to banish any possible "referential fallacy," keeping, so to speak, any intrusion of history away from the story. And behind this determination there may be, one suspects, the literary man's old complex toward—and longing for—pure science, together with some hope that linguistics and structuralism will at long last provide the critics with the key admitting them into the prestigious club of scientists.

I have quoted the passage from Todorov, however, for a different reason: because it also provides a plausible explanation of why the *Decameron* recently has been studied—or read—in several countries by writers of various aesthetic persuasions, sometimes not particularly

225

interested (or competent, for that matter) in Romance literatures, but always aiming at a general discussion about the nature and origin of narrative—and viewing the *Decameron* as an important piece of evidence in their inquiry.[2]

Actually, as we all know, the *Decameron* tells the story of ten charming young people whose main occupation is storytelling; and when their supply of tales, or rather their taste for storytelling, runs out, so does the plot of the *Decameron*, and it is Boccaccio's turn to start writing those same stories.

How could one dream of a better illustration of Todorov's definition of fiction? Indeed, the whole book could be seen as an extended, prophetic metaphor of that definition. As was to be expected, Todorov himself became aware of this, and in 1969 published his own *Grammaire du Décaméron*, in which he tried to combine *l'analyse du récit* practiced by other critics of the same school (Bremond, for example)[3] with the method invented by Vladimir Propp in the late 1920s: *nil sub sole novi*.

As Propp managed to draw from his meticulous classification of Russian fairy-tales a *Morphology of the Folktale*,[4] so Todorov uses the *Decameron* to build a new science he calls *narratologie* or narratology. This seems to consist in the adoption of some "primary categories"— such as noun, adjective, and verb—and some "secondary categories"— such as modal, logical, or temporal relationship—by means of which he can codify any given text. In our case, for instance, he might reduce each one of Boccaccio's one hundred stories into a formula, say: "$Xb (\rightarrow YcX) \, obl + (Y - cX) \, oPtX \rightarrow Xa \rightarrow Y - cX$," meaning that in a particular group of tales agent X commits a sin which compels agent Y to punish agent X, etc.[5]

Now Propp's operation was a clever and successful one, inasmuch as it proved the existence and the constant repetition with a number of variants and through a number of combinations, of certain basic elements and patterns in the collective, anonymous field of folktales— such as the trial of the hero, his journey toward an almost impossible goal, the themes of interdiction and transgression, and so on.

Applied to (or should we say against) the *Decameron*, the same approach leads to a surprising—or perhaps not so surprising—effect: that the referential fallacy, chased out through the door, comes back in again through the window. "Narratologic" formulae speak only of agents and of their elementary actions, interactions, motivations; not only is life, the banished referent, still there, but it appears needlessly simplified, as though the sophisticated characters of Boccaccio were stripped of their attire and their culture, and exiled from history into prehistory—or if you prefer, from the gay, animated life of fourteenth-century Florence to the anthropological timelessness of some *tristes tropiques*. And this is disappointing to say the least, because such a hasty rummaging in the *Decameron* as *in corpore vili* can only discredit what still seems to me a good idea, that of exploring Boccaccio's masterpiece as an outstanding early model of modern narrative.

Not only is the *Decameron*, like any other great literary achievement, at one and the same time both inside and outside of history, and not only does Boccaccio know that very well, but he also takes the trouble to tell the reader about the nature of his book—in the *Proemio* to be sure, but less in the *Proemio* than from within the tales themselves, through the very unfolding of their narratives.

On the one hand, Boccaccio's intention of linking the *Decameron* to his own life story, and to contemporary society as a whole, is evident from the outset. He offers his work, we read in the *Proemio*, to all young women in love, in order to pay to them, in narrative cash as it were, the debt of gratitude he contracted in his youth toward some wise friends, whose words consoled him when he was about to die of love.

There is, of course, a smile contained in this statement of intention, but it is no joke either. From the start, the project of storytelling is presented as the outcome of the author's biography, and also as the fulfillment of a cultural function, as a remedy or a compensation for the *peccato della Fortuna*, the injustice of Fortune, that has made women weaker than men against the power of love, and has given them no opportunity for distraction such as sport, business, or a political career.[6] At the end of the book the author will address women again: "piacevoli donne . . . in pace vi rimanete, di me ricordandovi, se ad alcuna forse alcuna cosa giova l'averle lette." ("may . . . peace, sweet ladies, remain with you always, and if perchance these stories should bring you any profit, remember me").[7]

But between the two ends of the *Decameron* the dear and fair ladies are far more than ideal readers, they stand for the concrete experience of life, as we see in the introduction to the fourth day. There, to the critics who reproached him for not staying in Parnassus with the Muses, Boccaccio answers:

le donne già mi fur cagione di comporre mille versi, dove le Muse
mai non mi furono di farne alcun cagione. Aiutaronmi elle bene, e
mostraronmi comporre que' mille; e forse a queste cose scrivere,
quantunque sieno umilissime, si sono elle venute parecchie volte a
starsi meco, in servigio forse e in onore della simiglianza che le
donne hanno con esse: per che, queste cose tessendo, né dal monte
Parnaso né dalle Muse non mi allontano quanto molti per avventura s'avvisano. [35–36]

[ladies have caused me to compose a thousand lines of poetry in the
course of my life, whereas the Muses never caused me to write any
at all. It is true that they have helped me, and shown me *how*; and
it is possible that they have been looking over my shoulder several
times in the writing of these tales, however unassuming they may
be, perhaps because they acknowledge and respect the affinity
between the ladies and themselves. And so, in composing these
stories, I am not straying as far from Mount Parnassus or from the
Muses as many people might be led to believe.]

This passage has been taken by many critics as an open confession of
realism, and in a way it is that.[8] But the Muses are indeed as necessary
as women to the success of Boccaccio's enterprise. If—as we discover in
the course of the book—the ten young people are in several cases already familiar with the stories they are listening to,[9] then it is not just
the plot, the suspense about the ending, which captures their attention
and their admiration. Even a well-known story may give great pleasure
provided it is well told—as happens today to us with the excellent
staging of a play that we may know by heart.

This possibility of increasing one's awareness of a reality more or less
familiar but always open to further exploration with the help of the
Muses, is in no place so beautifully stated as in the sixth day of the
Decameron. In no other *giornata* does storytelling appear to be, as here,
so subtle an interplay between words and facts, an activity peculiar to
civilized men and women—both an exquisite pastime and a way to
prove one's nobility without seeking religious or political investiture.
Furthermore, the *ars narrandi* formulated and exemplified by Boccaccio
in this giornata is in itself the best warning (as I shall try to show)
against the two tendencies that some critics succeed in combining
today: to make literature, or verbal strategy, the only content of

literature; and to make of a literary text an ethnological document, ignoring most of its historical and stylistic connotations in the name of a *grammaire universelle*.

On the sixth day, "the discussion turns upon those who, on being provoked by some verbal pleasantry, have returned like for like, or who, by a prompt retort or shrewd manoeuvre, have avoided danger, discomfiture or ridicule." So, as the whole *Decameron* tells about ten people whose chief pastime and raison d'être is storytelling, on the sixth day these ten people speak about characters who are interesting chiefly because they know how to speak. And the choice of the theme has immediate and remarkable consequences for the length, the setting, and the construction of the tales.

To be effective, witticisms must be witty and short, we are told by Filomena, the first storyteller of the day.[10] In fact, the tales of this *giornata* are the shortest in the whole book, with the exception of the last one, told by Dioneo. In order to be witty, clever retorts obviously require clever persons to make them; but no less necessary is a community of language and of customs between the author of the sally or *motto* and his victim, and between these and their audiences, and I use the plural because usually the witty exchange takes place in front of other characters in the story; and then, of course, there are the nine young people of the *brigata* who listen from outside the story but within the book.

What is needed, to use an expression fashionable in our semiotic days, is a common code to insure a prompt and faithful reception of the witty message. Now, out of ten stories, five take place in Florence, three (those of Oretta, no. 1, of Chichibio, no. 4, and of Giotto, no. 5) in the country just outside the city, and the remaining two (those of Filippa, no. 7, and of Friar Cipolla, no. 10) in other Tuscan towns not far from Florence— Prato and Certaldo, respectively.

Even today Florentines are often convinced that they are by far the wittiest people in Italy, and probably Boccaccio was not free from this foible. But in order to convince ourselves that chauvinism is certainly not the main reason for the pervasive "Florentinity" of the sixth day, it is enough to take notice of other significant features, such as the recurrence in several stories of the same *belle e laudevoli usanze* ("excellent and commendable customs"), like the parties of merry young people in the stories of Oretta, of Michele Scalza (no. 6), and of Guido Cavalcanti (no. 9); or the repetition of the same proverbial sayings, for instance, "as ugly as the ugliest Baronci," also in three tales; or again, the fact that the fictional time of the stories, that is, the time in which the events related in them are supposed to happen, is always close to the present of the narrators—that year, 1348, in which the stories are supposed to be told.

The result of all these devices is to diminish the distance, which is always well marked in the other days, between the universe of the tales—colorful, adventurous, sometimes coarse—and the universe of the frame, that is, of the ten refined storytellers, with its elegant and repetitious rituals. In fact, as has been remarked by some critics, the two stylistic levels come so close at the beginning of the sixth day as to produce a sort of two-way crossing or double overlapping. In the introduction to the giornata, before the young people start telling their stories, a violent quarrel breaks out between two of their servants about the greater or lesser probability, if any, that Florentine girls are still virgins when they marry—a quarrel that brings the comic, heavily allusive language of the people into the gracious and stylized world of the brigata. As if to balance this vulgar intrusion, the first, very short tale—the protagonist of which is a beautiful and noble Florentine lady walking with some friends in the countryside—clearly introduces into the realm of the *novelle* the leisurely, contemplative mood of the frame.

All this creates between the people of the brigata and the characters about whom they speak a close complicity that is a distinctive feature of the sixth day and is sustained throughout the ten stories. In the tenth, however, the gullible peasants of Certaldo and Friar Cipolla's abominable servant, Guccio Balena alias Guccio Porco, will provide a sharp contrast with the idyllic scene that follows immediately in the conclusion of the giornata, when the seven young ladies of the company bathe chastely naked in a delightful pool, far from the eyes of their male companions: and thus a clear borderline is finally reestablished between the two worlds.[11]

So far I have stressed the aspects of our giornata which make for a homogeneous linguistic and social background, conducive to the *leggiadri motti*. But this by no means implies repetitiousness or monotony. As in other days where the stories are closely bound together by the theme (that of tragic love in the fourth giornata, for example), a first element of variety is provided by the difference of the characters in terms of social position, culture, and intelligence.

At the top of the ladder, first in the admiration of Boccaccio and his ten storytellers, are the great artists: Giotto the painter (story no. 5), and Cavalcanti the poet and "natural philosopher" (no. 9); one step below are the noble and rich men of good taste, like Geri Spina (no. 2) and Currado Gianfigliazzi (no. 4), and also the great scholars like Forese da Rabatta (no. 5); not far after these come the commoners of parts and wit like Cisti the baker (no. 2), Michele Scalza the clubman, or even a clever friar like Cipolla; and at the bottom, dim-witted, bizarre servants like Chichibìo and Guccio.

As for the ladies, we go from Oretta, wife of Geri Spina (no. 1), *gentile e costumata donna e ben parlante* ("a lady of silver tongue and gentle breeding"); to Nonna de' Pulci (no. 3), *fresca e bella giovane e parlante e di gran cuore* ("a fine-looking girl in the flower of youth, well-spoken and full of spirit"); to Madonna Filippa (no. 7), *gentile donna e bella e di gran cuore* ("a gentlewoman lovely and big-hearted"); to Cesca (no. 8), still noble and pretty but an awful bore; down to the utterly repulsive Nuta, the sweaty and greasy maid courted by Guccio in Certaldo (no. 10)—a girl, says Dioneo, whose breasts were as big as dung baskets.

If I have cited Boccaccio's definitions of all these feminine characters, it is because here we begin to perceive the complex dialectic between reality and words that runs through the *giornata* and indeed the whole *Decameron*. We have heard that the Muses must help Boccaccio to write about women, which means—as we shall see better in a moment—that it is the elegance and variety of stylistic treatment which bestow literary interest on characters interesting in life and make their adventures "narrable." But once the narrative situation has been created, then different psychological realities may bear the same labels. On the one hand, characterizations like *gentile*, *costumata*, *bella*, *di gran cuore*, may express the same moral judgment applied to different cases: so that, for instance, the generous adultery of Madonna Filippa, whose potential for love far exceeds her husband's modest needs, is as praiseworthy as the jealous virtue of Nonna de' Pulci, the young Florentine bride publicly teased by the bishop.

Alternatively, applied to contexts utterly different, the same formulae become revealing and amusing just because of their sameness. Take Chichibìo, the Venetian cook who, after giving his sweetheart a leg of the crane that he was roasting, maintains to his master that cranes have only one leg; and when, taken the next day to the pond for a field verification, he sees the birds asleep standing on one leg, he shows them *prestamente* (swiftly) to the angry Currado. We find the same adverb when Giotto, teased by his neighbor and friend Forese, the great scholar who is just as ugly ("Giotto, supposing we were to meet some stranger who had never seen you before, do you think he would believe that you were the greatest painter in the world?"), answers *prestamente*: "Messere, credo che egli il crederebbe allora che, guardando voi, egli crederebbe che voi sapeste l'abicì" ("Sir, I think he would believe it if, after taking a look at you, he gave you credit for knowing your *ABC*'s"). And again Guido Cavalcanti, cornered and bantered by Betto Brunelleschi and his friends among the marble tombs near San Giovanni, says to them *prestamente*: "Signori, voi mi potete dire a casa vostra ciò che vi piace" ("Gentlemen, in your own house you may say whatever you like to me"), meaning that because of their ignorance they are mentally as good as dead, and therefore at home among the tombs. It is evident that *prestamente* introduces with equal efficacy the automatic response of the brainless and scared Chichibìo, and the sharp retorts of Giotto and Guido, which come from a thoughtful awareness of themselves and of the world.[12]

From the same perspective, we could notice the versatility of a stylistic pattern, the sequence of three adjectives tied together by assonances and alliterations. In story no. 8, Cesca is said to be *spiacevole, sazievole e stizzosa* ("disagreeable, petulant, and insipid"); in story no. 10 Cipolla describes his servant by multiplying the same pattern by three. Guccio, he says, is "tardo, sugliardo e bugiardo: / nigligente, disubidiente e maldicente: / trascutato, smemorato e scostumato" ("untruthful, distasteful, and slothful; / negligent, disobedient, and truculent; / careless, witless, and graceless"—p. 17). And a little further on in the same tale, his flirt, the buxom maid of Certaldo, is described by Dioneo as being *sudata, unta e affumicata* ("plastered with sweat, grease, and soot").

Now it seems clear to me that Cesca's sequence conveys the strong dislike of Emilia, the storyteller; for a character who, being a girl of her own age and social condition but unbearably tedious and fastidious, disgraces all Florentine ladies. In the nine adjectives used by Friar Cipolla for Guccio, on the contrary, we feel much indulgence and amusement, almost an owner's pride in his pet monster. Whereas the tricolon depicting Nuta, the scullery lass, is far more denotative than connotative: it tells just the way she is, and there is no reason she should not be that way, since she appears as attractive to Guccio as she may be distasteful to others.

An equally clever mixture of analogies and variations can be found in the *motti*, or witty sayings, the main theme of the giornata and the principal justification for the stories. In two cases the witticism does not conform to the standard model provided by today's theory of communication, which assumes the existence of a *sender* of the message, a *content* to the message, and a *receiver* of it. After the sleeping cranes, scared by Currado's shouting, have put down their second legs and run away, Chichibìo objects to his master:

> Messer sì, ma voi non gridaste *ho ho* a quella di iersera; che se così gridato aveste, ella avrebbe così l'altra coscia e l'altro piè fuor mandata, come hanno fatto queste. [18]

> [Indeed, sir . . . but you never shouted "Oho!" to the one you had last night, otherwise it would have shoved its second leg out, as these others have done.]

Currado laughs and forgives; but the fact is that Chichibìo is not immediately aware of the comic impact of his words: what he says, his message, becomes a *leggiadro motto* only when and because it is received by Currado.

If here we have a sally duly appreciated but involuntary, in tale no. 8 we find just the opposite, one that is perfectly intentional but not understood. One day Cesca, the waspish and dull girl, is complaining that at a party she had met only tedious people, and her uncle retorts: "Figliuola, se così ti dispiaccion gli spiacevoli, come tu di', se tu vuoi viver lieta, non ti specchiare giammai" ("If you can't bear the sight of horrid people, my girl, I advise you, for your own peace of mind, never to look at yourself in the glass"). But Cesca, concludes Emilia the storyteller,

> più che una canna vana e a cui di senno pareva pareggiar Salamone, non altramenti che un montone avrebbe fatto, intese il vero motto di Fresco; anzi disse che ella si voleva specchiar come l'altre; e così nella sua grossezza si rimase e ancor vi si sta. [10]

> [whose head was emptier than a hollow reed even though she imagined herself to be as wise as Solomon, might have been a

carcass of mutton for all she understood of Fresco's real meaning, and she told him that she intended to look in the glass just like any other woman. So she remained as witless as before, and she is still the same to this day.]

This time the message, sent intentionally, is never properly received, at least by its primary target: fortunately, the nine listeners of the brigata are there to glean it, outside of the tale but well within the book.

Between these two extremes are the characters who understand the *motto* addressed to them immediately, and those who need to have it explained. The servant Geri Spina sends to Cisti, the generous baker, to ask for some of his exquisite white wine, but who has taken along too big a bottle, is repeatedly told by Cisti: "Figliuolo, messer Geri non ti manda a me" ("Messer Geri has not sent you to me, my lad"); and when finally, instructed by Geri, he asks: "To whom is he sending me then?" Cisti answers: "To the Arno." But only the master will be able to interpret the baker's riposte to his servant: by going to see Cisti with such a large bottle, he had treated his wine as casually as if it were the Arno's water.

Again, there are those who, hit by a witty retort, take it *en connois-seurs* and if anything feel closer to their assailant; and those for whom the witticism resounds as a bitter, if well-deserved, lesson that they have to swallow in silence. The bishop of Florence, who teases in public a young and virtuous bride, Nonna de' Pulci (tale no. 3), is sharply reminded by her of a scandal that occurred recently in his own family, so that the bishop and his companion, a Catalan gentleman who had played a major role in that scandal, "senza guardar l'un l'altro, vergognosi e taciti se n'andarono, senza più quel giorno dirle alcuna cosa" ("without so much as looking at one another, rode away silent and shamefaced, and said no more to Monna Nonna that day").

The same tale provides the opportunity for another distinction: the *motti* may be gratuitous, provoked, or necessary. They are gratuitous when they spring from the leisurely and playful milieu of Florentine parties, and aim only to amuse, like the intimation (in story no. 6) that the members of the Baronci family—notoriously the ugliest people in Florence—must be also the noblest, because things created first are nobler and the ugliness of the Baronci proves that God made them before all others, when he was still clumsy and learning his trade. Sallies are provoked when told to pay a joker in the same coin, and the bite will be more or less stinging according to the gravity of the provocation. Finally, they may be necessary to avoid a serious danger, such as the whipping awaiting Chichibìo, or destruction, like the death sentence hanging over the pretty head of Madonna Filippa in tale no. 7. Publicly tried for adultery in a city, Prato, where this crime (if we are to believe the storyteller) calls for capital punishment, Filippa admits the fact, extols at length the merits of her lover, and finally entreats the mayor, who acts as judge, to ask her husband whether she has ever shunned his conjugal desires. And at the husband's negative answer, this is her reply:

> "Adunque" seguì prestamente la donna "domando io voi, messer podestà, se egli ha sempre di me preso quello che gli è bisognato e piaciuto, io che doveva fare o debbo di quel che gli avanza? debbolo io gittare ai cani? non è egli molto meglio servirne un gentile uomo che più che sé m'ama, che non lasciarlo perdere o guastare?" [17]

> ["Well then," the lady promptly continued, "if he has always taken as much of me as he needed and as much as he chose to take, I ask you, Messer Podesta, what am I to do with the surplus? Throw it to the dogs? Is it not far better that I should present it to a gentleman who loves me more dearly than himself, rather than allow it to turn bad or go to waste?"]

In one way, the forceful self-defense of Filippa threatened with death in front of the citizens of Prato can be linked with the sermon of Frate Cipolla when he is threatened with *scorno* and shame in front of the people of Certaldo. Perhaps it is not by accident that these two stories, in which a complex verbal strategy replaces the flashing *motto*, are also the only ones placed in cities other than Florence. But Filippa talks profusely because she knows exactly where she is going and she wishes to awaken the conscience of her fellow citizens: while Cipolla launches into the long story of his improbable travels and wondrous relics for much the opposite reason, because, after finding coals in the box out of which he had promised to produce the feather of the Archangel Gabriel, he wants to buy time and lull his audience into believing the explanation for the metamorphosis on which his brain is working in the meantmie.

In another way, it seems to me that Madonna Filippa's dogs ("What am I to do with the surplus? Throw it to the dogs?") occupy the extreme

end of calculated crudity and at the same time, so to speak, of con-
sumer-oriented good sense ("Is it not far better that I should present it
to a gentleman . . . rather than allow it to turn bad or go to waste?")—
the extreme end, I would say, of a rhetorical range, at the opposite end
of which we find the graciously allusive metaphor of the horse used by
Madonna Oretta.

To this lady a gentleman, while they are walking in the country with
some friends, had proposed a ride "gran parte della via che ad andare
abbiamo, a cavallo con una delle belle novelle del mondo" ("to carry
her on horseback with one of the most beautiful tales in the world")[13]—
that is, to alleviate the weariness of the long walk by telling her a story.
But he is such a poor storyteller that Oretta cannot stand him for very
long, and says: "Messere, questo vostro cavallo ha troppo duro trotto,
per che io vi priego che vi piaccia di pormi a piè" ("Sir, this horse of
yours trots too roughly, I beg you to put me down and allow me to go
on foot").

These, Boccaccio would probably say, are dogs and horses that
women borrow from the Muses when they have made friends with
them. But since such animals, in their respective stories, are neither
agent nor acted upon—in fact, do not even exist—I am afraid that they
would be of little use to the strict narratologist.

We have seen how all the tales are centered on or around Florence.
Even within this municipal microcosm, reality offers to the eye of the
storyteller an inexhaustible gamut of situations, cases, and characters
which can be organized by analogy (the common theme of the *leggiadri
motti*) or classified according to the social rank and the personal merit
of the protagonists, from Cavalcanti and Geri down to Chichibìo and
Guccio, but which become "narrable" only if and when the storyteller
finds one of the stylistic ciphers that each one of those contexts suggests.
I say *one* and *suggests*, rather than *the* and *requires*, because Boccaccio's
youthful narrators are not simply obeying the rhetorical principle of
stylistic convenience—that is, to put it in another way, because Boccaccio is not Dante.

For Dante matter and style are—or should be—locked together in a
relationship of necessity: *nomina sunt consequentia rerum*, the immutable order of things created must be paralleled and mirrored by that of
signs: so that, for instance, once the value of an inspiration has been
recognized, one ought simply to follow it ("I' mi son un, che quando

/ Amor mi spira, noto," *Purg.* 24.52–53). And conversely, when a specific way of life has been found wrong and left behind—say, the habit of exchanging injurious and bawdy sonnets, as in Dante's *tenzone* with Forese Donati—one should automatically repudiate the style connected with that experience. Let us remember, in *Inferno* 30, Dante's sheer curiosity for the masterful exchange of nasty retorts between Maestro Adamo and Sinon the Greek, and Virgil's biting reprimand to his pupil, possibly the harshest in the whole poem: "Or pur mira! / Ch'è per poco che teco non mi risso. . . . Ché voler ciò udire è bassa voglia" ("See here, / I am not far from falling out with you! . . . For liking to hear such things is a low taste").[14]

Clearly, for Dante there was only one way to write the *Commedia.* One could object that there was just one way to write the *Decameron* too: but for Boccaccio each storyteller of the brigata is free and faced with a double choice—the choice of the specific tale he or she is going to tell within a given theme, and the choice of the mode in which he or she is going to tell it—and each time he or she bears full responsibility for it before the other members of the company. Take, for example, the beginning of the tenth tale, where Dioneo suggests that Frate Cipolla was always welcome in Certaldo "forse non meno per lo nome che per altra divozione . . . con ciò sia cosa che quel terreno produca cipolle famose per tutta Toscana" ("doubtless due as much to his name as to the piety of the inhabitants, for the soil in those parts produces onions that are famous throughout the whole of Tuscany," p. 6). Here the principle that I have just recalled, *nomina sunt consequentia rerum*, finds a playful, paradoxical application, which in turn preludes thematically the anthropomorphic inventions in Cipolla's sermon, where among other startling relics are mentioned the clothes of the Holy Catholic Faith and the jawbones of the Death of Saint Lazarus— "e de' vestimenti della Santa Fé cattolica . . . e la mascella della Morte di San Lazzaro." The illusionistic, almost surrealistic, dynamics of the tale is announced from the outset by a conscious verbal decision of the storyteller, Dioneo.

No less significant is the different treatment given to the same situation in two stories: in both the second (Geri Spina and Cisti) and the ninth (Guido Cavalcanti), we have a leisurely walk through the most familiar streets of Florence. But in the case of Geri and his guests, the Roman ambassadors, the promenade reaches an eminently visual, pictorial climax in front of Cisti who, wearing a white doublet and a freshly laundered apron over it, sits by his door and, taking a small Bolognese jug out of a tin pail of fresh water, pours his precious white wine into "bicchieri che parevan d'ariento, sì eran chiari" ("wineglasses, that gleamed as brightly as if they were made of silver"), as in a miniature or a Flemish panel. Whereas Guido's solitary walk ends in a web of literary allusions, with the poet thinking fast and talking short, quite alive among the tombs, as though to recall and reverse the predicament in which Dante had found his father Cavalcante in the sixth circle of Hell.

This freedom and variety of verbal and iconographic invention, naturally, is not peculiar to the sixth giornata: but here better than anywhere else the author shows that such stylistic flexibility is the condition for capturing in a good story the mutable flavor of reality— that is, the condition of fiction itself. In this sense, no other tale is as revealing as the first one of this giornata. Filomena recounts that Oretta, wife of Geri Spina,

> per avventura essendo in contado, come noi siamo, e da un luogo ad un altro andando per via di diporto insieme con donne e con cavalieri, li quali a casa sua il dì avuti avea a desinare, ed essendo forse la via lunghetta di là onde si partivano a colà dove tutti a piè d'andare intendevano, disse uno de' cavalieri della brigata: "Madonna Oretta, quando voi vogliate, io vi porterò, gran parte della via che ad andare abbiamo, a cavallo con una delle belle novelle del mondo". Al quale la donna rispuose: "Messere, anzi ve ne priego io molto, e sarammi carissimo".
>
> Messer lo cavaliere, al quale forse non stava meglio la spada allato che 'l novellar nella lingua, udito questo, cominciò una sua novella, la quale nel vero da sé era bellissima, ma egli or tre e quattro volte replicando una medesima parola, e ora indietro tornando, e talvolta dicendo: "Io non dissi bene", e spesso ne' nomi errando, un per un altro ponendone, fieramente la guastava: senza che egli pessimamente, secondo la qualità delle persone e gli atti che accadevano, proffereva. Di che a madonna Oretta, udendolo, spesse volte veniva un sudore e uno sfinimento di cuore, come se inferma fosse stata per terminare; la qual cosa poi che più sofferir non poté, conoscendo che il cavaliere era entrato nel

pecoreccio né era per uscirne, piacevolmente disse: "Messere, questo vostro cavallo ha troppo duro trotto, per che io vi priego che vi piaccia di pormi a piè". [6–11]

[finding herself in the countryside like ourselves, and proceeding from place to place, by way of recreation, with a party of knights and ladies whom she had entertained to a meal in her house earlier in the day, one of the knights turned to her, and, perhaps because they were having to travel a long way, on foot, to the place they all desired to reach, he said: "Madonna Oretta, if you like I shall take you riding along a goodly stretch of our journey by telling you one of the finest tales in the world."

"Sir," replied the lady, "I beseech you most earnestly to do so, and I shall look upon it as a great favor." Whereupon this worthy knight, whose swordplay was doubtless on a par with his story-telling, began to recite his tale, which in itself was indeed excellent. But by constantly repeating the same phrases, and recapitulating sections of the plot, and every so often declaring that he had "made a mess of that bit," and regularly confusing the names of the characters, he ruined it completely. Moreover, his mode of delivery was totally out of keeping with the characters and the incidents he was describing, so that it was painful for Madonna Oretta to listen to him. She began to perspire freely, and her heart missed several beats, as though she had fallen ill and was about to give up the ghost. And in the end, when she could endure it no longer, having perceived that the knight had tied himself inextricably in knots, she said to him, in affable tones: "Sir, you have taken me riding on a horse that trots very jerkily. Pray be good enough to set me down."]

Placed exactly at the center of the *Decameron*, this extraordinary little tale seems to me truly to contain a *poetica in nuce* of the whole book, with a function similar to that performed, in some altarpieces of the fifteenth century, by the small object—a lamp, an egg—which hangs from the summit of the apse *en trompe-l'oeil* just above the head of the Virgin, and summarizes at the center the rhythm and the geometric tension of the whole composition. The remarks that Madonna Oretta suggests will also be the conclusions of this discussion.

First of all, a clear distinction is made between the potential beauty of a story ("una sua novella, la quale nel vero da sé era bellissima") and the responsibility of the narrator ("fieramente la guastava"). Second, the miserable failure of the knight makes Filomena wonder whether he is really a gentleman ("al quale forse non stava meglio la spada allato che 'l novellar nella lingua"): as if the traditional requirements of nobility, "valore e cortesia," or else "il pregio della borsa e della spada," as Dante had written in the *Purgatorio*, should by now be completed by, and tested against, another virtue, both individual and socially oriented, that of "ben parlare."[15] Third and even more interesting is the effect of the knight's failure on Oretta herself. As Boccaccio, by means of his book, is actually and actively consoling the fair ladies for "il peccato della Fortuna," likewise and conversely our gentleman, by telling his story so badly, provokes in Oretta a very physical malaise, making her literally sweat, and her heart sink as if she were going to die.

Once again we are reminded of the power of words over reality; literature and life could hardly be closer than they appear to be here. But this is not all because, fourth, the tale is at the same time the negative exposition of a craft as far as its plot goes, and the positive illustration of the same craft as far as its style goes. If the knight offers with his mistakes a perfect example of how a story ought never to be told, Filomena, who speaks so vividly about those mistakes, gives us an equally perfect example of how he should have acquitted himself of his task. What was so painful for Madonna Oretta is again pleasurable for the nine listeners and for us. Life and literature are once again quite distinct, although by no means alien to each other.

Many things in life are not understood or, to use Madonna Filippa's metaphor, go to the dogs—from the witty advice of Cesca's uncle, to the doomed heroism of Ghismonda and other women in love on the tragic fourth day. To write their story as deftly as Filomena tells that of Madonna Oretta is also to make sense of something that otherwise would be totally wasted, to salvage in terms of culture what has been lost in terms of life because of time, human malice, or just bad luck. That is why it is possible to envisage the *Decameron*, quite literally, as Boccaccio's answer to the plague (an event that obviously stands for a greater social and historical crisis), without detracting from its literary nature and poetic quality.

NOTES

1. I am translating—with the omission of a few words—from Tzvetan Todorov, *Littérature et signification* (Paris: Larousse, 1967), p. 49.

2. See, for instance, the first two chapters of Victor Shklovskiĭ, *Khudozhestvennaia proza; razmyshleniia i razbory* (Moscow: Sovetskiĭ pisatel', 1959), which I know in the Italian translation of A. Ivanov: *Lettura del "Decameron". Dal romanzo d'avventura al romanzo di carattere* (Bologna: Il Mulino, 1969), or Hans-Jörg Neuschafer, *Boccaccio und der Beginn der Novelle; Strukturen der Kurzerzählung auf der Schwelle zwischen Mittelalter und Neuzeit* (Munich: W. Fink, 1969). A critical hypostasis of the *novella* genre underlies most of the studies by various authors, edited by André Rochon in the volume *Formes et significations de la "beffa" dans la littérature italienne de la Renaissance* (Paris: Université de la Sorbonne nouvelle, 1972; on Boccaccio, pp. 11–44: Anna Fontes-Baratto, "Le thème de la *beffa* dans le *Décaméron*"). Some interesting pages are devoted to Boccaccio by Robert E. Scholes and Robert Kellogg, in *The Nature of Narrative* (New York: Oxford University Press, 1966), passim. For the most recent criticism on Boccaccio, see the review articles by Cesare De Michelis in *Studi sul Boccaccio* 6 (1971): 263–79, and "Rassegna boccacciana (Dieci anni di studi)," *Lettere italiane* 25 (1973): 88–129.

3. I am referring in particular to issue no. 8 (1966) of *Communications*, entirely devoted to "L'analyse structurale du récit," with articles by Roland Barthes, Claude Bremond, Gérard Genette, etc.

4. Vladimir Propp, *Morphology of the Folktale*, trans. Laurence Scott, with an introduction by Svatava Pirkova-Jakobson, 2d ed. rev. Louis A. Wagner (Austin: University of Texas Press, 1968).

5. *Grammaire du Décaméron* (The Hague: Mouton, 1969), p. 63. Much more rigorous and convincing—both for the wise choice of the giornata and for the competence of the author—is the study in the same direction by Cesare Segre, "Funzioni, opposizioni e simmetrie nella giornata VII del *Decameron*," *Studi sul Boccaccio* 6 (1971): 81–108.

6. See the *Proemio* in Giovanni Boccaccio, *Decameron*, ed. Vittore Branca (Florence: Le Monnier, 1951), 1: 3–7. I shall follow this edition in all my citations from the sixth giornata (2: 125–95), giving the paragraph numbers only in the case of the longer passages.

7. *The Decameron*, trans. with an introduction by G. H. McWilliam (Harmondsworth: Penguin Books, 1972), p. 833. This is the translation quoted throughout.

8. See, for example, Carlo Salinari in his commented edition of the *Decameron* (Bari: Laterza, 1972), 1: 286.

9. This is the conclusion to be drawn from the opening remark of Queen Elissa in the ninth tale of the sixth day: "Quantunque, leggiadre donne, oggi mi sieno da voi state tolte da due in su delle novelle delle quali io m'avea pensato di doverne una dire, nondimeno me n'è pure una rimasa da raccontare" ("although you have

deprived me of at least two of the stories that I thought of telling you today, I still have another in reserve").

10. In a long *prolago* to the first tale which—as was already noticed by Francesco Mannelli, the first commentator on the *Decameron* in the fourteenth century—repeats, often verbatim, Pampinea's introductory speech in the tenth tale of the first day; in both passages the regret the storyteller expresses at seeing that "oggi poche o non niuna donna rimasa ci è, la qual ne sappi ne' tempi opportuni dire alcuno [motto] . . . general vergogna di tutte noi" ("few if any women remain today who can produce a witticism at the right moment . . . to the universal shame of all of us") is perhaps reminiscent of Dante's regret about the scarce demand for laurel in his day: "Sì rade volte, padre, se ne coglie / Per triunfare cesare o poeta, / Colpa e vergogna dell'umane voglie," *Paradiso* 1.28–30 ["So rarely, father, is the foliage plucked / For triumph of a Caesar or a bard / —Ah shameful waywardness of our desires!—"]. *The Divine Comedy*, trans. Thomas G. Bergin and illus. Leonard Basking (New York: Grossman, 1969), 3: 3.

11. For the relationship between the Oretta and Cipolla tales and the *cornice*, see respectively Giovanni Getto, *Vita di forme e forme di vita nel "Decameron"* (Turin: G. B. Petrini, 1958), pp. 29–30, 139–42, and my study "Il sorriso di Messer Torello (*Decameron*, X, 9)," *Romance Philology* 23 (1969): 157–58.

12. For the frequent recurrence and extraordinary versatility of the key adverb *prestamente* in Boccaccio's masterpiece, see *Concordanza del "Decameron,"* ed. Alfredo Barbina (Florence: Barbèra-Giunti, 1969), s.v.

13. For this and the next short citation I prefer to give my own translation, more literal if inelegant.

14. *Inferno* 30.131–32, 148: Bergin trans., 1: 220–21.

15. For the notion of a new intellectual aristocracy implicit in Filomena's doubt, see Mario Baratto, *Realtà e stile nel "Decameron"* (Venice: Neri Pozza, 1970), pp. 74–76, where the first full appreciation of this tale also appears: "una novella . . . il cui effettivo contenuto è l'esercizio stesso del novellare." Certainly independent of Baratto's book, which he does not mention, is Guido Almansi, "Lettura della novella di Madonna Oretta," *Paragone-Letteratura* 270 (August 1972): 139–42. For Almansi, too, "si tratta . . . di una metanovella, cioè di una novella sull'arte di novellare"; but then the story itself ("una delle più fragili di tutta l'opera; banale, quasi insignificante l'episodio; inesistente la caratterizzazione dei personaggi, fiacca la battuta finale") is unnecessarily sacrificed on the altar of the *signifiant*: "La novella di Madonna Oretta è un aperto invito a una lettura formalistica del testo."

Only after completing this essay was I able to see Gilbert Bosetti, "Lecture 'structurale' de la sixième journée du Décaméron," *Bulletin d'Information du Centre de Documentation et de Recherches Bibliographiques de l'Université de Grenoble* 25–26 (June-December 1970): 36–46. In spite of a few curious distractions and misinterpretations, Bosetti's article is a remarkable attempt to analyze the sixth day in the light of Lacan's theories on metaphor and metonymy. Some of my observations are anticipated by his "structural" reading, and are organized in a totally different and more rigorous—if sometimes far-fetched—construction.

10

Alberti's Linguistic Innovations

Michael Vena

The Renaissance concept of *homo faber* was actualized even linguistically in the case of Leon Battista Alberti, who demonstrated in a quintessential way his capacity to rejuvenate the vernacular forms of tradition, just as he opened up entirely new prospects for the Renaissance. Cristoforo Landino, a fellow humanist, recognized the innovative character of Alberti's language in his opening lecture on Petrarca's sonnets at the Studio Fiorentino, and expressed his views on this matter very explicitly:

> I firmly believe that no man can be found who has displayed greater industry in enlarging our language than Battista Alberti. I ask you to read his books, which are numerous and touch on many subjects. Observe with what industry he has contrived to bring to us every elegance, every construction, every refinement that can be found among Latin writers.[1]

To be sure, one could hardly claim that, since Landino, critics have failed to recognize the wealth of Alberti's linguistic contributions. Nevertheless, they have failed to appreciate his full power to invigorate a whole stock of words and expressions, inherited mostly from Latin, which he introduced functionally into the stream of vernacular discourse, thereby elevating it. Such innovative qualities are only a part of the gamut of his artistic genius. Indeed, his importance as a central figure of the early Renaissance need hardly be stressed here, for he is certainly one of the most versatile personalities of the period: man of letters, philosopher, artist, scientist.

243

On Alberti as a universal man and on the wide range of his interests, there are well-known works by Girolamo Mancini, Paul Henri Michel, Giovanni Santinello, Joan Gadol, and of course Eugenio Garin and Paul Oskar Kristeller.[2] On the prose of Alberti and other vernacular humanists in the fifteenth century, there are some excellent studies by Bruno Migliorini, Giovanni Nencioni, Raffaele Spongano, Ghino Ghinassi, and Maurizio Dardano.[3] Lately, the most assiduous and productive cultivator of the Albertian field has been Cecil Grayson of Oxford, who has edited for Laterza the three volumes of Alberti's complete vernacular works.[4] In his notes on these texts and in various articles,[5] Grayson has given us many insights into particular aspects of Alberti's composition, such as orthography, phonology, and morphology.

We still lack, however, an exhaustive and well-articulated linguistic analysis that would fully reveal the committed awareness present in Alberti's literary output. Along the same lines, equally rewarding might be an attempt to correlate Alberti's linguistic theory with his own literary practice. We have nothing on Alberti comparable to Gianfranco Folena's study of Sannazaro, Ghino Ghinassi's of Poliziano, or Pier Vincenzo Mengaldo's of Boiardo.[6] Folena addressed himself, a few years ago, to the need for such research, and particularly to the value of a study of Alberti's bilingualism (Latin and Italian); he hoped that we would thus be able to establish the chronology and semantic history of a large stock, in particular, of learned vocabulary.[7] Since Grayson has now completed his third and last volume of Alberti's vernacular works, the time is ripe to begin a systematic study of one of the major protagonists in Italian linguistic history.

Within the framework of this essay, I shall dwell briefly on Alberti's views of the vernacular. I shall then deal with the lexical contributions Alberti incorporates into his literary production, with some emphasis on the physiognomy of such innovations. Finally, I shall conclude by stressing the correlation between these linguistic phenomena and the spiritual and intellectual experience which, through Alberti's expressive medium, helps shape the configuration of ideas of the early Renaissance. For the most part, my observations are based on the moral treatises of the author, collected in the second volume of the Grayson edition. Aside from their content dealing with matters of an ethical and civic nature, as well as with a general outlook on the world, these works bear witness to that linguistic symbiosis between Latin and Italian which constitutes an integral part of Alberti's humanism; they serve as background for our discussions on the lexical wealth which Alberti draws from his vast erudition and from contemporary experience.

Concerning Alberti's linguistic views, it is necessary for us to understand the context in which he faced the so-called linguistic crisis. There is a prevailing notion that after Boccaccio's death the vernacular remained conspicuously sterile for almost a century. Although we can accept such statements only with proper reservations, especially when we think of the vigor displayed by the literary genres in the vernacular of this period, it is an undeniable fact that vernacular prose did lapse into a role of secondary importance. Vernacular output simply cannot compare with the booming success that accompanied the resurgence of Latin and the enthusiasm generated by the humanists in their quest to recapture the ancient splendor of the Roman Golden Age by writing in Latin. But their triumph was short-lived. Their efforts, however praiseworthy, were bound to fail. As Raffaele Spongano points out, the evolution of their language is such that even those who declared themselves against the vernacular could not help seeing its image reflected in their Latin: "Di Roma usavano i vocaboli e la morfologia, ma non il modo di atteggiare il pensiero" ("from Rome they had inherited vocabulary and syntax, but not their frame of mind").[8]

Consequently, the development of the vernacular, which already had made vigorous progress with Dante, Petrarca, and Boccaccio, could not be interrupted. On the contrary, with a revival of literary taste for Latin, a sort of *transfusion of characters* and *exchange of experience*—if not a real marriage—was inevitable between the two languages. Therefore we cannot say that either language prevailed. Instead, we have a sui generis recurrence of the Horatian conception, "Graecia capta ferum victorem cepit" (Horace, *Epist.* 2. 1, 156), in that the conqueror and the conquered each fell under the spell of the other, but at the same time the subdued vernacular, precisely through this process of osmosis, took on new vigor and effectiveness.

While the process became institutionalized, animating the discussions of men of letters and scholars in general, there came on the scene the dynamic personality of Leon Battista Alberti, who deserves credit for upholding the merits of the literary vernacular during critical times. As Cecil Grayson puts it:

Convinced that the Tuscan language, despite its origin in the corruption of Latin was not in itself deficient as a medium, but only lacking in writers of merit who had used it or would use it, he wrote in the vernacular in the middle of the fifteenth century several major works of humanistic character and content, believing so to benefit a greater number of his fellow men.[9]

Aside from Alberti's many labors on behalf of the vernacular, there remain some writings of his that attest to his ideas and illustrate his study of this particular topic. We shall survey some of them.

From 1432 on, Alberti attended diligently to the elaboration of the first three books of his *Famiglia*, to which a fourth was added later. This treatise on the family is a work of distinctly humanistic character, dealing with topics of private and public morality: matrimony, education of the young, duties of a father, household management, friendship. In the proem to the third book we have a clear indication of his ethical as well as his civic commitments, to be considered here in linguistic terms. Specifically, he spells out the importance he gives to matters of language; he claims that by writing in the vernacular he will be of benefit to the largest possible number of fellow citizens, and that the vernacular idiom is the most suitable medium for communicating the merits of ancient and modern wisdom for the "bene e beato vivere" of every citizen in the state.

These thoughts are reiterated in his prefatory remarks to another treatise of sociopolitical import, *Teogenio*. Alberti here makes two important points. The first one, as in the proem, presents didactic considerations; in the second one, of an apologetic nature, Alberti wants to show his appreciation to Lionello D'Este who, unlike others, does not take issue with Alberti for writing in the lowly vernacular. This reflects the linguistic polemics of that period. In fact, it is significant that Alberti dedicates his work to Lionello, a great patron of the arts, who constituted, along with Alberti, Piero de' Medici, and Lorenzo, a nucleus of the most earnest supporters of vernacular literature in the fifteenth century. Lionello's court in Ferrara became one of the main centers of intellectual and artistic revival in Europe. He was instrumental in attracting to his court some of the best minds, among them (besides Alberti) the highly respected humanist teacher Guarino Veronese, who had much to do with the education of Alberti himself. In the dedicatory letter to *Teogenio*, Alberti writes:

Tanto t'affermo, io scrissi questi libretti non ad altri che a me per consolare me stessi in mie avverse fortune. E parsemi da scrivere in modo ch'io fussi inteso da' miei non littcratissimi cittadini. Certo conobbi a questa opera giovò, e sollevommi afflitto. E vedoli pur richiesti da molti più che se io gli avessi scritti latini.

[I'll tell you this much: I wrote these books for myself rather than for others, to console myself in my adverse fortune. And it seemed that I should write in a way that would be understood by my less well educated fellow-citizens. I knew for a fact it [writing in the vernacular] helped as far as this work goes, and that lifted my troubled spirit. And indeed I see them [these books] asked for by many, more so than if I had written them in Latin.][10]

As we can see, Alberti's reference to civic commitment is interwoven with the contemporary polemic on the use of language. This polemic seems to echo the controversies arising from the *certame coronario*, a poetry contest which Alberti himself organized. Undoubtedly, that competition had a precise purpose: it was meant to test the possibilities of the vernacular language as well as to forge a link between general cultural matters and the development of literature.[11] The topic of the *certame* was true friendship: it drew about a dozen participants and *gran concorso di popolo*. The winner was entitled to a silver crown fashioned in the shape of laurel fronds. This contest is very significant in that it represents, so far as we know, the first literary competition involving a prize in the history of Italian literature; it has therefore to be regarded as the true ancestor of famous contemporary prizes, such as the Strega, Viareggio, and Campiello. Far from being an idealized recognition like that conferred upon Petrarca on the Capitoline at Rome (around 1341), this contest subjected each participant to the verdict of a jury; the candidate excelling all rivals was to be judged on the basis of actual performance.

The prize was awarded to no one. I am inclined to regard this decision as indicating a Renaissance attitude of striving continuously toward an ideal which fulfillment could only impair. It is also consistent, I think, with Alberti's view that when a man reaches the top he has to think at once of the inevitability of descent or decline. Quite frankly, no winner could be as important to us now as the meaning of the competition itself and the indications we get from it of trends in Tuscan poetry of that period: on the one hand the popular tradition of Michele del Giogante, and on the other the classical inspiration of Leonardo Dati. Nor should we stop here. The main virtue of this enterprise was that Alberti conceived the establishment of a regular competition whose purpose would be tutelage over the future of Italian language and literature, and that he did so long before the birth of sixteenth-century academies—Crusca and others. We may surmise that such was also the intent of the proposed second *certame* which had envy as its subject, and that it was not a reaction to the polemics over the supposed failure of the first competition. Indirectly, Alberti gives an indication of such intent, or at least of his attitude toward it during the years immediately following the events, when in the *Profugiorum ab aerumna* he describes the *certame*:

> instituzione ottima, utile al nome e dignità della patria, atta a esercitare preclarissimi ingegni, accomodata a gran culto di buoni costumi e di virtù.

> [an excellent initiative, useful to the name and dignity of our homeland, suitable for training outstanding talents, dedicated to the encouragement of good manners and virtue.][12]

Alberti never received any official recognition as a forceful supporter of the vernacular language, although he enjoyed much fame and admiration among men of letters and artists of the Renaissance. One reason for attaining such degree of success may have been divined by Giorgio Vasari in his classic history of Renaissance men; Alberti combined creative and critical genius in the representational arts.[13] Accordingly, Vasari claimed, and he was not off the mark, that Alberti's theoretical works added luster to his practice, just as his knowledge of science and literature enhanced his position as an artist.

> But when theory and practice by chance coincide, there is nothing more seemly in our life—both because art aided by knowledge becomes much richer and more perfect and because the counsels and writings of learned artists gain more efficacy and more credence than the words or works of those who can merely exercise their gift.[14]

In Alberti's case, the combination of theory and practice did not stop with art treatises. To his tireless and varied endeavors on behalf of the vernacular, he added spontaneously the activity of codifier of the language. Not only does the artist in him live and develop, but also the objective scientific observer who devotes his attention to the details of Italian grammatical structure. The *grammatichetta vaticana*, which derives its title from the only manuscript (Vat. Reg. Lat. 1370), is the first grammar of the Italian vernacular language, and was compiled by Alberti. It was published for the first time in 1908 by Ciro Trabalza, who describes it as "the last link in a long chain" leading to the "supporters of the vernacular in the fifteenth century, among whom first place belongs to Alberti."[15] The question of the author has remained wide open for some time. More recently, Cecil Grayson and Carmela Colombo[16] have independently established the Albertian paternity of the *grammatichetta*. In his edition, Grayson points out the close relationship of Alberti's work to the Latin grammar, *Institutiones* of Priscian (ca. A.D. 500–530), and the regularity of the Latin grammatical system as it appears in Alberti. He also indicates that the *grammatichetta* incorporates, aside from syntax and phonetics, Latin grammatical terms of which we now have evidence in the vernacular.

Above all, this work provides additional proof, if not a full discussion of Alberti's views on language. He claims, along Flavio Biondo's line of thought, that Latin and Italian are not two different languages, but rather that the latter was born out of corrupted Latin and the influence of foreign invasions. Alberti has a distinct awareness of the evolution of language which is quite remarkable for the time. He dwells on the presence of neologisms, semantic variations, and word changes in the vernacular, which he partly attributes to "vizi del favellare," that is, the imperfections of casual speech. Finally, he concludes that the Tuscan language easily lends itself to such changes.

> E' vizi del favellare in ogni lingua sono o quando s'introducono alle cose nuovi nomi, o quando gli usitati si adoperano male. . . . Alieni sono in Toscana più nomi barberi, lasciativi da gente Germana, quale più tempo militò in Italia, come *elm, vulasc, sacoman, bandier* e simili. In qualche parte mutati saranno quando alle dizioni si aggiungerà o minuirà qualche lettera come chi dicesse *paire* pro *patre* . . . e quando si ponesse una lettera per un'altra, come chi dicesse; *aldisco* pro *ardisco*.[17]

[Imperfections of casual speech occur in every language, either when new words for things are introduced or when the familiar

words are not used properly . . . . Foreign in Tuscany are a number of words, left there by Germanic people who for some time
made war in Italy, such as *elm, vulasc, sacoman, bandier,* and the
like. In some part they may be changed when a letter is added to or
removed from the words, as in saying *paire* instead of *patre* . . .
and if one letter were substituted for another, as in saying *aldisco*
instead of *ardisco.*]

Alberti recognizes that there are diverse phenomena affecting the evolution of a language. Yet he also recognizes, nor should we neglect, the
humanistic conception admirably expressed by Cristoforo Landino,
that "it is necessary to be Latin for anyone who wants to be a good
Tuscan."[18] A firm indication of such theories is provided, I think, in
Alberti's vernacular writings, particularly in his prose. Accordingly, I
shall attempt to substantiate such a claim through an analysis of
Alberti's vocabulary.

In this essay the focal point of inquiry is the word, primarily in its
outward features. I shall regard the word as an inherited document, the
patrimony of everyone, from the man on the street to the great poet.
My conclusions may be of interest to historians of language. Linguistic
historians collect words individually, analyze them, determine their
meanings, and establish their origins only in relation to the wider cultural and linguistic patrimony of that period. I shall follow this procedure in my observations on the character of the vocabulary Alberti is
supposed to have introduced into the literary vernacular. It is important
to note that the real novelty of this lexicon has not been fully indicated
by any researcher thus far. The items we are dealing with represent the
"first example" of the word, or the first example in a particular semantic
variance, which the various historical-etymological dictionaries attribute to later authors or do not record at all. For the most part, they
are the latinisms—that is, words derived from classical Latin—which
occur abundantly in Alberti's works.

But along with such latinisms of humanistic taste, we find other words
of late Latin provenance, namely, from the Middle Ages or of popular
formation, which become enmeshed with the existing filaments of
Florentine language. As a result, the elevated language of tradition is
struck by a wave that we could broadly define as "bourgeois," antici-
pating, in its own unique way, circumstances that have brought about
language changes in the Italian cities of today. In this regard, it is

worth recalling that the problem of "urbanization" in Florence—
decried by Dante long ago: "new people and gains too quickly made"[19]
—corresponds to a fact which, even on a linguistic plane, in the Florentine concept of the word, will be a synonym for corruption. In the fifteenth century we witness certain trends that change literary Florentine,
either through forms coming from outside Florence or through a
phenomenon by which etymological forms are often replaced by analogical ones.

This last phenomenon makes it difficult at times for us to separate
the new from the inherited, especially in view of the general conception
of the period that Latin and vernacular Italian were substantially one
language and that it was enough to adapt the endings in order to transpose Latin words into the vernacular. It is, after all, a phenomenon that
reflects the humanistic "poetics" of returning to the authority of the
ancients in all branches of learning, and it certainly involves vocabulary,
as is demonstrated in this inquiry which illustrates the erudite and
bookish formation of the author. In reality, the entrance of Latin
vocabulary into the vernacular had illustrious precedents in the
trecento. Such a phenomenon takes on wider social dimensions in the
fifteenth century.

In the analysis of the new vocabulary which Alberti adopts functionally into the vernacular, we shall consider, for practical reasons,
three categories: adjectives, nouns, and verbs. It is necessary to stress
here that such a lexical study goes somewhat beyond an external determination of the author's linguistic fiber. The choice of lexical elements
gathered here illustrates his constant search for invigorating, challenging originality of expression which befits the totality of his humanistic
conception of the world and of reality. The words herewith presented
have not been recorded as being used for the first time in literary
language by Alberti but are attributed by historical-etymological dictionaries to *later* authors. As a general comment, we might even indicate that Alberti's smooth manipulation of new lexical matter seems
to indicate that his early vernacular writing is cast more in a colloquial
vein, whereas *Teogenio, Profugiorum ab aerumna,* and to a great extent
De Iciarchia deal with lofty matters of ancient wisdom and, as a result,
muster a much larger number of latinisms.

Adjectives

One of the most distinctive adjectival formations is that of the learned adjective. We have examples of standard classical adjectivalization (*primario, precipite*), abstract and qualifying adjectives (*pedissequo, albo*), adjectives derived from present participles (*prestante, ossequente*). A category whose frequency is quite high is that represented by adjectives with a suffix in *-abile, -ebile* (*inviolabile, indelebile*), but these are gradually replaced by the form in *-evole*; the frequency of the latter increases as Alberti continues to write in the vernacular, even though many of these adjectives in *-evole* are not new. Another series, equally noteworthy, is that of verbal adjectives formed upon past participles (*depurato, remisso, inserto*), while the learned adjective relating to a particular activity remains conspicuous throughout: allusion to a discipline (*matematico*), a text (*astronomico*), a literary genre (*lirico, comico, tragico*), a myth (*acidalio, olimpico*). Along the same lines it might be well to point out here that Alberti even attempts to transfer classical meter to vernacular poetry, as when he presents heroes and episodes of the pagan world in his hexameters for the *certame* (*Dite o mortali . . .*).

Speaking of poetry, we cannot overlook Alberti's contribution to the literary genres, particularly the pastoral eclogue and the elegy, not to mention the rest of his poetical compositions whose innovative character has been well pointed out by Grayson, Giovanni Ponte, and Piero Bigongiari.[20] There appears also in Alberti, another series, equally rich, of suffixes in *-oso* (*annoso, suspizioso*), but along with these orthodox latinisms, we notice the presence of analogical forms (*eccidioso, indegnoso, tremitoso*). There are very few compound adjectives representing for the most part cases in which the demarcation between Romance languages and Medieval Latin is not well defined (*maldestro, malfermo, malconsigliato*). Finally, we have a series of adjectives of a popular tradition which often give a sense of immediateness and informality to Alberti's language (*bitorzuto, flappo, muccilutoso, sauciato*). New adjectives in Alberti are derived mostly from nouns, a few from verbs. In rare cases, adjectives give rise to nouns.

Nouns

Alberti follows basically the same procedures in introducing nouns into his new language. We observe here, too, that a large part of his vocabulary is imported from classical Latin, and that represents the most considerable novelty. Some of these terms, merely decorative, have had a short life; they are rare items often accompanied by a familiar synonym or by synonymic iterations that normally explain the meaning of a new term (this may also be the case with adjectives and verbs). We find among such learned words a rather common and highly productive series, derivatives of participles with the suffix -*zione* (*comprobazione, enumerazione, gratificazione*). There is also a considerable series derived mostly from adjectives, with a suffix -*ta* (-*tate*) (*atrocità, venustà, superiorità, placabilità*). Another category, already conspicuous in Boccaccio's prose, is characterized by *nomina agentis* in -*tore*, less common -*trice*, of verbal derivation, which denotes a particular activity (Rohlfs, 1146) and now and then takes on the function of adjective (*delatore, ottrettatore, disturbatore, indagatrice*). Along with these words, however, we have *persuasore* and *effessore* which are indicative of the decidedly influential character of the Latin past participle in the formation of nouns. There follows, in that classification, the suffixal series of abstract nouns in -ANTIA, -ENTIA, changing in -*anza*, -*enza*, (*intolleranza, insolenza*); they are derivations from the present participle or analogical formations (Rohlfs, 1106, 1107).

On the other hand, the latinizing forms in -*izia*, -*izie* (*blandizie*) prove to be less common; these forms are replaced by the popular forms in -*ezza*. Within this large erudite family we may also note the suffixal formations in -*tudine* (*crassitudine, amplitudine, flessitudine*), abstract terms of the learned or reconstructed language (Rohlfs, 1149). Lastly, we observe the recurrence of some deverbatives (*obbligo*), some adjectival nouns (*intercenali*), some substantivized participles (*picchiata, affacciato*). These last two terms seem to show popular origin; and we should perhaps arrange in a category of popularisms such terms as *bade, brasil, scorzo, cuorio*, which conceivably belong to the patrimony of Medieval Latin, though the linguistic elaboration to which they have been subjected makes us doubt their Latin trappings. Rather, these words must indeed be examples of the living language of the people.

There are, in fact, various new formations of a popular character in Alberti, particularly some abstract derivatives formed mostly upon verbs, but also upon adjectives and nouns. In this category, we find that substantives with a suffix in -*mento* are very common. Such a suffix gives a sense of completeness or fulfillment to the word (Rohlfs, 1901, Folena) (*intricamento, motteggiamento, onestamento*). We find—rarely —that this formation may also have a concrete meaning, (*travamenti,* "structure of beams"). Another series is made up of abstract nouns derived mostly from qualifying adjectives, with a suffix in *-ezza* (*adattezza, ubriachezza*), which convey a feeling of provisional condition, and of nouns ending in *-aggine* (*disadattaggine*), which, on the contrary, give a sense of lasting condition. According to Rohlfs, this last suffix owes its origin to Latin -AGO, -AGINE, originally for the formation of collective nouns, often related to plants. We notice, however, that later *-aggine* has experienced an analogical development and has taken on a function of abstract quality (Rohlfs, 1058). The last suffix to be considered here is *-eggio* (*motteggio*) of Tuscan provenance (Folena, p. 187), probably derived from the verbal form *-eggiare*. Generally in Alberti, the suffix acquires a semantic value that substantially transforms the original meaning of the word. Alberti obviously enjoyed manipulating his language, particularly in shaping the connotation of diminutives and augmentatives in the living idiom (*occhiazzi, stagliuzzato*).

Verbs

As for neologisms in the verb, the fundamental characteristic lies in the new prefixes, even though they may constitute the most ephemeral part of Alberti's contributions to the lexicon. As in the case of suffixes and diminutives, we cannot underestimate the semantic weight of the prefix in Alberti, whether it be a mere reinforcer or a harmonizing element, or whether it is meant to express detachment or participation. Let us record some of the most frequent prefixes that normally have an origin in Latin (the Latin prefix is written here in small capital letters).

There are notable examples of prosthesis of the letter *a* (Latin AD) and the doubling of the initial single consonant: (*ammarginare, accurvarsi, asserenare.*) This is a distinct tendency of Alberti, the roots of which could perhaps be traced to dialect. We also have a counterpart to this phenomenon in many cases of apheresis wherein the omission of the prosthetic initial syllable (*noiare, dolorare*) clearly indicates the author's awareness and reasoned construction of certain language patterns. For the formation of verbs with this prefix, Alberti draws heavily on nouns and adjectives. The prefix IN is used both as a negative and as a preposition. The preposition, considered here, shows great versatility in the formation of verbs, whether it is used to indicate motion, beginning of a condition, arranging or supplying (*incorsare, inferire, inseminare, infuriare*). The Latin privative prefix EX gives *s* plus consonant, meaning motion from a place or exclusion (*sgangherato, slegare, sbarbare, sbroccare*). Within this category, we might accommodate some presumably learned reconstructions or examples of prosthesis of *e* (*escrescere, esterminio, escrucciare*). It should be noted also, on this matter, that the frequency of prosthesis of *i* before *s* plus consonant is quite high in Alberti. *Dis* (DE + EX) in a privative function expresses the idea of separation or cessation of condition or activity (*dismesso, discontentare*). *Con* or *co* (CUM) and the assimilation with the following consonant have mostly a frequentative character (*consequitare, colliquifarsi*), and we could make the same claim for SUB (*socquieto, succrescere, susservire*). PRAE and INTER denote temporal precedence, hence prevention; PER suggests an attempt at thoroughness; AB is used in a sense of dispersion; and OB is found almost always in a derogatory context.

We have dealt at length with the verbal prefix, but even among verbs we have to present a suffixal family having ample distribution in Alberti's works. It is the suffix *-eggiare*, derived from the Greek *-ιζω* and come down to us through ecclesiastical and Medieval Latin (Folena, p. 187; Rohlfs, 1160). Rohlfs points out that such a suffix is used to form verbs from adjectives and nouns; but in Alberti, we have derivations also from verbs which become frequentatives (*resteggiare, palpeggiare*). As Folena has indicated, this suffix is much more common in Tuscany than the learned suffix *-izzare*, though elsewhere the latter predominates in the literary language of the first centuries. In Alberti, the suffix *-eggiare* represents the norm, while *-izzare* is extremely rare; we may cite *dirizzare* in *Teogenio* and the geminative form of the same, *adirizzare*, in the *Famiglia* and in some of the *sentenze morali*.

This analysis allows us to conclude that rare latinisms, vernacularisms, neologisms (words with a new meaning), neoformations (adjectives in *-oso*, substantives in *-mento*, *-ezza*, etc.), the series involving prefixes and suffixes, and the technical terminology—all constitute the most typical physiognomy of the vocabulary that Alberti transposes into the vernacular. Such a contribution reflects living experience and contemporary linguistic taste, while it also coincides with the most significant revival of vernacular literary production in the fifteenth century.

Alberti embarks on a conscious and far-reaching program for

enriching and ennobling the vernacular. In order to be convinced, we should observe some devices he employs in his linguistic practice. Here we find latinisms coupled in peaceful coexistence with the most genuine vernacularisms. As an amiable Virgil, Alberti guides his readers by practical explanation of the rare or new word by a known synonym; or by way of hendiadys, in which a concept is completed in the two elements that compose it; or by synonymic iterations, borrowings, and restorations of Latin terminology integrated into the vernacular alongside expressions of oral tradition. From the items of the vocabulary we could catalogue as innovations, we shall choose certain ones, taken from just a few pages but recurring in all of Alberti's works, which exemplify the linguistic as well as the intellectual labor of the author directed toward a means of expression, aesthetically desired, as a reflection of equilibrium, measure, harmony—as a reflection, in short, of an ideal of perfection.

Let these examples suffice to support my claim that Alberti engages in a conscious effort to deal with the fabric of his new humanistic prose (the new words are italicized): *esredarlo*, privarlo dei beni paterni, p. 335, 2; tedio e *mattanamento*, p. 353, 5; risi e *motteggi*, 27, 7; una femmina *petulca*, arrogante, immodesta, 341,22; tanta mansuetudine e *placabilità* d'animo, 327,2; (sé adornò con quelli abiti e *insigni* trionfali), indosso la *pretesta* vesta regale, 307,11; *quassata* e aperta, 349,15; rode e *sbarba*, 29,71; rompe e *sfascina*, 32,146; per tuo *suffragio* e per benignità delli dii, 311, 26; di veneno simile all'*acconito* (aconito), 90, 34; svelta e lungi *asportata*, 89, 20; *cincischiànle*, diamoli nuova lima e forma, 93, 19; *crassitudine* e peso della terra, 103, 10; povertà . . . *egestà*, 71, 25.

When we observe the placing of these new words, we can easily appreciate the conscious process of Alberti's creative mind and his efforts to give dignity to the literary vernacular. He indulges in the use of Latin forms when dealing with lofty matters, while he adopts popularistic elements when his target is a more contingent and concrete reality. What appears remarkable, though, is the elegance and control he exerts in phrasing everything with discretion. As a result, in Alberti's language we find nothing artificial, nothing commonplace or excessively ossified by imitation. Instead, we have a language—literarily controlled—in which Alberti's taste for the novel, the invigorating, and the challenging finds its raison d'être in his search for an originality characteristic of his whole personality, a language that is part of his creative impulse as well as of his need for a concise and pleasing form of expression. It is the same characteristic displayed by Alberti in architecture, painting, science, and pedagogy.

The real triumph of humanism comes about with the literary production in the vernacular. This study of Alberti's vocabulary is only another indication of the universality of the man who incorporated ancient inspiration and modern commitment, who—I must say—absorbed the Middle Ages into the Renaissance, as is demonstrated by various aspects of his personality, explainable (if not separable) in a psychological context through the evolution of his thought: analysis of passions and of feminine psychology, celebration of love and friendship, glorification of man in the midst of nature, the moral management of household and state.

All of Alberti's production substantiates the temper of his balanced and clear thinking. In Alberti's world there is no place for overpowering passions that would upset the unity of his vision. He is horrified by any lack of control, any emotional or passionate act committed without the guidance of reason. Likewise in his linguistic practice, Alberti exercises full control over his prose, a control which he derives from long classical training while he remains receptive to the linguistic and cultural innovations. He was convinced that the ancients had taught us the substance of what there was to learn. For this reason he links the ancient and contemporary world in a pragmatic vision of his time and undertakes to mold a language to express it harmoniously.

Even in the matter of syntax, Alberti operates uniquely. In his "confezione" of the new humanistic vernacular, he breaks away from the tradition of language as it appears in the three major authors, Dante, Petrarca, and Boccaccio. Although he is aware of the literary language of his predecessors, Alberti does not rely upon Dante's *Convivio* as a model for his prose; he goes back to classical antiquity rather than to earlier Romance structures. Likewise, his syntax differs greatly from Boccaccio's and remains foreign to the canons of medieval rhetoric (present participles, verbs at the end of clause, gradualities of style used for a definite purpose). Alberti's prose is all new, robust, controlled by intimate architectural logistics, like the arches he designed and built.

I select from *Profugiorum ab aerumma* one of numerous passages that could be taken from Alberti's works, in which the articulation of sentence structure pervaded by a sense of Ciceronian symmetry (the high frequency of two adjectives modifying a noun, of two or three substantives in the same grammatical function, the syntagmatic duplication of the hypotaxis) contributes, in an almost discursive tone, to create a state of edifying serenity which Alberti derives from his rigid discipline and from a detached contemplation of the world and its events.

Come alle tempeste del verno ne addestriamo e apparecchiamo, coperti e difesi dalle veste, dalle mura, da nostri refugi e ridutti, e se pure el tedio delle nevi, la molestia de venti, le durezze de freddi ne assedia e ostringe, noi oppogniamo e vetri alle finestre, e tappeti agli usci, e precludiamo ogni adito onde a noi possa espirare alcuna ingiuria del verno; e se saremo robusti e fermi, vinceremo ogni sua asprezza e acerbità e rigore essercitandoci ed eccitando in noi quel calore innato e immessoci dalla natura a perseverar vita alle nostre membra; se forse saremo malfermi e imbecilli, ne accomandaremo al fuoco e al sole e alle terme; così alle volubilità e impeti e tempeste della fortuna bisogna addestrarsi e apparecchiarsi con l'animo, e precludersi dalle perturbazione ogni adito, ed eccitare a susservare in noi quello ignicolo innato e insito ne nostri animi quale v'aggiunse e infuse la natura ad immortale eternità. Addesterremo e apparecchieremo l'animo nostro contro a' commovimenti de' tempi e contro alle ruine de' casi avversi, in prima col premeditare e riconoscere noi stessi, poi col giudicare e statuire delle cose caduche e fragili, non secondo l'errore della opinione, ma secondo la verità e certezza della ragione.[21]

[Just as for the rages of winter we train and prepare ourselves, covered and protected by clothing, by walls, by our shelters and retreats, and even if the tediousness of snows, the vexation of winds, the harshness of chills besiege and compel us, we counteract by putting panes in windows, carpets at front-doors, and close off every access that might let in any assault of winter; and if we are strong and firm, we shall overcome all its roughness, sharpness, and inclemency by exercising ourselves and by stimulating that native warmth instilled in us by nature to ensure the life of our limbs; if we are perhaps sickly and weak, we shall rely on fire and on the sun and on hot baths; likewise, it is necessary to train and

prepare our spirit against the fickleness and impetuosity and rages
of fortune, close off access to any disturbance and stimulate that
native spark to endure which is inbred in our spirit, which nature
added and infused in us for immortal eternity. We shall train and
prepare our minds against the commotions of the times and
against the ravages of adversities, first by assessing and knowing
ourselves thoroughly, then by evaluating and determining those
things that are perishable and uncertain, not according to the
vagary of opinion, but according to the truth and certainty of
reason.]

This passage reflects the general spirit of the treatise, dealing with
"agreeable matters," learning, wisdom, and other "worthy topics"
such as music and architecture. The setting, too, provides much of the
inspiration for this edifying serenity: Alberti and his fellow Florentines
carried on such discourses under the cupola of Brunelleschi's dome.
Stylistically, we have a simile that proceeds by ample, clear, classical
forms; it denotes an atmosphere of calm and comfort, created by the
workings of nature, always seen by Alberti as a positive force seconding
the actions of virtuous and reasonable men. Alberti succeeds in creating
such a mood by means of word order and syntax, in an arrangement
that becomes a stimulating heuristic device. As in the case of his
vocabulary, Alberti enjoys treating skillfully and cleverly his syntactical
furnishings, his *masserizia linguistica*, as a way to experiment and in
an effort to harmonize.

Alberti creates *ex novo* a humanistic prose, based on the symmetry of
the sentence structure, as an expression of serenity, beauty, harmony—
a stylistic model measured in terms of proportion and comfort. Giovanni Nencioni refers to this prose as a "double wealth, traditional and contemporary, of Alberti's vernacular and its power to disorganize—as
Machiavelli would say—vocabulary and sentence structure borrowed
from Latin without being disorganized by them."[22] This new prose,
which Alberti elaborates in the middle of the fifteenth century, serves as
a point of departure for the refinement, natural decantation, and *concinnitas* which characterize the ensuing Renaissance. As indicated by
Nencioni, the innovative manner of Alberti's language corresponds in
part to Machiavelli's concept of a linguistic model, insofar as their
perspective of *imitatio* is concerned. But as an advocate of "nostra
Toscana lingua" Alberti differs from Machiavelli, whose polemical

intervention on behalf of the florentinity of the vernacular appears in his *Discorso o dialogo intorno alla nostra lingua*.[23]

Yet it is clear that Alberti was highly regarded through the sixteenth century, especially in the representational arts. Admiration for his personality among men of letters and artists is clearly shown in statements by Landino, Poliziano, Lorenzo, and Vasari; he certainly occupied a key position between the fourteenth and sixteenth centuries. Nonetheless, in the history of Italian language (and literature) he remains an isolated figure. Stylistically, *Il Cortegiano* and other prose writings of the cinquecento, under the influence of the Bembo school, remain much closer to Boccaccio. Also, Alberti's poetry conveys a mood altogether different from Petrarca's. In diversity, Alberti remains consistent in theory and practice to his linguistic mode of expression.

Alberti synthesized his aesthetic vision with remarkable consistency in a variety of ways. A practical outlook on things and a high moral value blend in his search for a link between "humanae litterae" and "res publica," between an ideal of life and empirical reality, for he has an ever-present awareness of his cultural mission and civic commitment. Hence, his intent is not to disparage but to vindicate the literary vernacular that results from the harmonizing of contemporary humanistic culture with the vernacular tradition. Alberti's undertaking, then, is one of elaboration and technical refinement, aimed at a level that is literarily controlled by the turn and proportion of phrases, providing a careful and decorous *medietas* of his linguistic and stylistic elements. Such elements reflect not only living experience but also a preference for a language that, in Giovanni Ponte's words, would give, along with the wealth of learned terms, "colorful adjectives and nouns of popular taste which without impairing the harmonic composition of the whole, concur in avoiding the danger of monotony."[24] Alberti's vernacular is intended as a means, but also and above all as an end aesthetically to be cherished.

Thus, in Alberti the Renaissance concept of *homo faber* is linguistically incarnate, and the link between theory and practice which he provides, symbolizes that idea made real. Out of a fusion of empirical experience and rational faculties, we find in Alberti the basic and essential premise to a sound and sagacious activity, responsive to man's commitment to be responsible to himself and others, especially when others lack such a sense of responsibility. That is why Alberti does not hesitate to establish a parallel between his own activity and the activities of others; in fact, through other speakers he even points to himself as a model for life. He seems to perceive how and when man's behavior may serve society; and if he represents a type of man almost perfect, of exceptional qualities, he does so because he is convinced that such a temper is necessary in the jungle of human society: in a perspective of shifting vicissitudes of good and evil, only the person who is in control of his actions can hope to save himself, though Alberti realizes that every human being has by necessity his own limitations. For Alberti, the personal experience attains high value only if we proceed according to a precise program, a preestablished order, and above all with a sense of proportion in the social and moral sphere. Thus he presents in himself the Renaissance enhancement of the earthly dignity of life, toward which every individual should strive continuously in order to lead a useful, active, serene, and virtuous existence—that is, to realize the humanistic concept of *man* as the *measure of all things.*[25]

NOTES

1. *Miscellanea di cose inedite e rare* (Florence: Baracchi, 1853), reprinted in Bruno Migliorini, *Storia della lingua italiana*, 4th ed. (Florence: Sansoni, 1971), p. 252. All English translations are mine, unless otherwise specified.

2. Girolamo Mancini, *Vita di Leon Battista Alberti* (Florence: Carnesecchi, 1911); Paul Henri Michel, *La pensée de L. B. Alberti* (Paris: Les belles lettres, 1930); Giovanni Santinello, *Leon Battista Alberti* (Florence: Sansoni, 1962); Joan Gadol, *Leon Battista Alberti: Universal Man of the Early Renaissance* (Chicago: University of Chicago Press, 1969); Eugenio Garin, *L'umanesimo italiano* (Bari: Laterza, 1965); Paul Oskar Kristeller, *The Classics and Renaissance Thought* (Cambridge: Harvard University Press, 1955).

3. Migliorini, pp. 233 ff.; Giovanni Nencioni, *Fra grammatica e retorica* (Florence: 1953), pp. 69–79; Raffaele Spongano, *Un capitolo di storia della nostra prosa d'arte* (Florence: Sansoni, 1941); Ghino Ghinassi, "Leon Battista Alberti fra latinismo e toscanismo: la revisione dei *Libri della Famiglia*," *Lingua Nostra*, vol. 22 (1961); Maurizio Dardano, "Sintassi e stile nei *Libri della Famiglia* di L. B. Alberti," *Cultura neolatina* 23 (1963): 1–36; "Sintassi dell'infinito nei *Libri della Famiglia* di L. B. Alberti," *Annali della Scuola Normale di Pisa, Lettere, Storia, Filosofia*, s 2, 32 (1963); pp. 83–135.

4. Leon Battista Alberti, *Opere volgari*, a cura di Cecil Grayson, 3 vols. (Bari: Laterza, 1960, 1966, 1973).

5. Cecil Grayson, "Appunti sulla lingua dell'Alberti," *Lingua Nostra*, vol. 16 (1955); see also his "The Humanism of Alberti," *Italian Studies*, vol. 12 (1957); and *A Renaissance Controversy: Latin or Italian* (Oxford: Clarendon Press, 1960).

6. Gianfranco Folena, *La crisi linguistica del Quattrocento e l'Arcadia di I. Sannazaro* (Florence: Olschki, 1952); Ghino Ghinassi, *Il volgare letterario nel Quattrocento e le Stanze del Poliziano* (Florence: Le Monnier, 1957); Pier Vincenzo Mengaldo, *La lingua del Boiardo lirico* (Florence: Olschki, 1963).

7. Gianfranco Folena, "Noterelle lessicali albertiane," *Lingua Nostra* 18 (1957): 6. This essay was already in the hands of the editors when Nicoletta Maraschio's study "Aspetti del bilinguismo albertiano nel *De Pictura*" appeared in *Rinascimento*, 2 (1972, but not available before 1974): 12.

8. Spongano, *Un capitolo di storia*, p. 3.

9. Grayson, "The Humanism of Alberti," p. 48.

10. Alberti, *Opere volgari*, 2: 55.

11. On this topic, see Pio Rajna, "Le origini del certame coronario," *Miscellanea Renier* (Turin, 1912), pp. 1027–56; Antonio Altamura, *Il Certame Coronario* (Naples, 1952). Most recently, Guglielmo Gorni viewed Alberti's hexameters for the *certame* as an effort to link contemporary poetry to the Virgilian eclogue. (By paying such homage to Virgil, Alberti was aiming at a revival of ancient poetry in vernacular literature—"Storia del Certame Coronario," *Rinascimento* 2 (1972): 135 ff.)

12. Alberti, *Opere volgari*, 2: 144.

13. Alberti, as everyone knows, dealt with perspective, experimenting possibly with a kind of *camera obscura*, and wrote treatises on painting (*De Pictura*), sculpture (*De Statua*), and architecture (*De Re Aedificatoria*).

14. Giorgio Vasari, *Vite dei più eccellenti pittori, scultori, ed architetti* (Florence, 1771), 2: 236.

15. Ciro Trabalza, *Storia della grammatica italiana* (Milan, 1908), p. 531. Also, "Una singolare testimonianza dell'Alberti grammatico," *Miscellanea Torraca* (Naples, 1912).

16. Alberti, *La prima grammatica della lingua volgare*, ed. Cecil Grayson (Bologna, 1964), p. 39. Carmela Colombo, "Leon Battista Alberti e la prima grammatica italiana," *Studi linguistici italiani* 3 (1962): 176–87.

17. Alberti, *La prima grammatica*, pp. 60–61.

18. In Migliorini, *Storia della lingua italiana*, p. 241.

19. Dante Alighieri, *The Divine Comedy*, trans. and ed. Thomas G. Bergin (New York: Appleton-Century-Crofts, 1955).

20. Grayson, "Alberti and the Vernacular Eclogue in the Quattrocento," *Italian Studies*, vol. 11 (1956). Giovanni Ponte, "Il petrarchismo di L. B. Alberti," *Rassegna della letteratura italiana*, vol. 7 (1958). Piero Bigongiari, "Le rime di Leon Battista Alberti," *Capitoli di una storia della poesia italiana* (Florence: Le Monnier, 1968), pp. 175 ff.

21. Alberti, *Opere volgari*, 2: 121.

22. Nencioni, *Fra grammatica e retorica*, p. 165.

23. Cecil Grayson raises some questions about the authorship of this "dialogue" and its date of composition in a provocative article, "Machiavelli and Dante"

Essays in Honor of Hans Baron (Chicago, 1971), reprinted in *Cinque Saggi su Dante* (Bologna: Patron, 1972), pp. 117–48. See also Fredi Chiappelli, *Machiavelli e la 'lingua fiorentina'* (Bologna: Boni, 1974).

24. Giovanni Ponte, "Leon Battista Alberti umanista e prosatore," *La rassegna della letteratura italiana* 68 (Florence: Sansoni, 1964): 268.

25. The words here underlined belong to Alberti (*Libri della Famiglia*, ed. Grayson, p. 132). It is a paraphrase from Protagoras, which the author might have read in Diogenes Laertius, but he does not mention either of them here. For general linguistic information as well as orientation, I have benefited from Folena's study (*La crisi linguistica*) and from Gerhard Rohlfs, *Grammatica storica della lingua italiana e dei suoi dialetti*, 3 vols. (Turin: Einaudi, 1966, 1968, 1969).

11

Headlong Horses, Headless Horsemen:
An Essay on the Chivalric Epics of Pulci,
Boiardo, and Ariosto

A. Bartlett Giamatti

Near the middle of the *Third Georgic*, Virgil offers images of the power of sexual passion. One of the most striking is the horse whose whole body trembles at the familiar scent:

> ac neque eos iam frena virum neque verbera saeva, non scopuli rupesque cavae atque obiecta retardant flumina correptosque unda torquentia montis.[1] [3.252–54]

> [No longer now can the rider's rein or the cruel lash stay his course, nor rocks and hollow cliffs, nor opposing rivers that tear up mountains and hurl them down the wave.]

The unchecked horse is the very principle of release, more powerful even than Nature at her most elemental. Because no curb can control him, he is Nature become unnatural, potency turned monstrous, as is made clear later, in the lines on the frenzied mares and their mysterious droppings —the "hippomanes," or horse madness, favored by witches (ll. 266–83). Yet, though these images of fertility run riot, the poet is able to establish images of restraint and instances of his own control. The figure of the unchecked horse allows Virgil to show how, like the farmer, he must impose limits in order to foster growth—else

265

without art, Nature will die of her unchecked impulse. Restraint and release, and all they mean for each other, are the essence of the image, as well as of the *Georgics*.[2]

Throughout the *Aeneid*, Virgil uses the metaphor of curbing, sometimes, as with Aeolus, who curbs the winds (1.54) or Dido, who will check the proud (1.523), without any extended implications. More interesting resonances occur at 4.135, where Dido's horse, resplendent in purple and gold, awaits her "ac frena ferox spumantia mandit" ("and fiercely champs the foaming bit"), the horse prefiguring the passion that will run unchecked after the episode in the cave thirty lines later. The madness here implicit in the barely restrained horse is explicitly exploited in book 11. There, at the battle outside Latium, the Trojans push the Latins back to their city walls. The gates are closed. Some roll in trenches, "immissis pars caeca et concita frenis/arietat in portas et duros obice postis" ("some, charging blindly with loosened rein, batter at the gates and stoutly barred doors," ll. 889–90). Out of this Latin self-destruction will eventually come a strain of Roman self-sacrifice, but at this moment blindness and madness are all we see in those who smash into their own locked gates.

However, the most potent image for frenzy and restraint in the poem occurs in book 6. Aeneas and his men approach the Sibyl. She first goads him into prayer, and then, possessed and shaking, she tries, says the poet, to loose Apollo from her breast.

> tanto magis ille fatigat
> os rabidum, fera corda domans, fingitque premendo.
>
> [6.79–80]
>
> [so much the more he tires her raving mouth,
> tames her wild heart, and moulds her by constraint.]

Apollo rides her like a horse; and after his message is chanted through her, the poet returns to the image again: "ea frena furenti / concutit et stimulos sub pectore vertit Apollo" ("so does Apollo shake the reins as she rages, and ply the spur beneath her breast," ll. 100–01).

The Sibyl as horse, Apollo as rider, is the most telling image for the relation of *furor* (l. 102) and *frenum*—that is, for the way energy is concentrated or significance compounded through restraint. And, like the image of the horse in *Georgic* 3, this one of the Sibyl and her divine rider is finally important because of the connection it establishes between the events described in the poem and the poet's activity. Here again the imposition of limit releases truth, as Apollo "fingit premendo," fashions or shapes her by restraint, just as the poet fashions his work of art by the laws of his craft. Whether reining in a horse in order to capture a pace, or disciplining the imagination in order to shape a work of art, the process is the same.

In the Sibyl and Apollo as horse and rider, there is another dimension as well. Energy comes from below, to be controlled by the higher part. This notion may go back to the centaur, our earliest image of the combined horse and rider, certainly our earliest of the power of the beast and the rationality of man.[3] The conjunction of beast and man, of energy and reason, as embodied in the centaur, is expressed through the image of Apollo riding the Sibyl, save that now god and man, not man and beast, are joined. Now on the vertical scale established by the image, what was bestial is human; what was human is divine. The image of the horse and rider has tremendous flexibility.

In his *Consolatio Philosophiae*, Boethius returns several times to the imagery of riding, specifically of curbing, always at crucial points in the book. In book 2, poem 8, on how love is the ruling principle of the universe, he says that if Love loosened the reins, then all now bound would make perpetual war:

> Hic si frena remiserat,
> Quidquid nunc amat inuicem
> Bellum continuo geret . . .[4]

The Universe, says Boethius, is bound into freedom by love—as again the paradox of meaningful release as a function of restraint is exploited in the image of the curbed horse. He makes the point again in book 3, poem 2: "Quantas rerum flectat habenas / Natura potens" ("how mighty Nature guides the reins of all things"), and at the end returns once again to the image to show that nothing is outside of God's plan: "Sic quae permissis fluitare uidetur habenis, / Fors patitur frenos ipsaque lege meat" ("Chance, too, which seems to rush along with slack reins, is bridled and governed by law"—book 5, poem 1). Boethius uses the imagery of reins and curbing to underscore the great theme of his book, which is the expansion of spiritual freedom because of the limits of Providence. But Boethius does more—he invests the imagery with a moral energy, a spiritual immediacy, that guarantees the life of the image after him.

Dante exploits the same imagery to great effect. In the *Convivio* (4.17.4), for instance, we read of Temperance, "che è regola e freno de la nostra gulositade" ("which is the rule and rein on our gluttony").[5] Perhaps the most interesting example, however, occurs early in book 4, where

> lo Imperadore . . . sia lo cavalcatore de la umana volontade. Lo quale cavallo come vada sanza lo cavalcatore per lo camp assai è manifesto, e spezialmente ne la misera Italia, che sanza mezzo alcuno a la sua governazione è rimasa. [*Convivio* 4.9.10][6]

> [The Emperor . . . is the rider of the human will. And how that horse goes without the rider over the field is most obvious, and especially in miserable Italy, that is left without means for its governance.]

Regardless of how the image is finally translated—whether Italy, or the Emperor, or the horse of the human will is referred to by the *sua* preceding *governazione*—the vision of the streaking, unchecked horse is an unforgettable metaphor for appetite run wild, a people completely leaderless.

In the *Commedia*, the image of the *freno*, the curb, is used fourteen times, once in the *Inferno* (for Phaeton, 17.107), once in the *Paradiso* (for Adam, another Phaeton, 7.26), and twelve times in the *Purgatorio*. These usages in the *Purgatorio* exploit every dimension—physical, ethical, and spiritual—of the image, and are appropriate to the *cantica* that is precisely about release through restraint. However, I would like to touch briefly on another passage where the image is used in a different way:

> Allor mi dolsi, e ora mi ridoglio
>   quando drizzo la mente a ciò ch'io vidi,
>   e più lo 'ngegno affreno ch'i' non soglio,
> perché non corra che virtù nol guidi;
>   sì che, se stella bona o miglior cosa
>   m'ha dato 'l ben, ch'io stessi nol m'invidi.
>   [*Inferno* 26.19–24][7]

> [The grief that seized me then I feel anew
>   When I recall the sight that met my eyes;
>   Remembering, I keep tighter rein on wit

Than is my wont, lest it may run unchecked
By virtue's guidance, so that if perchance
Some favoring star or nobler arbiter
Has blessed me with a talent, I myself
May not pervert it to my own dismay.]

Here, in his own voice, the poet sets up the crucial difference between himself as poet (and by extension in the episode proper, as pilgrim) and that other great voyager, Ulysses. As the canto unfolds, we see how, for all the similarities between them, Dante is distinct from Ulysses; for the poet has restrained his imaginative power to remain within God's (and virtue's) plan, whereas Ulysses has released the full force of his rhetorical power and, a Siren to his crew, has led his men away from reason's dictates. Dante restrains his "ingegno" so as not to deny himself its good; Ulysses releases his, without restraint, and loses all. Dante the poet shapes his utterance and thus shapes his moral being, figured in the pilgrim, whereas Ulysses misshapes his language in order to persuade and thus misshapes his men.

We see this process even more clearly when, at the end of the *Purgatorio*, Dante returns to the image. The mountain has been scaled, and the garden and its rivers passed through. If he had more space, he says, he would write of the sweet draughts that never satisfy:

> ma perché piene son tutte le carte
> ordite a questa cantica seconda,
> non mi lascia più ir lo fren de l'arte.
>
> [*Purgatorio* 33.139–41]

[But inasmuch as all the sheets ordained
For this my second Canticle are filled,
The curb of art lets me no further go.]

The curb applied *by* Dante in *Inferno* 26 is applied *to* Dante in *Purgatorio* 33. The change is significant, for the pilgrim has just achieved his greatest earthly freedom in the garden and, *rifatto* (*Purgatorio* 33.143), now ascends to Paradise, a release that is precisely the result of restraints he has assumed to perfect his moral being. Dante shows us how to curb in order to create, that is, he gives us an insight into the aesthetic process he is engaged in. But the aesthetic shaping is also, for Dante, a moral shaping: the poet shaping his pilgrim, God, his poet. And each creator (Dante or God) refrains his creature (pilgrim or poet) in order to reform him. The aesthetic and the moral are united in the imagery of curbing.

Dante has greatly extended the implications of Virgil's "fingit premendo" (*Aeneid* 6.80), Apollo's shaping the Sibyl by constraining her, as if she were clay and he were a sculptor. Dante has moralized this figure, and has brought out the latent self-consciousness in the riding image—the sense that, as a man refrains his horse, so he guides himself. The poets of the Renaissance epic, therefore, could find the multiple images of curbing a horse, loosing a horse, and riding in harmony, exploited in their ethical, moral and aesthetic dimensions by their great predecessors in the epic tradition. These are images that Pulci, Boiardo and Ariosto would return to often, for there is no figure more central to chivalric epic than the checked or unchecked horse and its rider. Nor is there a more apt image for the effort the epic poet is engaged in.

Luigi Pulci, Morgante[8]

In canto 13 of the *Morgante*, Rinaldo comes to the court of King Marsilio. Suddenly a messenger appears and, falling to his knees, recounts the following:

> che morte ha cinquecento o più persone
> un gran caval co' denti e colle penne,
> ch'era sfrenato, e fu già di Gisberto,
> e pareva un demòn là in un diserto.
>
> [stanza 51]

> [that five hundred or more people have been killed
> by a great horse with teeth and plumes
> that was unchecked, and came of Gisberto,
> and seemed a demon there in the desert.]

The horse is a symbol for the part of man we must govern most wisely. But even more, it represents the energy in life most dangerous to the established chivalric conventions and norms. We see this most clearly when Rinaldo sets his noble mount Baiardo to combat with the mad and wild horse. In the process, Rinaldo sets up an image of the two ways life can run—into pattern or sheer energy, into convention and containment or vital deformity and death. He sets up the dialectic that informs the *Morgante*. He also creates an image of the gap between the ideal and the actual; and in that gap the poem will reside.

Rinaldo watches the fight between the palfrey and the marauder for two hours. Then two stanzas sum up the episode, and much of the poem:

> Rinaldo un poco stette a vedere;
>   ma poi, veggendo che 'l giuoco pur basta,
>   e che co' morsi quel bravo destriere
>   e colle zampe Baiardo suo guasta,
>   dispose fare un colpo a suo piacere;
>   détto a quell' altro un pugno tra gli orecchi
>   col guanto, tal che non ne vuol parecchi;

> e cadde come e' fussi tramortito.
>   Baiardo si scostò, ch'ebbe paura.
>   Gran pezzo stette il cavallo stordito;
>   poi si riebbe, e tutto s'assicura.
>   Rinaldo verso lui presto fu gito,
>   prese la bocca alla mascella dura,
>   missegli un morso ch'aveva recato;
>   e quel cavallo umile è diventato.

>   [13.64–65]

> [Rinaldo sat awhile to watch;
>   but then, seeing the game had gone far enough,
>   and that with bites and hooves
>   that big horse was smashing up his Baiardo,
>   he resolved to strike a blow in his favor.
>   And while Baiardo was reeling,
>   he gave that other a fist between the ears
>   with his glove—such as few would want;

> and it fell as if it had fainted.
>   Baiardo ran to one side, he was afraid.
>   For a good while the horse lay stunned,
>   then it recovered and checked himself over.
>   Rinaldo quickly went to him,
>   took his mouth by the hard jaw,
>   put in a bit he had brought,
>   and that horse became docile.]

As the wild thing is killing Baiardo, the chivalric fiction, Rinaldo does what Pulci will always see man as having to do: he uses his hands to reshape the situation. We must respond to actualities, as events occur, says Pulci, and not trust to conventions or codes to do our living for us. Of course, every new adjustment, every insertion of the self into the maelstrom of events, creates, potentially, a new convention, a new pattern for behavior; but to understand this dialectic is to understand the game that is life. Here Rinaldo knows when his particular *gioco* (64) has gone far enough; we will see later how Pulci sees all existence in this fashion. Now, the wild horse has sufficiently threatened the order of things so that the order must be made to include him if it and we are to survive.

The horse is stunned by a blow from the mailed fist. Why not sooner? After all, five hundred have died. The answer is that Pulci, like all Renaissance writers, is interested in paradigms for behavior, not in continuous narrative realism. And after the mailed fist, the process of *frenare*, of curbing, begins. It is done by hand, by the shaping power of the human, the higher part fashioning out of the energy of the lower something that transforms them both: "fingit premendo." The wild horse becomes a *pecorin*, a *pecorella* ("lamb")—in both cases a *maraviglia* ("wonder," at 66,68)—and finally a symbol for the love between Rinaldo and Marsilio's daughter Luciana (68–69). From the stuff of murderous chaos, Rinaldo has wrought something quite new.

The episode of Rinaldo and the "cavallo sfrenato" encompasses a good deal of Pulci's manner and meaning. I intend to look briefly at two specific parts of the climax of the episode as a way of glimpsing some of the larger issues in the *Morgante*. First, let us return to the stunned horse: "e cadde come e' fussi tramortito" ("and it fell as if it had fainted," 65). The image of the supine horse is a constant in the poem, always associated with ghastly carnage. For instance, at the battle around Paris, the Christians are hemmed in by death:

> l'un sopra l'altro morto era caduto,
>   e gli uomini e' cavalli attraversati,
>   tal che miracol sarebbe tenuto
>   quanti furon poi morti annumerati.
>   Avea cinque ore o più già combattuto:
>   or pensi ognun quanti e' n'abbi schiacciati.
>
> [10.47]

[one on the other had fallen dead,
and the men and horses lay across each other,
so it would have taken a miracle
to reckon the number of those dead.
[They] had fought for five hours or more:
think of how many had been squashed.]

This vision of the reductiveness and anonymity of warfare is but a prefiguration of the scene at Roncesvalles. There Charlemagne sees:

i cavalieri armati
l'un sopra l'altro in su la terra rossa,
gli uomini co' cavalli attraversati;
e molti son caduti in qualche fossa,
nel fango in terra fitti arrovesciati;
chi mostra sanguinosa la percossa,
chi 'l capo avea quattro braccia discosto,
da non trovargli in Giusaffà sì tosto.

[27.198][9]

[the armed knights
[lay] one on the other on the red ground,
the men with the horses across them;
and many had fallen in ditches,
in the mud, rammed in the ground upside down;
those who show a bloody wound,
those with a head and four scattered limbs
that won't be found in Jehoshaphat very soon.]

Throughout the poem, the only natural consequence of men and horses mixed, of war, is deformity and death. And, throughout, with his savage wit, Pulci employs a striking figure for the shapelessness of men and beasts slaughtered together in battle: it is the image of the pudding or stew. In canto 7.56: "e' ne faccan gelatine e mortiti,"[10] ("they made a pudding or stew"), and later:

era a veder sotto questa rovina
morti costor come una gelatina.

[19.173]

[there was to be seen under this ruin
these dead as if in a pudding.]

> tutta la terra pareva coperta
> di gente smizzicata saracina,
> da poter far mortito o gelatina.
>
> [23.38]

> [all the ground seemed covered
> with chopped up Saracens
> as if to make a stew or pudding.]

The "stew" of battle is most forcibly described at Roncesvalles, which is:

> un tegame
> dove fussi di sangue un gran mortito,
> di capi e di peducci e d'altro ossame
> un certo guazzabuglio ribollito . . .
>
> [27.56]

> [a pan
> where there was a great stew of blood,
> of heads and little feet and other bones,
> a kind of boiled concoction . . .]

But the stew extends beyond the battlefield; shapelessness and dissolution underlie all of life. We understand this when we hear that splendid Tuscan word *guazzabuglio* ("concoction"), a word, we realize, that we have heard before.

At the end of his exuberant monologue to Morgante, Margutte compared his life to a book (18.140), but to a special kind of book:

> Io t'ho lasciato indietro un gran capitolo
> di mille altri peccati in guazzabuglio;
> ché s'i'volessi legerti ogni titolo,
> e' ti parrebbe troppo gran mescuglio.
>
> [18.142]

> [I left behind you a great composition
> of a thousand other sins in a concoction;
> for if I were to read you every title,
> it would strike you as too great a mixture.]

As Margutte goes on to say, his life is an endless story; but his final word will be: "che tradimento ignun non feci mai" ("I have never betrayed anyone," 142). Morgante is delighted:

> non crederrei con ogni sua misura
> ti rifacessi appunto più natura,
> né tanto accomodato la voler mio.
>
> [143–144]
>
> [I wouldn't have thought that Nature
> could have made you better to its own measure,
> nor better fitted to my desire.]

Here is the heart of Pulci's vision: all of life and Nature is made according to *misura*; and that measure, that perfect proportion, resides in gluttony (see 19.86, where "gelatina o solci" figure the stuff of existence) and in *mescuglio* and *guazzabuglio*. Life is the process of consumption and expansion, always tending to dissolution and deformity. Food, men, horses, words—all are part of the ever-expanding, fermenting mix, the ever-decaying, ever-swelling mingle of undigested elements, physical and linguistic, that is human existence. The only *misura* is finally *mescuglio* or *guazzabuglio*—Pulci sees no check, no rein, on appetite and so he hymns deformity. He celebrates monstrosity as the only principle of proportion. Finally, of course, the book of Margutte's life—crammed with splendid sin and with joy in excess, recounted in the tough, slangy, gamey gristle of proverbial Tuscan—is only an image of the larger book. The greater *guazzabuglio*, the thicker, more redolent *mortito*, is the *Morgante* itself, constantly expanding, cannibalizing older poems, growing to twenty-three cantos, then to twenty-eight, ending only with the perception that decay outstrips even the glory of excess, and that Hell is here in our daily lives. Despite efforts of convention, of social codes and constructs, the urges in human affairs to shapelessness, to becoming a stew, seem too great to check.

And yet Pulci does assert his control. He does imply throughout that he can contain the stew, or, at least, that one can gain some perspective on a world whose proportions are so deformed. The key to this attitude, which extends throughout the poem as much as the sense of life as a *mortito* does, can also be found in the episode of the *cavallo sfrenato* with which we began. We remember that after Rinaldo had watched the wild horse batter Baiardo for two hours, "veggendo che 'l giuoco pur basta" ("seeing the game had gone far enough," 13.64), he moved to stop the battle. Throughout the poem, battle—the cause of the shapeless stew of carnage—is also seen as a *gioco* ("game"). Over and over, the process whereby life loses its human form, the process that symbolizes the lack of form in human existence, is distanced and thus controlled by calling it a "game." The terms of the dialectic in the poem are, finally, undifferentiated confusion and decay (*mortito, mescuglio, gelatina, guazzabuglio*), and cool, skeptical formality, an acceptance of rules without any faith in them (*gioco* or *gioco netto*, or a "safe bet," a game where no risks are taken, a game everyone wants and no one has.)[11]

We know that the idea of play is profoundly important to Renaissance culture; it is at the heart of Erasmus's great satire:

> And he is unseasonable who does not accommodate himself to things as they are, who is "unwilling to follow the market," who does not keep in mind at least that rule of conviviality, "Either drink or get out"; who demands, in short, that the play should no longer be a play. [*The Praise of Folly*][12]

It is the essence of the wisdom of *Don Quixote*, as we know when Montesinos tells his cousin Durandarte that Quixote has come to render them *desencantados* ("disenchanted"), and Durandarte replies that if it doesn't happen, "cuando así no sea¡ oh primo!, digo, paciencia y barajar" ("even if it doesn't happen, oh cousin, have patience and shuffle the cards," pt. 2, chap. 23).[13] Here, the losing gambler's proverb makes it clear that life is bearable only so long as the game continues, that play is so crucial because we must sustain the capacity to maintain illusion. Yet Erasmus or Cervantes, or indeed Rabelais, after all, are only the heirs of Pulci, for no one understands better, in these terms, the necessity for play in human life than Margutte. We return to the beginning of that long speech to Morgante.

> Mentre ch'io ho danar, s'io sono a giuoco,
>   rispondo come amico a chiunque chiama;
>   e giuoco d'ogni tempo e in ogni loco,
>   tanto che al tutto e la roba e la fama
>   io m'ho giucato, e' pel già della barba:
>   guarda se questo pel primo ti garba.

Non domandar quel ch'io so far d'un dado,
    o fiamma o traversin, testa o gattuccia,
    o lo spuntone: è va per parentado,
    ché tutti siàn d'un pelo e d'una buccia.
    E forse al camuffar ne incaco, o bado,
    o non so far la berta o la bertuccia,
    o in furba o in calca o in bestrica mi lodo?
    Io so di questo ogni malizia e frodo.

                                                    [18.121–22]

[When I have money, if I am playing,
    I answer like a friend to whoever calls;
    and I play at all times, anywhere,
    so that for any and every stake
    I've played, until I'm stripped:
    see if being in your birthday suit pleases you.

Don't ask me if I know about dice,
    about snake-eyes, trey, Little Joe from Kokomo,
    boxcar or seven-out; it's in the blood;
    we're all the same under the skin.
    And do you think I don't give a crap about a good con,
    Or that I can't take anyone for a ride,
    Or can't play the shell game or steal your shirt?
    I know every trick there is.]

Play until you're skinned, says Margutte, until there is no more. The
game is all in the playing, not in believing that anything will come of it.
Life consists of seeing everything as a gamble, with no safe bets, a
gioco with no *gioco netto*. It is this attitude of total tolerance and total
skepticism that gives Margutte, and others, their ability to accept
deformity as a norm. Thus, war or any other system is a game if one
believes that fraud is the only truth and decay the only constant. Indeed, this attitude toward life can shape it, can give it form, if one is
willing arbitrarily to assert that what seems only a *mortito* or *guazzabuglio* is really just another pass with the dice, another trick in the endless
show. Margutte seems to speak, finally, for the poet whose poem is
the largest game of all, the poet who, even later, confesses that "ch'io
sono stato al monte di Sibilla,/che mi pareva alcun tempo un bel
gioco" ("For I have been to the Sibyl's mountain,/which once seemed to

me a good game," 24.112). This is the poet who admits that magic was his favorite game, that magic and its demons were his Parnassus and his Muses (113; also 28.141). Pulci sees making magic, like writing poetry, as the final game, the willed play of the mind over the void. The dialectic in the poem, and in the poet, between the desire to believe and the inability to believe, between the perception of shape as made by the mind and immersion in formlessness as experienced by the body, between Jehoshaphat and Caïna, is constant.

Finally, at the end, Pulci proffers several images for release and restraint that sum up this dialectic and its larger implications. These images all appear together in a remarkable stanza near the close of his poem. He is musing on the *Morgante* and its making:

> Ben so che spesso, come già Morgante,
>   lasciato ho forse troppo andar la mazza;
>   ma dove sia poi giudice bastante,
>   materia c'è da camera e da piazza;
>   ed avvien che chi usa con gigante,
>   convien che se n'appicchi qualche sprazza,
>   sì ch'io ho fatto con altro battaglio
>   a mosca cieca o talvolta a sonaglio.

[28.142]

> [I know that often, just like Morgante,
>   I've let things go a little too far;
>   but where there is a proper judge,
>   there is material for the salon and the square.
>   It follows that whoever has to do with a giant
>   will have to take on some of his traits,
>   though I have fought other [different] battles
>   at *mosca cieca* or *sonaglio* [blind man's bluff].]

Lasciare or *mettere troppa mazza* means getting carried away in story-telling, going too far. And here the poet is saying that, like Morgante, he has been guilty of excess, of surpassing limit, of running unchecked. The radical urge in the poem toward shapelessness is shaped here by a colloquial phrase, a phrase that also occurred earlier when Pulci was ruminating on his effort:

> e bisognòe qui andar pel segno ritto

(non so se troppa mazza altrove misse),
che l'aüttor che *Morgante* compose
non direbbe bugie tra queste cose.

[28.63]

[It is necessary here to go on the straight line
(I don't know if it has gone too far)
so that the author who writes the *Morgante*
wouldn't tell any lies among all these things.]

Again, the hint of having gone too far, the ironic worry that his magic releases lies instead of truth; but now this concern is played off against an image of restraint. "Andar pel segno ritto" refers to the carpenter's art, and to the ochre line, guiding a saw, that is made by snapping a string covered with dye against the wood. Pulci counters all the images of stews, of swelling language and imagination, of sheer size beyond measure, with a carpenter's image, an image like Rinaldo's placing the bit in the horse's mouth in canto 13, an image of the human hand controlling the shape of things and not relying on convention or custom to shape things for us.

The poet is literally a *fabbro*, an artisan making his momentary stays against confusion. It is an image whose power derives from its directness and plainness, and it is one that Pulci uses for his art at critical points in the poem. For instance, when he refers to one of his fictional sources, the author "Arnaldo," he speaks of him as one who "va pel fil della sinopia saldo/sanza uscir punto del segno ritto" ("goes by the straight line/without leaving at all what was marked," 27.80).[14] And when he speaks of his major fictional source, "Alfamennone," and the authority for the fantastic stories about Morgante, Pulci still asserts that he is following the truth: "Tanto è ch'io voglio andar pel solco ritto" ("so much do I want to follow the straight line," 19.153). Thus, whenever Pulci refers to his art he introduces the image of control to justify precisely the release of a new story. He knows that the lies in his poem, or in life, can only be effective when they are purveyed as the truth; he knows that the horror of shapelessness is made more acute, but also more bearable, when it is given explicitly artistic form. The dialectic between restraint and release, between *misura* and *mescuglio*, is finally for Pulci a way of talking about the very effort he is engaged in—the loosing of images that must contain rather than create chaos.

For Pulci, the identification between what his characters do and what he does was firmly made at 28.142, the stanza cited above, where Pulci allied himself with Morgante. There Pulci said that, like his character, he had "lasciato . . . troppo andar la mazza":

> ed avvien che chi usa con gigante,
> convien che se n'appicchi qualche sprazza,
> sì ch'io ho fatto con altro battaglio
> a mosca cieca o talvolta a sonaglio.

> [It follows that whoever has to do with a giant
> will have to take on some of his traits,
> though I have fought other [different] battles
> at *mosca cieca* or *sonaglio* [blind man's bluff].]

To understand this identification of poet and character, we must first know that *mosca cieca* or *sonaglio* are names for a child's game in which a player is blindfolded and cries out "Sonaglio," while the others form a circle around him and answer "Béccati quest'aglio." They then shove and hit the blindfolded player until he is able to grab one of his tormentors, who then enters the circle and takes the blindfold. This game is alluded to throughout the *Morgante* (2.11; 6.15; 7.12, 43; 10.147; 23.38) and here at 28.142. And it serves, in every case but the last, as a metaphor for battle. In short, *mosca cieca* is the specific game, the *gioco*, that underlies the concept of play and informs the poem. In the last allusion, at 28.142, the game refers not only to the matter of the poem and Morgante's place in it, but also to the composition of the poem and Pulci's role as maker.

And what it means is that, much as Morgante and Pulci have both participated in and celebrated excess, much as both saw life as a game and thus, up to a point, managed to remain untouched by the inevitable decay of existence, in the end Morgante, unlike Pulci, loses at *mosca cieca*. Finally, in the absurd game the world plays with us, Morgante— massive, vital and oddly human—is killed. He is killed by a crab that bites his heel (20.50 f.), precisely as the Tuscan proverb he once cited with a laugh says: "I granchi credon morder le balene" ("Crabs think they can bite whales," 19.7). The power in the proverb comes to life, and loosed, it kills. But this is what Pulci has been saying all along: that any form of energy—a proverb, a wild horse, a giant, a poem— can, if let loose, destroy normal expectations, assumptions, patterns, conventions. Any game, like chivalry, or magic, or writing, can get out of hand and result in a terrible "stew" of men and horses, or in heresy, or in an aimless and shapeless poem.

And that is how he has played *mosca cieca* differently from Morgante. Pulci has not, like Morgante, celebrated excess as an end in itself but rather as a means to fullness within measure. For, while Pulci celebrates energy—never more so than when it is fully actualized—he also celebrates it only this side of having it overwhelm all limits. He is, ultimately, the poet of the thin red line. Pulci has always known when to swell the story and when to cut it on the mark. Like Rinaldo, who knew when the "cavallo sfrenato" was going too far with Baiardo, who knew the game, Pulci has known when to explode and when to contract, when to expand a literary convention and when to follow it, when to embellish the older chivalric literature and when to embody its essence.

Pulci has played *mosca cieca* with the literary tradition; but because he knew when to change the players and how to keep the game going, it has not done him in. I think the model for Pulci's view of this process, in poetry and in life, is there near the middle of his poem, in canto 13, where we started. There, the unchecked horse, representing all the glorious, new energies that kill older forms, is transformed by the miraculous hand of the man into a symbol of peace, the lamb, and into a figure for love between man and woman. To transform murderous power into art is the only game Pulci finally can believe in. It is what his poem does, and it is what the figure of the unchecked horse finally comes to mean.

Matteo Maria Boiardo, Orlando Innamorato[15]

Pulci exulted in life's excess even as he sought to shape it before it became chaos. Boiardo's view is simpler, less ambiguous, and his poem is more orderly, less given over to what it would contain, perhaps less profound. Boiardo, too, knows that life (and art) tend instinctively toward deformity, but he takes no pleasure in the energies released by decomposition; he does not hunger for, as well as recoil from, the stew of human affairs. Boiardo deeply fears the impulse in life toward dissolution. He wants a universe of purpose, perspective, and proportion and he believes he can provide at least the model for such a world in his art, in his lovely creation of glistening knights and graceful ladies.

Pulci believed the death of old conventions released energy for new ones, thus the (futile) dialectic of his vision. Boiardo is much more aristocratic and conservative. He understands the limitations of chivalry; he will note the ironic discrepancy between surface and substance, between what we say and what we do—though not with the piercing clarity of his younger contemporary, Ariosto. But Boiardo does not find anything liberating or exhilarating in the decay of order and the pursuit of excess; rather, he laments the passing of the chivalric world and, in his way, seeks to memorialize it, shortcomings and all. As we will see, his terms for life and art are very similar to Pulci's, but the final emphasis is very different, and the vision is less hectic, more refined.

The best illustration of these similarities and differences, is found in Boiardo's attitudes toward love and limitation. Both the power of love and a proper sense of limit are established in the opening stanza of the poem:

> Signori e cavallier che ve adunati
> Per odir cose dilettose e nove,
> State attenti e quïeti, ed ascolatati
> La bella istoria che 'l mio canto muove;
> E vedereti i gesti smisurati,
> L'alta fatica e le mirabil prove
> Che fece il franco Orlando per amore,
> Nel tempo del re Carlo imperatore,
>
> [1.1.1]
>
> [Lords and knights here assembled
> To hear of things delightful and new,
> Pay attention, stay quiet and listen
> To the lovely history that moves my song,
> And see the boundless deeds,
> The high labor and the wondrous efforts
> That French Orlando did for love
> In the time of King Charles the Emperor.]

At the middle of the stanza are those "gesti smisurati," ("boundless deeds") those excessive, destructive deeds that are done for love. Boiardo's great themes are, finally, the destructiveness of passion, the life-enhancing quality of cool control. Of course, he will praise love, just as he described some of Orlando's deeds as "alta fatica . . . mirabil prova." But even as love is praised, there is always the hint of something else. For instance, in the famous stanzas on love as the universally unifying force, a very ambiguous note is sounded in the last couplet.

> Ché amore il senno e lo intelletto avanza,
> Né giova al provedere arte o pensiero.
> Giovani e vecchi vanno alla sua danza,
> La bassa plebe col segnore altiero;
> Non ha remedio amore, e non la morte;
> Ciascun prende, ogni gente ed ogni sorte.
>
> [1.28.2]

> [For love advances good sense and intellect,
> It helps to furnish art or high thoughts,
> The young and the old move to its dance,
> [as does] the meanest plebe with the haughty lord;
> There is no remedy for love, and none for death;
> It takes everyone, every person and every destiny.]

For all the splendid things love is, it is also like death, irresistible and remorseless. The stanza describes a dual perspective on love that is characteristic of the poem as a whole. One more example: later in the poem, we begin to hear an even more menacing note, one that, as we will see, resounds often in the last part of the poem.

> Amor primo trovò le rime e' versi,
> I suoni, i canti ed ogni melodia;
> E genti istrane e populi dispersi
> Congionse Amore in dolce compagnia.
> Il diletto e il piacer serian sumersi,
> Dove Amor non avesse signoria;
> Odio crudele e dispietata guerra,
> Se Amor non fusse, avrian tutta la terra.
>
> [2.4.2]

> [Love first found the rhymes and verses,
> The sounds, the songs, and every melody;
> And unknown people and disparate folk
> Join in Love in sweet company.
> The delight and the pleasure will be submerged

> Where Love does not hold sway;
> Cruel hate and spiteful war,
> If Love is not, will conquer the earth.]

Love is central to the world of the poem because it can effect so much: love can lead to high deeds or to "gesti smisurati"; it can bind society in harmony or it can falter and leave men "sommersi" ("sunk") in excess. Like Pulci, Boiardo knows that the force for life—he calls it love—can also be the agent of death, that the lovely world of proportion and purpose contains within it the potential for shapelessness, and that this potential is always just beneath the surface. But where Pulci rode out the impulse toward decay and dissolution in order to engage (and hence control) it, Boiardo, always aware of its power, hopes to check or rein it in from the very outset.

Thus, from the beginning the general instinct in everything to go beyond proper limits, to be "smisurato," is repeated as a warning, over and over. And all things participate in this instinct: Astolfo's helmet is "di valore ismesurato" ("of measureless value," 1.1.61); Ferraguto "amava oltra misura" ("loved beyond measure") and later makes "un salto smisurato" ("a boundless leap," 1.1. 72; 78); a giant is called "Argesto smisurato" ("measureless Argesto," 1.1.75), while later another, Malpresa, is "dismisurato" ("unmeasurable," 3.1.59). Later again, in the garden of Falerina, Orlando sees a tree "fuor di misura" ("beyond all measure," 2.4.48), with a harpy sitting in it: "Grandi ha le branche e smisurato artiglio" ("It had huge claws and measureless talons," 51). The creature "Turbosse oltra misura il conte Orlando" ("Disturbed Count Orlando beyond measure," 59). Characters, like Bradamante (3.5.51) or Ranaldo (1.5.5; 2.30.12) can give blows "tanto smisurato" or "oltra misura" or "fuor d'ogni misura," while at other times whole episodes are beyond measure. For instance, Turpin tells us, says the poet, of a "bestia smisurata" ("measureless beast," 2.28.33); but, he continues, "Io non ho prova che chiarir vi possa, / Perché io non presi alora la misura" ("I have no way of clarifying this / Because I did not take its measure," 36).

Thus everything—objects, animals, humans, even recorded history itself—tends to excess, and despite what he says here, Boiardo is constantly engaged in taking their measure, in checking and refraining the urge to swell to shapelessness. At times, his control consists of telling us exactly what the result of this impulse to swell will be. This is the apocalyptic strain in the poem, visions of dissolution and confusion that correspond to Pulci's view of existence as a grisly stew or his invocation of Caïna. For instance, we noted above the warning that without Love and its ordering power, all would be sunk or dissolved ("sumerso,' 2.4.2). This was, at that point, a warning of what was potential in human affairs. But at other points, the fear of losing a vision of harmony, of losing the capacity to assert a universe of proportion and purpose, becomes translated into a vision of actuality. The aristocrat feels the mob pressing in, and the fear of shapelessness is cosmic and real: Agramante's army passes from Africa to France:

> Chi potrebbe il tumulto racontare
> Da la gente sì strana e sì diversa,
> Che par che 'l celo e il mondo se sumersa?
>
> [2.28.54][16]

> [Who could tell the tumult
> Of people so strange and so diverse,
> That it seemed the heavens and earth would be sunk?]

Or again:

> Or torniamo alla gente africana
> E a questi re, che al campo sono entrati
> Con tal romore e grido sì diverso,
> Che par che il celo e il mondo sia sumerso.
>
> [2.30.7]

> [Now let us return to the African people,
> And to these kings, who have come on the field
> With such a noise and cries so diverse
> That it seems the heavens and earth will sink.]

As we will see, the only diversity or differentness that Boiardo can calmly envision is that created by and in his own work of art. Otherwise his poem, in something bordering on xenophobia, warns us against diversity of any other kind. The apocalyptic visions of the cosmos drowned in barbarians, of civility losing its shape, were prophetic; for when Charles VIII brought his French armies into Italy in 1494, Boiardo evidently could no longer sustain his poem. He stopped writing his epic, leaving it unfinished; the blow to his vision of what Italy ought to be was too great to encompass in poetry.

All of Boiardo's deep fears of diversity and decay, and his equally deep desires for order, are summed up in an episode in book 2, canto 30. This is really one of the climactic episodes of the poem, for the third book, ten years in the making, is truncated and elegiac in tone. The scene is the great battle between the armies of Charlemagne and Agramante. Charlemagne rallies the Christians by reminding them of their divinely inspired duty, and he exhorts them not to fear the foe's greater numbers. A bit of fire can ignite a great deal of straw. Then he cries:

> Se forïosi entramo alla battaglia,
> Non sosterranno il primo assalto apena.
> Via! Loro addosso a briglie abandonate!
> Già sono in rotta; io il vedo in veritate.
>
> [2.30.44]

> [If we enter the battle furiously [madly]
> They will barely be able to sustain the first assault;
> Go! After them with loosened bridles!
> Already they are in ruin. I see it truly.]

"A briglie abbandonate"—Charlemagne urges release, "sfrenatura," upon his cavaliers. He urges them to do precisely what the poet has been warning the reader against—to court excess as a means to restraint, expanding toward death as a way of retaining a hold on life. Boiardo's Charlemagne expresses Pulci's vision, that one asserts control by exploiting the energy of decay. Pulci urged this because he believed only in the final order of the dialectic of expansion and retraction; Boiardo's Charlemagne courts chaos because he believes in God's ordering hand. Boiardo has finally found a way of incorporating the terrifying energy (and imagery) of "sfrenatura" into his poem; and having done that, he then immediately offers a critique of what I have called Pulci's vision.

In the next stanza, Boiardo tells us what energy the language of excess releases. It is something we have seen and heard before:

> Qua se levò l'altissimo romore;
> Chi suona trombe e chi corni, e chi crida;
> Par che il cel cada e il mondo se divida.
>
> [2.30.45]

> [Here the most intense sound arose;

Some blew trumpets, some horns, some yelled;
It seems that the heavens fall and the earth yawns.]

Cacophony as an index of apocalypse: the same sight and sound we had
in 2.4.2, 2.27.21, 2.28.54, and 2.30.7 is here applied to the Christians
moving into battle. Boiardo is saying that Charlemagne's command
threatens the very order he wants to maintain. And when the Saracens
stream out in vast numbers, the full force of Boiardo's critique emerges:

Discesce il campo in mezo a poco a poco,
Fosso non vi è, né fiume, che confini,
Ma urtano insieme gli animi di foco,
Spronando per quel piano a gran tempesta;
Ruina non fu mai simile a questa.

[2.30.46]

[The field shrinks at the middle, little by little;
There is no trench, or river, as a boundary,
But the souls in flame scream together
Spurring on that plain like a huge storm;
Ruin was never anything like this.]

The battlefield shrinks as the armies move toward each other, but compression is an illusion. The reality is ghastly expansion, beyond all
limits, either man-made (trenches) or natural (rivers)—expansion
brought on by "spurring," by the activity of unrestrained desire for
dissolution in warfare. The result is not a human but an elemental
context, a "gran tempesta" of excess even beyond the limits of ruin.
Boiardo sees what Pulci saw, a stew or horrible mix, but Boiardo sees
no good in it, no promise of vitalizing energy if one sups at this table.
The inflamed souls, "gli animi di foco," finally become souls in flame,
souls in hell.

Le lancie andarno in pezzi al cel volando,
Cadendo con romore al campo basso,
Scudo per scudo urtò, brando per brando,
Piastra per piastra insieme, a gran fraccasso.
Questa mistura a Dio la racomando:
Re, caval, cavalier sono in un fosso,
Cristiani e Saracini, e non discerno
Qual sia del celo, qual sia de l'inferno.

[2.30.47]

[Lances go in pieces, flying toward the heavens,
Falling with noise to the plain below,
Shield screams on shield, sword on sword,
Armor plate on armor plate together, a great uproar;
This mixture I commend to God:
King, horse, knight are in a ditch,
Christians and Saracens, and I cannot tell
What is of heaven, what of hell.]

What Pulci called a *mescuglio*, Boiardo calls a *mistura* ("mixture");
and as Pulci's term had its own echoes in the *Morgante* in *mortito* and
guazzabuglio, so Boiardo's sets up its own peculiar resonances in the
Orlando Innamorato. This is no *mortito* in a poem that loves ingestion,
but a horrible *mistura* in a work that honors *misura*. It is significant
that Boiardo says "a Dio la racomando," ("I commend [it] to God"),
for he regards this awful mix of classes, races, and kinds as an affront
to God's purpose and plan. Boiardo, always anxious to believe in a
universe of proportion and hierarchy, is constantly disappointed.

He finally balances this grim *mistura* of Kings, horses, and cavaliers
at the end of book 2, with his own version of the benign and lovely mix
a man can make later in book 3.

> Còlti ho diversi fiori alla verdura,
> Azuri, gialli candidi e vermigli;
> Fatto ho di vaghe erbette una mistura,
> Garofili e vïole e rose e zigli:
> Traggasi avanti chi de odore ha cura,
> E ciò che più gli piace, quel se pigli;
> A cui diletta il ziglio, a cui la rosa,
> Ed a cui questa, a cui quella altra cosa.

> Però diversamente il mio verziero
> De Amore e de battaglie ho già piantato.

[3.5.1–2][17]

> [I have gathered various flowers, of green,
> Blue, yellow, white, and vermilion;
> I have made from lovely plants a medley,
> Carnations and violets and roses and lilies:
> Let him come forward who cares for the scent,
> And whatever pleases, let him take;

> Whoever likes the lily, whoever the rose,
> And to him this, to him that other thing,
>
> > Thus diversely my poetry
> > Of Love and battle I have already planted.]

Boiardo opposes the power of art to the energies of the battlefield. Here the *mistura* is a garden, where the diversity is of color and scent, under the control of the gardener-poet. The garden is an image of the poem, the poem (hopefully) an image of how things ought to be varied but orderly—like a garden. To say Boiardo retreats into art is an over-simplification, for art includes the potential for disaster, as the poem has. Rather, Boiardo retreats into images of the organic, or the natural, restrained. He chooses to emphasize the formal dimension of art, the impulse to control, rather than, with Pulci, to indulge the energy that lies under his hand. Boiardo is the poet of the curb rather than of the rider.

Boiardo's deepest desire is to conserve something of purpose in a world of confusion. He knows that chivalry is an outmoded system, but he wants to keep something of its value, its respect for grace and noble behavior, even while he relinquishes its forms and structures. Boiardo is trying, in short, to freeze the impulse to dissolve, the impulse that, with Pulci, he understands is instinctive to human life. Boiardo wants to check the urge to dissolution, to *sommergere*, that time seems inevitably to embody. He does not want to roll back the clock and re-gain the old world, but he does want to recapture the sense of control of oneself, if nothing else, that marked life under the old system. He wants to be able to praise something other than the giddy, headlong rush.

Boiardo makes his view of life explicit at the end of *Orlando Innamorato*. The last canto is only twenty-six stanzas long and is about the problems of control and the futility of desire in terms that we have come to regard as fundamental to the chivalric epic. Fiordespina is smitten with Bradamante, whom Fiordespina takes to be a male knight. To woo this knight, Fiordespina offers a gift, a splendid horse "forte e legiero" ("strong and nimble").

> un sol difetto avia,
> Che, potendo pigliar co' denti il morso,
> Al suo dispetto l'om portava via,

Né si trovava a sua furia soccorso.
Sol con parole si puotea tenire:
Ciò sa la dama e ad altri non vol dire.

[3.9.8]

[One defect alone he had,
That, taking the bit between his teeth,
In his contempt he ran off with the man,
Nor can he find help against [the horse's] fury;
Only with a word can he be held in:
The woman knows this [word] and doesn't want to tell [it to] others.]

Here Boiardo reintroduces the image of the *cavallo sfrenato* and celebrates the power of language, or art, to control sheer, brute force. It is a word alone that can stop this runaway, a word that can freeze the rush to decay.

Bradamante mounts, the horse takes off, Fiordespina follows:

E vede ben che la bocca ha sfrenata;
Ora tira di possa, ora tira piano,
Ma a ritenerlo ogni remedio è vano.

[3.9.19]

[And [Bradamante] sees well that the mouth is unchecked,
Now pulls with strength, now pulls gently,
But every effort to hold him in is vain.]

Try as she might, Bradamante cannot "ritenne il cavallo sfrenato" ("hold in the unchecked horse," 20). One word will stop this mad dash toward a mountain covered by tangled growth—that is, this dash away from order and into the thicket of confusion. But few know the word, and those who do tend to forget what it is. Fiordespina suddenly cries out to the helpless rider:

Non so come mi sia di mente uscito
Di farti noto che il destrier, che ti ha
Quasi condutto di morte al partito,
Qualunche volta se gli dice: "Sta!"
Non passarebbe più nel corso un dito;
Ma, come io dissi, me dimenticai
Farlo a te noto, e ciò mi dole assai.

[3.9.23]

[I don't know how it slipped my mind
To tell you that the horse, who has
Almost taken you to your death at the outset,
Whenever you say to him "Stop!"
Wouldn't go any farther than a finger's length;
But, as I said, I forgot
To tell you, and I am very sorry.]

Underneath what is funny and even ridiculous here, is a serious point. And that is once again we come back to love, the passion that leads one out of oneself; and, through love, we glimpse all the human passions that drive us out of control and send what we most value spinning toward death. The very obviousness of the words *Sta* or *Whoa* only serves to underscore the extremity of our need for something to stop the flight beyond *misura* to death, to stop the careening of history into chaos. And when in stanza 24 Bradamante finally cries "Sta!" to the horse of human impulse, the simple word works. The poet is able to envisage language as asserting control over matter, art as it can, in earnest or in game, regulate life. And yet while here we have an instance of what Boiardo always desires—the capacity of convention to curb sheer energy—the last stanza of the poem undercuts the victory man seems so narrowly to have won from time.

Mentre che io canto, o Iddio redentore,
Vedo la Italia tutta a fiama e a foco
Per questi Galli, che con gran valore
Vengon per disertar non so che loco;
Però vi lascio in questo vano amore
De Fiordespina ardente a poco a poco;
Un altra fïata, se mi fia concesso,
Racontarovi il tutto per espresso.

[3.9.26]

[While I sing, O my Redeemer,
I see Italy all in flames and fire,
Set by these Gauls, who with such valor
Come to ravage I don't know what place;
However, I leave you with this vain love
Of Fiordespina burning little by little;

> Another time, if it's given me,
> I'll tell you the rest explicitly.]

That is all. And the "Sta!" that stops the poem, the word that reins in the glorious beast that is the *Orlando Innamorato*, is not the news of Charles VIII but, finally, the "vano amore." That is the final word, and vision—the fruitless desire of Fiordespina for Bradamante. Boiardo comes to see the futility of trying to control human desire; he sees the inability of the old way of life to check the human passions that must, after all, exist in order to animate life. There is no final staying of the steed save in poems, and poems—like the magic word—will often be forgotten and will always, finally, make very little difference.

At the end of the fourth canto of book 2, Boiardo has occasion to refer in passing to his art:

> Perché se dice che ogni bel cantare
> Sempre rincresce quando troppo dura,
> Ed lo diletto a tutti vi vo dare
> Tanto che basta, e non fuor di misura.
>
> [2.4.86]

> [Because it is said that every lovely song
> Always palls if it lasts too long ·
> And I want to give delight to everyone,
> In the proper amount, and not beyond measure.]

Rincresce means not only "grows tiresome," but at its root means "grows weighty," "swells," "bloats." Even art is subject to its own laws of expansion; even language, for Boiardo the medium for establishing limitation, is subject to the urge to surpass limits. Art is not exempt from the very impulse it must control; the epic is finally an instance of the problem it describes. And the only recourse language has is to do what it says—is to fall silent after it has said "Stop!" The very meaning of his poem, that there is no way to check decay, in ourselves or our institutions, try as we might, dictated that Boiardo stop. There was no other way to end without reproducing chaos.

Ludovico Ariosto, Orlando Furioso[18]

In the fourth canto of *Orlando Furioso*, the putative hero, Ruggiero, is astride the splendid hippogriff: "Poggia l'augel, né può Ruggier frenarlo" ("The griffin soars, nor can Ruggiero [check it]," 49). The winged horse will not be curbed by the immature knight. The poem is, in many respects, about how Ruggiero grows up, how he grows into his role as founder of the Estensi, how he learns to check the forces outside and curb the energies within. This inability to refrain the hippogriff signals in Ruggiero a lack of vision, an imaginative weakness, an insufficiently developed perspective on the world. The winged horse, soaring over the earth, gives the broad, epic view of creation, and if one cannot control that medium for sight, one lacks insight in every sense. But what Ruggiero and so many others lack, Astolfo possesses in abundance. Astolfo is the master of perspective and control in this poem, and among other proofs of his privileged position we may note his handling of the same hippogriff.

> la sella sua, ch' appresso avea, gli messe;
> e gli fece, levando da più morsi
> una cosa et un' altra, un che lo resse;
> che dei destrier ch'in fuga erano corsi,
> quivi attaccate eran le briglie spesse.
>
> [22.28]

> [[He placed] the saddle on him, which lay near, and
>   bitted
> The steed, by choosing, all the reins among,
> This part or that, until his mouth was fitted:
> For in that place were many bridles hung,
> Belonging to coursers which had flitted.]

Like Pulci's Rinaldo at the scene of the horse fight, Ariosto's Astolfo offers us a version of the artist who disciplines the imagination by bridling the sheer energy it contains. As he chooses among the bits and bridles, Astolfo reflects the flexibility and shrewdness of the poet who must use not only what is at hand but also what is proper to the moment. Control of the winged horse figures control of one's intellective part, and that part of us, for Ariosto, is our destiny. For our intellect either accepts or transcends the codes and conventions, the social illusions, of life; it is the part that can destroy us or save us.

The image of the curbed or uncurbed horse occurs throughout the poem in a variety of ways. This is partly because there is in Ariosto a greater tendency than in Pulci or Boiardo to use the image for abstract purposes. We hear, for instance, about the curb of envy (27.82), of shame (30.71), of courteous modesty (42.98); we hear of breaking the rein of shame (29.30) or of patience (28.102); we hear of grief restrained (42.28). This tendency to exploit the metaphor in relation to abstract qualities or emotions is part of a larger intellectualizing impulse in the poem, a strain of abstract analysis that gives the poet's ironic scrutiny of human institutions such seeming distance and such power. This tendency toward abstraction also carries with it, and by no means always for ironic purposes, a moralizing streak, one that often emerges in the opening stanza of a given canto. For instance, Ruggiero rescues the naked Angelica:

> Quantunque debil freno a mezzo il corso
> animoso destrier spesso raccolga,
> raro è però che di ragione il morso
> libidinosa furia a dietro volga,
> quanto il piacere ha in pronto . . .
>
> [11.1]

> [Although a feeble rein, in mid-career,
> Will oft suffice to stop courageous horse:
> 'Tis seldom Reason's bit will serve to steer
> Desire, or turn him from his furious course,
> When pleasure is in reach.]

Or later, when a belovèd is threatened:

> Qual duro freno a qual ferrigno nodo,
> qual, s'esser può, catena di diamante
> farà che l'ira servi ordine e modo,
> che non trascorra oltre al prescritto inante,
> quando persona che con saldo chiodo
> t'abbia già fissa Amor nel cor costante,
> tu vegga o per violenzia o per inganno
> patire o disonore o mortal danno?
>
> [42.1]

> [What bit, what iron curb is to be found,
> Or (could it be) what adamantine rein,
> That can make wrath keep order and due bound,
> And within lawful limits him contain?

> When one, to whom the constant heart is bound,
> And linked by Love with solid bolt and chain,
> We see, through violence or through foul deceit,
> With mortal damage or dishonor meet.]

In both cases, the poet muses on the way powerful passions cannot be curbed by Reason's, or by a reasonable, rein; and in both cases, the sexual impulse, either as sheer lust in 11.1 or as Love, the spike (*chiodo*) in the heart, in 42.1, goads the character, as both will goad Orlando, to excess. In 42.1, Ariosto sees man as surpassing proper limit (1.4), much as Boiardo had invoked *misura* as his norm and Pulci had a sense of the game's limits, of the line the carpenter had to follow. Like his predecessors, Ariosto knows the urge to release will lead to shapelessness and decay. But he employs different terms.

Ariosto finally always sees *sfrenatura* as leading to fragmentation of the self, to the shattered or splintered personality—almost as if the self were a fragile artifact, susceptible to cracking under the pressure of convention and disillusionment. We get a glimpse of Ariosto's concept in 11.1, where he speaks of how a rein can the "animoso destrier spesso raccolga" ("[often gather in the lively beast]"). The idea of "gathering in" the horse, of integrating and consolidating the self, is at the heart of his vision. He is always concerned with the collected, as opposed to the dispersed or scattered, self.

Ariosto believes that to be collected or self-contained is the result of one's being flexible and adaptable; that one controls the self by serving no overmastering ideology, such as Chivalry or Petrarchan love or institutionalized religion. And he believes one is dispersed or "beside oneself" or, as he says, "di sé tolto," instead of "in sé raccolto," when one surrenders to the dictates of some social custom instead of acting as the time demands. Excess, or madness—and they are the same to this intensely practical but cerebral poet—occurs when we ignore our native *senno* ("[common] sense") for some system. Ariosto is not cynical—Pulci is much more so—he is only conservative. They are very different attitudes.

Like Pulci and Boiardo, Ariosto conveys his version of restraint and release, or what I have called the collected and dispersed self, through the radical image of curbing the horse. In fact, the poet establishes this image and attitude at the outset of the poem. Angelica flees Rinaldo:

La donna e il palafreno a dietro volta,
e per la selva a tutta briglia il caccia;
né per la rara più che per la folta,
la più sicura e miglior via procaccia:
ma pallida, tremando, e di sé tolta,
lascia cura al destrier che la via caccia.

[1.13]

[The affrighted damsel turns her palfrey round,
And shakes the floating bridle in the wind;
Nor in her panic seeks to choose her ground,
Nor open grove prefers to thicket blind.
But reckless, pale and trembling [and out of herself]
Leaves to her horse the devious way to find.]

The horse out of control is simply a symbol for human despair. When one is "beside oneself," *di sé tolto*, as Angelica is, one is *sfrenato* like the horse. How one rides is an index of one's spiritual state.

Orlando now becomes the focus of the poet's attention, in these terms, as Ariosto begins to point toward the middle of the poem and the core of the poem's meaning. Orlando is capable of acting in a rational, or collected, fashion, as Ariosto shows when Orlando rescues Olimpia from the ravenous Orc: "Orlando in sé raccolto, / la mira altier, ne cangia cor ne volto" ("collected in himself, the peer / Looks proudly on, unchanged in heart and cheer," 11.35). Here he is integrated, not shattered, because his own passions and beliefs are not at issue; whereas, when he encounters his own needs, he goes, if you will, to pieces. For instance, after defeating Manilardo, Orlando pursues Angelica again:

Il suo camin (di lei chiedendo spesso)
or per li campi or per le selve tenne:
e sì come era uscito di sé stesso,
uscì di strada.

[12.86]

[Through wood and field his courser did he goad,
Often inquiring for the royal dame:
Beside himself, he strayed beside the road.]

Just as he is beside himself, so is he off the road. The dashing or wan-

dering horse is the fragmented self. As we know, Orlando is capable
of self-possession, of riding a straight line. But in the hostile world
of Romance (and Renaissance Italy), dispersal, the crooked course,
is the norm.

Canto 23 is the middle canto of the completed poem and the center
of its meaning. All the energies and images of the *Orlando Furioso* tend
to flow into or out from this core. The cunning structure of the canto
would itself repay study, but suffice it to note here that Bradamante's
situation at the beginning of canto 23 accurately catches up Orlando's
predicament, in the terms we have been using, and projects his massive
agony to come. Bradamante wanders in the night, searching for her
beloved, Ruggiero:

> Spesso di cor profondo ella sospira,
> di pentimento e di dolor compunta,
> ch'abbia in lei, più ch'amor, potuto l'ira.
> —L'ira—dicea—m'ha dal mio amor disgiunto.
>
> [23.7]

> [With sorrow and repentance oft assailed,
> She from her inmost heart profoundly sighed,
> That Anger over Love should have prevailed.
> ["Anger," she said "has displaced me from my love."]]

Here the sinister echo in line 3 of Dante's Ugolino ("Poscia, più che
'l dolor, poté 'l digiuno" —"Till hunger over grief at last prevailed,"
Inferno 33.75) startles us and deepens our sense of disjunction, of the
way that madness, because of love, will only separate us farther from
those we love, and from ourselves. Here is all the rhetoric of the shattered self in half an octave.

Ariosto now brings Orlando to the fore, and shrewdly reintroduces
the crucial image of the horse and curb. Orlando fights mighty Mandricardo:

> Sta in sé raccolto Orlando, e ne va verso
> il suo vantaggio, e alla vittoria aspira:
> gli pon la cauta man sopra le ciglia
> del cavallo, e cader ne fa la briglia.
>
> [23.86]

[Firm in his stirrups self-collected stood
Roland, and watched his vantage to obtain;
He to the other courser's forehead slipt
His wary hand, and thence the bridle stript.]

As in the battle with the Orc (11.35), Orlando is self-possessed when confronted by an external force or foe. Ariosto implies again, as he does so often, that we are only really fragmented in our dealings with ourselves. Now the bridle is off Mandricardo's horse, as Orlando at least symbolically unleashes the forces of ruin, the energies of self-destruction. Orlando falls; Mandricardo's horse—"Il destrier c'ha la testa in libertade, / quello a chi tolto era il freno di bocca" ("[The horse whose head is free, / who had the bit removed from his mouth]," 88)—dashes off. By emphasizing the horse's *sfrenato* condition, Ariosto sets up an ironic contrast between the man who was sufficiently "in sé raccolto" to release the curb, and the horse from whom "tolto il freno era di bocca." The rest of the canto describes how the man loses himself and becomes the horse.

Mandricardo's runaway mount finally hurtles into a ditch: "Quivi si ferma il corridore al fine; / ma non si può guidar, che non ha freno" ("Here stopt the horse; but him he could not guide, / Left without bit his motions to restrain," 91). There can be no advancement without restraint—a basic paradox in the poem, and in all these Renaissance poems. But in the same octave Doralice offers her bridle to Mandricardo, who refuses (92), but who snatches the bridle from the approaching Gabrina, whose horse then runs madly away (93–94). What Ariosto leaves us with is the image of curbing and releasing violently expanded, of life as an endless chain of runaways, as potentially always out of control. All of this is preparing for Orlando's final agony.

Orlando now follows the strange course of Mandricardo's mount for two days, until he comes to a lovely, garden clearing, which in many ways reminds us of Alcina's isle-garden and of Ruggiero's arrival there (6.20–24). The reminiscence is appropriate, for in its way this place will be as different from what it appears to be as that one was. Here the pastoral spot will be the seat of madness, as Ariosto begins to concentrate his attack on those traditions and conventions that take us out of ourselves, that give us assumptions about life and the world that are false, and that the world does not or cannot sustain.

As he looks around, Orlando sees *scritti* (102; 106), *lettere* (103),

parole (106)—all the trees have inscriptions carved into them telling of
the passionate love between Medoro and Angelica. This is an assault
on the convention of Petrarchan love on two levels. First, Orlando's
(ultimately) *fin amors* and Petrarchan ideas about the aspiring lover and
the disdainful lady are shattered because the lady is supposed to reject
all amorous approaches, and here, as the inscriptions make very clear,
Angelica has succumbed. Orlando's assumptions about the conventions
of love and courtship are thus destroyed. But Ariosto also attacks the
love that is consummated, showing it not to be a tender, if realistic,
romance between the princess and the soldier, but rather, beneath the
elegant language of love, a crude transaction in physical needs. For
instance, stanza 108, one of the inscriptions, opens with clear Petrarchan echoes: "Liete piante, verdi erbe, limpide acque" (["Smiling
plants, green meadows, clear waters"]) but at the end it says of Angelica:

> "spesso ne le mie braccia nuda giacque;
> de la commodità che qui m'è data,
> io povero Medoro ricompensarvi
> d'altro non posso, che d'ognior lodarvi.'
>
> [["Often in my arms she naked lay;
> For the commodity that is here given me,
> I poor Medoro cannot recompense you
> Except to sing your every praise."]]

The description of Angelica naked does not destroy our illusions; it
is the attitude toward her, the language of the marketplace—*commodity,
poor, recompense*—that makes the girl meat and shows praise of her to
be the only coin in which he can pay her. Ariosto is attacking the social
myths and their conventional language because they lie.

   Indeed, lying is a fundamental point to this lovely wood of words out
of which madness comes. We feel more and more the presence of language on the trees, until the wood is a forest of verbal signs and Orlando
is trapped in it, unable to believe their significance but forced to believe
it, in either case the victim of the *scritti*. This is the dilemma Ariosto
sees all of us confronted with; as readers of the poem, we are faced, as
Orlando is, with words that are deceptive, inherently deceitful, the
medium for fictions, but words that also tell us a hard truth. And that
truth is that as people in the real world, we are faced (like Orlando in

the poem) with symbols, codes, and conventions that may not simply shatter us but may also give our lives meaning and coherence. In short, Orlando in the wood of words is Ariosto's image for the reader in the poem, for the reader in the world, and for the tragic predicament he faces: unwilling to believe what he must believe in, and, when forced to believe, shattered as a result.

Orlando gathers himself to lie to himself:

> Poi ritorna in sé alquanto, e pensa come
> possa esser che non sia la cosa vera.
>
> [144]

> [He somewhat [gathered himself in], and thought
> How possibly the thing might not be true.]

But it avails nothing. After spending a night in the same cabin they stayed in, hemmed in by even more inscriptions, trapped in the reality of their fiction, Orlando is told by a shepherd the *istoria* of Medoro and Angelica.[19] And then, in a literalization of the hard truth, Orlando is shown the gem Angelica gave the shephered when they left.

> Questa conclusion ful la secure
> che 'l capo a un colpo gli levò dal collo.
>
> [121]

> [A deadly axe was this unhappy close,
> Which, at a single stroke, lopt off his head.]

Orlando is truly beside himself; what happened to the horses of Mandricando and Gabrina—loss of control of the head—has happened to him. Ariosto then signals the release of grief (and madness) with the image we have been observing: "Poi ch'allargare il freno al dolor puote /(che resta solo e senza altrui rispetto)" ("[Then] he can give the rein to raging woe, / Alone, by other's presence unreprest," 122). He is the horse, unrestrained, something mad in his energy and not human. His radical dislocation is communicated by his headlessness, his condition that of a "cavallo sfrenato."

Then follows the great statement in the poem of the dispersed or divided self. Orlando cries out:

> Non son, non sono io quel che paio in viso:
> quel ch'era Orlando è morto et è sotterra;

la sua donna ingratissima l'ha ucciso:
sì, mancando di fé, gli ha fatto guerra.
Io son lo spirito suo da lui diviso,
ch'in questo inferno tormentandosi erra,
acciò con l'ombra sia, che sola avanza,
esempio a chi in Amor pone speranza.

[128]

[I am not—am not what I seem in sight:
What Roland was is dead and under ground,
Slain by that most ungrateful lady's spite,
Whose faithlessness inflicted such a wound.
Divided from the flesh, I am his sprite,
Which in this hell, tormented, walks its round,
To be, but in its shadow left above,
A warning to all such as trust in love.]

Now Orlando is not simply a victim of the fact things are not what they seem; he embodies that fact. Illusion is the essence of existence. And the result of this situation, and knowledge, is that man is radically divided against, and within, himself. Here is Ariosto's greatest appeal for prudence and self-possession and for a willingness to live within limitation, and his greatest warning against putting one's faith and hope in any system, verbal or cultural. For the end of such wholesome faith will only be despair and division.

Orlando is mad. And his madness grows, "Che fuor del senno al fin l'ebbe condotto" (["Until it had led far beyond good sense"], 137). Ariosto, typically, introduces that quality he values most, *senno*, good or common sense, by telling us it has been lost. In stanza 133, the essential, brute man emerges when Orlando strips off his armor, thus shedding chivalry, for once he is bereft of his reason, he must jettison the civilized trappings that symbolized, and also undermined, reason. Now Orlando is defined by his real needs, not by social norms, and like any of the runaway horses we have seen, he plunges on into the woods. The terrible weight of conventional assumptions has shattered this man, as, according to the poet, it will shatter any one of us. Like his predecessors, Ariosto has used the spectacle of the horse and the metaphor of curbing to show us the loss of control that invariably results from substituting something else for one's native *senno*.

The story of Orlando is resumed in canto 29, where many of these insights are clarified and extended. Orlando sees Angelica and Medoro and gives chase. She uses her magic ring to disappear and Orlando seizes her mare "ch'un altro avrebbe fatto una donzella" (["as another would have seized a girl,"] 68). Here the identification between sexual activity and riding, hinted at humorously elsewhere (8.49–50, 28.64) is made serious and explicit, and the mad fury of Orlando is given a powerful sexual source and meaning. As he rides her horse into the ground and kills it, it is clear that he has released on the mare the sexual energy that, according to social and "poetic" custom, he had to restrain with her mistress. And after the horse dies and he simply drags her over the ground, "Orlando non le pensa e non la guarda, / e via correndo il suo camin non tarda" ("Orlando nought the slaughtered mare regards, / Nor anywise his headlong course retards," 71). He has truly become the "cavallo sfrenato" once more, his human sexual fury spent, his bestial nature now unchecked. In canto 30, he finally rides another horse straight into the sea (12–14), as Ariosto exploits the imagery of dissolution and submersion we saw in Pulci and Boiardo, the fatal tendency in man to succumb to the rush of instinct and to lose all human shape. But the most powerful image is that of the huge, naked man dragging the dead mare. This is Ariosto's most arresting vision of man's sexual need spurring him beyond reason, and of chivalry as a burden, a dead weight to be borne even when it is without life or significance.

The *senno* Orlando lost at 23.132 is recovered by Astolfo at 34.66, on the Moon.[20] Astolfo brings Orlando's *senno* back to earth to where the mighty madman is bound fast. Orlando inhales from the proferred vial and sanity returns. Then Orlando, restored, wonders at his bound condition:

> Poi disse, come già disse Sileno
> a quei che lo legàr nel cavo speco:
> *Solvite me*, con viso sì sereno,
> con guardo sì men de l'usato bieco,
> che fu slegato.
>
> [39.60]

> [Then said, as erst Silenus said—when seen,
> And taken sleeping in the cave of yore—
> SOLVITE ME, with visage so serene,

With look so much less wayward than before,
That him they from his bonds delivered clean.]

Orlando echoes Virgil's Silenus (*Eclogue* 6.24: "Solvite me, pueri: satis est potuisse videri" ["Loose me, lads; enough that you have shown your power"]), a bucolic reminiscence that cures the madness acquired in a pastoral place. As we said before, our tragic predicament is that tradition and convention can sustain us as well as destroy us, cure as well as kill. There are no easy answers.

Now the great cry for release expands on all the former images of restraint, as Orlando has finally learned that external curbs are unnecessary if a man checks his internal energies himself. He who was like, and then was, a "cavallo sfrenato" can now be a Silenus freed, because he knows the only true and effective check is his own *senno*, his own sense of limit and inner government matched to the moment. As the former images of unrefrained energy find their proper answer in this example of the man who checks himself, so *senno* restored brings with it the "viso . . . sereno." Throughout the poem, *senno* is finally opposed to *sfrenatura*, *serenità* to the person *di sé tolto*.[21]

At the end of the *Orlando Furioso*, all we have learned through Orlando's plight in canto 23, and what went into and came out of that canto, is manifest in history. Ruggiero and Bradamante will found the Este line. But at their marriage, the forces of disunity, in Rodomonte, intrude to shatter the new integration of might and grace, Saracen convert and native Christian, male and female (46.101 f.). Ruggiero and Rodomonte then engage in a titanic struggle before the wedding guests, in a way dispersing the energy already so carefully gathered and woven—as in the poem—into the wedding tent and nuptial bed (46.77 f.). Rodomonte seizes Ruggiero by the throat and throws him to the ground. At this critical moment, when everything that was gathered in threatens to become dispersed, Ruggiero looks at his bride: "e turbar vide il bel viso sereno" ("[And troubled sees] that fair face serene," 125). The vision of secular serenity, the most we can hope for here below, inspires Ruggiero, and he reasserts himself. The battle is tremendous, but finally

Ruggier sta in sé raccolto, e metter in opra
senno e valor, per rimaner di sopra.

[133]

[Collected in himself, Ruggiero wrought
[sense and courage, to remain on top.]]

What we can have—not what we ought to have—energizes Ruggiero to collect himself and to rely on what is best within him, and not on what society prescribes for him. Angelica, "di sé tolto" by love in canto 1, is matched by Ruggiero, "in sé raccolto" for love in canto 46.

The ironies of this final resolution, of course, are clear, for much as Ruggiero is able to restrain, or gather and thus effectively release all his *virtù*, our last view is of the bridegroom embracing not the bride but his male enemy, not new life but death. Our final view is of how, at the beginning of Este history, only the past was reenacted when the future was meant to be projected, how war was the constant norm where peace was supposed to rule. Like Virgil, whose epic's last line his last line echoes, Ariosto sees hope as streaked by melancholy and futility, the civic order as always prey to the individual's impulse to decay. But this resolutionm—omentary, tenuous—and the story of Orlando, who learned how a man becomes headless and runs away, beside himself, into the forests of despair, and how he can come back, is the paradigm for man's excesses and for the self-imposed limitations that will be his salvation.

Later the chivalric epic would change. In Tasso, the impulse to dispersal and the need for limit would become part of the very structure of his epic as well as themes in it. In Spenser's *Faerie Queene* and Cervantes's *Don Quixote*, the necessity to refrain our instinct to transform would produce great, elegiac epic visions. But the radical issues are established in Pulci, Boiardo, and Ariosto, in those poets who understood first the limits of the world they so loved, who knew that we swell toward death in pursuit of what is most vital in us, who knew that artistic creation is, finally, a version of the problem of restraint and release that the work of art describes. These were the poets who understood how deep into our common humanity the simple image and act of restraining a horse could go.

NOTES

1. Text and translation from Loeb Library *Virgil*, ed. H. R. Fairclough, 2 vols. (rev. ed., London and Cambridge, Mass., 1965).

2. In Greek writing, the predominant images for horses out of control involve horses and chariots. Hippolytus, whose name means "loosened" or "liberated" horse, is the master image for the tragic end to unruly passions. For the ethical and erotic impulses of man, there is Plato's image of the two winged horses of the soul, the one "noble and good, and of good stock," the other quite the opposite (*Phaedrus*, 246b), and their charioteer (253c, 254a). Representations of *riding* are rare in Greek art and literature before 700 B.C.—Homer speaks of riding only twice, and then in similes (*Iliad* 15.679, *Odyssey* 5.371), though he does show chariot horses ridden under extraordinary circumstances (*Iliad* 10.512 f.). See J. K. Anderson, *Ancient Greek Horsemanship* (University of California Press, 1961), p. 10. Because ancient riders, Greek and Roman, had no stirrups, there are instances mentioned by historians of riders dying as a result of their inability to control their horses—Tacitus, *Agricola* 37.6; Plutarch, *Artaxerxes* 21 (Anderson, *ibid*, pp. 76-77). On the stirrup and its importance, especially to chivalry, see Lynn White, Jr., *Medieval Technology and Social Change* (Oxford University Press, 1962), pp. 1-38.

3. The ancients seemed to emphasize different parts of the centaur: Nessus, who would have raped Deianira, is the lower part; Chiron, already remembered in the *Iliad* (4.219) for his healing arts, is the upper, human part.

4. Text from the Loeb Library *The Theological Tracts,* ed. H. F. Stewart and E. K. Rand (Cambridge, Mass. and London, 1918); I have used the translation in the Library of Liberal Arts of Richard Green (Indianapolis and New York, 1962).

5. I use the two-volume edition of G. Busnelli and G. Vandelli in the series *Opere di Dante*, ed. M. Barbi (Florence, 1934). On Temperance, and spurring and curbing a horse (and the *Aeneid*), see also *Convivio* 4.26.5-11. Henceforth, all translations are mine unless otherwise noted.

6. See *Convivio* vol. 2, p. 101 for other versions of the image and explications.

7. Text from *La Divina Commedia*, ed. C. H. Grandgent, rev. C. S. Singleton (Cambridge, Mass.: Harvard University Press, 1972). Translation from *The Divine Comedy*, trans. and ed. T. G. Bergin (New York: Crofts Classics, 1955).

8. Luigi Pulci (1432–84). *Morgante* begun in 1461; cantos 1–23.47 printed in 1478; cantos 18.112–19.155 (Margutte episode) printed separately, 1480–81. Both publications were lost; other versions printed in 1481 and 1482, while Pulci was also working on a second poem, finished after 25 March 1482; the two poems published together as one, 7 February 1483. Text used is *Morgante*, ed. F. Ageno, *Letteratura Italiana, Storia e Testi* 17 (Milan-Naples, 1955). Translations mine. Ageno has a good bibliography, pp. xxviii-xxx; I would only add, in English, L. Einstein, *Luigi Pulci and The Morgante Maggiore, Litteraturhistorische Forschungen*, vol. 22 (Berlin, 1902), and G. Grillo, *Two Aspects of Chivalry, Pulci and Boiardo* (Boston, 1942), though this last is less helpful. For Pulci's cultural milieu and relevent bibliography, see E. A. Lebano, "Luigi Pulci and Late Fifteenth-Century Humanism in Florence," *Renaissance Quarterly* 27 (1974) 489–98. For a survey of the Italian epic including Pulci, Boiardo, and Ariosto, see the introduction to *Ludovico Ariosto Orlando Furioso*, trans. W. S. Rose, ed. S. A. Baker and A. B. Giamatti, Library of Literature (New York, Indianapolis, 1968); also, a survey of translations of these poets and others by K. J. Atchity, "Renaissance Epics in English," *Italica* 50, no. 3 (1973):435–39. Also see below, notes 15 and 18.

9. The contrast between Jehoshaphat (Joel 3:2), the scene of the resurrection of the dead (also *Morgante* 1.6; 3.43), and Roncesvalles, the "dolente valle" ("sorrowful valley"), "Caïna d'inferno" ("Caïna of Hell"), full of dead at 27.201, is another instance of the dialectic, of Pulci's constant desire to believe in something better and his awareness of decay beneath everything.

10. Ageno cites a codex where *mortito* is defined as being made "con un capo di porco e dodici piedi di castrone cotti nel vino rosso con coccole di mortine, garofani, cannella e pepe" ("with the head of a pig and twelve feet of a gelding cooked in red wine with myrtle berries, clove, cinnamon, and pepper"), *Morgante*, 7.56, p. 168. The animal parts in red wine are a ghastly analogue to the carnage of war. And was there not a punning echo of the *mortito* in the *cavallo*, who after Rinaldo struck him, fell "come e' fussi tramortito"? (13.65).

11. Warfare—and thus, in this world—life, as *gioco*: 3.49, 13.64, 19.37, 112, 20.68, 21.74, 22.138, 170, 27.27; for references to "fare il gioco netto," see 11.37, 13.62, 17.12, 64, 26.151, 28.21.

12. Desiderius Erasmus, *The Praise of Folly*, trans. H. Hudson (Princeton, 1941), p. 38. On play, see J. Huizinga's classic *Homo Ludens* (Boston, 1950), especially pp. 180–82.

13. *El Ingenioso Hidalgo Don Quixote de la Mancha*, ed. F. Rodríguez Marín (new ed., Madrid, 1948), 5, 174.

14. On Arnaldo, see 25.115, 28.26.

15. Matteo Maria Boiardo (1441–94). *Orlando Innamorato*, begun in the 1460s; books 1 (29 cantos) and 2 (31 cantos) published together in 1483; book 3 (9 cantos) published separately in 1495; all three books published together first in 1495. Text used: *Orlando Innamorato, Amorum Libri*, ed. A. Scaglione, Classici Italiani, 2 vols. (Turin, 1963). Translations mine. Scaglione has a useful bibliography in 1.37–41. Now there are the papers of the Boiardo Congress, Scandiano, Reggio-Emilia, 1969, in *Il Boiardo e la critica contemporanea*, ed. G. Anceschi (Florence, 1970). Criticism in English: Sir Antonio Panizzi published, with Italian text and English notes, Boiardo's *Orlando Innamorato* (4 vols.) and Ariosto's *Orlando Furioso* (4 vols.), with an introductory volume on romantic narrative (London, 1830–34); J. A. Symonds, *Renaissance in Italy, Italian Literature*, 2 vols. (London, 1881), now in Capricorn Books (New York, 1964), 1: 371–432, on "Pulci and Boiardo"; Vernon Lee [Violet Paget], *Euphorion: Being Studies of the Antique and Mediaeval in the Renaissance*, 2 vols. (London, 1884), discusses Boiardo in each volume; E. W. Edwards, *The Orlando Furioso and its Predecessor* (Cambridge, 1924). Of recent criticism in English, there is a fine chapter in R. Durling, *The Figure of the Poet in Renaissance Epic* (Cambridge, Mass.: Harvard University Press, 1965), and a study by A. Di Tommaso, *Structure and Ideology in Boiardo's Orlando Innamorato*, University of North Carolina Studies in Romance Languages and Literatures, vol. 23 (Chapel Hill, 1972). See also n. 8 above and n. 18 below for relevant items.

16. See the preparation for this event, at 2.28.21, when the court goes to battle, substituting for *danze* (dances) a cacophony of men, instruments, and dogs: "Par che '1 cel cada e '1 mondo abbia a finire" ("It seems that the heavens fall and the world comes to an end.")

17. Compare a similar stanza on his own art by Pulci, *Morgante* 28.140.

18. Ludovico Ariosto (1474–1533). *Orlando Furioso* was begun by 1509 and published in forty cantos, 1516; 2d rev. ed., forty cantos, 1521; 3d ed., forty-six cantos, 1532. Text used : *Orlando Furioso*, ed. L. Caretti, La Letteratura Italiana, Storia e Testi 19 (Milan-Naples, 1954); notes to *Orlando Furioso* in vol. 2, *Opere Minori*, ed. C. Segre. Translations are from the W. S. Rose translation, ed. Baker and Giamatti, with my emendations in brackets. I have not adopted Rose's spelling of proper names. There is a vast literature on Ariosto; the best review of Ariosto's critical "fortune" and a listing of basic bibliographies and monographs is in Mario Puppo, *Manuale critico-bibliografico per lo studio della letteratura italiana*, 5th rev. ed. (Turin, 1964), pp. 243–52; see also the entry "Ludovico Ariosto" by N. Sapegno in *Dizionario Biografico degli Italiani* (Rome, 1962), 4.172–88. For criticism in English, see the bibliography in the Rose translation, ed. Baker and Giamatti, pp. xlv-xlvi. Two recent full-length studies of Ariosto and his poem in English are: Robert Griffin, *Ludovico Ariosto*, Twayne World Authors Series (New York: Twayne Publishers, 1974) and C. P. Brand, *Ludovico Ariosto: Preface to the Orlando Furioso* (Edinburgh: Edinburgh University Press, 1974). Also see above, nn. 8 and 15 for relevant items.

19. *Istoria* (118; 120) is also the poem's word for itself—see 13.80 or 23.136—as the analogy between Orlando's predicament and the reader's is maintained throughout.

20. Earlier occurrences of *senno* at 4.65 and 27.8 contribute to the meaning of sensible, reasonable, and ethical behavior that the word acquires in the poem.

21. For *sereno*, see the serene air (4.43), sky (27.8), faces of God (17.6), Christians (43.199), or serene eyes obscured (1.79; 11.64)—all images of the integrated ideal we must strive for. This particular pattern of imagery has an important history, and implications, in the Renaissance epic: see A. B. Giamatti, "Spenser: From Magic to Miracle," in *Four Essays on Romance*, ed. H. Baker (Cambridge, Mass.: Harvard University Press, 1971), pp. 17–31.

12

The Timelessness of the *Scienza Nuova* of Giambattista Vico

A. Robert Caponigri

Half a century ago and more, an incident occurred that might well have served as the subject of one of those *aneddoti* Benedetto Croce loved to recount and recounted so deftly. In dedicating his seminal work on the philosophy of Giambattista Vico to the noted neo-Kantian philosopher and historian of philosophy, Wilhelm Windelband, Croce confided that his motive was the hope that a serious lacuna he had lamented both in Windelband's history and others as well, might be remedied. This was the absence of any presentation of the thought of Giambattista Vico. Some twenty years later, on the appearance of the second edition of his own monograph on Vico, Croce reported with evident pleasure, not only that Windelband had, in the fifth edition of his history, repaired that lacuna, but also that Croce's own work had, almost immediately on its appearance, been translated from the Italian into several other languages.[1]

Today such an omission would be unthinkable. Vico has moved from the periphery of the history of Western thought to its very center. His place as one of the seminal thinkers of modern times and the timeliness and significance of his great work, the *Scienza Nuova*,[2] for our own age are assured. How, one is led to ask, is this transformation to be explained? The explanation is clear. In the *Scienza Nuova*, Vico anticipated by two centuries contemporary man's most profound discovery concerning himself: the fact that he has a history—even more, that man

309

is his own history, because by creating history man discovers and actualizes his own humanity.

Contemporary man has come to this discovery of his historical character by a laborious path. The first stage on this path (one recalls the idols of Bacon and Vico's own *borie*—the self-conceits, the wells of arrogance, SNS 122–28) is deliverance from illusion, in this case, from the illusory promises of science. The growth of the modern spirit of science in the Renaissance[3] and the cultural transformations that followed, led modern man to believe that he had discovered in science the means of coming to know his own nature, of realizing his own highest potentialities, and of controlling not only the forces of nature but also the course of his own history. The illusory character of the promise of science revealed itself only slowly. Only slowly did the mastery over nature that science promised appear in its true light: as nature's mastery over man. Similarly, the self-knowledge that science promised man proved to be the alienation of man from himself, because science could reveal man to himself only as an object and therefore as something *other* than himself, never as himself.

Finally, science proved to be, not the directive and rectifying principle of history, but the destroyer of history. Scientific knowledge led man to forget history. The past became irrelevant, something to be displaced and forgotten, not remembered and preserved. The future became hazardous, despite all notions of planning based on scientific knowledge and technology, because science could not teach man wisdom and prudence, the true principles of man's historical action. The present became lost between future and past. Because it passed so rapidly into the past, the present, too, seemed to exist only to be forgotten. Because the present seemed so unsubstantial, it seemed to exist only to serve the future—a future that man in the present would never enjoy. Deliverance from illusion, however, if it really is deliverance, means awakening to reality. The reality to which contemporary man awakened from the illusions of science was history: his own history, his own character as historical, at once creator and creature of history.

In the light of this new understanding of himself, and in the new perspective which he had gradually gained on history, contemporary man realized the stature of Vico and the relevance of his *Scienza Nuova*. He recognized in Vico one who had anticipated his own disillusionment with the promises of science; in like manner, he perceived in the long-neglected doctrines of the *Scienza Nuova* anticipations of fresh insights into his historical character. He saw that, from the very threshold of the modern age, Vico had diagnosed the situation of modern man before that situation had even arisen.[4] On the very eve of the triumph of science, Vico had sensed the hollowness of its promises, the unwisdom of its truth. When the idea of science seemed to overshadow all rivals, Vico had intuited the alienation that science would bring to man and had confronted science with the only discipline that could bring man authentic self-knowledge and spiritual integrity. He defined this knowledge in the "science of humanity" which is the substance of the *Scienza Nuova*. As contemporary man has come to appreciate his own predicament, the power of Vico's vision and its contemporary relevance has grown steadily clearer.

The *Scienza Nuova*, in its widest scope, envisages nothing less than a science of humanity that might serve as the speculative basis for an integral humanism. Integral humanism may be defined as man's total presence to himself. The structure of that presence is complex. Vico conceived that structure, in the first place, as "wisdom." Humanism, as wisdom, is man's presence to himself as idea and power: "nosse, posse, velle" ("knowledge, capacity, will").[5] These dimensions of presence do not stand in opposition to each other. They constitute a concrete synthesis: wisdom is idea that is endowed with its own immanent, dynamic principles of self-actualization. Wisdom is, in Vico's words: "Egli è l'uomo . . . nel proprio esser d'uomo, che mente ed animo, or vogliamo dire intelletto e volontà. La sapienza dee compier all'uomo entrambe queste due parti e la seconda in séquito della prima" ("Man, in his proper being as man, consists of mind and spirit, or, if we prefer, of intellect and will. It is the function of wisdom to fulfill both these parts in man, the second by the way of the first," SNS 364). In this synthesis, idea is the radical principle of presence. Idea, moreover—and specifically the idea of man—is a normative idea for Vico. The ultimate object of the *Scienza Nuova* is to determine the idea of man as the principle of man's total presence to himself. Up to this point Vico seems to be in the direct line of Plato. Coincidence with Plato is, however, not a point of arrival but a point of departure for Vico's thought.

Plato, Vico believes, thought that to determine the idea of man meant to fix man's essence in a principle of unity, identity, and permanence apart from the processes in which human life is existentially involved.

Plato tried to establish the subjectivity of man independently of the organic processes in which man's physical and psychic life are delicately and intricately enmeshed; independently of the social and cultural processes which are the very substance of his concrete existence; and, finally, independently of the natural order in which organic, cultural, and social processes transpire. The error of Platonism (and of Western philosophy in general), from the point of view of an integral humanism, is to be found precisely here. "La filosofia," Vico writes, "considera l'uomo quale dev'essere, e sí non può fruttare ch'a pochissimi, che vogliano vivere nella repubblica di Platone, non rovesciarsi nella feccia di Romolo" ("Philosophy considers man as he should be and so can be of service only to very few who wish to live in the Republic of Plato, not to fall back into the dregs of Romulus," SNS 131).

But this is wrong, for "La filosofia, per giovar al genere umano, dee sollevar e reggere l'uomo caduto e debole, non convellergli la natura né abandonarlo nella sua corruzione" ("To be useful to the human race, philosophy must raise and direct weak and fallen man, not rend his nature or abandon him in his corruption").[6] The idea of man, conceived in the abstract and transcendent manner of Platonism, cannot be the principle of a concrete human wisdom or of man's total presence to himself. On the contrary, Vico believes, such an idea of man must only alienate man from himself and distort the self-knowledge which is the necessary basis of all human wisdom. The Platonic idea is the source, not of wisdom, nor of total presence, but of a profound absence and alienation in man.

Vico introduces a qualification that alters the Platonic position radically. This qualification is the insight that the idea of man must be sought in and through, not in opposition to, the concrete existential processes. The processes of culture and history are constitutive elements of the idea of man. These processes identify the conditions on which the idea of man is available, the conditions on which man's total presence to himself is possible. The idea of man is not the presupposition of those processes. Man does not have a "nature" that can be identified independently of those processes and on which those processes may be thought to depend. The nature of anything is its coming to be—its birth —in time. "Natura di cose altro non è che nascimento di esse in certi tempi e con certi guise, le quali sempre che sono tali, indi tali e non altre nascon le cose" ("The nature of things is nothing but their coming into being [*nascimento*] at certain times and in certain fashions. Whenever the time and fashion is thus and so, such and not otherwise are the things that come into being").[7] The idea of man must be derived from these processes. The insight conveyed in this *degnità* points to the speculative problem of the *Scienza Nuova* as a science of humanity.

Vico is not yet in a position to formulate this speculative problem of his "science of humanity" clearly. He has still to determine the dimension of concrete process to which the idea of man is most directly related and from which it may, therefore, be derived with greatest security. Man is an organism, man is in physical nature, man creates culture, man has a history. Which of these processes reveals the idea of himself to man most directly?

Physical nature is too wide a context for the idea of man for two reasons. In the first place, nature is the matrix of ideas other than that of man, ideas that are in contradiction to the idea of man, that alienate man from himself when he seeks to know himself in terms of those ideas. In the second place, whatever idea of man can be derived from or formulated in the context of physical nature, arises by a negative movement and therefore as an absence of man from himself. For example, the ideas of causation and of physical necessity arise within the context of physical nature. Insofar as these ideas are the principles under which the idea of nature itself is determined, the idea of man can arise within the context of nature only by negation. Man cannot render himself present to himself through these ideas of cause and physical necessity. He cannot think of himself as merely a dimension of a system of causation, nor as wholly determined in his being and action by physical necessity. He can define himself in the context of nature only by denying that these ideas apply to him or by imposing important limits on the manner and the degree to which they do apply. The sense of his own freedom—however that freedom is conceived—is too profound.

Consequently, any attempt on man's part to form the idea of hmself in the context of physical nature is abortive and generates absence from himself, not presence to himself. On the other hand, such definition of the idea of man by negation is not without meaning for man. The knowledge of what he is not is surely part of man's total presence to himself. As Vico says, man is "nosse, posse, velle finitum" ("finite knowledge, capacity, will"). He indeed completes this sentence by adding "quod tendit ad infinitum" ("which tends to the infinite").[8] The sense of limit which vibrates through that "finitum" is absolutely integral to man's idea of himself. Physical nature therefore remains, for Vico, the broadest context for the idea of man. It is not, however, the specific context for the positive formulation of that idea, and cannot provide the clue to the formulation of the speculative problem of the *Scienza Nuova*.

While the context of physical nature is too wide for the formulation of the idea of man, the organic context is too narrow. Since the organic order is a specification of the order of nature, it is subject to the same criticisms. Vico adduces a further reason, however, why the organic context is alien, or at least inadequate, to the idea of man. An idea of man can indeed be formulated within the organic context: the idea of man as individual, the instantiation of a genus or kind. This idea is too meager, however, to generate or sustain man's total presence to himself. On the contrary, the idea of man as individual must eventually prove to be a source of alienation and absence for man. The individual is only a repetition of the species; each individual lives out the total economy of the species in the solitude and isolation of his own existence. He is essentially solitary, and because solitary, generates no new forms of life. He repeats the eternal cycle; or, if that cycle is broken, as evolutionary theory would suggest, it is through no initiative of the individual, nor by any cooperative initiative of the individual with others of his kind.

The idea of man as individual makes him a solitary; it sets him in opposition to himself in the essentially group processes of culture and makes the relationship of individual and community unintelligible. This fact was brought home to Vico very clearly by the doctrine of jusnaturalism to which he had fallen heir. It is the basis of his opposition to that doctrine, as well as to all forms of contractualism, even in the form which had been put forward by the political theorists of the "Second Scholasticism," such as Suarez.[9]

The concrete processes of culture alone provide the context for the idea of man because only in that context are the conditions of total presence realized. In that context alone presence encounters no limiting absence. In culture, the alienation latent in nature is overcome because all cultural structures are modes of the presence of man to himself as defined against nature. The alienation implicit in the idea of man as individual is also transcended in this context, because the abstract confrontation between men as individuals is negated by the basic group structure of all cultural forms. As a consequence of these reflections, the speculative problem of the *Scienza Nuova* appears as the problem of the relation of the idea of man to cultural process.

An ambiguity still persists. Vico has not yet identified the specific character of cultural process. He has suggested that culture is essentially social. Sociality itself, however, does not suffice to specify the character of culture with respect to the idea of man. While sociality is a dimension of man's presence to himself in the context of culture, it is not the term which relates the idea of man to the concreteness of cultural process. The term that will establish this relation and, in doing so, will advance the precise formulation of the speculative problem of the *Scienza Nuova*, has yet to be fixed. Vico identifies this term as *time* and, by doing so, identifies the speculative problem of the *Scienza Nuova* as the speculative problem of history—of the relation of *time* and *idea*.

Vico first attempts to meet this problem of the relation of time and idea, not in the context of the science of humanity in its widest scope, but within the narrower confines of the science of jurisprudence. Within the field of jurisprudence, moreover, he identifies the problem of natural law as crucial. Vico believes that juridical institutions are the type of all cultural forms. Jurisprudence is the science of juridical institutions, and the problem of the natural law is the central speculative problem of jurisprudence. He is persuaded, consequently, that the solution of the problem of natural law will provide him with the key to the speculative problem of the science of humanity—the relation of the idea of man to the process of the formation of cultural structures through time: the problem of the relationship of time and idea.

The theoretical problem of natural law is the problem of finding the principle by which the ostensible opposition between positivity and ideality, between reason and authority, and between truth and certitude in the law may be mediated. Vico's point of departure is the social process of the interpretation and administration of law. This process is confronted immediately by the positive law—that is, a specific enactment of a concrete legislative will in determinate circumstances. The primary properties of positive law are *certitude* and *authority*. As Ulpian wrote: "Dura lex sed scripta," which Vico amends to "Lex dura est, sed certa est" ("The law is harsh but written"; "The law is harsh, but nonetheless it is certain").[10]

These properties, however, do not furnish an adequate basis for the interpretation and administration of law, to say nothing of the theoretical comprehension of it. The literal translation of law from the context of its enactment to that of its interpretation merely on the basis of its certitude and authority must result as often as not in injustice—the nullification of the reality of law. A mediatorial principle that might effect a valid translation is necessity. The maxims of the law exercise this function to a certain degree, but they add only a further positive dimension to the juridical situation. They have practical, not theoretical, value.[11] At the theoretical level appears the ideality of the law as opposed to its positivity. Against its mere authority, there appears its *ratio*, its rational principle; over against its mere certitude, its truth.[12]

These elements of law—authority and certitude, *ratio* and truth—are not in necessary correlation, in the order of positive law there is always the latent possibility of tension and even opposition between them; a positive law that has no valid *ratio*, a principle that is not realized or actualized in positive legislation, is always possible. As Vico translates—or better interprets—Ulpian's "Dura est, sed scripta," "Certa lex est, sed vera prorsus non est" ("The law is harsh but written"; "The law is indeed certain, but may not, for all that, be true").[13] This opposition, latent or actual, can be only a matter of fact; it cannot be a principle of the science of jurisprudence nor of the actual process of adjudication—the interpretation and administration of law. Vico's words are adamant "auctoritatem cum ratione omnino pugnare non posse; nam ita non leges essent [the positive laws] sed monstra legum" ("authority can in no way be at war with reason; if it were, those [positive] enactments would not be laws but legal monsters").[14]

The ideality of the law itself cannot be the principle of mediation; ideality denominates a higher immediacy of the law that stands over against the positivity of the law, as one immediacy over against another. Ideality and positivity are the dimensions of law that demand mediation, a principle that will determine the coincidence or deviation of ideality and positivity in any single instance of law; a principle which, in Vico's expression, may establish or effect the convertability of truth and certitude, authority and reason, in law (TI, pp. 147 ff.). The discovery of such a principle is the basic speculative problem of the theory of natural law. Vico's thesis is that this principle is time or history.

Vico develops the theory that time is the principle of mediation between the positivity and ideality, the certitude and the truth of law, by a comparison between jusnaturalism and Roman jurisprudence. This comparison, which occurs as early as the *De Studiorum Ratione* and persists to the *Scienza Nuova Seconda*, consistently yields the same conclusion: the superiority of Roman jurisprudence resides in its historical insight. Jusnaturalism errs because it mistakes the ideality of the law for the natural law. As a result, jusnaturalism can do no more than confront the immediacy of the positive law with a second immediacy—that of the ideality of the law. The two dimensions of law—positivity and ideality, truth and certitude—remain alien and extrinsic to each other in jusnaturalist theory. Roman jurisprudence, by contrast, identified time as the mediatorial principle between the ideality and the positivity of the law.

The central principle of Roman jurisprudence is the "sette dei tempi" ("divisions of the times," TI, pp. 46, 119–22). In the light of this principle, Roman jurisprudence could view the total process of the formation of positive law in history as the concretization of the ideality of the law according to the diversity of utility and necessity in diverse times. This Roman insight yields both a material and a formal, or interpretative, concept of natural law, in which positivity and ideality are mediated, generating the truth of the law as an immanent movement of its certitude. Materially, the natural law is a community of content, of command and prohibition, in positive law (SNS 141–46). Formally, as a principle of interpretation, the natural law directs attention to the time-structure of positive law as the clue to its relation to the ideality of the law.[15]

The terms *time* and *idea*, which constitute the inner formality of juridical structures, cannot be limited to the context of juridical institutions. The typical character that Vico assigns to juridical institutions with respect to all cultural structures makes the extension of these terms to the total cultural process inevitable. All forms of cultural life are dimensions of law in the sense that the law exhibits their essential structure. This is the reason why Vico calls the Roman law "un serioso poema" (SNS 1027). All cultural life, therefore, is the subject of universal jurisprudence, and the structure of the total cultural process is polarized around the same terms that characterized natural law: *time* and *idea* The total cultural process is viewed as a temporal-ideal process in which the ideal term is not merely a limited idea—such as the idea of justice or *aequum bonum* which informs the juridical process—but the universal idea of man, of humanity.

If this conception of cultural process is correct, man in his idea stands in the same relationship to himself as the ideality of the law stands to its positivity, the idea of humanity to the cultural process in which it is realized—in the relation, that is, of time and idea. Time and idea, consequently, represent, not a process in which man is involved only extrinsically and contingently, but the inward form of his own life, of his "nature" which is, in the dictum of Vico quoted above,[16] his coming to be in time. The ultimate reference of the time-idea polarity is man himself.

Vico's analysis reveals the basic term of a science of humanity—time and idea. It does not, however, yield the speculative *principle* but only the speculative *problem* of that science. If that science is not to remain at a purely positivistic level, bereft of true philosophical stature, a speculative concept of history must be formed. The speculative concept of history must make clear in principle the possibility of a time-ideal process. The speculative problem of the *Scienza Nuova* is that of finding the principle of mediation between time and idea—the formulation of a theory of history as the formal basis of a science of humanity.

The *speculative* problem of the *Scienza Nuova*, then, seems clear: to discover how a temporal process may be ideal and how the idea may be realized in time. That speculative concept, once formed, will become the basis of a genuine and effective historical method whose object will be the whole range of man's cultural experience. Vico formulates the speculative concept of history in two phases. In the first and negative phase he is concerned with the critique of the concept of nature and the basis of that concept—intellectualism. He discovers that the concept of nature is, historically, the source of the separation between time and idea that had so far made a genuine science of humanity impossible. In the second and positive phase, his purpose is to identify the principle of the unity of time and idea. He finds this principle to be man himself as "finitum quod tendit ad infinitum"—a "finite being whose whole tendency is toward the infinite."

To appreciate Vico's critique of the concept of nature, reference must be made to his famous formula "verum factum convertuntur" ("truth and fact are transposable").[17] A strong argument has been made for a "pragmatic" interpretation of this formula.[18] Such an interpretation would seem to receive little support from Vico's text. Truth, according to pragmatic theory, is consequential on action; the dualism between thought and action implicit in pragmatism is alien to Vico. His insight is that truth is a dimension of the subject and cannot be conceived as a property of objects in themselves, in other words, as being independent of the subject, as not having its ground in the subject. Giovanni Gentile, in his theory of mind as pure act,[19] would seem to offer the clearest insight into Vico's intention in this formula of convertibility, for Gentile makes clear the basic circularity which characterizes the actuality of mind.

Truth is the mode of presence of the subject to itself; but this mode of presence is complex. Subject is not immediately present to itself. Its self-presence is mediated and the term of this mediation is the object. The object, in its turn, is grounded in the actuality of the subject—not in the antecedent actuality, to be sure—but in the actuality of the subject in the act of rendering itself present to itself through the mediation of the object. It is this circularity, which establishes the integrity of mnd as total presence—that is, presence in which the dualism of subject and object is completely mediated, but in a mode of mediation in which the actuality of the two is not distorted into a "higher" immediacy but retained in a thoroughly mediated duality—that Vico intends by his formula of the conversion of truth and fact. And this formula, in turn, offers the basis for his critique of the concept of nature.

Vico's critique of the concept of nature involves a sharp dichotomy between the world of nature and the world of history. Nature, he states, as the result of God's creative act, is wholly accessible only to Him.[20] Man can have only a superficial knowledge of nature. The truth of history, by contrast, since it is the result of his own creative activity, must in principle be wholly accessible and available to man. Of history, and hence of himself, man can hope to achieve a knowledge "in depth."

Vico's critique of nature, consequently, reduces itself to a charge of "eternism." "Eternism" involves a conception of truth that separates temporal process and idea beyond any possibility of mediation. This separation of the ideal and the temporal is brought about by a transference of subjectivity that Vico finds illegitimate. Nature is not eternistic because it excludes the principle of the convertibility of truth and fact. Rather, nature is eternistic by reason of the character of the subjectivity to whose act truth is referred in the concept of nature. The subjectivity implicit in nature is *absolute* subject; nature involves total presence of absolute subject to itself. The presence of absolute subject to itself must be without temporal dimension; it must be that "species aeternitatis" under which Spinoza sought to view all things. The idea is contracted into instantial immediacy, the *totum simul* of classical scholastic metaphysics. In eternism the human subject, which is not absolute, is transcended—namely, is *no longer* the subjectivity to which truth, in the process of circularity described above, is referred. The human subject stands at the core of history. All its reality transpires in history. Time is of its essence, precisely because human subjectivity is "finitum quod tendit ad infinitum." This formula also indicates the specific form of the time of history, the time of human subjectivity. Time is the inner movement from absence to presence—from absence, which is the constitutive finitude of human subjectivity, to the *infinitum*, which is the plenum of human subjectivity, presence to itself. Eternism is fallacious because it renders history unintelligible to man, because it denies that tension between finitude and infinity which is the essence of the time of human subjectivity and of history and the inner form of the presence of man to himself.

The fallaciousness of eternism is amply documented in the history of Western philosophy. Plato, as Vico never ceases to point out, is its primary exemplar. The same fallacy, however, infests the thought of Spinoza and, later, of Hegel. Hegel documents his awareness of his displacement of subjectivity by the description he is said to have given of his *Logic*, namely, that it depicts God's knowledge of the world antecedent to His creation of it.

We must also note that Vico is not unqualifiedly opposed to the principle of eternism and does not become involved in "atheism" as a result of that opposition, as G. F. Finetti charged and as Croce supports him in that charge.[21] Vico opposes eternism only to the degree that it pretends to offer the principle of a science of humanity. Eternism, in his view, can be the principle of a theology—or better, as Antonio Rosmini indicated, of a theosophy. Theosophy is not a science *about* God from a human standpoint, as theology has always been, even when supported by revelation. Theosophy is God's own science of his own nature and of his creation. Moreover, the science in which theosophy consists is not a contemplative science determined by an object that is given to it; it is, rather, identical with the act by which God establishes his own being and by which the being of his creation is generated. Such a science as theosophy must be, is not impossible for man, as Rosmini emphasizes (and Vico would agree); but it would have to have some other basis than a science of humanity or a "natural" theology. Such a "theosophy" must have its basis in a revelation that would render God present in history, and hence a possible object of knowledge for man under the guise in which God's presence enters history. Now the "guises" of God's presence in history are two: Providence and direct revelation (incarnation). Vico recognizes both of these modes. Under the first guise, Providence, God forms an integral part of the field of the science of humanity. Vico says specifically, in his catalogue of the aspects of the *Scienza Nuova*, that under one of these aspects—and a most important one—it constitutes a "teologia civile ragionata della provvedenza" ("a rational civil theology of divine providence," SNS 385).

Whence, then, does the fallacy of eternism arise? This question also falls within the scope of Vico's critique of the concept of nature. Its source is to be found, he believes, in "intellectualism," in that "boria de' dotti" ("conceit of the learned") which he describes in the *Scienza Nuova* (SNS 127). Intellectualism is the assumption by man of the posture of absolute subjectivity. It is the attempt to see all things "sub specie aeternitatis," from the point of view of absolute presence as something already realized, or, as in the case of Hegel's alleged claim for his *Logic*, from God's point of view reached by an impossible leap of the mind. Intellectualism, because of its absolute and transcendental orientation, robs man of temporal perspective; as a result, it alienates him from history—his own history. The "dotti" of Vico's *degnitá*, possess a learning which has been won for them by a long historical struggle; from that pinnacle they look back only to deny the journey that brought them there. Thus they are led to assume one of two attitudes toward the past, both of which are false: either they idealize the past, and look to it as a golden age, a treasure of esoteric wisdom; or they disdain it completely. Vico's insight is surer. History is neither to be glorified nor disdained; it is to be understood as the path man has traveled to achieve his humanity.

In opposition to this fallacy of intellectualism, the source of eternism, Vico advances a positive principle for the mediation of time and idea. Stated in his own words, this principle is that "questo mondo civile egli certamente è stato fatto dagli uomini, onde se ne possono, perché se ne debbono, ritruovare i principi dentro le modificazioni della nostra medesima mente umana" ("the world of civil society has certainly been made by men and its principles are therefore to be found within the modifications of our own human mind," SNS 331). Taken in conjunction (and only in conjunction) with Vico's definition of man as "finitum quod tendit ad infinitum," this passage of the *Scienza* becomes the rubric of Vico's theory of history and its key.

When identifying the terms of the speculative problem of history—time and idea—Vico moved from the more restricted to the more inclusive areas in which these terms were realized—from juridical institutions to cultural forms, and finally to man himself. Time and idea define the terms of man's own being. Man stands, not outside of history, but within it. He is within it, not only as its creator, but as the author of his own being in the act of creating history. The force of the rubric cited above—"questo mondo civile egli certamente è stato fatto dagli uomini" ("the world of civil society has certainly been made by men")—is to show more clearly how man is present in history. Cultural institutions are in history contextually; the concept of history is necessary for their theoretical penetration. Man is in history radically, because he transacts his entire existence in terms of time and idea. The radical principle of historicity, consequently, is to be found in man. Man is the mediator between time and idea. History finds its formal principle—that is, the principle of mediation between time and idea—in man, and man finds his reality in history. The speculative problem of history may, therefore, be stated more precisely: how is man the mediatorial principle between time and idea?

The answer to this question is contained in Vico's definition of man as "finitum quod tendit ad infinitum." This "tendency to the infinite" is the source of man's character as mediatorial principle between time and idea. The terms which, in Vico's definition, this tendency holds in unity and in disequilibrium—finite and infinite—are the correlatives of time and idea, the terms of history.

As the correlatives of finite and infinite, time and idea may be identified as partial and total presence. Man is the formal principle of history as subject, which is in dynamic disequilibrium between partial and total presence to itself. History in its "objectivity," in the total process of culture and the multiplicity of cultural forms, is the content of that presence, the system of its phenomena. This phenomenal distention of the subject, in its turn, possesses the same dynamic disequilibrium as

its formal principle, man as subject of history, and defines in phenomenal terms the same movement from partial to total presence, the
radical order of history.

With the identification of man as subject of history, of presence as
the radical mediatorial term between time and idea, of time itself as the
distention of the subject between partial and total presence, the speculative problem of history has been solved in principle. The mediatorial
term between time and idea has been identified and the relationship of
these terms to that mediatorial principle established. The character of
that movement from partial to total presence in which history precisely
consists still remains to be identified. Vico undertakes to make this
identification in his analysis of "le modificazioni della nostra medesima
mente umana" (SNS 331).

These "modifications of our human mind" are neither "empirical"
nor "phenomenal." They are not to be derived in any way from the
content of history. Structuralizations of the content of history can yield
only the phenomenology of history—that is, the system of historical
phenomena, of their order as well as of their individual characteristics.[22]
No such structuralization can yield the ideal principles of history. The
modifications are, rather, the ideal articulations of presence, of a finite
presence which tends to the infinite, of a presence which is in dynamic
disequilibrium between partial and total presence. The rule, or law, of
these articulations of presence is synthesized in the fifty-third *degnità* of
the "Elementi" of the *Scienza Nuova*: "Gli uomini prima sentono
senz' avvertire, dappoi avvertiscono con animo perturbato e commosso,
finalmente riflettono con mente pura" ("Men at first feel without observing, then they observe with a troubled and agitated spirit, finally
they reflect with a clear mind," SNS 218).

The terms of this statement are synthetic; they indicate phases, not
of the theoretical nor of the practical dimensions of presence in abstraction from each other, but of presence as the primal unity beyond all
such distinctions. Vico calls this primal unity "wisdom." The fundamental articulations of presence are, therefore, to be given in terms of
wisdom: the vulgar or popular wisdom, which Vico says, "fu la sapienza
volgare di tutte le nazioni" ("was the vulgar wisdom of all nations,"
SNS 365; it consisted of "divinità d'auspici," or "reading the auspices")
and the wisdom of the philosophers. Nevertheless, the formal principle
of each mode of presence is theoretical: a mode of awareness. Con-

sequently, the articulation of presence as wisdom is established in theoretical terms, in other words in terms of that mode of awareness which corresponds to and provides the formal principle of each mode of wisdom.

The theoretical articulations of presence as wisdom are variously designated. From the point of view of the faculties that produce them, they are designated as fantasy and reason. From the point of view of the forms in which they are expressed, they are called myth and idea. Finally, from the point of view of the way in which the faculties operate in expression, they are designated as spontaneity and reflection. Fantasy, whose mode of production is spontaneity and whose expression is myth, is the formal principle of that wisdom that Vico calls, variously, "vulgar," "popular," or "poetic"; reason, whose mode of operation is reflection and whose expression is idea, is the formal principle of the wisdom of the philosophers. Most radically, however, these articulations are to be distinguished as the dispositions of man as the subject of history.

Poetic wisdom is the mode of partial presence; the wisdom of the philosophers, the mode of total presence of man as subject of history. Each wisdom finds concrete expression in the total economy of natural law, namely, in the total structure of culture, because each informs a proper language, an order of law, of polity, and so forth. The specific character of each component of culture—for instance language, polity, etc.—has a mode of presence as its formal principle. The forms of expression that function as formal principles of the diverse systems of wisdom are myth and idea.

Myth is the key to poetic wisdom and it may be related to that wisdom in two ways: genetically and interpretatively. Myth may be considered as it gives form to poetic wisdom and, from a historiographic point of view, as it allows poetic wisdom to be penetrated from the level of idea. For Vico, fantasy, the faculty that generates myth, is closely associated with memory; indeed, the association with memory is the key to the activity of fantasy. Myth operates through the generation of synthetic images. These images are not generalizations from repeated experiences; rather, time-depth is the essential structure of these images. Myths, therefore, are not generalizations but histories. Vico extended this observation on myth to all the tropes of poetic language:[23] each is a history. Because myth is the formal structural principle of poetic wisdom, the interpretation of myth provides the key to understanding the structures of culture—language, law, polity, etc.—governed by that wisdom. For myth to serve in this fashion, however, it is necessary first to determine the key to the interpretation of myth.

That key lies precisely in its time-depth structure. The first canon of mythology is that every myth is a history (TI 179). The full penetration of the myth, consequently, must represent the reconstruction of a moment of presence of the subject of poetic wisdom in which an entire time-career is synthesized. This observation is true whether the mythical structure is a historical institution, such as a system of law; or an iconographic structure, such as the poetic character of the lawgiver; or a complex iconic system, such as the Homeric poems. In each case, a time-image movement, a poetic history, is synthesized. The presence of man to himself in poetic wisdom must consequently be deciphered from these histories.[24]

Myth, precisely because of its historical, time-depth character, reveals a mode of presence of man as the subject of history. Myth reveals the partial presence to himself that man achieves through the creation of the structure of which myth is the language. The partial character of the presence achieved through myth springs from the spontaneity of myth. The image-structure ofy mth is generated spontaneously, under the impulsion of passion. In the myth, consequently, man, as subject of history, is present to himself only according to the immediate terms of the myth. He is enclosed within these immediacies and, to this extent, is absent from himself according to the limits that the properties of spontaneity and immediacy place upon the myth. Partial presence is also partial absence of man, the subject of history, to himself.

This ambivalent character of the partial presence of man in poetic wisdom, the limitation of presence by absence, accounts for the relation of poetic wisdom to the total presence implied in idea. Idea implies total presence of man to himself because reason, the principle of total presence, seeks the basis of partial presence in a principle of the whole, namely, in an "eternal and ideal history" (SNS 393). The agency of total presence is reflection. Through reflection, man is released from the immediacies and the limitations of partial presence and is enabled to envisage the whole of his history, the total idea of himself. The wisdom of reflection, flowing out as power into the world of concrete cultural forms and into the structures of rational or philosophical discourse, reflects this whole and stands as history of it, just as the structures of poetic wisdom reflect or express the immediacies among which they are formed.

As a result, the relationship between poetic and philosophical wisdom as modes of presence of man in history is complex. The two wisdoms stand, under one aspect, in contradiction to each other; under another aspect, they are premise and conclusion. Partial presence is always a contradiction of total presence simply because it is, at the same time, absence. Every myth is absurd from the point of view of reason. At the same time, myth is the premise, the ground, of the idea. Between image and idea there is radical opposition. The world of the one stands in opposition to the world of the other. Idea, nevertheless, arises on the basis of image. It does so, however, not as the simple clarification or extension of the image, but in some sense at least, as the negation of image—a negation which is, at the same time, fulfillment and realization. Together they constitute the presence of man to himself in history.

Poetic wisdom and the wisdom of philosophy, image, and idea, and the mode of presence proper to each, clearly stand as positivity and ideality, as *certum* and *verum* in relation to each other in the total structure of man's presence to himself. Like the positivity and ideality, the *certum* and the *verum* of law, poetic wisdom and the wisdom of philosophy demand a mediatory principle. That principle must be the true agency of man's total presence to himself in history. In Vico's view, it canot be an immanent principle. This is to say that this mediation of poetic and philosophical wisdom cannot be effected within the terms of human presence alone; there must be recourse to a transcendent principle. For Vico, that principle is *Providence*.[25]

Providence assures the direction of history—the time-ideal process of presence—toward its ideal goal: man's total presence to himself. Providence exercises this function by correcting the deviations, falsifications and alienations to which history is vulnerable because of the tension between partial presence and total presence inherent in it. Providence is itself a form of wisdom—that is, an idea and a power—the idea and power of a transcendent principle. It is the converse of man, the "infinitum quod generat finita" ("infinite principle that generates finite things"). The action of Providence in history is not transitory, an intervention. Providence is present in history functionally and constitutively, as the mediatory principle for the tension between the modes of human presence: partial and total.

As the mediatorial principle within history, Providence profoundly modifies the structure of human presence in history. The constitutive dynamic of human presence is an inward movement from partiality to totality. In this movement, however, human presence encounters contradictions and obstacles that it cannot overcome through its own power. These contradictions can be overcome only by reference to a third principle, another presence and wisdom. As a consequence, human presence in history presents the contradictory aspect of a movement toward totality in conflict with itself and one that can find this totality only in a transcendent principle of presence. Human presence achieves totality only by reference to the total presence implied in Providence. Only in God's presence as Providence can man achieve his total presence to himself in history. Only in the light of that transcendent presence can history lose its aspect of insuperable contradiction and can man's own presence be rescued from the incurable trauma of finitude.

Providence, consequently, is the ultimate principle of the mediation of time and idea, the ultimate and definitive element in Vico's theory of history. Providence mediates time and idea in the context of human presence in history and therefore mediates human presence itself; a science of humanity, in the last analysis, concerns the way in which total human presence is realized in the presence of God as Providence acting in history. The science of humanity proves, paradoxically, to be a science of God, a theology. Man's total presence to himself in history is to be measured by the degree to which he can discern the presence of God as Providence and decipher the true course of history, the "storia ideal eterna" ("ideal eternal history") which the "nations traverse in time" in the light of that transcendent presence.

The speculative concept of history as the theory of the synthesis of time and idea in the total presence of the human subject provides the theoretical basis of the science of humanity that is, at the same time, the theology of God's Providence. The establishment of this idea of the science of humanity still leaves in question the method by which such a science might be achieved. Vico establishes this method as the unity of philosophy and philology (TI, pp. 144 ff.).

The philological dimension of the science of humanity rests upon the expressive character of language. The modes of presence of man as the subject of history were characterized by Vico in two ways: as faculties and as modes of expression. The latter characteristic becomes dominant from the point of view of the science of humanity. The concrete forms of culture offer themselves for interpretation in the science of humanity as expressions of presence and, since presence is exhaustive in such expressions, as presence *simpliciter*. All culture is language; language comprises all the expressions of presence. In his presence to himself, man is his own word. Philology is, on the one hand, the science of expression, in the sense of the knowledge of the genesis of expressive forms and, on the other, the process of the interpretation of expressive or linguistic forms. Philology must therefore be the basic instrument of the science of humanity.

The task of philology as the instrument of the science of humanity is threefold. Its first charge is to identify, collect, restore, and place in context the actual symbols in which human presence has expressed itself. The sedulous collection of a *corpus inscriptionum* by a Muratori, a Mommsen, or a Renan, the laborious excavation of the archaeologist, the painstaking researches of the humanist in archives and libraries, the acute analyses of historical linguists, of the historians of jurisprudence, the sciences, and the arts—all are philology in the process of fulfilling its first task. The second task is the preparation of the theoretical schemata for the interpretation of structures of expression. This is the task to which Vico devotes himself in the portions of the *Scienza Nuova* which he calls *Elementi, Dei Principi,* and *Del Metodo.* The intimate relation of philology and philosophy begins to appear at this point. The schemata that must be established for the purposes of the science of humanity cannot be mere abstract classifications of expressions on some practical and contingent basis. Those schemata must be genuinely ideal and necessary and must have reference to the modes of presence—to which the expressive forms themselves refer—as those modes are distinguished ideally and of necessity.

The task of distinguishing the modes with reference to the subject of expression—man—is the first purpose of philosophy, and it appears within the process of philology. Philosophy, consequently, appears as a movement within the philological task. The process toward the idea, which is the specific movement of philosophy, is initiated as a response to the inward exigency of philology. The pattern of the relationship between philology and philosophy is established at this point. The categories of philosophy begin to take form within the matrix of philology as the theoretical structuralizations of the conditions for the interpretation of expressive forms. The forms or modes of human presence emerge as the inward ideality of concrete expressive forms. The third task is the actual interpretation of expressive systems. In this task, philology and philosophy work (under ideal conditions) in complete harmony and reciprocity. This is the task to which Vico devoted himself in those very portions of the *Scienza Nuova* dedicated to the reconstruction of poetic wisdom in all its dimensions (SNS, book 2).

At this point, a difficulty suggests itself which Vico does not confront directly. His failure to do so is the source of some of the obscurities and ambiguities that are frequently laid at his door. The difficulty is this: is man capable of interpreting his own history, of constructing a science of humanity, relying wholly on his own resources, without consulting a third principle? The drive of Vico's thought toward an "integral humanism" would suggest an affirmative answer. The integrity of that humanism would seem to be lessened by the necessity of recourse to any power other than man's own.

Vico's doctrine of Providence, however, would seem to counsel a negative reply. If the totality of man's presence to himself in history can be achieved only through the mediation of God's presence in history as Providence, as he holds, must not that same providential presence figure in the task of interpreting the logos of history? It cannot be denied that tension exists at this point in Vico's "science of humanity." That it appeared to him as a disruptive tension must, however, be doubted. Vico assumes, and not without considerable justification, that he has resolved this problem in principle by his very doctrine of Providence. The Providence of Vico is indeed a transcendent principle, but it is not entirely a principle of the "absolute other." Providence is a necessary principle of an integral view of history from a completely human point of view. His science, he tells us, must of necessity be a "teologia civile ragionata" ("rational civil theology") of Providence (SNS 385).

But whence are the clues for the interpretation of providential presence to be derived? Vico provides an answer for this question too, though many may find it less than satisfactory. I would submit that this clue lies in man's finitude—more precisely, in his capacity to dis-

cern the limits of his finitude and to employ this discernment as a hermeneutic device for distinguishing the voice of God and the action of
God in history from man's own voice and action. Such discernment
must be difficult to attain and is, consequently, rare; but difficulty and
rarity do not impugn its status in principle.

The reciprocity of the philological and philosophical dimensions of
the method of Vico's science of humanity is, in principle, complete.
The categories of philosophy arise only within the matrix of expressive
forms. These forms, in turn, take on depth and significance only as they
are illuminated by the inward operations of philosophy. The science of
humanity, on the basis of this reciprocity, will itself prove to be a wisdom, because it will yield, not an abstract idea of man (which would be
a form of absence), but the concrete presence of man to himself as idea
informing historical existence.

NOTES

1. Croce's work, *La filosofia di Giambattista Vico*, appeared in 1911 (Bari: Laterza). The first edition of Wilhelm Windelband's *Lehrbuch der Geschichte der Philosophie*, to which Croce is most probably alluding, appeared in 1892. Croce's remarks
on the lacuna are to be found in appendix 2 of *La filosofia di Giambattista Vico*, pp.
331–32 of the 1947 edition. Windelband's correction of the lacuna which Croce
deplored is to be found on pp. 450 and 622 of Heimsoeth's revised edition of the
Lehrbuch (Wilhelm Windelband, *Lehrbuch der Geschichte der Philosophie*, ed. Heinz
Heinsoeth, Tubingen, 1950). Cf. Benedetto Croce, *Bibliografia Vichiana*, enlarged
and revised by Fausta Nicolini, 2 vols. (Naples, 1948), 2: 815–16.

2. Giambattista Vico, *La Scienza Nuova Seconda*, 3d ed., ed. Fausto Nicolini,
2 vols. (Bari: Laterza, 1942; hereafter referred to as SNS ed. N). English translation
by Thomas G. Bergin and Max Fisch: *The New Science of Giambattista Vico* (Ithaca,
N.Y.: Cornell University Press, 1948; 2d ed., 1968; hereafter referred to as NSBF).
For an account of the evolution of this work, cf. A. Robert Caponigri, *Time and
Idea: The Theory of History in Giambattista Vico*, (London: Routledge and Kegan
Paul, 1953; hereafter referred to as TI), pp. 11–35. All references to *La Scienza Nuova*
will be to paragraph numbers which correspond in the Italian original and the English
translation by Bergin and Fisch.

3. Cf. A. Robert Caponigri, *History of Western Philosophy*, 5 vols. (Notre Dame
and London: University of Notre Dame Press, 1961–71), 3: 55–103.

4. Cf. Vico's "De nostri temporis studiorum ratione," in Giambattista Vico, *Le
orazioni inaugurali, il De Italorum sapientia e le Polemiche*, ed. G. Gentile and F.

Nicolini (Bari: Laterza, 1914), pp. 76–126. English translation by Elio Gianturco: *On the Study Methods of Our Time* (Indianapolis and New York: Bobbs-Merrill [Library of Liberal Arts], 1965).

5. Cf. Giambattista Vico, *Il Diritto Universale*, ed. Fausto Nicolini, 3 vols. (Bari: Laterza, 1936; hereafter referred to as DU), 1 sect. 10.

6. SNS 129. The theological idiom (i.e. *l'uomo caduto e debole*), dominant in DU, is continued here and is never abandoned by Vico.

7. SNS 147. Cf. also 148: "Le proprietá inseparabili da' subbietti devon essere produtte dalla modificazione o guisa con che le cose sono nate; per lo che esse ci possono avverare tale e non altra essere la *natura o nascimento* di esse cose" (italics mine).

8. DU, vol. 1, sect. 10, and cf. DU "Sinopsi" and "proemium" passim.

9. "Jusnaturalism" is the name given to the theory of natural law in the form it assumed in the seventeenth and eighteenth centuries, of which the principal representatives are Hugo Grotius (1583–1645), Thomas Hobbes (1588–1679), and Samuel Pufendorf (1632–94). Jusnaturalism differs from the traditional theory of natural law because it does not consider such law as participation in a perfect universal order that either *is* God himself (the Stoics) or *from* God (the Mediaevals), but as the necessary regulation of human relations, which man discovers by his own reason and which is therefore independent of the will, or even the existence, of God. Vico engages the principal representatives of jusnaturalism passim in his writings (cf. for example SNS ed. N 394–98). "Contractualism" is the doctrine that recognizes as origin or foundation of the state or civil community a convention or contract among its members who are conceived to have been, either ideally or actually, previously free of such obligation. Hobbes, Grotius, Pufendorf, Locke (1632–1704), and Rousseau (1712–78) are among its chief representatives, as is Spinoza (1632–77).

By the term "Second Scholasticism" is understood the revival of scholastic thought about the time of the Council of Trent. Francesco Suarez, S.J. (1548–1617) is among its chief exponents (cf. his *De Legibus*). Cf. Carlo Giacon, S.J., *La Second Scolastica*, 3 vols. (Milan: Bocca, 1944–50). On Vico and Suarez, see Elio Gianturco, "*Jus Gentium* According to Vico and Suarez," in *Revue de Littérature Comparée* (1936), pp. 167–72, and *idem*, "Suarez and Vico," in *Harvard Theological Review* 27 (1934): 207–10. On Vico and Grotius, see Guido Fasso, *Vico e Grozio* (Naples: Guida, 1971).

10. "Durum est, sed scriptum" Ulpian: *Dig.* I, 1 (*De justitia et jure*) 6; Vico: DU, vol. 1, sect. 82, Vico (l.c.) adds "tantumdem sonat: Certa lex, sed vera prorsus non est." Cf. SNS 322: "Onde ciò che in tali casi Ulpiano dice: lex dura est, sed scripta est, tu diresti, con piu bellezza latina e con maggior eleganza legale: 'lex dura est, sed certa est.'"

11. DU, vol. 1, sect. 84: "Qui tenet certa legum, pragmaticus legum est; qui tenet vera legum, philosophus est. Hinc in jurisprudentia nova apud romanos: 'Scire leges non est verba legum tenere, sed earum potestatem et vim.'" Cf. Ulpian: *Dig* I, 3 (*De legibus*), 17.

12. DU, vol. 1, sect. 83: "certum ab auctoritate uti verum ex ratione," etc.; cf. SNS ed. N 321, 322, 324, and 325.

13. DU, vol. 1, sect. 82. Cf. n. 13 above.

14. DU, vol. 1, sect. 83, and *ibi*: "rationem naturalem ab auctoritate requirere esse importunum."

15. Cf. TI, pp. 52, 155, and chaps. 2 and 8 passim.

16. Cf. n. 7 above.

17. Cf. Benedetto Croce, *La Filosofia di Giambattista Vico*, chap. 1.

18. Cf. Arthur Child, *Making and Knowing in Hobbes, Vico and Dewey* (Berkeley and Los Angeles, 1953); A. A. Grimaldi, *The Universal Humanity of Giambattista Vico* (New York: S. S. Vanni, 1958).

19. Cf. Giovanni Gentile, *Teoria generale dello spirito come atto puro Opere*, vol. 3 (Florence: Sansoni), esp. chap. 3.

20. SNS ed. N 331; "Questo mondo naturale . . . perché Iddio egli il fece, esso solo ne ha la scienza."

21. Cf. G. F. Finetti, *Difesa dell'autorità della sacra scrittura contro G. B. Vico* (Bari: Laterza, 1936), and Croce's introduction to that volume, pp. v-xvi. (Finetti's work dates from 1768).

22. Vico differs in this respect from such writers as Sorokin, Toynbee, Spengler, etc. Croce seems to err when he writes: "Il vero è che la forma mentale . . . del Vico, come turbava la pura trattazione filosofica con le determinazioni della scienza empirica e dei dati storici, così turbava la ricerca storica col miscuglio della filosofia e della scienza empirica" (*La filosofia di Giambattistia Vico*, 1947 ed., p. 157).

23. Cf. SNS ed. N 404–11: "Corollari d'intorno a' tropi, mostri e transformazioni poetiche." Cf. also 456–72.

24. SNS ed. N 156. Cf. DU, vols. 3, 4: "De Homero Eiusque Utroque Poemate," ed. Nicolini, pp. 675–700.

25. TI, pp. 91 ff.; Croce, *La filosofia di Giambattista Vico*, pp. 115 ff.

13

Leopardi First and Last

Lowry Nelson, Jr.

Since the great efflorescence of Italian literature in the late Middle Ages and the Renaissance, when the incumbency of tradition from classical antiquity and Provençal was established, Italian poets have felt the pressure of the past at increasingly complex levels. Perhaps one of the reasons for the neglect of Dante until the later eighteenth century was that the example of the *Divine Comedy* was too momentous to cope with: a cosmic poem in intricate verse whose language was as much a creation as any of the other aspects of the poem; a poem overwhelmingly exemplary, self-consistent, complex, and complete; a poem intensely personal and idiosyncratic, and yet so public as to be the literate reader's total possession. Even Dante's lyric poetry took on the character of private-public autobiography (the *Canzoniere* as well as *La Vita nuova*) in so systematic a way as almost to exclude imitation or rivalry on its own terms.

Petrarch's poetry is, of course, another matter. In the *Canzoniere*, which we may properly call, with precise petrarchan casualness, his *Rime sparse*, there is indeed a scheme; but it is quite new in encompassing both randomness and intensity, expressed in a new sort of language, and in creating a new tension between the private and the public. The scheme is variable and capacious, with many spaces for the reader to conjecture in and no grand necessity to march on or to adduce the next piece of evidence to fit into the all-sufficing whole. Moreover, the language, despite the fact that it is somewhat artificial, seems spoken and intimate—occasionally solemn, but meditatively rather than

333

forensically so. And in point of autobiography and the reader's fictive
identification, obviously Petrarch's world is more immediately engaging
than Dante's in its direct concern with the fluctuant fortunes of earthly
love and its familiar sentiment and pathos.

Though inadequate, such terms of comparison between Dante and
Petrarch give some basis for explaining the distant, brooding presence
of Dante in later Italian poetry and the immediate, intimate and
pervasive influence of Petrarch. Or to put it better, succeeding Italian
poets underwent an *experience* of Dante and an *experience* of Petrarch
in ways that were obligatory and complex; yet it was the experience of
Petrarch that in Italian poetry (not to mention European) was the more
continuous and far-reaching. For centuries it was at the school of
Petrarch that the novice Italian poet learned his lessons, and Leopardi
was no exception.[1]

Leopardi did not make his public start as an amorous petrarchan
sonneteer, but rather as the author of two patriotic canzoni reminiscent,
naturally, of Petrarch's "Italia mia," not to mention classical antiquity,
Dante, and seventeenth- and eighteenth-century Italian poetry. This is
not the place to recapitulate the long history of Italian patriotic poetry
that kept the very idea of an integral Italy alive. Yet some account of
the place within that tradition of Leopardi's "All'Italia" (with some
minor reference to the so-called twin canzone "Sopra il monumento di
Dante") will serve to characterize that poem of his early youth and thus
to provide, perhaps, some useful points of comparison and contrast with
Leopardi's last poem, "La Ginestra," which is the major subject of this
essay.

It is my purpose here glancingly to evoke the traditions of Italian
poetry within which two relatively "public" poems of Leopardi stand
and to deal with each poem in some detail. Clearly, I cannot do proper
justice to the full complexity of the traditions, in particular to the
Italian "pre-Romantic" poetry now so much discussed by scholars; but
I wish primarily to do some justice to Leopardi's two poems, first and
last, without becoming mired in the "humus" of antecedents, including
Leopardi's own juvenilia, and the vast and disproportionate attention
currently being given the *Zibaldone*, the *Pensieri*, and the second-rate
poetry.

Any discussion of the patriotic and hortatory (commonly referred to
in Italian criticism as "paraenetic") elements of Italian poetic tradition

must begin with Dante. His most famous and effective apostrophe to
Italia occurs in *Purgatory* 6: 76–151, on the occasion of Virgil meeting
Sordello; both of them were natives of Mantua and poets in "la
lingua nostra," that startling and moving conception of Romania and
the whole Latin and neo-Latin tradition of culture. The very gladness and
courtesy of their encounter are the occasion for an ironic and sarcastic
diatribe against the warring factions of Italy and the weak Holy Roman
emperors (Albert of Hapsburg, in particular), who have not established
secular authority able to "accompany" or counterbalance the papacy.
For our purposes, what is important is not only the impassioned tone
but also the personification of Italia as servile woman, no mistress of
provinces but madam of a brothel in which the lust is blood-lust. Yet
that personification does not function fully and consistently; rather, it
gives way to Rome as "vedova e sola" ("widow and alone") and finally
to Florence as a sick woman tossing on a feather bed.

By way of contrast, the personification of Italia in Petrarch's poem is
elaborated more fully and consistently.[2] Italia is seen as a wounded
body, yet a body that is also the topographical map of Italy, hence an
allegorical figure with great latitude between signifier and signified.
Indeed, the poet feels free to turn directly to his real audience, the local
warring lords who should make peace and unite against the Teutonic
invaders in defense of the *patria*: the female figure Italia has easily
merged into the more generic patria and at the end, in the envoi, the
audience is now the canzone itself that is sent off as message and messenger to plead for safe-conduct:

> di' lor: "Chi m'assicura?
> I' vo gridando: Pace, pace, pace."

> [Say to them: "Who will pledge my safety?
> I go crying 'peace, peace, peace.' "]

In effect, then, Petrarch has written, in a form most often associated
with love poetry, a circumspect diplomatic *démarche* to the political
leaders of an imaginary nation.

Without going into the different political circumstances that condi-
tioned Dante and Petrarch in their apostrophes, and without recapitulating the confused post-Napoleonic and pre-Risorgimental situation of Leopardi in 1818, we can still make certain claims for Leopardi's
patriotic poem as a poetic novelty of some success. Motifs that he uses

are, of course, to be found in Alfieri and Foscolo, not to mention a whole tribe of minor poets and poetasters. Among the latter is Vincenzo Da Filicaia (1642–1707), whose most lasting fame is the fact that he has a tomb in Santa Croce in Florence.[3] In a truly turgid canzone, "All'-Italia," and in a set of six sonnets under the same title, Italia is indeed personified. Yet only in the fifth sonnet ("Quando giú dai gran monti bruna bruna/Cade l'ombra") is there a hint of dramatic pathos, as Italia is directly addressed:

> E in cosí buie tenebre non vedi
> L'alto incendio di guerra, onde tutt'ardi?
> E non credi al tuo mal, se agli occhi credi?
>   Ma se tue stragi col soffrir ritardi,
> Soffri, misera, soffri; indi a te chiedi
> Se sia forse vittoria il perder tardi.

[And in such gloomy darkness do you not see the high conflagration of war from which you are all afire? And do you not believe your ill fortune if you believe your eyes? But if by suffering you delay your slaughters, suffer, poor wretch, suffer; then ask of yourself if losing late may perhaps be victory.]

There is some tepid pathos in this. Though parallels are sometimes drawn to Leopardi's canzone from elsewhere in Filicaia's poetry (the poems on the Siege of Vienna and on Sobieski), they seem weak and generic or to have a common source in Homer or Virgil.

More to the point is a poem by the good minor Baroque poet Fulvio Testi (1593–1646) whose epistolary poem "Sopra l'Italia" Leopardi includes in his Chrestomathy.[4] It is a meditation on the ruins of Rome (in a lineage familiar from Hildebert of Lavardin to Castiglione to Du Bellay and beyond), which lie amid plowed fields and pastures as witness to the Roman corruption through Eastern luxuries, and as a portent that unless Italia rouses herself she may be invaded and occupied even by Persians and Thracians, traditional enemies more properly of Greece than of Rome. Enough remains, perhaps, of ruined Rome to inspirit the modern, divided Italians if they were at all worthy.

> Ben molt'archi e colonne in più d'un segno
> Serban del valor prisco alta memoria;
> Ma non si vede già, per propria gloria
> Chi d'archi e di colonne ora sia degno.

[A great many arches and columns in more than a trace preserve
the exalted memory of ancient valor; but no longer is there to be
seen anyone who through his own glory might be worthy of arches
and columns.]

Again Italia is personified:

> E non t'avvedi, misera, e non senti
> Che i lauri tuoi degeneraro in mirti?

[But do you not realize, poor wretch, and do you not sense that
your laurels have degenerated into myrtles?]

The customary pathos is there, as well as the inevitably appropriate
images of arches and columns, of which the iconography in poetry and
painting is vast. Testi is also author of a full-blown poetic prosopopeia,
"L'Italia," whose pathos is undercut by its practical purpose of exalting
the martial valor of the then duke of Savoy.

In regard to patriotic poetry just preceding Leopardi, at least some
mention should be made of the ingratiating tergiversator and copious
poetaster, Vincenzo Monti, who in 1805 composed a sort of "vision" on
the occasion of Napoleon's coronation as king of Italy, "Il Beneficio."[5]
In his vision the poet creates a highly sentimental figure of Italia holding
on to her ragged dignity and reminding the nations she was once their
queen. Her sons, in response to her call for help, turn their swords on
each other. Who should appear but Napoleon, like Zeus from Olympus.
The rest, with Dante appearing and speaking some of his own lines, is
bombasted fustian.

These, then, are some of the texts known to the nineteen-year-old
Leopardi. Apart from the generally ennobling example of Dante and
Petrarch, and more indirectly in this particular case, of Alfieri and
Foscolo, they could afford him small reason for emulation and only
weak precedent in the matter of conception. A truly effective combination of consistent and vivid personification, pathos, the Greek as well
as the Roman model, and the figure of the poeta-vates is left to Leopardi's "All'Italia," which is inevitably and fruitfully conscious of the
tradition that evokes it, and which achieves a precocious and quite
successful originality.

In contrast to the companion poem, "Sopra il monumento di Dante,"
which, in its unrelieved hortatory and grandiloquent posturing, is what
one might expect of a gifted adolescent, "All'Italia" creates, by selec-

tive detail and precise, dramatically conceived episodes, a nobly modulated evocation of Italia, past, present, and in perspective. After centuries of invasion, occupation, and division into small states, and after
the upheavals of Napoleonic imperialism that provoked so many
abortive allegiances and cruel proscriptions, Italy in Leopardi's youth
seemed set in the divisions imposed and sanctioned by the Treaty of
Vienna (1815): in brief, the states of Piedmont, Tuscany, Modena, the
Kingdom of the Two Sicilies, the Papal State, and Austrian occupation
of northeastern Italy. Not only were Italian patriots conscious of invidi-
ous division and weakness (though, of course, "unification" was hardly
a universal desire among the enormously diverse regions and the in-
articulate masses), but they were also burdened with the recent memory
of Italians fighting in foreign wars for an infinity of motives and by
simple coercion.

All the more effective, then, the evocation in 1817 of the figure of
Simonides, poet-celebrant of the Hellenes, for once all united against a
common invading enemy, the Persians. Obviously, it was precisely the
illusory hopes aroused by Napoleon's unprecedented state-making and
unmaking during the years from 1796 to 1815, and the solemn atmosphere of rhetorical heroicizing, that could sanction and revivify, with an
urgent if only imaginative calculus of possibilities, the age-old notion of
a unified Italy. In the relative calm of Leopardi's day, a new perspective
seems to have been possible: a new modulation of fervor and lament, a
new hope derived from the vast historical scope that Leopardi must
have learned poetically from Foscolo in the *Sepolcri*, not from the stale
laudations or lamentations of the glorious past evoked in pedantic
imitation of classical Roman poetry.

Granted, it is difficult to distinguish generically between the earnest,
learned allusiveness and the classicizing language of Foscolo on the one
hand, and the corresponding mechanical paraenesis of a Da Filicaia or
a Monti on the other. Within Leopardi's work that represents a problem
too: the distinction between the stiff, conventional elevated style with
contorted syntax and archaisms, and the still conventional elevated style
whose success may seem to come from nearly the same means. Why
not, indeed, say that it is a central problem in the whole history of
Italian poetry since Dante? The critic is at some disadvantage here, in
that to make his points convincingly he must or should induce in the less
experienced reader a numbing knowledge of the traditional, mediocre

verse in the elevated line, from out of the echo chamber of *aulicità* or grandiloquence.

To give some example from the early Leopardi, we may cite and inspect the beginning of "Sopra il monumento di Dante":

> Perché le nostre genti
> pace sotto le bianche ali raccolga,
> non fien da' lacci sciolte
> dell'antico sopor l'itale menti
> s'ai patrii esempi della prisca etade
> questa terra fatal non si rivolga.
> O Italia, a cor ti stia
> far ai passati onor; che d'altrettali
> oggi vedove son le tue contrade,
> né v'è chi d'onorar ti si convegna.

[While peace may gather our peoples under its white wings, Italic minds will not be loosened from the bonds of ancient somnolence if this fated land does not confront again the patriotic examples of the primeval age. O Italy, may you take it to heart to do honor to [our] forebears; for your regions are now widowed of such as they, nor is there anyone whom it would be fitting for you to honor.]

It is perhaps not so much that contorted syntax and archaisms are present here, but that they abound, clamoring all at once for attention, as the reader performing the text puts each in a provisional niche with an urgent market. Then he must transpose or somehow translate, and in doing so arrives at a simple sense that almost renders both the poet's and the reader's effort vain: though the Restoration effected in 1815 has brought peace to the Italian people, their minds will not awaken unless they think back on the good old Roman times.

Some of the crabbedness of the verse doubtless derives from a sort of *trobar clus* against the censor, but that is no aesthetic excuse or redeeming poetic value in this case: the closet-patriot is hardly a fit celebrant of soldierly self-sacrifice. This poem shows how hard it was to compose a good and brave poem in an often meretricious genre. Leopardi's other poem, "All'Italia," shows in what ways the difficulty can be met with surprising success, how the burden of the past can be borne with some grace and strength.

It is, then, within the hortatory patriotic tradition, the tradition of *aulicità* and paraenesis, that we are constrained to approach the poem. What we find at the beginning is a rapid panorama of the imposing ruins, not for the purpose of sentimentally evoking past grandeur and making the usual explicit and obvious comparisons to the pusillanimous, inglorious present or merely the solemnly corrosive passage of time; and for the sake of a genre-scene of flocks amid crumbling ramparts, in the evocative style of Piranesi or Canaletto. Instead, we encounter a fervent speaker who sees at a glance what is there and what is missing. "Erme" in "erme torri degli avi nostri" is, as one of Leopardi's favorite words, a sparing touch of pathos.

> O patria mia, vedo le mura e gli archi
> e le colonne e i simulacri e l'erme
> torri degli avi nostri
> ma la gloria non vedo . . .

[O my fatherland, I see the walls and the arches and the columns and the images and the desolate towers of our forefathers, but glory I do not see . . .]

The objects are seen in a hurried catalogue whose paratactic sweep is all the more impressive if we think that each would serve a conventional poet to pursue forced inspiration through *amplificatio*. And the speaker is there, unaided and in propria persona, not one of a crowd of well-meaning tongue-cluckers. Rather than the usual clutter of symbolic plants and weapons, we encounter the laurel and the iron with which the forehead and the breast of Italia are no longer girded.

> . . . non vedo il lauro e il ferro ond'eran carchi
> i nostri padri antichi. Or fatta inerme,
> nuda la fronte e nudo il petto mostri.

[. . . I do not see the laurel and the iron with which our ancient fathers were laden. Now made defenseless, you show your forehead naked and naked your breast.]

The prosopopeia of Italia that follows is certainly a familiar device, though here it is freshened by an unblenching description of her face abjectly between her knees, and by the consistency of the personification that seems to call out for chivalrous rescue. Fortunately,

though, she says nothing in her own voice (far from speaking rancor-
ously like a once fashionable grande dame, as in Monti's poem), nor
does she appear suddenly as a topographical map of Italy in uneasy
neopetrarchan allegory. Instead, the poet becomes aroused to speak as
her impassioned advocate and to call on heaven and earth to answer
his anguished question, "chi la ridusse a tale?" ("who brought her to
this pass?"); and in effective passion he calls out for arms:

> nessun pugna per te? non ti difende
> nessun de' tuoi? L'armi, qua l'armi: io solo
> combatterò, procomberò sol io.

[No one battles for you? None of your own defends you? Arms,
arms here! I alone shall fight, alone shall I fall prostrate for you.]

His blood may become fire in "italici petti"—a conventional phrase, a
bit pompous perhaps, but far preferable in its Foscolian sonority to
"itale menti," "itali pregi," and "itali ingegni," which clutter the
poem on Dante's monument. Why is there no one else to do battle? It
is not simply a deplorable decline in martial valor among the moderns
(the usual moralizing and tiresome reproach), but the hard, sad fact
that Italians are forced to fight for others and against others' enemies.
The poet hears and seems to see the somber foreign battles he tersely
and impressively describes. Those Italian soldiers cannot say on dying
"alma terra natia, / la vita che mi desti ecco ti rendo" ("nourishing
native land, the life you gave me I here return"), as could the ancient
Hellenes, for once united against the invading barbarian.

  With considerable power, the scene is set for a prototype or archetype
of the poet-celebrant to appear: not the blind Homer only *foreseen* by
Cassandra in Foscolo's *Sepolcri*, but the poet Simonides, contempora-
neous singer of the Hellenic wars against the Persians. With bardic
solemnity (which owes something to Ossian) Simonides mounts the
heights above Thermopylae and, looking out on the sky, the sea, and
the land, sings his impassioned tribute to the dead at that forlorn
battleground that served to warn the Hellenes and challenged the
surge of Xerxes and his army. Not only is the courage of the young
band of Greek soldiers stressed but also their grace:

> Parea ch'a danza e non a morte andasse
> ciascun de' vostri, o splendido convito:

> ma v'attendea lo scuro
> Tartaro, e l'onda morta . . .

[It seemed as if each of you were going to a dance or to a resplendent feast and not to death; but awaiting you was dark Tartarus
and the dead wave . . .]

The tone here is one of hortatory pathos kept in check by understatement and concrete description that well convey an early Greek in
contrast to an oratorical Roman tone or, in more precise terms, a tone
that suggests Virgilian battle, Foscolian Hellenism, and indeed certain
fragments of Simonides himself.[6]

The range of the poem is expansive both geographically and historically, and also in the poetic resonances that echo from so bold an entry
into the lists of an age-old tradition. The scene of battle is evoked and
described in the present tense with considerable force and concision. At
the end the Greek warriors, finally overcome by their wounds, fall one
upon the other, and the poet cheers them with "Oh viva, oh viva"
("Evviva, evviva" in the first version), which Leopardi defends in a
note that claims such colloquial exclamations were not considered
indecorous by the ancients. Such a poetic self-defense against his potential critics underscores the success with which he hoped to go, and
indeed did go, however cautiously, beyond the frigid proprieties of his
time.

The poem ends in calm reverence for the dead warrior-patriots, as
the poem's Simonides declares their immortal fame and wishes that his
own blood might have soaked the same earth—a conventional sentiment which, in its direct simplicity, occasions no embarrassment. But
since that sacrifice is not for him, at least the gods may grant that his
modest fame will last as long as theirs.

> Deh foss'io pur con voi qui sotto, e molle
> fosse del sangue mio quest'alma terra.
> Che se il fato è diverso, e non consente
> ch'io per la Grecia i moribondi lumi
> chiuda prostrato in guerra,
> così la vereconda
> fama del vostro vate appo i futuri
> possa, volendo i numi,
> tanto durar quanto la vostra duri.

[Ah would that I too were with you down under here and that this nourishing earth were soft with my own blood. But if fate is contrary and grants not that I, struck down in war, close my dying eyes for Greece, so may the modest fame of your bard among those to come, the gods willing, last as long as yours may last.]

It is a poet's hope expressed with proper modesty: their fame is clearly great and he, the poet, has rightly celebrated it. "Quanto la vostra [fama]" is therefore not a weak reference but one that must again be taken as understatement, which so often has the force of eloquence in Greek poetry.

Naturally, the author of this poem, "All'Italia," is wholly bound up in the figure of his own creation, Simonides, just as the fate of Greek patriotism is, by cultural or learned tradition, bound up with that of the Italians. The full set of possible parallels is left for the reader's meditation, as the poem, ending in Simonides' words (indeed, almost half given over to his role), seems to invite the reader to return to the beginning "O patria mia"; for ancient Greece is Leopardi's cultural patrimony almost as intensely as Italy and the whole Latin tradition are his immediate patria. Ancient Greece, the ruins of Rome, the modern pitiable state of Italia, and the paralyzing dilemma of the patriot with no effective battle to fight for liberty of the fatherland—all are rendered vividly and as parts of some undetailed argument or plan of action. The lack of a program and an explicit moral is part of the honesty of the poem, whose tensions are unresolved and unresolvable. The distancing through the ancient Greek example, the alternation of sustained and decorous pathos, vivid though vain action, and understatement, create not so much a portentous and paraenetic sermon as a dramatic and noble meditation on the fate of Italy, with no foreclosure of hope for the future yet with somber uncertainty.

"All'Italia" begins Leopardi's career as a poet but, if we may be allowed to discount his other patriotic and satirical verse, he therewith paid a kind of tribute to a national poetic tradition and thereafter went his own personal, at times almost solipsistic, way as a poet of solitary meditation and remembrance up to his final poem, "La Ginestra." A brief sketch of that momentous poetic career between his first and last poems (excluding juvenilian exercises) can hope only to suggest some reasons why a comparison of first and last need not be a useless or meretricious telescoping.

Continuing in various versions of the celebratory Greco-Roman style, Leopardi composed several poems balancing life, accomplishment, fame, and death (even stoical suicide): "A un vincitore nel pallone" (1821), "Bruto Minore" (1821), and "Ultimo canto di Saffo" (1822). Their varying tones of evanescent triumph, clearsighted regret, and nobility in contemplation of death, are rendered in terms of calm, circumstantial pathos, far from the youthful, committed fervor of "All'Italia."

More important artistically are the so-called first idylls: the unexampled little poem of secular ecstasy, "L'Infinito" (1819),[7] and the more elaborated genre scenes of tender hope and melancholy, "La sera del dí di festa," "Alla luna," "Il sogno," and "La vita solitaria" (1820–21). Later gusts of poetic inspiration in the 1820s created such masterpieces of remembrance and regret as "A Silvia" (1818) and "Le ricordanze" (1829), as well as other genre pieces, "Il sabato del villaggio" and "La quiete dopo la tempesta" (both 1829), in which tenderness skirts the edge of sentimentality and the universal moral that death cures all cares threatens, however understated, to become too insistent and repetitive.

It was in the mid 1820s, mostly in 1824, that Leopardi composed his best essays and dialogues, which he called *Operette morali*. At times they are tinged with Lucianic satire and diatribe, but most often—as in "Federico Ruysch e le sue mummie," "Storia del genere umano," and "Torquato Tasso e il suo genio familiare"—they are poised between disillusionment and ingenuous hope—or better, a kind of hoping for hope that is quintessentially Leopardian. The poem that best reflects that poise is "'Canto notturno di un pastore errante dell'Asia," which shares with many of the *Operette morali* in dialogue form, an artistically salutary distancing and a making-strange in the Russian sense of *ostranenïe*.

A lonely, wandering shepherd in the limitless wilderness of nature asks of the distant but seemingly companionable moon all the simple questions about the purpose of life. We are *toto caelo* removed from conventional apostrophes to the moon's beauty and evocations of pleasurable moods in gardens or quiet towns, not to mention allusions to classical moon myths—all of which Leopardi had shown he could manage well, and even brilliantly. With a sort of ingenuous generosity, the shepherd answers for the silent moon:

> Ma tu per certo,
> giovinetta immortal, conosci il tutto.

[But you, immortal girl, surely know all.]

As for himself, he knows and senses that all the eternal movements of the universe may bring contentment to someone else, but to him life is suffering:

> Questo io conosco e sento,
> che degli eterni giri,
> che dell'esser mio frale,
> qualche bene o contento
> avrà fors'altri; a me la vita è male.

He turns to his flock and artlessly asks how their rest can be restorative and tranquil while he, if he lies down, is tormented by tedium and vexation:

> perché giacendo
> a bell'agio, ozioso,
> s'appaga ogni animale;
> me, s'io giaccio in riposo, il tedio assale?

At the end he imagines that if he had wings he might be happy in that freedom of flight; but then, perhaps all creatures of whatsoever kind, are born to misfortune: "forse . . . è funesto a chi nasce il dí natale." Again, the danger of a flatly pessimistic moral is barely averted by the ingenuous tone successfully sustained throughout and by that finally hesitant and moving *forse*.

In this regard, and in contrast to the "Canto notturno," it is relevant to mention two late poems in which the interrogative mode is superseded rather harshly by direct and crushing answers. "A se stesso" (1833) is a brief, bleak call for death and a declaration of nature's ugly malevolence and "l'infinita vanità del tutto." In "Il tramonto della luna" (1836) even the nocturnal light of the moon fades; though day comes again, lost youth can have no further dawn and age has only the tomb. With such despondency Leopardi might well have ended his actual wracked life and his poetic career with the word *sepoltura*.

Leaving aside much paraenetic, occasional, argumentative, and satirical verse that has been, along with his best works, so much and too often undiscriminatingly discussed, and simply on the basis of those works mentioned so far and briefly characterized and evaluated, let us turn to Leopardi's last major poem, "La Ginestra," in order to put it in the perspective of his earlier literary achievement and to judge it on its literary merits.[8]

In my discussion I have been sparing in citation of the literary and ideological traditions that were incumbent and inherent in Leopardi's time: the Enlightenment and its aftermath, from Voltaire and the *philosophes* to Rousseau and beyond. By intention I have avoided what I consider a misleading and confusionary temptation to posit a system of thought on Leopardi's part and to make selective and supposedly conclusive references to the farrago of the enormous and intriguing notebook he compiled betwen 1817 and 1829 (with a few last entries up to 1832). Leopardi was not a systematic thinker, though his occasional reflections and jottings are sometimes striking. His notebook, the *Zibaldone*, serves best as a quarry for his intellectual biography, his critical views, and his taste, and now and then as a clue to his method of composition; yet surely it cannot substitute for what is or is not in the poems themselves. To the fact that he read and speculated widely over a period of twelve years or so we have testimony in the *Zibaldone*. But that his poetic utterance is somehow controlled or determined by his notebook or that he stuck to certain positions sketched at various times therein, without regard to the fluctuations of memory and poetic imagination, is a notion that cannot be plausibly sustained. We run the risk, in submitting our judgment to whatever jotting may seem related in those 4,500 manuscript pages, of misreading or over-reading the individual poems. A philosophical system cannot be summed up in a lyric. Indeed, the danger is that in lyric form an explicit world-view may lose conceptual and necessarily discursive nuance and end up as a banality of commonplaces.

For a sympathetic reading and evaluation of "La Ginestra" it would seem proper to lay stress not on the philosophical or ideological propositions (which are, in summary, hardly original or intellectually compelling) but rather on the poetic texture and structure, the diction and sound, the varying syntax and tone, the role of the reader in response to his fictive role as it is written in the poem itself. On the other hand, it is, of course, entirely legitimate to note parallels and antecedents in Leopardi's own previous poetry, and even to posit some scheme of smooth development or "inevitable" unity after the fact (the fact of the poet's death and thus the completion of his work, which then we may view as a whole).

But there are excesses and disadvantages and distortions to be incurred along that line as well. I take only a partial risk by stressing first and last—mostly the differences which seem illuminating—and by lightly referring to the "great" and the "first" idylls. It does not serve my purpose, if it is legitimate, to deal here with the poems I leave out, for example, "Palinodia," "Il pensiero dominante," "Aspasia," the two sepulchral poems, and the "Paralipomeni della Batracomiomachia." By leaving them out, I stress that the two poems I deal with most fully can stand usefully as independent and as contrasting with each other—all by way of illuminating Leopardi the major poet (both *major* poet and major *poet*). What I earnestly wish to avoid are false claims, misplaced erudition, and the veiled apology for supposed failure which Leopardi himself so scornfully disdained.

Seven strophes, seven movements of mood, constitute the poem and interplay in ways that would take inordinately long to explicate in this context; thus a simpler, linear account would seem preferable here, an account that tries to discuss the poem as performed, or more punctiliously as performance, after the fact of first reading. For convenience, the movements or strophes are: one (ll. 1–51); two (ll. 52–86); three (ll. 87–157); four (ll. 158–201); five (ll. 159–236); six (ll. 237–96); seven (ll. 297–317). All are clearly indicated by pauses in the text and by individual inner consistency. Throughout the poem is the speaking voice of the poet, generally alone in a point of vantage, meditating, as in the "idylls," and on occasion hortatory, in distant echo of "All'Italia," but then also peremptory and derisive in a new and disconcerting tone for Leopardi's major poetry. Always we are "here" with the poet:

> Qui su l'arida schiena
> del formidabil monte
> sterminator Vesevo . . .

[Here on the parched back of the fearful, destroying mountain Vesuvius . . .]

Present danger, the mindless cruelty of Natura,[9] the indifference of age-old existence, past eruptions attested by the petrified lava—all seem somehow balanced by the humble endurance, the selfless beauty, and

the unaccountably generous scent of the ginestra that alone grows in
this hostile place, as it does in the countryside around decayed Rome.
Once here were pleasant farms and grainfields, but now only the ginestra, "contenta dei deserti," as we are told at the beginning, seems to
live through it all, as if out of compassion for all-encompassing ruin.

> Or tutto intorno
> una ruina involve,
> dove tu siedi, o fior gentile, e quasi
> i danni altrui commiserando, al cielo
> di dolcissimo odor mandi un profumo,
> che il deserto consola . . .

[Now one ruin encompasses all about, where you reside, O gentle
flower, and as if pitying the harms of others, you send to heaven a
scent of sweetest smell that consoles the wilderness . . .]

The casual wanderer may soberly take note.

But then, suddenly, comes a burst of scorn for those who exalt man's
estate in the bosom of "loving" Natura, calling on them to come and
see what a slight or slightly stronger movement can senselessly do to
destroy. Here Leopardi addresses not the vulgarized Leibnizians (as
did Voltaire in *Candide ou l'Optimisme*), but rather the neoteric Rous-
seauvians and the armchair primitivists who, as Lois Whitney has
shown,[10] could also entertain, without a sense of contradiction, aspira-
tions to infinite human progress—in the banal and modish phrase taken
from his cousin Terenzio Mamiani and mockingly quoted here: "le
magnifiche sorti e progressive" (in effect, "the ever grander fortunes of
mankind"). The moral is drawn abruptly, didactically, scornfully; and
to read the poem we must put up with the sudden vehemence.

Indeed, the poem itself becomes something like a lava flow and
inundates the next two sections, issuing from an eruption comparable
to Dante's famous sudden and lengthy invective, already cited, against
"serva Italia" (*Purgatory* 6.76 ff.). Our expectations for the canzone
form and for Leopardi's previous use of it hardly prepare us for this
torrent. Only in the high-mindedly dramatic "All'Italia" is there anything like it in Leopardi; it is the tradition of *saeva indignatio* from
Persius and Juvenal to Swift and Voltaire that gives it some literary
sanction. Yet Leopardi's naked scorn and mockery in canzone form

may still seem new, upsetting, perhaps excessive, and artistically even an embarrassment.

Be that as it may, for a time we shall follow the crushing flow. Again, it is *this* place (*qui*), but here the present age must see itself mirrored, the age that falsely turns away from the rational thought and civility achieved by the Renaissance to again enslave free thought in brutish illusions. Addressing the present age, the poet says, in paraphrase: the bright wits whom ill-luck made you their father, fawn on your childish antics, though at times they vapidly mock you. But the poet Leopardi will not die without openly declaring his contempt even if he risks oblivion as a mocker of his own time.

The watchword of the modish is *libertà*, yet they wish thought (*pensiero*, which often in Leopardi means "imagination") to be their slave. In other words, *liberty* has become a cant-word (attrition partly of the Napoleonic illusions and disillusions); it has become a slogan that hides the truth of our existence in dogmas of infinite social progress and happiness (all based on an erroneous belief in the benignity of human nature and Natura); whereas true liberty and freedom of thought must acknowledge that man is puny and Natura cruel or indifferent. Man is little, really nothing in the vastness of the cosmos, and can find wisdom only by recognizing his littleness. It is only civility, or civilization (*civiltà*), that can guide the people's destinies (*i pubblici fati*) toward something better.

Civiltà takes on great richness, especially when one realizes that the poem acknowledges no real father (as in *patria*) or real mother (as in sentimental, "romantic" nature). What remains is a kind of civil brotherhood and the honest hard truth of man's real fate to endure in decency till death. But the age does not accept such a view, caught as it is between "soft" primitivism and prideful progress.

> Così ti spiacque il vero
> dell'aspra sorte e del depresso loco
> che natura ci diè . . .

[Thus you disliked the truth about harsh fortune and the depressed place that Natura gave us . . .]

Again the cowardly age has turned its back on the light that reveals the harsh truth:

> Per questo il tergo
> vigliaccamente rivolgesti al lume
> che il fe' palese . . .

Here we hark back to the epigraph at the beginning of the poem, which
is quoted in Greek from John 3:19: "But men preferred darkness to
light," and the verse continues, "because their deeds were evil." At all
events, the scriptural phrase is ironically made to refer to the light of
eighteenth-century rationalism and stoicism, not to that of supernatural revelation or the comfort of an afterlife. (Of his great contemporaries, Leopardi often seems most in tune with the later Byron.) The
age reserves the epithet *magnanimous* only for those knaves and fools
who exalt the human condition up beyond the stars:

> magnanimo colui
> che se schernendo o gli altri, astuto o folle,
> fin sopra gli astri il mortal grado estolle.

Throughout this movement, then, the crabbedness and sputtering scorn,
in their apparently confused vehemence, would seem to stem from the
vastly confused variety of optimistic views held at the time in horrendous colloidal suspension—later to be precipitated out in the meliorists,
religious revivalists, progressivists, utopians, social prophets, positivists, and so on indefinitely.

After this invective, this scattering scorn and vituperation, comes the
third movement with its still impassioned but more reasoned account
of human failings and pretensions. While the truly high and noble
spirit acknowledges his human limitations, those who are falsely high-
minded scribble absurd claims and promises which natural disasters
habitually obliterate. Nature in a humanly noble sense, and in reference
to humble, harmless things, stands in utter contrast to Natura, the
inhuman cosmos that cruelly and indifferently prevails around us.

> Nobil natura è quella
> che a sollevar s'ardisce
> gli occhi mortali incontra
> al comun fato, e che con franca lingua,
> nulla al ver detraendo,
> confessa il mal che ci fu dato in sorte,
> e il basso stato e frale . . .

[Noble nature is that which dares to raise its mortal eyes up to meet the common fate, and which with honest tongue, subtracting nothing from the truth, professes the evil that was given as our lot and the low and frail condition . . .]

The other "nature," which I distinguish as Natura, is the true guilty party:

> che de' mortali
> madre è di parto e di voler matrigna

[who is mother of mortals by parturition and stepmother by desire].

It is she who is the real enemy of mankind (*l'umana compagnia*), who must band together in fraternal love, giving aid in the common war (*guerra comune*) we are forced to wage against our "natural" enemy, stepmother Natura. But then, men carry battle to their own camp, forgetful of the true enemy, and fight rabidly among themselves. There is yet some hope, however, that once again the truth will be understood by the common folk (*il volgo*), after the vaunted delusions of omnipotent human progress and the notion of gentle, nursing nature are dispelled; people will then be able to return to the root of the matter through wisdom (*verace sapere*), frank and upright relationships ("l'onesto e il retto/conversar cittadino"), justness (*giustizia*), and pious concern (*pietade* in the Roman sense).

All these words have their richness in a simple morality derived from no religion, no higher calling, no categorical imperative, but rather from lowly prudence (*probità*) purged of prideful illusions (*superbe fole*). At first men were drawn together in *social catena* by horror at impious Natura; now rational, humble truth has been revealed (though pretentiously rejected by mongers of progress and optimism), and men may again turn away from their folly and return to making the best of things as they really are. Against the frenzy of foolish progress, meaningless wars for false causes, religious and patriotic delusions, the poet sets a gentler, humbler, though still somber hope. Invective against the vainglorious age subsides gradually into some slim but reasonable vision of simple people living in decency and prudent concord: a great comedown from grandiose pretensions; poetically, an extremely difficult and perhaps unsuccessful modulation from high and violent indignation to a sort of Horatian or even Wordsworthian *mediocritas*.

After these two violent and argumentative movements, barely controlled or contained, we return to the place where the speaker views outward nature in its calm nocturnal beauty. The cosmic meditation and anguish are not stilled by the scene: what gradually happens through the rest of the poem is that the fullness of nature-Natura's indifferent beauty and terror, and the inexorable fate of man, whatever his momentary feelings and thoughts, are brought into some equilibrium based on acknowledgment and clearsighted acceptance, movingly symbolized in the ginestra.

But first the poet searches the night sky and the vast view of the bay of Naples from his point of vantage, for some measure of infinity. It is night and he is sitting in a somber landscape of solidified lava. The stars flaming in the sky and reflected in the sea seem to be the world, the universe (*il mondo*). They are mere points to the eye, yet they are immense, as we know from *il vero* or the rational science of truth; just as to the stars the earth and sky are only a point in their midst, and just as man is nothing on this earthly globe. Then there are the nebulae, those stellar mists to which our stars, our "universe," are nothing. For the early Leopardi of "L'Infinito" such reflections might lead to a "sweet foundering" in the sea of his own imagination. But that ecstatic possibility is long since past. He is now facing the consequences of the infinitesimal, the infinite in reverse, of man and his world: at best a "point of nebulous light." The whole passage is eloquent and intricate, deriving its power from a nearly overwhelming concatenation of comparisons. All man's fables of his own identity and importance, the myths of divine epiphanies and interventions on earth, the new myths of "progress," are vanity of vanities. Indeed, the new notions are superstitition like the old. Overpowered, we are caught between derision and pity:

> qual moto allora,
> mortal prole infelice, o qual pensiero
> verso te finalmente il cor m'assale?
> Non so se il riso o la pietà prevale.

[What emotion then unhappy mortal race, or what thought toward you at last assails my heart? I know not whether laughter or pity prevails.]

So the poem fluctuates, almost unbearably, almost inartistically, between the two emotions: cosmic pessimism and unavailing compassion. Mockery or satire, urbanely modulated, might have been a poetic strategy, as with Persius or Swift; but Leopardi had tried that mode in 1835, in his "Palinodia al marchese Gino Capponi," and had verbosely and awkwardly failed.

Thus, Leopardi rejects the vastness of new Romantic myth in the grand manner of Foscolo, not to mention Hölderlin and Keats, who of course based themselves on ancient literary tradition; or the manner of Goethe and Shelley, not to mention Blake, who created a modern cosmic mythology with man still at the center. All that range of myth and assumption Leopardi rejected, doubtless in part because it was beyond him, but also, and most important, because for him it was hopelessly vain. There are no gods, they do not visit earth, the whole imaginable pantheon is a figment of man on this tiny earth, this little grain of sand ("questo oscuro/granel di sabbia"). Nor is the grand egocentricity of Rousseau or the "egotistical sublime" of Wordsworth, whose own minds seemed to them so momentous in the universe, for him. No, Leopardi, from his fearful cosmic vision of nullity and vanity, can only turn to see disaster in indifferent flux, it matters little whether among the nebulae, among the gods, or in an anthill.

In the fifth movement Leopardi makes the obvious comparison between a colony of ants crushed by a little apple that drops out of mere inevitable ripeness, and the tremendous explosion of a volcano that just as indifferently, but to our senses "infinitely" more momentously, snuffs out human life. In neither case is the disaster ennobling or remediable. But the comparison is made in grand Homeric fashion, conjoining small to great, for a torrential length of twenty-eight lines. It is partly the Homeric precedent and partly the previous tenor of the poem that should help dispose us to accept the seeming incongruity. After the terrible, destroying flood of lava seems to inundate the slender lines of the canzone, we confront head-on the hard moral that Natura has no special preference for men over ants, but that man lies somewhat less in the way of destruction only because his lineage is less fecund and widespread. The eruption is described in all its violence, but it is not particularized in this movement as the most famous and destructive eruption of A.D. 79 that buried Pompeii and the surrounding countryside. Yet the suddenness and violence of the description give it a poetically convincing air that it would not have had if it were simply another

set-piece, like Voltaire's or Varano's poems on the Lisbon earthquake
of 1756. After the shock of that description, the poet can then return
to the fully particularized setting on the side of the ominous volcano
and, in simple, homely terms, evoke the contemporary scene of the
ruined countryside, the humble peasants who struggle to live there,
and again the grand panorama of land and sea—all under the unpredic-
table menace of destruction.

In this sixth strophe the scale is reduced: the menace now is not so
much another general explosion as the imminent possibility of a local
burst of lava that could at any time destroy a little family and all its
possessions. After nearly eighteen hundred years, the *villanello*, or
humble peasant tending his vines, still raises his fearful gaze to the
death-dealing peak:

> ancor leva lo sguardo
> sospettoso alla vetta
> fatal . . .

And at night he may lie awake, jumping up now and then to keep a
fearful eye on the course of lava that may boil up from the unexhausted
womb and suddenly light up the vast region from Capri to the port of
Naples and Mergellina. If he should hear it approaching, signaled by
the seething of the water in his well, he will waken his children and wife
and flee, perhaps to look back and see all that he owns covered by
the burning flow.

These humble folk are more pathetic than the rich palaces of Pompeii now being excavated, like buried skeletons, for greed or historical
"piety." The wandering tourist may see the broken colonnades and the
still-smoking double peak and so contemplate the ruins of empire.
The ruined scene may, in fact, still be lit up by the lava.

> E nell'orror della secreta notte
> per li vacui teatri,
> per li templi deformi e per le rotte
> case, ove i parti il pipistrello asconde,
> come sinistra face
> che per vòti palagi atra s'aggiri,
> corre il baglior della funerea lava,
> che di lontan per l'ombre
> rosseggia e i lochi intorno intorno tinge.

[And in the horror of the secret night, by the deserted theaters, by the disfigured temples and by the broken houses where the bat hides its young, like a sinister torch that gloomily might stray through empty palaces, runs the glow of the funereal lava, which at a distance reddens through the shadows and stains the places round about.]

Rather than sudden terror, this is a scene of continuing sinister presence, superficially reminiscent of the graveyard and the *upupa* of Foscolo, not to mention other lurid descriptions in so-called pre-Romantic poetry. But one must allow that Vesuvius, with its numerous eruptions of greater and lesser intensity, its continual menace, and the then newly exposed ruins of Pompeii, Stabia, and Herculaneum, is something historically and actually more concrete and impressive than a merely imaginatively conjured scene of bubbling lava and deserted ruins with an ornamental bat.

In other words, the closeness of the mimesis of reality, the historical actuality, and the descriptive force, all confer on the passage something beyond conventional "gothic" or "pre-Romantic" sensationalism. Once again we are not permitted to miss the lesson, but it comes in muted form: our idea of antiquity is nothing in the eternal process of nature, and nature there, ironically, is always green:

> sta natura ognor verde, anzi procede
> per sí lungo cammino
> che sembra star.

[Nature stays at all times green, rather she proceeds by so long a road she seems to stay still.]

Leopardi takes his casual word *sta* and then elaborates that nature "stays" or "stands" but only seems to stand because in truth she proceeds by an unimaginably long road: empires fall, cultures disappear, and she sees nothing to hold her interest. Yet man arrogates to himself the boast of eternity:

> ella nol vede:
> e l'uom d'eternità s'arroga il vanto.

So in this, the sixth movement, we have returned to the pathos of the humble human (as in some of the "idylls") and of the unprotected innocent. There is no grand lament for past glories and magnificence, no vaunting of the *patria* as heir to antiquity, no salvation through national political means of governance, state, or martial heroism. Humility and endurance are the prime virtues, and there is no sanction from myth or religion or other vanities and illusions. The poem has, in its widely modulating moods, made all that scorchingly and glaringly clear. The paraenetic rhetoric of impassioned declamation in some of Leopardi's earliest poems, the fervor and despair of some of the middle poems, the gentle pathos here and there, are somehow brought together under the aegis of a sovereign pessimism, meaning expectation of the irremediable worst. There can be no appeal to a sentient, omniscient, purposive power because there is none. Ultimately, despite appearances, nature and Natura are one.

In the face of the unappealable and inconsolable, the true measure and example cannot be religion, the political state, the ancients, the self-perpetuating poetic-patriotic-religious tradition. Only the ginestra, the true and only nature we humanly perceive as opposed to cruel, cosmic Natura, can be a true measure and example in its humble endurance free from cowardice or frenzied pride, stronger and wiser for that than man. Here, Leopardi shows himself to be a "hard" primitivist and anti-progressivist, a true pessimist (as Schopenhauer was later to testify) who can only mingle scorn with pity and who knows there is no appeal.

At the end of this poem, then, the poet addresses the humble plant tenderly:

> E tu, lenta ginestra
> che di selve odorate
> queste campagne dispogliate adorni,
> anche tu presto alla crudel possanza
> soccomberai del sotterraneo foco
> che ritornando al loco
> già noto, stenderà l'avaro lembo
> su tue molli foreste.

[And you, slow ginestra, who adorn with your fragrant woods these despoiled fields, you too will soon succumb to the cruel sway of the subterranean fire which, returning to the already familiar place, will spread its greedy edge over your pliant forests.]

Selve and *foreste* may seem out of proportion to a small heatherlike plant, yet the poem has had much to say about proportions. When the lava comes once again, the ginestra will bend its head before the overwhelmingly deadly mass, but not in cowardly and useless supplication. It will, by its very gentleness, avoid the extremes of being madly erect or utterly supine before its future oppressor. It is wiser and less infirm than man in not thinking its frail stems immortal either by decree of some fate or by its own deluded belief:

> ma più saggia, ma tanto
> meno inferma dell'uom, quanto le frali
> tue stirpi non credesti
> o dal fato o da te fatte immortali.

So the poem ends in humble, hopeless finality but with a lowly dignity— or rather wisdom. The plant is the paragon of wisdom; it *is* wisdom. We are not invited to return to our egos (as often occurs in Romantic poets who use flowers or the landscape as ego-projections); if anything, we should leave them and ask for nothing, no satisfaction, no comfort, but simply endure like the flower of the wilderness, the "fiore del deserto" of the title. It is not its prosopopeia but the ginestra itself that is in focus at the end.

This disturbing poem is unbalanced between its extremes of harsh rhetoric and the tender quasi-personified plant; between the addresses to self-deluded man in his pride and to the lowly plant that asks nothing. Yet the alternatives Leopardi might have taken are safer and tamer. It could have been a somber, stoical meditation, a final affirmation of specifically religious consolation for man's hard fate, a simple moral exhortation to be somehow like a plant, or a scornful, mocking satire against mankind or deified Natura. That it is not quite any of these may well give us a sense of unease. The poet, however, chooses to advocate no consolation; he chooses instead to advocate the cold light of reason and the minimal virtue of endurance amid unremitting and mindless disaster—cold comfort indeed. Since reasonable arguments go unheeded in this age, he must utterly expose human vanity and pride. In doing so he imitates, in effect, the molten force of the all-consuming lava and the rough, barren, craggy aspect of its petrified waves and ridges, now grown cold but still witness to the prospect of further burning disaster. The contradiction between malevolent Natura and the gentle creatures of nature remains unresolved: there is no pretense at resolving it. Exegetes who for sentimental or rationalistic motives wish to do the resolving for Leopardi expose themselves to his scorn and mockery from beyond the grave. The second part of Goethe's *Faust* and Hugo's *La Légende des siècles* would surely have appalled him, though one can imagine him being in sympathy with *In Memoriam* and a good deal of twentieth-century poetry.

"La Ginestra" is a solemn poem that exceeds the bounds of the traditional canzone, even in the paraenetic mode we have earlier sketched, from Petrarch to "All'Italia." Its lesson is hard and shorn of habitual hopes and illusions. Its respites are piercingly poignant. All in all, a terrible, terrifying vision. Probably the poem is a grand failure. We, as readers, also fail in often not reading it whole, in often not wanting to read it whole. But there it is, with its crabbed scorn, its mocking anger, its gentle despair, and its hard, unphilosophically stoic beauty. We turn elsewhere in Leopardi (to "All'Italia" and the "idylls") and to Foscolo's *Sepolcri*, as well as to Petrarch, the presiding *numen* of language, in order to know what Leopardi here forthrightly and almost pitilessly rejects and denies to both himself and us. Would that it were otherwise, we may think. But it is not. There it is.

BIBLIOGRAPHICAL NOTE

The most convenient, complete, and up-to-date edition of Giacomo Leopardi is *Tutte le opere*, edited by Walter Binni with the collaboration of Enrico Ghidetti, in two volumes (Florence: Sansoni, 1969). There the reader will find all the texts responsibly presented with a long introduction, a bibliography, and thorough analytic indexes. Still very useful are the editions of Francesco Flora (Milan: Mondadori, 1937–49) and the truly critical one (in the textual sense) of the poems and the *Operette morali* by Francesco Moroncini (Bologna, 1927–29). Mario Fubini's old, commented edition of the *Canti* (Turin: UTET, 1930) is still useful. Currently, the most convenient and informative commented edition of the *Canti* is that of Niccolò Gallo and Cesare Gàrboli in the Nuova Universale Einaudi series (Turin, 1972): the notes and apparatus are reliable and informative; only the occasional critical comments may seem flimsy or overblown. There are numerous other editions and, of course, single poems are continuously anthologized.

Fortunately there exists a good account of Leopardi's critical fortune so far as the *Canti* are concerned: Alberto Frattini, *Critica e fortuna dei "Canti" di G. Leopardi* (Brescia: La Scuola Editrice, 1957, rev. ed., 1964). To the same author we owe the best brief general introduction readily available in Italian: *Giacomo Leopardi* (Rocca San Casciano: Cappelli, 1969). Also useful is Emilio Bigi's historical and bibliographical survey of criticism in *I classici italiani nella storia della critica*, ed. Walter Binni (Florence: La Nuova Italia, 1967), 2:353–407. An excellent sketch of Leopardi's whole career is to be found in Natalino Sapegno's *Compendio di storia della letteratura italiana* (Florence: La Nuova Italia, 1947; rev. 1965), 3:202–56. Also informative are his *dispense*, *Storia della poesia di Leopardi* (Facoltà di Lettere, Università degli Studi di Roma, academic year 1953–54), in two volumes, mainly for Leopardi's early intellectual and poetic development.

Francesco De Sanctis's great *Storia della letteratura italiana* (1870–71; ed. Benedetto Croce [Bari: Laterza, 1912, and often reissued]) does not reach as far as Leopardi; but he left essays and the major portion of a book on Leopardi, which are both impassioned and quite sound (in *Opere complete*, general editor Carlo Muscetta, vol. 3, ed. Walter Binni [Bari: Laterza, 1953]). De Sanctis's love for the early patriotic poems of Leopardi stems from the high patriotic fervor of his own time (the Neapolitan ferment from about 1830 to 1848 and beyond); he is an excellent critic of the "idylls" but he never came to terms with "La Ginestra." Not many others have. Certainly not Croce, whose whole theory of *poesia* would predispose him against the "didactic" and paraenetic in much of Leopardi's poetry: see the characteristic short essays on Leopardi in *Poesia e non poesia* (Bari, 1922) and in *Poesia antica e moderna: interpretazioni* (Bari, 1940). Later Italian critics have often been stung or embarrassed by Croce's occasionally derogatory remarks. They could, if they would, take comfort from his odd praise of the poet Vigny, who too often seems didactic, without verve, and a bit dowdy now.

In the welter of books and articles on Leopardi recently published, one notes the insistent claims, *pace* Croce, for Leopardi's greatness not only as poet but as linguist, existentialist, and philosopher—or at least *philosophe*. Such claims often seem lacking both in critical preciseness and proper international perspective. The studies in which they are set forth may simply be exercises within the assumed parameters of Italian academic expectations and performance: a phenomenon familiar in most countries as part of a general inflation and overproduction of critical, academic discourse.

Also, one notes a growing, perhaps overgrowing, interest in eighteenth-century intellectual and literary "background," in pre-Romanticism, however that may be defined. It is certainly a great gain that scholars like Mario Fubini and Franco Venturi have explored and expounded so well the intense and interesting activity of eighteenth-century ideologues and *littérateurs*, establishing the high level of native culture and seeing it in its proper international perspective. Recently, however, there has been a tendency to claim too much originality for the Italian settecento. As far as Leopardi is concerned, the first hefty volume of the *acta* of the Centro Nazionale di Studi Leopardiani (Florence: Olschki, 1964) contains some good essays but a great deal of unproportioned ballast.

A sometimes good, sometimes merely hortatory critic whose great claims for Leopardi have aroused emulation is Walter Binni, whose fine edition has been mentioned and whose *La nuova poetica leopardiana* (Florence: Sansoni, 1971, a new and enlarged edition of a work first issued in 1947) is quite important but disappointing in its imprecise formulation and its idiom of Italian academic jargon which defies brief exemplification. At least Binni devotes a whole chapter to "La Ginestra" and is thus one of the few critics to confront the poem extensively; the results are rather fuzzy, however. As for "background" in poetry of the eighteenth century, the best thing of all is the volume, edited by Bruno Meier, with a fine, long introduction by Mario Fubini, in the Riccardo Ricciardi series: *Lirici del settecento* (Milan-Naples, 1959). Fubini's bibliographic note, with its strictures on Binni's "isms," is also a valuable contribution to that volume. A good specialized study on Italian eighteenth- and nineteenth-century taste, which takes proper account of Leopardi in the last section, is Renzo Negri, *Gusto e poesia delle rovine in Italia fra il sette e l'ottocento* (Milan: Ceschina, 1965), a commendably well-informed and generally well-written book on the subject in its full European context.

As for volcanoes, and Vesuvius in particular, perhaps the best reference as a start is the article in the *Enciclopedia italiana*. For other indications, see the excellent essay by G. M. Matthews, "A Volcano's Voice in Shelley," *ELH* 24 (1957): 191–228. Also the Leopardian volcanologist should look up the numerous references to current earthquakes and eruptions in Italy to be found in *Antologia* (1821–33), the great magazine which surely was a source of multifarious information for many men of letters, including Leopardi, to whom later scholars attribute an often unrealistic degree of "first-hand" erudition. In point of both ruins and volcanoes, not to mention the Lisbon earthquake, it would seem disproportionate to attempt a particular array of "sources" for Leopardi beyond the common literary and historical tradition and the undeniable assumption that Leopardi read Voltaire, Bettinelli, and Baretti (all with well-known texts on Lisbon), Rousseau and Ossian, Foscolo, and whoever else a well-read genius would plausibly have read and known.

For his reading, one must of course refer to the *Zibaldone* for the years he kept it and also to the two chrestomathies of verse and prose that he compiled and published. See the *Crestomazia italiana: la poesia* (Turin: Einaudi, 1968), well edited by Giuseppe Savoca. Finally, perhaps the best long account of Leopardi's intellectual setting is *L'Ideologia letteraria di Giacomo Leopardi* (Naples: Liguori, 1968) by the distinguished and wide-ranging scholar Salvatore Battaglia.

In English J. H. Whitfield's *Giacomo Leopardi* (Oxford, 1954) is informative. The best general introduction to his life in any language is *Leopardi: A Study in Solitude* (London, rev. ed. 1953) by the admirable Marchesa Iris Origo. Interesting confrontations are to be found in Karl Kroeber's *The Artifice of Reality: Poetic Style in Wordsworth, Foscolo, Keats, and Leopardi* (Madison, Wisc., 1964). In German the best general volume is still the vaguely unsatisfactory *Leopardi* by Karl Vossler (Munich, 1923).

Citation could go on indefinitely since the critical corpus is vast and growing. If in my essay I do not engage other critics of these poems in some sort of fraternal dialogue, it is because I must honestly conclude that there are few real *punti d'appiglio*.

NOTES

1. I use the word *experience* instead of the usual *influence* with its hydraulic or astral overtones, because a poet has an idiosyncratic, active, and selective experience of reading another poet. It is implausible, even subliminally, to think of poets as passive receptacles.

2. Poem no. 128 in *Le rime*, ed. Ferdinando Neri, in the Riccardo Ricciardi series: Francesco Petrarca, *Rime, trionfi, e poesie latine* (Milan-Naples, 1951), pp. 183–88.

3. The texts cited from Da Filicaia and Testi are in Carlo Calcaterra, *I lirici del seicento e dell'Arcadia* (Milan-Rome: Rizzoli, 1936).

4. *Crestomazia italiana poetica* (Milan: Stella, 1828). See my Bibliographical Note for reference to Savoca's edition.

5. For the text, see Vincenzo Monti, *Tragedie, poemetti, liriche*, ed., Gino Francesco Gobbi (Milan: Hoepli, 1927), pp. 458–70.

6. See the two fragments translated by Leopardi in 1823–24 from, as he seems to have known, Simonides of Amorgos—not, apparently, Simonides of Ceos. They are included in the *Canti*, ed. Niccolò Gallo and Cesare Gàrboli (Turin: Einaudi, 1972), pp. 311–18. Generically about the inevitable passage of time, neither of them is appropriate or useful in regard to "All'Italia." The real Simonides of Ceos is the one whose martial fragments Leopardi has in mind.

7. See my forthcoming essay, "Leopardi's 'L'Infinito,' " in the *Studi in onore di Natalino Sapegno* (Rome: Bulzoni, 1974–).

8. *Ginestra* is a plant rather like heather or furze, called in English "broom" (hence the small article of domestic utility). For obvious reasons, I prefer to use the word *ginestra* even in an English context when referring to the plant outside the poem's title. On similar problems of translation, see Mario Praz's fine essay "Nomi di fiori," in *Machiavelli in Inghilterra ed altri saggi*, 2d ed. (Rome: Tumminelli, 1943), pp. 329–44.

9. Leopardi's use of the word *natura* may cause confusion. Mainly it has four senses: nature as all of existence; human nature; nature as benign flora and fauna, at times including man; and Natura as a malevolent or indifferent presiding deity or cosmic force. Only the last two senses directly concern us here. The benign sense, I translate as "nature"; the malign sense I capitalize and leave latinate as "Natura." In a strange way the two can even blend.

10. See Lois Whitney, *Primitivism and the Idea of Progress* (Baltimore, 1934), passim.

14

Strategies of the Anti-hero: Svevo, Pirandello, and Montale

Gian-Paolo Biasin

> Literature as well as criticism—the difference between them being delusive—are condemned (or privileged) to be forever the most rigorous and, consequently, the most unreliable language in terms of which man names and modifies himself. [Paul de Man, *Blindness and Insight*]

The figure of the hero in literary history has undergone a steady decline, so that instead of the classic hero of the Greeks it has been possible to speak of modern and contemporary heroes who are "mediocre" or "middling" (Luckàcs), "passive" (Garber), "unheroic" (Giraud), "intellectual" or "impossible" (Brombert), "vanishing" (O'Faolain), or "with a thousand faces" (Campbell).[1] It seems, therefore, preferable to do away entirely with the term *hero* and to use its opposite, *anti-hero*, which contains a reference to a lost past as well as to a problematic present.

But at first sight, the use of the metaphor implicit in the word *strategies* in connection with *anti-hero*, might seem a paradox, a contradiction in terms—at least to the extent to which the anti-hero is the exact opposite of the hero, who is the traditional referent for such a soldierly terminology as *strategy*. One needs only to think of Napoleon, hero and strategist par excellence, and the model for a whole generation of Romantic poets as well as of neoclassical artists.

However, the metaphor is necessary. When it was applied to the

363

hero, *strategy* had an active, aggressive connotation; when applied to the anti-hero, it has a passive, self-defensive quality which, by itself, might suffice to characterize a historical shift manifested and documented particularly in and by the contemporary novel—although the simple mention of such works as Brecht's *The Good Soldier Schweik* or Norman Mailer's *The Armies of the Night* (just to remain in a very specific semantic area) would suffice to enlarge the scope of the problem greatly. *Strategy* points to the environment, not only to the subject; and this environment is definitely hostile, if not cruel and violent. The anti-hero, if he wants to survive, *must* have a strategy; he must somehow use the weapons provided by the environment for his own ends. Besides, he, too, contains within himself certain elements of violence that are not too far removed from the notion and the practice of strategy.

But above all, since the anti-hero, exactly as the hero, is simply a character, he cannot be anything else than part of the "strategy" of the author—a point that must be always kept in mind, especially in the case of the contemporary novel and its literary as well as cognitive contributions. Walter Benjamin says that the critic is a strategist in the literary struggle: so is the author, obviously; and this struggle involves the reader, too.

If the environment is hostile and violent, the subject finds himself placed in a rapport of disharmony with it—a rapport for which contemporary sociology as well as literary criticism have a common, although not always precise, definition: alienation. In fact, the alienated man can be considered the twentieth-century man par excellence, and as such he plays a central role in literature: he becomes the anti-hero, who is now ironic, as in Svevo's *La coscienza di Zeno*; now intellectually rebellious, as in Pirandello's *Uno, nessuno e centomila* or Sartre's *La nausée*; now indifferent, as in Moravia's *Gl'indifferenti* or Camus's *L'étranger*; now not even existing, as in Calvino's latest stories—not to mention many other variations on the theme.

Perhaps the roots of contemporary alienation are to be found in the Romantic attitude of the "fallen angel" in a debased, unworthy world, an attitude that found its philosophical expression in Hegel's phenomenology and its most recent formulation in Morse Peckham's notion of "negative Romanticism." It is mainly psychological and ontological. But there is little doubt that the contemporary meaning of *alienation* derives directly from Marx and his description of capitalist society, where all human relations, within a class or between classes, become dehumanized, and the notions of "reification" and "fetishism of commodities" acquire a predominant role. Alienation in the Marxian sense should be juxtaposed to anomie, the concept developed by Durkheim, the positivists, and the behaviorists, for whom man is incapable of adapting himself to the changing conditions of society, and should be so adapted by society itself, through "social engineering" or even, today, through psychoanalysis. Both Marxian alienation and anomie are very important for the understanding of the contemporary "existential" situation.

There is no doubt that alienation in its various forms has an enormous relevance for contemporary literature; it is, in fact, a "prime theme" of literature. But, as the intelligent British Marxist David Caute recently suggested:

> Consider two types of alienation, the one a noxious disease, the other an antidote, a vaccine to the virus. . . . 1. *Entfremdung*—noxious and disabling, social and economic, political and psychological alienation; 2. *Verfremdung*—a philosophy and technique of literature, particularly drama, primarily associated with Brecht and involving detachment, non-empathy and disillusion. Art recognising itself as art. Alienated art.[2]

In contemporary Italian literature the major thrust toward a representation of the theme of alienation and at the same time toward an overcoming of it (precisely through the strategies of the anti-hero), has occurred mainly at the beginning of this century, in the 1920s, and more specifically in a short, intense period, when three major works in both the novel and poetry appeared: Italo Svevo's *La coscienza di Zeno* (1923), Luigi Pirandello's *Uno, nessuno e centomila* (1925), and Eugenio Montale's *Ossi di seppia* (1925; the second edition in 1928 included "Arsenio," written in 1926–27). A few diachronic considerations are in order before proceeding to the synchronic analysis of these works.

With *La coscienza di Zeno*, Svevo concluded his oeuvre, begun in 1892 with *Una vita* and continued in 1898 with *Senilità*, and marked a significant turning point in the development of the Italian novel—doubly significant, in fact, because it represented a new and powerful *vision du monde* after the ones established mainly by Manzoni and

Verga in the nineteenth century, and because, given precisely its novelty and power, it introduced modernism in Italian literature in a manner comparable to what Joyce did for English and Proust for French. It might be appropriately remembered that Svevo's fame was first of all European rather than Italian, thanks to Joyce's enthusiastic support, which led to the presentation of Svevo by Valéry Larbaud and Benjamin Crémieux in France, and by Eugenio Montale in Italy in 1925.

In that same year, Pirandello's *Uno, nessuno e centomila* represented the culmination of his creative activity both as novelist and playwright: it is the last novel he wrote, after working on it sparingly for more than a dozen years and developing some of its themes and ideas in the theater, notably, *Sei personaggi in cerca d'autore* and *Enrico IV* (1922). It brings to the extreme consequences the existential intuitions of *Il fu Mattia Pascal* (1905); it foreshadows the further, irrationalistic development of his latest plays; it is, in short, a *summa* of Pirandello's revolutionary contribution to contemporary literature, both in the theater (an almost obvious assertion is that Brecht, Ionesco, and other contemporary playwrights would have been impossible without him), and in the novel (his accomplishments here were for a rather long time obfuscated by his extraordinary success on the stage, but are now increasingly recognized as fundamental ones, along with Svevo's).

Montale's *Ossi di seppia* plays an equally fundamental role in the history of its author, of Italian poetry, and of contemporary poetry in general. It is the first book published by the young Montale, and it establishes the basis for his subsequent works, notably *Le occasioni* (1939) and *La bufera* (1957), but also *Satura* (1971) and *Diario del '71 e del '72*. It breaks with the predominant Petrarchan and Dannunzian tradition of Italian poetry, and powerfully inserts the problems and the language of conscience and analytical reason into an area where sentiments or irrationality dominated—even in the poetry of the other two great figureheads of hermeticism, Giuseppe Ungaretti and Salvatore Quasimodo. It had an enormous impact on a whole generation, and can be—actually has been—linked in many respects with T. S. Eliot's *The Waste Land*, that other milestone of contemporary poetry.

Svevo, Pirandello, and Montale are particularly representative of a major development in Italian literature in the 1920s (the period when, according to Giacomo Debenedetti, contemporaneity begins): they are the poets of the modern conscience. As such, their works are fundamental to understanding contemporary alienation through their respective antiheroes—Zeno, Moscarda, and Arsenio; and through the strategies of their authors they are three fundamental specimens of what Caute calls "alienated art, dialectical writing":

> What artistic writing can do is to move with a special freedom, creating new spaces of awareness, associating and juxtaposing features of reality, of consciousness, of myth, of aspiration and of belief in patterns and structures which could not be justified by academic or scientific criteria. Like philosophy, it has a special mission to operate in the empty space between the known and the unknown, the verifiable and the speculative. And, like philosophy again, it enjoys a special exploratory relationship with man's most extensively employed means of communication—language.[3]

Here Caute seems to use an approach that can be usefully linked with L. A. White's notion of "the science of culture" or "culturology," where the cognitive role of art in general and literature in particular is not only recognized but given a precise, scientific status.

While Caute uses the science of culture for ideological (that is, Marxist) purposes, the Italian critic Renato Barilli uses it for historicistic and literary ends, that is, for presenting Svevo and Pirandello as the two greatest innovators and founders of the contemporary novel through "una narrativa volta a collaborare all'istituzione globale di una nuova cultura" ("a narrative bent on collaborating in the total institution of a new culture"): "Si tratta di una cultura fondamentalmente posta al di là di quella borghese" ("It is a culture which is fundamentally posited *beyond* the culture of the bourgeoisie"), and whose major philosophic representatives can be said to be Bergson, Husserl, and Dewey.[4] Through a detailed historical and ideological analysis, Barilli persuasively demonstrates that Svevo and Pirandello want to "project," to plan, to indicate a new and better mankind—precisely "in the empty space between the known and the unknown, the verifiable and the speculative."

Similar conclusions, of course, can be applied to Montale's poetry as well. But it is important to stress that both Caute's and Barilli's approaches in reaching these conclusions (Marxistic ideology for the former, White's culturology for the latter) are used here as means toward a specific end of literary criticism: the discovery of structural similarities among different "characters" and works, the perception of their emblematic value, the exploration of their status as *literary* devices. In other words, the context here is that of a thematic, symbolic criticism whereby Zeno, Moscarda, and Arsenio appear as fundamental specimens of the anti-hero. The identity cards of these emblematic characters contain precious elements which reveal their strategies, as well as those of their authors. A brief analysis of some of these significant elements will follow.

Zeno Cosini

Even in Zeno Cosini's name, as Renata Minerbi Treitel has shown, there is a hint to the concept of alienation: Zeno means "stranger," Cosini seems to point to "meaningless little things," and therefore to an acknowledgment and a criticism of "reification."[5] But the real aspect of him that matters is his *coscienza*, his moral and psychoanalytic "conscience," his temporal "awareness," his totalizing "knowledge" or "con-science"—which is shown to be impossible. In other words, the emphasis is placed on interiority and contemplation rather than on behavior or action; individual values are placed above social ones. Zeno is a bourgeois who does not really accept the bourgeois order; he does not work, has no financial preoccupations, and therefore can devote his time to the whims of his contemplative nature. He is perplexed, undecided, awkward to the point of being almost "Chaplinesque" (as some critics have defined him), seemingly incapable of action, a "diseased" person perpetually searching for "health" but secretly proud of his sick condition, which privileges him above the "normal" state of the others.

In narrative terms, Zeno's alienation is shown and superseded through characteristic thematic devices:

(1) Smoking the last cigarette, which is the brilliant lack of solution to a chain of insoluble dichotomies: thought / life, will / thought, and—especially important for Svevo and the modern novel in general—chronological time / inner *durée*.

> Penso che la sigaretta abbia un gusto piú intenso quand'è l'ultima. Anche le altre hanno un loro gusto speciale, ma meno intenso. L'ultima acquista il suo sapore dal sentimento della vittoria su se stesso e la speranza di un prossimo futuro di forza e di salute. Le altre hanno la loro importanza perché accendendole si

protesta la propria libertà e il futuro di forza e di salute permane, ma va un po' piú lontano.

Le date sulle pareti della mia stanza erano impresse coi colori piú varii ed anche ad olio. Il proponimento, rifatto con la fede piú ingenua, trovava adeguata espressione nella forza del colore che doveva far impallidire quello dedicato al proponimento anteriore. Certe date erano da me preferite per la concordanza delle cifre. Del secolo passato ricordo una data che mi parve dovesse sigillare per sempre la bara in cui volevo mettere il mio vizio: "Nono giorno del nono mese del 1899." Significativa nevvero? Il secolo nuovo m'apportò delle date ben altrimenti musicali: "Primo giorno del primo mese del 1901." Ancora mi pare che se quella data potesse ripetersi, io saprei iniziare una nuova vita. [pp. 606–07]

[I am sure a cigarette has a more poignant flavor when it is the last. The others have their own special taste too, peculiar to them, but it is less poignant. The last has an aroma all its own, bestowed by a sense of victory over oneself and the sure hope of health and strength in the immediate future. The others are important too, as an assertion of one's own freedom, and when one lights them one still has a vision of that future of health and beauty, though it has moved a little further off.

The dates on my walls displayed every variety of color and I had painted some of them in oils. The latest resolution, renewed in the most ingenuous good faith, found appropriate expression in the violence of its colors, which aimed at making those of the preceding one pale before it. I had a partiality for certain dates because their figures went well together. I remember one of last century which seemed as if it must be the final monument to my vice: "Ninth day of the ninth month, in the year 1899." Surely a most significant date! The new century furnished me with other dates equally harmonious, though in a different way. "First day of the first month in the year 1901." Even today I feel that if only that date could repeat itself I should be able to begin a new life.] [pp. 11][6]

(2) The death of the father, which not only is a perfect example of the psychoanalytic ambivalence underlying the most "normal" sentiments, but also establishes Zeno as narrator, with an almost obvious reference

to the "parricide word" that is placed by Jacques Derrida at the very
origin of any *écriture*:[7]

> Su quel sofà piansi le mie piú cocenti lacrime. Il pianto offusca le
> proprie colpe e permette di accusare, senz'obbiezioni, il destino.
> Piangevo perché perdevo il padre per cui ero sempre vissuto. Non
> importava che gli avessi tenuto poca compagnia. I miei sforzi per
> diventare migliore non erano stati fatti per dare una soddisfazione
> a lui? Il successo cui anelavo doveva bensí essere anche il mio
> vanto verso di lui, che di me aveva sempre dubitato, ma anche la
> sua consolazione. Ed ora invece egli non poteva piú aspettarmi e
> se ne andava convinto della mia insanabile debolezza. Le mie
> lacrime erano amarissime.
>
> Scrivendo, anzi incidendo sulla carta tali dolorosi ricordi,
> scopro che l'immagine che m'ossessionò al primo mio tentativo di
> vedere nel mio passato, quella locomotiva che trascina una se-
> quela di vagoni su per un'erta, io l'ebbi per la prima volta ascol-
> tando da quel sofà il respiro di mio padre. [p. 634]

[My bitterest tears were shed on that sofa. Tears throw a veil over
our faults and allow us to accuse Fate without fear of contradiction. I wept because I was losing my father for whom I had always
lived. It did not matter that I had been so little with him. Had not
all my efforts to become better been made in order to give satisfaction to him? It is true that the success I strove for would have been
a personal triumph for me as against him who had always doubted
me, but it would have been a consolation to him as well. And now
he could wait no longer and was going away convinced of my
incurable incapacity. The tears I shed were indeed bitter.

While I sit writing, or rather engraving these tragic memories on
my paper, I realize that the image that obsessed me at the first
attempt to look into my past—the image of an engine drawing a
string of coaches up a hill—came to me for the first time while I
lay on the sofa listening to my father's breathing.] [p. 41]

(3) The relationships with the wife (Augusta), who is the perfect
embodiment of the bourgeoisie, and with the lover (Carla), who is
romantic and possessive: both of them are necessary to establish
Zeno's own detachment and superiority:

—Com'è che ti concedesti a me? Come meritai una cosa simile?
. . .

—A me pare che tu mi abbia presa,— e sorrise affettuosamente per provarmi che non intendeva di rimproverarmi.

Ricordai che le donne esigono si dica che sono state prese. Poi, essa stessa si accorse di aver sbagliato, che le cose si prendono e le persone si accordano. . . .

Lì, accanto a Carla, rinacque intera la mia passione per Augusta. Ora non avrei avuto che un desiderio: correre dalla mia vera moglie, solo per vederla intenta al suo lavoro di formica assidua, mentre metteva in salvo le nostre cose in un'atmosfera di canfora e di naftalina. [p. 770]

["What made you give yourself to me? What had I done to deserve it?"——

"I thought it was you who had taken me," she said, smiling affectionately at me to show that she did not mean it as a reproach.

I remembered that women always insist on the fiction that they have been raped. But she soon saw she had made a mistake, for you may take things, but people must give themselves——.

As I lay there beside her, my love for Augusta revived in all its force. I only had one wish now: to hurry home to my wife, just in order to see her working like a busy bee, putting all our clothes away in camphor and naphthaline.] [p. 190]

(4) The story of his commercial association, which is a delightful mockery of the capitalist system *from within*, beginning with the commercial letters thrown up in the air and left to the chance of falling one way or the other in order to be answered or not, and ending with the buying and selling of a completely unmystical (that is, literally demystified) *incense*—a perfect instance of a "gratuitous act";[8]

(5) The use of psychoanalysis as a means of narrating a story and of diversifying Zeno from the others, with the implicit but clear criticism both of the society made up of these others, and of psychoanalysis intended purely as a therapy: *disease* becomes a positive value:

Io soffro bensì di certi dolori, ma mancano d'importanza nella mia grande salute. Posso mettere un impiastro qui o là, ma il resto ha da moversi e battersi e mai indugiarsi nell'immobilità come gl'incancreniti. Dolore e amore, poi, la vita insomma, non puo essere considerata quale una malattia perché duole. . . .

Naturalmente io non sono un ingenuo e scuso 'il dottore di vedere nella vita stessa una manifestazione di malattia. La vita somiglia un poco alla malattia come procede per crisi e lisi ed ha i gionalieri miglioramenti e peggioramenti. A differenza delle altre malattie la vita è sempre mortale. Non sopporta cure. Sarebbe come voler turare i buchi che abbiamo nel corpo credendoli delle ferite. Morremmo strangolati non appena curati. [pp. 953–54]

[Of course I have pains from time to time, but what do they matter when my health is perfect? I may have to put on a poultice now and then for some local ailment, but otherwise I force my limbs to keep in healthy motion and never allow them to sink into inertia. Pain and love—the whole of life, in short—cannot be looked on as a disease just because they make us suffer.

I am not so naïve as to blame the doctor for regarding life itself as a manifestation of disease. Life is a little like disease, with its crises and periods of quiescence, its daily improvements and setbacks. But unlike other diseases life is always mortal. It admits of no cure. It would be like trying to stop up the holes in our body, thinking them to be wounds. We should die of suffocation almost before we were cured.] [pp. 396–97]

(6) The final apocalypse, which is a "pharmakon," in the form of a prophecy significantly directed against contemporary military strategists: an enormous explosion caused by some sort of "Doomsday Machines" will free the earth from "parasites and disease," sweep it clean, and make it ready for a better mankind.

Stylistically, Svevo's dialectical writing, his literary strategy of the anti-hero, is achieved especially through the following devices: (1) the interposing of a note by a "Dr. S." between Zeno's diary, the author, and the reader, thereby providing an ideal "distance" to and from the narrator—the highly *unreliable* narrator, whose words can never be taken at face value:

Sembrava tanto curioso di se stesso! Se sapesse quante sorprese potrebbero risultargli dal commento delle tante verità e bugie ch'egli ha qui accumulate! [p. 599]

[He seemed to feel intense curiosity about himself. But he little knows what surprises lie in wait for him, if someone were to set about analyzing the mass of truths and falsehoods which he has collected here.] [p. 5]

(2) the choice of a plain, "business Italian," which is very discursive and nonpoetical, but highly communicative and therefore "didactic"[9]— the perfect linguistic instrument needed to illustrate the author's project, his *vision du monde*; (3) the awareness of the narrator that he is telling simply a story, not the truth—in other words, the self-awareness of art recognizing itself as art and positing the necessity of its being art (in this case a novel rather than a sociological or medical treatise).

Vitangelo Moscarda

There is no particular meaning in the name of the protagonist and narrator of Pirandello's novel; but it is fair that it be so, because like his predecessor, Mattia Pascal, he is only a name to which "one, none and one hundred thousand" entities correspond. His individuality is completely lost in the dehumanized relations of his society, yet this dehumanization is necessary for his highest self-awareness. Like Zeno, Moscarda is a bourgeois who does not accept the bourgeois order at all. He, too, does not work and has no financial preoccupations, so that his contemplative nature can come to the fore from the very beginning. He, too, is often perplexed and undecided, seemingly incapable of action, awkward, a "madman" juxtaposed to the "sane" others and finally emerging *above* them. When he does decide and does act, his decision and action will be "gratuitous," scandalous, and revolutionary.

In narrative terms, Moscarda's alienation is shown through thematic devices that closely parallel the ones used by Svevo for Zeno, and that perform an analogous function in the structure of the novel. (1) Looking at himself in the mirror, which is the very image of the *dédoublement de soi*, of the chain of dichotomies—contemplation / action, thought/ life, will/thought, self/other, and mad/sane; it might be worth remembering that the mirror-image has become almost a *topos* of contemporary art, from the novel (as in Malraux's *La condition humaine*— Clappique—or in Sartre's *La nausée*—Roquentin) to painting (as in Picasso's *Les demoiselles d'Avignon*). Here is Pirandello's version:

> Ma, all'improvviso, mentre così pensavo, avvenne tal cosa che mi riempì di spavento più che di stupore.
>
> Vidi davanti a me, non per mia volontà, l'apatica attonita faccia

di quel povero corpo mortificato scomporsi pietosamente, arric-
ciare il naso, arrovesciare gli occhi all'indietro, contrarre le labbra
in su e provarsi ad aggrottar le ciglia, come per piangere; restare
così un attimo sospeso e poi crollar due volte a scatto per lo scop-
pio d'una coppia di sternuti.

S'era commosso da sé, per conto suo, a un filo d'aria entrato chi
sa donde, quel povero corpo mortificato, senza dirmene nulla e
fuori della mia volontà.

—Salute!—gli dissi.

E guardai nello specchio il mio primo riso da matto. [p. 1300]

[But all of a sudden, as my thoughts ran like this, something
happened to change my stupor to a looming terror. I beheld in
front of my eyes, through no will of my own, the apathetically
astonished face of that poor mortified body piteously decompos-
ing, the nose curling up, the eyes turning over inward, the lips
contracting upward, and the brows drawing together as if for
weeping—they remained like that, in suspense for an instant, and
then without warning came crumbling down, to the explosive
accompaniment of a couple of sneezes. The thing had happened
of itself, at a draught of air from some place or other, without that
poor mortified body's having said a word to me, and quite beyond
any will of my own.

"To your health!" I cried.

And I beheld in the mirror my first madman's smile.] [pp. 39–
40][10]

(2) The absence of the father (Moscarda is an orphan), with affective
"ambivalence" and with "parricide words" that are even stronger—and
certainly more dramatic—than Zeno's own:

La nostra nascita staccata, recisa da lui, come un caso comune,
forse previsto, ma involontario nella vita di quell'estraneo, prova
d'un gesto, frutto d'un atto, alcunché insomma che ora, sì, ci fa
vergogna, ci suscita sdegno e quasi odio. E se non propriamente
odio, un certo acuto dispetto notiamo anche negli occhi di nostro
padre, che in quell'attimo si sono scontrati nei nostri. Siamo per
lui, lì ritti in piedi, e con due vigili occhi ostili, ciò che egli dallo
sfogo d'un suo momentaneo bisogno o piacere, non si aspettava:

quel seme gettato ch'egli non sapeva, ritto ora in piedi e con due occhi fuoruscenti di lumaca che guardano a tentoni e giudicano e gl'impediscono d'essere ancora in tutto a piacer suo, libero, *un altro* anche rispetto a noi. [pp. 1327–28]

[Yet our birth was an involuntary thing in the life of that stranger, the indication of a deed, fruit of an act, something in short that actually causes us shame, arousing in us scorn and almost hatred. And if it is not properly speaking hatred, there is a certain sharp contempt that we are now conscious of in our father's eyes also, which at this second happen to meet our own. We to him, as we stand upright on our feet here, with a pair of hostile eyes, are something that he did not expect from the satisfaction of a momentary need or pleasure, a seed that he unknowingly cast, a seed standing upright now on two feet, with a pair of popping snail's eyes that stealthily survey him and judge him and prevent him now from being wholly what he would like to be, free, *another man* even with respect to us.] [pp. 96–97]

(3) The relationships with the wife (Dida), a very concrete and nasty embodiment of the bourgeoisie, and with the lover (Anna Maria), romantic and possessive, both necessary to define his "nonidentity" (he is Gengè for the former and Vitangelo for the latter), and therefore to establish his final detachment and superiority—exactly as was the case with Zeno;

(4) The story of his disengagement from his father's bank, which is a complete, literal rejection of one of the key institutions of capitalist society;

(5) The use of madness as a means of diversifying Moscarda from the others, in order to criticize the system of social roles and the related bourgeois values attached to them. Witness the scene when Moscarda tells the two bankers, who believe him to be mad, to kneel in front of madmen: "Andate, andate là, dove li tenete chiusi: andate a sentirli parlare! li tenete chiusi perché cosi vi conviene!"—p. 1355. ("Then go—go there where you keep those people locked up; go, go and listen to them talk! You keep them locked up because it's more convenient for you"—p. 150).

(6) The final, private, "pantheistic" dispersion into nature of the character, who has given up all his belongings, his social position, even

his name—a dispersion which has the same function as Zeno's public apocalypse—that is, to point to the possibility of another, better world, different from the present one and projected into a hypothetical future.

Stylistically, Pirandello's dialectical writing, his literary strategy, is achieved—significantly in a novel which is the epitome of his theater— through the following devices: (1) the fragmentation of the story into short chapters, much à la Tristram Shandy, as Giovanni Macchia has pointed out:[11] these short chapters are self-enclosed scenes doing away with the traditional plot and breaking the "story" continuously, show- ing it to be precisely that, a story; (2) the choice of a mddle Italian idiom, highly communicative and didactic, furthering a cognitive operation; (3) the rhetorical addresses of the narrator to the readers, such as the following:

> Difatti, non andavo forse incontro al signor Vitangelo Moscarda per giocargli un brutto tiro? Eh, signori, sì, un brutto tiro (scusa- temi tutti questi ammiccamenti; ma ho bisogno d'ammiccare, d'ammiccare così, perché, non potendo sapere come v'appajo in questo momento, tiro anche, con questi ammiccamenti, a in- dovinare). [p. 1345]

> [Was I not, in all truth, setting out to play a dirty trick upon Signor Vitangelo Moscarda? Yes, good people, that is what it was! a dirty trick (you will have to excuse all these winks on my part, but I have need of winking, to wink like this, since, not being aware just what impression I am making upon you at this moment, I may be able thus to obtain a hint).] [p. 131]

These rhetorical addresses encourage an "active, personal response,"[12] and provide space for it within the fiction itself: again, the self-aware- ness of art as such.

Arsenio

This old-fashioned name (ironically hinting at virility and juxtaposed to Eusebio, the author's favorite nickname) would seem to recall a poetical character like T. S. Eliot's Prufrock rather than novelistic characters like Zeno and Moscarda, especially given the facts that poetry and novels are traditionally considered heterogeneous, and that Montale in the 1920s was at the beginning of his literary career, while Svevo was concluding his own and Pirandello was in his full maturity.[13]

Yet the linking, if not the comparison, of Arsenio with Zeno and Moscarda, seems not only advisable but necessary.[14] Arsenio's identification card cannot be as complete as Zeno's and Moscarda's, precisely because he is a lyrical and not a novelistic character. He is a character nevertheless, and a very emblematic one, as an embodiment of Montale's major themes and as a catalyzer of culture. In Gianni Pozzi's words, Arsenio is

> la figura drammatica di un personaggio travolto dalla sua incertezza metafisica, come dai nembi dell'uragano, puntualizzazione e rappresentazione di una esistenza assieme individuale ed emblematica, cosciente ma non pacifico simbolo dell'angoscia esistenziale di un'epoca, di una generazione, di una situazione umana.

> [the dramatic figure of a character overwhelmed by his metaphysical incertitude as well as by the storm; he is the precise representation of an individual and at the same time emblematic existence; he is the conscious, although not peaceful, symbol of the existential anguish of an epoch, a generation, a human situation.][15]

Like Zeno and Moscarda, Arsenio is shown to be a bourgeois character, who, however, does not seem to accept the bourgeois order—or at least to fit into it properly. He is on the elegant seashore of some Riviera resort, and it is fair to assume that he does not have serious financial preoccupations; he is alone, absorbed in his own thoughts, undecided, perplexed, seemingly incapable of action and awkward in his strolls through pebbles and seaweeds, precisely "Chaplinesque," like Zeno. Besides, perhaps like a character by Musil, he is shown to be very "atmospheric," if not "without qualities."

In narrative terms (as far as a "narrative" can be extracted from a poem), Arsenio's alienation is portrayed or conveyed through the following images: (1) the waiting for a "tempesta" ("storm"), for "un'altra orbita" ("another orbit"),[16] for something that will terminate his senseless wandering, something posited beyond his present condition of "ore / uguali, strette in trama" ("equal hours, tied in a weft") and of apathy and difficulty of living, symbolized by the "buio che precipita" ("impending darkness"); (2) the absence of the father: Arsenio is alone, "in faccia al mare" ("facing the sea")—the same Mediterranean Sea called "Padre" ("Father") in "Mediterraneo," the poem in *Ossi di seppia* where Montale describes himself directly, without an alter ego, as "uomo che tarda/all'atto" ("a man slow to act"), and where he also states: "E questa che in me cresce/è forse la rancura/che ogni figliuolo, mare, ha per il padre" ("This, which is growing within me/is perhaps the rancour/that each son, o sea, has for his father"); (3) the "delirio d'immobilità" ("delirium of immobility"), which expresses a dramatic dichotomy between life and the absolute, between Arsenio's thought and life; it can be compared with Zeno's time, described by Montale himself as "stagnante eppure continuamente in moto" ("stagnating, yet always moving"),[17] as well with Moscarda's present tense—a series of snapshots; this "delirium of immobility" is counterpointed by equivalent images throughout *Ossi di seppia*, notably in "In limine," "I limoni," and "Mediterraneo VII"—"Il tuo delirio sale agli astri ormai" ("Your delirium goes up to the stars by now"); (4) the final cosmic image, "la cenere degli astri" ("the ash of the stars"), which reflects both the inner conscience of Arsenio and the macrocosm, and thematically as well as structurally corresponds to Zeno's apocalypse and to Moscarda's annulment in nature.

Stylistically, Montale's literary strategy of the anti-hero, or of the poet who does not want to be "laureate," who prefers his own *diminutio anti-aulica*, is carried through the poetical devices which have become almost commonplace in contemporary poetry, according to the fundamental analysis of Hugo Friedrich:[18] (1) the use of the oxymoron (such as "immoto andare," "motionless going") as a sign of the contradictory nature, absurdity, and vanity of the whole reality; (2) the use of the insistent imperatives (with the related *tu* form), which mark the difficult relationship of the poetical character with the others and the world (the indicative, by contrast, would be the sign of his harmony with them and with it); (3) the choice of "objective correlatives" to indicate inner states of conscience, as well as to portray the fragmentation of external reality, its loss of unity and of meaning; (4) the use of a "broken" poetical language (negativity, dissonance), corresponding to the "break" in the society and the world today, and instituting the self-awareness of poetry as poetry, in sharp contrast with D'Annunzio's "poeticity."

Zeno, Moscarda, and Arsenio are three emblematic characters because they are anti-heroes envisaged by their respective authors not simply as "mirrors" of crisis (alienated "consciences"), but as "projects" of a different and better idea of man (conscious "alienations"). Through their structual affinities they carry a precise symbolic meaning, they are part of a literary and cognitive strategy common to Svevo, Pirandello, and Montale, as well as to the few true innovators of contemporary European literature.

It might be said that Zeno's apocalypse, Moscarda's pantheistic epiphany, and Arsenio's cosmic storm, are a sort of "dystopia" or anti-utopia, analogous to the political allegories of Zaymatin, Huxley, or Orwell, of which Caute wrote that they are "didactic because they are warnings as well as prophecies."[19] It seems important and significant that such a message should come through the strategies of individual figures like Zeno, Moscarda, and Arsenio: "Literature, as an act of *revolt*, is historically structured and attuned to represent the *individual* constituent in the parliament of the collective culture . . . . The last individualist is born not only out of the logic of liberalism, but out of the very womb of the novel"—and of poetry as well, for that matter. Both in the case of the novel and of poetry, in fact, "it is a question of a literary construction of dystopia recognizing and exploring by means of internal alienations its own nature as sign, symbol and book."[20]

Only at a superficial level do the strategies of the anti-hero lead to some sort of self-destruction; while conveying what Frank Kermode called "the sense of an ending,"[21] on the contrary, they bring about a renewed assertion of man, no longer with a capital *M*, no longer at the center of the universe, but still man, who carries with him one of his highest values—the written, victorious word.

NOTES

1. Victor Brombert, ed., *The Hero in Literature* (Greenwich, Conn.: Fawcett Premier, 1969), pp. 11–21 and passim. On the contrary, cf. Sergio Pacifici, "Italo Svevo's Antiheroes," *The Modern Italian Novel from Manzoni to Svevo* (Carbondale: Southern Illinois University Press, 1967), pp. 149 83.

2. David Caute, *The Illusion* (New York: Harper Colophon, 1971), p. 164.

3. Ibid., p. 102.

4. Renato Barilli, *La linea Svevo-Pirandello* (Milan: Mursia, 1972), pp. 13–14.

5. Renata Minerbi Treitel, "Zeno Cosini: The Meaning Behind the Name," *Italica* 8, no. 2 (Summer 1971): 234–45.

6. Italo Svevo, *La coscienza di Zeno*, in *Romanzi* (Milan: Dall'Oglio, 1969), and *Confessions of Zeno*, trans. Beryl De Zoete (New York: Vintage Books, n.d.). Subsequent references will be to these editions.

7. Jacques Derrida, "La pharmacie de Platon," *La dissémination* (Paris: Seuil, 1972), pp. 69–197.

8. Geno Pampaloni, "Italo Svevo," in Emilio Cecchi and Natalino Sapegno, eds., *Storia della letteratura italiana*, vol. 9, *Il Novecento* (Milan: Garzanti, 1969), pp. 493–532; on p. 523 he describes Zeno's "gratuitous act": "molto più complesso e direi moderno di quello di Gide" ("more complex and even modern than Gide's"), since it is "oggettiva condizione dell'uomo nell'irrealtà" ("the objective situation of man in unreality"): Zeno "*riceve* dalla vita risposte immotivate" ("*receives* unmotivated responses from life").

9. Barilli, *La linea Svevo-Pirandello*, p. 12.

10. Luigi Pirandello, *Uno, nessuno e centomila*, in *Tutti i romanzi* (Milan: Mondadori, 1959²), and *One, None and A Hundred-thousand*, trans. S. Putnam (New York: Dutton, 1933). Subsequent references will be to these editions.

11. Giovanni Macchia, "Luigi Pirandello," in *Storia della letteratura italiana*, 9: 439–92, on pp. 464–65; now in *La caduta della luna* (Milan: Mondadori, 1973), pp. 265–66.

12. Caute, *The Illusion* p. 182. But he also adds, on p. 211: "Far from proposing that all the world is a stage, dialectical theatre insists that a stage is a stage attempting to say something about the world while remaining conscious of its own nature as a stage. . . . In these respects Pirandello's work is somewhat foreign to dialectical theatre."

13. Cf. Marco Forti, *Le proposte della poesie e nuove proposte* (Milan: Mursia, 1971), p. 147, n. 16.

14. The similarity of the theme contemplation/action in Svevo and Montale is briefly analyzed by Ettore Bonora, *La poesia di Montale* (Turin: Tirrenia, 1965), 1: 59; Silvio Ramat, *Montale* (Florence: Vallecchi, 1965), pp. 67–68, likens Arsenio's "skepticism" to Zeno's. Cf. also Barilli, *La linea Svevo-Pirandello*, pp. 249–50: "I 'momenti eccezionali' pirandelliani sono perfettamente omologhi alle epifanie di Joyce, alla *madeleine* proustiana, ai 'talismani' di Montale" ("Pirandello's 'exceptional moments' are perfectly homologous with Joyce's epiphanies, Proust's *madeleine*, and Montale's 'talismans'"). In general terms, for Giacomo Debenedetti (*Il romanzo del Novecento* [Milan: Garzanti, 1971], p. 419), "se il personaggio 'uomo' del romanzo moderno è un estraneo, egli adombra anche il personaggio del poeta ermetico: ne raffigura l'atteggiamento, il comportamento" ("if the character 'man' of the modern novel is a stranger, he also foreshadows the character of the hermetic poet, representing his attitude and behavior").

15. Gianni Pozzi, *La poesia italiana del Novecento* (Turin: Einaudi, 1965), p. 167.

16. Eugenio Montale, *Ossi di seppia* (Milan: Mondadori, 1965), pp. 131–33. The (literal) translations are mine.

17. Eugenio Montale, "Italo Svevo nel centenario della nascita," in Eugenio

Montale-Italo Svevo, *Lettere, con gli scritti di Montale su Svevo* (Bari: De Donato, 1966), p. 169. Debenedetti (p. 541) speaks of Zeno's "insensato muoversi che non fa azione" ("senseless moving which does not make for action").

18. Hugo Friedrich, *La lirica moderna* (Milan: Garzanti, 1961).

19. Caute, *The Illusion*, p. 261.

20. Ibid., pp. 261–63.

21. Frank Kermode, *The Sense of an Ending* (New York: Oxford University Press, 1967), p. 98: "And of course we have it now, the sense of an ending. It has not diminished, and is as endemic to what we call modernism as apocalyptic utopianism is to political revolution."

15

Pavese's *Diario*: Why Suicide? Why Not?

Giose Rimanelli

Poetry is what drama is about. It is the hard core of the dramatic experience—everything else is peripheral documentary. As a young writer in Italy after the Second World War, I first knew Cesare Pavese as a novelist, a literary critic, a translator, and a publisher.[1] After his suicide in a hotel room in Turin in August 1950, I came across his first book of poetry, *Lavorare stanca* (*Work Is Wearying*), and only then realized that Pavese was a poet with a vocation for death and a feeling for life. In 1952, when the first edition of his diaries was published—with the significant title *Il mestiere di vivere* (*The Business of Living*)[2]—I found out about his odd love affair with death, and about his ability, in the words of A. Alvarez, to "transform disaster into art,"[3] much like the American poet Sylvia Plath, who committed suicide in London in 1963.

It was not until January 1974, however, while watching a dramatization of the works of Plath in Brooklyn, that it occurred to me that Pavese, like her, may have transformed art into disaster. For the words of both writers eat into the memory like shallow phrases, while their insights seem deep. Why should the following sentences taken from Pavese's *Mestiere*—so bland, so conventional—also seem so right?

Chi non ha avuto sempre una donna, non l'avrà mai. [MV 291]

[If a man has not always had a woman, he will never have one.]
[BB 286]

Finchè vorrai essere solo, ti verranno a cercare. Ma se allunghi la mano, non vorranno saperne. E così via. [MV 292]

383

[As long as you want to be alone, they come looking for you, but if you hold out your hand, they ignore it; that's how it goes.]
[BB 286]

Tu ricordi meglio le voci che non i visi delle persone. Perchè la voce ha qualcosa di tangenziale, di non raccolto. Dopo il viso non pensi alla voce. Data la voce—che non è niente—tendi a farne persona e cerchi un viso. [MV 292]

[You remember people's voices better than their faces. There is something indicative, spontaneous, about a voice. Given the face, you do not think of the voice; given the voice—by no means negligible—you try to envisage the person and look forward to seeing the face.] [BB 286]

Qualcosa finisce. Te ne accorgi dal fatto che, quando ti abbandoni o ti siedi a fumare, sei inquieto e ansioso. Temi cose della pratica? No. Temi il tuo vuoto. [MV 294]

[Something is coming to an end. When you relax and sit smoking, you find you are troubled and anxious. Are you afraid of the practical things in life? No. What you fear is the vacuum within you.]
[BB 288]

But Pavese died a suicide and, just as for Plath, death was a terrible game for him, and life an awful toil, a burden, a *mestiere* to learn and to endure. The *Diario* is important for the complete understanding of the man and the writer. But by itself it is still an "object" that sears. One feels almost a sense of self-righteousness when reading it, like watching another perform an obscene act. However, with the passing of the years, Pavese's presence has grown monolithic in our consciousness and, by rereading him, we have also learned how to respect him.

Pavese's diaries embrace an arc of fifteen years, the period of his artistic production and maturity. From 1935 to 1950 the thin red line runs from his political banishment to his literary success to his suicide. In the beginning it is possible that the *Diario* was born as a receptacle for notes on aesthetics, destined only for the author's eyes—as a guide to the development of his poetics. Then, little by little, the notes took on a more private tone and the writing of them became a trade, a job, a *mestiere*, an occupation, and also a refuge and a mirror for Pavese himself—"l'altro da sé," his other self to whom he could tell everything without lying.

The *Diario* begins with the sentence "Finito confino" ("Today my imprisonment ends," MV 30); and it closes:

> Basta un pò di coraggio.
> Più il dolore è determinato e preciso, più l'istinto
> della vita si dibatte, e cade l'idea del suicidio.
> Sembrava facile, a pensarci. Eppure donnette l'hanno
> fatto. Ci vuole umiltà, non orgoglio.
> Tutto questo fa schifo.
> Non parole. Un gesto. Non scriverò più.
>
> [MV 378]

> [All it takes is a little courage.
> The more the pain grows clear and definite, the more
> the instinct for life asserts itself and the thought of
> suicide recedes.
> It seemed easy when I thought of it. Weak women have
> done it. It takes humility, not pride.
> All this is sickening.
> Not words. An act. I won't write any more.]
>
> [BB 366]

Yet *Il mestiere di vivere* is not simply a journal. There are no references to the fashionable world or details to recount. Instead it is made up of a series of *pensées*, moments of an inner development which, upon being transferred to the page with immediacy, confirm that every word was in its time lived by the author and linked intimately to the unfolding of his life and of his literary work. Pavese was trying to justify himself vis-à-vis himself and others, "nella realtà quotidiana," in daily life.

A publisher's note in the first printing of the *Diario* states that the manuscript was found among Pavese's papers, complete with title and an analytic index: "1935–1950 / *il mestiere di vivere* / di Ce. Pavese." This suggests that Pavese himself had given some thought to its eventual publication, and that thereby his private confession might become a public one. His drama, therefore, while still so different from that of an André Gide or a Julian Green—remarkable *diaristi* of this century—

takes its place among the human-intellectual speculations of the latter, with the *Carnets* of Albert Camus, the *Diaries* and letters of Franz Kafka, and Sylvia Plath's autobiographical *The Bell Jar*. It is, in short, another testimony of the intellectual individual of our time seared by the irreconcilable conflict between feeling and reason, the conscious and the unconscious, life as action and life as stillness, destiny. In an entry of the *Diario* dated 14 July 1950, he writes frantically:

> Lo stoicismo è il suicidio. Del resto sui fronti la gente ha ricominci-ato a morire. Se mai ci sarà un mondo pacifico, felice, che cosa penserà di queste cose? Forse quello che noi pensiamo di can-nibali, dei sacrifici aztechi, dei processi delle streghe. [MV 376]

> [Stoicism is suicide. People are dying in battle again. If ever there is a peaceful, happy world, what will it think of these things? Perhaps what we think about cannibals, Aztec sacrifices, witch-craft.] [BB 364]

The first pages of the *Diario* are notes on the creative process. Pavese, not at all sure of what he wrote about his poetry in 1934, and later published as an appendix to the "Solaria" edition of his book of poems, *Lavorare stanca*, wanted to clarify and deepen his poetics. He wrote this part during the months of his political banishment to Brancaleone Calabro. However, his return to Turin effected the turn of the screw, the change. Here he learned that a former girl friend of his university days, to whom he was emotionally attached, had been married only a day before his arrival. He was devastated by moral and spiritual feelings of futility and failure—the more so because

> con tutta la debolezza ch'era in me, quella persona mi sapeva legare a una disciplina, a un sacrificio, col semplice dono di sé. E non credo che questa fosse la virtù di Pierino, perchè il dono di lei mi alzava all' intuizione di nuovi doveri, me li rendeva *corpo* dinanzi. Perchè abbandonato a me, ne ho fatta l'esperienza, sono *certo* di non riuscirci. Fatto una carne e un destino con lei, ci sarei riuscito, ne sono altrettanto certo. Anche per la mia stessa viltà: sarebbe stato un imperativo al mo fianco.
>
> Invece, che cosa ha fatto! Forse lei non lo sa, o se lo sa non gliene importa. Ed è giusto perchè lei è lei ed ha il suo passato che le traccia l'avvenire. [MV 34]

[In spite of all my weaknesses, that lady managed to make me conform to discipline, to self-sacrifice, by her simple gift of herself to me. By so doing she raised me to an intuition of new tasks, made them take shape before my eyes. Because, left to myself as I know from experience, I am *convinced* I shall not succeed. Made one flesh and one destiny with her, I should have succeeded. Of that I am equally certain. Even because of my cowardice, she would have become a spur in my flank.

Instead, what has she done! Perhaps she does not know, or, if she does, it means nothing to her. And that is fair enough, for she is herself, with her own past that marks out her future.] [BB 48]

This relationship, however, is to be understood as an attempt on Pavese's part to plant himself in society, to normalize his existence, which already for some time had been tormented with complexes of timidity, hedonism, solitude, and ideas of suicide.

A. Alvarez swiftly declares that Pavese's suicide was born, not made. In fact, as with Sylvia Plath, birth seems to hold the secret.[4] From some of Pavese's early poetry, or poetic undertaking, we see that even during his pre-university years he was tormented and tempted by the idea of suicide. Davide Lajolo, Pavese's biographer, indicates the following as strictly autobiographical:

> Sono andato una sera di dicembre
> per una stradicciuola di campagna
> tutta deserta, col tumulto in cuore.
> Avevo dietro me una rivoltella.
> Quando fui certo d'essere ben lontano
> d'ogni abitato, l'ho rivolta a terra
> ed ho premuto. Ha sussultato al rombo,
> d'un rapido sussulto che mi è parso
> scuoterla come viva in quel silenzio.
> Davvero mi ha tremato tra le dita
> alla luce improvvisa ch'è sprizzata
> fuor della canna. Fu come lo spasimo,
> l'ultimo strappo atroce di chi muore
> di una morte violenta. L'ho riposta
> allora, ancora calda, entro la tasca
> e ho ripreso la via. Così, andando,

tra gli alberi spogliati, immaginavo
il sussulto tremendo che darà
nella notte che l'ultima illusione
e i timori mi avranno abbandonato
e me l'appoggerò contro una tempia
per spaccarmi il cervello.[5]

[One December evening I walked along a deserted country path, my heart in tumult. I carried with me a revolver. When I was sure I was far away from any inhabited place, I pointed it at the ground and pressed the trigger. It leaped at the roar, a sudden leap that seemed to me to shake it as though alive in that silence. It truly trembled between my fingers at the sudden light which shot from its barrel. It was like the spasm, the last atrocious shudder, of one who dies a violent death. Then, I returned it, still hot, to my pocket, and I resumed the path. Thus, moving between the naked trees, I imagined the tremendous leap it will make in the night when the last illusion and fears will have abandoned me, and I'll place it against a temple to shatter my brain.]

Now, no matter how much this poem reveals a romantic attitude, it is more than a romantic poem or an act of bravado. Words like *tumulto* in the heart, *spasimo, strappo atroce, sussulto tremendo, ultima illusione*, etc., express a felt state of mind—a struggle " of all the days, of all the hours against inertia, dejection, fear."[6] The failure of his love relationship, which struck him as an enormous joke, induced Pavese to re-evaluate all his actions, past and present. The introspections to which he fell victim now began to assume an existential character. And since any misfortune "is either due to error, not bad luck, or it arises out of our own culpable inadequacy" (BB 64), he tried to define himself and to discover within himself the cause of his problems.

In practice, these are examinations of conscience that will be repeated in the entire *Diario*, and with greater frequency in the years from 1936 to 1940—years in which Pavese sought the exact standards by which to measure himself: "The lesson is this: to build in art, or build in life, banish sensuousness from art, as from life; exist tragically" (BB 50). Pavese finds himself in an important phase of his life, in that key point at which life is woven into art and the two spheres will never again be separated. Why banish *il voluttuoso* ("sensuousness"), and why exist *tragicamente* ("tragically")? These are not simple propositions. One becomes aware of the fact that, for Pavese, to live sensuously means to live instinctually, to abandon oneself to events and to passions without posing questions to oneself. It means not to be really conscious.

Hedonists, in fact, approach life without reservations, totally exposed; they try to dissipate themselves in the pursuit of sensation or some absolute principle. It is for this very reason, perhaps, that they end up finding themselves always, or almost always, in a disarmed state in comparison to others: those who act according to a scheme, a moral code. The latter, not accepting the "act," or the "moment" as an end in itself, have the capacity to transform experience into consciousness. Placed before a hierarchy of values, in the end they choose among these values and construct their own lives on the basis of this choice. On the other hand, the man who lives sensuously or unconsciously is nothing but a boy who is not master of himself. Pavese considers himself an adolescent. Thus he writes: "so far in life my tendency has been to advocate enjoying things as they are, rather than to agitate to reform" (BB 30). But he who enjoys does not possess. And although childhood and adolescence are spontaneous experiences and authentic living, they remain the age of impotence because they are not translated into fullness.

Pitiless self-analysis, that constant self-auscultation, are phases of a process of spiritual maturation during which the passive "I" that gives, arrives at the point of transforming itself into an active "I" that selects and receives. For the moment Pavese rejects suicide because "non è più un agire, è un patire" ("it is no longer an action, only a submission," MV 37). To face problems, to live with them, or to try to resolve them— this is the challenge of the virile man.

On the other hand, however, if becoming adult means to immerse oneself in history—that is to say, to accept the problems and values of a whole society and make a self-adjustment—then Pavese becomes aware that he must struggle against an insurmountable obstacle. His struggle was waged between thought and feeling, reason and emotion, between the rational and the irrational. In other words, maturity coincides with the discovery of the "I," when man becomes conscious of himself. But if this knowledge comes "per identificazione amorosa" ("through a loving recognition," MV 142), which is still equivalent to a state of inferiority, no real contact with others has been established. We become aware of the fact that maturity—that is to say, the mastery of our own feelings—is essentially separation, "l'isolamento che basta a se stesso" ("isolation that is sufficient unto itself," MV 136).

In childhood, rather, in the intoxication of youth, "si prova il brivido della conoscenza universale" ("one feels the never-ending thrill of universal knowledge," MV 142), for the very reason that we believe in others and establish friendship and love in the most absolute sense. It follows that if every person represents a monad, human brotherhood is a form of communion. In other words, the adult desires to remain conscious, and the other person can be approached only if a kind of common agreement takes place between the two. The reason for this is that the morality imposed by society does not correspond to the reality of facts. It does not facilitate union: all that remains is a path in between, leading to communication. Society, finally, falsifies and impoverishes the feelings by justifying a kind of behavior that is then translated into indifference. Hence, for Pavese, day-to-day practical life reveals itself to be only an accumulation of interests that favor the shrewd.

In this practical life (at least on the basis of some caustic observations), women would be the greatest practitioners of shrewdness:

> Se una donna non tradisce, è perchè non le conviene. [MV 116] [If a woman does not betray you, it is because it does not suit her convenience.] [BB 121]

> L'unico modo per conservarti una donna—se ci tieni—è metterla in una situazione tale che il mondo, il rispetto umano, l'interesse, ecc. le impediscono di andarsene. Chi cerca di conservarsela per pura forza di dedicazione e di sincerità è un ingenuo. Avere la legittimità dalla propria: è il modo con cui si stabilizzano le rivoluzioni e si tengono le donne. Liberarsi da ogni nobile gusto, e accettare di essere *a righteous citizen*, un grasso borghese. Guarda come si sono messi a posto principalmente le tue conoscenze. Chiavar bene e mangiare meglio; piace a tutti.

> Ed è gente che si stupirebbe moltissimo se tu mettessi in dubbio che si sacrifica per gli ideali. La vita pratica è astuzia, nient'altro. Tutto si riduce alla sacramentale astuzia della fidanzata che non deve *dargliela* al moroso, altrimenti lui la pianta. [MV 97]

[The only way to make a woman stay with you—if that is what you want—is to place her in such a position that public opinion, the respect of her own circle, and her self-interest, all prevent her from going away. A man who thinks he can bind her to him merely by his devotion and sincerity is a fool. Make sure accepted customs are on your side: that's the way to settle revolutions or keep women. Cast aside every noble impulse and settle down as a righteous citizen, a fat bourgeois. Look how all your acquaintances have found themselves good positions, enjoying their screwing, and their meals even more. That pleases everybody.

And such people would be extremely surprised if you were to cast any doubt on their willingness to sacrifice themselves for their ideals. The practical way of life is a matter of shrewdness, nothing else. Like the high-minded shrewdness of the engaged girl who feels she ought not to give herself to her lover, lest he should jilt her.] [BB 105]

Obviously Pavese was still resentful of his unfortunate amorous experiences with women when he wrote this. But it is not exactly a vendetta against the female sex; rather, it is a documentation of the failure of his dialogue with life. His search, which should have culminated in the awareness of the duties he assumed, and which should have persuaded Pavese to participate in society, actually drove him still further away from both prospects. No longer accepting the common morality, which had revealed itself to be an amalgam of shrewdness and hypocrisy, he built for himself a system based on the Christian principle of charity:

> Idiota e lurido Kant—se dio non c'è tutto è permesso. Basta con la morale. Solo la carità è rispettabile. Cristo e Dostojevskij, tutto il resto sono balle.   [MV 84]

> [Foolish and dirty Kant: if God does not exist, everything is permissible. Enough of morality; only compassion [charity] is a creed worthy of respect. Christ and Dostoievsky. All the rest is nonsense.] [BB 94][7]

Pavese descended even more deeply into his subconscious, making a god of it, like Boehme and Jung. In other words, Pavese, in rejecting a philosophy that denied the existence of God, rejected it above all because it denied an absolute value to every ethic—thus precluding every form of community from man and, consequently, of charity. Charity, Pavese discovers, reflects the tendency toward order and cosmology. Soon, however, he had to realize his mistake on this point too. Charity requires a conscious annihilation of the personality, and for him this was too high a price to pay. He ran the risk of falling once more into that childish ingenuousness which he had sought so desperately to overcome. On the other hand, the price he paid for remaining in his solitude was exceedingly high: "Passavo la sera seduto davanti allo specchio per tenermi compagnia" (MV 127) ("I spent the whole evening sitting before a mirror to keep myself company," BB 132).

With the passing of time, Pavese succeeded in forgetting himself and assuaging the pain of memories, at least to the extent that time allowed him to achieve a certain calm and a certain orientation in his studies. He wrote his first stories and seriously interested himself once more in ethnology. But perhaps work was only a pretext, a palliative. In 1940 he got himself involved in another love affair. Now he was better prepared and approached the obstacle with caution. This time the girl was Fernanda Pivano, a former student of his during the time of his temporary teaching post at the Liceo Massimo d'Azeglio of Turin. Lajolo describes her as "a young lady now fully developed, beautiful, much courted, loquacious, elegant, and happy."[8] Indeed, indeed. I met Signora Pivano in 1954 and I remember her as an elegant woman, intelligent, and of slightly faded beauty. For this reason, perhaps, she was more intense, but I would not be able to say how happy she was. She inquired about my American background and my grandfather, a dixieland jazzman who is described on the jacket cover of my first novel, and I couldn't help remembering Pavese, who courted her without saying anything to her, who tried to win her intellectually, and who unexpectedly twice asked her to marry him, only to be refused on both occasions.

But this time it was not the woman's fault. Perhaps it had not been the woman's fault the first time either. Nor, perhaps, was it the fault of the American actress, Constance Dowling, the last time. I remember the third time I saw Pavese in Rome in 1950, at the Caffè Greco, on elegant Via dei Condotti. Constance was with him. I had met her at a party about a month before at the home of an American actress, because at that time I was frequenting motion-picture people. With me was the poet Rocco Scotellaro, who knew Pavese better than I did through the friendship of the writer-painter Carlo Levi. But that encounter turned out to be an embarrasing occasion for all concerned. The custom at the Caffè Greco, known all too well to its clientele, is that upon entering one goes to sit at a table occupied by "una faccia familiare," a person one knows. Miss Dowling invited us to sit at their table, but Pavese remained silent, visibly annoyed.

We left quickly and lost our way while strolling through those tangled little streets between Piazza di Spagna and Via del Corso. In the neighborhood of the Hotel d'Inghilterra, on Via del Leoncino, we again ran into Pavese and Miss Dowling, who were trying to make their way to the Corso. The woman greeted us with a surprised, yet cordial "Ciao" while Pavese darted a helpless glance at us. I blushed. I felt miserable. I thought that my chances of being published by Einaudi, then run by Pavese, were ruined because of that stupid incident, and Scotellaro felt the same: he, too, had a book in Turin, at the mercy of Pavese's acceptance or rejection.[9] "He must think we're spying on him," said Scotellaro. "He's in Rome incognito, and he doesn't like Rome, nor gossips." I replied: "If that's the case, the hell with him. Why does he show up at the Greco?" But evidently she had dragged him there.

At any rate, Pavese knew that the deficiency in communication was his failing, not the other's. The wound was reopened, but he had expected it. Now his suffering derived not so much from the failure in himself as from the fact that it once more revealed his weakness:

> La lezione più atroce di quest'altro calcio è che non eri per nulla cambiato, per nulla *corretto*, dai due anni di meditazione. Ciò per toglierti anche il conforto che tu possa ancora uscire da questo pozzo con la meditazione. [MV 195]

> [The bitterest lesson of this new kick fate has given you is that you have not changed at all or *corrected* anything by your two years of meditation. You have even lost the consolation of thinking that you might still be able to get out of this slough through meditation.] [BB 196]

In short, Pavese had tried to remain always fully aware of himself, to take the initiative, to be superior; but he had not succeeded and had fallen once more into the usual error. The problem of the preceding years still remained with him: how to approach others. Further, the alternatives, the possible solutions, were still the same: stoic isolation or Christian annihilation. These failures with women have considerable importance in themselves because they support the need for self-knowledge. To understand the reason for a sorrow is tantamount to fleeing from despair.

The years from 1940 to 1945 were decisive for Pavese the man and the writer. He moved to Rome in order to open a branch of the Einaudi publishing house there. He wrote his first long stories in Rome. He was drafted into the army but discharged because he suffered from asthma. After the armistice of September 8, 1943, Pavese took refuge in Serralunga di Crea, a small town in the Monferrato, instead of joining his Communist friends in the underground and taking part in the partisan struggle. He spent his time reading and meditating, and discovered his "method" in the vocation of the myth. He wrestled with himself between mysticism and ethnology, two things that revealed themselves to him as being incompatible. Up to then the ethical imperative of love had acted in Pavese as communion with the other. But in Serralunga love became an undoing of the personality which, after the act of mortification, becomes a regenerative force. These are the phases that lead to ecstasy:

> Lo sgorgo di divinità lo si sente quando il dolore ci ha fatto inginocchiare. Al punto che la prima avvisaglia del dolore ci dà un moto di gioia, di gratitudine, di aspettazione . . . Si arriva ad augurarsi il dolore. [MV 257–58]

> [We feel this same glow of divinity when suffering has brought us to our knees, so much so that the first pang can give us a sense of joy, gratitude, anticipation. . . . We reach the point of wanting pain.] [BB 255]

The configuration of the myth made steady progress. For the mentality of primitive man, the gesture has the value of a rite; and as a symbolical expression it therefore presupposes another reality. For the ascetic possessed by God, his vision—his world of essences, his life as a series of encounters that are repeated continually in the same way—is at times exhausting because it involves an extremely emotional participation. Revelation occurs by way of the senses. The mystic humbles himself; in short, he annihilates himself in the single desire to become one with the Absolute. It is the transport of St. Teresa of Avila, entirely permeated with a sexual imagery.

But Pavese believes that "qualunque sofferenza che non sia insieme conoscenza è inutile" ("any suffering that does not also teach you something is futile," MV 139). The myth, in point of fact, is a manifestation of the irrational, the unconscious. It is an involuntary, childish manifestation that Pavese interprets by using Freud: the unconscious is the same as impotence. But if the fundamental encounter, which through repetition is transformed into myth, occurs during childhood—if the life of the adult remains pre-fixed in time—man is deprived of free will. Myth having become consciousness, discloses fate. In a very important page of the *Diario*, Pavese wrote:

> Da bambino s'impara a conoscere il mondo non—come parrebbe —con immediato e originario contatto alle cose, ma attraverso i segni delle cose: parole, vignette, racconti. Se si risale un qualunque momento di commozione estatica davanti a qualcosa del mondo, si trova che ci commuoviamo perchè ci siamo già commossi; e ci siamo commossi, perchè un giorno qualcosa ci apparve trasfigurato, *staccato* dal resto, per una parola, una favola, una fantasia che vi si riferiva. [MV 230]

> [As a child one learns to know the world not—as it would seem— by immediate initial contact with things, but through signs of things: words, pictures, stories. If anything in the world inspires a moment of ecstatic emotion, we find that we are moved because, on some day or other, it seemed to us transfigured, detached from everything else, by a word, a fable, a fancy that we connect with it.] [BB 229]

For clarity's sake one might say that man, as it were, makes himself happen (unconsciously) and then rediscovers himself by way of analysis. The myth is a tribal archetype and at the same time an objectification of feelings. Hence it functions as a contact, as a form of communion between the "I" and the collectivity. The chief difference between myth and mysticism is that mystical experience is not translated into knowledge. God is unknowable, and at any rate He represents an extrahuman dimension. No religion would manage to survive without the presupposition of faith. Pavese's thought is an assertion of faith in the real. He is a noncontemplative mystic who perceives the spiritual only through experience. It is from this experience that the revelation—myth —is born from which he derives the ethic of fate. Thus, he made the following entry in the *Diario*:

> Il semplice sospetto che il subcosciente sia Dio—che Dio viva e parli nel nostro subcosciente ti ha esaltato. [MV 279]

> [The very suggestion that the subconscious may be God, that God lives and speaks in our subconscious mind, has exalted you.] [BB 276]

At the end of the war Pavese joined the Italian Communist Party. But his attitude remained ambiguous: after trying to assimilate religion and communism into his thinking, he was forced to reject them. God— if He exists—is too distant from us. And communism is history, it situates the Absolute in hope, in generations of struggles and sacrifices. On the other hand, Pavese does not know what to do with a reality that does not have a radical link with his essence, his subconscious, etc.

Pavese achieved the status of a writer of the first rank in Italian literature following the publication of *Il compagno* (*The Comrade*) and *La casa in collina* (*The House on the Hill*). And all people turned to him, all needed him. At that time I wrote him a letter (1948), requesting permission to use—if nobody else was using it—a typewriter belonging to the Einaudi offices in Rome in order to type a copy of one of my early novels. (Although he had returned to Turin, Pavese was still officially responsible for the branch in Rome.) He replied promptly that he had no objection to my using a typewriter, but that the decision would have to be made by the new director of the branch, the critic Carlo Muscetta.

For those who knew him, and for those who did not know him, Pavese was already a kind of myth. But he was increasingly more alone: "Ti fai casa di un ufficio, di un cine, di due mascelle serrate" ("For you, home means the office, the cinema, and your own clenched jaws," MV 294). It was in this state of mind that he met the American actress with whom he lived his last adventure. He wrote to Lajolo that "an unexpected lark from America" had arrived for him. And he added:

"But she will soon go away, I feel it, I will hear her wings flap, without even having the strength to make an attempt, to utter a shout to call her back."[10]

One day in 1952 I was a guest at the house of Maria Livia Serini, on Via dei Quattro Venti, in Rome—the Turinese girl to whom Pavese was linked by a bond of affectionate friendship, and to whom, for about two years, he dictated a couple of his novels. It was a happy gathering, there had been much drinking, and now the group of friends was preparing to wind up the festivities at a restaurant in the Trastevere quarter. While the others were listening to records, I took *Dialoghi con Leucò* (*Dialogues with Leucò*) down from the shelves and read Pavese's dedication to Maria Livia. At first she said nothing, but then the expression on her face changed and she exclaimed: "Take the book with you, take all the Pavese you find here. But please don't talk about him. It makes me mad and sad." From that day on our friendship was somewhat solidified in the remembrance of Pavese. We always talked about him, he was never so alive. Yet at the end of every discussion she gave utterance to the question that still tormented her: "Why did he do it?" And I: "Well, why suicide? Why not?"

Pavese did not kill himself over any woman. Perhaps he conceived of suicide as the ultimate expression of his very being, a gesture for which his life was but a preparation. "If I commit suicide, it will not be to destroy myself but to put myself back together again," once wrote Antonin Artaud.[11] And it is also not enough to assert that the central problem of Pavese's life was an impossible maturity, or the lack of a bond with the *other*, the world of causes and effects.[12] It is clear on the other hand, that Pavese interpreted life and reality dualistically. And an attentive reading of the *Diario* confirms that he considered his task to be the clarification and possibly the reconciliation of the two extremes: sensuousness and existing tragically, extroversion and introversion.

For Pavese, knowing was a form of arriving at the secret of knowledge. In order to reveal himself to himself, in a first phase he tried to objectify himself. For example: "Se potessimo trattare con *noi stessi* come trattiamo con *gli altri*," ("If only we could *treat ourselves* as we treat *other men*," MV 121); "L'arte di sostituire noi a ciascuno, e sapere quindi che ciascuno s'interessa soltanto di sé" ("The act of putting ourselves in another man's place and so learning that each is concerned only with himself,"MV 115), etc. But all this becomes still more evident if the myth is interpreted as a means and not an end. Once having unmasked his myths, and consequently reduced them to fate, Pavese transformed himself into a character. In fact, his tendency to use the second person to address himself, the third person to talk about himself to others, and finally his interest in dreams, were all symptoms of a split personality. They concealed his need to *see himself* act. There was a cognitive process even in this seeing himself act. Only when fate emerges from it does freedom vanish.

What is fate? It represents the objectivization of an entire life, and therefore of the present. Pavese observed that fate is not things that happen according to a scheme. Rather, each of us, if he has the strength, interprets the things that have occurred, arranging them according to a meaning. For Pavese, each life is a closed world.[13] This is because each person creates his own fate, which will be discovered in maturity. The mind (in childhood) decides the facts that will come into being, whereas man is free of every determinism. Nevertheless, the man who has reduced the myths into consciousness is fatally separated from himself and from his world. In practice, objectivization leads to alienation. "Sono triste, inutile, come un dio" ("I am sad, useless, like a god," MV 326). Hence Pavese's need for contact, which in the years of maturity became an utter fixation. But the conjunction, the communion, never occurred:

> Tu sei solo, e lo sai. Tu sei nato per vivere sotto le ali di un altro, sorretto e giustificato da un altro, che sia però tanto gentile da lasciarti fare il matto e illudere di bastare da solo a rifare il mondo. Non trovi mai nessuno che duri tanto; di qui, il tuo soffrire i distacchi—non per tenerezza. Di qui, il tuo rancore per chi se n'è andato; di qui la tua facilità a trovarti un nuovo patrono—non per cordialità. Sei una donna, e come donna sei caparbio. Ma non basti da solo, e lo sai. [MV 314]

> [You are alone, and you know it. You were born to live under the wings of someone who would sustain and justify you, someone kind enough to let you play the fool and imagine yourself capable of remaking the world singlehanded. You never found anyone who could endure so much; hence your suffering when friends depart, not because of any tenderness for them; hence your resentment toward the one who has gone; hence your facility for finding

a new ally—not out of cordiality. You are a woman, and like a
woman you are obstinate. But alone you are not enough, and
you know it.] [BB 305–06]

The arrival of Constance Dowling was another illusion, and Pavese
knew it. But he gave himself up to it. This blonde woman, refined,
precarious, vivacious, and distant (there are so many like her in the
United States, a cross between mother-father figure, hard work and
fatalism), for him symbolized the past, his childhood, his dreams of an
America learned through literature, and so on. But by transforming
woman into myth, which means letting-go, a status of inferiority (i.e.,
impotence), he ended up by possessing nothing. And when he was in
possession—that is to say, when woman is not myth—he felt himself
absent, detached. Pavese, in short, would have liked to possess himself
and the woman at the same time; but he was too overcome by himself.
His conquest, his maturity in the end constituted defeat.

The poems after *Lavorare stanca* are connected with the *Diario*, and
they are all dated, with the exception of one—*La casa*—which still
suggests the old style. These poems, therefore, are first of all to be
interpreted in relation to that spiritual development which had been
assuming specific contours in Pavese during the war years. But they are
also important from a technical point of view. They represent a renewal
of rhythms in comparison with those of 1934. Now the poet no longer
invents characters, he no longer narrates but expresses only his emotion. If in *Lavorare stanca* he presents the exterior life of the character
and his relation to the landscape, thus falling into naturalistic description, with the poems of 1945 and 1950 he gave up description, the images became epithets, attributes that transfigured the woman-goddess
into a cosmic symbol.

> Sei la vita e la morte.   You are life and death.
> Sei venuta di marzo   You came in March
> sulla terra nuda—   on the naked earth—
> il tuo brivido dura.[14]   your shudder endures.

Instead of the epic-narrative, here we have lyrical poetry. Necessarily,
the rhythm is different. It is no longer slow and calm, but impatient,
dry, hammering. Words assume an importance they did not have in
Lavorare stanca. They contain a violent emotional charge even without

being onomatopoeic. They are metaphorical, mythic, hallucinatory words that have the same power of ineluctability and of hieratic evocation that we find, for example, in litanies or prayers. The poet's experience is in the present, but he literally creates the woman while seeking her name.

A group of poems written in 1945 opens with the following lines:

Terra rossa terra nera,	Red land black land,
tu vieni dal mare,	you come from the sea,
dal verde riarso,	from the parched green,
dove sono parole	where are ancient words
antiche e fatica sanguigna	and blood-red toil
e gerani tra i sassi—	and geraniums among stones—

Here the recurrent images constitute a leitmotif even if a story is not being unfolded, and we glimpse a certain but almost imperceptible structure in them. Pavese, however, defines woman from the time of the very first poems. The designation "tu vieni dal mare" ("you come from the sea") immediately discloses the mythic level. It is Aphrodite who is being defined. She is continually being associated with earth, the countryside, the process of nature which renews itself cyclically but remains the same in repetition. Woman is immobilized. She becomes an archetype

di stagioni e di sogni	of seasons and crushed dreams
che alla luna si scopre	which on the moonlight reveals
antichissimo, come	as very old, like
le mani di tua madre,	the hands of your mother,
la conca del braciere.	the pot of the brazier.

She is something that no one has ever possessed, who is self-sufficient, who has no need of others. But at the same time, for the "I" she is something more, an intimate myth, his entire childhood:

Sei la cantina chiusa,	You are the closed cellar,
dal battuto di terra,	hardened by the earth,
dov'è entrato una volta	where the barefoot child
ch'era scalzo il bambino	entered one day
e ci ripensa sempre.	and thinks of it always.

But the woman is dark, like the cellar—and impenetrable, inscrutable.

As long as they are lovers they will always be enemies, because one will try to possess the other. The complete union will be effected only in death, when they are beyond human individuality.

Two poems from the collection of *La terra e la morte* (*Earth and Death*) probably do not belong to this group, or at least not to that theme of sentimental adventure. They are "Tu non sai le colline" ("You don't know the hills") and "E allora noi vili" ("And so we cowards"). In the first poem the "I" defines his hills; in the second, perhaps, the war, a collective experience. They are autobiographical poems, written in Rome from October 27 to December 3, 1945. Pavese was under the influence of another infatuation, the third in his life. All three were important. On November 27 he wrote in his *Diario*:

> E' venuto la terza volta, quel giorno. E' l'alba, un'alba di nebbia diffusa, viola fresco. Il Tevere ha lo stesso colore. Malinconia non greve, pronta a sfumare sotto il sole. Case e alberi, tutto dorme.
>
> Ho visto l'alba, non è molto, dalle sue finestre della parete accanto. Era la nebbia, era il palazzo, era la vita, era il calore umano.
>
> Dorme Astarte-Afrodite-Mèlita. Si sveglierà scontrosa. Per la terza volta è venuto il mio giorno. Il dolore più atroce è sapere che il dolore passerà. Adesso è facile umiliarmi. E poi? [MV 287]

> [It came to you for the third time, that day. It is dawn, a dawn of scattered cloud, pale mauve. The Tiber has the same color. Sadness, but not overbearingly so, ready to be cheered by the sun. Houses and trees, everything's sleeping. I watched the dawn a while ago, from her side windows. There was haze, stillness, and a human warmth. Astarte-Aphrodite-Mèlita is still sleeping. She will wake in a bad mood. For the third time, my day has come. The keenest pang of my grief is to know that grief will pass. Now it is easy to feel humiliated. What next?] [BB 282–83]

The woman sleeps at dawn because "per te l'alba è silenzio"[15] ("for you the dawn is silence"), while the poet has spent a sleepless night. The thought is clear: the woman who is sleeping is self-sufficient; she is free. There is no one yet who tames her by possessing her, nor is she interested in possession. For Pavese this constitutes a new failure. But he tried to console himself with the reflection:

Com'è grande il pensiero che veramente *nulla a noi è dovuto.*

Qualcuno ci ha mai promesso qualcosa? E allora perchè attendiamo? [MV 287]

[What a great thought it is that truly *nothing is owed to us*. Has anyone ever promised us anything? Then why should we expect anything?] [BB 283]

The other group of poems, *Verrà la morte e avrà i tuoi occhi* (*Death will come and he will have your eyes*) in a certain sense repeats Pavese's experience of 1945. They are sustained by the same meter, and images and words are used there as in the first poems. They are a reflection of the mythic return. This time, too, Aphrodite has "come from the sea." And Pavese, on March 9, 1950, noted: "Battito, tremore, infinito sospirare. Possibile alla mia età?" (MV 370) ("My heart throbs; I tremble, I cannot stop sighing. Is it possible at my age?" [BB 359]).

The difference is that this time the woman is "vita e morte" ("life and death"). The encounter that occurred in March coincided with germination, and had the meaning of a rebirth. For Pavese it was an awakening, a hope with a question mark: "Eppure ho un senso di fiducia, di (incredibile) tranquilla speranza" ("Yet I feel confident and [incredibly] serenely hopeful," MV 370). He knows that it will not last, but he snatches at every mad idea that it might. Meanwhile the poems are suffused with a tender light, and this atmosphere surrounds the woman who has become spring, who transforms night into morning, who is "acqua chiara" ("clear water"), "dolce frutto" ("sweet fruit"), "anemone o nube" ("anemone or cloud"). But at the same time she is "radice feroce" ("a fierce root"): "Il tuo passo leggero / ha riaperto il dolore" ("Your light step has reopened the pain"). Communion is impossible.

Pavese's suicide is usually interpreted as a symbolical gesture in terms of these poems. It does not seem to me, however, that this idea of sacrifice, the consummation of a rite of union with the woman-goddess-mother, is valid. The thought of suicide accompanied Pavese from the time he was eighteen. Lajolo writes:

At eighteen he had already written (in a letter to a friend): *Pavese è morto*, Pavese is dead. And if shortly afterwards he declared that he must return to the struggle, it was only to dedicate the rest of his life to poetry. His struggle, he explained, consisted solely in per-

severing in order to reach the heights of "la solitudine dei geni,"
"the solitude of geniuses." The "blows and the kicks" ("i pugni ed
i calci") were not an excuse for resignation; and for this reason in
the final poetry, anticipated in the pre-university poetry, death
returns as the protagonist, that same death before which he will
immolate himself, evoking it once more in the final, most desolate
lines:

> Verrà la morte e avrà i tuoi occhi
> questa morte che ci accompagna
> dal mattino alla sera, insonne,
> sorda, come un vecchio rimorso
> o un vizio assurdo.

> [Death will come and he will have your eyes—
> that death that is with us
> from morning to night, sleepless,
> deaf, like an old remorse
> or an absurd vice.]

It is the same "vizio assurdo" ("absurd vice"), Lajolo concludes, that
tortured Pavese in these early days and crept into his blood like a
disease. It was his syphilis—as he wrote—a kind of suicide fever which,
barely expulsed, quickly returned, incurable.[16]

We may add that, obviously, Pavese had managed to overcome his
many crises because, in point of fact, he had succeeded in transforming
the woman into a "means" of a cognitive process. This process came to
an end in 1950. In order to go forward Pavese would have had to deny
himself—that is to say, to accept the emptiness of a demythified life. It
was this that he was afraid of. Clearly he knew that the fate that hovered
about him was sterility. Therefore suicide came to represent a choice—
why suicide? why not? It was the only way to escape fate. And it also
represented a gesture of deep, infinite resignation.

NOTES

1. I was introduced to Pavese one evening in March 1950, at the Roman branch of
the Einaudi Publishing House, then in Via Uffici del Vicario. He was standing alone

in the middle of a large room, a slim, tall man wearing thick eye-glasses and an off-white trench-coat. He was reading a newspaper that he was holding close to his eyes, almost covering his face and head. I said "hello" and he just smiled. Half an hour later I met him again at the Giolitti Bar, downstairs; he was still alone and I said "hello" again. He offered to pay for my espresso and asked where I was living. I talked of a manuscript of mine, the novel *Tiro al piccione* (translated into English by Ben Johnson, Jr. with the title *The Day of the Lion* [New York: Random House, 1954]), and he asked me to send it to him in Turin. I did, through Carlo Muscetta, then head of the Roman branch of Einaudi.

In May, Muscetta received Pavese's opinion about the book, now published in Pavese's *Lettere 1924–1950*, ed. Lorenzo Mondo with the collaboration of Davide Lajolo and Italo Calvino (Turin: Einaudi, 1966), 2: 521. Pavese's political position at that time, both in terms of judging my book and in assessing his own awareness in the writing of the novel *La casa in collina* (*The House on the Hill*), which was sharply criticized by many Communist friends, has been accurately analyzed by Gian-Paolo Biasin in *The Smile of the Gods*, a thematic study of Cesare Pavese's works (Ithaca, N. Y.: Cornell University Press, 1968), pp. 163–88, and p. 307 n. I corrected the Einaudi galley proofs of *Tiro al piccione* in January 1951, but the book was never released. A year later I took it to Elio Vittorini in Milan, who had already read it at Pavese's request, and liked it. He suggested that I go to see Remo Cantoni at Mondadori, and give his name as a reference. The book was published by Mondadori in March 1953.

2. *Il mestiere di vivere—Diario 1935–1950* (Turin: Einaudi, 1952) was edited and translated by A. E. Murch under the title *This Business of Living—Diary 1935–1950* (London: Peter Owen, 1961), and by the same translator (with Jeanne Molli, introduction by Frances Keene) was published in the United States under the title, *The Burning Brand—Diaries 1935–1950* (New York: Walker & Company, 1961). All translations are mine. When I quote, however, from *The Burning Brand*, I refer to it by the initials BB and the page number; when quoting directly from *Il mestiere di vivere*, I give the initials MV and the page number. Though some of the translations from A. E Murch are wrongheaded, I chose to correct them only slightly.

3. Under the title *The Savage God: A Study of Suicide* (New York: Bantam Books, 1972), British literary critic A. Alvarez wrote a worthy report about suicide and literature, stating in his preface (p. xii): "I offer no solution. I don't, in fact, believe that solutions exist, since suicide means different things to different people at different times. For Petronius Arbiter it was a final stylish grace note to a life devoted to high style. For Thomas Chatterton it was the alternative to slow death by starvation. For Sylvia Plath it was an attempt to get herself out of a desperate corner which her own poetry boxed her into. For Cesare Pavese it was as inevitable as the next sunrise, it was an event which all the praise and success in the world could not put off."

4. Alvarez examines Pavese's case as follows (p. 121): "The life of the suicide is, to an extraordinary degree, unforgiving. Nothing he achieves by his own efforts, or luck bestows, reconciles him to his injurious past. Thus, on August 16, 1950, ten days before he finally took sleeping pills, Pavese wrote in his notebook: 'Today I see clearly that from 1928 until now I have always lived under this shadow.' But in 1928 Pavese

was already twenty. From what we know of his desolate childhood—his father dead when he was six, his mother of spun steel, harsh and austere—the shadow was probably on him much earlier; at twenty he simply recognized it for what it was. At thirty he had written flatly and without self-pity, as though it were some practical detail he had just noticed: 'Every luxury must be paid for, and everything is a luxury, starting with being in the world.' A suicide of this kind is born, not made."

5. Davide Lajolo, *Il "vizio assurdo": Storia di Cesare Pavese*, 2d ed. (Milan: Il Saggiatore, 1960), pp. 75–76.

6. Ibid., p. 84.

7. Pavese must be mistaken in his reference to Kant, since the concept he attributes to him here is actually more Nietzschean, as argued by Kirilov in Dostoevsky's *The Possessed*.

8. Lajolo, *Il "vizio assurdo,"* p. 252.

9. Rocco Scotellaro was a protégé of Carlo Levi, the internationally known author of *Cristo si è fermato ad Eboli* (*Christ Stopped at Eboli*). Scotellaro, who was born in Lucania in 1923 and died in Naples in 1953, was at that time waiting for the publication of his first book of poems, *E' fatto giorno*, by Einaudi of Turin. That publication never materialized. The book was published posthumously, in 1954, by Mondadori (Milan).

10. Lajolo, *Il "vizio assurdo,"* p. 113.

11. *Artaud Anthology*, ed. Jack Hirschman (San Francisco, 1965; Great Horwood, 1967), p. 56.

12. Armada Guiducci, *Il mito Pavese* (Florence: Vallecchi, 1967), p. 39. See also Carlo Salinari's "La poetica di Pavese," in *Preludio e fine del realismo in Italia* (Naples: Morano Editore, 1967), and Ruggero Puletti's *La maturità impossibile* (Padua: Rebellato, 1961).

13. In his *Death and Sensuality: A Study of Eroticism and the Taboo* (New York: Walker and Company, 1962), p.12, Georges Bataille writes: "Beings which reproduce themselves are distinct from one another, and those reproduced are likewise distinct from each other, just as they are distinct from their parents. Each being is distinct from all others. His birth, his death, the events of his life may have an interest for others, but he alone is directly concerned in them. He is born alone. He dies alone. Between one being and another, there is a gulf, a discontinuity."

14. Cesare Pavese, *Poesie edite e inedite,* ed. Italo Calvino (Turin: Einaudi, 1962).

15. Ibid., p. 168.

16. Lajolo, *Il "vizio assurdo,"* p. 89.

16

Ungaretti's "Lindoro di deserto":   Jongleur of the Self[1]

Glauco Cambon

Ungaretti would not have become the father of the new Italian poetry if he had not shared, either directly or through an independent affinity, certain basic experiences of European and American poetry: *symbolisme*, imagism, futurism, expressionism. Thus we see him repeatedly focus his poetical utterance on a single image or on a cluster of images free of any explanatory nexus (as happens in poems like "Attrito," "Solitudine," "Dolina notturna," "Dormire," "Inizio di sera," "Soldati," and "Stasera," to mention only a few). Sometimes the imagery takes a turn for the violent and eccentric, in Futurist style. At other times, visual imagery thins out to the verge of symbolic abstraction, and utterance seems about to founder in a mystical silence (as is the case with "Destino," "Mattina," "Dannazione," "Preghiera"). Or else it will expand into a hieratic kind of narrative, something between elegy and epos (and this applies to "I fiumi" above all, but also to "Popolo" and to "In memoria," one of *L'Allegria*'s high points). And very often, untainted by preciosity, Ungaretti's words will yield a secret essence, will heighten one another through phonetic or etymological interplay—an experiment, needless to say, anticipated by Gerard Manley Hopkins and paralleled by August Stramm,[2] the German expressionist who died on the Russian front in World War 1 after endeavoring to achieve an extreme lyrical essentialness in his native medium by dropping suffixes, laying bare word-roots, or mixing them

407

into new coinages, with the result that a mythic spell suffuses his diction in ways oddly germane to the climate of *L'Allegria.*

There is no denying the rich gamut of Ungaretti's early poetics, which can encompass a whimsical elvishness and a solemn austerity, from "Lindoro di deserto" to "I fiumi" or "In memoria"; and such richness would have been impossible without the playful instinct, the *allegria,* of the jongleur, of the acrobat walking a tightrope between joy and nostalgia, ecstasy and ennui. In "I fiumi," we can glimpse its re-flection, within the poem's stern verbal scene, in the image of the acro-bat, which picks up the surprising circus theme of stanza 1; the image radiates holiness. In this, Ungaretti certainly had an ally and inspirer in Aldo Palazzeschi, the juggler of poetry, who was also to show his mettle in the most delightfully mischievous works of fiction modern Italian literature has to offer. Behind Palazzeschi, our poet pointed out,[3] loomed Laforgue, whose irony has helpfully affected several first-rate poets in our century.

But by saying this we do not dispute Ungaretti's originality, since the "origins" of his poetry, as Luciano Rebay[4] showed in his diligent study, are connected with some of the paramount developments in modern European literature. Ungaretti, in Leone Piccioni's opinion,[5] did come to the Italian literary scene as an unspoiled outsider starting from scratch; but in his case *unspoiled* does not mean untutored, and one should remember that his providential intervention in the living history of Italian poetry was directly stimulated by *La Voce.* The freedom he was seeking, which was so dear to his Egyptian friend Mohammed Sceab, found its expression also (or above all) in the sense of playful-ness, in the far from facile discovery of whatever magic can be elicited from words by matching "distant, wireless images."

By playing, the child discovers the world, and so does the poet. It is a very serious game, and Hopkins knew it when he ran through the alliterative keyboard of his language; James Joyce knew it, and so did Hart Crane, Wallace Stevens, Rainer Maria Rilke, and Emily Dick-inson; so did Stéphane Mallarmé when he decided to "let the words themselves take the initiative" and went on to write *Un Coup de Dés.* In the same way, Giuseppe Ungaretti realized that, to put images and words at liberty (with the backing of the great Futurist imps), he had to stake all of himself in the game.

When the child plays, his very freedom leads him to invent strict rules, and this is how one might mythically describe the course of Ungaretti's poetics from *L'Allegria* to *Sentimento del Tempo*. Yet the greatest moment is still the moment of dawn, the moment of freedom which becomes open form, the getting in touch with one's own possibilities:

> Allibisco all'alba
>
> Ora specchio i punti di mondo
> che avevo compagni
> e fiuto l'orientamento
>
> Mi copro di un tepido manto
> di lind'oro[6]
>
> [I startle into astonishment at the dawn
>
> Now I mirror those points of the world
> which were once close to me
> and I scent my orientation
>
> I $\left\{ \begin{array}{l} \text{don a warm mantle} \\ \text{am covered with a warm fleece} \end{array} \right.$
> of pure gold]

The poet who came from the desert, who finds that anywhere the world can be a desert, dons Lindoro's mask to face it, and in the presence of danger, in the "ghirigoro di nostalgie" ("arabesque of nostalgias") he discovers his joy, he conquers "desolation," he freely plays with the revealed happiness of words.

And so the poem unfolds from sound to sound, from pause to pause, from image to image; it actually takes shape before our eyes and in our ears through the oddest byways. The wolf who "scents his orientation" (in *Sentimento del Tempo* he will become a "nostalgic wolf," "un nostalgico lupo") puts on the sun for a garment and changes into a sheep, accepts the world once more, leans "into the arms . . . of good weather" ("in braccio mi sporgo / al buon tempo"), returns to childhood. The emotional change from *no* to *yes* shows in the pun on "lind'oro;" and it is at this rhythmical juncture that the only perfect rhyme of the whole poem emerges:

> Il sole spegne il pianto

> Mi copro di un tepido manto
> di lind'oro

> [The sun extinguishes my weeping

> I am covered with a warm fleece
> of pure gold

> I don a warm mantle
> Lindoro's own]

A rhyme, to be sure, charged with semantic overtones. Yet the positive outcome of verbal exploration had already been foreshadowed by the opening couplet, where the play of interlocking phonic echoes evokes a cradle in motion:

> Dondolo di ali in fumo
> mozza il silenzio degli occhi

> [A swaying of wings that fade in smoke
> cuts short the silence of my eyes]

The surprise of awakening is all contained in this beginning and in its immediate sequel:

> Col vento si spippola il corallo
> di una sete di baci

> [The wind shreds the coral
> of a thirst for kisses]

The world is translated into an elemental subjectivity, into a set of instinctual reactions. Meanwhile, however, a series of liquid, soft sounds takes shape to insinuate final acceptance. These sounds soon precipitate their semantic substance in what could be called the third strophic moment of the poem:

> Allibisco all'alba

It is a one-verse strophic unit which rehearses to a point of total clarity the subjective phenomenology of the previous lines; the poem might even start here, after all. But if it did, it would not be the same thing; for this "beginning" is the conclusion of a phonic process delineated by reiteration of the syllable *al*, which eventually rounds itself out in the word *alba*—a word Ungaretti cherished, as witness his similarly inventive play on it in the strongly vocalized beginning of "O notte":

> Dall'ampia ansia dell'alba
> svelata alberatura
>
> [By the vast anxiety of the dawn
> revealed forest]

Alba: that is a word like an element, an absolute opening of the voice, and thus a liberation, a start. It represents the culmination of words like *ali*, *corallo*, *allibisco*, which attract to their phonic Gestalt the sparse "*l*"'s constellating the first lines. The verb *allibisco*, by adding the labial consonant to *al*, precipitates the formative movement of the whole phonic series toward its resolution in *alba*; *alba* is in fact its crystallization in noun form. Three lines beyond, occurs the word *mondo*, condensing a semantic development which took its departure from *alba* itself: the rise of consciousness from sleep marks at the same time the return of objective reality, however intensely colored by memory—by a sorrowful memory of harmony lost ("i punti di mondo/ che avevo compagni," "those points of the world / which were once close to me"). Of crucial importance is the use of a verb like *specchio*, "I mirror,"[7] to indicate the advent of *reflection* after initial amazement and dismay (*allibisco*); naturally the verb entails its direct object ("i punti di mondo"), unlike the aptly intransitive *allibisco* which denoted the dawning of consciousness—namely, a consciousness still self-involved. The displaced self is trying to find its bearings (hence the use of *fiuto* as a verb loaded with animal connotation, the response of instinct to a dismal situation); orientation, in fact, will come from the Orient, with sunrise, since the sun "extinguishes the weeping" ("spegne il pianto") by casting full light on the overall predicament of man among other men:

> Sino alla morte in balia del viaggio
> Abbiamo le soste di sonno
>
> [Until death at the mercy of the journey
> We have our pauses of sleep]

The only plural form to be found in the poem is that verb *abbiamo*,

which instantly focuses the whole lyric by widening the speaker's scope
to include the shared lot of *others*.

But it is exactly this desolate wisdom—the complete awakening—that
gives the cue for a reconciliation with reality, an *allegria*, and such a
further dialectical development finds its phonic counterpart in the
emphatic iteration of the sound-cluster *so*:

> Abbiamo le *so*ste di *so*nno
> Il *so*le spegne il pianto

The harmony precariously restored, the recovered orientation of the
self, is expressed in the two verbs that respectively govern the two last
clauses (and strophic units): *mi copro* ("I cover myself, I don") and
mi sporgo ("I lean out"). Phonically and semantically, the poem's movement comes to a head in *mi sporgo*, which echoes from afar *specchio*
and *spegne* along with the whole constellation of plosive labials (*punti*,
compagni, *pianto*, *tepido*, *copro*); these seem to suggest a thickened,
solidified reality in counterpoint to the initial play of liquid consonants,
which did their part to present reality as if in solution. *Mi sporgo* ("I
lean out") is an existential gesture, a decision for the world, in the
world, since the world offers protection and not only danger ("in
braccio . . . al buon tempo," "in the arms . . . of good weather").

To put it more prosaically, the persona gets dressed ("mi copro . . .
di un tepido manto / di lind'oro") and goes outdoors (leaves the shell).
The whole world (*mondo*) is by now a mantle (*manto*), a golden fleece,
at least on this day, in this moment which the self savors to prolong
it; and then the very sky (the "good weather") is about to take the shape
of a sustaining, paternal godhead ready to embrace its creature. The
scholar of myth, Usener, would call it an *Augenblicksgott*, a momentary
godhead; and indeed, the Italian language here makes for a pun no
less vivid than the one extracted from the name *Lindoro*—for *buon
tempo* means not only good weather, but also a favorable moment or
temporal interval, toward which the self reaches out from his station in
contingency in order to enjoy it while it lasts, in what becomes a new-
fangled *carpe diem*.

If time is duration, it is duration in fleetingness, and in it the juggler
finds his element. Whether he dons the mask of Lindoro, of the acrobat,
or of the sentimental clown, he plays on words with the grace of a
master who is used to hazard. Here I am not referring only to semantic

acrobatics or "hothouse imagery" (to say it with Marcel Raymond and Joan Gutia)[8] such as meets us at the outset, where a synaesthetic conglomerate like "silence of the eyes" ("silenzio degli occhi"), especially if it is a silence "cut short" (*mozzato*) by a "swaying of wings that fade in smoke" ("dondolo di ali in fumo"), wavers between some hidden higher sense and nursery-rhyme nonsense (but see Dante's "chi per lungo silenzio parea fioco," in *Inferno* 1.63, which did intrigue Ungaretti). Nor do I have in mind just the lacelike words "si spippola il corallo / di una sete di baci" ("the coral is shredded / of a thirst for kisses"), where the visual metaphor depicting the shredding of clouds in the pink sky of dawn tilts the statement toward denotative rarefaction to climax in freely subjective language (its resolution following immediately in the lines "Mi si travasa la vita / in un ghirigoro di nostalgie"—"My life is transfused / into an arabesque of nostalgias," which make good those semantic hazards). I am thinking above all of the swaying, plurilinear total structure, within which one can isolate several overlapping members that, if so detached from the context, would become as many independent poems, quite similar to more than a few of the numerous short lyrics in Ungaretti's verse diary.

By way of example, here is some experimental anatomy. The first member we could with impunity carve out of the versatile context, is the one consisting of the first five lines as gathered into three strophic units:

Dondolo di ali in fumo
mozza il silenzio degli occhi

Col vento si spippola il corallo
di una sete di baci

Allibisco all'alba

[A swaying of wings that fade in smoke
cuts short the silence of my eyes

The wind shreds the coral
of a thirst for kisses

I startle into astonishment at the dawn]

The suspended final clause thereby obtained recalls several others that Ungaretti chose to seal short composition—like impressionistic epiphanies which, rather than "conclude" (i. e. close), seem to *open* onto the subsequent silence, and thus to imply a possible ad lib sequel. This is the case in "Notte di maggio," "Stasera," "Dannazione," "Universo," "Allegria di naufragi" (which actually takes its departure from a silent prologue); it is also the case in "Mattina," "Noia," "Inizio di sera," and several quick entries in "Fine di Crono" (for instance, "Una colomba"), and "Sogni e Accordi" from *Sentimento del Tempo*.

It was Jules Laforgue who said of Gustave Kahn's lyrics that they seemed to him "des commencements de poèmes infinies." Many of Ungaretti's compositions, because they bank on the implicit, are something like that: pure beginnings. It isn't just a matter of his *symboliste* heritage, but even more of the amount of free integration that the verse-diary form demands and allows beyond the individual pages or moments it encompasses. To continue with our experiment, a second composition to be hypothetically detached from the whole of "Lindoro di deserto" will overlap with the previous one:

> Col vento si spippola il corallo
> di una sete di baci
>
> Allibisco all'alba
>
> Mi si travasa la vita
> in un ghirigoro di nostalgie

We already saw that the couplet here raised to the status of a conclusion does resolve on a subjective level the psychophysical phenomenology of the preceding couplet ("Col vento, etc."); between the two couplets, then, we get as a rhythmical and semantic hinge the phonically outstanding line "Allibisco, etc." Now if these five lines were to appear by themselves, as an autonomous piece, in the pages of *L'Allegria*, I daresay nobody would question their structural integrity; and in this regard it helps to recall that Ungaretti himself often adopted the procedure experimentally applied in the present context, when in the course of textual revisions he finally split into two independent poems what had originally been one composition: witness "Levante" and "Nebbia," "La notte bella" and "Universo," "Il capitano" and "Primo amore." My purpose, of course, is not to invalidate the basic unity of the poem in question, but only to test its structural physiognomy, which would hardly invite this kind of manipulation unless it were so challengingly peculiar. So, then, here is a third fragment we can raise to independent status:

> Mi si travasa la vita
> in un ghirigoro di nostalgie
> Ora specchio i punti di mondo
> che avevo compagni
> e fiuto l'orientamento
>
> Sino alla morte in balia del viaggio
>
> [My life is transfused
> into an arabesque of nostalgias
>
> Now I mirror those points of the world
> which were once close to me
> and I scent my orientation
>
> Until death at the mercy of the journey]

This confessional and gnomic nucleus could very well go into the section of L'Allegria that bears the title "Girovago," thanks to a clear thematic affinity which my experimental carving brings out by making the last line quoted a conclusion.

Yet it is just here that, by going on and thereby rejecting the option described, lyrical discourse turns around to come eventually to a head in an affirmation, albeit precarious; and from now on the dismembering operation I have been essaying for purposes of structural verification would prove of less consequence; for the last four strophic units of the poem, from "Abbiamo le soste di sonno" ("We have our pauses of sleep") to the end, seem much more closely tied to one another, semantically hinging as they do on the line that goes "Sino alla morte, etc." This line, indeed, reaches the bottom of "desolation," and so makes it impossible for the sequel to go any way but up, if stasis is to be avoided. It is true that we could see what happens if we make that very line the beginning of an independent utterance which would encompass what is left of the whole poem:

> Sino alla morte in balia del viaggio
>
> Abbiamo le soste di sonno
>
> Il sole spegne il pianto

Mi copro di un tepido manto
di lind'oro

Da questa terrazza di desolazione
in braccio mi sporgo
al buon tempo

[Until death at the mercy of the journey

We have our pauses of sleep

The sun extinguishes my weeping

I don a warm mantle
of pure gold
Lindoro's own

From this terrace of desolation
I lean out into the arms
of good weather]

Now a close look will tell us that the incisiveness of that opening line
is not enough to rescue the passage from the dangerous aftermath of
amputation. The line in question is an absolute, peremptory statement
unqualified by any verb with its correlates of tense and mood; it is, then,
suspended outside time, in a nonhistorical stance banking on nominal
style, so that the following clauses relate to it as limitations, partial
negations of its desolate message. But the lack of a concrete reference
at the very outset makes itself felt. Abstraction, gratuitous allegory,
looms on the horizon, a threat the passage as such can elude only by
staying within its global context, which supplies it with the specific
weight of chronologically focused sensory data.

What our analytical experiment has ascertained is the relative degree
of autonomy inherent in various verse clusters of "Lindoro di deserto."
Attention should be paid to the fact that these nuclei, or compositional
members, are not externally juxtaposable but conspicuously dovetail-
ing, because they share entire lines as structural elements. This way,
paradoxically, their being isolable as semantic units confirms the free
unity of the poem—something comparable to the swaying structures, or
mobiles, of Alexander Calder. For the internal autonomy of the several
decontextualized members is underscored, both by the customary
emphatic pauses (bridged though they may be by the suppression of

punctuation), and by the exclusion of any modal particle. Such particles, if used, would somehow constrain the various strophic phrases and deprive them of the full resonance accruing to them in the specific version chosen by the author: which is why he saw fit to leave out, in the final part, certain conjunctions or adverbs one might easily inject in the context as logical connectives: for instance, *ma, almeno, e inoltre, così*, ("but," "at least," "and besides," "thus"). The only salient adverb is "ora" ("now"), in the eighth line, and it imparts to the poem its temporal individuation; it actually appears in the central strophic unit, which also contains the only hypotactic phrasing and the only appeal to the past to be found throughout the composition: "che avevo compagni."

It is here, as we have seen, that consciousness achieves its full awakening—since "Lindoro di deserto" does parallel other poems of Ungaretti's by dramatizing an awakening (and decades later we shall find that other awakening, the "Canzone" of *La Terra Promessa*). Each strophic phrase emerges from a silence and dives into a silence. Each of the structural members I have experimentally isolated points to an ideal or virtual semantic direction, only to discard it for another, so that a possible graph of the poem should take a plurilinear rather than a monolinear shape (this is one reason why I thought of comparing it to Calder's mobiles). And between the global structure and the several members that one can isolate within it at different stages of autonomy (the last one is obviously less "autonomous" than the previous ones), a system of formal relationships obtains which corresponds to those to be descried between the entire book and its sections and individual poems.

"Lindoro" is a verbal microcosm mirroring the macrocosm of *L'Allegria* because it allows for several semantic possibilities, virtual projections of meaning, subtending its unity to the internal "discontinuities" (as Genot would put it).[9] "Lindoro" *flows* in its experiential moment, within which several implicit moments emerge; *L'Allegria* flows in its diarylike dimension. Lindoro's acrobatics is something other than the ritual ceremony of "I fiumi"—it is, in fact, its antitype—but in this case divergence is no incongruity, for the same voice is overheard throughout the most whimsical modulations. "Lindoro" comes to rest on the note established by the reflexive verbs "mi copro" and "mi sporgo," which denote existential gestures, elemental motions of the psyche (as well as of the body); in the same way, the symbolic action of "I fiumi" is woven by a set of analogous verbs (mostly reflexive): "mi tengo," "mi sono disteso," "ho riposato," "ho tirato su / le mie quattr'ossa," "mi sono riconosciuto."

This is the keynote of *L'Allegria*, whether we try to grasp it through linguistic analysis or by an existential approach of the Jungian, or at least psychoanalytical, typological kind. The poet himself, annotating his definitive edition, said that *L'Allegria* is the book of the self—of the self, I beg to add, that seeks and posits itself as a presence in the world, and in such a process will alternately emerge from the cosmic matrix: "mi sporgo" ("I lean out"), "mi desto" ("I wake up"), "m'avviene di svegliarmi" ("I happen to wake up"), "ho tirato su, etc." ("I have raised up"), "mi vedo" ("I see myself"), "mi sento" ("I feel myself"), "porto la mia anima" ("I carry my soul"), "mi trovo / languente" ("I find myself / languishing"), "mi riconosco" ("I recognize myself"); or reimmerse itself in it: "mi sono fatto / una bara / di freschezza" ("I have made for myself / a casket / of freshness"), "mi sento diffuso" ("I feel myself diffused"), "mi sono disteso / in un'urna d'acqua" ("I have lain down / in an urn of water"), "mi sono colto / nel tuffo / di spinalba" ("I have picked myself / in the dash / of hawthorn"), "piombo in me / E m'oscuro in un mio nido" ("I plunge into myself / And darken in a nest of mine"), "Appisolarmi là" ("There to doze off"), "E in questa uniforme / . . . mi riposo / come fosse la culla / di mio padre" ("And in this uniform / I rest / as if it were the cradle / of my father"),"M'illumino" ("I am illumined"), "Mi desterò" ("I shall awaken"). Between the two alternating phases which mark the self's death and rebirth: "nascendo / . . . tornato da epoche troppo vissute" ("emerging into birth/. . . on the return from overlived ages") there intervenes a third one, as we saw —namely, consciousness committed to establishing its foundation in the real, in permanence even through the flux of time: "Sto" ("I stand"), "Resto docile" ("I remain docile"), "e come portati via / si rimane" ("and as if carried away / we remain"), "Fermato a due sassi / mi trovo" ("Clinging to two rocks / I find myself"), "Si sta come" ("We stay like"), "e forse io solo / so ancora / che visse" ("and I alone perhaps / still know / that he lived").

This bird's-eye view of the verbal cosmos of *L'Allegria*, which was suggested by the linguistic parallelism between a final motif of "Lindoro" and the very backbone of "I fiumi," helps to confirm the character of

what Matthew Arnold, perhaps, would have called the "high seriousness" of Ungaretti's poetry; yet such a high seriousness is counterpointed by play, or is actually fulfilled through the earnest play of the
acrobat who acts as the jongleur of the self.

NOTES

1. From a book on Ungaretti's poetry to be published by Einaudi in Turin, under
the title *Misura e Mistero: Poesia di Ungaretti.*
2. One fairly available source for a telling choice of Stramm's poetry in its historical context is the anthology of Expressionist verse edited by Kurt Pinthus for Ro-
wohlt Verlag: *Menschheitsdämmerung, ein Dokument des Expressionismus,* originally
published in Berlin in 1920 with the subtitle *"Symphonie jüngster Dichtung,"* and then
in Hamburg in 1959 with new notes and introduction. In his new introduction, the
anthologist himself mentions Ungaretti's poetry as germane to Expressionist poetics.
On *Menschheitsdämmerung,* I published extensive review articles in *Aut-Aut,* vol.
63 (May 1961), and in *Comparative Literature,* vol. 13 (Winter 1961). See in particular Stramm's poem "Abendgang" on p. 145 of the anthology, for a clear example
of the phenomena discussed here.
3. G. Ungaretti, *Vita d'un uomo, tutte le poesie* (Milan: Mondadori, 1969), pp.
547–48 (in "Prima lezione" on the canzone of *La Terra Promessa*).
4. Luciano Rebay, *Le origini della poesia di Ungaretti* (Rome: Edizioni di Storia e
Letteratura, 1962).
5. Leone Piccioni, *Vita di un poeta— Giuseppe Ungaretti* (Milan: Rizzoli, 1970).
6. Ungaretti, *Vita,* p. 24. *Lindoro* is the name of a Pierrot-like figure *avant lettre*
in Goldoni's plays.
7. Compare this with "anima deserta" and "specchio impassibile" in "Distacco,"
as well as with the necromancy of mirrors in "Ti svelerà (*Sentimento del Tempo*)
and "Canto" (ibid.).
8. Joan Gutia, *Linguaggio di Ungaretti* (Florence: Le Monnier, 1959). He avowed-
ly borrows the term from Marcel Raymond's *De Baudelaire au surréalisme* (Paris:
Corti, 1939, 1952), where Ungaretti, by the way, is mentioned—at least in the new
edition of 1952 I have at hand (pp. 44 and 189).
9. Gérard Genot, *Sémantique du discontinu dans L'Allegria d'Ungaretti* (Paris:
Editions Klincksieck, 1972).

Bibliography
of the Writings of
Thomas Goddard Bergin
(as of March 1, 1974)

Mary Ann F. Rizzo

BOOKS

Giovanni Verga. New Haven: Yale University Press, 1931. Reprint, 1969.

Modern Italian Short Stories (ed.). Boston: D. C. Heath, 1938. Revised edition, 1959.

Luciano Zuccoli: ritratto umbertino. Rome: Società Editrice del Libro Italiano, 1940.

Anthology of the Provençal Troubadours (ed., with R. T. Hill). New Haven: Yale University Press, 1941. Revised edition, 1973.

Three French Plays (ed., with T. Andersson). New York: American Book Company, 1941.

Spanish Grammar (textbook, with G. Dale). New York: Ronald Press, 1943.

The Autobiography of G. B. Vico (trans. with M. Fisch). Ithaca: Cornell University Press, 1944. Revised edition (Great Seal Books), 1963.

Parco Grifeo (verse). Ithaca, N. Y.: privately printed, 1946.

Machiavelli's "The Prince" (trans.). New York: F. S. Crofts, 1947.

The New Science of G. B. Vico (trans. with M. Fisch). Ithaca: Cornell University Press, 1948. Revised abridged edition, Garden City: N.Y.: Doubleday & Company, 1961. Revised abridged edition, 1970.

Dante's "Inferno" (trans.). New York: Appleton-Century-Crofts, 1948.

Dante's "Purgatorio" (trans.). New York: Appleton-Century-Crofts, 1953.

421

Dante's "Paradiso" (trans.). New York: Appleton-Century-Crofts, 1954.

Taming of the Shrew (ed.). New Haven: Yale University Press, 1954.

Divine Comedy (trans.). New York: Appleton-Century-Crofts, 1955.

The Poems of William of Poitou (trans.). New Haven: privately printed, 1955.

Translations from Petrarch (comp., ed., trans.). Edinburgh-London: Oliver and Boyd, 1955.

Liriche di Rambaldo de Vaqueiras (ed., trans.). Florence: Sansoni, 1956.

Paradiso IX. Rome: Signorelli, 1959.

The Poet and the Politician (Essays of S. Quasimodo: trans., with S. Pacifici). Carbondale: Southern Illinois University Press, 1964.

Bertran de Born: Liriche (trans., ed.). Varese: Magenta, 1964.

Italian Sampler (trans.), Montreal: Casalini; Florence: La Nuova Italia, 1964.

Dante, New York: Orion Press; Boston: Houghton-Mifflin, 1965.

Approach to Dante (English ed. of above). London: The Bodley Head, 1965.

The Sonnets of Petrarch (comp., ed., trans.). New York: Limited Editions, 1965.

Concordance to the Divine Comedy (ed. with E. H. Wilkins et al.). Cambridge, Mass.: Harvard, The Belknap Press, 1965.

Sonnets and Odes of Petrarch (ed., trans.). New York: Appleton-Century-Crofts, 1966.

Perspectives on the Divine Comedy. New Brunswick: Rutgers University Press, 1967. Paperback edition, Bloomington: Indiana University Press, 1970.

From Time to Eternity (essays on Dante; ed.), New Haven: Yale University Press, 1967.

A Diversity of Dante. New Brunswick: Rutgers University Press, 1969.

The Divine Comedy (trans., rev. trans.). New York: Grossman, 1969.

Dante: His Life, His Times, His Works (ed., trans.). New York: American Heritage Press, 1970.

Cervantes: His Life, His Times, His Works (ed.), New York: American Heritage Press, 1970.

Petrarch. New York: Twayne Publishers, 1970.

Dante's Divine Comedy. Englewood Cliffs, N. J.: Prentice Hall, 1971.

On Sepulchres (trans. of Ugo Foscolo's "Carmen dei sepolchri").
Bethany, Conn.: Bethany Press, 1971.

Invito alla Divina Commedia. Bari: Adriatica editrice, 1971.

CONTRIBUTIONS TO BOOKS

Articles on Alvaro, Benelli, Bontempelli, Cicognani, Deledda, Farina,
Nencioni, Niccodemi, Novelli, and Tozzi in *Columbia Dictionary of
Modern European Literature,* edited by Horatio Smith. New York:
Columbia University Press, 1947, and subsequent revisions.

"Dante and Romance Letters." In *Humanities for our Time,* edited by
Walter Agard, et al., pp. 87–116. Lawrence: University of Kansas
Press, 1949.

Articles in *Dizionario Letterario Bompiani.* Milan: Valentino Bompiani editore, 1957.

"G. C. Belli: Tre mmaschi e nnuovi femmine"; "Giacomo Leopardi:
a Silvia"; "Umberto Saba: Ulisse." In *The Poem Itself, 45 Modern
Poets in a New Presentation,* edited by Stanley Burnshaw, pp. 282–
83, 278–81, and 304–05. New York: Holt, 1960.

"Giuseppe Villaroel." In *Giuseppe Villaroel: Cinquant'anni di attività
letteraria,* edited by Comune di Catania, pp. 75–76. Florence: Olschki editore, 1962.

Translations of "William IX Count of Poitiers, Bernart de Ventadorn,
Peirol, and Dalfin d'Alvernhe, Peire Cardinal." In *Anthology of Medieval Lyrics,* edited by Angel Flores. The Modern Library, 1962.

Translations of "Umberto Saba." In *Contemporary Italian Poetry,*
edited by Carlo Golino (1962).

"Dante—Hell; Topography and Demography." In *Essays on Dante,*
pp. 76–93. Bloomington: Indiana University Press, 1964.

Article on Dante in *Groliers Encyclopedia International,* vol. 5 (1964).

Translation of three poems by "Rocco Scotellaro." In *Modern European Poetry.* New York: Bantam Classics, 1966.

Verse translations of "Brutus Minor" and "Aspasia." In *Leopardi:
Poems and Prose,* edited by Angel Flores (1966).

Verse translation of "The Goat by Umberto Saba." In *Selections from
Italian Poetry,* edited by A. Michael de Luca and William Giuliano
(1966).

"On the Personae of the Comedy." In *American Critical Essays on the*

Divine Comedy, edited by R. J. Clements, pp. 117–42. New York: New York University Press, 1967.

"Italian Literature." In *Modern Literature,* vol. 2, edited by Victor Lange, pp. 3–64. Englewood Cliffs, N. J.: Prentice Hall, 1968.

Translation of "Petrarch's *Bucolicum Carmen I: Parthenias.*" In *Petrarch to Pirandello, Studies in Italian Literature in Honour of Beatrice Corrigan,* edited by Julias A. Molinaro, pp. 3–18. Toronto: University of Toronto Press, 1973.

ARTICLES IN PERIODICALS

"Textbooks Available for the Study of Italian in America," *Italica* 6 (1929): 41–43.

"Raimbautz's D'una Dona m Tuelh e m Lays" (with Benjamin P. Bourland), *Italica* 12 (1935): 99–101.

"Luciano Zuccoli, ritratto umbertino. Profilo," *Tempo Nostro* 5 (1936): 45.

"Achille Campanile," *Italica* 15 (1938): 179–81.

"Umberto Fracchia," *Italica* 15 (1938): 225–27.

"Remarks on some Recent Lyrics," *Italica* 16 (1939): 58–63.

"Riccardo Bacchelli," *Italica* 17 (1940): 64–68.

"Bruno Cicognani," *Italica* 19 (1942): 22–25.

"Greetings to Inventario," *Books Abroad* 21 (1947): 34–35.

"Luigi Russo," *Books Abroad* 22 (1948): 142–43.

"Italian Fiction Today," *Yale Review* 39 (1950): 709–22.

"Portuguese Epic in Octaves," *Saturday Review of Literature* 33 (1950): 31.

"To Christ Crucified" (translated from the Spanish), *Christ Church Chronicle* 73 (1951): 1.

"Literature: a European Bookshelf," *Saturday Review of Literature* 35 (1952): 21.

"Gaucelm Faidit: a semblan del rei ties" (with Raymond Thomas Hill), *Romanic Review* 44 (1953): 81–88.

"Moravian Muse," *Virginia Quarterly Review* 29 (1953): 215–25.

"Luigi Russo," *Books Abroad* 28 (1954): 26.

"Belli's Sonnets," *Books Abroad* 28 (1954): 27.

"Literary Scene in Western Europe, 1953," *Classic Features* (1954).

"Italy, 1955," *Current History* 29 (1955): 78–84.

"Umberto Saba, Poems" (trans. with F. M. Clapp), *Italian Quarterly* 1 (1957): 3.

"Giuseppe Villaroel," *Italian Quarterly* 3 (1960): 38–39.

"Giuseppe Villaroel, Poems" (trans.). *Italian Quarterly* 3 (1960): 40.

"Marco dell'Arco," *Cesare Barbieri Courier* 3 (1960): 8–9.

"Reflections on a Centennial: The Italian Risorgimento," *Yale Review* 50 (1961): 491–503.

"A Poem" (by T. G. Bergin), *Cesare Barbieri Courier* 5 (1962): 12.

"Vittorio Bodini, Poems" (trans.), *Italian Quarterly* 7 (1963): 20–21.

"Giuseppe Gioacchino Belli," *Cesare Barbieri Courier* 6 (1964): 9–11.

"Dante's Provençal Gallery," *Speculum* 40 (1965): 15–30.

"On the Personae of the Comedy," *Italica* 42 (special Dante issue, 1965): 1–7.

"The Women of the Comedy," *Cesare Barbieri Courier* 7 (1965): 34–41.

"The Changing Portrait (Dante)," *Books Abroad* 39 (1965): 1–6.

"On the Personae of the Comedy," *La Parola del Popolo (Chicago) Omaggio a Dante* 58 (1965): 66–68.

"Dante's Comedy—Letter and Spirit," *Virginia Quarterly Review* 41 (1965): 525–41.

"Dante" (poem), *Yale Review* 55 (1965): 86.

"Da Emerson a Santayana," *Fiera Letteraria* (1965).

"Two Poems by Giuseppe Zappulla" (trans.), *Cesare Barbieri Courier* 8 (1966): 7.

"A Translation from Leopardi: Memories," *Umanesimo I* (1967).

"Luigi Pirandello, pathfinder and more," *Books Abroad* 41 (1967): 413–17.

"Saba and his 'Canzoniere,' " *Books Abroad* 42 (1968): 503 08.

"Gli Affetti di un disperato" (trans.), *Forum Italicum* 2 (1968): 305–09.

"Three Latin Poems by Petrarch" (trans.), *Cesare Barbieri Courier* 9 (1969): 17–18.

"An Anniversary: Cesare Barbieri Courier," *Italica* 47 (1970): 119–20.

"Ungaretti traduttore," *Books Abroad* 44 (1970): 571–76.

"The Divine Comedy, Target of Translators," *Pen Club Magazine* (1970), 26–61.

"Bucolicum Carmen III: The Amorous Shepherd, Francesco Petrarca" (trans.), *Forum Italicum* 5 (1971): 598–603.

"The Enjoyable Horrendous World of Aldo Palazzeschi," *Books Abroad* 46 (1972): 55–60.

"Dante," *Italian Quarterly* 16 (1972): 97–115.

"Giuseppe Ungaretti, 'Dormire,' 'Girovago,' 'Natale' " (trans.), *Forum Italicum* 6 (1972): 292–95.

"Vittorio Bodini, poet, critic, mediator," *Books Abroad* 47 (1973): 73–76.

REVIEWS

Edmund G. Gardner, *The Story of Italian Literature. Italica* 5 (1928): 49–50.

Thomas Caldecot Chubb, *The Life of Giovanni Boccaccio. Saturday Review of Literature*, August 30, 1930, p. 86.

F. Winwar (trans.), *The Decameron of Giovanni Boccaccio. Saturday Review of Literature*, August 30, 1930, p. 86.

Filostrato of Giovanni Boccaccio. Saturday Review of Literature, June 13, 1931, p. 89.

John Purves (ed.), *A First Book of Italian Verse. Italica* 9 (1932): 62–63.

J. L. Bickersteth, *Form, Tone and Rhythm in Italian Poetry. Italica* 11 (1934): 113–14.

Ignazio Silone, *Fontamara. New York Times Book Review*, September 23, 1935.

Mario Puccini, *Sull'orlo. Italica* 13 (1936): 128–29.

Ugo Betti, *Le Case. Books Abroad* 11 (1937): 364.

Le Avventure notturne. Books Abroad 11 (1937): 364–65.

Il Libro degli animali. Books Abroad 11 (1937): 365.

Riccardo Bacchelli, *Iride. Books Abroad* 12 (1938): 107–08.

Nino Salvaneschi, *Il Sole nell'anima. Books Abroad* 12 (1938): 368–69.

Dino Terra, *Qualcuno si diverte. Books Abroad* 12 (1938): 369.

I Medici e i Lorena negli ultimi due secoli del granducato di Toscana. Books Abroad 12 (1938): 499.

Arturo Marpicati, *Quando fa sereno. Books Abroad* 12 (1938): 500.

Ignazio Silone, *Pane e vino. Books Abroad* 12 (1938): 502.

Goffredo Sajani, *La Tua, la mia Engadina! Books Abroad* 12 (1938): 502.

Alberto Viviani, *Novità' dell'oltre mondo. Books Abroad* 12 (1938): 502–03.

B. Russo, *Politica estera e coloniale. Books Abroad* 13 (1939): 107.

P. G. Fiori, *Lorenzo il magnifico. Books Abroad* 13 (1939): 109.

Giorgio Imperatori, *Goethe e gli scrittori d'Italia. Books Abroad* 13 (1939): 112.

Massimo Bontempelli, *Miracoli. Books Abroad* 13 (1939): 113–14.

Giovanni Necco, *Realismo e idealismo nella letteratura tedesca moderna. Books Abroad* 13 (1939): 245–46.

Virgilio Brocchi, *Il Tramonto delle stelle. Books Abroad* 13 (1939): 247.

Vito Magliocco, *Detroit, U.S.A. Books Abroad* 13 (1939): 374.

Vito Magliocco, *La Pubblicità in America. Books Abroad* 13 (1939): 374.

Renzo Scrtoli Salis, *La Politica dei mandati internazionali. Books Abroad* 13 (1939): 374.

Michele Saponaro, *Vita amorosa ed eroica di Ugo Foscolo. Books Abroad* 13 (1939): 375.

Leone Vivanti, *Il Concetto della indeterminazione. Books Abroad* 13 (1939): 376–77.

Vittorio Emanuele Bravetta, *Il Fratello di Romolo e Remo. Books Abroad* 13 (1939): 378.

Tia Celletti, *Tre Tempi. Books Abroad* 13 (1939): 378.

Cesare Zavattini, *I Poveri sono matti. Books Abroad* 13 (1939): 379.

V. G. Rossi, *Oceano. Books Abroad* 13 (1939): 379.

Gaetano Firetto, *Torquato Tasso e la Contrarriforma. Books Abroad* 13 (1939): 499.

Apriano E. Oppo. *Forme e colori nel mondo. Books Abroad* 13 (1939):500.

Ugo Betti, *Uomo e donna. Books Abroad* 13 (1939): 501.

Fantasia davanti a Palazzo Dario. Books Abroad 13 (1939): 501–02.

Alessandro Varaldo, *La trentunesima perla. Books Abroad* 13 (1939): 503.

Bruno Brunelli, *Figurini e costumi nella corrispondenza di un medico del '700 (Antonio Vallisnieri). Books Abroad* 14 (1940): 85.

Vincenzo Cardarelli, *Il Cielo sulle città. Books Abroad* 14 (1940): 86.

Arnaldo Frateili, *Clara fra i lupi. Books Abroad* 14 (1940): 90.

Gertrude Alli Maccarani, *Momenti. Books Abroad* 14 (1940): 433.

F. M. Trevisani, *La Cristina. Books Abroad* 17 (1943): 389.

Carlo Levi, *Cristo si è fermato ad Eboli. Books Abroad* 21 (1947): 101.

Anna Maria Armi (trans.), *Francesco Petrarca: Sonnets and Songs. New York Times Book Review*, March 9, 1947, p. 28.

Franco Venturi, *Dalmazza Francesco Vasco (1732–1794)*. *Romanic Review* 38 (1947): 180–82.

Leo Ferrero, *Angelica*. *Italica* 24 (1947): 179–81.

Rodolfi de Mattei, *Ritratti di antenati*. *Books Abroad* 21 (1947): 353.

Attilio Momigliano, *Cinque Saggi*. *Books Abroad* 21 (1947): 354.

Bonino Mombrizo, *La Legende de Ste. Catherine d'Alexandrie. Poeme italien du XVe siècle*. *Romanic Review* 39 (1948): 74–75.

Giovanni Papini, *Lettere agli uomini del Papa Celestino sesto*. *Books Abroad* 22 (1948): 317.

Bruno Cicognani, *Barucca*. *Books Abroad* 22 (1948): 422–23.

Leonardo Olschki, *The Genius of Italy*. *Saturday Review of Literature*, July 16, 1949, pp. 25–26.

Giuseppe Prezzolini, *Repertorio bibliografico della storia e della critica della letteratura italiana dal 1933 al 1942*. *Romanic Review* 40 (1949): 301–03.

Riccardo Bacchelli, *The Mill on the Po*. Translated by Frances Frenaye. *Herald Tribune Book Review*, September 17, 1950, p. 5.

Bruno Brunelli, *Il Pensiero politico italiano dal Romagnosi al Croce*. *Books Abroad* 24 (1950): 412.

Guido Errante, *Marcabru e le fonti sacre dell'antica lirica romanza*. *Romanic Review* 41 (1950): 211–13.

J. E. Shaw, *Guido Cavalcanti's Theory of Love. The Canzone d'Amore and other Related Problems*. *Romanic Review* 41 (1950): 277–81.

Giulio Natali, *Vittorio Alfieri*. *Books Abroad* 25 (1951): 64.

Francesco Brundu, *Il Salto delle pecore*. *Books Abroad* 25 (1951): 165.

Flora Volpini, *La Fiorentina*. *Books Abroad* 25 (1951): 167.

Dante Arfelli, *The Unwanted*. Translated by Frances Frenaye. *Herald Tribune Book Review*, August 19, 1951, p. 4.

Elio Vittorini, *The Twilight of the Elephant*. Translated by Cinina Brescia. *Herald Tribune Book Review*, August 26, 1951, p. 4.

Vasco Pratolini, *A Hero of our Time*. *Herald Tribune Book Review*, October 14, 1951, p. 6.

Alessandro Manzoni, *The Betrothed*. Translated by Archibald Colquhoun. *Herald Tribune Book Review*, October 28, 1951, p. 4.

Alberto Moravia, *The Conformist*. Translated by Angus Davidson. *Herald Tribune Book Review*, November 4, 1951, p. 8.

Giuseppe Berto, *The Brigand*. Translated by Angus Davidson. *Herald Tribune Book Review*, December 9, 1951, p. 12.

Werner P. Friederich, *Dante's Fame Abroad. Italica* 29 (1952): 139–40.

Carlo Coccioli, *Heaven and Earth. Herald Tribune Book Review*, July 13, 1952, p. 8.

Alberto Moravia, *The Fancy Dress Party*. Translated by Angus Davidson. *Herald Tribune Book Review*, August 3, 1952, p. 6.

Elio Vittorini, *The Red Carnation*. Translated by Anthony Bower. *Herald Tribune Book Review*, August 3, 1952, p. 6.

Alba de Cespedes, *The Best of Husbands. Saturday Review of Literature*, November 8, 1952, p. 52.

D'Annunzio dramaturge. Romanic Review 43 (1952): 65–67.

Giuseppe Marotta, *Tutte a me. Books Abroad* 27 (1953): 79.

Luisa Santandrea, *I Vent'anni ritornano. Books Abroad* 27 (1953): 80.

Marino Moretti, *I Grilli di Pazzo Pazzi. Books Abroad* 27 (1953): 191.

Giovanni Verga, *The House by the Medlar Tree*. Translated by Eric Mosbacher. *Saturday Review of Literature*, May 2, 1953, pp. 31–32.

Adolfo Angeli, *Le tre Fiamme. Books Abroad* 27 (1953): 299–300.

Goffredo Parisi, *The Dead Boy and the Comets*. Translated by Marianne Ceconi. *Herald Tribune Book Review*, September 13, 1953, p. 8.

Little Novels of Sicily. Herald Tribune Book Review, September 20, 1953, p. 8.

Ugo Moretti, *Rogue Wind*. Translated by Giuseppina T. Salvadori and Bernice L. Lewis. *Saturday Review of Literature*, October 3, 1953, p. 26.

Ignazio Silone, *A Handful of Blackberries*. Translated by Darina Silone. *Saturday Review of Literature*, October 10, 1953, p. 62.

Eca de Queiroz, *Cousin Bazilio*. Translated by Roy Campbell. *Saturday Review of Literature*, November 7, 1953, p. 23.

Giovanni Guareschi, *The House that Nino Built*. Translated by Frances Frenaye. *Herald Tribune Book Review*, pt. 1 (November 15, 1953), p. 4.

Francis Fergusson, *Dante's Drama of the Mind: A Modern Reading of the Purgatorio. Yale Review* 43 (1953): 150–51.

Tito Ferruccio Barbieri, *2 × 2 = 5. Books Abroad* 28 (1954): 79.

Aldo Palazzeschi, *Roma. Books Abroad* 28 (1954): 219–20.

Livia de Stefani, *La Vigna di uve nere. Books Abroad* 28 (1954): 347.

Archibald Colquhoun, *Manzoni and His Times. Herald Tribune Book Review*, August 8, 1954, p. 3.

David Magarshack, *Turgenev, A Life. Classic Features* (1954).

Rocco Fumento, *Devil by the Tail. Classic Features* (1954).

Paride Rombi, *Perdu. Classic Features* (1954).

Mario Tobino, *Le libere Donne di Magliano. Books Abroad* 29 (1955): 92.

Francesco de Sanctis, *La Poesia cavalleresca e scritti vari. Books Abroad* 29 (1955): 344.

Riccardo Bacchelli, *Nothing New under the Sun. Herald Tribune Book Review*, September 11, 1955, p. 6.

A. Robert Caponigri, *Time and Idea: The Theory of History in Giambattista Vico. Italica* 32 (1955): 200–03.

Andre Beaucler, *The Last of the Bohemians—20 Years with Leon-Paul Fargue. Westchester Forecast* (1955?).

Ernest Hatch Wilkins, *History of Italian Literature. Modern Philology* (1955?).

Americo Castro, *The Structure of Spanish History. Yale Review* (1955?).

V. S. Pritchett, *The Spanish Temper. Yale Review* (1955?).

Sebastian Juan Arbo, *Cervantes.* Translated by Ilsa Barea. *Saturday Review of Literature*, January 21, 1956, pp. 46–47.

Dorothy L. Sayers, *Introductory Papers on Dante. Speculum* 33 (1956): 319–22.

Luciano Anceschi and Sergio Antonielli, *Lirica del Novecento. Books Abroad* 30 (1956): 217.

Giulio Natali, *Ugo Foscolo. Books Abroad* 30 (1956): 219.

Marino Moretti, *Uomini Soli. Books Abroad* 30 (1956): 328.

Herbert Kubly, *Easter in Sicily. Saturday Review of Literature*, November 10, 1956, p. 19.

Natalia Ginzburg, *A Light for Fools.* Translated by Angus Davidson. *Saturday Review of Literature*, January 5, 1957, p. 14.

Richard Wright, *Pagan Spain. Saturday Review of Literature*, March 16, 1957, pp. 60–62.

Giovanni Guareschi, *Don Camillo Takes the Devil by the Tail.* Translated by Frances Frenaye. *Herald Tribune Book Review*, June 2, 1957, p. 8.

Edith Templeton, *The Surprise of Cremona. Saturday Review of Literature*, July 6, 1957, p. 14.

Morris L. West, *Children of the Shadows. Saturday Review of Literature*, August 3, 1957, p. 16.

Four Volumes of Short Stories, by Frank O'Connor, Alberto Moravia,

Samuel Yellen, and Daniel Culley. Moravia review by TGB. *Saturday Review of Literature,* September 21, 1957, p. 18.

Dorothy L. Sayers, *Further Papers on Dante. New York Times Book Review,* September 22, 1957.

Gerald Brenan, *South from Granada. Saturday Review of Literature,* October 19, 1957, p. 59.

Italo Calvino, *The Path to the Nest of Spiders.* Translated by Archibald Colquhoun. *Herald Tribune Book Review,* November 17, 1957, p. 6.

Domenico Vittorini, *The Age of Dante. Italian Quarterly*—Dante Shelf, 1 (1957): 79.

Francesco de Sanctis, *De Sanctis on Dante.* Edited and translated by Joseph Rossi and Alfred Galpin. *Italian Quarterly*—Dante Shelf, 1 (1947): 80.

Bernard Stambler, *Dante's Other World: The Purgatorio as a Guide to the Divine Comedy. Italian Quarterly*—Dante Shelf, 1 (1957): 81.

Dorothy L. Sayers, *Further Papers on Dante. Italian Quarterly*—Dante Shelf, 1 (1947): 84.

Ippolito Nievo, *The Castle of Fratta.* Translated by Lovett F. Edwards. *Herald Tribune Book Review,* January 5, 1958, p. 3.

Mario Soldati, *The Confession.* Translated by Raymond Rosenthal. *Saturday Review of Literature,* February 15, 1958, p. 22.

Livia de Stefani, *Black Grapes. Herald Tribune Book Review,* April 20, 1958, p. 4.

The Penguin Book of Italian Verse, edited and with Introduction by George R. Kay. *Italian Quarterly* 2 (1958): 69–70.

Giovanni Guareschi, *My Secret Diary 1943–1945.* Translated by Frances Frenaye. *Herald Tribune Book Review,* June 29, 1958, p. 7.

Franco Solinas, *Squarcio the Fisherman.* Translated by Frances Frenaye. *Herald Tribune Book Review,* July 27, 1958, p. 3.

Dorothy L. Sayers, *Introductory Papers on Dante. Speculum* 33 (1958): 319-22.

Cesare Pavese, *Among Women Only.* Translated by D. D. Paige. *Herald Tribune Book Review,* June 28, 1959, p. 4.

Giovanni Verga, *The She-Wolf and other Stories.* Introduction and translated by Giovanni Cecchetti. *Italica* 36 (1959): 235–36.

Charles T. Davis, *Dante and the Idea of Rome*. *Italian Quarterly—Dante Shelf*, 3 (1949): 59.

Joseph Anthony Mazzeo, *Structure and Thought in the Paradiso*. *Italian Quarterly—Dante Shelf*, 3 (1959): 62.

Charles Singleton, *Dante Studies II*. *Italian Quarterly—Dante Shelf*, 3 (1959): 64.

Maurice Valency, *In Praise of Love*. *Italian Quarterly—Dante Shelf*, 3 (1959):67.

Italo Calvino, *The Baron on the Trees*. Translated by Archibald Colquhoun. *Herald Tribune Book Review*, October 11, 1959, p. 3.

Danilo Dolci, *Report from Palermo*. Translated by P. D. Cummins. *Herald Tribune Book Review*, November 15, 1959, p. 3.

Italo Calvino, *Italian Fables*. Translated by Louis Brigante. *Herald Tribune Book Review*, November 22, 1959, p.13.

Erich von Richthofen, *Veltro und Diana. Dante mittelalterliche und antike Gleichnisse nebst einer Darstellung ihrer Ausdrucksformen*. *Romance Philology* 13 (1959): 185–88.

Ernest Hatch Wilkins, *Studies in the Life and Work of Petrarch*; *Petrarch at Vaucluse*; *Petrarch's Eight Years in Milan*. *Speculum* 34 (1959): 706–14.

Maurice Valency, *In Praise of Love*. *Renaissance Quarterly*, vol. 12 (1959).

Gavin Maxwell, *The Ten Pains of Death*. *Herald Tribune Book Review*, January 17, 1960, p. 4.

Alberto Moravia, *The Wayward Wife and other Stories*. *Herald Tribune Book Review*, February 7, 1960, p. 5.

Antonio Barolini, *Our Last Family Countess and Related Stories*. *Herald Tribune Book Review*, March 20, 1960, p. 7.

Anthony Rhodes, *D'Annunzio. The Poet as Superman*. *Herald Tribune Book Review*, March 27, 1960, p. 7.

Giuseppe di Lampedusa, *The Leopard*. Translated by Archibald Colquhoun. *Herald Tribune Book Review*, May 1, 1960, p. 1.

P. M. Pasinetti, *Venetian Red*. *Herald Tribune Book Review*, May 8, 1960, p. 4.

The Selected Writings of Salvatore Quasimodo. Edited and translated by Allen Mandelbaum. *Herald Tribune Book Review*, July 10, 1960, p. 8.

Carlo Cassola, *Fausto and Anna*. Translated by Isabel Quigley. *Herald Tribune Book Review*, July 17, 1960, p. 7.

Ruth Stephen, *My Crown, My Love*. *Herald Tribune Book Review*, October 16, 1960.

Mercedes Salisachs, *The Eyes of the Proud*. Translated by Delano Ames. *Herald Tribune Book Review*, October 30, 1960.

Peter van Paassen, *Life and Times of Girolamo Savonarola*. *New York Times Book Review* (1960?).

Mario Soldati, *The Real Silvestri*. Translated by Archibald Colquhoun. *Herald Tribune Book Review*, January 22, 1961, p. 34.

Kateb Yacine, *Nedjma*. Translated by Richard Howard. *Herald Tribune Book Review*, February 26, 1961, p. 30.

Danilo Dolci, *Outlaws*. Translated by R. Munroe. *Herald Tribune Book Review*, March 5, 1961, p. 32.

James Morris, *The World of Venice*. *Herald Tribune Book Review*, April 2, 1961, p. 32.

Georges Conchon, *The Measure of Victory*. Translated by Elisabeth Abbot. *Herald Tribune Book Review*, May 14, 1961, p. 27.

Ignazio Silone, *The Fox and the Camellias*. Translated by Eric Mosbacher. *Herald Tribune Book Review*, May 28, 1961, p. 25.

Zoe Oldenbourg, *Destiny of Fire*. Translated by Peter Green. *Herald Tribune Book Review*, June 4, 1961, p. 27.

Elio Vittorini, *The Dark and the Light: Erica and La Guribaldina*. Translated by Frances Keene. *Herald Tribune Book Review*, June 18, 1961, p. 30.

Wido Hempel, *Giovanni Vergas Roman I Malavoglia und die Wiederholung als erzählerischer Kunstmittel*. *Italica* 38 (1961): 251–53.

Cesare Pavese, *The Burning Brand—Diaries 1935–1950, The House on the Hill*. *Herald Tribune Book Review*, December 10, 1961.

M. A. Mazzeo, *Medieval Cultural Tradition in Dante's Comedy*. *Modern Philology* (1961?).

Ugo Pirro, *A Thousand Betrayals*. *Herald Tribune Book Review*, January 14, 1962.

Giuseppe di Lampedusa, *The Leopard*. *Herald Tribune Book Review* (Paperback Section), January 14, 1962.

Miguel de Cervantes, *Six Exemplary Novels*. *Herald Tribune Book Review* (Paperback Section), January 14, 1962.

Alberto Moravia, *Mistaken Ambitions. Herald Tribune Book Review* (Paperback Section), January 14, 1962.

Alberto Moravia, *Three Novels: The Conformist; A Ghost at Noon; The Fancy Dress Party. Herald Tribune Book Review* (Paperback Section), January 14, 1962.

J. A. Mazzeo, *Medieval Cultural Tradition in Dante's Comedy. Italian Quarterly*—Dante Shelf, 6 (1962): 94.

Irma Brandeis, *The Ladder of Vision. Italian Quarterly*—Dante Shelf, 6 (1962): 96.

Irma Brandeis, *Discussions of the Divine Comedy. Italian Quarterly*—Dante Shelf, 6 (1962): 100.

Rocco Montano, *La Poesia di Dante. Italian Quarterly*—Dante Shelf, 6 (1962): 100.

Denys Hays, *The Italian Renaissance in its Historical Background. Yale Review* 51 (1962): 459–60.

Erich Auerbach, *Dante, Poet of the Secular World. Yale Review* 51 (1962): 460–62.

Ernest Hatch Wilkins, *Life of Petrarch. Yale Review* 51 (1962): 462–63.

Juan Garcia Hortelano, *Summer Storm. Herald Tribune Book Review,* May 6, 1962.

Carlo Cassola, *Bebo's Girl. Saturday Review of Literature,* July 7, 1962.

Curzio Malaparte, *Benedetti Italiani. Books Abroad* 36 (1962): 314.

Rodolfi Celletti, *Marta. Herald Tribune Book Review,* August 12, 1962, p. 6.

Bianca Garufi, *Il Fossile. Books Abroad* 36 (1962): 420–21.

Ugo Moretti, *Nuda ogni sera. Books Abroad* 36 (1962): 421.

Jose Luis de Villalonga, *The Pleasure Seeker.* Translated by Richard Howard. *Herald Tribune Book Review* October 7, 1962, p. 8.

Giuseppe Dessi, *The Deserter.* Translated by Virginia Hathaway. *Herald Tribune Book Review,* October 14, 1962, p. 10.

Vasco Pratolini, *Two Brothers.* Translated by Barbara Kennedy. *Herald Tribune Book Review,* October 21, 1962, p. 14.

David Stackton, *A Dancer in Darkness. Herald Tribune Book Review,* November 11, 1962, p. 10.

Jan Westcott, *Condottiere. Herald Tribune Book Review,* November 18, 1962, p. 12.

Federico de Roberto, *The Viceroys.* Translated by Archibald Colquhoun. *Herald Tribune Book Review,* November 25, 1962, p. 12.

Giuseppe di Lampedusa, *Two Stories and a Memory*. Translated by Archibald Colquhoun. *Saturday Review of Literature*, December 8, 1962, pp. 23–24.

Fabrizio Onofri, *Roma 31 dicembre*. *Books Abroad* 37 (1963): 69.

Lorenza Mazzetti, *The Sky Falls*. *Saturday Review of Literature*, March 23, 1963.

Joseph Jay Deiss, *The Great Infidel*. *Herald Tribune Book Review*, April 14, 1963, p. 9.

Eca de Queiroz, *The Sin of Father Amaro*. Translated by Nan Flanagan. *Herald Tribune Book Review*, April 21, 1963, p. 10.

Michele Prisco, *La Dama di Piazza*. *Books Abroad* 37 (1963): 195.

Saverio Strati, *Avventure in città*. *Books Abroad* 37 (1963): 195–96.

Oreste del Buono, *Image of Love*. Translated by Helen R. Lane. *Herald Tribune Book Review*, May 12, 1963, p. 10.

Joao Guimaraes Rosa, *The Devil to Pay in the Backlands*. Translated by James L. Taylor. *Herald Tribune Book Review*, May 19, 1963, p. 8.

Charles S. Singleton, *Journey to Beatrice*. *Speculum* 38 (1963): 501–04.

Luigi Malagoli, *Saggio sulla Divina Commedia*. *Books Abroad* 37 (1963): 324.

Giulio Vallese, *Da Dante ad Erasmo, Studi di letteratura umanistica*. *Books Abroad* 37 (1963): 325.

Zoe Oldenbourg, *Cities of the Flesh, or The Story of Roger de Montbrun*. *Herald Tribune Book Review*, September 8, 1963.

Vittorio Bodini, *La Lune dei Borboni e altre poesie*. *Books Abroad* 37 (1963): 444.

Giovanni Cecchetti, *Leopardi e Verga*. *Italica* 40 (1963): 376–78.

Vasco Pratolini, *La Costanza della Ragione*. *Books Abroad* 38 (1964): 63–64.

Guido Aristarco, *Il Mestiere del critico*. *Books Abroad* 38 (1964): 67.

Carlo Cassola, *An Arid Heart*. *Saturday Review of Literature*, January 25, 1964.

Tommaso Landolfi, *Gogol's Wife and other Stories*. Translated by Raymond Rosenthal. *Herald Tribune Book Review*, February 2, 1964, p. 17.

Morris Bishop, *Petrarch and His World*. *Yale Review* 53 (1964): 468–70.

Aldo Scaglione, *Nature and Love in the Late Middle Ages*. *Yale Review* 53 (1964): 470–72.

Antonio Barolini, *A Long Madness*. *Saturday Review of Literature*, May 9, 1964.

Alba de Cespedes, *Rimorso*. *Books Abroad* 38 (1964): 303–04.

Aldo S. Bernardo, *Petrarch, Scipio and the Africa*. *Speculum* 39 (1964): 486–89.

Sergio Solmi, *Scrittori negli anni*. *Books Abroad* 38 (1964): 419–20.

Giovanni Arpino, *L'Ombra delle colline*. *Books Abroad* 39 (1965): 74–75.

Alfonso Gatto, *Il Vaporetto*. *Books Abroad* 39 (1965): 76.

Erich Auerbach, *Dante, Poet of the Secular World*. Translated by Ralph Mannheim. *Italian Quarterly*—Dante Shelf, 9 (1965): 21.

T. K. Swing, *The Fragile Leaves of the Sybil*. *Italian Quarterly*—Dante Shelf, 9 (1965): 21.

Allan Gilbert, *Dante and his Comedy*. *Italian Quarterly*—Dante Shelf, 9 (1965): 22.

Dino Bigongiari, *Essays on Dante and Medieval Culture*. *Italian Quarterly*—Dante Shelf, 9 (1965): 24.

Roberto Sorelli, *Dante, Scriba Dei*. *Italian Quarterly*—Dante Shelf, 9 (1965): 26.

Odes. Translated by H. Vere-Hodge. *Italian Quarterly*—Dante Shelf, 9 (1965): 27.

Aldo Vallone, *La Prosa della Vita Nuova*. *Italian Quarterly*—Dante Shelf, 9 (1965): 28.

Essays on Dante, Edited by Mark Musa. *Italian Quarterly*—Dante Shelf, 9 (1965): 29.

Vasco Pratolini, *Bruno Santini*. *Herald Tribune Book Review*, March 28, 1965, p. 17.

Guido Botta, *Tenerezza e noia*. *Books Abroad* 39 (1965): 335–36.

Giorgio Bassani, *The Garden of the Finzi-Continis*. Translated by Isabel Quigley. *Saturday Review of Literature*, July 24, 1965, p. 46.

Marzieh Gali, *Avignon in Flower 1309–1403*. *Herald Tribune Book Review*, August 22, 1965, p. 11.

Luciano Bianciardi, *It's a Hard Life*. Translated by Eric Mosbacher. *Saturday Review of Literature*, October 2, 1965, p. 59.

Eugenio Donadoni, *Studi danteschi e manzoniani*. *Books Abroad* 39 (1965): 421–22.

Lucio Mastronardi, *Il Meridionale di Vigevano*. *Books Abroad* 39 (1965): 429.

Centenary Essays on Dante, by Members of the Oxford Dante Society. *Speculum*, vol. 40 (1965).

Bonaventura Tecchi, *Gli Onesti*. *Books Abroad* 40 (1966): 78.

Pier Paolo Pasolini, *Poesia in forma di rosa*. *Books Abroad* 40 (1966): 80.

Rocco Montano, *Storia della poesia di Dante*. *Italian Quarterly—Dante Shelf*, 10 (1966): 68.

Remo Fasani, *Il Sacro Poema*. *Italian Quarterly—Dante Shelf*, 10 (1966): 71.

William de Sua, *Dante into English*. *Italian Quarterly—Dante Shelf*, 10 (1966): 72.

Gilbert E. Cunningham, *The Divine Comedy in English, Vol I*. *Italian Quarterly—Dante Shelf*, 10 (1966): 72.

Divine Comedy. Revised translation by Geoffrey L. Bickersteth. *Italian Quarterly—Dante Shelf*, 10 (1966): 74.

Dante, ed. John Freccero. *Italian Quarterly—Dante Shelf*, 10 (1966): 76.

Paget Toynbee, *Dante Alighieri, His Life and Works*. Edited by Charles Singleton. *Italian Quarterly—Dante Shelf*, 10 (1966): 77.

Erich Auerbach, *Literary Language and its Public in Late Latin Antiquity and in the Middle Ages*. *Italian Quarterly—Dante Shelf*, 10 (1966): 78.

Mario Casella, *Introduzione alle opere di Dante*. *Italian Quarterly—Dante Shelf*, 10 (1966): 78.

Egidio Guidubaldi, *Dante europeo*. *Italian Quarterly—Dante Shelf*, 10 (1966): 78.

Charles Speroni, *Dante*. *Italian Quarterly—Dante Shelf*, 10 (1966): 93.

Giovanni Nicosia, *Il grande Tumolo*. *Books Abroad* 40 (1966): 201.

Mario Pomilio, *La Compromissione*. *Books Abroad* 40 (1966): 329.

The Poetry of Panuccio del Bene, ed. Mark Musa. *Italica* 43 (1966): 314–15.

Remo Fasani, *Il Sacro Poema*. *Speculum* 41 (1966): 742–43.

Rocco Montano, *A Translation from Leopardi*. *Memories. Umanesimo I* (1967), pp. 21–26.

The World of Dante: Six Studies in Language and Thought. Edited by S. Bernard Chandler and J. A. Molinaro. *University of Toronto Quarterly* 36 (1967): 389–91.

Dante's Lyric Poetry, edited and translated by Kenelm Foster and Patrick Boyde. *Italian Quarterly*—Dante Shelf, 11 (1967): 89.

Dantis Aligherii Epistolae, compiled by Paget Toynbee, edited by Colin Hardie. *Italian Quarterly*—Dante Shelf, 11 (1967): 91.

Centenary Essays on Dante, by Oxford Dante Society. *Italian Quarterly* —Dante Shelf, 11 (1967): 92.

The Mind of Dante, ed. Uberto Limentani. *Italian Quarterly*—Dante Shelf, 11 (1967): 94.

The World of Dante: Six Studies in Language and Thought, edited by S. Bernard Chandler and J. A. Molinaro. *Italian Quarterly*—Dante Shelf, 11 (1967): 100.

A Dante Symposium, edited by William de Sua and Gino Rizzo. *Italian Quarterly*—Dante Shelf, 11 (1967): 103.

Thomas Caldecot Chubb, *Dante and His World. Italian Quarterly*— Dante Shelf, 11 (1967): 106.

Gilbert E. Cunningham, *The Divine Comedy in English, Vol. II. Italian Quarterly*—Dante Shelf, 11 (1967): 107.

Vasco Pratolini, *Allegoria e derisione. Books Abroad* 41 (1967): 459–60.

Thomas Caldecot Chubb, *Dante and His World. Virginia Quarterly* (1967).

Letters from Petrarch, edited and translated by Morris Bishop. *Speculum* 43 (1968): 123–25.

Alba de Cespedes, *La Bombolona. Books Abroad* 42 (1968): 91.

Giuseppe Dessì, *Lei era l'acqua. Books Abroad* 42 (1968): 91–92.

Fabio Tombari, *Il Gioco dell'oca. Books Abroad* 42 (1968): 93.

Virgilio Lilli, *Microsaggi. Books Abroad* 42 (1968): 95–96.

Riccardo Bacchelli, *Rapporto segreto. Books Abroad* 42 (1968): 251.

Raffaele Carrieri, *Io che sono cicala. Books Abroad* 42 (1968): 254–55.

Giancarlo Majorino, *Lotte secondarie. Books Abroad* 42 (1968): 255.

Luigi Malerba, *The Serpent. Saturday Review of Literature*, May 18, 1968.

Carlo Cassola, *Storia di Ada. Books Abroad* 42 (1968): 416.

Mario Spinella, *Sorella H, libera nos. Books Abroad* 43 (1969): 245.

Andrea Zanzotto, *La Beltà. Books Abroad* 43 (1969): 246–47.

Sergio Solmi, *Dal Balcone. Books Abroad* 43 (1969): 247.

Pietro Paolo Gerosa, *Umanesimo cristiana del Petrarca: influenza agostiniana; attinenze medievali. Speculum* 44 (1969): 638–40.

Italo Svevo, *Confessions of Zeno. Saturday Review*, September 13, 1969.

Alfredo Luzi, *La Vicissitudine sospesa. Books Abroad* 44 (1970): 93.

Riccardo Bacchelli, *L'Afrodite: un romanzo d'amore. Books Abroad* 44 (1970): 94.

Giovanni Arpino, *Il Buio e il miele. Books Abroad* 44 (1970): 97.

Aldo S. Bernardo, *A Diversity of Dante. Italian Quarterly*—Dante Shelf, 14 (1970): 105.

Giuseppe Zagarrio, *Quasimodo. Books Abroad* 44 (1970): 642.

Daniel Vogelmann, *Cose. Books Abroad* 44 (1970): 645.

Joseph Carey, *Three Modern Poets: Saba, Ungaretti, Montale. Books Abroad* 44 (1970): 646–47.

Leonida Repaci, *Storia dei Rupe. Il tra guerra e rivoluzione. Books Abroad* 45 (1971): 97–98.

Nelo Risi, *Di Certe Cose. Books Abroad* 45 (1971): 100.

Mario Soldati, *L'Attore. Books Abroad* 45 (1971): 298.

Pirandello; Letteratura e teatro. Books Abroad 45 (1971): 498.

Leone Piccione, *Vita di un poeta; Giuseppe Ungaretti. Books Abroad* 45 (1971): 501–02.

Dante Alighieri, The Paradiso. Translated by John Ciardi. *Yale Review* 60 (1971): 614–15.

Dante Alighieri, The Divine Comedy—Inferno. 2 vols. Translation and commentary by Charles S. Singleton. *Yale Review* 60 (1971): 615–17.

Robert S. Lopez, *The Three Ages of the Italian Renaissance. Renaissance Quarterly* 24 (1971): 232–33.

Giovanni Santillo, *Studi sull'umanesimo europeo. Renaissance Quarterly* 24 (1971): 233.

Riccardo Bacchelli, *Versi e rime. Primo Libro—La Storia del mattino. Books Abroad* 46 (1972): 96–97.

Leonardo Sinisgalli, *Il Passero e il lebbroso. Books Abroad* 46 (1972): 97.

Giacinto Spagnoletti, *Palazzeschi. Books Abroad* 46 (1972): 281.

Michele Tondo, *Salvatore Quasimodo. Books Abroad* 46 (1972): 281.

Marino Moretti, *Tre Anni e un giorno. Books Abroad* 46 (1972): 283.

Aldo Palazzeschi, *Storia di un'amicizia. Books Abroad* 46 (1972): 463–64.

Luigi Malagoli, *L'Anti-Ottocento. La Rivoluzione poetica in Italia. Books Abroad* 46 (1972): 647–48.

Attilio Bertolucci, *Viaggio d'inverno. Books Abroad* 46 (1972): 651.

Patrick Boyde, *Dante's Style in His Lyric Poetry. Renaissance Quarterly* 25 (1972): 440–42.

Enrico Falqui, *Novecento letterario italiano. I—storici e critici, da Croce a Gargiulio; II—dizionaristi, bibliografi e antologisti; III—narratori e prosatori, da d'Annunzio a C. E. Gadda. Books Abroad* 47 (1973): 126–27.

Francisco Navarro Ledesma, *Cervantes: The Man and the Genius*, translated and revised by Don and Gabriela Bliss. *New York Times Book Review*, February 18, 1973, p. 20.

Giovanni Giudice, *O Beatrice. Books Abroad* 47 (1973): 545.

MISCELLANEOUS

Scholarly

"On Translating Dante." Paper read at the Annual Meeting of the Dante Society, May 17, 1955, and published in *73rd Annual Report of the Dante Society* (1955), pp. 3–22.

"Dante." R.A.I. program prepared and transmitted for three minutes (July 1955).

Preface to *Memoirs of Lorenzo da Ponte* (New York: Orion Press, 1959).

Preface to T. K. Swing, *The Fragile Leaves of the Sybil* (1962).

"Los Cuatros mundos de Dante Alighieri." Lecture given in Puerto Rico and published in *Atenea* (January 1966).

"Una concordanza americana alla Commedia dantesca." Transmitted over "Voice of America," with copies for distribution (December 28, 1967).

"Twentieth-Century Italian Poets," condensed from an address before the Italy-America Society, New York City, and recorded in *Spoleto Festival Recordings* (1969).

Petrarch's *Bucolicum Carmen*, translated with notes. New Haven: Yale University Press, 1974.

Non-Scholarly

"Brindisi, 1943." *Italica* 23 (1946): 352–55.

"Salerno-Naples, February-March, 1944." *Italica* 24 (1947): 57–61.

"Allied Military Administration of Italy, 1943–1945, C. R. S. Harris." In *United States Naval Institute Proceedings* (January 1959).

"For a Space Prober," poem launched with TRAAC Satellite and published in *APL Technical Digest* (November 15, 1961).

"Inaugural Sestina," poem in Editor's Window of *Yale Alumni Magazine*, vol. 27 (June 1964).

"Elm Street Lost" (pseud. Tom Goddard), poem published in *New Haven Journal Courier*, June 27, 1964.

"The Octopus" (pseud. Tom Goddard), poem published in *New Haven Journal Courier*, June 27, 1964.

"The Residential Colleges at Yale." Address given at the University of Massachusetts and published in *Mass. Alumnus* (Summer 1964).

"Heaven" (pseud. Homer N. Bigstag), poem published in *New Haven Journal Courier*, August 15, 1964.

Master Pieces. New Haven: privately printed, 1965.

"Insurgent Love Can Rally Volunteers" (pseud. Tom Goddard), poem published in *New Haven Register*, July 31, 1965.

"A Letter and a four line jingle." *Time Magazine*, August 20, 1965.

Sonnets "Almanac for Academics," illustrated by Dr. Herbert Thoms. Hamden, Conn.: Shoestring Press, 1965.

Letter on "Viking Map" in Graduate Fence of *Yale Alumni Magazine*, vol. 29 (November 1965).

Interview, "Continuing Concern about the War in Vietnam." *Yale Alumni Magazine*, vol. 30 (February 1967).

"Football 1969; The Saga of the Unsung." *Yale Alumni Magazine*, vol. 33 (December 1969).

"Department Comments—T.G.B.," in *Yale Alumni Magazine*, vol. 33 (March 1970). This was the beginning of his regular monthly column. The title was changed with volume 34 (October 1970) to "Time and Change." This column continues to appear monthly.

WORK IN PROGRESS

Scholarly

Supplementary chapter of E. H. Wilkins's *History of Italian Literature*, with some revision thereof. Cambridge, Mass.: Harvard University Press, 1974.

Petrarch's *Africa* (with Alice S. Wilson), translated with notes. New Haven: Yale University Press. Forthcoming.

Boccaccio. New York: Viking Press. Forthcoming.

Various entries in new *Columbia Dictionary of European Literature*. New York: Columbia University Press. Forthcoming.

Non-Scholarly

Yale Football, 1952–1973. Forthcoming.

Squares and Tesseracts, edited by Kenneth John Atchity. Collected poems. Forthcoming.

Index

443